In Praise of Dharmadhātu

The Nitartha Institute Series

published by Snow Lion Publications

Nitartha Institute was founded in 1996 by The Dzogchen Ponlop Rinpoche, under the guidance of Khenchen Thrangu Rinpoche and Khenpo Tsültrim Gyamtso Rinpoche, the leading contemporary teachers of the Karma Kagyü tradition of Tibetan Buddhism. The Institute, under the aegis of Nitartha *international*, aims to fully transmit the Buddhist tradition of contemplative inquiry and learning; it offers Western students training in advanced Buddhist view and practice, as taught by the Karma Kagyü and Nyingma lineages of Tibet.

The Institute is pleased to ally with Snow Lion Publications in presenting this series of important works offering a wide range of graded educational materials that include authoritative translations of key texts from the Buddhist tradition, both those unique to the Kagyü and Nyingma lineages and those common to the wider scope of Indo-Tibetan Buddhism; modern commentaries by notable lineage scholar-practitioners; manuals for contemplative practice; and broader studies that deepen understanding of particular aspects of the Buddhist view. The initial releases are from the Kagyü tradition and will be followed by publications from the Nyingma tradition.

This publication is an Intermediate Level Nitartha book.

IN PRAISE OF DHARMADHĀTU

Nāgārjuna and
the Third Karmapa, Rangjung Dorje

Translated and introduced by Karl Brunnhölzl

SNOW LION PUBLICATIONS
ITHACA, NEW YORK ✦ BOULDER, COLORADO

Snow Lion Publications
P.O. Box 6483
Ithaca, NY 14851 USA
(607) 273-8519
www.snowlionpub.com

Printed in USA on acid-free recycled paper.

Typeset by Stephanie Johnston based on a design by Gopa & Ted2, Inc.

ISBN-10: 1-55939-286-X
ISBN-13: 978-1-55939-286-0

Library of Congress Cataloging-in-Publication Data

Brunnhölzl, Karl.
In praise of dharmadhātu : Nāgārjuna and the Third Karmapa, Rangjung Dorje / translated and introduced by Karl Brunnhölzl.
p. cm.
Includes English translation of Raṅ-byuṅ-rdo-rje's Tibetan commentary on Dharmadhātustava.
Includes bibliographical references and index.
ISBN-13: 978-1-55939-286-0 (alk. paper)
ISBN-10: 1-55939-286-X (alk. paper)
1. Nāgārjuna, 2nd cent. Dharmadhātustava. 2. Raṅ-byuṅ-rdo-rje, Karma-pa III, 1284-1339. 3. Mādhyamika (Buddhism) I. Raṅ-byuṅ-rdo-rje, Karma-pa III, 1284-1339. Dbu ma chos dbyiṅs bstod pa'i rnam par bśad pa. English. II. Title.

BQ2910.D487B78 2007
294.3'85--dc22

2007035243

Contents

Abbreviations:

AC	Rangjung Dorje's autocommentary on his *Profound Inner Reality*
AS	*Asiatische Studien*
D	Derge Tibetan Tripiṭaka
Döl	Dölpopa's commentary on the *Dharmadhātustava*
DSC	Rangjung Dorje's commentary on the *Dharmadhātustava*
EDV	Rangjung Dorje's *Explanation of the Dharmadharmatāvibhāga*
GL	Gö Lotsāwa's commentary on the *Uttaratantra*
J	Johnston's Sanskrit edition of the *Ratnagotravibhāgavyākhyā*
JIABS	*Journal of the International Association of Buddhist Studies*
LG	Lodrö Gyatso's commentary on the *Dharmadhātustava*
MHTL	Lokesh Chandra's *Materials for a History of Tibetan Literature*
MM	Rangjung Dorje's *Aspiration Prayer of Mahamudra*
N	Narthang Tibetan Tripiṭaka
NT	Rangjung Dorje's *Treatise on the Distinction between Consciousness and Wisdom*
NY	Rangjung Dorje's *Treatise on Pointing Out the Tathāgata Heart*
P	Peking Tibetan Tripiṭaka
PEW	*Philosophy East and West*
RT	Rongtön's commentary on the *Dharmadhātustava*
SC	Śākya Chogden's commentary on the *Dharmadhātustava*
SS	Sönam Sangbo's commentary on the *Dharmadhātustava*
TBRC	The Tibetan Buddhist Resource Center (www.tbrc.org)
TOK	Jamgön Kongtrul Lodrö Tayé's *Treasury of Knowledge*
WZKS	*Wiener Zeitschrift für die Kunde Südasiens*
ZMND	Rangjung Dorje's *Profound Inner Reality*

An Aspiration
by H.H. the Seventeenth Karmapa, Orgyen Trinlé Dorjé

You realize that whatever appears dawns within the play of the mind
And that this mind is the dharmakāya free from clinging.
Through the power of that, you supreme siddhas master apparent existence.
Precious ones of the Kagyü lineage, please bring about excellent virtue.

Through the heart of a perfect Buddha having awoken in you,
You are endowed with the blossoming of the glorious qualities of supreme insight.
You genuine holder of the teachings by the name Dzogchen Ponlop,
Through your merit, the activity of virtue,

You publish the hundreds of flawless dharma paintings
That come from the protectors of beings, the Takpo Kagyü,
As a display of books that always appears
As a feast for the mental eyes of persons without bias.

While the stream of the Narmadā[1] river of virtue
Washes away the stains of the mind,
With the waves of the virtues of the two accumulations rolling high,
May it merge with the ocean of the qualities of the victors.

This was composed by Karmapa Orgyen Trinlé Dorjé as an auspicious aspiration for the publication of the precious teachings called "The Eight Great Texts of Sūtra and Tantra" by the supreme Dzogchen Ponlop Karma Sungrap Ngedön Tenpé Gyaltsen on April 18, 2004 (Buddhist Era 2548). May it be auspicious.

1 The image here alludes to this river being considered as very holy by Hindus—even its mere sight is said to wash away all one's negative deeds (it rises on the summit of Mount Amarakaṇṭaka in Madhya Pradesh in central India, and after a westerly course of about eight hundred miles ends in the Gulf of Cambay below the city of Bharuch).

Foreword
by H.H. the Seventeenth Karmapa, Orgyen Trinlé Dorjé

In Tibet, all the ravishing and beautiful things of a self-arisen realm, such as being surrounded by ranges of snow mountains that are adorned by superb white snowflakes, being filled with Sal trees, abundant herbs, and cool clear rivers, are wonderfully assembled in a single place. Through these excellencies, our country endowed with the dharma is the sole pure realm of human beings in this world. In it, all parts of the mighty sage's teachings, the teacher who is skilled in means and greatly compassionate, are fully complete—the greater and lesser yānas as well as the mantrayāna. They are as pure and clean as the most refined pure gold, accord with reasoning through the power of things, dispel the darkness of the minds of all beings, and are a great treasury that grants all desirable benefit and happiness, just as one wishes. Without having vanished, these teachings still exist as the great treasure of the *Kangyur*, the *Tengyur*, and the sciences as well as the excellent teachings of the Tibetan scholars and siddhas who have appeared over time. All of these teachings equal the size of the mighty king of mountains, and their words and meanings are like a sip of the nectar of immortality. Headed by the Dzogchen Ponlop Rinpoche with his immaculate superior intention of cherishing solely the welfare of the teachings and sentient beings, many people who strive with devotion, diligence, and prajñā to preserve the teachings at Nitartha *international* undertook hardships and made great efforts over many years for the sake of preventing the decline of these teachings, increasing their transmission, and preserving them, and, in particular, for the special purpose of spreading and increasing in all directions and at all times, like rivers in summertime, the excellent stream of explanations and practices of the unequaled Marpa Kagyü lineage—the great family of siddhas. By way of these efforts, the book series of "The Eight Great Texts of Sūtra and Tantra," which encapsulate the essential meanings of the fully complete teachings of the victor, was magically manifested in such a way that many appear from one. Based on this, while being in the process of making efforts myself in the preparatory stages of accomplishing the protection of the teachings and sentient beings, from the bottom of my heart, I strew the flowers of rejoicing and praise on this activity. Together with this, I make the aspiration that, through this excellent activity, the intentions of the noble forefathers may be fulfilled in the expanse of peace.

This was written by Karmapa Orgyen Trinlé Dorjé at Gyütö on July 19, 2002 (Buddhist Era 2547).

Foreword
by The Dzogchen Ponlop Rinpoche

More than 2,500 years ago in ancient India, a young prince named Siddhārtha found himself dissatisfied with the illusions of a royal life that had been painstakingly maintained by his father, King Śuddhodana. One day, Siddhārtha set out with a keen sense of quest. He wanted to understand what life really is and how the world around him really worked. This curious adventure eventually became his journey to enlightenment.

His pursuit did not start with sacred or supramundane experiences; it started with a very simple and straightforward desire to find the truth. Siddhārtha did not begin his journey by discovering great faith in god or religion, nor did he stumble upon a charismatic guru. Rather, he relied on his simple desire and keen intellect—his inquisitive mind. This led him to discover the basic truth about life and the world, and, through this discovery, he became known as the Buddha, the Awakened One.

After attaining enlightenment, the Buddha gave three main groups of teachings called the three "wheels of dharma." First, at the Deer Park in Sarnath, he turned the wheel of dharma on the four noble truths. Second, at Vulture Peak Mountain in Rajagṛha, he turned the wheel of dharma on prajnāpāramitā or transcendent wisdom. Finally, at Vaiśālī and other places, he turned the wheel of dharma on buddha nature and other topics.

According to the literature of the mahāyāna tradition, these three sets of teachings became the basis for what would later be called the journey of the "three yānas."[1] All traditions of Buddhism throughout the world emerged from these three.

To help future students understand and realize the vast and profound words of the Buddha, two great Indian masters, Nāgārjuna (c. 150–250 CE) and Asaṅga (c. fourth century), the pioneers of the mahāyāna tradition, wrote numerous treatises and commentaries to elucidate the Buddha's intention. The master Nāgārjuna transmitted the lineage of the profound view of emptiness that originated from Manjuśrī, while the master Asaṅga transmitted the lineage of vast bodhisattva practices that came from Maitreya.

Nāgārjuna was born into a Brahmin family in southern India in Vaidarbha.[2] His birth was predicted in various sūtras, such as the *Laṅkāvatārasūtra (Descent into Laṅka Sūtra)*. At the age of seven, his parents sent him to Nālandā University in northern India, where he met the great master Saraha. At Nālandā, Nāgārjuna studied sūtras and tantras under Saraha, Ratnamati, and many other masters and, eventually, became the university's abbot.

It is recorded in the mahāyāna histories that Nāgārjuna discovered the collection of prajñāparamitā sūtras that had been lost for many generations from the land of nāgas. He also is said to have brought back nāga clay, and built many temples and stūpas with it.

At one time, when Nāgārjuna was traveling to teach, he met some children playing on the road and prophesied that one of them, then named Jetaka, would one day become a king. When Nāgārjuna returned many years later, the boy had in fact grown up and become a king in South India named Udayibhadra (Tib. bde spyod bzang po). Nāgārjuna taught the king for three years and then went to Śrī Parvata, the holy mountain overlooking the modern-day Indian land of Nāgārjunakoṇḍa, where he wrote the *Ratnāvalī* (*Precious Garland*; Tib. rin chen 'phreng ba) and the *Suhṛllekha* (*Letter to a Friend*; Tib. bshes pa'i spring yig) for the king. In this way, Nāgārjuna taught throughout India. He spent the later part of his life in Śrī Parvata, where he wrote most of his texts known as the "Praises."

Respected as an unsurpassed master by all Buddhist schools, Nāgārjuna elucidated the Buddha's three turnings of the wheel of dharma through his writings known as the Three Collections.

The Collection Of Speeches: In this first collection, Nāgārjuna offers advice to both householders and to the ordained sangha on how to follow the path. His *Suhṛllekha (Letter To A Friend)* is an example of such a treatise. These instructions are connected to the Buddha's teachings of the first turning of the wheel of dharma.

The Collection Of Reasoning: The second collection is the most renowned series of Nāgārjuna's writings. In it, he presents the *Madhyamaka* or Middle Way philosophy, regarded as the highest teachings on the view of emptiness. There are six texts in this collection, and among them the *Mūlamadhyamakakārikā* (*Fundamental Wisdom of the Middle Way*; Tib. dbu ma rtsa ba shes rab) is the principal treatise. Through his teachings in this collection, Nāgārjuna elucidates the Buddha's second turning of the wheel of dharma, the prajñāpāramitā sūtras.

The Collection Of Praises: In this final collection, Nāgārjuna clarifies the concept of *tathāgatagarbha* or buddha nature and explains the Buddha's third turning of the wheel of dharma through writings such as the *Paramārthastava*

(*Praise To The Ultimate Truth*; Tib. don dam par stod pa) and *Dharmadhātustava* (*In Praise of Dharmadhātu*; Tib. chos dbyings bstod pa).

Besides these Three Collections, Nāgārjuna also wrote many other texts and commentaries, such as his commentary on the *Guhyasamājatantra*. He was not only an accomplished scholar but also a realized meditation master, and is thus counted among the eighty-four mahāsiddhas of India.

The *Dharmadhātustava* is a well known text from the collection of praises and is studied in depth in the Tibetan Buddhist tradition. It is regarded as one of Nāgārjuna's most important texts because of its use of many examples to clearly explain the theory and nature of *tathāgatagarbha*.

Many Tibetan masters authored commentaries on this praise. Among them are Kunkhyen Rangjung Dorje, the Third Karmapa of the Kagyü lineage, and Panchen Śākya Chogden of the Sakya tradition.

I am very happy that Dr. Karl Brunnhölzl has completed an English translation of Nāgārjuna's *Dharmadhātustava* along with its commentary by the Third Karmapa, Rangjung Dorje. Karl is well trained in Buddhist studies and meditation, and is both a wonderful teacher of the Nalandabodhi sangha and an accomplished translator. He has done an excellent job of researching and translating this text and providing further material for reflection on the text's key topics. This book will serve as a great resource for those who wish to explore the teachings on buddha nature.

There are many texts on buddha nature from the tradition of Asaṅga, but this is the first time that a detailed presentation of Nāgārjuna's approach to buddha nature has been brought to English language readers. Therefore, this work is a great contribution to the establishment of genuine Western Buddhism.

Through this, may all beings discover and realize the true nature of their minds, the completely awakened wisdom of the Buddha.

Dzogchen Ponlop Rinpoche
Nalanda West
Seattle, Washington
July 31, 2007

1 The three yānas or "vehicles" are 1) the śrāvakayāna or vehicle of the hearers, 2) the pratyekabuddhayāna or vehicle of the solitary realizers, and 3) the bodhisattvayāna or vehicle of bodhisattvas, the spiritual aspirants of the mahāyāna.

2 Also spelled Vidharba. This was a kingdom in the modern-day Indian states of Maharashtra and Andhra Pradesh.

Preface

There is without a doubt no shortage of books—in Tibetan, Chinese, Japanese, and several Western languages—on Nāgārjuna's classical Madhyamaka texts as well as his *Ratnāvalī* and *Suhṛllekha*. However, so far, there exists no comprehensive discussion of the texts that the Tibetan tradition refers to as his "collection of praises"[1] in general and the *Dharmadhātustava* in particular. To begin to address this lack, the present book explores the scope, contents, and significance of Nāgārjuna's scriptural legacy in India and Tibet, especially his collection of praises. The main discussion of the *Dharmadhātustava* contains an overview of the text's structure and basic themes, an English translation, and exemplary passages from Indian and Tibetan works to illustrate the topics for which this text was considered to be important. The *Dharmadhātustava's* themes are deepened through a translation of its earliest and most extensive Tibetan commentary by the Third Karmapa, Rangjung Dorje, supplemented by relevant excerpts from other Tibetan commentaries. Additional resource materials to provide a broader background include short biographies of Nāgārjuna and Rangjung Dorje, a Buddhist "history" of luminous mind and buddha nature, and some remarks on the Third Karmapa's view. The appendices identify the already existing translations of some of the praises attributed to Nāgārjuna in the Tibetan *Tengyur* and present English renderings of all the remaining ones.

Throughout the texts presented here, the dharmadhātu is not understood as some mere emptiness or abstract nature of all phenomena but as the true state of our mind, luminous nonconceptual wisdom, or the present moment of mind's fundamental awareness and vast openness being inseparable. Thus, although it will be clear that Nāgārjuna's *Dharmadhātustava* fully accords with his classical Madhyamaka works, the emphasis here is not so much on philosophical considerations or reasonings to establish emptiness or freedom from reference points, but on the actual experience of the dharmadhātu's vivid wakefulness free from anything to hold on to or pinpoint. Even for someone like Nāgārjuna, whose fame seems to be almost exclusively based on his mind-boggling reasonings that leave nothing intact, this is not so surprising as it may seem at first. Like any other Buddhist master, his first and foremost concern is not philosophical or logical sophistication but liberation from saṃsāra. As is often said in the Buddhist teachings, "Mind is the king," and liberation is absolutely no exception to that. In other words, nirvāṇa or buddhahood is not just the end of the world as we know it, resulting in some vacuum or blank emptiness, but a living experience of penetrating insight, free from suffering and full of compassion, which takes place in and is realized by an enlightened mind's unlimited vision. So Nāgārjuna's *Dharmadhātustava* constantly points to that liberating and liberated experience, through both metaphor and reasoning. The text draws a sketch of our Buddha heart and its journey on the path of a bodhisattva, just to arrive at what it has always been, then being called "buddhahood." This sketch is embellished with a variety of colors by different commentators, painting a rich picture of what makes all beings Buddhas-to-be.

In particular, as far as the view of Karmapa Rangjung Dorje is concerned, this book may be considered as complementary to the presentations of Madhyamaka as found in my *The Center of the Sunlit Sky*, which are mainly based on Karmapa Mikyö Dorje's view. The Kagyü tradition says that its specific view on Madhyamaka was established by the Eighth Karmapa, while its distinct position on the teachings on buddha nature (and the tantras) was laid out by the Third Karmapa. As the following will show, the Yogācāra tradition as a whole may well be included in what was elucidated by the Third Karmapa. In this way, these two Karmapas provide a comprehensive presentation of the two great traditions of the mahāyāna.

In relying on the sources mentioned, it should be clear that anything in this book that sounds wonderful and is beneficial for touching our Buddha heart may well be appreciated as reflecting the words and realizations of great masters and scholars. Everything else, including all mistakes, can as usual be said to expose the obscurations of the translator and compiler.

Speaking of great masters and scholars, my sincere gratitude and appreciation go to Dzogchen Ponlop Rinpoche, who taught the *Dharmadhātustava* together with the Third Karmapa's commentary at Nitartha Institute's annual program in 2005. He encouraged me to publish these two texts ("if it's not too much work") and granted his guidance for the translation. Many thanks go to Jeff Cox and Sidney Piburn from Snow Lion for their readiness and efforts to publish this book, and to Sudé Walters and Steve Rhodes for being great editors. I am very grateful to Stephanie Johnston for taking the pains to read through the entire manuscript, offering many helpful editorial suggestions, and doing the layout. Also, I greatly appreciate the generous financial support by Tsadra Foundation and Nitartha Institute, which made this work possible. Last, but not least, I am deeply grateful to Mette Harboe for letting her Buddha heart shine, and to Sengé, who taught me how to take a break, tickling both my patience and my mind.

I offer this work with the wish that it may chime in with the constant wake-up calls from the enlightened hearts in all beings, be they suffering or liberated. May it be a humble contribution to the enlightened activities of all the Karmapas, especially during these times of strife and paranoia obscuring our mind's basic peace and self-confidence.

Brabrand, in the windy expanse of the Danish peninsula Jutland,
June 2006

Nāgārjuna and His Works

Who Was Nāgārjuna?

THIS MAY look like a very stupid question, since every Buddhist seems to know this great master very well. However, while legends abound, there is hardly anything that is known with certainty about Nāgārjuna's life (probably second century) as far as "hard historical data" go. Usually, the Indian and Tibetan traditions are not much interested in these kinds of "facts" anyway, the main purpose of presenting "life stories" of great masters in these traditions being to edify and inspire the reader to follow their examples. In that vein, to give just a rough picture by primarily following Tibetan accounts, it is said that Nāgārjuna was prophesied by the Buddha in many sūtras and tantras.[2] Born into a Brahman family at Vidarbha in southeast India, he is reported to have been ordained by Rāhulabhadra and received the name Śrīmān.[3] He undertook a thorough study of all the then available scriptures of the hīnayāna and mahāyāna and defeated the Buddhist monk Śaṃkara and the Saindhava Śrāvakas, who criticized his teachings and the mahāyāna, as well as many non-Buddhists in debate. Eventually, he was invited to the land of the nāgas, taught the dharma there, and obtained the prajñāpāramitā sūtras from Takṣaka, their king. For the rest of his life, he propagated and commented extensively on these texts, thus becoming the founder of the Madhyamaka system. Nāgārjuna spread the teachings of the mahāyāna far and wide and also built many temples and stūpas. He seems to have spent the middle period of his life mostly in the kingdom of Andhra in the eastern part of middle India. There, he was supported by a king of the Sātavāhana dynasty,[4] to whom he wrote his *Suhṛllekha* and *Ratnāvalī*, and who is said to have eventually attained the same siddhi of long life as Nāgārjuna.[5]

In the latter part of his life, he mainly stayed in the neighboring areas of Amarāvatī, Dhānyakaṭaka,[6] Nāgārjunakoṇḍa, and Śrī Parvata, where he engaged in tantric practices and is said to have attained the first bhūmi of a bodhisattva. It so happened that the above Sātavāhana king had a son called Śaktimān, who very much wanted to become king himself. His mother told him that his father could only die once Nāgārjuna was dead, because their powers of long life were connected. She told him to ask Nāgārjuna for his head, since, as a bodhisattva, he could not refuse that request. Śaktimān went to Śrī Parvata and Nāgārjuna granted him his head, but it could not be cut off by any weapons. Nāgārjuna knew that, due to an incident in one of his past lives, in which he had killed an insect with a blade of kuśa grass, the only way to behead him was with such kuśa grass.[7] After Śaktimān had done so, Nāgārjuna's mind went to Sukhāvatī. Śaktimān buried Nāgārjuna's head and body many miles apart, fearing their reunion. It is said that the body and the head have been moving toward each other ever since, and that when they unite Nāgārjuna will live again and promote the benefit of sentient beings. Finally, the *Mahāmeghasūtra* says, he will become the Tathāgata *Jñānākaraphrabha[8] in the worldly realm *Prasannaprabhā. Among his many disciples, the chief one was Āryadeva.[9]

As for the reasons for being named Nāgārjuna, there are three accounts. One says that, once, when he was teaching the dharma in a park, several nāgas rose up around him to form an umbrella, shielding him from the hot sun. This event made him known as the lord of nāgas, to which "arjuna" was added, since he spread the teachings of the mahāyāna as fast as the mythological archer Arjuna[10] could shoot his arrows. The second account says that Nāgārjuna received his name because he subdued the nāgas through his practice of mantra. Thirdly, the Chinese biography by Kumārajīva says that Nāgārjuna received his name because he was born under an arjuna tree and perfected his prajñā through receiving mahāyāna sūtras from a great nāga in the ocean.

What Did Nāgārjuna Write or Not Write?

This is certainly not the place to provide a comprehensive overview of all the many works ascribed to Nāgārjuna that are preserved in Sanskrit, Tibetan, and Chinese, nor to settle the disputes about which of them were actually written by him. In the following, I will mainly focus on references to Nāgārjuna's praises in Indian sources and how the Tibetan tradition describes the significance and interrelations of what it calls Nāgārjuna's three scriptural collections—"the collection of speeches,"[11] "the collection of (Madhyamaka) reasoning,"[12] and "the collection of praises."

Beginning with references to Nāgārjuna's scriptural legacy in general by Indian Buddhist masters, Candrakīrti's (sixth/seventh century)

Madhyamakaśāstrastuti (stanza 10) enumerates only eight works by Nāgārjuna: (1) *Mūlamadhyamakakārikā*, (2) *Yuktiṣaṣṭikā*, (3) *Śūnyatāsaptati*, (4) *Vigrahavyāvartanī*, (5) *Vidalā (Vaidalyaprakaraṇa)*, (6) *Ratnāvalī*, (7) *Sūtrasamucchaya*, and (8) *Saṃstuti* (praises).[13] However, this list does not even include all the texts that Candrakīrti quotes in his own works (see below). Interestingly though, he explicitly refers here to Nāgārjuna's praises in general. Mostly, the Indian tradition agrees with the above list, but many other masters, such as Bhāvaviveka (sixth century), Avalokitavrata (seventh century?), Śāntarakṣita, Haribhadra (both eighth century), Kamalaśīla (740–795), Prajñākaramati (tenth century), Atiśa (982–1054), Maitrīpa (c. 1007–1085), and Sahajavajra (eleventh/twelfth century), refer to and/or quote varying numbers of additional works by Nāgārjuna, such as the *Akutobhayā*,[14] the *Suhṛllekha*, the *Bodhicittavivaraṇa*,[15] the *Mahāyānaviṃśikā*, the *Dharmadhātustava*, the *Niraupamyastava*, the *Lokātītastava*, the *Acintyastava*, the *Paramārthastava*, the *Cittavajrastava*, the **Bodhisaṃbhāraśāstra*,[16] the *Vyavahārasiddhi*,[17] and—among his tantric works—the *Pañcakrama*.

As for Nāgārjuna's authorship of his praises as testified by Indian sources, Atiśa's *Ratnakaraṇḍodghātanāmamadhyamakopadeśa* lists the *Dharmadhātustava*, *Lokātītastava*, *Cittavajrastava*, *Paramārthastava*, **Nirvikalpastava*,[18] and *Acintyastava* as Nāgārjuna's works.[19]

In particular, the *Dharmadhātustava* is quoted and explicitly attributed to Nāgārjuna in Bhāvaviveka's *Madhyamakaratnapradīpa*[20] and Nāropa's (988–1069) *Sekoddeśaṭīkā*.[21] It is also cited in Ratnākaraśānti's (early eleventh century) *Sūtrasamucchayabhāṣya*[22] and Dharmendra's *Tattvasārasaṃgraha*.[23] Atiśa's *Dharmadhātudarśanagīti* incorporates many verses from well-known Indian Buddhist works, among them several by Nāgārjuna, including nineteen (!) verses from the *Dharmadhātustava*.[24]

As for Nāgārjuna's four praises that are referred to as a set called *Catuḥstava*, there is a synoptical commentary on them by Amṛtākara, the *Catuḥstavasamāsārtha*.[25] The general term *Catuḥstava* is explicitly used in Prajñākaramati's *Bodhicāryāvatārapañjikā*.[26] In particular, the text quotes the *Lokātītastava*,[27] *Niraupamyastava*,[28] and *Acintyastava*.[29] The *Bodhicāryāvatārapañjikā* by Vairocanarakṣita (eleventh century) also uses the term *Catuḥstava*, with the quotes stemming from the *Niraupamyastava*.[30] Dharmendra's *Tattvasārasaṃgraha* cites all four praises, some several times.[31]

The *Lokātītastava* is furthermore quoted in Candrakīrti's *Prasannapadā*[32] and *Madhyamakāvatārabhāṣya*,[33] Haribhadra's *Abhisamayālaṃkārāloka*,[34] Jayānanda's (eleventh century) *Madhyamakāvatāraṭīkā*,[35] and Sahajavajra's *Tattvadaśakaṭīkā*.[36] The *Niraupamyastava* is also cited in Candrakīrti's *Prasannapadā*[37] and *Śūnyatāsaptativṛtti*,[38] Atiśa's *Bodhipathapradīpapañjikā*,[39] Jayānanda's *Madhyamakāvatāraṭīkā*,[40] Maitrīpa's *Tattvaratnāvalī*[41] (which explicitly attributes it to Nāgārjuna), and the *Pañcakrama* (attributed in the Tibetan tradition to Nāgārjuna).[42] The *Acintyastava* is found in Bhāvaviveka's *Madhyamakaratnapradīpa*,[43] Śāntarakṣita's *Tattvasiddhi*,[44] Maitrīpa's *Pañcatathāgatamudrāvivaraṇa*,[45] and Sahajavajra's *Tattvadaśakaṭīkā*[46] too. The *Paramārthastava* is quoted in Bhāvaviveka's *Madhyamakaratnapradīpa*[47] and Atiśa's *Bodhipathapradīpapañjikā*.[48] The *Pañcakrama* contains a passage that resembles verse 9 of this praise.[49]

The *Cittavajrastava* is quoted in the *Ādikarmapradīpa*[50] by Anupamavajra (eleventh/twelfth century). The *Kāyatrayastotra* is cited in its entirety in Nāropa's *Sekoddeśaṭīkā*[51] and explicitly attributed to Nāgārjuna in Jñānaśrīmitra's (c. 980–1040) *Sākarasiddhiśāstra*.[52] Vibhūticandra's (twelfth/thirteenth century) *Bodhicaryāvatāratātparyapañjikāviśeṣadyotanīnāma* quotes from the **Nirvikalpastava*, with the stanzas corresponding to the *Prajñāpāramitāstotra*.[53] In addition, several Indian texts quote from a now lost **Nirālambastava* (Tib. dmigs su med par bstod pa; *In Praise of the Nonreferential One*). This title appears in Dharmendra's *Tattvasārasaṃgraha*, which attributes it to Nāgārjuna and cites a verse from it.[54] Atiśa's *Bodhipathapradīpapañjikā* attributes another verse to Nāgārjuna, which ends in "I pay homage to the nonreferential one."[55] The *Pañcakrama* also contains three verses with the same ending.[56]

The Tibetan tradition ascribes about 180 texts in the *Tengyur* on both sūtras and tantras to Nāgārjuna.[57] According to the (later) Tibetan tradition, his works on the sūtras are grouped into three main sets: the collection of speeches, the collection of (Madhyamaka) reasoning, and the collection of praises. In due order, these are often said to comment on the Buddha's three turnings of the wheel of dharma.[58]

The collection of speeches is usually said to include the *Ratnāvalī* (by some placed within the collection of reasoning) and the *Suhṛllekha*. Three further treatises on (worldly) knowledge and ethical conduct attributed to Nāgārjuna may be counted here as well.[59]

The collection of reasoning is said to contain either five or six texts. Everybody seems to agree that the first five are the following:

1) *Mūlamadhyamakakārikā*
2) *Yuktiṣaṣṭikā*
3) *Śūnyatāsaptati*
4) *Vigrahavyāvartanī*
5) *Vaidalyaprakaraṇa*.

If six texts are counted as belonging to this collection, either the *Ratnāvalī* or the *Vyavahārasiddhi* is added (for details, see below).

In the collection of praises, the Tibetan *Tengyur* attributes the following eighteen works to Nāgārjuna:

Dharmadhātustava (Tib. chos dbyings bstod pa)
Niraupamyastava (dpe med par bstod pa)
Lokātītastava ('jig rten las 'das pa'i bstod pa)
Cittavajrastava (sems kyi rdo rje'i bstod pa)
Paramārthastava (don dam par bstod pa)
Kāyatrayastotra (sku gsum la bstod pa)
Sattvārādhanastava (sems can la mgu bar bya ba'i bstod pa)
Prajñāpāramitāstotra (shes rab kyi pha rol tu phyin pa'i bstod pa)[60]
Acintyastava (bsam gyis mi khyab bar bstod pa)
Stutyatītastava (bstod pa las 'das par bstod pa)
Niruttarastava (bla na med pa'i bstod pa)
Āryabhāṭṭarakamañjuśrīparamārthastuti ('phags pa rje btsun 'jam dpal gyi don dam pa'i bstod pa)[61]
Āryamañjuśrībhāṭṭarakakaruṇāstotra (rje btsun 'phags pa 'jam dpal gyi snying rje la bstod pa)
Aṣṭamahāsthānacaityastotra (gnas chen po brgyad kyi mchod rten la bstod pa)
Aṣṭamahāsthānacaityastotra (gnas chen po brgyad kyi mchod rten la bstod pa)[62]
Dvādaśakāranayastotra (mdzad pa bcu gnyis kyi tshul la bstod pa)
Vandanāstotra (phyag 'tshal ba'i bstod pa)
Narakoddharastava (dmyal ba nas 'don pa'i bstod pa)[63]

The question regarding which of all these texts were actually written by Nāgārjuna or not has already received some attention in Tibet and is still discussed extensively by many modern scholars, naturally with no unanimous answers.[64] In any case, there is no doubt that Nāgārjuna—even if only his generally accepted works are taken into account—displays a wide range of resourceful ways to express the Buddhist teachings in their entirety. Thus, as much as some people might like to do so, it is impossible to restrict his approach solely to negative or deconstructive rhetoric, as typically found in his classical Madhyamaka works. Even these texts sometimes "deviate" from such a style, let alone some of his other texts, in which he uses affirmative terminologies—even with regard to the ultimate—and notions that are anything but typical Madhyamaka. The major examples for Nāgārjuna's positive descriptions of the nature of phenomena, the luminous nature of mind, the notion of "fundamental change of state," and so on that are found in his praises will be given below,[65] so a few further sources shall suffice here. For example, the *Mūlamadhyamakakārikā* speaks about the characteristics of ultimate reality. Providing the characteristics—even if they are phrased negatively—of anything, let alone of something like the ultimate, is sure enough not what Nāgārjuna does otherwise in this text, usually concluding that everything is neither this nor that, empty, and lacking any nature. In the following verse, most of the characteristics of ultimate reality are phrased in the negative, but the first one does point out that the subsiding of all discursive mental activity and its reference points still is and must be one's own personally experienced insight.

Not known through something other, peaceful,
Not referential through any reference points,
Without conceptions, and without distinctions:
These are the characteristics of true reality.[66]

Nāgārjuna's *Yuktiṣaṣṭikā* says that this is the only state that is true and reliable:

The victors have declared
That nirvāṇa alone is real,
So which wise one would think
That the rest is not delusive?[67]

His *Bodhicittavivaraṇa* explicitly states this to be the supreme state of mind, which is not just indifferent or neutral, but blissful and irreversible:

The mind is arrayed through latent tendencies.
Freedom from latent tendencies is bliss.

This blissful mind is peacefulness.
A peaceful mind will not be ignorant.
Not to be ignorant is the realization of true reality.
The realization of true reality is the attainment of liberation.

This is also explained
As suchness, the true end,
Signlessness, the ultimate,
The supreme bodhicitta, and emptiness.
. . .
This precious mind without afflictions
Is the single supreme gem.
It cannot be harmed or snatched away
By robbers like afflictions and māras.[68]

Similar to the *Dharmadhātustava*, the *Mahāyānaviṃśikā* declares final enlightenment—nonabiding nirvāṇa—to be the revelation of stainless luminosity that is ever-present and unchanging throughout ground, path, and fruition:

> Those who see dependent origination
> To be the true actuality
> Thus see the world as empty,
> Free from beginning, middle, and end.
>
> Through this, they see that, for themselves,
> There is neither saṃsāra nor nirvāṇa—
> Stainless changeless luminosity
> Throughout beginning, middle, and end.[69]

The **Bodhisaṃbhāraśāstra* says that such enlightenment entails limitless qualities:

> The kāyas of a Buddha have infinite qualities.
> The two accumulations for enlightenment are their root.
> Therefore, the accumulations for enlightenment
> Do not have any limit either.[70]

The *Sūtrasamucchaya* quotes several sūtras that assert the existence of the dharmadhātu or the Tathāgata heart as permanent, immutable, peaceful, and eternal.

Nāgārjuna also says a few other things that a radical Mādhyamika is not supposed to say, such as considering outer objects as being just aspects of mind (even using some of the same arguments and examples as the Yogācāras), and accepting such teachings as a valid step on the path. The *Bodhicittavivaraṇa* states:

> With regard to a single external referent,
> Different consciousnesses operate.
> Just that which is a pleasant form [for some]
> Is something else for others.
>
> With regard to a single female form,
> A mendicant, a passionate person, and a dog
> Entertain the three different thoughts
> Of a corpse, an object of desire, and a morsel.
>
> . . .

As the entities of apprehender and apprehended,
The appearances of consciousness
Do not exist as outer objects
That are different from consciousness.

Therefore, in the sense of having the nature of entities,
In all cases, outer objects do not exist.
It is these distinct appearances of consciousness
That appear as the aspects of forms.

Due to mental delusion,
People see illusions, mirages,
Cities of gandharvas and so on—
Forms and such appear just like that.

The teachings on the aggregates, constituents, and so on
Are for the purpose of stopping the clinging to a self.
By settling in mere mind,
The greatly blessed ones let go of them too.[71]

His *Mahāyānaviṃśikā* says:

All of this is merely mind,
Coming about like an illusion.
Through this, good and bad actions,
As well as good and bad rebirths [occur].

Through the wheel of mind stopping,
All phenomena come to a standstill.
Therefore, the nature of phenomena is identityless.
Hence, the nature of phenomena is completely pure.[72]

The *Bodhicittavivaraṇa* discusses the ālaya-consciousness and denies that it is really existent, but does not dismiss it altogether, even affirming its illusory function in saṃsāra:

Likewise, the ālaya-consciousness
Is not real but appears as if it were real.
When it moves to and fro,
It retains the [three] existences.[73]

As for the details of the path of bodhisattvas, such as proper ethical conduct, bodhicitta, the pāramitās, and the ten bhūmis, Nāgārjuna's *Ratnāvalī*, *Suhṛllekha*, *Bodhicittavivaraṇa*, and **Bodhisaṃbhāraśāstra* provide extensive explanations. The *Ratnāvalī* also discusses the thirty-two major marks of a Buddha, including their causes, at length. As will be seen below, all of these elements are also contained in succinct form in the *Dharmadhātustava*.

To summarize, Christian Lindtner says in his *Nāgārjuniana*:

> In my view the decisive reason for the said variety of Nāgārjuna's writings is to be sought in the author's desire, as a Buddhist, to address himself to various audiences, at various levels and from various angles. This motive would of course be quite consistent with the mahāyāna ideal of *upāyakauśalya* [skill in means] (cf. BS 17). Thus MK [*Mūlamadhyamakakārikā*], ŚS [*Śūnyatāsaptati*] and VV [*Vigrahavyāvartanī*] were intended to be studied by philosophically minded monks. VP [*Vaidalyaprakaraṇa*] was written as a challenge to Naiyāyikas. YṢ [*Yuktiṣaṣṭikā*], VS [*Vyavahārasiddhi*] and PK [*Pratītyasamutpādahṛdayakārikā*] are contributions to Buddhist exegesis. CS [*Catuḥstava*] is a document confessing its author's personal faith in the Buddha's deśanā, while SS [*Sūtrasamucchaya*], BV [*Bodhicittavivaraṇa*], BS [**Bodhisaṃbhāraśāstra*], SL [*Suhṛllekha*] and RĀ [*Ratnāvalī*] on the whole addressed themselves to a wider Buddhist audience, monks as well as laymen.
>
> I will therefore take it for granted that Nāgārjuna never changed his fundamental outlook essentially, and, accordingly, look upon his writings as expressions of an underlying unity of thought conceived before he made his début in writing.[74]

The underlying unity of Nāgārjuna's outlook is also highlighted by the fact that a considerable number of Indian Mādhyamikas—such as Bhāvaviveka, Candrakīrti, Haribhadra, Śāntarakṣita, Prajñākaramati, Atiśa, Jayānanda, Maitrīpa, and Sahajavajra—frequently refer to and quote several of his praises and other texts (and not only the passages in these that speak about emptiness). In particular, none of these masters obviously saw any fundamental incompatibility between the texts in the collection of reasoning and the collection of praises.[75]

On Nāgārjuna's influence on later Buddhism, especially Madhyamaka, Lindtner says:

> I do not think that it is possible to name one single later Mādhyamika in India—Prāsaṅgika or Svātantrika—who does not expressly acknowledge, or at least indicate (through allusions, quotations etc.) Nāgārjuna as his authority par excellence, second only to Śākyamuni himself, of course.[76]

It goes without saying that, if possible at all, Nāgārjuna's significance as the towering figure of mahāyāna Buddhism—being called a "second Buddha"—was even greater throughout the Tibetan tradition.

Various Views on Nāgārjuna's Scriptural Legacy and Its Scope

In the Indian Buddhist tradition, apart from very frequent references to and quotations from Nāgārjuna's works, actual overviews or classifications of them appear to be almost nonexistent. In addition to the abovementioned short list in Candrakīrti's *Madhyamakaśāstrastuti* (the five texts of the collection of reasoning, the *Ratnāvalī*, the *Sūtrasamucchaya*, and the praises), his *Yuktiṣaṣṭikāvṛtti* gives a brief account of the interrelation between Nāgārjuna's four major Madhyamaka texts. Candrakīrti brings up the question why Nāgārjuna does not praise the Buddha in the *Śūnyatāsaptati* and the *Vigrahavyāvartanī* but does here in the *Yuktiṣaṣṭikā* (just as in his *Mūlamadhyamakakārikā*). Candrakīrti answers by saying that the *Vigrahavyāvartanī* and the *Śūnyatāsaptati* are elaborations on *Mūlamadhyamakakārikā* I.3 and VII.34, respectively, in order to answer objections to these verses. Since these two texts thus have no independent line of teaching, they contain no extra praise either. The *Yuktiṣaṣṭikā*, however, just as the *Mūlamadhyamakakārikā*, was composed by way of mainly analyzing dependent origination. Therefore, it is not something like an elaboration on the *Mūlamadhyamakakārikā*.[77]

Atiśa's *Ratnakaraṇḍodghātanāmamadhyamakopadeśa*[78] gives the most extensive Indian layout of Nāgārjuna's works, explicitly listing forty-five texts and indicating an even greater number by repeatedly saying "and so on." Atiśa explains that, for the sake of those who are at the lowest level of the bodhisattva's stage of engagement through aspiration, Nāgārjuna composed the greater and lesser texts on producing incense (P5808, 5809) and so on. For physicians, he wrote the *Yogaśataka* (P5795) and others. For those who have entered the mahāyāna, he composed the *Bodhicittotpādavidhi* (P5361/5405), **Bodhisattvāvatāraprakāśa*, *Sūtrasamucchaya*, and so on. In addition, he wrote the *Mūlamadhyamakakārikā* and its elaborations, the *Vigrahavyāvartanī* and *Śūnyatāsaptati*. The branches of these are said to be the *Yuktiṣaṣṭikā*,

Mahāyānaviṃśikā, Bhāvasaṃkrānti (P5472), *Bhāvanākrama, Akṣaraśataka* (P5234), *Vaidalyaprakaraṇa, Bodhicittavivaraṇa, Dharmadhātustava, Paramārthastava, Prajñāpāramitāstotra* (called **Nirvikalpastava*), *Acintyastava, Lokātītastava, Cittavajrastava, Śālistambasūtraṭīkā* (P5486), and the *Pratītyasamutpādahṛdayakārikā* with its commentary. For the sake of those with sharpest faculties who serve as the vessels for the secret mantra of the mahāyāna, Nāgārjuna composed texts on the meaning of the *Guhyasamājatantra*, that is, the **Guhyasamājamaṇḍalābhiṣekavidhi, Guhyasamājamaṇḍalavidhi* (P2663), *Piṇḍīkṛtasādhana* (P2661), *Sūtramelāpaka* (P2662), and *Pañcakrama* (P2667). He is also said to have written commentaries on the *Catuḥpīṭatantra* and the *Mañjuśrīnāmasaṃgīti* as well as many sādhanas.[79] Interestingly, Atiśa does not mention the *Suhṛllekha* and *Rājaparikathānāmaratnāvalī* here, but his *Bodhipathapradīpapañjikā* lists the latter.[80]

In contrast to the Indian tradition, Tibetan works offer a rich variety of accounts and classifications of Nāgārjuna's scriptural legacy. In the introduction to his commentary on the *Mūlamadhyamakakārikā*, the early Tibetan Mādhyamika Majawa Jangchub Dsöndrü[81] (died c. 1185) gives an interesting survey:

> In general, as for the treatises composed by this master, there are (1) those that elucidate the causal pāramitāyāna, (2) those that elucidate the fruitional vajrayāna, and (3) the one that teaches these two to be equivalent.
>
> 1) The first include three [types]. There are (a) those that mainly teach the view: the sixfold collection of reasoning; (b) those that mainly teach conduct: the **Bodhisaṃbhāra* (the extensive one), the *Sūtrasamucchaya* (the medium one), and the *Suhṛllekha* (the brief one); and (c) [the one that teaches] view and conduct equally, the *Rājaparikathānāmaratnāvalī*.
>
> (a) As for the first one being definitely sixfold, the focus of the view or prajñā is to unmistakenly determine the nature of all phenomena—emptiness—or the two realities. There are the two main texts, which are like the body and teach all sections of this topic in a complete way, and the four treatises that are the branches or elaborations presented in order to eliminate wrong ideas only about [certain] parts of said topic. As for the first [of these] being definitely two, some explain that the *Mūlamadhyamakakārikā* teaches dependent origination as being free from the eight extremes of reference points, such as arising and ceasing, while the *Yuktiṣaṣṭikā* teaches that it

is free from the four extremes of reference points, that is, the pair of arising and ceasing and the pair of existence and nonexistence. However, the explanation that they, in due order, teach the nature [of phenomena]—emptiness—in a negating way through negative determination and teach this nature—emptiness—in an affirmative way through positive determination on a merely conventional level appears to penetrate [the purport of] these texts. As for the treatises that are the branches being definitely four, the *Vigrahavyāvartanī* is an elaboration to eliminate [the objection that Nāgārjuna's] own words contradict his refutation of arising from something other in [the *Mūlamadhyamakakārikā*'s [first chapter on] examining conditions. . . . The *Śūnyatāsaptati* is taught to refute that the characteristics of conditioned phenomena—arising, abiding, and ceasing—in [the *Mūlamadhyamakakārikā*'s seventh chapter on] examining conditioned phenomena are established by a nature of their own. . . . The *Vaidalyaprakaraṇa* [answers] . . . the objection, "If entities are without nature, this is contradictory to [such] a nature being established through valid cognition" . . . through examining [the notion of] valid cognition itself. The *Vyavahārasiddhi* [answers] . . . the objection, "If entities are without nature, then, just like the horns of a rabbit, presentations of what is conventional are not justified" through saying that dependent origination is a suitable corrective for [an absolutized understanding of] the lack of nature . . . Therefore, this manner [of identifying the main and elaborating texts within the collection of reasoning] dispenses with all the statements of earlier [masters, such as] some arriving at six by adding the *Ratnāvalī* [and leaving out the *Vyavahārasiddhi*]; [some] saying that it is called a "collection or group of reasoning," but that there is no definitive number of six [texts in it]; and [others] stating that the treatises that [make up] the collection of reasoning, which teaches the lack of nature, are [only] five. This said manner is also clearly stated in [Candrakīrti's] commentary on the *Yuktiṣaṣṭikā*. For the reason that [Nāgārjuna] pays homage [to the Buddha] in [the beginning of] this text but not in the others such as the *Vigrahavyāvartanī*, the *Yuktiṣaṣṭikā* is a main text, just like the *Mūlamadhyamakakārikā*, while the others are elaborating treatises . . . [82]

(2) Those [texts] that elucidate the vajrayāna are the *Pañcakrama* and so forth.

> (3) The one that teaches these two [pāramitāyāna and vajrayāna] to be equivalent is the *Bodhicittavivaraṇa*, since it is a commentary on the words of the *Guhyasamāja* root tantra (in which Vairocana calls the ultimate "the greatness of bodhicitta"), commenting on the characteristics [of bodhicitta].[83]

Particularly noteworthy in Majawa's classification of Nāgārjuna's works is the complete absence of his praises.

The Third Karmapa, Rangjung Dorje's (1284–1339) commentary on the *Dharmadhātustava* says the following about the three collections of Nāgārjuna's texts on the sūtras:

> From among those [texts], in particular, he composed three types of commentaries on the collection of the sūtras. The [first type] consists of the collection of speeches, which is composed in such a way that the accomplishment of mundane and supramundane purposes and the definite distinction between what is to be relinquished and what is to be adopted are noncontradictory in terms of the presentations of the labels of the mahāyāna and the hīnayāna. . . .[84]

> You may wonder, "Well, how could these words here [in verse 2 of the *Dharmadhātustava*] that 'the fruition of nirvāṇa—dharmakāya—[becomes manifest] through the cause of saṃsāra having become pure' be appropriate? Aren't these two mutually exclusive in the sense of not coexisting? Moreover, how could it be appropriate in this [context] that saṃsāra and nirvāṇa exist? This contradicts [Nāgārjuna's] statement that all phenomena are without nature, which he makes in [his] collection of reasoning, refuting [any such nature] through enumerating many [reasonings]." What is to be explained here is as follows. . . .[85]

> Therefore, once all conceptions of apprehender and apprehended within [primary] minds and mental factors have become pure and are at peace, what is called "buddha wisdom" is made to appear. The *Acintyastava* says:

> What is dependent origination
> Is precisely what you maintain as emptiness.

Also the genuine dharma is like that
And even the Tathāgata is the same.

It is also held to be true reality, the ultimate,
Suchness, and the elementary substance.
It is true and undeceiving.
Through realizing it, [one] is called a Buddha.[86]

Therefore, due to [the stained dharmadhātu as] the cause of saṃsāra having become pure, there is no contradiction in referring to it with the term "nirvāṇa." In the collection of reasoning, [Nāgārjuna] negates the clinging to characteristics, but he does definitely not refute the teachings on the way of being of the Buddha and the dharma, wisdom, great compassion, or the wonderful enlightened activity of the Buddhas. Nevertheless, the blinded wisdom eyes of ordinary beings conceive of that as something else. . . . This [text] here occasions the teaching on the very own essence of the purity of consciousness that is stained by apprehender and apprehended [in just an adventitious way].[87]

Butön Rinchen Drub's (1290–1364) *History of Buddhism* first discusses Nāgārjuna's texts of the collection of reasoning:

As for the commentaries on the intention of the middle [cycle of] the Buddha's words, there are two [types]: those that elucidate the aspect of the view and those that elucidate the aspect of conduct. First, . . . those [works] that teach on the meaning of what the sūtras explicitly discuss (or the essential meaning) are the six [texts] of the collection of reasoning. [Among] these six, it is said that the *Śūnyatāsaptati* teaches that all phenomena are natural emptiness, dependent origination free from [all] extremes of reference points. The *Prajñānāmamūlamadhyamakakārikā* refutes what is other than that, that is, a reality of arising and so on. These two are the main or principal [works]. The *Yuktiṣaṣṭikā* proves that [emptiness] through reasoning. The *Vigrahavyāvartanī* removes the flaws that others [adduce] when disputing that [emptiness]. The *Vaidalyaprakaraṇa* teaches the manner of disputing with others, that is, the dialecticians. The *Vyavahārasiddhi* teaches that, despite [phenomena's] ultimate lack of a nature, on the level of seeming [reality], the conventions of the world are justified and established.[88]

Later in his text, Butön lists a great number of major and minor works by Nāgārjuna. He does not go into any details with regard to the praises but explicitly considers them to be Madhyamaka works:

> As for his treatises, in the field of knowledge that consists of the inner [Buddhist teachings], [among] those that mainly teach on the view, the cycle of Madhyamaka praises teaches the middle free from extremes through scriptures, while the collection of reasoning teaches it through reasoning. [Among] those that mainly teach on conduct, the *Sūtrasamucchaya* teaches this through scriptures, while the **Mahāyānavyutpanna*[89] teaches it through reasoning. The *Svapnacintāmaṇiparikathā* awakens the disposition of the śrāvakas. The *Suhṛllekha* mainly teaches on the conduct of householders, while the **Bodhisaṃbhāra* mainly teaches on the conduct of the ordained. As for the section of the tantras, the **Tantrasamucchaya* is a summary of view and conduct. The *Bodhicittavivaraṇa* determines the view. The *Guhyasamājasādhana*, the *Piṇḍīkṛtasādhana*, the *Sūtramelāpaka*, and the [*Guhyasamāja*]*maṇḍalavidhi* in twenty verses teach on the generation stage. The *Pañcakrama* and so on teach on the completion stage . . . The *Ratnāvalī* teaches the union of view and conduct of the mahāyāna for kings . . .[90]

The commentary on the *Dharmadhātustava* by the Jonang scholar Nyagpowa Sönam Sangbo[91] (1341–1433), a disciple of Dölpopa Sherab Gyaltsen[92] (1292–1361), briefly states:

> The collection of speeches [is] for unraveling the vast meanings
> of the variety of dharmas,
> The collection of reasoning for unraveling the profound meaning
> of the intention of the middle [turning of the wheel of dharma],
> And the collection of praises for unraveling the profound meaning
> of the intention of the final [turning of the wheel of dharma].[93]

The Blue Annals by Gö Lotsāwa (1392–1481) mentions, mostly without author, several times the collection of reasoning[94] and many of Nāgārjuna's other texts on sūtras and tantras, with the notable absence of the *Bodhicittavivaraṇa*, the *Vyavahārasiddhi*, the *Mahāyānaviṃśikā*, the **Bodhisaṃbhāra*, and almost all the praises. Gö Lotsāwa's text begins with the *Kāyatrayastotra* in both Sanskrit and Tibetan but gives neither its title nor author. Also without author, it mentions the *Cittavajrastava* and the *Dharmadhātustava* once each, the latter when reporting that the Third Karmapa wrote a commentary on it.

Śākya Chogden's[95] (1428–1507) *The Origin of Madhyamaka* says the following about Nāgārjuna's three cycles of teaching:

> It is explained that the protector Nāgārjuna uttered his lion's roar three times on this earth. It is well known that Nāgārjuna first composed the treatises of the collection of speeches, which mainly explain the aspect of vast conduct. Next, he composed the treatises of the collection of reasoning, which mainly explain the dharma of the profound view—emptiness in terms of cutting through superimpositions by studying and reflecting. Finally, he composed the *Bodhicittavivaraṇa*, *Cittavajrastava* and so on, which mainly explain emptiness as experienced through meditation.[96]

The same author's *Distinction between the Two Traditions of the Great Charioteers* points to the collections of reasoning and praises being complementary, with the first serving to cut through all reference points and the latter speaking about making this a living experience.[97]

Śākya Chogden's contemporary, Gorampa Sönam Senge[98] (1429–1489), composed a general outline of Madhyamaka, called *Illuminating the Definitive Meaning*, which quotes and closely follows Majawa's above presentation in many respects but also speaks about Nāgārjuna's praises in detail. Unlike most other sources mentioned, it provides a clear and comprehensive explanation of the three collections of speeches, reasoning, and praises.

> In general, this master has composed many treatises that elucidate all five fields of knowledge. From among these, the topic at hand is the knowledge of the inner reality [that is, Buddhism]. [Nāgārjuna] taught both its view and conduct by way of scripture and by way of reasoning. The first [approach is found in his] *Sūtrasamucchaya* and the second in the following three collections:
> 1) the collection of reasoning
> 2) the collection of praises
> 3) the collection of speeches.
>
> 1) The spiritual friend Majawa holds, "..."[99] This needs a bit of scrutiny. [Candrakīrti's] commentary on the *Yuktiṣaṣṭikā* speaks about the ways in which the *Vigrahavyāvartanī* and the *Śūnyatāsaptati* elaborate [on the *Mūlamadhyamakakārikā*], but there appears no mentioning of a way in which the other [texts] are elaborations.

Also, as for the *Vyavahārasiddhi*, it was not translated into Tibetan, and master Candrakīrti's *Prasannapadā*, when speaking about the way of looking at the scriptural tradition of master Nāgārjuna, mentions the other five but not this [text]. Therefore, it appears that it was not counted within the collection of reasoning in India either. Some later [masters] say that it is not justified to arrive at six [texts in this collection by adding] the *Ratnāvalī*, since it belongs to the collection of speeches.

Therefore, [the question of what the collection of reasoning contains] is to be treated as follows. [It consists of] three [types of texts]: (a) those that negate the objects of negation imputed by others, (b) those that present [Nāgārjuna's] own system, the body of Madhyamaka, and (c) those that remove objections by way of elaborating on that.

a) The first is the *Vaidalyaprakaraṇa* for the following reasons. . . . It says that it refutes the philosophical systems of opponents in order to relinquish their pride, but not that it elaborates on [Nāgārjuna's] own texts. In the text itself, there only appears a refutation of the Naiyāyikas' sixteen terms of dialectics and their meanings, but nothing else.

b) The second [type] includes both the *Mūlamadhyamakakārikā* and the *Yuktiṣaṣṭikā*. As for their difference, there are three [explanations]. Some explain that the *Mūlamadhyamakakārikā* teaches dependent origination as being free from the eight extremes of reference points, such as arising and ceasing, while the *Yuktiṣaṣṭikā* teaches that it is free from the four extremes of reference points, that is, the pair of arising and ceasing and the pair of existence and nonexistence. Others say that [the former] is a refutation of our own [Buddhist] factions and other factions in common, while [the latter] is a refutation of our own factions in particular. Yet others say that they respectively teach the nature [of phenomena]—emptiness—in a negating way through negative determination and teach this nature—emptiness—in an affirmative way through positive determination on a merely conventional level. Majawa says that this latter [position] appears to penetrate [the meanings of] the texts. As for the meaning of "by way of negative determination or positive determination," the intention behind this statement was that the former emphasizes the negation of a nature, while the latter emphasizes, through examples such as illusions and mirages, the teaching that [there are] appearances despite this lack of nature. c) The third [type] includes two [texts], the *Vigrahavyāvartanī* and the *Śūnyatāsaptati* . . .[100]

2) The collection of praises is threefold: (a) praises to the ground, (b) praises to the path, and (c) praises to the fruition.

a) The praises to the ground include the *Cittavajrastava* (P2013), a praise to [mind's] lucidity, that is, the bearer of the nature [of phenomena, the dharmadhātu]. . . . This is a praise to mind as such, which is the ground of everything in saṃsāra and nirvāṇa. The *Dharmadhātustava* (P2010) is a praise to the dhātu, which is the nature of phenomena. [Its first verse] . . . eliminates the qualm of whether the dharmadhātu that is not liberated from adventitious stains is suitable as an object of praise, while the following is a praise to the dharmadhātu that [only] becomes the cause of saṃsāra, if it is not seized through [the proper] means.

b) The praises to the path include the *Sattvārādhanastava* (P2017), which is a praise to great compassion, the means. [Its colophon informs that] it is what the Bhagavat said to the sixteen great śrāvakas in the scripture called *Bodhisattvapiṭaka[sūtra]*.[101] [Nāgārjuna] extracted it from there and then inserted it [in the form of these verses] into the collection of praises. The *Prajñāpāramitāstotra* (P2018) is a praise to prajñā, the mother of the four kinds of noble ones. Ngog Lotsāwa used that very same expression for it, while Nagtso [Lotsāwa] referred to it by the expression "In Praise of Nonconceptuality" (*rnam par mi rtog pa'i bstod pa*).

c) The praises to the fruition include the *Kāyatrayastotra* (P2015), which is a praise to each one of the three kāyas separately. The praises that eulogize by way of teaching the view's own essence without distinguishing between the three kāyas are the *Paramārthastava* (P2014), the *Niraupamyastava* (P2011), the *Acintyastava* (P2019), the *Lokātītastava* (P2012), the *Stutyatītastava* (P2020), and the *Niruttarastava* (P2021). Some appear to add here also the two *Aṣṭamahāsthānacaityastotras* (P2024 and P2025) and the two praises to Mañjuśrī (P2022 and P2023).

3) The collection of speeches includes both the *Rājaparikathā-nāmaratnāvalī* and the *Suhṛllekha*.[102]

The History of the Dharma by the Karma Kagyü master Pawo Tsugla Trengwa[103] (1504–1566) mostly follows Butön's outline, without any mention of the praises:

> The *Śalistambakasūtraṭīkā* instructs on the teachings of the Buddha in general. The collection of praises teaches on the Madhyamaka that is the fruition, while the collection of reasoning teaches on the Madhyamaka that is the path. The *Śikṣasamucchaya* teaches on conduct. The **Mahāyānavyutpanna* is a compendium of the sūtras. The *Svapnacintāmaṇiparikathā* encourages the śrāvakas [to enter] into the mahāyāna. The *Suhṛllekha* is for householders, while the *Ratnāvalī* is for [everybody] in common. The **Tantrasamucchaya* teaches on the view and conduct of mantra. The *Bodhicittavivaraṇa* teaches on its view. The *Piṇḍīkṛtasādhana*, the *Sūtramelāpaka*, and the [*Guhyasamāja*]*maṇḍalavidhi* in twenty verses teach on the generation stage. The *Pañcakrama* and so on teach on the completion stage . . .[104]

All that Tāranātha (1575–1635) says about Nāgārjuna's texts in his *History of Buddhism in India* is that he composed five fundamental treatises to silence the contesting śrāvakas who believed in external reality. As for the *Kāyatrayastotra*, Tāranātha takes Nāgāhvaya (meaning "the one called Nāga," which is exactly how Nāgārjuna is referred to in the above prophecy in the *Laṅkāvatārasūtra*) to be a distinct person and attributes this praise to him.[105]

Based on the *Mahābherīsūtra*, the introduction to the mahāyāna in Chapter Ten of the *Exposition of Philosophical Systems*[106] by the Gelugpa scholar Jamyang Shéba[107] (1648–1721) speaks of three proclamations of the dharma by Nāgārjuna. First, he is said to have spread the teachings according to the *Mahābherīsūtra*. Secondly, he recovered the prajñāpāramitā sūtras, taught on the sūtras discussing emptiness, and composed the fivefold collection of reasoning, thus founding the Madhyamaka system. Thirdly, he composed the *Ratnāvalī* and, upon his return to South India, brought with him the *Mahābherīsūtra*, the *Śrīmālādevīsūtra*, the *Tathāgatagarbhasūtra*, and the *Sarvabuddhaviṣayāvatārajñānālokālaṃkārasūtra*. He mainly taught the *Mahābherīsūtra* and also wrote the *Dharmadhātustava*.[108] Jamyang Shéba concludes by stating the standard Gelugpa position on [Nāgārjuna's] third cycle of teachings, in particular the *Dharmadhātustava*:

> Here, I declare that the *Dharmadhātustava* conforms to the style of teaching in the *Uttaratantra*[109] and the *Dhāraṇīśvararājaparipṛcchā-sūtra*. These [texts say that] all sentient beings have the basic element of becoming enlightened, present this [element] as emptiness, and establish that there is a single yāna ultimately. Therefore, they are in accord with the middle [turning of the] wheel [of dharma], but since they take the Buddha to be permanent in terms of continuity and to not have passed into nirvāṇa in terms of the definitive meaning, [Nāgārjuna's] third proclamation of the dharma is taken to be distinct from his second.

Chapter Twelve of Jamyang Shéba's work—which treats the Prāsaṅgika system—says that the treatises on which these Mādhyamikas rely start with Nāgārjuna's works, as they are listed in Candrakīrti's *Prasannapadā*. Among Nāgārjuna's praises that are directed toward the ultimate, Jamyang Shéba explicitly lists the *Dharmadhātustava*, *Lokātītastava*, *Kāyatrayastotra*, *Niruttarastava*, *Stutyatītastava*, *Acintyastava*, and *Cittavajrastava* (the words "and so on" at the end of this list seem to indicate that there are more praises by Nāgārjuna).[110]

Except for the basic description of the collection of reasoning and Gorampa's above presentation of all three collections, there are no clear—let alone unequivocal—statements in the above sources as to which texts exactly make up Nāgārjuna's three scriptural collections. This situation is confirmed in the *Presentation of Philosophical Systems*[111] by Jamyang Shéba's main disciple, Janggya Rölpé Dorje (1717–1786), despite the latter relying on the former's presentation:

> It is explained that this great master uttered the great proclamation of the dharma three times. [However,] a clear explanation of what these three great proclamations are neither appears in the early scriptural tradition nor in the words of Lord [Tsongkhapa] and his spiritual heirs. Some scholars of other factions explain that his first proclamation of the dharma refers to his defeating some groups of the śrāvakas, such as the monk Śaṃkara. The second proclamation of the dharma refers to his composing of the treatises that teach on profound emptiness, such as the collection of Madhyamaka reasoning. The third proclamation of the dharma refers to his composing [works] that are based on the *Mahābherīsūtra* and others, such as the *Dharmadhātustava*. These teach that the permanent Tathāgata heart—the basic element, the dharmadhātu—pervades all sentient beings. This appears indeed to be based on several passages in the

> *Mahābherīsūtra* and the *Mahāmeghasūtra*. The truly venerable Jamyang Shéba Dorje takes this manner [of presentation] to be a justified position. He explains that [Nāgārjuna's] latter two proclamations of the dharma accord in that their subject is the middle [cycle of] the Buddha's words. However, the third proclamation of the dharma teaches extensively on the way in which the Buddha is permanent in terms of continuity and, in terms of the definitive meaning, did not pass into nirvāṇa. Therefore, it is taken to be a [proclamation] that is distinct from the second proclamation of the dharma.[112]

As far as the collection of praises is concerned, the explanation in *The Treasury of Knowledge* by Jamgön Kongtrul Lodrö Tayé (1813–1899) almost literally follows Gorampa's presentation but omits the *Stutyatītastava* and the *Niruttarastava*:

> As for identifying the three collections, most Tibetans maintain the following. The collection of speeches contains two [texts]: the *Suhṛllekha* (delivered as a message to a king from far away) and the *Ratnāvalī* (given as an actual speech [before a king]).
>
> As for the collection of reasoning, four [texts]—the *Mūlamadhyamakakārikā*, the *Yuktiṣaṣṭikā*, the *Śūnyatāsaptati*, and the *Vigrahavyāvartanī*—represent the collection of reasoning that refutes anything to be proven, that is, all extremes of reference points. The fifth—the *Vaidalyaprakaraṇa*—refutes the means to prove such, that is, dialectic reasoning.
>
> The collection of praises contains two that pertain to the phase of the ground: the praise to the bearer of the nature [of phenomena, the dharmadhātu,][113] as being [mind's] lucidity and [the praise to that nature itself,] the *Dharmadhātustava*. It also contains two praises that pertain to the phase of the path: the one to the means, great compassion, and the one to prajñā, the mother of the four kinds of noble ones.[114] [The praises] that pertain to the time of the fruition include the praise to each one of the three kāyas separately[115] and the praises by way of the view's own essence, without distinguishing between them, that is, the *Paramārthastava*, the *Niraupamyastava*, the *Acintyastava*, the *Lokātītastava*.

> Candra[kīrti]'s *Prasannapadā* also [lists the same five texts of the collection of reasoning and adds] "*Parikathāratnāvalī* and *Saṃstuti*."[116] The latter being elaborations, this means that the five [texts in] the collection of reasoning are explicitly enumerated [in his text too]. Therefore, there is no great disagreement [between Candrakīrti and what was presented above]. Earlier [Tibetan masters], such as Ku Lotsāwa [Dode Bar],[117] assert a sixfold collection of reasoning by adding the *Vyavahārasiddhi* to the [above] fivefold collection of reasoning. The precious Lord [Tsongkhapa] and others [ask why] it is not enumerated in the *Prasannapadā*, if there is such a text. Also, it would be reasonable for it to be quoted by the direct disciples of noble [Nāgārjuna], but it is not quoted anywhere.[118] Therefore, they say that the collection of reasoning is sixfold by adding the *Ratnāvalī*.
>
> As for this [enumeration], the *Mūlamadhyamakakārikā* teaches in detail through a great number of reasonings that all phenomena are determined to be emptiness, while not teaching on the aspect of means. The*Yuktiṣaṣṭikā* presents the main body of Madhyamaka, and also the other three texts [in this collection] teach nothing but emptiness. The *Ratnāvalī* teaches in detail on the two kinds of identitylessness and also instructs on the aspect of means as is appropriate. Therefore, the *Mūlamadhyamakakārikā*, the*Yuktiṣaṣṭikā*, and the *Ratnāvalī* represent the treatises that are the fully complete main body [of these teachings], while the other three are like branches that elaborate on the *Mūlamadhyamakakārikā*.[119]

In the introduction to his commentary on the *Dharmadhātustava*, the Sakya master Lodrö Gyatso[120] (born nineteenth century) says:

> As for the words of noble Nāgārjuna, there is the explanation that the collection of speeches comments on the intention of the first [cycle of the Buddha's] words, the collection of reasoning comments on the middle [cycle of the Buddha's] words, and the collection of praises comments on the final [cycle of the Buddha's] words. Such an [explanation] is completely fine. But here, [it is said that] the collection of reasoning teaches mainly on the ground (the view), the collection of speeches teaches mainly on the path, and the collection of praises teaches mainly on the fruition. From among these, the main [text] in the collection of praises is the *Dharmadhātustava*.[121]

The colophon of his commentary states:

> The *Abhisamayālaṃkāra* and the collection of reasoning teach the inseparability of the two realities, being just like space free from reference points. The three middling texts of Maitreya, the collection of speeches, and the collection of praises teach the union of the two accumulations, being just like two wings. The collection of praises and the *Uttaratantra* mainly teach the notion of the basic element of the two kāyas, the fruition of union. Therefore, with regard to the single essence of the path, these texts just bring out clearly the notions of lucidity and emptiness, respectively.[122]

To summarize what has been said on Nāgārjuna's praises, compared to the list of eighteen praises that the *Tengyur* attributes to him, all Indian and even the Tibetan masters mentioned above give considerably shorter lists. Atiśa enumerates only six praises (P2010, 2012–2014, 2018–2019), Jamyang Shéba seven (2010, 2012, 2013, 2015, 2019–2021), Jamgön Kongtrul nine (P2010–2015, 2017–2019), and Gorampa eleven (P2010–2105, 2017–2021).[123] These four authors all agree on not considering P2022–2028. The others either do not mention Nāgārjuna's praises at all or summarily just speak of "the collection of praises."

Who or What Is Praised in Nāgārjuna's Praises?

Apart from what was said in Gorampa's and Jamgön Kongtrul's above descriptions of the contents of some of Nāgārjuna's praises, formally speaking, in one way or another, most of them pay homage to Buddha Śākyamuni. The *Niraupamyastava*, *Lokātītastava*, *Paramārthastava*, *Acintyastava*, *Stutyatītastava*, *Niruttarastava*, and *Vandanāstotra* all praise the Buddha directly, and the *Dvādaśakāranayastotra* does so by enumerating his twelve great deeds. As their name says, the two *Aṣṭamahāsthānacaityastotras* pay homage to the eight kinds of stūpas in commemoration of eight major deeds of Buddha Śākyamuni in certain locations (although the order, the names, and the accounts of these eight often differ both between the two praises and from the standard set of eight stūpas). The *Kāyatrayastotra* eulogizes the Buddha's three kāyas in general. The *Dharmadhātustava* and *Cittavajrastava* praise the ultimate nature of the mind. Judging by their names, one would expect the *Āryabhāṭṭarakamañjuśrīparamārthastuti* and *Āryamañjuśrībhāṭṭarakakaruṇāstotra* to be praises to Mañjuśrī, but in the true sense of the word, this is only the case with the former one,[124] while the latter is more a desperate cry for this bodhisattva's help (see Appendix III). The same goes for the *Narakoddharastava*, supplicating the Buddha to save sentient beings from the sufferings of saṃsāra. According to the Tibetan colophon in the *Tengyur*, the *Sattvārādhanastava* is Nāgārjuna's versified summary of a discourse on the importance of acting for the benefit of sentient beings out of compassion, which Buddha Śākyamuni himself delivered to the sixteen great śrāvakas in a chapter of the *Bodhisattvapiṭakasūtra*.[125]

However, when looking at the actual contents of these praises, especially in the major ones—*Niraupamyastava*, *Lokātītastava*, *Paramārthastava*, *Acintyastava*, *Stutyatītastava*, *Niruttarastava*, and partly in the *Dharmadhātustava* and *Kāyatrayastotra*—we find exactly the same approach and terminology as in Nāgārjuna's much more well-known Madhyamaka works, which are unequivocally accepted as his. Thus, the majority of the verses in his praises could equally be found in the texts included in the collection of reasoning. In other words, Nāgārjuna praises the familiar notions of emptiness, dependent origination, nonarising, freedom from reference points, the lack of any nature, and identitylessness. To give just a few typical examples, the *Lokātītastava* says:

> An entity does not arise as being existent [already],
> Nor as being nonexistent, nor as being both existent and nonexistent,
> Neither from itself, nor from something other,
> Nor from both—so how is it born?
> . . .
> It is not tenable for a result
> To arise from a perished cause,
> Nor from a nonperished one—
> You consider arising as being like a dream,
> . . .
> Dialecticians hold that suffering
> Is created by itself, created by something other,
> Created by both, or without a cause,
> But you say that it arises in dependence.
>
> What dependent origination is
> Is exactly what you consider to be emptiness.
> Your incomparable lion's roar is
> That there is no independent entity.
>
> In order to relinquish all imagination,
> You taught the nectar of emptiness.

However, those who cling to it
Are also blamed by you.

Being motionless, contingent,[126] empty,
Illusionlike, and arisen from conditions,
All phenomena are elucidated by you,
O protector, as lacking a nature of their own.[127]

The *Niraupamyastava* declares:

O blameless one, you have realized
That the world of beings, just like an echo,
Is free from unity and mutiplicity
And lacks transmigration and destruction.

Lord, you have realized that saṃsāra
Is free from permanence and extinction
And lacks characteristics and what is to be characterized,
Just like a dream or an illusion.[128]

The *Acintyastava* states:

What has arisen from conditions
Is said by you to be unarisen.
What is not born by a nature of its own
You elucidated to be empty.

If there is existence, there is nonexistence,
Just as there is short when there is long.
If there is nonexistence, there is existence.
Therefore, both do not exist.

"Existence" is the view of permanence.
"Nonexistence" is the view of extinction.
Therefore, you have taught this dharma
Free from the two extremes.

Hence you have said that all phenomena
Are free from the four possible extremes,
Unknowable for consciousness,
Let alone being within the sphere of words.

What is beyond both being and nonbeing,
But has not gone anywhere at all,
What is neither knowledge nor knowable,
Neither existent nor nonexistent,

Neither one nor many,
Neither both nor neither,
Without base, unmanifest,
Inconceivable, indemonstrable,

Neither arising nor ceasing,
Neither extinct nor permanent—
That is similar to space,
Not within the sphere of words or wisdom.

What is dependent origination
Is exactly what you consider to be emptiness.
Of the same kind is the genuine dharma,
And also the Tathāgata is like that.

Emptiness is not different from entities,
And there is no entity without it.
Therefore, you have declared as empty
Phenomena that originate dependently.[129]

The *Paramārthastava* says:

Due to the nature of nonarising,
There is no arising for you,
Neither going nor coming, O protector,
I pay homage to you devoid of any nature.[130]

The *Niruttarastava* declares:

In you, there is neither knowing nor nonknowing,
Neither a yogin nor an ordinary person,
Neither meditation nor nonmeditation—
I pay homage to the unsurpassable.[131]

Even the *Dharmadhātustava*, which otherwise speaks about the dharmadhātu in more positive terms, clarifies:

Since dharmadhātu's not a self,
Neither woman nor a man,
Free from all that could be grasped,
How could it be labeled "self"?
. . .
"Impermanence," "suffering," and "empty,"
These three, they purify the mind.
The dharma purifying mind the best
Is the lack of any nature.
. . .
Virtuous throughout beginning, middle, end,
Undeceiving and so steady,
What's like that is just the lack of self—
So how can you conceive it as a self and mine?
. . .
As long as we still cling to "self" and "mine,"
We will conceive of outer [things] through this.
But once we see the double lack of self,
The seeds of our existence find their end.

Since it is the ground for buddhahood, nirvāṇa,
Purity, permanence, and virtue too,
And because the childish think of two,
In the yoga of their nonduality, please rest.
. . .
Free from latent tendencies, you're inconceivable.
Saṃsāra's latent tendencies, they can be conceived.
You're completely inconceivable—
Through what could you be realized?
. . .
The nonbeing of all beings—
This nature is its sphere.
The mighty bodhicitta seeing it
Is fully stainless dharmakāya.[132]

In general, the texts of Nāgārjuna and his followers exhibit a basic layout in terms of the three stages of no analysis, slight analysis, and thorough analysis. As Āryadeva's *Catuḥśataka* says:

First, one puts an end to what is not meritorious.
In the middle, one puts an end to identity.

Later, one puts an end to all views.
Those who understand this are skilled.[133]

First, the skandhas, the four realities of the noble ones, and so on are taught in accordance with worldly conventions in order to turn away from nonvirtue and practice virtue. The stage of "slight analysis" (that is, analysis through reasoning) refers to negating any personal and phenomenal identity and speaks about nonarising, emptiness, and the like. Finally, "thorough analysis" refers not to any further stage of examination beyond the second, but to letting go of all views and reference points, including emptiness. The praise with the significant title *Stutyatītastava* (*In Praise of The One Beyond Praise*) also clearly presents these three stages:

The skandhas, dhātus, and āyatanas
You have indeed proclaimed,
But any clinging to them too
You countered later on.
. . .
In order to relinquish all views,
O protector, you declared [entities] to be empty.
But that too is an imputation,
O protector—you do not hold that this is really so.

You assert neither empty nor nonempty,
Nor are you pleased with both.
There is no dispute about this—
It is the approach of your great speech.[134]

There are many more similar verses in Nāgārjuna's praises, but the ones above should sufficiently illustrate the point of the underlying unity of thought in both the collection of reasoning and the collection of praises. In addition, to a certain extent, but—as the above examples should have made clear—by far not exclusively or even predominantly, some of these praises also express buddhahood and the nature of phenomena in more positive or affirmative terms, which are not found in the collection of reasoning. For example, the *Paramārthastava* says:

You do not dwell in any of all the dharmas,
But have gone to the reaches of the dharmadhātu,
Having attained the supreme profundity—
To you, the profound, I pay homage.[135]

The *Niruttarastava* states:

> Having left behind this shore and the yonder,
> You illuminate the supreme nature of all that can be known
> Through the power of your miraculous display of wisdom—
> To the unsurpassable, I pay homage.
> . . .
> Your luminous single wisdom
> Determines all knowable objects without exception,
> Thus being equal and beyond measure—
> To the unsurpassable, I pay homage.[136]

The *Niraupamyastava* says:

> You know the single taste
> Of what is defiled and purified.
> Since the dharmadhātu is without distinction,
> You are completely pure in all respects.
> . . .
> O faultless one, you have vanquished the afflictions
> Right down to their very roots, their latent tendencies,
> But you have procured the nectar
> Of the afflictions' very nature.
> . . .
> Since the dharmadhātu is without distinction,
> There is no difference between the yānas, O lord—
> Your declaration of three yānas
> Is for the sake of introducing sentient beings.
>
> Your body is eternal, immutable, peaceful,
> Made up of dharma, and victorious,
> But because of people to be guided,
> You have demonstrated passing [into nirvāṇa].[137]

With respect to ultimate reality, the *Acintyastava* even states:

> It is also held to be true reality, the ultimate,
> Suchness, and the basic substance.
> This is the undeceiving reality.
> Through realizing it, [one] is called a Buddha.
> . . .

It is also said to be a nature of its own, the primordial nature,
True reality, the basic substance, and the real thing.[138]

The *Cittavajrastava* says:

I bow to my own mind
That dispels mind's ignorance
By eliminating the mind-sprung web
Through this very mind itself.

Sentient beings with their various inclinations
Picture different kinds of gods,
But our precious mind cannot be established
As any other god than complete liberation.[139]

The style of such passages is no doubt reminiscent of the teachings on buddha nature as they are found, for example, in Maitreya's *Uttaratantra*. However, the most consequent and comprehensive example of this approach among Nāgārjuna's praises is certainly the *Dharmadhātustava*, with its many examples of how the dharmadhātu—the luminous nature of the mind—abides within adventitious stains but is completely untainted by them. One of these examples says:

A garment that was purged by fire
May be soiled by various stains.
When it's put into a blaze again,
The stains are burned, the garment not.

Likewise, mind that is so luminous
Is soiled by stains of craving and so forth.
The afflictions burn in wisdom's fire,
But its luminosity does not.[140]

The final manifestation of this ever-present and unchanging luminosity with all its qualities, such as infinite compassion, prajñā, and the capacity to promote the benefit of all sentient beings, is said to be "the fundamental change of state." This is nothing but the completely unobscured dharmadhātu, which is then called "dharmakāya."

The abode of buddhadharmas
Fully bears the fruit of practice.

> This fundamental change of state
> Is called the "dharmakāya."[141]

Also, the text explicitly declares that the Buddha's teachings on emptiness are neither contradictory to nor invalidate this luminous nature of the mind:

> The sūtras that teach emptiness,
> However many spoken by the victors,
> They all remove afflictions,
> But never ruin this dhātu.[142]

The *Kāyatrayastotra*'s first verse on the dharmakāya declares:

> What is neither one nor many, the foundation of great and excellent benefit for oneself and others,
> Neither an entity nor the lack of an entity, of equal taste like space, of a nature difficult to perceive,
> Untainted, changeless, peaceful, unequalled, all-pervading, and free from reference points—
> To the incomparable dharmakāya of the victors, which is to be personally experienced, I pay homage.

This is elaborated in the autocommentary as follows:

> The dharmakāya is . . . the foundation of great and excellent benefit for oneself and others, which refers to being the foundation for attaining the excellences of the higher realms and liberation. You may wonder, "If the nature of the dharmadhātu—being free from one and many, beginning and end—is explained as emptiness, how can it be the foundation for the great and excellent welfare of oneself and others?" There is no problem. Just as it, through the power of the latent tendencies of ignorance, manifests in the form of the container and its content [the outer world and the beings therein], it [can as well] serve as the foundation for the welfare of oneself and others, just as our consciousness in dreams [can manifest in different ways]. "Then the nature of the dharmadhātu without beginning and end would become the latent tendencies of ignorance." No, it is rather like being impregnated with [some scent,] such as musk. This is what the true nature of phenomena is like. Moreover, through meeting a spiritual friend and finding the excellent path, the adventitious latent tendencies of ignorance are removed and

> [the dharmadhātu] becomes completely pure, just as gold or copper becomes free from stains. In this, there is no adopting of qualities or relinquishing of flaws, since it is said:
>
> There is nothing to be removed from it
> And not the slightest to be added.
> Actual reality is to be seen as it really is—
> Who sees actual reality is released.
>
> Thus, being associated with certain conditions, [the dharmadhātu seems] to be afflicted, but the unborn is never seen to be born. . . . It is untainted in that it is free from the stains of desire and such. It is changeless in that it does not shift from its own nature. It is peaceful in that all afflictions have come to rest. It is to be personally experienced by sentient beings, just as [it is pointless] to ask a young woman about her bliss [of making love for the first time].[143]

Naturally, in the case of someone like Nāgārjuna, who is primarily famous—or notorious—for not leaving any of our cherished belief systems intact, no matter how subtle they may be, the use of such overtly affirmative or even "un-Buddhist" terms may seem strange, if not contradictory. However, it should be more than clear that he does not use these terms to refer to any absolutely or truly existing entity that is left as something identifiable after everything else has been annihilated by Madhyamaka reasonings. Rather, far from being mutually exclusive, what Nāgārjuna's two approaches attempt to elucidate is that, despite there being nothing to pinpoint in the dharmadhātu as the nature of the mind, it can still be experienced directly and personally in a nonreferential way. It is precisely in this way that Śākya Chogden's *Distinction between the Two Traditions of the Great Charioteers* explains Nāgārjuna's two collections of reasoning and praises to be complementary:

> In the collection of reasoning, [the dharmadhātu] is [explained] in terms of cutting through superimpositions by studying and reflecting. In the collection of praises, it is [described] in terms of making this a living experience through meditation. Some people say, "These two scriptural systems are contradictory. For, what is ascertained in the collection of reasoning is not explained as what is to be brought into experience in the collection of praises, let alone what is explained in the latter as what is to be made a living experience being explained as ultimate reality in the collection of reasoning—even its sheer existence is refuted there." There is nothing wrong

> here for the following reasons. To cut through superimpositions by way of the knowledge of studying and reflecting in the collection of reasoning is for the sake of putting an end to the conceptions that cling to any characteristics of what is to be experienced [in meditation]. Then, there is no flaw at all in teaching that the dharmadhātu is experienced once [such conceptions] have been stopped in this way. . . . "But then, isn't one thing ascertained through the view and something else brought into experience through meditation?" No, since it is absolutely unreasonable that, once one meditates after all the hosts of reference points have been put to an end through the view, the meditating mind experiences something other than just dharmadhātu wisdom.[144]

In other words, the more positive expressions in the collection of praises only start being used and making sense after one's mind has already been stripped of everything that obscures what these terms speak about—mind's true nature free from adventitious stains. Nāgārjuna talks about what we encounter after his collection of reasoning has helped our mind cutting its way through the dense jungle of its own ignorance. Of course, this does not mean to finally find something within that very jungle of reference points, but to just "arrive" at what mind clear of its ignorance has naturally been all along anyway. Thus, without anybody looking at anything, the astounding panorama enjoys itself. To repeat the first verse of the *Cittavajrastava*:

> I bow to my own mind
> That dispels mind's ignorance
> By eliminating the mind-sprung web
> Through this very mind itself.

Clearly, just like most Buddhist masters, Nāgārjuna does not regard enlightenment as some empty dark nothingness, but the wide-awake awareness of mind completely free from all illusory ignorance, obscuration, and suffering.

As for the seemingly contradictory facts of Nāgārjuna realizing that, ultimately speaking, there is nothing to be praised nor someone who praises, but is nevertheless composing praises with great enthusiasm, the *Stutyatītastava*'s first verse says:

> The Tathāgata who has traveled
> The unsurpassable path is beyond praise,
> But with a mind full of respect and joy,
> I will praise the one beyond praise.

The concluding verses of the *Paramārthastava* elaborate on this as follows:

> Through such praises, you may be extolled,
> But what has really been praised here?
> All phenomena being empty,
> Who is praised and who praises?
>
> Who would be able to praise you
> Who are free from arising and declining
> And for whom there is neither middle nor end,
> Neither perceiver nor perceived?
>
> Having praised you who are without coming and going,
> The Well-Gone One[145] free from going,
> May the world, through this merit,
> Walk on the path of the Well-Gone One.[146]

Again, Nāgārjuna never tires of speaking clearly against any reifying tendencies, through which we might be carried away from the actual experience of mind's nonreferential luminosity. However, on the plane of seeming reality, for a Buddhist like Nāgārjuna, proceeding towards true reality and realizing mind's nature does not merely depend on the sharpness of prajñā seeing through all our hang-ups, but on the union of this prajñā with the proper means. No matter how sophisticated our reasonings or how refined our insight may be, there is no way around also opening our hearts, giving rise to positive mental imprints (aka accumulating merit), and cultivating compassion for others. Therefore, praises from the depth of our heart, touching—or being touched by—our innermost being, serve very well as skillful and relevant means to precisely these ends. In fact, they are just like the spontaneously uttered dohās of other great siddhas. Thus, what the above verses say should be equally applied to the scope of all other praises by Nāgārjuna too.

In this vein, a great part of the contemporary scholarly doubts about whether Nāgārjuna's praises were actually authored by this otherwise relentless deconstructor of each and every thing are simply based on the fact that the notion of spiritual devotion (Skt. bhakti) or even ecstasy—though not unknown, but almost forgotten, in the West—seems alien, "unphilosophic" or even threatening to the "modern critical minds" of many Western scholars. On the other hand, no Indian (or Tibetan) has any problem with spiritual devotion at all. Rather, it has always been and continues to be a common and crucial natural element in all Indian spiritual traditions. Also in mahāyāna Buddhism, there is a clear tradition of devotional literature, as testified by the many famous works of great poets such as Rāhulabhadra, Aśvaghoṣa, Mātṛceṭa, and Āryaśūra. The term *bhakti* is even explicitly mentioned in some of their texts, and so it is in Nāgārjuna's praises, for example, in his *Paramārthastava* (verse 2) and *Niraupamyastava* (verse 23). Thus, even for modern Indian scholars such as T. R. V. Murti, Nāgārjuna's praises are just an expression of the wholehearted pursuit of his spiritual path:

> There is no reasonable doubt with regard to *Catuḥstava* . . . being the work of Nāgārjuna. These are feeling verses of the highest devotion; they show that Nāgārjuna, like Śaṅkara, had the religious strain also well-developed in him. Both these great Ācāryas have the same felicity of language and the capacity to express their thoughts even in shorter pieces.[147]

To summarize, as Pawo Rinpoche Tsugla Trengwa says in his commentary on the *Bodhicaryāvatāra*, there are many positions on ultimate reality, such as holding it to be a nonimplicative negation, saying that it is an implicative negation, or stating it in a very affirmative way as being something permanent and stable. However, each of these presentations implies a certain purpose. In some situations, the ultimate may be explained as a nonimplicative negation in order to remove people's clinging to it as being really established in any possible way. In other contexts, it may be explained as an implicative negation in order to dispel the clinging to it as being a nonimplicative negation. At yet other times, it may also be described as something permanent and stable that is not empty of qualities in order to remedy clinging to the ultimate as just a nonexistent. Thus, it should be clear that all these explanations do not really contradict each other. However, if they are put forward in any way that involves clinging to them, they are a far cry from the ultimate, since affirmations and negations are nothing but imputations by minds that cling to existence and nonexistence, respectively. In light of the actual nature of phenomena, all clinging—no matter to what—is simply mistaken.

A Brief "History" of Luminous Mind[148]

A Terminological Map for the Dharmadhātustava *and Its Commentaries*

To better understand the *Dharmadhātustava* and its significance, it seems indispensable to address at least some of the key notions in this work and its commentaries. Many of these terms and their meanings are rather complex and are often used in different ways in different contexts or in other texts. Thus, it is only possible to give a very basic introduction pertinent to the texts in question.

The Eight Consciousnesses

Starting with the model of the eight consciousnesses, to be sure, it is taught in many sūtras and is not something "invented" by the Yogācāra School. The eight consciousnesses are the ālaya-consciousness, the afflicted mind (Skt. *kliṣṭamanas*, Tib. nyon yid), the mental consciousness (Skt. *manovijñāna*, Tib. yid kyi rnam shes), and the five sense consciousnesses. The ālaya-consciousness is nothing but the sum of the virtuous, unvirtuous, and neutral tendencies that make up the continuum of a sentient being. Thus, it is not like a container that is different from its contents, but more like the constant flow of the water that is called a river. In other words, there is no other underlying, permanent substratum or entity apart from the momentary mental impulses that constitute this everchanging flow. Due to various conditions—mainly the stirring of the afflicted mind (comparable to wind or a strong current)—the various appearances of the five sense consciousnesses and the (mainly conceptual) mental consciousness together with their seemingly external and conceptual objects emerge from the ālaya-consciousness in every moment. Right after each moment of this dualistic interaction of subjects and objects, the imprints created by them merge back into—or are "stored"—in the ālaya, just like waves on the surface of a river. In this way, the ālaya-consciousness is both a cause for saṃsāric appearances and a result, that is, their imprints. This does not mean that the ālaya actively creates anything, it is just the sum of the dynamic process of various causes and conditions interacting, otherwise known as dependent origination. In this way, it is equivalent to fundamental ignorance and the karma accumulated by it, serving as the basis for all saṃsāric appearances and representing the sum of all factors to be relinquished in order to attain liberation. Thus, it ceases upon the attainment of buddhahood. Because of all of this, it is not to be misconceived as an ātman or a creator.

To wit, when just the term *ālaya* appears, close attention to the context must be paid, since it can either refer to the ālaya-consciousness or, especially in the tantras, to the fundamental ground of all being, equivalent to the luminous nature of mind or the Tathāgata heart. For example, the *Ghanavyūhasūtra* uses the term *ālaya* in this way:

> The various seeds are the ālaya,
> And the virtuous Sugata heart is also such.
> The Tathāgatas have taught
> This Heart with the term ālaya.
> The Heart is proclaimed as the ālaya,
> But the mentally feeble do not understand this.[149]

Similar passages can be found in the *Laṅkāvatārasūtra*. Especially in the tantras, the term ālaya is often used for buddha nature or ultimate nonconceptual wisdom (for more details, see Sparham 1993).

The afflicted mind—being always associated with a set of four afflictions (ignorance, the views about a real personality, self-conceit, and attachment to the self)—is what mistakes the empty aspect of the ālaya-consciousness as being a self and its lucid aspect as what is "other." This is the starting point of fundamental subject-object duality, which then ramifies into the appearances of the remaining six consciousnesses and their objects, all of them being constantly filtered and afflicted through this basic self-concern. Thus, these consciousnesses are accompanied by the three primary mental afflictions—desire for what seems pleasurable, aversion toward what seems unpleasurable, and indifference toward what seems neither—as well as countless secondary mental disturbances based on these afflictions. Karmic actions—trying to obtain what seems desirable and get rid of what seems not—ensue, inevitably leading to various kinds of suffering sooner or later. Thus, the wheel of saṃsāra spins.[150]

Especially the Yogācāra School speaks about the triad of "mind" (Skt. citta, Tib. sems), "mentation" (Skt. manas, Tib. yid), and "consciousness"

(Skt. vijñāna, Tib. rnam shes). Here, "mind" indicates the ālaya-consciousness. "Mentation" either designates just the afflicted mind or the seventh consciousness as consisting of both the afflicted and the immediate mind. "Consciousness" stands for the five sense consciousnesses and the mental consciousness. As for the Sanskrit term *manas*, it has a wide range of meanings, primarily being one of the many Sanskrit words for "mind" in general, also meaning "conceptual mind," "thought," and "imagination."[151] There is a definite lack of proper equivalents for most of the rich Sanskrit and Tibetan terminologies used for mind and its many facets, but there is also a need for distinct terms when going into the subtleties of mapping out mind in Buddhist texts. This is why *manas (yid)* is rendered here by the English technical term "mentation." *The Oxford English Dictionary* defines it as "mental action or a mental state," suggesting mind being in a state of operation, which is how the Sanskrit and Tibetan terms are mainly used (at least in the present context). Rangjung Dorje's commentaries on his *Profound Inner Reality* and the *Dharmadhātustava* further divide "mentation" into the "afflicted mind," the "immediate mind," and "pure mentation" (for details, see the translation of the latter text below).[152]

The World Is Imagination

The related terms *vikalpa (rnam rtog), kalpanā (rtog pa), parikalpa (kun rtog),* and their cognates all have the basic sense of "constructing," "forming," "manufacturing," or "inventing." Thus, in terms of mind, they mean "creating in the mind," "forming in the imagination," and even "assuming to be real," "feigning," and "fiction." This shows that their usual translation as "thought" or "concept" is not wrong, but often far too narrow. Fundamentally—and this is to be kept in mind throughout Buddhist texts—these terms refer to the ongoing constructive yet deluded activity of the mind that constantly brings forth all kinds of dualistic appearances and experiences, thus literally building its own world.[153] What is usually understood by "conceptual thinking" is just a small part of this dynamic, since it also includes nonconceptual imagination and even what appears as outer objects and sense consciousnesses—literally everything that goes on in a dualistic mind, conscious or not. This meaning of deluded mental activity is particularly highlighted by the classical Yogācāra terms *abhūtaparikalpa* ("false imagination," lit. "imagination of what is unreal") and *parikalpita* ("the imaginary"), the latter being what is produced by false imagination. Thus, in this more general sense, I often use "imagination" for the above terms as well. This is also what Nāgārjuna means in verse 5 of his *Cittavajrastava*:

[For] the mind that has given up imagination,
Saṃsāra impregnated[154] by imagination
Is nothing but an imagination—
The lack of imagination is liberation.

Obviously, this does not refer to saṃsāra being just (conceptual) thinking or that the mere lack of such thinking is nirvāṇa.

Mind Has Three Natures

This leads us to "the three natures," the imaginary nature (Skt. parikalpitasvabhāva, Tib. kun brtags kyi rang bzhin), the other-dependent nature (Skt. paratantrasvabhāva, Tib. gzhan dbang gi rang bzhin), and the perfect nature (Skt. pariniṣpannasvabhāva, Tib. yongs grub kyi rang bzhin).[155] There are a large number of sometimes very different presentations of what these three natures are in both Indian and Tibetan texts. To give just a brief and general idea, the other-dependent nature is the mistaken imagination that appears as the unreal entities of subject and object, because these are appearances under the influence of something other, that is, the latent tendencies of ignorance. It appears as the outer world with its various beings and objects; as one's own body; as the sense consciousnesses that perceive these objects and the conceptual consciousness that thinks about them; as the clinging to a personal self and real phenomena; and as the mental events, such as feelings, that accompany all these consciousnesses. Thus, false imagination is what bifurcates mere experience into seemingly real perceivers that apprehend seemingly real objects. This very split into subject and object—the imaginary nature—does not exist even on the level of seeming reality, but the mind that creates this split does exist and function on this level.

The imaginary nature covers the entire range of what is superimposed by false imagination onto the various appearances of the other-dependent nature, from the most basic sense of subject-object duality via a self and really existent phenomena up through the most rigid beliefs about what we and the world are. In other words, what appear as one's own body and mind form the bases for imputing a personal self. What appear as other beings, outer objects, and the consciousnesses that relate to them provide the bases for imputing really existent phenomena. In detail, the imaginary nature includes the aspects that appear as conceptual objects (such as the mental image of a form), the connections of names and referents (the notion that a name is the corresponding referent and the mistaking of a referent for the corresponding name), all that is apprehended through mental superimposition (such as direction, time, outer, inner, big, small, good, bad, and so on), and all nonentities, such as space. All of these exist only conventionally, as nominal objects for the dualistic consciousnesses of ordinary sentient beings. They are not established as anything real.

The perfect nature is emptiness in the sense that what appears as other-dependent false imagination is primordially never established as the imaginary nature. As the ultimate object, this emptiness is the sphere of nonconceptual wisdom, and its nature is phenomenal identitylessness. It is called "perfect," because it never changes into something else, is the supreme among all dharmas, and is the focal object of prajñā during the process of purifying the mind from adventitious stains. Due to its quality of never changing into something else, it is also named suchness. Since the dharmas of the noble ones are attained through realizing it, it is called "dharmadhātu." Just as space, it is without any distinctions, but conventionally, the perfect nature may be presented as twofold—the unchanging perfect nature (suchness) and the unmistaken perfect nature (the wisdom that realizes this suchness).

At times, the perfect nature is also equated with the luminous nature of mind or buddha nature. In this vein, the Seventh Karmapa, Chötra Gyatso (1454–1506), says in his *Ocean of Texts on Reasoning*[156] that the perfect nature can be classified as (1) the path of purification and (2) the focal object of this path. (1) The causal aspect of this path is the naturally abiding disposition. It consists of the uncontaminated seeds in the ālaya, which are "the latent tendencies of listening"[157] to the genuine dharma and thus serve as the cause for the dharmakāya. However, since they abide in the mind stream from the very beginning through the nature of phenomena, they are merely revived through listening, therefore not created newly. Thus, Asaṅga's explanation implies that the mere fact of the nature of phenomena—suchness or emptiness—is not the naturally abiding disposition. Rather, this disposition consists of these latent tendencies of listening, in other words, the factor of prajñā. The reason is that the latent tendencies of listening render the six inner āyatanas of individual sentient beings distinct from each other. In this way, the naturally abiding disposition is also called "the distinctive feature of the six āyatanas."[158] This means that, through the latent tendencies of listening that serve as the cause for the path of the mahāyāna, the six inner āyatanas that exist within the continua of those persons who have revived these latent tendencies are made distinct from the inner āyatanas of sentient beings who do not have such tendencies. For these tendencies are the indicator that the persons who are endowed with them are the ones who have the disposition of the mahāyāna. The same goes for the latent tendencies of listening that serve as the causes for the paths of the śrāvakas and pratyekabuddhas, respectively. Why are the latent tendencies of listening included in the perfect nature? They are neither the imaginary nor the other-dependent natures, since they constitute the remedy for being afflicted and so on. The actual paths that result from such tendencies are the paths of the three yānas, such as the thirty-seven dharmas concordant with enlightenment and the six pāramitās. It is said that, during the path, these pure tendencies abide together with the impure tendencies of the ālaya-consciousness like a mix of milk and water, from which practitioners extract just the milk, leaving the water behind.[159] (2) The focal object of these paths is also included in the perfect nature, since it is the cause for purification and does not originate from the seeds of affliction. Rather, the dharma is the result that is the natural outflow of having realized the completely pure dharmadhātu. Thus, it belongs to neither the imaginary nor the other-dependent natures.

In brief, the imaginary nature is like mistakenly apprehending the visual appearances that are caused by blurred vision to be floating hairs or dark spots. Since such are nothing but superimposition, they do not exist at all. Therefore, the imaginary nature is called "the lack of nature in terms of characteristics." The other-dependent nature consists of dependently originating appearances, just like the sheer visual appearances seen by this person with blurred vision. These appear in an illusionlike manner but are without any nature of their own and do not really arise. Therefore, the other-dependent nature is called "the lack of nature in terms of arising." The perfect nature is "the ultimate lack of nature," which has two aspects. First, although there is no personal identity, the perfect nature is what functions as the remedy for the notion of a personal identity. Just as an illusory ship to cross an illusory ocean, it serves as the means to cross the ocean of saṃsāra to the other shore of nirvāṇa. In terms of dependent origination, this remedial aspect is actually contained within the other-dependent nature, but since it is the cause for realizing the ultimate, it is included in the category of "the ultimate lack of nature." The second aspect of the perfect nature is the one due to which enlightenment is attained through actively engaging in it. This aspect is undifferentiable from phenomenal identitylessness. Like space, it is omnipresent and not established as anything whatsoever. It can be compared to the free space that is the natural object of unimpaired eyesight, once blurred vision has been cured, and it is realized that what appeared as floating hairs never actually existed anywhere. This aspect is "the ultimate lack of nature" per se.

On the level of seeming reality, it can be said that the imaginary is nominally existent, while the other-dependent is substantially existent in the sense of something that performs functions. The perfect nature does not exist in any of these two ways, but it exists in a way of being without reference points. Thus, the imaginary nature is also called "the emptiness of the nonexistent," the other-dependent "the emptiness of the existent," and the perfect "the ultimate emptiness."

A Fundamental Change of State

The Sanskrit term *āśrayaparivṛtti* (Tib. gnas yongs su gyur pa) is often translated as "transformation." In general, there are a great number of scriptures (from the Pāli canon up through the tantras) in which this term is used with reference to a variety of different things or processes (see Davidson 1985). For some, the word "transformation" may be appropriate, but—as also the *Dharmadhātustava* and its commentaries show clearly—the whole point in terms of the dharmadhātu, natural purity, buddha nature, or the luminous nature of the mind is that there is absolutely no transformation of anything into anything else. Rather, the revelation of mind's primordially pure nature as fruitional enlightenment only appears as a change of its state from the perspective of deluded mind—seeming to be obscured before and then unobscured later. But this does not refer to any change in nature, just as the sun first being covered by clouds and then being free from clouds would not be called a transformation of the clouds into the sun, or even any transformation of the sun itself. Thus, when this process of uncovering mind's fundamental nature is sometimes described in Buddhist texts as if there were a transformation of something impure (such as mental afflictions) into something pure (such as wisdom), this is just a conventional or expedient way of speaking.

Specifically, there is the classical Yogācāra format of how a change of state occurs in terms of the eight consciousnesses on the one side and the four wisdoms and the three kāyas on the other side, but this does not indicate that the former are actually transformed into the latter. Rather, just as in the above example of the clouds and the sun, by virtue of the former vanishing, the latter become manifest. Still, conventionally speaking, it is said that the ālaya-consciousness manifests as mirrorlike wisdom. Most fundamentally, once the emptiness in these consciousnesses has become pure, the dharmadhātu is completely pure. This may also be understood as the fundamental space of the dharmadhātu in which these changes of state take place, all the while being inseparable from it. As for the relationship between the four wisdoms and the three kāyas, mirrorlike wisdom represents the dharmakāya, the wisdom of equality and discriminating wisdom make up the sambhogakāya, and all-accomplishing wisdom is the nirmaṇakāya.[161]

The Expanse of the Basic Element of Being

When used in terms of ultimate reality, the Sanskrit words *dharmadhātu* or just *dhātu* are understood in two main ways, which are reflected by two different Tibetan words that translate the latter term. In its most general way, *dhātu* in *dharmadhātu* refers to the ultimate nature of all phenomena—being equivalent to emptiness—which is usually translated into Tibetan as *dbyings* ("expanse," "space" or "vastness"). If *dhātu* signifies specifically the nature of the mind of sentient beings in the sense of buddha nature as the most basic element of their entire being, it is typically rendered as *khams* (lit. "element"). To be sure, these two meanings and their Tibetan renderings are not necessarily regarded or employed in a mutually exclusive way. Still, generally speaking, they represent the understanding of (dharma)dhātu in Madhyamaka texts and the texts on buddha nature, respectively. Obviously, in the *Dharmadhātustava* and its commentaries, the term is clearly used in the latter way.

Self-Awareness and Personal Experience

The Tibetan tradition sometimes presents a threefold division of awareness (Tib. rig pa):

(1) awareness of something other (Tib. gzhan rig)
(2) self-awareness (Tib. rang rig)
(3) awareness of the lack of nature (Tib. rang bzhin rig pa).

The first means that mind is aware of something that seems to be other than itself, such as outer material objects. The second refers to mind being aware of itself in a nondual way, that is, without any identifiable difference between mind as the perceiving subject and mind as the perceived object. The third is the direct realization of the true nature of all phenomena, that is, that they are without nature. Obviously, (1) pertains only to ordinary beings. Awareness (2) is found in both ordinary beings and noble ones (those who directly perceive the nature of phenomena) in a general sense, though the profundity of nondual experience differs. Awareness (3) only occurs in noble beings from the path of seeing onward. It is also called "the wisdom that realizes identitylessness," "yogic valid cognition," or "personally experienced wisdom" (Skt. pratyātmavedanīyajñāna, Tib. so so rang rig pa'i ye shes). The latter term emphasizes that this wisdom is one's own unique, immediate, and vivid experience, not just some imagined idea of something one has heard or read of. Mind realizing the nature of all phenomena includes mind being aware of its own ultimate nature, which is the unity of awareness and emptiness. The nature of such a realization is to be free from the triad of something that is aware, something of which it is aware, and the act of being aware, while at the same time being an incontrovertible transformative experience in the noble ones' own minds (Skt. pratyātmāryajñāna, Tib. 'phags pa'i so so rang gi ye shes). It is in this sense that many Tibetan masters, such as the Seventh Karmapa, have explained this wisdom as the most sublime expression of the principle that mind is able to be aware of itself in a nondual way, that is, free from any aspects of subject and object. However, this kind of realization is to be clearly distinguished from the ordinary notion of self-awareness (2), which basically means that all beings are aware of their own direct experiences, such as being happy or sad.

This difference is reflected in the rather specific Buddhist use of the Sanskrit words *svasaṃvid*, *svasaṃvedana*, and *svasaṃvitti* (*rang rig*; self-awareness) on the one hand and *pratyātmagati*, *pratyātmādhigama*, and *pratyātmavid* (one's own experience/realization) with the latter's derivatives, such as *pratyātmavedya* and *pratyātmavedanīya* (all translated into Tibetan as *so so rang rig*). More literally, *pratyātmavedanīyajñāna* means "the wisdom of what is to be personally experienced/realized (that is, the true nature of phenomena)." Of course, there is some overlap in the semantic range of these two groups, and the words in the first may also sometimes be used in the second sense. However, the emphasis in the latter group is clearly on one's own firsthand knowledge or experience of something, be it emptiness, the dharmadhātu, or the nature of one's mind.[162]

In themselves, the corresponding Tibetan expressions *rang rig* and *so so rang rig* do not mirror this distinction and are often taken to mean just the same. If the Tibetan tradition gives a distinct explanation of the meaning of *so so* in *so so rang rig pa'i ye shes*, it is usually done in two ways. First, so so refers to the fact that the final unmediated realization of the nature of our mind can only be accomplished by our mind's wisdom itself and not by anything extrinsic to it, such as a teacher's instructions or blessings. In other words, the only way to really personally know what the wisdom of a Buddha or bodhisattva is like is to experience it in our own mind. In this sense, such wisdom is truly inconceivable and incommunicable, which is part of what the term "personally experienced wisdom" indicates, since it is one's very own "private" experience unshared with others. Of course, in this context, it should be clear that "personal" or "private" does not refer to an individual person in the usual sense, since the wisdom of the noble ones encompasses the very realization that there is no such person or self. Nevertheless, it is an experience that occurs only in distinct mind streams that have been trained in certain ways, while it does not happen in others. The second explanation of so so is that, just like a mirror, this wisdom clearly sees all phenomena in a distinct way without mixing them up.

In the *Dharmadhātustava*, the term *so so rang rig* (suggesting a word from the second group of Sanskrit words above) appears in three verses (29, 46, and 56). Both it and the corresponding *so so rang rig pa'i ye shes* are also used frequently in the commentaries.

Having the Heart of a Tathāgata

The term *tathāgatagarbha* is not only found in the so-called "*tathāgatagarbha* sūtras" (for these, see below) but even in at least one of the prajñāpāramitā sūtras. The *Adhyardhaśatikaprajñāpāramitāsūtra* includes the classical phrase, "all sentient beings contain/possess the Tathāgata heart" (*sarvasattvās tathāgatagarbhāḥ*).[163] The term does not appear in the Pāli canon but in several other early mahāyāna texts, such as the *Laṅkāvatārasūtra*.

As for the meaning of this Sanskrit compound, it is definitely not as straightforward as it may seem at first glance. In brief, its first part (*tathā*) can be taken as either the adverb "thus" or the noun "thusness/suchness" (as a term for ultimate reality; several texts gloss *tathāgatagarbha* as "suchness"). The second part can be either read as *gata*—"gone"—or *āgata*—"come, arrived" (the Tibetan *gshegs pa* can also mean both). However, in the term tathāgata, both meanings more or less come down to the same. Thus, the main difference lies in whether one understands a *Tathāgata* as (a) a "Thus-Gone/Thus-Come One" or (b) "One Gone/Come to Thusness," with the former emphasizing the aspect of the path and the latter the result. The final part of the compound—*garbha*—literally and originally means embryo, germ, womb, the interior or middle of anything, any interior chamber or sanctuary of a temple, calyx (as of a lotus), having in the interior, containing, or being filled with. At some point, the term also assumed the meaning of "core," "heart," and "pith,"[164] which is also what its usual Tibetan translation *snying po* means. Technically speaking, the compound *tathāgatagarbha* can be understood as either a *bahuvrīhi* or a *tatpuruṣa* compound, meaning "containing a Tathāgata (as core)" or "the core of a Tathāgata," respectively. The first is the most natural reading and is also supported by numerous passages in the scriptures.[165]

Given that both the compound *tathāgatagarbha* and its parts are so rich in meaning, there is clearly no English word that can appropriately translate it. Nevertheless, instead of just using the Sanskrit, my personal choice of rendering *garbha* as "heart" is based on this word—in its metaphorical sense—also referring to the pith or core of something and appearing evocative enough to point to buddha nature as being "our true heart." Nevertheless, from among the above meanings of *garbha*, the ones that signify the space within some enclosure or sheath seem to lend themselves best to a nonreifying notion of buddha nature as the open and luminous space of the nature of mind within the cocoon of adventitious stains that obscure it. However, this image should not lead one to misconceive buddha nature as being some tiny or in any way dimensionally limited space within every sentient being.[166]

Interestingly enough, in interpreting the meaning of *garbha*, the Tibetan and the Chinese Buddhist traditions went in opposite directions. The Tibetan term *snying po* clearly stands for the interior nucleus or most essential part of something. The Chinese *ts'ang* means womb or enclosure, indicating something that includes or pervades, which later even culminated in the notion that buddha nature pervades everything animate as well as inaminate. Finally, it should be noted that translations such as "Tathāgata embryo" or "Tathāgata potential" are highly misleading. For, as all the teachings on and examples for buddha nature explain again and again, the whole point is that it is completely without change, let alone any growth or development, throughout all the phases of sentient beings, bodhisattvas, and Buddhas.[167]

Luminous Mind

Finally, let's look into the *Dharmadhātustava*'s main theme of "naturally luminous mind" (*prakṛtiprabhāsvaraṃ cittam*) being defiled by and then freed from adventitious stains (*āgantukamala*). Throughout the Buddhist sources in which this notion appears, the word *prabhāsvara-* (which means clear, brilliant, shining) often alternates and/or is equated with terms such as (*pari-, vi-*)*śuddha* and *vimala*, thus being understood as "pure" or "stainless." Therefore, the rendering "luminous" does not—at least not primarily—refer to some notion of light but to mind's intrinsic purity, even if it seems to be tainted by temporary extrinsic defilements. This is also confirmed by the contemporary Kagyü and Nyingma master Dzogchen Ponlop Rinpoche, who states that the notion of buddha nature refers primarily to the natural purity of mind. As for "adventitious stains," *āgantuka* means "anything added or adhering," "incidental," "accidental," and also "newcomer," "stranger," or "guest." Thus, these stains are not "at home" in buddha nature, nor do they belong there but are rather strange new kids on the block or unwelcome guests. The sūtras also say that "adventitious" refers to phenomena that can be purified or are removable. Most fundamentally, however, "adventitious" indicates that these stains are completely unreal, mere fictions of the dualistically mistaken consciousnesses of ordinary beings. This means that, in actual fact, there is nothing to be removed. "Removing" or "purifying" indicates that it is sufficient to realize that nothing of what appears as so solid and real to us right now is actually there or happening. This is similar to realizing, when mistaking a garden hose for a snake, that there isn't and never was any snake as that hose apart from us mistaking it for a snake and then panicking. Obviously, the process of realizing the same with regard to buddha nature and its adventitious stains—aka as saṃsāric suffering—is not as easy and swift as just giving that hose a second, closer look. Rather, we need to run a thorough and exhaustive check on all our most ingrained habits and patterns of first making up and then dealing with ourselves and our world.

As for the expression "the clear light (nature) of mind," which is found in most English translations and commonly used especially among Western followers of Tibetan Buddhism, it is usually based on the Tibetan *'od gsal ba*, which can mean "clear or bright light," "lucidity," "luminosity," or "lustre" (it can also be their respective adjectives). I am not fundamentally arguing with the above translation, since it—on the positive side—surely has the benefit of being evocative and inspirational in tone. However, as countless incidents show, it is more often than not misunderstood in the sense of mind being some source of light (either in a sense of "love and light" or even in a visual sense), which is definitely not what is meant by it.[168]

Luminous Mind and Tathāgatagarbha

Before discussing the actual text of the *Dharmadhātustava*, it seems appropriate to trace its key notion of naturally luminous mind being temporarily obscured by and then free from adventitious stains in Buddhist scriptures. Showing that it appears throughout a wide range of texts—both in terms of history and topics—will help to clarify that the occurrence of this theme and how it is presented in Nāgārjuna's text is in no way something unusual or new in the Buddhist tradition.[169] Statements that mind is luminous and only obscured by adventitious stains are already found several times in the Pāli canon. Examples include a passage from the *Aṅguttara Nikāya*:

> O monks, the mind is luminosity, and yet it is defiled by adventitious defilements. An ordinary being who has not heard about this does not realize it as it really is. Therefore, I say that an ordinary being who has not heard about this does not possess the cultivation of mind. O monks, the mind is luminosity, and yet it is freed from adventitious defilements. The noble śrāvaka who has heard about this realizes it just as it really is. Therefore, I say that the noble śrāvaka who has heard about this possesses the cultivation of mind.[170]

This is also quoted in Buddhaghoṣa's *Aṭṭhasālinī* (68.23 and 140.25), his commentary on the Theravādin abhidharma text *Dhammasaṅghanī*.

Furthermore, the *Dhammasaṅghanī* states:

> O monks, sentient beings are defiled by defilements of the mind. Through the purity of the mind, sentient beings are purified.[171]

Aṭṭhasālinī 68.22 and *Papañcasūdanī* I 232.12 cite this passage, and masters of various early schools, such as the Mahāsāṃghikās, Mahiśāsakas, Andhakas, and Vibhajyavādins, elaborated on its theme. Thus, it is found in the *Śāriputrābhidharma*[172] (doctrinally related to both the Mahiśāsakas and the Vibhajyavādins) and also in Vasumitra's doxographical work *Samayabhedoparacanacakra* (Chin. *I pu tsung lun lun*):

> The essence of the mind is naturally pure, but if it is defiled by adventitious defilements, it is called "impure."[173]

According to Hsüan-tsang's (seventh century) *Vijñāptimātratāsiddhi*,[174] the notion of a "stainless consciousness" (*amalavijñāna*) was originally a teaching of the Vibhajyavādins (more precisely, the Mahāsāṃghika-Ekavyāvahārika-Lokottaravādin-Kaukkuṭikas), who speak about the natural purity of the mind being merely obscured by adventitious stains.

Many early postcanonical texts on abhidharma use the notions of *bhavaṅga* and *vīthimutti*, referring to the state of mind in meditation when it is free from any activity of thinking or outwardly oriented perception. Written from a Theravāda perspective, the *Kathāvatthu* attributed to Moggaliputta Tissa says that mind in *bhavaṅga* is in its natural state (*pakaticitta*),[175] which the commentaries describe as luminous (*pabassara*) and natural (*pakati*).[176]

Finally, in the context of commenting on the *Abhidharmakośa*'s first verse of paying homage to the Buddha as the one who has overcome the mental darkness with regard to all that can be known, pulls beings out from the swamp of saṃsāra, and teaches in just the way things really are, Yaśomitra's *Abhidharmakośavyākhyā* quotes the following stanza (as he does when explaining VII.36):

> I perceive their very subtle
> Seed for liberation,
> Just like gold hidden within stones
> Containing [this precious] element.[177]

As for the sūtras of the māhayāna, the *Lalitavistarasūtra* reports that Buddha Śākyamuni, right after having become the Awakened One, uttered the following verse:

I have found a nectarlike dharma,
Profound, peaceful, free from reference points, luminous, and unconditioned.
Whoever I would teach it to could not understand it.
Thus, I shall just stay silent in the middle of the forest.[178]

Another passage speaks about the state of mind of a bodhisattva in profound meditative equipoise:

> The minds of bodhisattvas who rest like that in meditative absorption are completely pure, fully cleansed, luminous, without defilements, free from secondary defilements, supple, workable, and unmoving.[179]

The nature of what the Buddha taught is described as follows:

> What is taught to be always like the sky, nonconceptual, luminous, and free from middle and extremes is said to be this wheel of dharma.[180]

The notion of luminous mind also appears in several places in the prajñāpāramitā sūtras. For example, the *Aṣṭasāhasrikāprajñāpāramitāsūtra* says:

> The mind is no-mind. The nature of the mind is luminosity.[181]

and:

> Subhūti, these minds are natural luminosity. It is thus that the Tathāgata, based on this prajñāpāramitā, fully knows reality just as it is—that the undefiled minds of these sentient beings immeasurable [in number] are in fact undefiled.[182]

The *Pañcaviṃśatisāhasrikāsūtra* explains that mind's luminosity refers to its natural unaltered purity:

> ". . . Thus, the mind is no-mind. The nature of the mind is luminosity." Śāriputra asked, "What is mind's luminosity?" Subhūti said, "Venerable Śāriputra, it is the mind neither being associated with nor dissociated from desire, neither being associated with nor dissociated from hatred, ignorance, upsurges, obscurations, contami-

> nations, entanglements, or wrong views. This, Śāriputra, is mind's luminosity."[183]

And about the all-pervasiveness of this luminosity:

> Since form is natural luminosity, it is completely pure and undefiled. Since feelings, discriminations, formations, and consciousness are natural luminosity, they are completely pure and undefiled. Since [everything] up through omniscience is natural luminosity, it is completely pure and undefiled.[184]

The *Suvikrāntavikrāmiprajñāpāramitāsūtra* states that prajñāpāramitā is free from mind, it being mind's natural luminosity, which is completely pure by nature. In this, there is no arising of mind.[185]

The *Samādhirājasūtra* says:

> In whose name and form subtle discrimination operates,
> In that name and form, the mind will be without craving
> and luminous.[186]

Also the *Daśabhūmikasūtra* speaks of "mind's luminosity" (*cittaprabhāsvaratā*).[187]

It is to be noted that all these quotes are found in sūtras that are among the most essential scriptural foundations of the Madhyamaka School and not from so-called "Yogācāra sūtras" or the *tathāgatagarbha* sūtras. Of course, especially the latter—such as the *Śrīmālādevīsūtra*, *Aṅgulimālīyasūtra*, *Dhāraṇīśvararājaparipṛcchasūtra*, *Tathāgatagarbhasūtra*, *Mahāparinirvāṇasūtra*, *Mahāmeghasūtra*, *Sāgaramatiparipṛcchasūtra*, *Gaganagañjaparipṛcchasūtra*, *Ratnadārikāparipṛcchasūtra*, and *Ratnacūḍaparipṛcchāsūtra*—abound with statements on luminous mind and adventitious stains. To give just a few examples, the *Laṅkāvatārasūtra* frequently speaks about mind's nature being pure luminosity, such as:

> As for the Tathāgata heart that the Bhagavat taught in the sūtra collection, the Bhagavat said that it is completely pure natural luminosity. Thus, since it is completely pure right from the beginning, this primordial complete purity is endowed with the thirty-two major marks and exists within the bodies of all sentient beings.[188]

The *Saddharmapuṇḍarīkasūtra* says:

> The genuine ones among bipeds, the Buddhas,
> Know the nature of phenomena to be always luminous.
> Thus, I teach a single yāna.[189]

And about the Buddha's wisdom:

> The power of my wisdom is like that—
> It is very luminous and without all extremes.[190]

The sūtra's final part praises its qualities in terms of the pure bodies and mental faculties of bodhisattvas (such as being able to instruct others by knowing all teachings, the minds of beings, and so on). The concluding verse states:

> Their mental faculties will be completely pure,
> Lucid, luminous, unsullied,
> Fully knowing dharmas of many kinds,
> Be they bad, virtuous, or in between.[191]

The *Sāgaramatiparipṛcchasūtra* uses the example of a blue beryl, which is first covered by mud for a thousand years and then extracted from it and cleansed. During all that time, the beryl has never lost its natural purity.

> Likewise, Sāgaramati, bodhisattvas know the natural luminosity of the mind of sentient beings, but also see that it is defiled by adventitious defilements. The bodhisattvas think: "These defilements have not entered the natural luminosity of the mind of sentient beings. These defilements are adventitious, arisen from false imagination. May I be able to teach the dharma in order to remove these adventitious defilements of sentient beings!"[192]

Needless to mention, the Buddhist tantras and their commentaries speak extensively about luminous mind and adventitious stains in many ways.

As for Indian mahāyāna treatises, naturally, the works by Maitreya and many other Yogācāra texts treat this topic in great detail. For example, the *Uttaratantra* says:

> The luminous nature of the mind
> Is changeless, just like space.
> It is not defiled by adventitious stains,
> Such as desire, born from false imagination.[193]

The *Madhyāntavibhāga* declares:

> What is afflicted and what is purified
> Refer to being with stains and without stains.
> Purity is asserted to be like the purity
> Of the element of water, gold, and space.
> . . .
> It is neither defiled nor undefiled,
> Neither pure nor impure,
> Because of mind's luminosity
> And the adventitiousness of defilements.[194]

The *Mahāyānasūtrālaṃkāra* states:

> Mind is held to be always luminous by nature,
> Contaminated [only] by adventitious flaws.[195]

The *Dharmadharmatāvibhāga* says:

> To penetrate the nature
> [Of the fundamental change of state]:
> It is suchness without stains,
> So that adventitious stains do not appear,
> While suchness does appear.
> . . .
> Examples for the fundamental change of state
> Are space, gold, and water.[196]

Vasubandhu's *Dharmadharmatāvibhāgabhāṣya* explicitly identifies this fundamental change of state with natural luminosity.[197] Also Sthiramati's *Abhidharmasamucchayaṭīkā* agrees that mind's fundamental change of state is a change of state of suchness, coming about due to the elimination of the adventitious defilements of naturally luminous mind.[198]

Naturally, all the various commentaries and subcommentaries on Maitreya's above texts by Asaṅga, Vasubandhu, Sthiramati, Asvabhāva, and so on elaborate on this topic. In addition, Asaṅga's *Ratnagotravibhāgavyākhyā* quotes a Prakrit verse, saying that the Buddha uttered it while having the pure disposition (*viśuddhagotra*) and the basic element of the Tathāgata (*tathāgatadhātu*) in mind:

> Just as within stony debris
> Pure gold is not seen,
> And then is seen through being purified,
> The Tathāgata [is seen] in the world.[199]

An interlinear gloss on verse 28 of Sajjana's (eleventh/twelfth century) *Mahāyānottaratantraśāstropadeśa* (a brief summary of the *Uttaratantra* in 37 verses) equates buddha nature with luminous mind.

Also, many commentaries on the *Abhisamayālaṃkāra*, usually in the section on the dharmadhātu as the "disposition" (*gotra*),[200] speak of it or mind as being naturally luminous and only covered by adventitious stains, such as Dharmamitra's (eighth/ninth century) *Prasphuṭapadā*, Ratnākaraśānti's *Śuddhimatī* and *Sāratamā*, Prajñākaramati's *Abhisamayālaṃkāravṛttipiṇḍārtha*, and Abhayākaragupta's (eleventh/twelfth century) *Marmakaumudī* and *Munimatālaṃkāra*. In this context, Vasubandhu's huge commentary *Bṛhaṭṭīkā*[201] on the three largest prajñāpāramitā sūtras may also be mentioned. On *Abhisamayālaṃkāra* IV.15b, Haribhadra's *Abhisamayālaṃkārālokā* explains:

> As for these [states of mind] being "naturally luminous," if one examines through valid cognition the nature of the impure states of mind that have become so in the state of ordinary beings by virtue of the cause that is mistakenness, one realizes them to have the essential nature of being unarisen and so on. Through having merged with this [realization], by virtue of [mind's] capacity to not revert from [its state of] the remedies having arisen and to eliminate adventitious desire and so on, said [states of mind] are naturally luminous, and it is nothing but their nature to be utterly pure.[202]

Furthermore, Asaṅga's *Yogācārabhūmi* states:

> In brief, the Bhagavat taught that a sentient being is a [mind] that has defilements from a long time in the past, yet is without a creator. At present, it is momentary and naturally luminous. He taught that, in the future, it will be [further] defiled through heedlessness or purified by heedfulness.[203]

His *Viniścayasaṃgrahaṇī* repeatedly speaks about this topic:

> Consciousness is not defiled by its nature, because the Bhagavat has said that it is natural luminosity.[204]

Kambala's (fifth/sixth century) autocommentary on his famous *Navaślokī* discusses naturally luminous mind and adventitious stains a number of times, clearly speaking against reifying the former:

> You may think, "This naturally luminous mind, which is free from apprehender and apprehended and is completely pure, since the stains of ignorance (such as desire) are relinquished, actually exists." In order to eliminate such clinging to the existence of this mind, it is taught to be like the reflection of the moon in water . . . "Clear" means being free from the turbidities of latent tendencies . . . Since perfect wisdom dispels the darkness of ignorance, pacifies the burning heat of the afflictions, and is not tainted by the stains of latent tendencies, it resembles the moon. Although this [moon of wisdom] appears in that way, it is not found as something that is directly perceptible, because what dawns in such a pure mind stream is not apprehendable as a real entity. The reason for this is that, from empty phenomena, nothing but empty phenomena come forth. Since that wisdom is unarisen from the very beginning, it is like the reflection of the moon in water. Thus, since it has the nature of the dharmadhātu, any clinging to entities or nonentities does not exist. Hence, it is not found as something that is directly perceptible.[205]

His *Ālokamālā* proclaims:

> The victors who have relinquished the obscurations
> Have declared, in brief, that saṃsāra
> Is the mind with stains, such as desire,
> And liberation consists of being devoid of these.
> . . .
> When their insight into themselves
> Is obscured by stains born from being covered,
> Just as crystals, minds appear
> As having another nature.
> . . .
> Saying, "In the end, everything vanishes"
> Is a rhetorical device for childish beings—
> Something else shines forth
> That cannot be expressed or analyzed.

There, dwelling in a place with nothing [to hold on to],
That brightly shining space
Illuminates the emptiness
Of itself and of emptiness.[206]

Dignāga's (c. 480–540) *Prajñāpāramitāpiṇḍārthasaṃgraha* states:

The consciousness of ordinary beings
Is pure by nature
And expressed by the term "Buddha,"
Just as a bodhisattva is [called] a victor.

Its own innate nature is enshrouded—
Being under the sway of ignorance,
It appears otherwise, just like an illusion,
While the fruition is like quitting a dream.[207]

Several texts by Paramārtha (c. 500–569) speak about the *amalavijñāna* ("pure consciousness") as a ninth kind of consciousness. It refers to the unconditioned, changeless, permanent mind unaffected by any impurities, identical with suchness as the ultimate. This *amalavijñāna* is the foundation of the Buddhist path, while the ālaya-consciousness is the foundation of all defilements. Paramārtha also equates this *amalavijñāna* with mind's luminosity and says that it is unmistaken and free from both the imaginary and the other-dependent natures (which comprise the manifestations of mistaken consciousness), thus being reminiscent of typical *shentong* positions.[208]

Dharmakīrti's (c. 600–660) *Pramāṇavārttika* says:

Mind is naturally luminous,
The stains are adventitious.[209]

His *Pramāṇaviniścaya* declares:

Also what is directly experienced by this self-awareness is nothing but the nature of this [awareness]. Since it has this nature, it is something very luminous itself. Therefore, it is expressed as "illuminating itself, like a lamp."[210]

Jñānaśrīmitra's *Sākārasiddhiśāstra* speaks several times about (the dhātu of) mind's natural purity and adventitious stains or reference points (*āgantuprapañca*).[211]

The notion of luminous mind is also found in many Madhyamaka texts. Bhāvaviveka's *Madhyamakahṛdaya* says:

> Unborn, without aspect,
> Changeless, luminous,
> Unequalled, infinite,
> Nonconceptual, without characteristics,
>
> Just like space, without anything to look at,
> It is seen by great beings.[212]

His *Madhyamakaratnapradīpa* states:

> For the time being, it operates as momentary [primary] minds and mental factors. Since these [moments] also have very subtle parts—due to being distinguished by their beginning, their present time, and their end—they are in fact without appearance. Therefore, they are not established as mind or mental factors but as the nature of the dharmadhātu. In this, you should rest. As the great Mother says:
>
> > Mind is not mind, since mind's nature is luminosity.[213]

The text also presents a number of similar quotes:

> It is primordially natural luminosity, unborn as any nature whatsoever, not established as subject and object, or knowing and what is known, nothing whatsoever, not dwelling in any extremes, not within the range of any expressions or reference points, inconceivable, unthinkable, and beyond thought. Therefore, do not mentally engage, but meditate by abandoning mindfulness and mental engagement.[214]

It even quotes Nāgārjuna twice as saying:

> Everything internal and external is mind as such,
> Being just like an illusion.
> This mind is explained as luminosity,
> Nirvāṇa, all-empty,
> And dharmakāya.[215]

Avalokitavrata's *Prajñāpradīpaṭīkā* says:

> The essence of mind is natural luminosity. To put an end to this [mind being ensnared by itself] means the freedom from adventitious stains and the fundamental change of state.[216]

and

> Since mind is naturally luminous, it is undefiled and pure. Since the defilements are adventitious, it is not undefiled and not pure.[217]

Śāntarakṣita's *Tattvasaṃgraha*[218] and his autocommentary on the *Madhyamakālaṃkāra*[219] also speak about naturally luminous mind and adventitious stains. Kamalaśīla's first *Bhāvanākrama* says:

> Once the mind has become stabilized on its focus through calm abiding, if one examines this [mind] through prajñā, the brilliance of perfect wisdom will dawn. At this point, just as darkness is dispelled through bright daylight, obscurations are eliminated. Like one's eyes and light [in producing a visual perception], both [calm abiding and superior insight] are mutually compatible with regard to the emerging of perfect wisdom. It is not that they are incompatible in the way that light and darkness are. The nature of meditative concentration is not darkness.[220]

The same master's *Madhyamakāloka* states:

> This statement, "All sentient beings possess the Tathāgata heart" teaches that all are suitable to attain the state of unsurpassable completely perfect buddhahood, since it is held that the term Tathāgata expresses the dharmadhātu, characterized by personal and phenomenal identitylessness, as being natural luminosity.[221]

Candrakīrti's *Madhyamakaprajñāvatāra* proclaims:

> Without identifying anything, without being distracted,
> Without characteristics, and luminous—thus meditate.[222]

Further examples include Ratnākaraśānti's *Triyānavyavasthāna*, *Madhyamakālaṃkāravṛtti-Madhyamapratipadāsiddhi*, *Prajñāpāramitopadeśa*, *Madhyamakālaṃkāropadeśa*, and his commentary on the *Khasamatantra*.[223]

Even Indian masters whom the Tibetan tradition clearly considers as Prāsaṅgikas explicitly speak about luminous mind and adventitious stains.

For example, both Candrakīrti's *Prasannapadā* and *Catuḥśatakaṭīkā* quote the same passage from a sūtra:

> All phenomena are naturally luminous, since prajñāpāramitā is completely pure.[224]

The same author's *Madhyamakāvatārabhāṣya* quotes two sūtras, one on the twelfth unshared quality of a Buddha—complete liberation—and the other on the termination of all mental contaminations:

> The complete liberation of Buddhas is called "complete liberation," since it is being free from all attachment and clinging . . . Naturally luminous mind is known just as it is. Therefore, through a single moment of prajñā, they fully and completely awaken into unsurpassable completely perfect enlightenment. . . .[225]

> "The termination of mental contaminations of a Tathāgata" means to be completely pure, stainless, utterly pure, luminous, and having overcome all ties due to latent tendencies.[226]

The only Indian commentary on this text of Candrakīrti, Jayānanda's (eleventh/twelfth century) *Madhyamakāvatāraṭīkā*, says that the second bhūmi is presented from the perspective of realizing that the dharmadhātu is the supreme, since it is naturally luminous.[227] Regarding the above passage on "complete liberation," the text comments as follows:

> Since mind is primordially unborn, it is of the nature of emptiness. Therefore, since it is not tainted by the stains of the afflictions, mind is naturally luminous. Accordingly, this natural luminosity's knowing in a nonreferential manner is complete liberation. Therefore, the knowing of naturally luminous mind is expressed as "complete liberation."[228]

Later, the text says:

> As for "having the characteristic of adventitious defilements," since suchness is naturally luminous, they are to be known as being adventitious, just as clouds in space . . . As for "having the characteristic natural luminosity," it is not tainted by these defilements, just as space [is not tainted] by clouds.[229]

Prajñākaramati's (tenth century) commentary on the *Bodhicaryāvatāra* comments on verse II.1:

> As for "the jewel of the genuine dharma," it has the characteristics of scripture and realization. "Stainless" means that, through threefold virtue, it is pure of the three spheres and naturally luminous, since it is in every respect not the locus of any stains and [since] the so-called "defilements" are adventitious.[230]

Commenting on verse VI.40, the text states that the mental flaws of sentient beings, such as hatred, are adventitious and something other than these beings' nature, since the nature of beings is naturally luminous mind and thus reliable.[231]

As mentioned above, Atiśa's *Dharmadhātudarśanagīti* incorporates nineteen verses from the *Dharmadhātustava*, and its second verse says:

> In due order, I will describe
> Those who behold the dharmadhātu and the others who do not.
> Profound peaceful suchness free from reference points,
> Unconditioned luminosity,[232]
> Is unborn, unceasing, and primordially pure.

His *Ratnakaraṇḍodghātanāmamadhyamakopadeśa* says the following on Madhyamaka meditation:

> As for the mind, it has no color and no shape. It is natural luminosity that is primordially unborn. The very knowledge that discriminates this is also luminosity. In this interval, consciousness is nothing whatsoever, does not abide as anything, is not established as anything, and has not arisen as any aspect, and all discursiveness without exception is completely at peace. This meditative concentration of space-vajra that is without appearance and in which all the dust of characteristics has vanished is like the very center of the sky that is lit up by the autumn sun.[233]

His *Madhyamakopadeśa* agrees:

> What is without form is the mind. As for that [mind], the past mind has [already] ceased and perished. The future mind has not [yet] arisen or originated. As for the present mind, it is very difficult to examine: It has no color and is without any shape. Since it is just like

> space, it is not established. In other words, it is free from unity and multiplicity, or it is unarisen, or it is natural luminosity. . . . Once all specific characteristics and general characteristics are established as nonexistent [through discriminating prajñā], this prajñā itself is without appearance and is luminous, not being established as any nature whatsoever. Thus, all flaws, such as dullness and agitation, are eliminated. In this interval [of meditative concentration], consciousness is without any thought, does not apprehend anything, and has left behind all mindfulness and mental engagement. For as long as the enemies or robbers of characteristics and thoughts do not arise, consciousness should rest in such a [state].[234]

Commenting on *Bodhicaryāvatāra* IX.27cd—an opponent's claim that saṃsāra needs mind or self-awareness as its support—Vibhūticandra's (twelfth/thirteenth century) *Bodhicaryāvatāratātparyapañjikāviśeṣadyotanī* says that mind does not qualify that way:

> Since mind is naturally luminous, it has the nature of being completely pure and is not what is to be relinquished.[235]

The same author's *Amṛtakaṇikodyotanibandha* speaks about mind's natural luminosity and adventitious stains, quoting *Uttaratantra* I.63.[236]

As for the Indian and Tibetan masters of the Kagyü lineage, they all refer to luminous mind over and over again, so just a few examples shall suffice. Tilopa's *Mahāmudropadeśa* ("Ganges Mahāmudrā") says:

> Just as the bright and clear heart of the sun
> Cannot be obscured by the darkness of a thousand eons,
> The luminous heart of your own mind
> Cannot be obscured by this saṃsāra of [infinite] eons.[237]

Nāropa's *Summary of the View*[238] states:

> Thus, it is taught, "Realize that luminous mind
> Is the mind of wisdom,
> And do not seek for enlightenment outside of that."
>
> Still, this mind becomes tainted
> By the adventitious stains of thoughts.
> Like water, like gold, and like the sky
> It can be pure or impure.[239]

The last stanza of Maitrīpa's *Madhyamakaṣaṭka* says:

> Luminosity free from the four extremes,
> Which has the character of the deity,
> Is of the nature of nondual bliss,
> Sheer dependent origination.

Marpa sang about his dream on Saraha's instructions:

> At this moment, I woke up,
> Caught by the iron hook of this unforgettable memory.
> In the dark dungeon of the sleep of ignorance,
> The vision of wide-awake wisdom opened up.
>
> Just as when the sun shines in a cloudless sky,
> The dark gloom of delusion lightened up and vanished.
> I thought, "Even if I met the Buddhas of the three times face to face,
> From now on, I have nothing to ask."[240]

Milarepa's song on distinguishing the expedient from the definitive in the context of Mahāmudrā says:

> Through realizing that delusion has no ground,
> The water-moon of awareness is immaculate and clear.
> The cloudless sun of luminosity
> Lights up the darkness of ignorance to its very brink.[241]

Gampopa instructs:

> Connate mind is the actual dharmakāya.
> Connate appearances are the light of the dharmakāya.
> Connate thoughts are the waves of the dharmakāya.
> Connate inseparability is what the dharmakāya is all about.

The Third Karmapa, Rangjung Dorje's *Aspiration Prayer of Mahāmudrā* says:

> Within the ground of purification—mind as such, lucid and empty in union—
> May the means to purify—the great vajra-yoga of Mahāmudrā—
> [Purify] what is to be purified—the adventitious stains of delusion—
> And the result of purification—the stainless dharmakāya—manifest.[242]

The Seventh Karmapa says the following in his *Ocean of Texts on Reasoning* on how the approaches of Nāgārjuna and Asaṅga are both grounded in luminous mind:

> Therefore, the great Yogācāra-Mādhyamikas who follow noble Asaṅga and his brother, through ascertaining that the dualistic appearances of apprehender and apprehended, which obscure true reality, are not established in the way they [appear], mainly teach the wisdom that realizes self-aware self-luminous mind. Noble Nāgārjuna and his spiritual heirs, by thoroughly analyzing the clinging to real [existence] and its objects that obscure true reality through the great [Madhyamaka] arguments, mainly teach that the nature of luminous mind abides as emptiness. In this way, they ascertain that [any such clinging and its objects] are without nature. Both systems do not differ in teaching the final true reality, since this very nature of luminous mind primordially is emptiness, and this emptiness primordially abides as having the essential character of luminosity.[243]

To conclude this "history" of luminous mind, I would like to quote one of the most comprehensive, insightful, and subtle discussions of the dharmadhātu as the "disposition" and Tathāgata heart—given mainly from the ultimate perspective—which is found in the Eighth Karmapa, Mikyö Dorje's (1507–1554) commentary on the *Abhisamayālaṃkāra*, called *The Noble One Resting at Ease*.[244] It not only covers the understanding of the Tathāgata heart in both the sūtrayāna and the vajrayāna, but also clarifies the position of the Third Karmapa and eliminates misconceptions. Mikyö Dorje's presentation culminates in a penetrating analysis of the *Uttaratantra*'s famous verse I.28, which is usually presented as a threefold proof for all sentient beings possessing buddha nature (since the dharmakāya radiates, suchness is undifferentiable, and they have the disposition).

The Eighth Karmapa on the Dharmadhātu as "Disposition" and Tathāgata Heart

In general, the meaning of "disposition" is as follows. In the hīnayāna, the disposition for enlightenment is presented as "having little desire and being content." But these are just indications that the disposition exists due to the signs of this disposition, whereas they are not clear teachings of the disposition that fully qualifies as such.

Hence, the meaning of "disposition" that is taught here is that it is an adequate substantial cause for its result to come about. Such a cause is classified as twofold: the causes for saṃsāra and nirvāṇa. The cause that is taught here is the disposition that is the cause for nirvāṇa. According to the followers of the mahāyāna, it is asserted that this very causal disposition abides as a seminal aspect based on the ālaya. The causal disposition for nirvāṇa is founded on the ālaya-wisdom, and the causal disposition for saṃsāra is founded on the ālaya-consciousness.[245]

Thus, these two causal dispositions are founded separately on the pure and the impure ālaya, respectively. However, the assertion that does not clearly differentiate between pure and impure ālayas, but presents the causal dispositions for both saṃsāra and nirvāṇa as based on a single ālaya as the bearer of such a property, is a mistaken understanding of the meaning of the abhidharma scriptures. The *Abhidharmasūtra* says:

> The dhātu of beginningless time
> Is the matrix of all phenomena.
> Since it exists, all beings
> And also nirvāṇa are obtained.

Thus, it is declared that both saṃsāra and nirvāṇa are justified, since all phenomena, by way of the three characteristics,[246] are present within the ālaya that is the dhātu of beginningless time. Here, the meaning of the sūtras is that one needs to differentiate between these two factors of wisdom and consciousness with respect to the ālayadhātu that does not reach a limit of beginning in time. Those who do not know this represent the impure system of gaining but an understanding of limited letters with respect to this phrase, "The dhātu of beginningless time is the matrix of all phenomena." Therefore, the necessity of making this distinction between consciousness and wisdom within the dhātu of beginningless time has been stated by the invincible protector [Maitreya] in his *Dharmadharmatāvibhāga*:

> The lack of a fundamental change of state
> Has four shortcomings—
> The flaw of lacking a support in which afflictions do not operate,
> The flaw of lacking a support for engaging in the path,
> The flaw of lacking a basis of designation
> For persons in nirvāṇa,
> And the flaw of lacking a basis of designation
> For the distinctive features of the three enlightenments.

Their opposites are the benefits involved,
Which are to be known as fourfold. [247]

In [its] commentary [by Vasubandhu] the following appears:

> At this point, it is not justified that mind is this very [basis], because the arising of remedies and the ceasing of antagonistic factors are simultaneous, and because contrary phenomena are not justified in the same basis, just as a cold and a warm sensation are not justified in the same basis.[248]

Therefore, it is clearly declared that there are four flaws, if there is no such support that does not allow for any operation of the factors to be relinquished and [allows for] the operation of their remedies and so forth—the ālaya-wisdom as the basis of the fundamental change of state—and that there are four benefits, if it exists. Hence, the distinction between consciousness and wisdom within the ālaya is the assertion of the Buddha Bhagavat.

If, according to the tradition of some people, the causal disposition for both saṃsāra and nirvāṇa is presented as nothing but the ālaya-consciousness, the order of all principles of the dharma of the mahāyāna is mixed up from its very foundation. Since the ālaya-consciousness is canceled upon becoming a Buddha, the ālaya-consciousness is no [longer] existent. But the change of state of the ālaya-consciousness into ālaya-wisdom (which is its opposite) must be presented as the wisdom that has changed state. But then it follows that, according to you [who hold this position], it is not suitable for wisdom that has changed state to arise, once the ālaya-consciousness is canceled. The reason for this is that the canceled ālaya-consciousness is something that is [already] canceled, while a shift from this ālaya-consciousness to wisdom (which has changed state by having cast away the ālaya-consciousness) is impossible within the sphere of knowable objects. A presentation that the mere factor of cancellation of the canceled ālaya-consciousness exists as the nature of the wisdom that has changed state contradicts reasoning—a phenomenon that has become nonexistent is in no case suitable as a cause for something existent.

Those present-day followers of [Mahā]mudrā, whose confusion is even a hundred thousand times bigger than this, exclaim, "Through refining the ālaya-consciousness into something pure, it turns into the result of mirrorlike wisdom." This is not justified for the following reasons: Something like this does not appear in any of the traditions of the mahāyāna, and what does not appear [there also] does not appear in the sense of something that is obtained through reasoning. A presentation of the ālaya-consciousness as the cause and mirrorlike wisdom as its result is not something that is obtained through reasoning. Rather, with respect to the mode of being of causes and results in terms of [such] causes and results in the abhidharma that actually fulfill these functions[249] (that is, what produces and what is produced), the ālaya-consciousness and mirrorlike wisdom are not adequate as a cause and a result that fully qualify as such. Also, since the very nature of the ālaya-consciousness is [nothing but] the adventitious stains, it is presented as impure. No matter how it may be refined by something else, it will not turn into something pure. It is not possible among knowable objects that something impure turns into something pure, or that something pure turns into something impure.

Some assert that there is the mere factor of lucid and aware mind, and that this is what comprises all the seeds of saṃsāra as well as the seeds of nirvāṇa. This is not tenable. That just one single [phenomenon] should function as the seminal cause for all of saṃsāra and nirvāṇa is not something that appears in the Buddhist tradition. That such does not appear [in this tradition is shown by the fact that] this is put forward as the assertion of non-Buddhists ("just one single awareness-consciousness, which is the cause or seed of both bondage and liberation") by the great guardians of the Buddha's teaching, glorious Dignāga and Dharmakīrti, and then refuted.

Most Tibetans in this land of snow say, "The twofold distiction between ālaya-consciousness and [ālaya-]wisdom is the system of the Mere Mentalists," and also, "The twofold distinction between ālaya-wisdom and [ālaya]-consciousness does not appear in any system whatsoever." Their own words are self-contradictory, because if [this distinction] appeared in the system of the Mere Mentalists, it contradicts not appearing in any system at all.

Therefore, in the manner of presenting the contaminated latent tendencies of saṃsāra as being within the ālaya-consciousness [as their] foundation, what cycles [in saṃsāra], what makes it cycle, and where it cycles are all not something beyond the ālaya-consciousness per se. Some may argue, "But in that case, a single such factor [—the ālaya-consciousness—] is not suitable as three factors (what cycles and so on)." As for this point, I accept that it is not suitable that way. Nevertheless, although a presentation of three [factors] through a single one and so on contradict reasoning, whatever happens from the perspective of mistakenness happens this way precisely through the issue of ignorance.

Such an ālaya-consciousness is classified as twofold: the seminal aspect and the maturational aspect. The [contaminated] seeds are input newly under the influence of the force of conditions—they are not something previously existing that is intrinsic through the nature of phenomena.

As for the manner in which uncontaminated seeds are input based on the ālaya-wisdom, the actual ālaya-wisdom is "the Sugata heart," "the vajra of mind," and "the naturally abiding disposition." These are synonyms for the emptiness that actually fulfills this function, which are taught briefly by Lord Maitreya in *Madhyāntavibhāga* [I.15].[250] Uncontaminated seeds are not something that must be input newly under the influence of conditions, but they are declared in the mantrayāna to be "the seeds of all aspects that are intrinsic by virtue of the nature of phenomena." In particular, they appear in the great texts of Lord Maitreya under the names "the latent tendencies of listening," "the distinctive feature of the six āyatanas," and "uncontaminated seeds."

These latent tendencies of listening are associated with ālaya-wisdom. You may wonder, "What kind of activity do they perform?" The noble master Asaṅga, who is capable of differentiating between the expedient and the definitive [meaning], has declared the following in his *Mahāyānasaṃgraha*:

> [Supramundane wisdom] originates from the natural outflow of the completely pure dharmadhātu, that is, the seeds which are the latent tendencies of listening. One may wonder, "What are these latent tendencies of listening anyway? Are they of the nature of the ālaya-consciousness, or are they not? If they were of the nature of the ālaya-consciousness, how should they be suitable as the seeds of its remedy? And if they are not of its nature, then look what the matrix of these seeds of latent tendencies of listening is." What these latent tendencies of listening in dependence on the enlightenment of Buddhas are, which matrix they enter, and that they enter the maturational consciousness[251] in a manner of coexisting with it—all this is like [a mixture of] milk and water. They are not the ālaya-consciousness, because they are the very seeds of its remedy.[252]

Small latent tendencies turn into medium latent tendencies, and these medium latent tendencies then turn into great latent tendencies, all this by virtue of being associated with listening, reflection and meditation that are performed many times. The small, medium and great latent tendencies of listening are to be regarded as seeds of the dharmakāya. Since they are the remedy for the ālaya-consciousness, they are not of the nature of the ālaya-consciousness. [In the sense of being a remedy,] they are something mundane, but since they are the natural outflow of the supramundane—the utterly completely pure dharmadhātu—they are the seeds of supramundane mind. Although this supramundane mind has not originated yet, they are the remedy for being entangled [in saṃsāra] through the afflictions, the remedy for migrating in the lower realms, and the remedy that makes all wrongdoing vanish. They are what is in complete concordance with meeting Buddhas and bodhisattvas.

Though beginner bodhisattvas are mundane, [these latent tendencies] should be regarded as being included in the dharmakāya and [those of] śrāvakas and pratyekabuddhas as being included in the vimuktikāya.[253] They are not the ālaya-consciousness but included in the dharmakāya and vimuktikāya, respectively. To the extent that they gradually shine forth in a small, medium, and great way, to that same extent the consciousness of complete maturation wanes and changes state too. If it has changed state in all aspects, the consciousness becomes devoid of seeds and is also relinquished in all aspects.

You may wonder, "How is it that the ālaya-consciousness, which abides together with what is not the ālaya-consciousness like water and milk, can wane in all aspects?" It is stated: "This is like geese[254] drinking milk from water. It is similar to the change of state when, being free from mundane desire, the latent tendencies of what is not meditative equipoise wane, while the latent tendencies of meditative equipoise increase."[255]

Hence, what is called "the latent tendencies of listening" is what allows one to listen to all the twelve branches of a Buddha's speech. It is the capacity of uncontaminated consciousness that is active through the power of the nature of phenomena. The factor of this capacity is what bears the name "latent tendencies of listening that are sustained by enlightenment." It is what is not suitable to blend with the mind streams of sentient beings. Here, these latent tendencies are said to be "latent tendencies" in terms of allowing the enlightened activity of the dharmakāya, which is based on enlightenment, to engage the mind streams of sentient beings. But there are no latent tendencies whatsoever that fully qualify as such in the enlightened activity of the dharmakāya, which has the character of the twelve branches of a Buddha's speech and is the natural outflow of the supramundane, completely pure dharmadhātu. It is declared to be the natural outflow that is free from all characteristics of latent tendencies.

One may think, "The explanation of small latent tendencies turning into medium latent tendencies, and these medium latent tendencies then turning into great latent tendencies and so on, is [a description of] such an increase in the sense that latent tendencies exist that fully qualify as such." This is not the case. What is called "latent tendencies of listening, which are the natural outflow of the completely pure dharmadhātu," does not represent an increase of latent tendencies. Rather, it is the power of the decline of the factors to be relinquished—the antagonistic factors—that appears as if the latent tendencies of listening, which are the natural outflow of the completely pure dharmadhātu, increase from small to medium and so on.

Here, the meaning of "Though being mundane, . . ." [in the above quotation] is said to be as follows. Though [the latent tendencies of listening] are the remedy for what is mundane, they are not contained in mundane mind streams but are the natural outflow of the supramundane dharmadhātu. The gist of "natural outflow" is that it addresses the definite need for something that is other than the completely pure dharmadhātu itself and [at the same time] outside of everything that exists within the class of impure phenomena whose nature is [the dharmadhātu]. So, from the perspective of this factor of the natural outflow being associated with a mind stream, it is both presented as a bodhisattva and yet this factor is also included in the dharmakāya. During this time, there are two [modes of engagement] in one single body of a yogin that appears as the other-dependent nature: the mode of engagement of the continuum of consciousness and the mode of engagement of the capacity of wisdom. Noble Nāgārjuna says [in his *Dharmadhātustava*]:

Just as from a mix of milk and water
That is present in a vessel,
Geese just sip the milk, but not the water,
Which remains just as it is.

Just so, being covered by afflictions,
Wisdom dwells within this body, one [with them].
But yogins just extract the wisdom
And leave the ignorance behind.[256]

Now one may think, "Since the causal disposition is explained as the unconditioned dharmadhātu, an unconditioned phenomenon is not suitable as the disposition. Disposition has the meaning of cause, and the presentation of causes and results is given based on conditioned phenomena. Hence, [the dharmadhātu] is not suitable as the causal disposition." Wishing to eliminate such a qualm, some say, "The mistake that an unconditioned phenomenon is not suitable as cause does not exist [here], because there is a twofold reason to present an unconditioned phenomenon as the causal disposition. It is presented in a twofold way through support and through focus. First, it is justified that an unconditioned phenomenon—which has the mode of supporting—functions as "causal disposition." Bodhisattvas are labeled due to their six āyatanas, and these are supported by the mental consciousness. Since in the end this is supported by the dharmadhātu, it is justified that the unconditioned dharmadhātu functions as "causal disposition" from the perspective of presenting it as support. The *Uttaratantra* teaches such through the two verses [starting with]:

[Likewise,] skandhas, dhātus, and faculties . . .[257]

Secondly, the presentation as causal disposition through focus [is justified] because bodhisattvas meditate by focusing on the nature of mind—the dharmadhātu. Therefore, at the time of the final freedom from stains, the dharmadhātu of mind becomes suchness free from stains."[258]

The explanation in the *Uttaratantra* that these rest on or are supported by the [following ones] is merely a presentation from a conventional perspective that, by the implication of all phenomena being emptiness, they are suitable to arise, suitable to appear, and [may relate as] support and supported. That the nature of the mind—or the unconditioned dhātu free from stains—could be supported by or resting on another phenomenon is primordially impossible. Therefore, it is neither justified that the very dharmadhātu supports something else, nor that the dharmadhātu itself is supported by something else. Furthermore, [these two verses] speak explicitly only of a being supported by or resting on the purity of mind, but they do not explain a being supported by the nature of the mind, the dhātu without stains. To identify "the purity of mind" in this context as the dharmadhātu is not necessarily so. Since the mind that is improper mental engagement never existed in this way, it does not change into something other than just its pure mode of being. Hence, this is the meaning of "resting."

In general, in order for [some things] to function as cause [and result], they must be mutually connected as support and supported. Also, such a support and supported must come together, but it is impossible that the dharmadhātu and the mental consciousness come together or that [one] supports [the other]. Even if there were such a coming together, it would not be a proof that justifies an unconditioned phenomenon as the disposition. Rather, that would be a proof of justifying a compound of a conditioned and an unconditioned phenomenon as the disposition. Furthermore, if something given supports a phenomenon, it is difficult to prove that it is the cause for that phenomenon, or even a cause at all. Neither is necessarily the case.

Moreover, it is justified to present the dharmadhātu as the Tathāgata once it has become free from stains through having meditated on the path by focusing on the nature of phenomena. However, a presentation of an unconditioned phenomenon as the disposition merely due to this is something uncertain. Rather, once the purpose of meditating by focusing on these[259] has been fulfilled, it is certain in every respect that an unconditioned phenomenon cannot be presented as the disposition.

Also, in general, since an unconditioned phenomenon that is contained in the mind streams of sentient beings is not possible, there is also no focusing of bodhisattvas on it or them being supported by the actual dharmadhātu that fully qualifies as such, because the dhātu that is the nature of phenomena is not suitable to support or to be focused on. Moreover, if the cause of the result of some phenomenon is not established as having the character of this specific [resultant] thing, then it contradicts reasoning that it could become the cause of that [result] by focusing on a cause other than this cause, or by [the result] being supported by [that other cause]. Hence, such is never the case.

You may say, "But what then is the presentation of an unconditioned phenomenon as the disposition in your own system?" This presentation of the unconditioned dharmadhātu as the cause for buddhahood is not to present it as a cause by way of the existence of a connection between a cause and a result that fully qualify as such. Rather, this unconditioned dharmadhātu is [presented as a cause] in terms of perfect buddhahood and the unconditioned dharmadhātu being one in nature, while separable as different isolates.[260] When [presenting it] in this way, the nature of the cause for perfect buddhahood and the nature of the cause that is the dharmadhātu is not different. Hence, the cause for perfect buddhahood is not different from the nature of the cause that is the dharmadhātu, and therefore it is called "the cause for buddhahood." When it is associated with stains, the name "result" is not used for this kind of nonduality of dharmadhātu and perfect buddhahood, but instead it is labeled by the name "cause." Once it has become free from stains, perfect buddhahood is taught by the name "result."

According to the definitive meaning, both [notions] that are taught here—what is taught by the name "cause" and what is taught by the name "result"—are of the same nature. Therefore, these two do not exist as an actual cause and its specific result that are different from each other. For, rather, their modes of being as described are inseparable in terms of the distinctive feature of true reality.

Nevertheless, according to the expedient meaning, the dharmadhātu is presented as the cause and perfect buddhahood as the result. This involves the intention that something pure does not originate from a completely impure cause, but that something pure originates or exists based on something pure only. Thus, the purpose in this sense is [established] in terms of it being easy for [such] an understanding to emerge within the perspective of those whose minds are trained in the presentation of causes and results. Otherwise, the mistake of the consequence that cause and result are the same would be accrued, since the very cause that is the unconditioned dharmadhātu is explained as "original Buddha" in the mantrayāna. Hence, it is an expedient meaning that the result of perfect buddhahood is produced by the unconditioned dharmadhātu.[261] This kind of expedient meaning is indeed a teaching adapted to the mental perspective of those to be guided. However, since the single actuality of the unconditioned dharmadhātu is taught in many ways, such as being a cause in some contexts and being a result in other contexts, it is necessary to distinguish the expedient meaning and the definitive meaning without mixing them.

As for "the distinctive feature of the six āyatanas of bodhisattvas," other Tibetans say, "Some distinctive features of the six āyatanas of bodhisattvas who are on the path have the capacity to produce uncontaminated phenomena." But I assert that the distinctive feature of the six āyatanas, that is, the consciousness that is not shared by the six āyatanas of bodhisattvas, is something that is to be taken as something distinctive that is other than the six āyatanas. The meaning of this is clearly explained by the protector Maitreya. What is called "uncontaminated consciousness" is the unconditioned naturally abiding disposition, which is definitely the cause for perfect buddhahood and exists in all beings without beginning, right from the start. Due to three ways in which such a single disposition becomes revealed when it meets with distinctive features of conditions, there are also three [types of] possessors of the disposition. The meeting with conditions is based on the distinctive feature of the unfolding disposition. The understanding of the unfolding disposition is as follows: The disposition, which through the power of the nature of phenomena, consists of the conditions for presenting the unconditioned disposition as the great enlightenment [of Buddhas], the conditions for presenting it as the medium enlightenment [of pratyekabuddhas], and the conditions for presenting it as the lesser enlightenment [of śrāvakas], is labeled as the "unfolding disposition."

In brief, the natural disposition is the support that exists from the very start, while the unfolding disposition abides as the disposition that consists of the [thirteen] accomplishments,[262] which are distinguished by the particular phenomena supported [by the naturally abiding disposition] and enable the arising of the kāyas that [promote] the welfare of others or not. The gist of such an explanation is as follows. The naturally abiding disposition is the very nature of the mind associated with stains. The factor of the gradual process of all its stains becoming exhausted or the factor of already having relinquished them is presented as the unfolding disposition. This leads to presenting the display of the two kāyas—which are one's own and [the welfare] of others—as the results of these two dispositions.

Those who assert that there exist both an empty and a nonempty aspect in this dharmakāya—one's own welfare—and that it exists as conditioned as well as unconditioned may well claim to have trained their minds in distinguishing the two realities according to the system of Lord Maitreya. However, any assertions that the dharmakāya and the dharmadhātu are conditioned and empty in the sense of a nonimplicative negation and so on [are not tenable] for the following reasons: Let alone in the distinction between the two realities as asserted by Lord [Maitreya], even in any [other] system of any [master] who founded a [Buddhist] tradition, a dharmadhātu and a dharmakāya that are conditioned phenomena are not asserted. [In all of these traditions,] it is impossible to present the dharmadhātu and the dharmakāya as the factor that is a nonimplicative negation, that is, as empty [in the sense] of never having existed primordially right from the start. Moreover, the dharmakāya and the dharmadhātu are never ever presented as seeming reality. Thus, this manner of exegesis is explained the same way in all authentic traditions of the mahāyāna.

Some people proclaim loudly, "The presentation of the disposition that is explained in [texts] such as the *Mahāyānasūtrālaṃkāra* and the *Abhidharma-samucchaya* is the system of the Mere Mentalists, but not the system of the Mādhyamikas." If this were the case, as a consequence, all scriptural traditions of the mahāyāna would be forcefully pushed into the camp of the Mere Mentalists alone, and thus the Mādhyamika camps would suffer tremendous losses. [Rather,] in the system of the Mere Mentalists as well, the naturally abiding disposition is accepted as the Buddha heart. They say, "It is possible among beings—those who possess the Buddha heart—that some do not reach nirvāṇa in the form of great enlightenment. Therefore, there are those who possess the disposition that is the cut-off disposition." However, they declare that there is no sentient being whatsoever that does not have the Buddha heart.

Basically, the Mere Mentalists assert this naturally abiding disposition here as lucid and aware experience, while the Mādhyamikas do not assert that. The Mere Mentalists assert that there are sentient beings who do not attain perfect enlightenment at all, while the others do not assert that. The Mere Mentalists assert that the disposition for great enlightenment does not exist in the mind streams of arhats of the hīnayāna, while the others assert that it does exist. The Mere Mentalists assert that arhats of the hīnayāna lack the cause for rebirth in existence, while the others assert that they do not lack it. These [are their assertions] to be understood without confusing them.[263]

In this context, in order to make one understand what the exact principle of the supreme yāna is, one must understand what true reality—the nature of phenomena—is. In the mantrayāna, this is explained as the principal of the divisions of all dispositions, the lord of the circle of the ultimate mandala, the unbroken continuum within all aspects of ground, path, and fruition, which is [always] devoid of the three poisons and whose nature is not impermanent. This actual mode of being is declared to be "the Tathāgata heart" by Lord Maitreya. His intention was that this Heart is the dharmakāya endowed with twofold purity, and that, by labeling a part with the name of the whole, sentient beings have one dimension of this Buddha heart endowed with twofold purity, that is, its "natural purity."[264] It is in this way that he spoke of "sentient beings having the disposition of the Buddhas."

In brief, no matter which reasoning one might put forward to prove that the Buddha heart exists in the mind streams of sentient beings, it is impossible to establish a direct connection between the reason and the predicate [in such a reasoning]. Also, as far as the assertion by others that sentient beings possess the Heart is concerned, it is [only] suitable to assert that they possess [such a heart] in the sense of the factors to be relinquished. However, in that case, the factors to be relinquished are nothing but mistakenness, which never existed from the start. The assertion that either a connection of identity or a causal connection is established[265] between this Heart and sentient beings, as well as the assertion that they are some kind of support and supported that actually fulfill these functions, are not in accord with the Buddha and the successor to his throne, the protector Maitreya, and so forth. Therefore, they should be discarded. Also the many different presentations of the disposition that are given in other scriptural traditions are [simply] pointing to a mere fraction of this actual disposition.

You may wonder, "Then what is such a Heart?" It is the very nature of true reality, which cannot be separated from what consists of the unsurpassable qualities. In terms of its own nature, it is [always] endowed with twofold purity. However, provisionally and from the perspective of dialecticians, the Heart that actually fulfills this function is presented as what is free from adventitious stains, and its being free from adventitious stains is asserted as perfect buddhahood at the time of fruition. But it is stated, "As for that where the imputed Heart exists, it exists in the basic element associated with its husks."[266] During that time [of the Buddha heart existing in ordinary sentient beings], since it exists in the basic element that is associated with its husks, it does not necessarily exist in the basic element itself. [Here,] the "imputed Heart" is identified as the nature of phenomena (dharmatā) existing in what is the completely pure nature of the dhātu.

The Heart that fully qualifies as such is the dharmatākāya.[267] Therefore, each of the bhūmis of the mahāyāna will be seized during the phases when this very [Heart] is coming free from each corresponding portion of stains. Those who see each of these portions [of freedom] are presented as the jewel of the ultimate saṅgha. Seeing this is not [in a way that] a bodhisattva's stream of consciousness sees the Heart. Rather, due to the fact that many facets of personally experienced wisdom exist in this very Heart, the various collections of consciousness that obscure it cease as the respective [obscurations on each of the bhūmis]. This is labeled with the name "seeing."

A Heart like this is not contained in the mind streams of any sentient being whatsoever, nor is it blended with any mind streams. By focusing on this Heart of the mind streams of sentient beings, the obscurations are purified, and even when liberation is accomplished, they do not have any connection to this Heart. At this point, [it is said that] "sentient beings have accomplished the path and thus attained the dharmakāya." [However,] this too is [just] in terms of convenient conventional expressions, because a fully qualified presentation of being endowed with the attainment of the [dharmakāya] through the [accomplishment of the path], as it is given in the abhidharma, cannot be applied to this.

Some fools say, "The Omniscient Karmapa Rangjung [Dorje] asserts the intention of the *Mahāyānottaratantra* to be that the Tathāgata heart exists in the dharmadhātu of the mind of sentient beings in an inseparable manner." This wise being did not assert such. In his autocommentary on *The Profound Inner Reality* he makes a twofold classification [of mind as such], saying, "what is pure is expressed as mind, and what is impure is [also] expressed as mind."[268] By explaining that those who possess impure mental impulses are sentient beings, he elucidates that the dharmadhātu does not exist in such sentient beings. He presents these very sentient beings as being the adventitious stains that are produced by false imagination, which mistakenly strays from the dharmadhātu. By giving the pure mind names such as "ordinary mind," "original protector," and "original Buddha," he says that it is exactly this [mind] that possesses the mode of being inseparable from the buddha qualities.[269] This kind of [pure mind] is also the [Buddha] heart that actually fulfills this function.

Now you may wonder, "What does this pure mind refer to?" It is "the luminous nature of the mind." The meaning of "luminous" is that mistaken mind is naturally pure. The teaching that such a naturally pure Heart exists in sentient beings is not meant literally. Rather, what is taught by "buddhahood exists in sentient beings" is that, by taking the naturally luminous Heart as the basis, impure sentient beings exist in it as that which is to purified. However, it is again [only] under the influence of other-dependent mistakenness that sentient beings exist as that which is to be purified, whereas, according to the definitive meaning, that which is to be purified—the adventitious stains—do not exist right from the start.

As for the meaning of "adventitious stains," it is inadequate in all respects to explain that "adventitious" refers to the assertion that something previously nonexistent originates newly or to the assertion that something previously existent is suitable to become separated off later. The meaning of "adventitious" is not having come from some time before, nor to cease at some later time, nor to arise as something that newly comes about. Nevertheless, due to various causes of mistakenness making their connections, these [stains] are adventitious in the sense of being transitory [appearances]. In other words, they are nullities that have the nature of being unreal, false, and nonexistent.

Also, "existing" in "[sentient beings] existing as that which is to be purified" does not refer to an existence as in the existence that is distinguished as the counterpart [of nonexistence] in the dichotomy of existence and nonexistence. Rather, the existence that is taught here has the meaning of existing or not existing as what performs a function. So, all these sentient beings are entities because they are able to perform a function.[270] If they exist [in this way], they are necessarily impermanent, and if they are impermanent, there is no need for any causes that make them perish other than the causes that produced them. Therefore, they abide as something that definitely perishes. Since they abide as something that definitely perishes in this way, a sentient being will pass into nirvāṇa upon its individual form of saṃsāra having become exhausted. It is in this sense that it is declared, ultimately speaking, that there is not even a single sentient being that absolutely never passes into complete nirvāṇa within this great basic element of sentient beings. This is the definitive meaning.

Whatever is an impermanent entity is necessarily something that arises from causes and conditions, and what arises from causes and conditions does not arise through a nature of its own. If something does not arise through a nature of its own, it does not exist permanently, and something that does not exist permanently is also not produced by permanent causes and conditions that give rise to it. For this reason, results that are produced by impermanent [causes] are similar to these very impermanent causes, thus being of concordant type [in being impermanent]. All phenomena of this concordant type are not phenomena that actually qualify as existing in the manner of being established by a nature of their own in terms of their own essence. Consequently, they are all called "the seeming," since what does not exist by a nature of its own is mistaken as existing [in that manner]. This mode is what obscures the basic state of natural emptiness." What is said here is the intention of the Karmapas who successively arrive as noble Avalokiteśvara intends, through assuming human births.

Nowadays some people say, "The intention of the Omniscient Rangjung Dorje is that the Tathāgata heart that is not empty of qualities, such as the [ten] powers, exists in sentient beings. This is clearly explained by the mighty victor, [the Seventh Karmapa,] Chötra Gyatso." This is [just] putting to melody what others say, but it is not our own [Kagyü] system.[271] You may wonder, "Which other great ones assert such a system?" In Tibet, the land of snows, there are indeed also many others who assert something like that, but the one who explains it by excessively promoting it is Dölpopa Sherab Gyaltsen. He declares that "such a Heart, which is free of all flaws and endowed with all qualities, exists in sentient beings. Through it existing in sentient beings, sentient beings do not have to be it. Therefore, one must make a difference between existing and being [something], without mixing them."[272]

I say that this statement, "Buddhahood exists in sentient beings" is flawed. In general, in a proof that a single subject [in question] either has a distinct property or is this very property, the establishment of a connection between the predicate of the probandum and the reason in such a way that they are inseparable in their own essence represents a "nature reason." Or, in a proof that something exists in the basis that is the subject [in question], the establishment of a causal connection between the predicate of the probandum and the reason is necessary.[273]

However, [considering the above statement] in terms of the first [type of proof], if "sentient beings" are taken as the subject, and "are Buddhas" is taken as the predicate of the probandum, then [the possibility] to connect these with a reason that is formulated with "exist" is generally excluded through valid cognition.[274] In particular, this [type of proof] is also not justified in your own system because, according to you, it is neither asserted that Buddhas are sentient beings, nor that sentient beings are Buddhas.

Furthermore, in [your own] system, you cannot take "sentient beings" as the subject and "Buddha" as the predicate of the probandum and then connect them with a reason that is formulated with "exist." For, to connect [two phenomena] in such a way that the one is or has the other, in general, one needs something that is not negating [what one tries to connect] through being contrary to it. But in your system, it is not proper to connect sentient beings and Buddhas through a reason that is formulated with "exist," since you claim that they, just like light and darkness, are contrary in the sense of not coexisting [in a single locus]. That means you cannot connect them in this way, because it simply comes down to not finding any reason at all that could serve as such a [correct] subject property.[275]

In brief, to be the probandum or to exist in it depends on a connection being established. However, for a connection to be established, the unmistaken positive and negative concomitances[276] must be established. Consequently, this [statement], "Buddhahood exists in sentient beings" is uncertain, since it does not rest upon any positive or negative concomitance whatsoever that is unmistaken through valid cognition.

[You may want to reformulate this by] saying, "In sentient beings who are endowed with buddhahood (the subject), buddhahood exists." Here, the nature of the subject is not established. That which is buddhahood or the Heart is unconditioned, and it is impossible that conditioned sentient beings are endowed with this unconditioned Heart. However, if we just assume that they were endowed with it, would they then be endowed with it in a contradictory manner or be endowed with it in a connected manner? [Obviously,] you do not assert that they are endowed with it in a contradictory manner.

But if they were endowed with it in a connected manner, the Heart and sentient beings who obscure it would [again] not be beyond being connected either by identity or in a causal manner, while the Bhagavat has declared in the collection of sūtras of definitive meaning that these two cannot be expressed as being either the same or different. Hence, the above thesis is not tenable.

The gist of this—the meaning of the statement by the victors and their children that "buddhahood exists in sentient beings"—is declared to be as follows: "Buddhahood exists in sentient beings, without [the two] being connected, in the manner of a Heart [or core] within the cocoon of beginningless afflictive obscurations, and in such a way that this Heart is not something whose own nature is nonexistent." As for the meaning of this, it is tenable to say, "Its intention is that the Heart exists as [or in] the Heart."

Some later great ones [in Tibet] say, "As for the meaning that the Buddha heart exists in sentient beings, it is declared that 'Buddhahood exists in sentient beings' with the following in mind: 'In different individual sentient beings, individual kinds of buddhahood that serve as the Hearts [of these beings] exist.'" Through being explained in this way, it indeed strikes the intelligence of some people as being tenable. However, the existence of individual kinds of buddhahood as the Hearts of individual sentient beings is also difficult to discriminate as being the definitive meaning. The buddhahood that serves as the Heart [of these beings] cannot be expressed as existing as many individual kinds that are either the same or different, because the suchness of this Heart cannot be differentiated as being good or bad due to a difference in its support ([existing in] a Buddha or a sentient being) and because this undifferentiable Heart is free from being one or many.

This is why some people put forth the following [proof]: "[Verse I.28 of the *Uttaratantra*] is taught as the means to prove the existence of the Heart that actually fulfills this function in sentient beings:

Since the perfect buddhakāya radiates,
Since suchness is undifferentiable,
And because of the disposition,
All beings always contain the Buddha heart.[277]

Therefore, the existence of the actual Buddha heart is established through these three reasons according to their order. During the time of [sentient beings], in all beings (the subject), the Buddha heart exists, because the disposition exists at this time." [However,] in such a formulation, the mode of positive concomitance (if the disposition exists, the Heart exists) is not established for the following reason. If the disposition is also presented as merely the latent tendencies of listening, the Heart refers to actual buddhahood. But while the latent tendencies of listening occur even on the level of [practicing the path due to just] having confidence,[278] the dharmakāya and the Buddha heart do not necessarily exist on that [level].

Furthermore, it may be said, "[In] these [sentient beings] (the subject), the [Buddha heart] exists, because the suchness of sentient beings and the Buddha heart are undifferentiable." Here, a part of the reason does not apply to the subject, since it is declared in this system of the *Mahāyānottaratantra* that suchness and the Buddha heart are equivalent and just different names, but that suchness does not exist in sentient beings.

Also, even if [the reason] "since the perfect buddhakāya radiates" is given for the same subject and predicate of the probandum as before, it does not go beyond being a reason that does not apply [to the subject], because it is impossible that the perfect buddhakāya radiates from the continua of sentient beings.

This is why the statement that the [Tathāgata heart] exists in [sentient beings] because of the [above] kinds of reasons must be understood through the triad of intention, purpose, and [logical] invalidation of the explicit [statement].[279] This is said clearly in this text [—the *Uttaratantra*—] itself.[280]

Some great ones say, "The intention behind [this statement] is that buddhahood exists in the continua of sentient beings as something suitable to come forth, just as in the example of butter existing in milk as something that is suitable to come forth [from it]." This example of those who put it that way is not justified either. That butter comes forth from milk is invalidated even by reasoning that is based on direct perception. So just as this example is [not] established, its meaning is not established either.

Thus, to explain the dharmadhātu [and nothing else] as the disposition as well as [the fact] that the fruitions of the three yānas emerge in dependence on just this [dharmadhātu] is what persists as the definitive meaning. Noble Asaṅga declared:

> You may wonder why [suchness] is called "dharmadhātu." Because it is the cause for all dharmas of śrāvakas, pratyekabuddhas, and Buddhas.[281]

Consequently, the threefold difference in terms of fully complete or not fully complete realization [of śrāvakas, pratyekabuddhas, and Buddhas, respectively] occurs through the three different [ways of] engaging in this very dharmadhātu as a yāna. However, [Asaṅga] did not state that realization's own nature is anything other than this cause that is the dharmadhātu.

Here, some may say, "Then it follows that also the realization of realizing personal identitylessness does not go somewhere else beyond the cause that is the dharmadhātu." [To this, there is] the widely known answer and the answer for those who [really] want to know. As for the first, if I [already] accept that there are no other phenomena apart from the dharmadhātu, why should I not accept [the above consequence]—I do accept it. As for the second, if this consequence refers to the existence of the factor of personal identitylessness in the dharmadhātu, I accept it. But if this consequence refers to the factor of realization through the prajñā that realizes the identitylessness of the continuum of the person that is connected to the continuum of a śrāvaka, then there is no entailment in it.

Some Tibetans present the nature of the dharmadhātu as consciousness that is lucid and aware. They explain the assertion that, by focusing on nothing but this, it functions as the support for the [various] types of realization of the three yānas as being the system of the Yogācāras. They say, "If the dharmadhātu is realized, this is not necessarily the realization of phenomenal identitylessness," and "When the result of any of the yānas comes forth in dependence on the dharmadhātu, it is not certain that the dharmadhātu must be realized [for this to happen]." There are indeed [such statements], but [for now] I leave them as bases to be examined.

You may say, "The gist of [your] explanation in this way presents the disposition that actually fulfills this function as the [Buddha] heart. Hence, in that case, since there are three [kinds of] possessors of the disposition, is this Heart itself presented as these three [kinds of] possessors of the disposition?" It is not. Though this Heart in itself does not go beyond just the single disposition of the Tathāgatas, the classification as three [kinds of] possessors of the disposition is [made] due to the existence of three different [kinds of] noble persons. However, it is not that there is something to be classified in the disposition of the Tathāgatas itself. Then you may think, "In that case, different noble persons are impossible altogether." What is taken as the basis of designating noble persons are the qualities of awareness and liberation of these noble ones.[282]

In brief, nowadays, those who boast about being the proclaimers of the definitive meaning say, "The disposition of the Buddhas is what relinquishes the respective portions of the factors to be relinquished in individual beings to be guided who are the three [kinds of] possessors of the disposition. Through that, they [respectively] attain the realization of some aspects or of the entirety of all aspects of the buddha disposition of the Buddhas. This is the justification for the three [kinds of] possessors of the disposition. Also, the attainments of these three types of enlightenment come forth due to the buddha disposition granting its power." In the first [parts] of such an explanation, there is nothing major that is untenable, but a phrase like "granting the power of the Heart" did not appear anywhere in India or Tibet before.

If both the words and their meaning are examined, [this kind of] Heart does not exist. Since the Heart is unconditioned, it is impossible to involve the conditioned activity of granting its power.

Some people may think, "Because all radiating of the enlightened activity of the dharmakāya from this very Heart accomplishes activity, the above [statement] is not untenable. Thus, it is tenable." To say this [just exposes] your flaw of not having been trained [thoroughly]. In terms of its own nature, the activity of the Buddha's dharmakāya is not a conditioned activity. At the time of such activity engaging with sentient beings, the [actual] accomplishing of that activity is something that takes place in the continua of sentient beings with pure karma, meaning that it comes about through the power of entities. Since that activity is accomplished in the continua of these [beings] during that time, there is no need for the existence of efforts or conditioned activities within the actual enlightened activity of the dharmakāya itself.

All accomplishments in the thirteen accomplishments taught here [in the *Abhisamayālaṃkāra*] are not just fruitless toils but meaningful results. Through having performed the activity of accomplishing the purification of adventitious stains in the Buddha heart, once the stains have become pure, [it can be said that] "the result of buddhahood is attained." This result is what bears the names "disposition," "support," or "cause" during the phase [of being in the process] of accomplishing it. That in this case there is no cause or result that fully qualifies as such has already been explained above.

In terms of the definitive meaning, exactly this disposition of the Heart is actual buddhahood. From the point of view of what appears to the sentient beings who obscure this very [Heart] and other beings to be guided, it appears as if they have become Buddhas, which is just seeming buddhahood. At this point, once the adventitious stains have become pure, it appears as if this very buddhahood needed to become completely perfect omniscient buddhahood again. But in terms of the definitive meaning, this very Buddha heart is buddhahood by its sheer presence. Therefore, it does not need to become buddhahood again, and nothing else is able to make it become buddhahood either. Thus, if examined and analyzed, apart from this very buddhahood being buddhahood, it is impossible for even a single noble person to become a Buddha anywhere else in any of the three times.

Precisely this actuality dawned in the minds of the Tagbo Kagyü guru of yore and was put into song. As Lord Tüsum Kyenba sang:

> If there is no change in buddhahood,
> There is no aspiration to attain all these fruitions.

Some later people in the land of snows say, "By presenting the thirteen accomplishments as something that arises as the nature of dharmadhātu wisdom, they are something supported in that manner. This is like, for example, presenting the six dhyānabhūmis[283] as the supports for minds on the uncontaminated path." To this, I say:

> However you differentiate "existing" and "being [something],"
> The continua of beings do not possess
> A connection to the Buddha heart.
> However supreme sentient beings may be,
> They are what is to be purified for luminosity to become fully clear.[284]
> However it may be covered by obscurations,
> The Heart does not move
> From buddhahood to anywhere else.

This much is for sure.[285]

Is Buddha Nature an Eternal Soul or Sheer Emptiness?

From all of this, it should be clear that the teachings on buddha nature do not refer to the existence of some solid eternal nucleus of buddhahood enclosed in sentient beings, deep down in the wild tangle of intense afflictions that obscure it. Rather, the explanation by the Eighth Karmapa fits very well with the above-mentioned meanings of *garbha* that signify the space within some enclosure or sheath, pointing to a nonsolidifying understanding of buddha nature as the open yet luminous space of the nature of the mind within the merely fictitious cocoon of adventitious stains. However, as the Karmapa extensively discussed, buddha nature is not just some small core or space that is literally and only located "within" every sentient being. In fact, it is the other way round—our whole existence as sentient beings is in itself the sum of adventitious stains that just float like clouds within the infinite, bright sky of buddha nature, the luminous, open expanse of our mind that has no limits or boundaries. Once these clouds dissolve due to the warm rays of the sun of wisdom shining within this sky, nothing within sentient beings has been freed or improved, but there is just this radiant expanse without any reference points of cloudlike sentient beings or cloud-free Buddhas.

Similar to the space within a glass becoming one with the infinity of all space, once the glass is broken, one cannot say that the space within these clouds is the same or different from all of space. Of course, as long as the clouds are there, from their perspective, the space within them seems to be different from the space without. But once the clouds are gone, the question of whether the space that had been within them is the same as or different from all other space simply does not apply anymore, because the very reference point that seemed to allow for such a distinction in the first place—the clouds—is gone. Likewise, once the adventitious stains—or, more personally speaking, we as sentient beings—have dissolved, it is a moot question whether "our" dharmadhātu (or buddha nature) and "all the rest" of the dharmadhātu (or the buddha natures of all Buddhas) are the same or different, since what is called a sentient being is nothing but the very mistakenness that makes up such a distinction.

To wit, when it is said that the Tathāgata heart is perfect in itself, primordially pure, and unchanging, and that buddhahood means just the removal of adventitious stains, one cannot help but notice striking similarities with the doctrine of *abhivyakti* ("manifestation" or "revelation"), which is found in both the Upaniṣads and the Sāṃkhya School. In the Upaniṣadic Pāśupata doctrine, *abhivyakti* refers to liberation as the manifestation of the perfections of the innate Śiva through the removal of stains. For the Sāṃkhyas, it means that the entire diversity of the world is nothing but a manifestation of the single, eternal, and unchanging primordial cosmic substance. In the same vein, the view that there is no difference between the Tathāgata heart as the cause of the dharmakāya and the result being nothing but its manifestation as dharmakāya seems to come very close to the Sāṃkhya School's central assertion that nothing can be produced that does not exist already (*satkāryavāda*)—an assertion that is generally refuted by all Buddhist schools and one of the favorite targets of the Mādhyamikas in particular (the result already being fully present in the cause). Needless to mention, the Tathāgata heart even being described as a self (*ātman*), permanent, blissful, and pure makes people wonder what the difference is compared to Vedic notions of *ātman* and *brahman*. In terms of the Buddhist path, the notion of all beings actually being Buddhas in the first place may lead some into an attempt of ignoring the stains and afflictive states of mind (which are said to be adventitious and unreal anyway) and pretend to be enlightened already, thus avoiding any serious practice in order to remove said stains and afflictions.

In Indian texts, there is no evidence that any Buddhist considered the teachings on buddha nature as "non-Buddhist." However, there never evolved any fixed set of "classical" doctrinal positions on it, the only Indian treatise devoted to this subject alone and treating it somewhat systematically being the *Uttaratantra* with its commentary by Asaṅga.[286] It should also not be forgotten that the primary scope and purpose of texts like the *Uttaratantra* and the *Dharmadhātustava* is to highlight the fact that all sentient beings are capable of attaining complete buddhahood. In this way, they are more inspirational and devotional in both style and content, rather than trying to lay out some distinct philosophical system in every detail. The task of further expounding on the notion of the Tathāgata heart, clearly setting it off from the above-mentioned doctrines and misunderstandings, and integrating it with the rest of the Buddha's teaching—in particular emptiness as taught in the prajñāpāramitā sūtras—was only taken on much later by Tibetan commentators. In this process, however, many masters who did not subscribe to the notion of buddha nature meaning nothing but emptiness—or at least being a teaching of expedient meaning—were severely criticized by others and even accused of having "heretic" views like the Sāṃkhyas or supporting the Vedic notion of *ātman*. Śākya Chogden's commentary on the *Dharmadhātustava* explains the difference as follows:

> If one has the remedies to relinquish the stains, there is no need to search for enlightenment somewhere outside or far away. But if one does not use these remedies, enlightenment is not near, since the mere existence of the dharmadhātu is not enlightenment. You may wonder, "But isn't it necessary to assert this dharmadhātu wisdom as natural buddhahood?" That is indeed so, but this in itself does not qualify as actual buddhahood, since the three kāyas are not complete. "But aren't the three kāyas complete naturally?" They are indeed complete, but that too does not qualify as actual buddhahood, since these are not the kāyas that serve as the ultimate welfare of others. Therefore, what is called "natural buddhahood" refers to the cause of actual buddhahood. Otherwise, if actual buddhahood existed just through what is called "natural buddhahood," one would assert the philosophical system of the Sāṃkhyas. For then, during the time of sentient beings, buddhahood would reside in them in a nonmanifest way and would [just] need to be made clearly manifest through the power of the path later.[287]

When asked about this, the senior contemporary Kagyü master Thrangu Rinpoche said that, if you do not practice these teachings on buddha nature, the mere view is just like the Sāṃkhya position. Thus, from a practical point of view, no matter how sophisticated the terminological or philosophical distinctions with regard to the Buddha heart may be formulated or conceived, for Buddhists, the whole point of these teachings is to personally connect with the experience and realization that they try to convey through the Buddhist path, that is, nothing less than discovering this Heart in themselves and become Buddhas.

In the same vein, Mipham Rinpoche's *Exposition of the Madhyamakālaṃkāra* quotes numerous passages from the Vedas and other Indian non-Buddhist texts that resemble Buddhist statements on Yogācāra, Madhyamaka, and buddha nature almost to the letter, and then concludes:

> Since Dzogchen is the final one of the very profound [teachings], it is difficult to realize. Therefore, the vast majority of meditations that are cultivated by way of meditating in a foolish way—which means either not having completed cutting through one's doubts through studying and reflecting or lacking the essential points of profound pith instructions—will be very close to these [non-Buddhist systems just mentioned]. Without finding certainty in primordial purity (*ka dag*), just mulling over some "ground that is neither existent nor nonexistent" will get you nowhere. If you apprehend this basis of emptiness that is empty of both existence and nonexistence as something that is established by its essence separately [from everything else], no matter how you label it—such as an inconceivable self, Brahmā, Viṣṇu, Īśvara, or wisdom—except for the mere name, the meaning is the same. Since the basic nature free from the reference points of the four extremes, that is, Dzogchen—the luminosity that is to be personally experienced—is not at all like that, it is important to rely on the correct path and teacher. Therefore, you may pronounce "illusionlike," "nonentity," "freedom from reference points," and the like as mere verbiage, but this is of no benefit whatsoever, if you do not know the [actual] way of being of the Tathāgata's emptiness (which surpasses the limited [kinds of] emptiness [asserted] by the tīrthikas) through the decisive certainty that is induced by reasoning. . . . In this way, Buddhist and non-Buddhist philosophical systems cannot be distinguished through mere words, but as far as the profound essential point is concerned, they are as different as the earth is from the sky. Hence, after his arrival in Tibet, Atiśa said that, in the India of his days, it is difficult to distinguish Buddhist and non-Buddhist philosophical systems. The same has happened for Buddhism and Bön in Tibet."[288]

As for the Gelugpa position on buddha nature, since it is still around, it seems inevitable to address it here. According to the Gelugpa School, buddha nature means nothing but sentient beings' emptiness, which is held to be a nonimplicative negation in the sense of the sheer lack of real existence (Tib. bden grub). Like so many Gelugpa positions, this is an interesting concept and, fundamentally, there is no problem with it, except that it is simply not tenable on the basis of any Indian text on buddha nature, nor through reasoning. At the same time, it is highly insufficient from a soteriological point of view. To keep this really brief, let alone what the *Uttaratantra* and the other treatises quoted above say again and again, the *Mahāparinirvāṇasūtra* states:

> Whenever you search for what is called "the emptiness of emptiness," nothing whatsoever is found. Even the Nirgranthas[289] have what is called "nothing whatsoever," but liberation is not like that . . . Liberation is the uncontrived basic element—this is the Tathāgata.[290]

Also many other sūtras, such as the *Śrīmālādevīsūtra*, *Aṅgulimālīyasūtra*, *Dhāraṇīśvararājaparipṛcchasūtra*, and *Tathāgatagarbhasūtra* suggest everything but the above Gelugpa position of the Tathāgata heart being nothing but emptiness, let alone a nonimplicative negation. The contemporary Western authority Lambert Schmithausen and others show in great detail that this interpretation of buddha nature has no foundation in the Indian texts on *tathāgatagarbha*. Schmithausen says:

> To summarize, it should be clear that the *Tathāgatagarbha* interpretation of the dGe-lugs-pas favored by Ru[egg], as interesting as it is in itself, is hardly less tenable from a historical point of view than the opinion of the dGe-lugs-pas that also the Ālayavijñānam of the Yogācāras is eventually nothing other than emptiness.[291]

On the more technical side, also in the Gelugpa system, a nonimplicative negation is categorized as a generally characterized phenomenon, which is defined as "that which is not able to perform a function."[292] So if buddha nature—and thus buddhahood—is nothing but a nonimplicative negation, by definition, it could not have any qualities, let alone those of a Buddha, such as unlimited prajñā, compassion, omniscience. Nor could it perform even so much as a wink of enlightened activity. In other words, if buddha nature means nothing but the sheer absence of real existence, how can any absence ever be something like buddhahood with all its wisdom, qualities, and enlightened activities? This is especially absurd, since the performance of enlightened activity for the welfare of all sentient beings is the whole and only point of becoming a Buddha in the first place—otherwise, one may as well just strive for the personal and inactive liberation of an arhat. In all texts on buddha nature, the enlightened activity upon its manifestation as dharmakāya is emphasized over and again as one of its most crucial elements. As Zimmermann says:

> Regarding the attainment of awakening, the authors of the TGS [*Tathāgatagarbhasūtra*] do not tire of emphasizing that this leads to the performance of the tasks of a Buddha. They obviously consider this fact as an automatic consequence of the manifestation of one's buddha nature, and in several passages it alone is stated to be a characteristic of buddhahood. This in itself demonstrates that efficaciousness was a main category in the earliest stage of *tathāgatagarbha* thought. The reason for describing a tathāgata primarily in terms of dynamic activity may well lie in an attitude of worldly engagement predominating over mainly theoretical concerns.[293]

Furthermore, according to the Gelugpa position, there is every reason to wonder why stones and cars do not become Buddhas too, since a buddha nature that is nothing but emptiness in the sense of a nonimplicative negation applies to all inanimate phenomena in just the same way. In addition, in the Gelugpa system, the teachings on buddha nature are regarded as being of expedient meaning, while emptiness (as said nonimplicative negation) is held to be the definitive meaning. Thus, when it is said at the same time that buddha nature means nothing but the emptiness of sentient beings, this leads to the consequence that buddha nature must either be of definitive meaning too or emptiness—at least the one of sentient beings—must be of expedient meaning. Let's not go into the details of the absurdity of there being two emptinesses—the expedient one of sentient beings and the definitive one of everything else (which would moreover make it impossible for sentient beings to realize that definitive emptiness based on anything in their own continua).

In addition, any nonimplicative negation is by definition an existent and an object of conceptual consciousness only. Thus, buddha nature—emptiness as such a negation—can only be realized by a conceptual consciousness, but never by nonconceptual yogic direct perception. This would mean that even the highest wisdom of a Buddha is still conceptual, and yogic perception (the only ultimately infallible form of insight in Buddhism) never happens. Even if it did arise anyway, it would have to realize something other than the emptiness that is a nonimplicative negation. But this simply means that it then would be mistaken, since it does not realize what is claimed to be the sole ultimate. In addition, since—according to the Gelugpas—such a nonimplicative negation already *is* the actual ultimate, there would be no need to abandon it and proceed to a direct realization.[294]

Furthermore, if buddha nature referred to nothing other than the emptiness that is a nonimplicative negation, why would the Buddha have bothered to greatly elaborate on merely this emptiness in many sūtras of the third turning of the wheel of dharma (which is moreover considered to be of expedient meaning by the Gelugpas), when he had already taught the emptiness of all phenomena at length and in a very straightforward manner in the prajñāpāramitā sūtras of the second turning? If—as per the Gelugpas—the third turning only teaches Mere Mentalism, then it is definitely contradictory that this very turning teaches the same emptiness (buddha nature being nothing but a nonimplicative negation) as the prajñāpāramitā sūtras, which the Gelugpas themselves consider to be of definitive meaning. On the other hand, if the third turning indeed teaches this emptiness, then it must be of definitive meaning too. Also, as mentioned above, even the *Adhyardhaśatikaprajñāpāramitāsūtra*—a part of the second wheel of dharma that is of definitive meaning—says that "all sentient beings contain the Tathāgata heart." So is this then a statement of definitive meaning, or is the sūtra of expedient meaning?

There are anecdotes of Gelugpas who, upon being asked in conversation whether a Buddha has wisdom or not, became more or less offended by such a "heretical" question. At the same time, in formal debate, they would strictly deny that a Buddha has wisdom. Similarly, it may be safely assumed that none of them would say "no" to the question, "Do you aspire to become a Buddha?" But does that mean that they are really inspired by the notion of wanting to become a nonimplicative negation? Okay, enough of that for now.

As for the arguments that the teachings on buddha nature are just of expedient meaning, they are usually based on *Uttaratantra* I.157, which says that the existence of the Buddha heart in all sentient beings is taught in order to eliminate the five flaws of faintheartedness, denigrating inferior beings, clinging to what is not the ultimate, denying the ultimate, and being excessively attached to oneself. Karmapa Mikyö Dorje's *Lamp That Elucidates the System of the Proponents of Other-Empty Madhyamaka*[295] states that the existence of buddha nature is taught in order to awaken all sentient beings' disposition for buddhahood and to relinquish the five flaws. Then, the Karmapa addresses the above argument in good Prāsaṅgika style by drawing the absurd consequence that, if these teachings were only of expedient meaning, there would be no need to give up these five flaws. In other words, we would have every reason to be fainthearted, lacking confidence in ever attaining enlightenment, since we do not have any buddha nature to even start with. Therefore, any trust in our buddha nature would just mean to fool ourselves. Also, we would be fully entitled to look down on inferior beings because none of them really have buddha nature, let alone any of its qualities. On the reverse side, we would be justified in being proud and self-satisfied upon achieving any "new personal" qualities. Also, everybody who denies the possibility of enlightenment would be perfectly right, since the nonexistence of buddha nature means the nonexistence of the dharmakāya. Thus, such people would just express the way things truly are. On the other hand, since there would be nothing other than just the delusions and obscurations that manifest as saṃsāra, it would be justified to take these illusory appearances as the only reality there is. Consequently, any attempt at practicing the Buddhist path would be pointless. It may be added that, if the teachings on buddha nature are understood as an expedient meaning, that is, as mere skillful means to address some specific flaws, it would follow that each and every teaching of the Buddha, including those on emptiness, is of expedient meaning. For, it is common for all instructions of the Buddha to be given for specific purposes and as remedies for specific problems. Consequently, there would be nothing in the Buddha's teachings that is of definitive meaning. On the other hand, there are also passages in the scriptures that clearly present the teachings on emptiness and identitylessness as remedial and expedient and those on buddha nature as fruitional and definitive. For example, the *Mahāparinirvāṇasūtra* says that teaching buddha nature after identitylessness is like first smearing bitter bile on a mother's breasts in order to prevent her baby from drinking milk while it has to digest a medicine (identitylessness) against a disease (clinging to any kind of identity). Once the baby is cured, it is allowed to drink the milk (buddha nature).[296]

To be sure here, the above absurd consequences by the Karmapa in no way imply that he affirms any reified existence of buddha nature. As his discussion in *The Noble One Resting at Ease* presented earlier shows in detail, he indeed agrees that the statement, "the Buddha heart exists in sentient beings" is of expedient meaning. He even explains the same for the result of perfect buddhahood being actually produced by the unconditioned dharmadhātu. But this does not mean that all teachings on the Buddha heart are of expedient meaning, as evidenced by the Karmapa's clarifications as to what their definitive meaning is.

To summarize, when not just clinging to the words but understanding what is conveyed by these words, let alone Nāgārjuna's *Dharmadhātustava*, in Indian Yogācāra texts too, there is no reifying interpretation of *tathāgatagarbha*. The teachings on buddha nature were never designed as a doctrinal or ontological alternative to or replacement of emptiness. *Tathāgatagarbha*—the luminous nature of the mind—is not regarded as a monistic absolute beside which all other phenomena have a mere status of emptiness. Rather, it is the natural state of our mind, in which no self-delusion is ever at work. The default example used throughout *tathāgatagarbha* texts for this nature of the mind being without reference points, inexpressible, and indemonstrable is space. Still, in order to clarify that the ungraspable expanse of the mind is not just a mere inert vacuum, but that this expanse is vivid sheer experience—the natural unity of expanse and wisdom—these texts also give many examples for the luminous aspect of mind's nature and its boundless inseparable qualities.

Nāgārjuna

THE *DHARMADHĀTUSTAVA*

An Overview of the Basic Themes of the Dharmadhātustava

GIVEN THIS long and rich "history" of luminous mind being covered by adventitious stains only, the subject of Nāgārjuna's *Dharmadhātustava* and how it is taught is not at all unusual, except for when one has one's own set agenda of what he is supposed to say as a "true" Mādhyamika and what not. In fact, since pretty much everybody else in the Buddhist mahāyāna world speaks on luminous mind and *tathāgatagarbha*, the question seems not to be why Nāgārjuna would teach on this subject, but rather why he would not.

As for the text of the *Dharmadhātustava*, only six of its verses (18–23) are preserved in Sanskrit, as quoted in Nāropa's *Sekoddeśaṭīkā*.[297] The Tibetan translation in 101 verses was prepared by Kṛṣṇa Paṇḍita and the Tibetan translator Nagtso Lotsāwa Tsültrim Gyalwa[298] during the middle of the eleventh century. The *Tengyur* editions of Peking (P2010; ka, fol. 73a.7–77a.8), Derge (D1118; ka, fol. 63b.5–67b.3), and Narthang (ka, fol. 70a.1–74b.7) show a number of variations, but only a few are significant (see translation). The Chinese Buddhist canon contains two translations of the *Dharmadhātustava* (Taishō 413 and 1675), translated by the famous tantric master Amoghavajra (705–774) and Dānapāla from Uḍḍiyāna in the early eleventh century, respectively. Differing from the Tibetan, Taishō 413 has 125 verses (its verses 91–112 and 116–119 are not found in the Tibetan) and also shows a number of variant readings. Taishō 1675 is not a literal translation but a freer rendering of the meaning in eighty-seven verses.[299]

As for the contents of the *Dharmadhātustava*, what was said above about the combination of affirmative and negative approaches in Nāgārjuna's praises no doubt applies the most to this text. In a way, one may say that it blends the style of the second and the third turnings of the wheel of dharma, striking a balance between all phenomena's lack of nature and mind's true nature. Many of its verses are in accord with both the teachings on emptiness as in Nāgārjuna's Madhyamaka works and the instructions on buddha nature as found in the *tathāgatagarbha* sūtras and Maitreya's *Uttaratantra*.

The latter is especially true for the examples that illustrate the *Dharmadhātustava*'s main theme—luminous mind or dharmadhātu being obscured by adventitious stains but essentially untainted by them, revealing all its qualities in full, once these stains are removed. The text contains twelve such examples: (1) butter within milk (verses 3–4); (2) a lamp within a vase (5–7); (3) an encrusted beryl (9–10); (4) gold in its ore (11); (5) rice grains in their husks (12–13); (6) sun and moon covered by five obscurations (18–19); (7) a soiled fireproof garment (20–21); (8) water deep in the earth (23); (9) a baby in the womb (27); (10) the same water being cold or warm (36–37); (11) milk mixed with water (62–63); and (12) the waxing moon (74–76). There are two more examples that illustrate there being no result without a cause: seeds in general (16–17) and sugar cane seeds in particular (69–73). The example of the banana tree (14–15) is a somewhat mixed metaphor applied to both of the just-mentioned senses, since the example itself says that a sweet fruit grows from something without pith, while its application in the next verse states that saṃsāra without pith being freed from the peel of the afflictions is the fruition of buddhahood. Together, the thirty verses on these examples and their meanings make up almost one third of the text.

The text also says repeatedly that the dharmadhātu or mind covered by adventitious stains is saṃsāra, while its being uncovered is nirvāṇa (1, 2, 37, 46–48, 56, 64, 79–80, and 88). From the perspective of sentient beings, there are three phases of the dharmadhātu: (1) being fully obscured by afflictions, it is called a sentient being; (2) being in the process of becoming gradually unobscured, it is called a bodhisattva; and (3) being completely unobscured, it is called buddhahood or dharmakāya (74–76). In the same vein, enlightenment is neither near nor far, being just a matter of realizing the ever-present dharmadhātu or not (49, 61), which occurs through or as the personal experience of one's own awareness or wisdom (1, 29, 46, 56, 61). At the same time, in classical Madhyamaka diction, the dharmadhātu is characterized as unarisen and unceasing (8); free from self and mine as well as all characteristics, such as gender (24–25); equal to the sky (87); completely inconceivable; and beyond the spheres of speech and the senses (89–90). All phenomena are said to be empty, nonexistent, merely dependently arising and ceasing, being *madhyama*—the very center (30–33). Conceptions about self, mine, or any other characteristics of phenomena are the very obscurations (28, 64). Similarly to the *Uttaratantra*, verse 22 addresses the question of the relationship between the Buddha's teachings on emptiness and the Tathāgata heart, stating that emptiness serves as the remedy for afflictions, but never invalidates the luminous nature of the mind. This is confirmed by verse 26, saying that emptiness or the lack of nature is what purifies the mind best. In terms of the practical application of this not only in formal meditation but throughout one's life, verses 38–45 speak of directly realizing the dharmadhātu through penetrating to the very essence of the five sense consciousnesses and the mental consciousness, including their objects, which is strikingly similar to what is said in this respect in Mahāmudrā and Dzogchen instructions. Further topics of the text include how Buddhas appear to sentient beings (51–55); that the dharmadhātu is the fundamental basis for everything in saṃsāra and nirvāṇa (2, 57–59); the ten pāramitās as the means to reveal the dharmadhātu (66–68); the progression of the ten bhūmis of bodhisattvas (78–87); and the fruition of buddhahood as the final "fundamental change of state," including its interaction with bodhisattvas on the tenth bhūmi (88–101).

In brief, the notion of dharmadhātu that Nāgārjuna presents here is clearly not sheer emptiness (let alone emptiness in the sense of a nonimplicative negation), nor just the nature of phenomena as the ultimate object to be realized. Rather, the dharmadhātu is understood as the natural state of luminous pure mind. This is personally experienced wisdom (the ultimate subject without any duality of subject and object), in other words, buddhahood full of enlightened qualities, which represents infinite benefit for both oneself and others.[300]

Translation: In Praise of Dharmadhātu[301]

I pay homage to Youthful Mañjuśrī.[302]

I bow to you, the dharmadhātu,
Who resides in every sentient being.
But if they aren't aware of you,
They circle through this triple being. [1]

Due to just that being purified
What is such circling's cause,
This very purity is then nirvāṇa.
Likewise, dharmakāya is just this. [2]

While it's blended with the milk,
Butter's essence appears not.
Likewise, in the afflictions' mix,
Dharmadhātu is not seen. [3]

Once you've cleansed it from the milk,
Butter's essence is without a stain.
Just so, with the afflictions purified,
The dharmadhātu lacks all stain. [4]

Just as a lamp that's sitting in a vase
Does not illuminate at all,
While dwelling in the vase of the afflictions,
The dharmadhātu is not seen. [5]

From whichever of its sides
You punch some holes into this vase,
From just these various places then,
Its light rays will beam forth. [6]

Once the vajra of samādhi
Has completely smashed this vase,
To the very limits of all space,
It will shine just everywhere.[303] [7]

Unarisen is the dharmadhātu,
And never cease it will.
At all times without afflictions,
Stainless through beginning, middle, end. [8]

A blue beryl, that precious gem,
Is luminous at any time,
But if confined within its ore,
Its shimmer does not gleam. [9]

Just so, the dharmadhātu free of stain,
While it's obscured by the afflictions,
In saṃsāra doesn't shine its light,
But in nirvāṇa, it will beam.[304] [10]

If this element exists, through our work,
We will see the purest of all gold.
Without this element, despite our toil,
Nothing but misery we will produce. [11]

Just as grains, when covered by their husks,
Are not considered rice that can be eaten,
While being shrouded in afflictions,
It is not named "buddhahood." [12]

Just as rice itself appears
When it is free from all its husks,
The dharmakāya clearly manifests,
Once it is free from the afflictions.[305] [13]

"Banana trees don't have a pith"—
That's used as an example in the world,
But their fruits—their very pith—
In all their sweetness we do eat. [14]

Just so, when saṃsāra without pith
Is released from the afflictions' peel,
Its fruition, buddhahood[306] itself,
Turns into nectar for all beings. [15]

Likewise, from all seeds there are,
Fruits are born that match their cause.
By which person could it then be proved
That there is a fruit without a seed? [16]

This basic element, which is the seed,
Is held to be the basis of all dharmas.
Through its purification step by step,
The state of buddhahood we will attain.[307] [17]

Spotless are the sun and moon,
But obscured by fivefold stains:
These are clouds and smoke and mist,[308]
Rahu's face[309] and dust as well. [18]

Similarly, mind so luminous
Is obscured by fivefold stains.
They're desire, malice, laziness,
Agitation and doubt too.[310] [19]

A garment that was purged by fire
May be soiled by various stains.
When it's put into a blaze again,
The stains are burned, the garment not. [20]

Likewise, mind that is so luminous
Is soiled by stains of craving and so forth.
The afflictions[311] burn in wisdom's fire,
But its luminosity does not. [21]

The sūtras that teach emptiness,
However many spoken by the victors,
They all remove afflictions,
But never ruin this dhātu. [22]

Water dwelling deep within the earth
Remains untainted through and through.
Just so, wisdom in afflictions
Stays without a single stain. [23]

Since dharmadhātu's not a self,
Neither woman nor a man,
Free from all that could be grasped,
How could it be labeled "self"? [24]

In all the dharma that's without desire,
You see neither women nor a man.
"Men" and "women" are just taught
For guiding those plagued[312] by desire. [25]

"Impermanence," "suffering," and "empty,"
These three, they purify the mind.
The dharma purifying mind the best
Is the lack of any nature. [26]

In a pregnant woman's womb,
A child exists but is not seen.
Just so, dharmadhātu is not seen,
When it's covered by afflictions.[313] [27]

Through conceptions of a self and mine,
Discriminations of names, and reasons,
The four conceptions will arise,
Based on the elements and their outcome.[314] [28]

Even the Buddhas' aspiration prayers
Lack appearance and characteristics.
Immersed in their very own awareness,[315]
Buddhas have the nature of permanence. [29]

Any horns there on a rabbit's head
Are just imagined and do not exist.
Just so, all phenomena as well
Are just imagined and do not exist. [30]

Also the horns of an ox do not exist[316]
As having the nature of particles.
Just as before, so it is after—
What's to be imagined there? [31]

Since [things] dependently originate
And in dependence too will cease,
If not even one [of them] exists,
How can fools imagine them? [32]

How the dharmas of the Sugata
Are established as the very middle[317]
Is through the ox- and rabbit-horn examples. [33]

The forms of sun, moon, and the stars
Are seen as reflections upon water
Within a container that is pure—
Just so, the characteristics are complete. [34]

Virtuous throughout beginning, middle, end,
Undeceiving and so steady,
What's like that is just the lack of self—
So how can you conceive it as a self and mine? [35]

About water at the time of spring,
What we say is that it's "warm."
Of the very same [thing], when it's chilly,
We just say that it is "cold." [36]

Covered by the web of the afflictions,
It is called a "sentient being."
Once it's free from the afflictions,
It should be expressed as "Buddha." [37]

In dependence upon eye and form,
Appearances without a stain occur.
From being unborn and unceasing,
The dharmadhātu will be known. [38]

In dependence upon sound and ear,
Pure consciousness [comes forth],
All three dharmadhātu without signs.
Linked with thought, this will be hearing. [39]

Smelling in dependence upon nose and smell
Is an example for the lack of form.
Likewise, it's the nose's consciousness
That conceptualizes dharmadhātu. [40]

The nature of the tongue is emptiness,
And the dhātu of the taste is void—
Being[318] of the dharmadhātu's nature,
Consciousness is nonabiding. [41]

From the nature of a body pure
And the characteristics of the tangible conditions,
What is free from such conditions
Is to be expressed as "dharmadhātu." [42]

Once conception and its concepts are relinquished
With regard to phenomena whose principal is mind,
It's the very lack of nature of phenomena
That you should cultivate as dharmadhātu. [43]

What you see and hear and smell,
What you taste and touch, phenomena as well—
Once yogins realize them in this way,
The characteristics are complete. [44]

Eyes and ears and also nose,
Tongue and body and the mind as well—
The six āyatanas fully pure.
This is true reality's own mark. [45]

Mind as such is seen as two:
Worldly and beyond the world.
Clinging [to it] as a self, it is saṃsāra—
In your very own awareness, true reality. [46]

Since desire is extinguished, it is nirvāṇa.
Hatred and ignorance are extinguished [too].
Since these have ceased, it's buddhahood itself,
The very refuge for all beings. [47]

Due to realization and its lack,
All is in this very body.
Through our own conceptions, we are bound,
But when knowing our nature, we are free. [48]

Enlightenment is neither far nor near,
And neither does it come nor go.
It's whether it is seen or not
Right in the midst of our afflictions. [49]

By dwelling in the lamp of prajñā,
It turns into peace supreme.
So the collection of the sūtras says:
"By exploring[319] your self, you should rest!" [50]

Children blessed by tenfold powers' force,
[See them] like the crescent of the moon,
But those beings with afflictions
Do not see Tathāgatas at all. [51]

Just as ghosts with thirst and hunger
See the ocean to be dry,
Those obscured by ignorance
Think that Buddhas don't exist. [52]

What's the Bhagavat supposed to do
For inferiors and those whose merit's low?
It's just like the supreme of jewels
Put in the hand of one who's blind. [53]

But for beings who acquired merit,
The Buddha dwells before their eyes,
With the thirty-two marks shining bright
In their luminous and glorious light. [54]

Though the protector's rūpakāya
May remain for many eons,
For guiding those in need of guidance,
It is just this dhātu that is different. [55]

Ascertaining the object of the mind,
Consciousness will engage in it.
Once your very own awareness becomes pure,
You will dwell right in the bhūmis' nature. [56]

The great and mighty ones' supreme abode,
Akaniṣṭha that's so beautiful,
And consciousness, all three of them,
Fuse into a single one, I say. [57]

As for knowing all among the childish,
The diversity among the noble,
And the great and mighty, infinite in time—
What's the cause of time in eons? [58]

For sustaining the duration,
During eons truly infinite,
Of [all] beings' outer realms
And for creatures' life-force to remain,
This is what's the inexhaustive cause. [59]

In that whose fruition's inexhaustible,
Through the special trait of nonappearance,
Engage in full for prajñā's sake. [60]

Don't think enlightenment is far away,
And don't conceive it as close by.
With the sixfold objects not appearing,
It's awareness of reality just as it is. [61]

Just as from a mix of milk and water
That is present in a vessel,
Geese just sip the milk but not the water,
Which remains just as it is.[320] [62]

Just so, being covered by afflictions,
Wisdom dwells within this body, one [with them].
But yogins just extract the wisdom
And leave the ignorance behind. [63]

As long as we still cling to "self" and "mine,"
We will conceive of outer [things] through this.
But once we see the double lack of self,
The seeds of our existence find their end. [64]

Since it is the ground for buddhahood, nirvāṇa,
Purity, permanence, and virtue too,
And because the childish think of two,
In the yoga of their nonduality, please rest. [65]

Generosity's multiple hardships,
Ethics gathering beings' good,
And patience benefitting beings—
Through these three, the dhātu blooms. [66]

Enthusiastic vigor for all dharmas,
Mind that enters meditative poise,
Prajñā as your permanent resort—
These too make enlightenment unfold. [67]

Prajñā that is joined with means,
Aspiration prayers very pure,
A firm stand[321] in power, wisdom too—
These four dharmas make the dhātu flourish. [68]

"To bodhicitta, I pay no homage"—
Saying such is evil speech.
Where there are no bodhisattvas,
There will be no dharmakāya. [69]

Some dislike the seeds of sugar cane
But still wish to relish sugar.
Without seeds of sugar cane,
There will be no sugar. [70]

When these seeds of sugar cane
Are well guarded, fostered, and refined,
Molassis, sugar, candy too
Will then come forth from them. [71]

With bodhicitta, it is just the same:
When it's guarded, fostered, and refined,
Arhats, conditioned realizers, Buddhas too
Will then arise and spring from it. [72]

Just as farmers guarding
Seeds of rice and others,
Thus, the leaders guard all those
Who're aspiring to the supreme yāna. [73]

Just as, on the fourteenth day of waning,
Just a little bit of moon is seen,
Those aspiring to the supreme yāna
Will see a tiny bit of buddhakāya. [74]

Just as when the waxing moon
Is seen more in every moment,
Those who've entered on the bhūmis,
See its increase[322] step by step. [75]

On the fifteenth day of waxing,
Eventually, the moon is full.
Just so, when the bhūmis' end is reached,
The dharmakāya's full and clear. [76]

Having generated this mind truly
Through continuous firm aspiration
For the Buddha, dharma, and the saṅgha,
Irreversibility shows time and again. [77]

Through the ground of darkness[323] all relinquished
And the ground of brightness[324] firmly seized,
It is ascertained right at this point.
Therefore, it is designated "Joy." [78]

What's been tainted through all times
By the stains of passion and so forth
And is pure [now], without stains,
That is called "The Stainless One." [79]

Once the afflictions' web pulls back,
Stainless prajñā brightly shines.
This dispels all boundless darkness,
And thus is The Illuminating. [80]

It always gleams with light so pure
And is engulfed by wisdom's shine,
With [all] bustle being fully dropped.
Hence, this bhūmi's held to be The Radiant. [81]

It triumphs in science, sports, and arts and crafts,
The full variety of samādhi's range,
And over afflictions very hard to master.
Thus, it is considered Difficult to Master. [82]

The three kinds of enlightenment,
The gathering of all that's excellent,
Arising, ceasing too exhausted[325]—
This bhūmi's held to be The Facing. [83]

Since it's ever playing with a web of light
That's configurated in a circle
And has crossed saṃsāra's swampy pond,
This is labeled "Gone Afar." [84]

Being cared for by the Buddhas,
Having entered into wisdom's ocean,
Being without effort and spontaneous—
By the hordes of māras, it's Immovable. [85]

Since those yogins have completed
Their discourses teaching dharma
In all awarenesses discriminating perfectly,
This bhūmi is considered Excellent Insight. [86]

The kāya with this wisdom's nature,
Which is stainless, equal to the sky,
Holds [the dharma] of the Buddhas.
From it, the "Cloud of Dharma" forms. [87]

The abode of buddhadharmas
Fully bears the fruit of practice.
This fundamental change of state
Is called the "dharmakāya." [88]

Free from latent tendencies, you're inconceivable.
Saṃsāra's latent tendencies, they can be conceived.
You're completely inconceivable—
Through what could you be realized? [89]

Beyond the entire sphere of speech,
Outside the range of any senses,
To be realized by mental knowing—
I bow to and praise whatever's suitable. [90]

In this manner of gradual engagement,
The highly renowned children of the Buddhas,
Through the wisdom of the cloud of dharma,
See phenomena's empty nature.[326] [91]

Once their minds are cleansed completely,
They have gone beyond saṃsāra's depths.
They rest calmly on a throne,
Whose nature is a giant lotus. [92]

Everywhere they are surrounded
By lotuses that number billions,
In their many jeweled petals' light,
And with anthers of enthralling beauty. [93]

They overflow with tenfold power,
Immersed within their fearlessness,
Never straying from the inconceivable
Buddhadharmas without reference point. [94]

Through all their actions[327] of outstanding conduct,
Their merit and their wisdom are complete—
This full moon's surrounded everywhere
By the stars that are its retinue. [95]

In the sun that is the Buddhas' hands,
Stainless jewels shine their light.
Through empowering their eldest children,
They bestow empowerment on them. [96]

Abiding in this yoga that's so great,
With divine eyes, they behold
Worldly beings debased by ignorance,
Distraught and terrified by suffering. [97]

From their bodies, without effort,
Light rays are beaming forth,
And open wide the gates for those
Who are engulfed in ignorance's gloom. [98]

It's held that those in the nirvāṇa with remainder
Into the nirvāṇa without remainder pass.
But here, the actual nirvāṇa
Is mind that's free from any stain. [99]

The nonbeing of all beings—
This nature is its sphere.
The mighty bodhicitta seeing it
Is fully stainless dharmakāya. [100]

In the stainless dharmakāya,
The sea of wisdom finds its place.
Like with variegated jewels,[328]
Beings' welfare is fulfilled from it. [101]

This completes In Praise of Dharmadhātu *composed by the great Ācārya*[329] *Nāgārjuna. It was translated by the Indian Upādhyāya Kṛṣṇa Paṇḍita and the [Tibetan] translator*[330] *Tsültrim Gyalwa.*[331]

The Significance of the Dharmadhātustava *in the Indo-Tibetan Tradition*

The full significance of the *Dharmadhātustava* in the Indian mahāyāna tradition is impossible to assess at present. The fact is that there is no preserved Indian commentary on it, nor any reports that one ever existed. Also, since there has been no exhaustive research as to in how many and in which Indian sources the text appears, there are only a handful of known quotations or explicit references to it. For example, Bhāvaviveka's *Madhyamakaratnapradīpa* cites seven verses of the *Dharmadhātustava* and explicitly attributes them to Nāgārjuna. Verses 91–96 appear in the context of bodhisattvas passing from the tenth bhūmi to buddhahood:

> When mighty [bodhisattvas] in their last life on the tenth bhūmi look at sentient beings, they see that there is no decrease [in their number] and think . . . "Without having manifested the dharmakāya, I am not able to lead sentient beings out [of saṃsāra]. Therefore, I will manifest the dharmakāya." After that [thought], they are empowered by the Tathāgatas of the ten directions and thus attain the qualities of a Buddha, such as the ten powers, in a complete way. This very point is stated by master [Nāgārjuna in his *Dharmadhātustava*] . . . Right upon that, just as the sunlit autumn sky at noon free from dust, all the dust of characteristics is no more. Being free from mind, mentation, and consciousness, in the expanse of suchness, everything without exception is nondifferent and of one taste. This is called buddhahood. . . . Buddhahood means to have awoken from the sleep of ignorance, while the bodhicitta of the nature of phenomena—great self-sprung wisdom—knows and fully realizes the entire maṇḍala of knowable objects in a single instant.[332]

In the context of outlining the three kāyas, Bhāvaviveka's text quotes verse 101 and comments:

> In brief, what consists of the buddha qualities (such as the powers, the fearlessnesses, and unshared [qualities]) and is nondual with and not different from prajñāpāramitā is the dharmakāya. What springs from its blessings and is supported by that basis of the [dharmakāya] is the sambhogakāya. What comes from its blessings and appears in accordance with the inclinations of those to be guided is the nirmāṇakāya.[333]

Nāropa's *Sekoddeśaṭīkā* quotes verses 18–23, explictly saying that they come from Nāgārjuna's *Dharmadhātustava.* These verses include two examples for luminous mind being obscured but unaffected by adventitious stains (like the sun and moon by the five obscurations, such as clouds and smoke, and the fireproof garment by dirt), and an example for wisdom remaining stainless within the afflictions (water deep within the earth). Verse 22 says that the sūtras on emptiness terminate the afflictions but never ruin the dharmadhātu. Nāropa explains that the afflictions that vie with the mind do not simply come out of the blue in a sudden or random way. Otherwise, the lack of desire could suddenly turn into having desire. He illustrates this with the example of copper being corroded. If the corrosions would arise suddenly or randomly, the copper would have been free from them all the time before and then become corroded in an instant. Also, if the corrosions had been around on their own for a long time and then the copper would arise later, where would they have come from in the first place? If they could arise without the copper, then it would also be possible that flowers grow in the sky. Rather, the shine of copper is present in it all the time, but just not manifest due to the corroding stains. Similarly, despite being empty of any nature of their own, the afflictions do not randomly come about without mind's luminosity as their fundamental basis in the first place. However, they never really stain it either but just coexist with it. Emptiness refers to what smoke and so on are, and wisdom is that which is to be experienced personally. Following Nāgārjuna's verses, Nāropa also quotes Āryadeva as saying that, once mental darkness has departed, mind's luminosity is instantly very clear, having the nature of ever-present illumination. This is the characteristic of ultimate reality—the nature of wisdom being luminosity—which is seen by the eye of wisdom.[334]

Ratnākaraśānti's *Sūtrasamucchayabhāṣya* quotes verse 27 in the context of there being just a single yāna, since all beings possess the Tathāgata heart:

> Since the dharmadhātu is the actuality of the disposition, they are inseparable. Therefore, all [beings] are such that they possess the Tathāgata heart, the result of that consequently being just a single yāna. It is taught in the form of various yānas as means for realization that entail progressive stages. Also, since this disposition does not appear by virtue of afflictions and so on, [the Buddha] spoke temporarily of five dispositions, since he said:
>
> > Just as gold within stony debris
> > Does not appear to the eyes,
> > And then appears through being purified,
> > It is said that the Tathāgata [is seen] in the world.[335]

Also noble Nāgārjuna states [in his *Dharmadhātustava*]:

> In a pregnant woman's womb,
> A child exists, but is not seen.
> Just so, dharmadhātu is not seen,
> When it's covered by afflictions.[336]

Dharmendra's *Tattvasārasaṃgraha* quotes verse 8 of the *Dharmadhātustava* in the context of establishing that the unborn and profound nondual wisdom of the mahāyāna is inexpressible and cannot be pinpointed as "this is it." It is free from existence, nonexistence, permanence, extinction, not the sphere of śrāvakas, and free from all reference points.

> It always abides perfectly as the nature of the dharmadhātu, being a subtle self-awareness. Therefore, it is the sphere of the very subtle vision of the Buddhas. As [Kambala's] *Ālokamālā* explains:
>
> > Since this self-awareness is subtle,
> > The subtle seeing of the Buddhas beholds it.
> > Although it dwells within ourselves, [fools] like me
> > Do not see it because of their ignorance.[337]
>
> Likewise, [the *Dharmadhātustava*] explains:
>
> > Unarisen is the dharmadhātu,
> > And never cease it will.
> > At all times without afflictions,
> > Stainless through beginning, middle, end.

These quotes are followed by further extensive citations from several texts by Nāgārjuna, including his *Paramārthastava*, *Acintyastava*, *Mūlamadhyamakakārikā*, and **Nirālambastava*, as well as from the prajñāpāramitā sūtras.[338]

As mentioned above, Atiśa's *Ratnakaraṇḍodghātanāmamadhyamakopadeśa* just lists the *Dharmadhātustava* as one of the many works by Nāgārjuna,[339] but his *Dharmadhātudarśanagīti* incorporates nineteen verses from the *Dharmadhātustava*. Atiśa's own work starts with verse 1 of Nāgārjuna's text, paying homage to the dharmadhātu in all sentient beings. The next two verses say that he will describe those who do or do not behold the dharmadhātu—unborn pure luminosity free from reference points, which is the natural nirvāṇa realized by nonconceptual wisdom. The following eighteen verses consist of most of the *Dharmadhātustava*'s examples for luminous mind being covered by adventitious stains (such as butter in milk, a lamp inside a vase, an encrusted beryl, gold in its ore, rice grains in their husks, a fireproof garment, and a baby in the womb); its verse 22 on the sūtras on emptiness; verse 24 on the dharmadhātu not being a self; and verses 30–32 on all phenomena as being just imaginary. After this, Atiśa continues by saying that the nature of the dharmadhātu is space, being without birth, aging, abiding, and ceasing, thus being unconditioned. At the same time, it is inseparable from the qualities of a Buddha and accordingly bears their disposition. His verse 25 says:

> Since [the view] is inseparable from the dharmadhātu,
> It does not make sense for there to be different views.
> However, I speak a little bit about the different views
> That [arise] due to [people's] differences in insight.

In accordance with the above description of the dharmadhātu in both affirmative and negative terms, Atiśa's subsequent presentation of the various Buddhist and non-Buddhist schools treats both the classical Madhyamaka approach to this dharmadhātu and what is taught on it in the *Dharmadhātustava*, the *Uttaratantra*, and many other Yogācāra works as equally valid. The former primarily focuses on the dharmadhātu as being the freedom from reference points that is to be realized, while the latter emphasizes the nonconceptual wisdom that realizes this freedom as well as the qualities that this realization entails. In this way, the two approaches appear not as mutually exclusive but more like two sides of the same coin. Thus, Atiśa concludes his respective presentations of Madhyamaka and Yogācāra as follows:

> If the middle is completely liberated from extremes,
> Since there are no extremes, there is no middle either.
> The view without middle and extremes
> Is the perfect view.
>
> This is the unsurpassable view
> With which the intelligent constantly familiarize.
> Whoever enters this view
> Will attain omniscience.
> . . .
> Leave behind these characteristics
> And cultivate spacelike wisdom.
> The nature of the mind is undefiled.

As long as the seeds of defilement are not exhausted,
The condition of the ālaya-consciousness is [made up] solely by them.

Once they have been exhausted, the undefiled dhātu
Is the vimuktikāya.
Just like the sun and its rays, it is always
The abode of the buddha qualities,
And thus the dharmakāya of those who grant refuge.[340]

As for the significance of the *Dharmadhātustava* in Tibet, an exhaustive search for citations in the entire literature of the Tibetan Buddhist tradition obviously lies beyond the scope of this book. Still, no doubt there are many known sources throughout all Tibetan schools that quote or refer to the *Dharmadhātustava*, though its significance in these schools differs greatly. Naturally, the text is dealt with more frequently in those schools that emphasize the teachings on buddha nature and/or—at least in parts—subscribe to the view of "other-emptiness," such as the Kagyü, Nyingma, and Jonang traditions (there is no known Nyingma commentary though). In addition, since half of the presently known Tibetan commentaries on the *Dharmadhātustava* were written by Sakya authors—four of them during the fourteenth to sixteenth centuries—the text must have been regarded highly in parts of that school at least during that time as well. Given the subject of the *Dharmadhātustava* and the manner in which it is taught, it is no surprise that quotations from this text are usually very rare, if not totally absent, in works by Gelugpa authors. In particular, in their texts I have not come across any citations of the *Dharmadhātustava*'s verses that speak about buddha nature in positive terms, such as the examples for luminous mind and adventitious stains in the beginning of the text. The following is a provisional attempt to present an overview of the range of topics for which Tibetan commentators thought this text to be relevant, focusing primarily on Kagyü sources.

To begin with the Third Karmapa, apart from his commentary on the *Dharmadhātustava*, he quotes nineteen verses from this text in his autocommentary on *The Profound Inner Reality*. In Chapter One, quoting verse 37, he says that mind in its impure phase is referred to by the names "mind," "mentation," and "consciousness," while it is designated as the kāyas and wisdoms once it has become pure.[341] Chapter Five speaks about yogic direct perception being present in all six consciousnesses and their objects, citing verses 43–47.[342] Chapter Nine quotes verses 16–22 as support that the Tathāgata heart is not only taught in vajrayāna and Yogācāra texts but also in Madhyamaka scriptures.[343] Finally, the commentary's conclusion teaches on the fruition of the wisdom-kāya and its enlightened activity, citing verses

88–90 and 99–101.[344] In his commentary on the *Dharmadharmatāvibhāga*, the Third Karmapa quotes verses 36–37 in support of explaining the nature of the complete change of state. He says that adventitious stains are nothing but one's own stainless and naturally luminous mind as such, but by virtue of this mind being ignorant of itself, cognizance appears in a dualistic way as if it were a separate apprehender and apprehended. Miragelike mental constructs arise and these false imaginations obscure luminous suchness. But once these obscurations do not appear, suchness will appear, just as water appears clear and transparent once it has become pure of silt. Luminosity and natural emptiness are not tainted by the nature of mental constructs, since these are nothing but nonexistents that appear.[345] There are also a number of similarities/allusions to certain verses of the *Dharmadhātustava* in Rangjung Dorje's *Treatise on Pointing Out the Tathāgata Heart*.

Gö Lotsāwa's introduction to his commentary on the *Uttaratantra* presents four ways in which the Tathāgata heart is taught. These are (1) suchness; (2) the true nature of the mind, the basic element of awareness; (3) the ālaya-consciousness; and (4) sentient beings. From among these, he says, (2) is taught in many texts by Nāgārjuna, such as the *Dharmadhātustava*, *Cittavajrastava*, and *Bodhicittavivaraṇa*, as well as in many sūtras of the third turning of the wheel of dharma.[346] Throughout his commentary, Gö Lotsāwa quotes forty-nine verses (!) of the *Dharmadhātustava* and also comments on most of them,[347] sometimes linking his explanations to Mahāmudrā and its key notion of ordinary mind (*tha mal gyi shes pa*). He also clearly states that the dharmadhātu—mind beyond affirmation and negation—is not a nonimplicative negation. In terms of practice, he emphasizes that the Tathāgata heart cannot be found anywhere else than right within one's own mental afflictions.

The Seventh Karmapa's commentary on the *Abhisamayālaṃkāra* quotes *Dharmadhātustava* verse 22 together with *Uttaratantra* I.154–155 as supports for the dharmadhātu's stains being adventitious, while its enlightened qualities are inseparable. The teachings on emptiness serve as an antidote against the afflicting stains but never affect the dharmadhātu itself.[348]

The same author's *Ocean of Texts on Reasoning* refers to the *Dharmadhātustava* at least once. This occurs in the context of describing the ultimate reality of "Great Madhyamaka" as naturally luminous dharmadhātu or *tathāgatagarbha*, which is never tainted by the stains of apprehender and apprehended. It is the natural prajñāpāramitā, which is the sphere of personally experienced wisdom and whose actuality is taught as the ultimate reality in the Madhyamaka scriptural tradition. This is said to be treated both in Nāgārjuna's Madhyamaka texts and his other works, such as the *Dharmadhātustava*, with the latter extensively ascertaining mind as such, which is lucid and empty in an inseparable way and the utter peace of all reference points. It is also explained in the texts of Asaṅga, Vasubandhu, Dignāga, and Dharmakīrti.[349]

One of the main students of the Seventh Karmapa, Karma Trinlépa Choglé Namgyal[350] (1456–1539), in his commentary on the Third Karmapa's *Profound Inner Reality*, refers to the *Dharmadhātustava* twice. The first is in the context of discussing the unfolding disposition, explaining that this term is used from the perspective of it looking as if enlightened activity unfolds through accomplishing the roots of virtue. However, the accomplishing of these roots of virtue itself is not the unfolding disposition. With this in mind, the *Dharmadhātustava* says that certain factors serve to unfold the basic element (verses 66–68), but it does not say that these are the actual basic element. The second reference is indirect, through quoting Rangjung Dorje's DSC on verses 24–26 as support for explaining the meaning of "dharmadhātu" as the entirety of dualistic phenomena, such as saṃsāra and nirvāṇa, or factors to be relinquished and their remedies, being of equal taste with the essence of nonduality.[351]

The Eighth Karmapa, Mikyö Dorje's *Lamp That Excellently Elucidates the System of the Proponents of Other-Empty Madhyamaka*[352] discusses buddha nature becoming progressively revealed from its cocoon of adventitious stains during the path. It says that liberation happens once self-aware wisdom gains mastery over the Tathāgata heart that naturally abides within one's own mind stream. However, liberation does not just mean that our clinging to identity turns into identitylessness. Such would be liberation through a mere nonexistence, just like the horns of a rabbit. This definitive meaning of the mahāyāna, which is taught in the final turning of the wheel of dharma, the Karmapa says, is summarized by the invincible Lord Maitreya in the nine examples and their meanings in his *Uttaratantra* and is also explained extensively through the *Dharmadhātustava*'s examples of a lamp inside a vase (verses 5–7) and the moon becoming full (verses 74–76).

As for the Eighth Karmapa's commentary on the *Abhisamayālaṃkāra*, the general presentation of the dharmadhātu as the "disposition"—which includes verses 62–63 of the *Dharmadhātustava*—was already presented above. In the introduction to this commentary, the Karmapa discusses the Buddha's three turnings of the wheel of dharma and their classifications by different masters. At the end, he presents the question of whether the third "wheel of prophecy" in Maitreya's classification and the third "wheel that puts an end to all views" in Nāgārjuna's come down to the same essential point. He quotes the Third Karmapa as saying that these two cycles share the same essential point in a general way through the implication that any final dharma cycle must necessarily be one that teaches freedom from reference points. On the other hand, in terms of a particular feature being included or not, these two cycles do not come down to the same essential point. For, Nāgārjuna's "wheel that puts an end to all views" speaks about nothing but the mere freedom from reference points, while "the wheel of prophecy" explains that the distinctive feature of what is to be experienced by personally experienced wisdom is the wisdom free from reference points. One may wonder then whether Nāgārjuna and his spiritual heirs do not assert this wisdom free from reference points. Such is not the case, since this wisdom is taught extensively in Nāgārjuna's collection of praises and Āryadeva's *Bodhisattvayogacāryacatuḥśataka*.[353] Later, the commentary's extensive discussion of the way in which realization evolves progressively on the ten bhūmis quotes the *Dharmadhātustava*'s verses 74–76 on the moon becoming full as a support.[354] The text's fifth chapter on the instantaneous training at the end of the tenth bhūmi, when discussing the qualities attained through the vajralike samādhi, repeats lines 76cd and cites verse 7.[355]

The Eighth Karmapa's commentary on Candrakīrti's *Madhyamakāvatāra*, *The Chariot of the Tagbo Siddhas*, quotes lines 82cd of the *Dharmadhātustava* to illustrate the fifth bhūmi. More importantly, in the context of what various Buddhist schools take as the basis onto which the notion "person" is imputed, the Karmapa says that, in the common approach of the sūtras, the Vaibhāṣikas and Sautrāntikas regard the five skandhas as this basis, while the Yogācāras pick the ālaya-consciousness. For them, a "Buddha" is either imputed onto mirrorlike wisdom (the essence of the ālaya-consciousness) or the perfect nature (the dharmadhātu empty of the imaginary and other-dependent natures). The *Abhisamayālaṃkāra* identifies "Buddha" as emptiness, the dharmadhātu free from reference points. Some Mere Mentalists explain the latter as nondual self-aware self-luminous consciousness, while the Mādhyamikas explain it as the freedom from reference points in which naturally pure emptiness and dependent origination are inexpressible as either being the same or different. In the uncommon approach of the vajrayāna, the basis of imputation is the kāyas and the wisdom of the stainless connate Sugata heart, which are present throughout ground, path, and fruition. This point, the Karmapa says, is also taught implicitly and in a hidden manner in the unsurpassable scriptural traditions of Madhyamaka that teach the definitive meaning of the sūtras, such as Maitreya's *Uttaratantra* and Nāgārjuna's *Dharmadhātustava* (quoting verse 37).[356]

The Fifth Shamarpa, Göncho Yenla's[357] (1525–1583) commentary on the *Abhisamayālaṃkāra* quotes from three verses of the *Dharmadhātustava*. Lines 8cd support the statement that, from the perspective of the disposition's own nature, it is endowed with twofold purity. Therefore, ultimately, one cannot say that sentient beings have the Buddha heart, because they are nothing but the ālaya-consciousness, which is mistakenness and has never been established right from the start. Nor is it the case that sentient beings are Buddhas, because adventitious stains are not permanent but certain to perish. Nevertheless, from the perspective of convention, at the time of the ground, it is suitable to speak of the sheer existence of one part of this Heart—its aspect of natural purity—in sentient beings, without it however being contained in, mixed with, or connected to the mind streams of these beings.[358] Lines 75ac are used to illustrate the progressive growth of the paths of liberation after the adverse factors of the culminating training have been relinquished.[359] Lines 76cd are quoted in the context of explaining the final full dawning of instantaneous personally experienced wisdom, which is primordially stainless and, during the vajralike samādhi at the end of the tenth bhūmi, overcomes the very last and most subtle adventitious stains.[360]

The Eighth Situpa, Chökyi Jungné's[361] (1699–1774) commentary on Karmapa Rangjung Dorje's *Aspiration Prayer of Mahāmudrā* quotes ten verses from the *Dharmadhātustava*. Referring to verses 17 and 22, the text says that the basis for everything in saṃsāra and nirvāṇa is the purity of mind, that is, the basic element or Tathāgata heart. This is the ground of purification but not what is to be purified, since in its own essence, there is not even an atom of a phenomenon to be purified. Verse 19 shows that mind has an impure and a pure aspect, the latter being lucid and empty. Since mind's purity is natural luminosity, it cannot be tainted by adventitious stains.[362] Once the means of purification have cleansed what is to be purified, the result of purification is just this fundamental nature of the ground, in which all adventitious stains consisting of apprehender and apprehended are completely relinquished, it thus becoming manifest as the dharmakāya. This is illustrated by verse 37.[363] What is explained as being relinquished is the aspect of mind that is taught by the triad of mind (the ālaya-consciousness), mentation, and consciousness (the six operating consciousnesses). But pure mind is expressed here as the dharmadhātu, great bliss, which is free from arising, abiding, and ceasing. Also omniscient wisdom is not different from the dharmadhātu and thus completely beyond the phenomena of impure mind. Since what are called "purified phenomena" are not established as something outside of this pure mind, through the progression of the mind streams of the beings to be guided becoming slightly pure and then mostly pure, nirmāṇakāyas and sambhogakāyas appear for them, respectively. This manner of ascertaining that all phenomena of saṃsāra and nirvāṇa are one's own mind comes from countless mahāyāna sūtras, tantras, and the commentaries on their intention. The quotations that follow this explanation include verses 46–47 from the *Dharmadhātustava*.[364] However, as for the statements that the Buddha sees the dharmadhātu just as it is, and that mind is self-aware and self-luminous, the following must be understood. Not seeing even an atom of something that could serve as a characteristic within the dharmadhātu free from all reference points is expressed as "the great seeing of wisdom." This being free from something to be aware of and something that is aware, or something to be made luminous and something that makes it luminous, is termed both "awareness" and "luminous." One must understand this secret essential point and not take said statements as being equivalent to the seeing of worldly people and so on. Otherwise, mind being aware of itself by itself is self-contradictory, accruing the flaws that are exposed in the *Laṅkāvatārasūtra*, the *Bodhicaryāvatāra*, and other texts. However, the nature of the mind is not to be taken as utterly nonexistent or completely unobservable either. If the basic element of naturally pure mind were nonexistent, even on the level of what is merely seeming, it would be untenable for the appearances of saṃsāra and nirvāṇa to occur, since one only speaks of saṃsāra or nirvāṇa due to the distinction of whether this fundamental ground is realized or not. This is clearly expressed in verses 11, 16, and 17 of the *Dharmadhātustava*.[365] Many Kagyü instructions on Mahāmudrā meditation emphasize that it is essential to forego pursuit of thoughts about the past, the future, or the present. Indeed, there are some people who say about this, "Your Mahāmudrā is to stop all mental engagement in terms of the three times. Therefore, it is the meditation of the Chinese Hvashang."[366] However, these people just talk without having examined the issue, since this Kagyü lineage does not hold that one should rest within a state of thoughts having ceased through deliberately stopping all mental engagement. Rather, as just explained, it holds that the present mind is preserved in an uncontrived way. Still, these people may think, "Even if that is the case, you are not beyond the flaw mentioned, since all thoughts in terms of the three times will cease on their own through preserving the present mind in an uncontrived way." This just shows that those who think like that are very attached to their thoughts and thus cannot let go of them. Since there seem to be very many people who have such a pure view, they are more than welcome to join in relishing their thoughts and have no need to analyze this here. As for us, Chökyi Jungné concludes, we have never embarked on any path other than the one taught by the Sugatas and traveled by the mighty siddhas. This is followed by a number of supporting quotes on nonconceptual samādhi from the sūtras, tantras, and treatises, which include *Dharmadhātustava* verse 43.[367]

Jamgön Kongtrul Lodrö Tayé's commentary on Rangjung Dorje's treatise *Pointing Out the Tathāgata Heart* cites eleven verses from the *Dharmadhātustava*. Verse 17 illustrates that the dharmadhātu is the basis for all beings and phenomena, and that its purification finally results in buddhahood. Verses 18–19 show that, just as the sun and the moon, the Tathāgata heart is endowed with the qualities of natural luminosity but temporarily obscured by adventitious stains. These stains do not taint the nature of this Heart, but it becomes unclear by their mistakenly appearing as if they were obscurations. Jamgön Kongtrul explains the five obscurations in these verses in almost literally the same way as Rangjung Dorje's own commentary on them.[368] Verse 46 is quoted in support for its being only by virtue of mind as such being realized or not that Buddhas and sentient beings, ultimate and seeming, saṃsāra and nirvāṇa, and so on appear, respectively, and are labeled in these ways.[369] Verse 22 is adduced in the context of asking why the Tathāgata heart, which can only be perceived as it is by Buddhas, is taught to ordinary beings. The reason is said to lie in counteracting the five flaws of faintheartedness and so on as presented in *Uttaratantra* I.157. Some people take this instruction on the purpose of the teachings on buddha nature as a proof for them to be of expedient meaning. However, in that case, all teachings on emptiness would be of expedient meaning too, since they were given in order to put an end to the clinging to identity, singularity, and single units. These people may think that this is a different case, since emptiness is the basic nature of all phenomena. But if even the sheer emptiness that they maintain, which is still within the sphere of the minds of ordinary beings, is regarded by them as the basic nature, why would the actual nature of phenomena that is beyond such minds—the nature of luminosity—not be that basic nature? Therefore, all that is said in the middle turning of the wheel of dharma on emptiness is that it is just this inconceivable expanse that lacks the characteristics of being conditioned (such as arising, abiding, and ceasing), but this is not a teaching that the basic element does not exist.[370] Verse 48 (together with *Mahāyānasaṃgraha* X.5 on the change of state of the skandha of form and a quote from the *Hevajratantra*) is given to rebut the following objection. Though it is reasonable for buddhahood to be nothing but mind's stains having become pure, the body is what comes about from the conditions that are one's parents, thus being of an impure and perishable nature. Consequently, it is unreasonable for unconditioned qualities to arise from something conditioned. There is no such flaw, Lodrö Tayé says, since this very body, which appears as the creative display of the mind, has the nature of the rūpakāyas with all their qualities. However, these only manifest upon the relinquishment of their being obscured by mind's own mistaken imagination.[371] Verses 9–10 are given as corresponding to the progressive purification of the dharmadhātu as illustrated by the gradual cleansing of a beryl in the *Dhāraṇīśvararājaparipṛcchasūtra* and other texts.[372] Verse 16 is adduced to reject the wrong view that the buddha qualities arise from a nature of phenomena that is understood as nothing but emptiness, that is, without any cause.[373] Verse 101 underlines that enlightened activity is without thoughts but still occurs in a spontaneous and effortless way.[374] Finally, verse 24 is quoted in the context of explaining how the dharmadhātu is dissimilar from the notion of a self as imputed by the tīrthikas.[375]

The same author's commentary on the Third Karmapa's *Distinction between Consciousness and Wisdom* cites three verses from Nāgārjuna's text. Verse 2 illustrates that it is nothing but the manifestation of the unchanging, primordially and naturally abiding nature of the five wisdoms and the four kāyas that is called "buddhahood." Verses 18–19 are quoted upon saying that what obscures this Buddha heart is impure imagination.[376]

In the introduction to his commentary on the *Uttaratantra*, Lodrö Tayé follows Gö Lotsāwa's above fourfold layout of how *tathāgatagarbha* is taught. He says that it is presented as (1) emptiness free from reference points, (2) the luminous nature of the mind, (3) ālaya-consciousness, and (4) bodhisattvas and ordinary beings. From among these, (2) is taught in the middle and last wheel, the tantras, the *Uttaratantra*, *Mahāyānasūtrālaṃkāra*, *Dharmadhātustava*, *Cittavajrastava*, and *Bodhicittavivaraṇa*.[377] The only quote of the *Dharmadhātustava* in this commentary is verse 11, serving to illustrate the justification for the teachings on the manner of purification in order to manifest the naturally pure dharmadhātu, which is due to the existence of this dharmadhātu as the basic ground in which the stains are to be purified (this being the fourth vajra-point of the *Uttaratantra*, based on the order of these topics in the *Dhāraṇīśvararājaparipṛcchāsūtra*).[378]

As for non-Kagyü Tibetan sources that deal with the *Dharmadhātustava*, let's start with the Sakya tradition. Its most famous representative and central authority, Sakya Paṇḍita Kunga Gyaltsen[379] (1182–1251), refers to Nāgārjuna's text in one of his final works, a commentary on some difficult points of the *Hevajratantra*, called *Stainless Precious Garland*.[380] He starts by saying that the causal tantra refers to the true nature of one's own mind—wisdom—being naturally stainless and pure, that is, free from all stains of imagination. But this wisdom is obscured by adventitious stains (afflictive and cognitive obscurations), with the term "adventitious" standing for what can be purified, like the oxidation on the surface of pure gold.[380] Later, he says that the meaning of all classes of tantra is contained in five topics: fundamental change of state, wisdom-kāya, nonabiding nirvāṇa, nonduality, and uninterrupted activity. On the first, the text comments as follows:

> In terms of essence, or the nature of phenomena, there is no fundamental change of state, since the nature of phenomena is free from reference points. With this in mind, Nāgārjuna explained in his *Mūlamadhyamakakārikā* and so on that there is no fundamental change of state. In terms of qualities, there is a fundamental change of state, since the inconceivable buddhadharmas, such as

> the eighteen unshared qualities, are attained. With this in mind, Nāgārjuna explained in his *Dharmadhātustava* that there is a fundamental change of state. Therefore, if these two teachings of the noble one are understood in this way, they are not contradictory. Consequently, the manner of fundamental change of state should be understood in this way.

Then, the text speaks about four ways of fundamental change of state: (1) the change of state of the five skandhas into mastery over the major and minor marks, pure buddha realms, and so on as described in the *Mahāyānasaṃgraha*;[382] (2) the change of state of the four maṇḍalas; (3) the change of state of body, speech, and mind into the three kāyas; and (4) the change of state of the eight consciousnesses into the five wisdoms. This is followed by rejecting the positions that Buddhas do not have wisdom and that wisdom is primordially nonexistent, affirming that Tathāgatas possess the wisdom of suchness and variety[383] as well as the three kāyas, with the latter and the five wisdoms being inseparable.[384]

As mentioned above, Gorampa's *Illuminating the Definitive Meaning* briefly refers to the *Dharmadhātustava* when discussing Nāgārjuna's three scriptural collections. Another one of his works on the correct view[385] refers to the Sakya authority Rendawa Shönu Lodrö[386] (1349–1412) as rejecting the Jonang School's claim that Nāgārjuna taught *rangtong* in his collection of reasoning but *shentong* in his collection of praises. According to Rendawa, in the collection of praises, there is not a single word that indicates something ultimately existent. Rather, the collection of praises rejects all extremes in just the same way as Nāgārjuna's Madhyamaka treatises. The first chapter of Gorampa's versified *Supplement to Differentiating the Three Vows*[387] extensively treats the topic of buddha nature, establishing it as the union of lucidity and emptiness, free from all reference points. After presenting Maitreya's stance on it, verses 8–10 state:

> In the collection of reasoning, noble Nāgārjuna
> Determined through reasoning the manner of dependent origination
> Being empty of the reference points of the four extremes,
> And then said that emptiness is suitable to perform functions.
>
> In the collection of praises, he eliminated
> That this emptiness is just nothing at all,
> And said that it is suitable to perform functions,
> Since the spontaneous presence of saṃsāra and nirvāṇa is mind
> as such.

Therefore, as for the manner of asserting the ground
Of the Madhyamaka system in the mahāyāna,
These two system-founders—the regent [Maitreya] and [Nāgārjuna],
Who was prophesied by the victor—accord in their intention.

In verses 47–49ab, Gorampa cites verses 1–2 of the *Dharmadhātustava* to support his rejection of the claim that the two kinds of purity—natural purity and purity of adventitious stains—are mutually exclusive. Later, when refuting the Jonang claim that the dharmadhātu is buddhahood even when not purified of stains, Gorampa says that this contradicts the treatises of Maitreya and Nāgārjuna, quoting *Uttaratantra* I.47 and *Dharmadhātustava* 12–13 and 36–37 (verses 73d–79), which clearly differentiate between the phases of the dharmadhātu being with and without stains.

More importantly still, there are five known Sakya commentaries on the *Dharmadhātustava* by Rongtön Sheja Künrig[388] (1367–1449), Sönam Gyaltsen[389] (1312–1375), Śākya Chogden (1428–1507), Lowo Khenchen Sönam Lhündrub (1456–1532),[390] and Lodrö Gyatso (born nineteenth century). Among the three that are available at present, Rongtön's very brief interlinear commentary does not offer any detailed or general explanations. Śākya Chogden's commentary starts by discussing the significance of the *Dharmadhātustava* by giving "the reasons why this treatise must be explained in clear and precise terms":

> The wrong ideas that need to be eliminated here are as follows. [1] One may think that the conventional term "dharmadhātu wisdom" does not appear in the yāna of characteristics. [2] The dharmadhātu of both sentient beings and Buddhas, which is explained in that [yāna], may be expounded as being nothing but the aspect of emptiness that is a nonimplicative negation. [3] One may identify the naturally abiding disposition, the svabhāvikakāya, and the nonabiding nirvana all three solely from the aspect of emptiness that is a nonimplicative negation, but not know how to explain them from the aspect of luminous aware experience. [4] [Instead,] one may explain that this aspect of luminous aware experience at the time of the ground is nothing but consciousness and not know how to explain it as wisdom. [5] Even those who know how to explain the above in such a way may claim that this very wisdom is actual buddhahood and dharmakāya. They may claim that, for this reason, all sentient beings are Buddhas and hold that they possess the qualities of the definitive meaning, such as the major and minor marks, the powers, and so forth. They may assert that the actual

> Sugata heart exists at the time of the ground. Not understanding that just this luminous aware experience is explained as the heart of sentient beings at the time of the ground and as the Buddha heart at the time of the fruition, they may claim such [an experience] to be the Buddha heart at all times. Not understanding that just this [luminous aware experience], through dividing it in three phases, is given the names "sentient being," "bodhisattva," and "Buddha," they may explain it as "Buddha" throughout all these phases.
>
> [6] Others, who do not understand that the explanation of the true nature of mind with stains as "the Heart" is an explanation from the aspect of wisdom, explain it to be the aspect of emptiness alone. They think that wisdom is taught to be really established in this text here and say that the [ways in which] venerable Nāgārjuna and venerable Asaṅga identify the naturally abiding disposition and the Sugata heart are totally incompatible. In particular, they do not explain that the dharmadhātu—which is to be praised by this text—is wisdom, but explain it to be nothing but emptiness. These are the wrong ideas that have arisen [about this text and its topic].
>
> The purpose of composing this explication here is to eliminate these ideas and then give rise to certainty in what the essence of dharmadhātu is, how it abides in the phases of saṃsāra and nirvāṇa, and the ways in which our apprehending of characteristics labels it in each of these phases and so forth.[391]

Lodrö Gyatso's commentary presents a thorough explanation of Nāgārjuna's verses and elaborates on a number of related topics. These include buddha nature not being invalidated through the teachings on emptiness; the nature of yogic consciousness in ordinary beings and bodhisattvas; the union of the two realities; buddhahood not being attained through viewing it as a nonimplicative negation; and the relationship between the texts of Nāgārjuna and Maitreya, being essentially equal.[392]

In the Jonang tradition, there are two commentaries on the *Dharmadhātustava* by Dölpopa and Sönam Sangbo (1341–1433). Sönam Sangbo's text is the only available commentary on this text that mentions the term "other-empty" at all (though just once), but otherwise frequently follows Rangjung Dorje's commentary (sometimes literally). Interestingly, Dölpopa's short commentary does not use said term either and exhibits only a few traces of his otherwise typical version of the *shentong* view. Dölpopa's main text that presents this view, *The Mountain Dharma Called The Ocean of Definitive Meaning*, quotes twenty verses from the *Dharmadhātustava* (1–10, 18–23, 27, 36–37, and 45),[393] saying that this text by Nāgārjuna, through many examples, extensively teaches on the Tathāgata heart, which is equivalent to the dharmadhātu, the dharmakāya, naturally luminous mind, self-sprung wisdom, and so on. Two other texts by Dölpopa, *A General Commentary on the Teachings*[394] and *The Fourth Council*,[395] allude to Nāgārjuna's text by referring to the masters who taught, through examples such as a lamp inside a vase, that the luminous Tathāgata heart is present within adventitious afflictions.

Tāranātha's (1575–1635) *Scriptural Foundation of The Ornament of Other-Emptiness*[396] cites seven verses of the *Dharmadhātustava* (1–2, 9–10, 22, and 52–53). His *Essence of Other-Emptiness* says that the Great Madhyamaka that is known in Tibet as "other-emptiness"[397] is elucidated by the texts of Maitreya as well as by Asaṅga and Vasubandhu. It is also very clearly present in Nāgārjuna's *Dharmadhātustava*. Thus, the position of both supreme noble ones—Asaṅga and Nāgārjuna—is "other-emptiness."[398]

The contemporary Jonang scholar Dzamtang Khenpo Lodrö Tragba's[399] (1920–1975) *Fearless Lion's Roar*[400] states that Maitreya, Asaṅga, and Vasubandhu teach through integrating the final view of all three yānas. In accordance with this, noble Nāgārjuna, through verse XV.7 of his *Mūlamadhyamakakārikā* ("Through his knowledge of entities and nonentities, in the instruction for Kātyāyana, the victor has refuted both [their] existence and nonexistence") establishes that even the first turning of the wheel of dharma teaches Madhyamaka free from the two extremes. Through verse 35 of his *Yuktiṣaṣṭikā* ("The victors have declared that nirvāṇa alone is true, so which wise one would think that the rest is not delusive?"), he also taught the final view of the middle turning to be the definitive meaning that is the Madhyamaka of "other-emptiness." In his commentaries on the last wheel, the collection of praises—the *Dharmadhātustava*, *Paramārthastava*, *Niraupamyastava*, *Lokatītastava*, and so on—and in some texts on the vajrayāna, he explains this excellently in accord with the view of the profound essential point of the supreme *Kṛtyayuga* teachings[401] and the works by Maitreya and his followers.

As for the Nyingma School, Lochen Dharmaśrī's (1654–1717) *Commentary on Ascertaining the Three Vows*[402] says the following about the difference between the views in the middle and the final turning of the wheel of dharma that are to be made a living experience through meditation:

> According to the explicit teaching of the middle wheel as commented on by Nāgārjuna in his collection of reasoning, since the definitive meaning is presented as a nonimplicative negation, not meditating on anything whatsoever is explained as meditating on

emptiness, and not seeing anything whatsoever is realizing true reality. According to the intention of the final turning as commented on in the works by Maitreya and those by Asaṅga and Vasubandhu as well as in Nāgārjuna's collection of praises, it is this very wisdom without the duality of apprehender and apprehended that is explained as what is to be made a living experience through meditation, and this also accords in intention with the profound collections of the secret mantra.

Furthermore, the text says that the Nyingma tradition appears to accord with Nāgārjuna as far as the way of taking the bodhisattva vows goes, but that such is not definite in terms of the view. The Nyingma view is surely not in contradiction to Nāgārjuna's collection of praises, but it mainly accords with Asaṅga's and Vasubandhu's way of exegesis, since it does not take the nonnominal ultimate as a nonimplicative negation but as emptiness that is an implicative negation, and since it holds the final turning of the wheel of dharma to be of definitive meaning.[403]

Ju Mipham Gyatso (1846–1912) says in one of his texts that his own system is *rangtong*.[404] His *Elimination of Doubts about the Genuine Dharma*[405](a reply to criticism of his commentary on the *Madhyamakālaṃkāra*) clarifies that he does not have the burden of needing to establish the *shentong* view, since he follows Rongzom Paṇḍita Chökyi Sangbo[406] (1012–1088) and Longchenpa, who both accord with the texts of Nāgārjuna, and that even someone inferior like him is one-pointedly inclined toward these. He continues that he felt forced to write his reply due to the words of others who regard *shentong* like an enemy. It was probably for the same reason that he wrote his *Lion's Roar Proclaiming Other-Emptiness*. This text says that when one ascertains the philosophical system of "other-emptiness," one must first ascertain that all phenomena lack a nature of their own, just as it is taught in Nāgārjuna's texts. If one does not understand this, one can neither ascertain the way in which the seeming is empty of its own nature, nor the way in which the ultimate is empty of something other. Therefore, in the beginning, freedom from reference points—the object that is to be personally experienced—is to be ascertained. Thereafter, one ascertains the nonconceptual wisdom that is the subject that realizes this ultimate object (freedom from reference points). In this way, both the object and the subject for which the way things appear and how they actually are concord, are called "the ultimate," while the objects and subjects for which the way things appear and how they actually are discord, are called "the seeming." Under analysis through the valid cognition that examines the conventional, there exist differences in terms of being deceiving or undeceiving and of being mistaken or unmistaken. Thus, what is undeceiving and unmistaken is presented as the ultimate and the opposite as the seeming. The well-known way of presenting the two realities as emptiness and appearance as well as the just-explained way of presenting them in terms of the way things appear and how they actually are, have both been taught in the sūtras and the great treatises since the very beginning—they were not newly created by the proponents of other-emptiness. They are taught in the *Dharmadharmatāvibhāga*, the *Uttaratantra*, and Nāgārjuna's *Dharmadhātustava* (quoting verses 20–22).[407]

Mipham Rinpoche's *Synopsis of the Sugata Heart* describes buddha nature as follows:

> The actuality of the dhātu of the two realities in union, which is free from the entire web of reference points and to be personally experienced, is called "naturally pure dharmadhātu" and "emptiness." All sūtras of the mahāyāna and the commentaries on their intention say that this is the buddha disposition that fully qualifies as such and the svabhāvakāya endowed with twofold purity. Therefore, it is not tenable to assert this naturally abiding disposition as anything but unconditioned. Being unconditioned, it is furthermore not reasonable for this [dharmadhātu] to, through its very own nature, perform the activity of producing another result and then cease. Consequently, it is not tenable to assert the qualities of the dharmakāya as anything but a result of freedom.[408] That it is like this is said by the regent, the great [bodhi]sattva on the tenth bhūmi, in his *Uttaratantra* and is also very clearly stated by the glorious protector, noble Nāgārjuna, in his *Dharmadhātustava*. Hence, by following these scriptures, our own tradition asserts the unconditioned dharmadhātu as the disposition. This dhātu is the basic nature of all phenomena, its essence is without arising and ceasing, and it has the character of appearance and emptiness inseparable, not falling on either side.[409]

The text continues with an extensive discussion of the threefold proof in *Uttaratantra* I.28 that all beings have buddha nature, explaining the first line—"since the buddhakāya radiates"—as follows:

> The ultimate perfect buddhakāya—the dharmakāya with its qualities that equal [the vastness of] space—clearly shows or radiates or manifests later from what was previously an ordinary being, that is, the mind stream of a person that has been associated with the entire set of fetters. Since there is such [a manifestation of the dharmakāya], the Tathāgata heart exists in the mind streams of

sentient beings from right now [up through the point when this manifestation happens]. There is a common and an uncommon justification for how this is established. As for the first one, if there are sentient beings who manifest this wisdom-dharmakāya, their minds necessarily have the disposition of being suitable to become Buddhas, while the same is not tenable for what completely lacks this disposition. As the *Dharmadhātustava* [verse 11] says:

> If this element exists, through our work,
> We will see the purest of all gold.
> Without this element, despite our toil,
> Nothing but misery we will produce.[410]

Later, the text emphasizes that the second and third turnings of the wheel of dharma, as well as the systems of Nāgārjuna and Asaṅga, share the same essential point, which equally pertains to the vajrayāna.

> Following what the Omniscient Longchen Rabjam[411] maintains, the emptiness taught in the middle turning of the wheel of dharma as well as the kāyas and wisdoms taught in the last one must definitely be taken as the union of appearance and emptiness. Consequently, since there is nothing to discriminate or to eliminate with regard to the two cycles of definitive meaning in the middle and last turnings, both are to be taken as the definitive meaning. Then, there is not only no contradiction such that one of these turnings must be taken as being of expedient meaning, if the other is [exclusively] taken as the definitive meaning, but by considering them to be a union, this kind of Tathāgata heart is regarded as the meaning of the "causal tantra," thus emerging as the essential point of the pith instructions of the vajrayāna. Therefore, one needs to understand that these teachings of the Buddha come down to the same essential point. All noble ones, such as Nāgārjuna and Asaṅga, are single-minded with regard to this ultimate point, since this is clearly realized through texts such as the *Dharmadhātustava* and *Bodhicittavivaraṇa*, as well as [Asaṅga's] commentary on the *Uttaratantra* and so on. As master Nāgārjuna says [in verse 22 of his *Dharmadhātustava*]:
>
> > The sūtras that teach emptiness,
> > However many spoken by the victors,
> > They all remove afflictions,
> > But never ruin this dhātu.

> Accordingly, having scrutinized through analysis for the ultimate, the final outcome of this is the inseparability of the two realities. Since this vajralike point is the dhātu that is indivisible through dialectical minds, there is no basis for engaging in disputes with regard to the ultimate.[412]

A commentary on Ju Mipham Gyatso's famous *Lamp of Certainty*[413] by his student Troshul Jamdor[414] quotes four verses of the *Dharmadhātustava*. Verse 22 is found as support for the primordially pure dharmadhātu and its self-radiance—the wisdom-kāya—being inseparable by nature, which results in the latter not being negated on the path or invalidated through analysis for the ultimate either. Moreover, just as gold is purified through fire, the more this wisdom is analyzed, the clearer its empty nature is seen, the two obscurations are purified, and the aspect of lucid appearance is seen as the emerging of the self-radiance of emptiness.[415] Verses 74–76 are cited to underline the gradual increase and perfection of the realization of the nature of the dharmadhātu, just as the waxing moon, by bodhisattvas on the path of the mahāyāna. This is said to apply all the more to śrāvakas and pratyekabuddhas, who cannot simply suddenly leap into the supreme realization of the mahāyāna by following their respective paths. Otherwise, those with comparatively dull faculties would be the people with the potential for instantaneous realization, while those with sharp faculties would only have the potential of a strictly gradual progression.[416]

Pöba Tulku Dongag Denbé Nyima[417] (1900/1907–1959), an important commentator on Mipham Rinpoche's works, says the following in his *Notes on the Essential Points of [Mipham's] Synopsis [of the Sugata Heart]*:[418]

> Concurring with the meaning taught in the sūtras that instruct on the disposition, the basic element, through the example of cleansing a gem, the *Uttaratantra*, the *Dharmadhātustava*, and so forth, according to what is found through the valid cognition of pure vision[419] by way of whether there is invalidation through the valid cognition of pure vision or not, take the sūtras that teach the final definitive meaning—the Sugata heart—to be of definitive meaning. Therefore, the final [cycle of] the Buddha's words that teaches on the topic of the Sugata heart—the nature of appearance and emptiness inseparable, the ultimate in which the way things appear and how they actually are concord—is asserted as being of definitive meaning, since this [Sugata heart] is what is found through the valid cognition of pure vision.[420]

The Nyingma School of Tibetan Buddhism by the late supreme head of the Nyingma lineage, H.H. Düjom Rinpoche (1904–1987), cites verses 20–21 of the *Dharmadhātustava* on the fireproof garment, saying that the ostentatious arising and ceasing of seeming reality does not harm true reality.[421] Furthermore, the text says twice that the Tathāgata heart or dharmadhātu abides in the minds of sentient beings in a way that is unaffected by all unreal adventitious stains, just as a precious gem in a swamp, each time quoting verse 23.[422] On the three kāyas as the fruition of the dharmadhātu, which is not just a nonimplicative negation, verse 101 is adduced.[423] Düjom Rinpoche also quotes verses 15–18ab from Atiśa's *Dharmadhātudarśanagīti*, which in fact—as mentioned above—are verses 27, 24, 26ab, and 22 of the *Dharmadhātustava*. He says that Atiśa (and thus Nāgārjuna) has determined that the unconditioned dharmadhātu—which is empty of imaginary karma and defilements but inseparable from the enlightened qualities—is the disposition or Tathāgata heart.[424] The text also refers a number of times to the collection of praises in general. Once the conclusive nonnominal ultimate reality has been determined in accordance with the collection of reasoning, there is no reason to deny that, according to the intentions of the texts of Maitreya and the collection of praises, the kāyas and wisdoms of a Buddha are naturally present and unconditioned, since they do not differ in nature from the dharmadhātu.[425] It is in the texts of Maitreya and in Nāgārjuna's collection of praises that the meaning of Great Madhyamaka (*shentong*)—the supreme among all philosophical systems in the sūtrayāna—is revealed.[426] Finally, Düjom Rinpoche says that the conclusive intention of Nāgārjuna and Asaṅga abides without contradiction in the nature of the Great Perfection, this intention comprising Nāgārjuna's collection of reasoning (the commentaries on the second turning of the wheel of dharma) as well as his collection of praises, mainly the *Dharmadhātustava*, and the commentaries by Maitreya, Asaṅga, Vasubandhu, and so on (all commentaries on the third turning).[427]

As for the Gelugpa School, there is mention of a presently unavailable early commentary by Nyendön Śākya Gyaltsen[428] (born fourteenth century). The above-quoted works by Jamyang Shéba and Janggya Rölpé Dorje are among the sources of the later default Gelugpa position on the collection of praises in general and the *Dharmadhātustava* in particular. To provide one of the rare quotes of this text in Gelugpa works, the contemporary scholar Kensur Padma Gyaltsen's[429] *Eye-opening Golden Spoon That Instructs on the Profound Meaning*[430] typically quotes verses 74–76 just to illustrate the gradual nature of realization and qualities appearing on the path.[431]

A rather peculiar example of Gelugpa texts that quote the *Dharmadhātustava* is a polemical work by Séra Jetsün Chökyi Gyaltsen (1469–1546), called *An Answer to the Karmapa*, which disputes some parts of the Eighth Karmapa's commentary on the *Abhisamayālaṃkāra*. In Séra Jetsün's section that rejects "nondual wisdom is the ultimate basic nature, exists ultimately, is a permanent entity, and is the final true intention of the third turning of the wheel of dharma, the texts by Maitreya, Asaṅga, and Vasubandhu, and—in particular—Nāgārjuna's collection of praises" and so on, he quotes eight verses from the *Dharmadhātustava*[432] (and many verses from other praises by Nāgārjuna). However, both the selection and interpretation of these verses are highly tendentious, solely geared toward making a case for orthodox Gelugpa positions. There is no room here to go into the highly complex details of showing that the Karmapa's explanations are often mispresented and/or oversimplified, while the "refutations" are limited only to default buzz-words and do not take into account the Karmapa's frequent emphasis that at times he moves to another level of discourse altogether (as described below in the section on the Third Karmapa's view, distinguishing between a conceptual "philosophical system" and a wider outlook from the perspective of direct realization in meditative equipoise).[433] Three examples of this shall suffice here. First, by only quoting verses 30 and 43–44 of the *Dharmadhātustava*, Séra Jetsün concludes that the entire collection of praises fully accords with the collection of reasoning and the Madhyamaka system in general in saying that the ultimate basic nature is nothing but all phenomena's lack of a nature, and that therefore emptiness must be a nonimplicative negation. Also, nondual wisdom is said to therefore not exist ultimately, which simply disregards the *Dharmadhātustava*'s verses (such as 23, 46, 63, 80–81, 87, and 101) that explicitly suggest wisdom's ultimate existence. Of course, Séra Jetsün does not mention any of the verses here that speak of the examples for the luminous nature of mind existing unaffected within the obscurations (such as 3–15, 18–22, 27, 36–37, and 74–76) either. Secondly, lines 1cd are given as the only "scriptural proof" that śrāvakas and pratyekabuddhas realize emptiness. The same two lines are moreover claimed as teaching that nondual wisdom is not the ultimate basic nature. Thirdly, verses 20–21 are given as scriptural support for the existence of wisdom and luminosity at the level of a Buddha (contrary to Séra Jetsün's claim, this is not something the Karmapa denies in the first place). At the same time, as stated above, it is denied that nondual wisdom exists ultimately, which of course begs the question how it exists then at the level of buddhahood. The standard Gelugpa answer is that it is a part of seeming reality, the only ultimate existent being emptiness. It should be obvious that this entails a number of problems, such as how a part of seeming reality could exist in the mind of a Buddha (the level of buddhahood being the very final level of ultimate reality), or how a Buddha's wisdom as a perceiving subject that belongs to seeming reality could ever realize any ultimate reality, such as emptiness.

To summarize, as will also be clear from the parts of the commentaries on the *Dharmadhātustava* translated below, the Tibetan tradition (with the exception of the Gelugpa School) regards the *Dharmadhātustava* as an indication that Nāgārjuna not only taught on emptiness but also on naturally luminous mind, the Tathāgata heart, and nonconceptual wisdom. Some, like Dölpopa and Tāranātha, consider this as clear evidence that Nāgārjuna is a *shentongpa*, his final view being "Great Madhyamaka" or "other-empty Madhyamaka." Others, like the Third Karmapa and Śākya Chogden, point out that the teachings in Nāgārjuna's collections of reasoning and praises are complementary and share the same essential point, with the same applying to the relationship between the Madhyamaka tradition of Nāgārjuna and his followers on the one hand and the Yogācāra tradition of Maitreya, Asaṅga, and Vasubandhu on the other.

Rangjung Dorje

THE THIRD KARMAPA, RANGJUNG DORJE, & HIS COMMENTARY ON THE *DHARMADHĀTUSTAVA*

A Short Biography

KARMAPA RANGJUNG DORJE was born on January 27, 1284 into a family of Nyingma tantric practitioners in the area of Mangyül Tingri Langkor[434] in Tsang, Central Tibet. His father was Dönba Chöbal[435] and his mother Jomo Yangdren.[436] From the age of three onward, he would sit on rocks or other seats and teach his playmates. He also proclaimed himself to be the Karmapa. At the age of five, he visited the Second Karmapa's main disciple and lineage holder, the great Drugba Kagyü siddha Urgyenpa Rinchen Bal[437] (1230–1309), who had already had a dream about his arrival. He tested the young Karmapa, who then reported details of the meeting between Rinchen Bal and the Second Karmapa, Karma Pakshi. Rinchen Bal returned all the Karmapa's possessions, including the Black Crown, bestowed the lay vows upon him, and gave him the name Rangjung Dorje, which had been Karma Pakshi's secret name. Thereafter, he began offering the Karmapa empowerments and instructions. At seven, Rangjung Dorje was ordained as a novice by Tropuwa Künden Sherab,[438] with whom he also studied the vinaya. Two years later, he arrived at the Karmapas' main seat in Tsurpu, where, over the next nine years, he received the entire transmissions of both the Kagyü and Nyingma lineages from his principal tutor, the great siddha Nyenré Gendün Boom,[439] as well as other teachers, such as Lopön Sherab Bal,[440] Gyagom Yeshe Ö,[441] and Namtsowa Mikyö Dorje.[442] After a retreat on the slopes of Mount Everest at age eighteen, Rangjung Dorje received full monastic ordination from Shönu Jangchub[443] and Gendün Rinchen.[444]

In the following years, he studied extensively with many great masters of all Tibetan traditions, thus gaining mastery of most of the Buddhist transmissions from India to Tibet. This included studying Madhyamaka, Yogācāra, the five texts of Maitreya, abhidharma, and pramāṇa at the famous Kadampa monastic college of Sangpu[445] with Śākya Shönu[446] (then abbot of its "lower" monastic seat) and Lodrö Tsungmé (mid-thirteenth to mid-fourteenth century); detailed expositions and empowerments of the *Kālacakratantra* and many other "old" and "new" tantras from Nyedowa Kunga Döndrub[447] (born 1268) and Tsültrim Rinchen;[448] teachings on medicine from Lama Baré;[449] and the *Vima Nyingtig*[450] as well as the *Six Dharmas of Niguma* from the most eminent exponent of Dzogchen at the time, Rigdzin Kumārarāja (1266–1343), the main teacher of the great Nyingma master Longchen Rabjam (1308–1368). With the latter, Rangjung Dorje also shared a mutual teacher-student relationship.

Throughout his life, the Third Karmapa spent considerable time in solitary meditation retreats but also traveled throughout Tibet, giving teachings and often acting as a mediator in local conflicts. He also had many visions of great masters of the past and deities. During a retreat in his early twenties at Karma Yangön,[451] he experienced such a significant encounter with Vimalamitra and Padmasambhava, both melting into a point between his eyebrows. At this moment, he realized all the Dzogchen tantras of the Nyingma lineage. Thereafter, he wrote several volumes on Dzogchen, the most important being the Karma Nyingtig,[452] thus unifying the teachings of the Kagyü Mahāmudrā and the Nyingma Dzogchen. Through this and the teachings he had received mainly from Rigdzin Kumārarāja, the Karmapa became both a tertön ("treasure-revealer") and a lineage holder in the Nyingma Dzogchen tradition. In 1310, he met with the famous Sakya master Yagdön Sangyé Bal[453] (1348–1414). Thereafter, he stayed in retreat on the slopes of Mt. Everest and at the hermitage of Gampo Sanglung[454] in Tagbo.[455] Altogether, he stayed for three years in Tagbo and Kongbo,[456] teaching, meditating, founding hermitages, and visiting holy places. In 1318, at the hermitage of Tsurpu Gung,[457] he had visions of the outer and inner spheres of the Kālacakra teachings, upon which he composed a treatise on a revised system of astrology, which is transmitted to this day as the Tsurpu tradition of Tibetan astrology. In the same year, he founded the hermitage of Upper Dechen[458] in the Tsurpu Valley, where he also wrote several of his most famous treatises, such as *The Profound Inner Reality* and *The Distinction between Consciousness and Wisdom*.

Rangjung Dorje is reported to have met Dölpopa once between 1320 and 1324 and prophesied that the latter would come to realize an especially sublime view unlike his present one.[459] It was soon after that Dölpopa formulated his system of "other-emptiness." In 1324, Rangjung Dorje returned for one year to Kongbo, teaching and establishing several monasteries and retreat facilities. While staying at Gogtreng[460] in Kongbo—a place where Padmasambhava had meditated—he composed his autocommentary on *The Profound Inner Reality* in 1325. In 1326, the Karmapa quelled a feud between the Central Tibetan kingdom of Tsal and the Khampas. He proceeded to eastern

Tibet, restored Karma Gön,[461] and had an iron bridge built over the Sogchu[462] River in 1328.

Continuing the relationship of the Mongol imperial court with the Second Karmapa, Rangjung Dorje was invited to China by the emperor Toq Temür of the Yüan dynasty in 1331. He entered China in 1332, to learn that the emperor had just died. His nephew and successor Irinjibal (aka Ratnaśrī) urged the Karmapa to continue his journey, but he also died soon after Rangjung Dorje's arrival at the court in Ta'i-tu. The Karmapa assisted in the complex matters of installing the next emperor Togan Temür—Irinjibal's elder brother—and bestowed many teachings upon him. Having promised the emperor to return in two years, Rangjung Dorje left the court for Tibet in 1334. He visited Wu-t'ai-shan (the holy mountain of Mañjuśrī)[463] and several places in Kham on the way, arriving in Tsurpu late in 1335. Upon being reinvited to the Mongol court, the Karmapa departed from Tsurpu in August 1336 and arrived in Beijing in 1337. During the eighth Tibetan month of that year (August-September), he prophesied a severe earthquake, making the emperor and his court camp on an open plain, thus saving many people. During the last two years of his life at the court, Rangjung Dorje functioned as spiritual and political advisor to the emperor, taught the dharma, and established some monasteries. In the summer of 1338, at a meeting of Mongol officials, he announced, "I, a yogin, am like a cloud. May all who wish to grasp the meaning of my teachings do so swiftly." On June 21 in 1339, Rangjung Dorje passed away, and it is said that his image appeared in the full moon on the night of that day.

As for the Karmapa's scriptural legacy, besides the texts mentioned, further important works that are still available are his autocommentary on *The Profound Inner Reality*, *The Aspiration Prayer of Mahāmudrā*,[464] an *Instruction Manual on Uniting with Connate Mahāmudrā*,[465] *Pointing Out the Three Kāyas*,[466] *The Nonduality of Prāṇa and Mind*,[467] a commentary on the *Hevajratantra*, commentaries on Saraha's three cycles of Dohā, Tilopa's "Ganges Mahāmudrā," and the Cakrasaṃvaratantra, several texts on the Cakrasaṃvaratantra, the *Kālacakratantra*, and Cutting Through (*gcod*), *The Treatise on Pointing Out the Tathāgata Heart*, and, of course, his commentary on the *Dharmadhātustava*.[468]

Rangjung Dorje's main disciples were Gyalwa Yungdönba[469] (1284–1365), who was his successor as a lineage holder, the First Shamarpa, Tragba Sengé[470] (1283–1349), and Yagdön Sangyé Bal.

Some Preliminary Remarks on Rangjung Dorje's View

In the Tibetan tradition and Western scholarship alike, the Third Karmapa is often unequivocally identified as a major—if not the main—Kagyü *shentongpa*, that is, a proponent of the view of "*Shentong*-Madhyamaka." No doubt a lot of research on the details of his view still needs to be done, but the fact is that not even the terms *shentong* or *rangtong* can be found in his works, let alone any discussions of them or what they refer to. This is particularly noteworthy with respect to those of the Third Karmapa's texts that clearly present his view and in which one would expect to find these terms and their explanations, if they had any significance for him. Therefore, to avoid looking at Rangjung Dorje's view through the filter of the somewhat "loaded" categories of *rangtong* and *shentong*, in the following, I will first present a preliminary outline of his view that is primarily based on his own writings and, only thereafter, address the question of what a *shentongpa* is exactly.

The methodological basis for looking at any philosophical or religious text, without merely trying to find confirmations of one's own or others' pre-established interpretations of such scriptures, is aptly stated by L. Schmithausen:

> I presuppose that the texts I make use of are to be taken seriously, in the sense that one has to accept that they mean what they say, and that what they mean is reasonable within its own terms.[471]

In this vein, the following sketch of the Third Karmapa's view suggests that, based on his own writings, he cannot be claimed as a one-sided adherent of the view of *shentong* as opposed to *rangtong*, since his explanations are squarely based in both the classical Yogācāra and Madhyamaka systems, providing a synthesis that emphasizes both their complementarity and their sameness with regard to the essential points. This balanced approach is moreover confirmed by a number of later Kagyü authorities (for details, see below).

My outline is based on seven of Rangjung Dorje's texts (including their commentaries) that speak in varying detail about his view, exhibiting a striking consistency in its basic traits that seems to justify a sketch of his position. These seven texts are the following:

(1) *The Profound Inner Reality* (ZMND)
(2) its autocommentary (especially on Chapters One, Six, and Nine) (AC)
(3) *The Distinction between Consciousness and Wisdom* (NY)
(4) *Pointing Out the Tathāgata Heart* (NT)
(5) the commentary on the *Dharmadhātustava* (DSC)
(6) *Explanation of the Dharmadharmatāvibhāga* (EDV)
(7) *The Aspiration Prayer of Mahāmudrā* (MM)

In the Kagyü tradition, the first four texts are considered as a unity, with the Karmapa's magnum opus—ZMND with its AC—being an extensive general commentary on the tantras. Its first chapter is a general discussion of the nature and origin of saṃsāra, as well as the nature of the mind—the Tathāgata heart—as the basis for nirvāṇa. Chapter Six includes the change of state of the eight consciousnesses into the five wisdoms. Chapter Nine contains a presentation of the two realities and the progressive steps of the path of both the sūtras and tantras. To be sure, ZMND and AC are primarily works on the tantras, but the just-mentioned explanations in them apply in general and are also found in the same way in NT, NY, and DSC. This clearly suggests that they indeed represent Rangjung Dorje's basic position as being the view that underlies sūtras and tantras in common.

NT and NY are works that supplement ZMND and AC, respectively, elaborating on buddha nature and the characteristics of the eight consciousnesses and the four (five) wisdoms, with the former changing their state into the latter (both works are also referred to in AC).[472]

As will be seen in the translation of DSC below, it also contains an extensive discussion of the two realities in the context of ground, path, and fruition, drawing on numerous sources from both the Yogācāra and Madhyamaka traditions, as well as a demonstration that these two traditions are not mutually exclusive but come down to the same essential point.

EDV is primarily a commentary on the *Dharmadharmatāvibhāga*, saying that—among the five texts of Maitreya—this one describes the manner of practically engaging in the Tathāgata heart. EDV clearly treats all these five texts as a unity and states that it is based on the works of both Asaṅga and Nāgārjuna, which is reflected in its many quotations from all these texts. Among all of Rangjung Dorje's works, EDV gives the most detailed presentations of the three natures, nonconceptual wisdom, and the notion of complete change of state. It also extensively explains the four "yogic practices" (*prayoga*) found in many mahāyāna texts (for details, see below), and—like DSC and NT—the relinquishment of the four conceptions in terms of factors to be relinquished, remedies, suchness, and fruition, as explained in the *Avikalpapraveśadhāraṇī*.

Of course, MM does not give a systematic presentation of the view but still highlights some crucial points.[473]

As for a tentative chronology of these texts, EDV's colophon says that it was written in a Tibetan Monkey Year at Upper Dechen, which can only be 1320.[474] The colophon of ZMND has a Tibetan Year of the Dog, which according to Jamgön Kongtrul's commentary ("Water Male Dog Year") is 1322. As for AC, its colophon gives 1325 as the year of composition. DSC was probably written in 1326 (possibly in 1327).[475] There is no date available for NT, while the colophon of NY says that it was authored at Upper Dechen in a Year of the Pig, which can only be 1323.[476] In any case, since both it and NT are referred to by Rangjung Dorje in his AC, they must have been composed before the latter and, given their overall context, in all likelihood after ZMND. Consequently, it seems that Rangjung Dorje laid out his basic view by way of these interrelated texts between 1320 and 1326/7, starting with EDV, followed by ZMND, NT, NY, AC, and finally DSC.

To present some key elements of Rangjung Dorje's view, his ZMND starts by explaining the purpose of its composition as being the realization of the stainless Tathāgata heart, which abides throughout the three phases of impurity (sentient beings), both impurity and purity (bodhisattvas on the path), and utter purity (Buddhas). AC comments that these phases represent ground, path, and fruition, or ground-tantra, means-tantra, and fruition-tantra. The stainless Tathāgata heart is the subject of the vajrayāna, which is most difficult to realize. "Vajra" refers to changeless buddhahood and "yāna" is what makes bodhisattvas proceed there. In other words, since the indestructible Tathāgata heart is the basis from which nothing in saṃsāra and nirvāṇa moves away, it is the vajrayāna. Since it is the very nature of buddhahood, it is called "Buddha heart." It entails the four inconceivable points that are also presented in the *Śrīmālādevīsutra* and the *Uttaratantra*. AC says:

> The [inconceivable] point of the "basic element" is that the Buddha heart is not tainted by any stains, but does not become buddhahood until all afflictive and cognitive stains have been relinquished. The [inconceivable] point of enlightenment is that [the basic element] is associated with these stains since beginningless time, but because these stains are adventitious, they are not established as any real substance. The [inconceivable] point of the qualities [of enlightenment] is that the sixty-four qualities of buddhahood exist in all sentient beings right now in a complete way, but if they are not triggered through the condition of the immaculate dharma (the natural outflow of the utterly stainless dharmadhātu), their power does not come forth. [The inconceivable point of enlightened activity is that] there is no difference in enlightened activity's [effortless, spontaneous, and nonconceptual] operation in terms of all sentient beings and Buddhas being the same or different. Thus, being free from all expressions yet serving as the basis for all expressions is being inconceivable . . . Though it is said that this mode of being is difficult to realize by śrāvakas, pratyekabuddhas, and even bodhisattvas who have newly entered the [mahā]yāna, for the time being, it shall be taught by way of an example. When a big precious gem of blue beryl is encrusted . . .

> Not understanding these reasons, [others] explain that the fruition exists [already] right now, that the afflictions are not to be relinquished, that new remedial wisdom cannot be produced, and that natural purity is the partial aspect of nothing but a nonimplicative negation.[477] Such explanations are a far cry from the vajrayāna. Therefore, one should know that this inconceivable matrix—the very essence of what dependently originates (such as ultimate and seeming, Buddhas and sentient beings, appearance and emptiness)—is contained in the three phases [of sentient beings, bodhisattvas on the path, and Buddhas] . . . In detail, I have already explained this in my *Treatise Determining the Buddha Heart.*[478]

The first chapter of ZMND begins with presenting the process of saṃsāric delusion as mind being unaware of its own nature:

> The cause is beginningless mind as such.
> Though it is neither unbalanced nor biased,
> Due to the unimpeded play of that very [mind],
> Empty in essence, lucid in nature,
> And unimpeded in manifesting, it appears as everything.
> That very [mind], being ignorant of itself,
> Is stirred by formational mentation.
> Due to being stirred like waves on water,
> Referents and apprehenders appear as two.
> [Mind] itself projects onto itself and grasps [at that].
> Due to the factor of mind moving outward,
> Objects are taken to be referents, and the consciousnesses arise.

Since these lines on how mind falls into delusion are essential and the basis for all following explanations as well as for Rangjung Dorje's commentary on the *Dharmadhātustava*, it seems appropriate to present the most crucial comments in AC:

> The general terminology of all yānas speaks of "mind as such." However, [this mind] has to be understood as being twofold—pure and impure. As for teaching [mind's] pure [aspect] as mind, the *Uttaratantra* . . . expresses the Buddha heart as mind, and this has the meaning of it being the basis of everything in saṃsāra and nirvāṇa. . . . The *[Aṣṭasāhasrikā]prajñāpāramitāsūtra* says:
>
> > The mind is no-mind. The nature of the mind is luminosity.

. . . To express [mind's] impure [aspect] as mind refers to what is taught as the "ālaya-consciousness." . . . This [ālaya-consciousness] embraced by false imagination consists of the minds and mental factors in the three realms, is the root of all obscurations, and is to be overcome by buddha wisdom. . . . As for the so-called "ālaya," if the term "consciousness" is not [explicitly] stated, since it is suitable [in certain contexts] to express suchness as "ālaya" too, [the term] "consciousness" is added [here]. . . . It is fine to use the conventional term "purified phenomena" due to the ālaya-consciousness having become pure, but it is not suitable to explain the ālaya-consciousness as being the cause for the buddha wisdom of nirvāṇa. "But isn't it that also the conceptuality that is based on the correct view of the immaculate dharmas being inseparable from the enlightenment of a buddha is input into the ālaya-consciousness? How are these purified phenomena produced?" They rely on the above-stated purity of mind, the dharmakāya, the Tathāgata heart, . . . which is explained in detail in *Mahāyānasaṃgraha* [I.45–49].[479] . . . Some may think that the unfolding disposition arises newly, but this is not the case. To present the naturally abiding disposition—the dharmadhātu—as the eight consciousnesses, such as the ālaya-consciousness, is a presentation and classification in terms of false imagination. Accordingly, the very own stainless essence of these eight collections [of consciousness] exists as the nature of the four wisdoms, and this is the presentation by way of correct imagination. Due to the previous stains having been overcome through the immaculate dharma that is based on the enlightenment of a Buddha, the mistakenness of the eight collections does not exist [anymore later]. Therefore, this is given the name "the wisdom of the fundamental change of state." For this reason, . . . [mind] without stains should be regarded as being wisdom and [mind] with stains to be consciousness. . . .

Having explained pure and impure mind in this way, [the meaning of] "beginningless" [in the first line of the verse above] is as follows. Since a beginning and an end in time are conceptual superimpositions, [mind's] own essence—be it with stains or stainless—is free from being the same as or other than dependent origination. Since there is no other beginning than that, this is called "beginningless time." In the very moment of being aware (*rig pa*) of our realizing [mind's] own essence, it is liberated, while not being aware (*ma rig pa*) of it is the beginning of mistaken mind, which is called "ignorance." . . . [Moreover,] there have been infinite [moments in] past times apart from just this [present] moment [of not realizing mind's nature], which are connected as a continuum [all the way up to this moment]. Therefore, to express this [infinite continuum of ignorance] through the term "beginningless" is fine too. However, thoughts that, right from the beginning, mind with stains exists as something permanent or that it arises out of nothing are just instances of the views about a true personality. If [mind] were permanently connected with the stains, they would be impossible to relinquish. [The other possibility means that] mind would arise without a cause. Since [such thoughts] entail these flaws, they also contradict reasoning. . . . Since this mind is inexpressible as being either the same or different with regard to Buddhas and sentient beings, it is not unbalanced. Since it does not fall into bias, such as permanence or extinction, it is unbiased. Therefore, this is the teaching on the very nature of mind.

As for how mind manifests, that very mind, due to the unimpeded play of its own essence through momentary consciousnesses, [while] its nature abides as emptiness and natural lucidity (which is the basis for everything), the individual manifestations of the collections of mental factors and the seven collections of consciousness appear in an unimpeded and momentary way from that [nature]. Therefore, during the phase of [mind] being impure, it is taught as "mind," "mentation," and "consciousness." Once it has become pure, it is expressed by the names of the three kāyas and the wisdoms. This is also stated by noble Nāgārjuna in [verse 37 of] his *Dharmadhātustava*:

> Covered by the web of the afflictions,
> It is called a "sentient being."
> Once it's free from the afflictions,
> It should be expressed as "Buddha."

. . . As for this mind being ignorant of itself, of what is it ignorant, through what is it ignorant, and in which way is it ignorant? It is ignorant of its own naturally pure essence. Through what [is it ignorant]? It is ignorant [of its own essence] through the unimpeded creative display of its own essence appearing as if it were [distinct] subjects and objects. In which way is it ignorant? Due to being stirred by formational mentation, it seemingly appears as

> causes and conditions, based on which it is rendered afflicted. This gives rise to ignorance, and through false imagination, it becomes the basis and the conditions of saṃsāra. Since this [mentation] manifests as mutual causes and conditions in relation to the ālaya[-consciousness], just like water and waves, it is incessantly stirring and forming. Therefore, it is ignorance. This is explained as "mentation." . . . This being associated with afflictions [—the afflicted mind—] . . . is the root of all the mistakenness of circling in the three realms. . . .
>
> What happens due to the above-mentioned movement of mind and mentation, which is like waves on water? . . . Referents (the six objects) and the six consciousnesses that apprehend [them], though not really existing as something different ultimately, arise such that they appear as two . . . Due to the factor of mind moving outward, objects are taken to be referents, and the consciousnesses arise. Those who do not know that all phenomena are mind entertain the thought that, though these consciousnesses are their own minds, outer objective referents are produced by subtle particles or hidden entities. In order to demonstrate that this is not the case, the manner of [mind] itself projecting [the aspects of subject and object] onto itself and grasping [at them as self and other] is to be taught.[480]

Later in that chapter, AC comments on the four conditions that give rise to everything produced by mind: the ālaya-consciousness as the causal condition; the sense faculties as the dominant conditions; forms, sounds, and so forth as the object-conditions; and the immediate mind as the immediate condition. Ultimately, the text says, these conditions are tenable as sheer dependent origination, but they are all nothing but expressions for particular events of imagination.[481]

Rangjung Dorje's extensive discussion of the two realities in the ninth chapter of AC[482] states that all notions of ground, path, and fruition are just superimpositions. What exists ultimately is naturally pure mind, the Buddha heart endowed with the two realities, free from the entire web of imaginary reference points. The text then comments on the passage from the *Vajrajñānasamucchayatantra* in ZMND (also found in DSC's complementary section on the two realities), which is phrased here as follows: The seeming is dualistic appearance, with its reality being like a reflection of the moon in water, while the ultimate is the eighteen emptinesses,[483] with its reality being nondual wisdom. Discussing the two realities largely in classical Madhyamaka style, Rangjung Dorje cites Nāgārjuna's *Mūlamadhyamakakārikā*, *Akutobhayā* (a rather long quote that also includes the passage in DSC's section on the two realities), *Mahāyānaviṃśikā*, and *Bodhicittavivaraṇa*, as well as Maitreya's *Madhyāntavibhāga* and *Uttaratantra*, and the *Guhyasamājatantra*. He addresses the objection that the explanation of the two realities as the Buddha heart is fine in Yogācāra and vajrayāna texts, but that the Madhyamaka texts teach the lack of nature of all phenomena and thus do not contain any instructions that the Buddha heart exists. Cautioning that one should not be mistaken about the words of the Mādhyamikas, Rangjung Dorje replies that precisely this Buddha heart is taught at length in the *Dharmadhātustava*, quoting its verses 16–21.

DSC's introductory section on the two realities starts with objections to verse 2 of the *Dharmadhātustava*, saying that it is not tenable that the fruition of nirvāṇa (dharmakāya) manifests through the cause of saṃsāra having become pure, since these two are mutually exclusive. Also, any form of existence of saṃsāra and nirvāṇa contradicts Nāgārjuna's statements in his collection of reasoning that all phenomena are without nature. Rangjung Dorje answers by first quoting the *Uttaratantra* and Asaṅga's commentary on it, identifying those who do not see the inconceivable object of the Buddhas (the Tathāgata heart) as ordinary beings, tīrthikas with views about a self, śrāvakas, pratyekabuddhas, and even beginner bodhisattvas whose minds are distracted from the correct realization of emptiness[484] through conceptualizing suchness and the fruition. Thus, the factors to be relinquished and their remedies must be understood in terms of both the Madhyamaka system of the two realities and the Yogācāra system of the three natures (supported by quotes from both traditions).

As for the two realities, it is the nature of dualistic appearances to appear like a reflection of the moon in water, which is seeming reality. Ultimate reality means that precisely these mere appearances are naturally free from all reference points. In this way, the two realities are completely free from being the same or different. At the same time, both are just conventional, and neither is independently real. The point of Madhyamaka is to bring every kind of clinging to reality, unreality, entities, and nonentities to an end. In this way, since the seeming is deceiving and illusionlike, it is merely false imagination that appears as the abodes, objects, and bodies of sentient beings, all consisting of the eight consciousnesses. Since these consciousnesses arise in dependence on false imagination, they are not real. But since they originate dependently and appear, they are not totally nonexistent either and thus called "other-dependent." As for the discriminations and labels on the basis of these other-dependent appearances, they are like a mirage and thus called "the imaginary nature," since what is nonexistent is imagined as existent. The root of such mistakenness is the stainless dharmadhātu being unaware of itself, but there is nothing in all of this that is really established. When these teachings on the two realities are practiced as the path, they represent the two accumulations, and their fruition is the union of the two kāyas.

Therefore, since the stained dharmadhātu as the "cause" of saṃsāra has become pure, there is no problem in calling it "nirvāṇa." In the collection of reasoning, Rangjung Dorje says, Nāgārjuna negates the clinging to characteristics, but he definitely does not refute the teachings on the way of being of the Buddha and the dharma, wisdom, great compassion, or enlightened activity. The *Dharmadhātustava* is a teaching on the very essence of pure mind, which is stained by apprehender and apprehended in just an adventitious way.

After its presentation of the two realities, AC[485] gives an overview of the gradual nature of the teachings of the Buddha, in which respectively coarser notions have to be progressively replaced by more subtle notions, extensively citing Nāgārjuna's *Bodhicittavivaraṇa* and Maitreya's *Mahāyānasūtrālaṃkāra*. That means, notions such as minute material particles or hidden objects, as held by the Vaibhāṣikas and Sautrāntikas, respectively, are of course mistaken from the perspective that all seemingly external objects are just mental appearances emerging from the ālaya-consciousness. Nevertheless, as a remedy for misconceptions that there is an ātman or a creating agent, the Buddha taught about minute particles in his presentation of the skandhas, dhātus, and āyatanas. Similarly, the realization that all phenomena are nothing but appearances in the mind, which come about through the causes and conditions represented by the eight consciousnesses, has its value in that the just-mentioned wrong views are relinquished through it. However, the notion that all phenomena are nothing but mind needs to be abandoned too. This makes one see true reality, which is either taught as mind too being unborn (the identitylessness of all phenomena) or as the dharmadhātu free from the duality of apprehender and apprehended. Thus, all levels of the Buddha's teachings are justified as expedient progressive means leading to the final realization of ultimate reality.[486]

EDV and the sixth chapter of AC (in brief)[487] as well as NY (in great detail) present the classical Yogācāra format of how the eight consciousnesses change state into the four wisdoms and the three kāyas. This means that the ālaya-consciousness manifests as mirrorlike wisdom, the afflicted mind as the wisdom of equality, the mental consciousness as discriminating wisdom, and the five sense consciousnesses as all-accomplishing wisdom. Mirrorlike wisdom represents the dharmakāya, the wisdom of equality and discriminating wisdom make up the sambhogakāya, and all-accomplishing wisdom is the nirmaṇakāya. However, AC adds that, though the change of state of the mental consciousness represents the sambhogakāya, both the change of state of the aspect of this consciousness that perceives outer objects[488] (which shows as the display of pure buddha realms) as well as the change of state of its conceptual part (unimpeded wisdom and enlightened activity at all times) are aspects of the nirmāṇakāya. NY then identifies the conceptuality that changes state into discriminating wisdom as the immediate mind.[489] AC and NY agree that both the part of the mental consciousness that perceives outer objects and the five sense consciousnesses change state into all-accomplishing wisdom. AC says that "dharmadhātu wisdom" refers to the very essence of these four wisdoms, that is, the utter purity of being free from all reference points (in other words, it is the fundamental luminous expanse of mind's nature—the dharmadhātu—in which the above changes of state take place, while always being inseparable from it). NY explains that the three kāyas and their activities (the fundamental change of state of the eight consciousnesses) are the maṇḍala of the dharmadhātu free from reference points. The svabhāvakāya means that everything in saṃsāra and nirvāṇa is primordially free from being one or different.[490]

As for NT and NY, both contain all of the above elements in greater or lesser detail, often having a more experiential tone geared toward meditation. The whole structure of NT greatly relies on the *Uttaratantra* and the *Mahāyānasūtrālaṃkāra*, even literally incorporating six verses from the former and several from the latter (as well as two from Nāgārjuna's *Mahāyānaviṃśikā*).[491] Like the *Dharmadhātustava*, DSC, ZMND, and AC, NT speaks about the Tathāgata heart as the ground of everything in saṃsāra and nirvāṇa, being naturally pure and merely obscured by adventitious stains (thus existing as the three phases of sentient beings, bodhisattvas, and Buddhas). Just as AC, it says that delusion always starts right now and repeats ZMND's above explanation on how mind is mistaken about itself. Similar to DSC, it presents the three natures and false imagination. It treats the thirty-two qualities of the dharmakāya and the thirty-two of the rūpakāyas, agreeing with the *Dharmadhātustava* and AC that all these qualities are within one's own body. Like DSC and EDV, it speaks about the freedom from the fourfold clinging to characteristics as per the *Avikalpapraveśadhāraṇī*. Ultimately, since there is no arising, there is no liberation either. Thus, both Buddhas and sentient beings are just like space.

The layout of NY is primarily based on Maitreya's *Mahāyānasūtrālaṃkāra* and Asaṅga's *Mahāyānasaṃgraha*,[492] thus being squarely placed in classical Yogācāra presentations.[493] At the same time, this short text says three times (!) that all phenomena do not arise from themselves, from something other, from both, or without a cause. It also states that phenomena are nothing but dependent origination, with this very dependent origination being empty of a nature of its own, free from being one or different, and unaffected by being real or false, just like an illusion or the moon in water, thus incorporating typical and crucial Madhyamaka elements. All seemingly outer objects are said to be just appearances in one's own mind, while adding the typical Madhyamaka stance on the teachings on "mere mind," that is, them being given in order to eliminate any idea of an external creating agent. The text also presents ZMND's above explanation on how mind is mistaken about itself, discussing the details of the eight consciousnesses. The presentation of the change of state of these eight into the wisdoms and kāyas corresponds to and elaborates on what is said in AC. It concludes by stating that buddhahood is the manifestation of the five wisdoms and the four kāyas, with the dharmadhātu (wisdom) representing the svabhāvakāya. The ālaya-consciousness is what possesses the stains of mind, mentation, and consciousness, while its stainlessness is called the Tathāgata heart.

Like parts of NT, MM is more oriented toward meditative practice, but it also contains most of the above-mentioned elements, such as the identification of what ground, path, and fruition are (verse 6). It speaks about appearances being mind, mind being empty yet displaying unimpededly, and mind free from object and subject being the luminosity to be realized (verses 9 and 18). In terms of the view, verse 7 is central:

> Within the ground of purification—mind as such, lucid and
>   empty in union—
> May the means to purify—the great vajra-yoga of Mahāmudrā—
> [Purify] what is to be purified—the adventitious stains of delusion—
> And the result of purification—the stainless dharmakāya—
>   manifest.[494]

Rangjung Dorje's treatment of the three natures, mainly found in EDV and DSC, greatly accords with how these were explained above in the introduction. In particular, EDV connects them with the threefold lack of nature, explicitly states that both the imaginary and the other-dependent natures are not really established, and says that the complete change of state of the other-dependent is the perfect nature.[495] In general, the Tathāgata heart is equated with the stainless nature of phenomena, nonconceptual wisdom, dharmakāya, the perfect nature, and prajñāpāramitā.

To summarize, all these texts by Rangjung Dorje share many of the same quotes or paraphrases from both Madhyamaka and Yogācāra works to support the same points. Moreover, throughout all his presentations, the Third Karmapa obviously not only sees no contradiction between Madhyamaka and Yogācāra but clearly suggests that they supplement each other and essentially come down to the same point. This matches his explicit statements at the end of DSC on how the masters of these two systems may sometimes make dissimilar statements but always agree on the vital meaning (the ultimate nature), and that the correct view, realization, and fruition of all yānas are to be understood as just one. In the same vein, as for the fruition of buddhahood in terms of the three kāyas and so forth, in his AC, Rangjung Dorje quotes extensively from the *Mañjuśrīnāmasaṃgīti*, *Uttaratantra*, *Dharmadhātustava*, and *Madhyamakāvatāra*, saying that he does so in order to eliminate the wrong ideas of people who think that the presentations of the fruition of buddhahood in the mantrayāna, by Asaṅga, Nāgārjuna, Candrakīrti, and others do not accord.[496]

In brief, there can be no doubt that Rangjung Dorje's explanations are always equally based on the major Yogācāra texts by Maitreya, Asaṅga, and Vasubandhu as well as the Madhyamaka texts by Nāgārjuna, Candrakīrti, Bhāvaviveka, Jñānagarbha, and so on. This balanced approach of the Third Karmapa not only has some Indian precursors (such as Kambala, Ratnākaraśānti, Jñānaśrīmitra, Abhayākaragupta,[497] and, to some extent, Śāntarakṣita and Kamalaśīla)[498] but is also repeatedly confirmed by later Kagyü masters. Thus, if one wants to use the categories of *rangtong* and *shentong* at all, one could say that Rangjung Dorje's view takes them to be anything but mutually exclusive and represents a creative synthesis of them. For example, this is exactly what a song on view, meditation, conduct, and fruition by the Sixth Shamarpa, Chökyi Wangchug[499] (1584–1630) says:

> Indeed, the learned set up mere presentations
> Of "self-empty" and "other-empty,"
> But the great victor, glorious Rangjung [Dorje],
> Holds these two to be noncontradictory.[500]

Likewise, a song about the view by the Thirteenth Karmapa, Düdül Dorje[501] (1733–1797)—and he of all should know what the Third Karmapa's view is—states:

> Secondly, [the system of] Asaṅga and his brother who follow the
> final wheel [of dharma]
> Is known as "False Aspectarian Mere Mentalism" in the land of
> the noble ones
> And as "other-empty Madhyamaka" in Tibet.
> The meaning of these two names is the same.
>
> This is the completely pure system that,
> Through mainly teaching the luminous aspect of the mind,

Holds that the fruitions—kāyas and wisdoms—exist on their own accord.
As for its necessity, it is asserted that it is taught in order to
Relinquish any arising of fear of emptiness and to awaken those with indefinite disposition.

When commenting on its meaning, venerable Rangjung [Dorje] says
That it is one with the system of Candrakīrti.
Others assert that the ultimate is existent and really established
And that emptiness is really established.

As for the mahāyāna's sūtra portion, both the middle and the final wheel [of dharma]
Have the purport of the Sugata heart, the unity of emptiness and luminosity.
The middle [wheel] explains this mainly by teaching emptiness,
While the final [wheel] elucidates it mainly by teaching luminosity.
I understand that, in actuality, these are not contradictory.[502]

The beginning stanzas of paying homage in a commentary on the *Uttaratantra*—which is based on Rangjung Dorje's lost summary of this text—by Dashi Öser[503] (born 1474), a close disciple of the Seventh Karmapa and teacher of the Eighth, state:

I pay homage to the dharma lord Rangjung Dorje,
Who commented on the intention of the victor and his regent Maitreya
By combining in a noncontradictory manner
The essential points of the intentions of both Asaṅga and Nāgārjuna.[504]

As presented above, the Eighth Karmapa's commentary on the *Abhisamayālaṃkāra*—this commentary itself being allegedly a *shentong* text—strongly denies the ascription of one of the most classical *shentong* positions to the Third Karmapa:

Some fools say, "The Omniscient Karmapa Rangjung [Dorje] asserts the intention of the *Mahāyānottaratantra* to be that the Tathāgata heart exists in the dharmadhātu of the mind of sentient beings in an inseparable manner." This wise being did not assert such. In his

> autocommentary on *The Profound Inner Reality* he makes a twofold classification [of mind as such], saying, "what is pure is expressed as mind, and what is impure is [also] expressed as mind."[505] By explaining that those who possess impure mental impulses are sentient beings, he elucidates that the dharmadhātu does not exist in such sentient beings. He presents these very sentient beings as being the adventitious stains that are produced by false imagination, which mistakenly strays from the dharmadhātu. By giving the pure mind names such as "ordinary mind," "original protector," and "original Buddha," he says that it is exactly this [mind] that possesses the mode of being inseparable from the buddha qualities.[506]

The Eighth Karmapa's commentary also discusses the question of whether the ways in which the third turning of the wheel of dharma as classified by Maitreya and Nāgārjuna, respectively, come down to the same essential point. He refers to the Third Karmapa as saying that these two cycles share the same essential point in a general way in that they both teach freedom from reference points. In particular though, Nāgārjuna speaks only about the mere freedom from reference points, while Maitreya explains the personally experienced wisdom free from reference points. However, Nāgārjuna and his spiritual heirs do not reject this wisdom, since it is taught in Nāgārjuna's collection of praises and Āryadeva's *Catuḥśataka*.[507] The exact same passage is also found in Jamgön Kongtrul Lodrö Tayé's *Treasury of Knowledge*.[508]

In the same vein, it is interesting and noteworthy that none of Jamgön Kongtrul's commentaries on ZMND, NT, and NY ever mention the terms "self-empty" or "other-empty." This is all the more striking for a number of reasons. First, Jamgön Kongtrul otherwise identifies Rangjung Dorje repeatedly as a *shentongpa*.[509] Secondly, ZMND, NT, and NY lend themselves easily to an interpretation purely from the point of view of *shentong*. Thirdly, Jamgön Kongtrul never hesitates to give such an interpretation in the same contexts in his own works and usually clearly presents himself as a *shentongpa*, frequently relying on Tāranātha, who was one of the most outspoken proponents of this approach. However, in contradistinction to all that, in his commentaries on the above three texts, Jamgön Kongtrul faithfully follows Rangjung Dorje's approach of a synthesis of classical Yogācāra and Madhyamaka, supporting it with many further quotations that identify the sources (mostly Yogācāra) of Rangjung Dorje's compositions and often exactly correspond to the citations that Rangjung Dorje himself uses in his AC, DSC, and elsewhere.

To come to the question of whether someone is a *shentongpa* or not, in order to be able to make any sense of it, let alone answering it, the underlying issues of what exactly *shentong* means and what a *shentongpa* is need more attention. This seems to be very obvious, but more often than not the terms *rangtong* and *shentong* and their differences are referred to with the tacit implication of their meaning and scope being totally clear and unequivocal for everybody. In fact, however, what is called "the *shentong* tradition" is anything but a monolithic system (as is true for most Buddhist "schools"). For various masters, *shentong* obviously means something very different, as evidenced by their giving their own distinct views on its meaning and its relation to *rangtong*. Certain Tibetans use the term *shentong* to refer to a doctrine with set positions (which can differ greatly as well). Others speak about it in the sense of a philosophical or an experiential outlook. Some refer to it as a tradition of how to practice meditation (*sgom lugs*), and others take it to be a combination of theory and practice, that is, view and meditation. Some even argue that *rangtong* and *shentong* represent sūtrayāna and vajrayāna, respectively.[510]

To give a few examples of how *shentong* can be presented, the contemporary Jonang scholar Khenpo Lodrö Tragba's *Synopsis of Philosophical Systems*[511]—basically following Dölpopa—gives his definitions for *rangtongpa* and *shentongpa*:

> Someone who says that a nonimplicative negation whose object of negation is "being really established" is the ultimate emptiness, is therefore called a "*rangtongpa*." . . . Someone who says that (1) the basis of emptiness—the ultimate, nondual wisdom—is not empty from its own side but empty of what is other—all reference points, such as apprehender and apprehended—and (2) that [all] phenomena that consist of what is seeming and adventitious are not only empty of the ultimate—whose essence is other—but that these seeming [phenomena themselves] are also empty of a nature of their own is therefore called a "*shentongpa*."

The same author's *Fearless Lion's Roar* clarifies the relationship between the seeming and the ultimate:

> The final mode of being is not just a sheer emptiness in the sense of everything being nonexistent and not established. Rather, within the ground that is the nonimplicative negation of being empty of [all] reference points of the seeming, the ultimate suchness of luminosity—which is an implicative negation—abides primordially.[512]

Jamgön Kongtrul Lodrö Tayé's *Treasury of Knowledge* explains his version of the *shentong* view by combining classical Indian Yogācāra presentations (as in Maitreya's *Madhyāntavibhāga* and *Mahāyānasūtrālaṃkāra*), the explanations in the *Uttaratantra*, and many of the *shentong* positions held by the Tibetan masters Dölpopa, Tāranātha, and Śākya Chogden. The essential point here is that the perfect nature (also referred to as buddha nature, emptiness, dharmadhātu, or nondual wisdom) is only empty of what is other than it—both the imaginary and the other-dependent natures—but not empty of its own nature with all its enlightened qualities, thus being really existent ultimately.

> From the point of view of cutting through reference points, [the following is taught]. On the level of seeming [reality], consciousness that appears as various appearances—mere false imagination—exists. Since the apprehending part and the apprehended part that appear within this [false imagination] are merely something mentally imputed, they are not existent even on the conventional level. Thus, seeming reality is free from the two extremes. Through accepting the mere existence of false imagination on the level of seeming [reality], it is free from the extreme of nonexistence and the extreme of extinction. Through lying beyond all dependent and imputed phenomena—such as an apprehending and an apprehended aspect, it is free from the extreme of permanence and the extreme of existence. Wisdom free from reference points really exists within consciousness (false imagination) as being the mode of the true nature of this [consciousness]. In the phase with stains, consciousness—that which bears this true nature—exists within the nature of phenomena as separable adventitious stains, that is, as the nature of stains that do not really exist and are the factors to be relinquished. Thus, it is said that ultimate reality is also free from the two extremes. It is beyond the extremes of existence, nonexistence, permanence, and extinction, because emptiness is really established, and all phenomena that consist of the duality of apprehender and apprehended—such as imagination—do not really exist.

> The seeming is merely an appearance of mistakenness and
> empty of a nature of its own.
> The nature of phenomena is unchanging and not empty of
> a nature of its own.
> . . .
> The imaginary does not exist, while the other-dependent exists
> seemingly.
> The perfect does not exist [on the level] of the seeming, but it
> exists ultimately.

One may wonder, "Is it not said in the sūtras that also the dharmadhātu is empty?" Generally speaking, it is empty or emptiness, but that does not mean that it has to be empty of its own nature. It is called "emptiness" because it is empty of everything that has characteristics other than wisdom itself, that is, [empty] of the reference points of apprehender and apprehended.

Here, as for the three characteristics—the imaginary, the other-dependent, and the perfect [natures]—the imaginary [consists of] all nonentities, such as space; the aspects that appear as conceptual objects, such as form; the connections of names and referents, that is, clinging to a name as being the [corresponding] referent and to mistake a referent for the [corresponding] name; and all that is apprehended through mental superimposition, such as outer, inner, end, middle, big, small, good, bad, direction, time, and so on. The other-dependent [nature] is mere consciousness that appears as the entities of apprehender and apprehended, because these are appearances under the influence of something other, that is, the latent tendencies of ignorance. The perfect [nature] is self-luminous self-awareness free from all reference points. Its synonyms are the nature of phenomena, dharmadhātu, suchness, and the ultimate. The imaginary and the other-dependent are equal in that they do not really exist, that they are appearances of mistakenness, and that they are something seeming and false. Nevertheless, it is necessary to classify them separately through their characteristics. The imaginary does not even exist on the level of the seeming, while the other-dependent exists on the level of the seeming. The perfect does not exist on the level of the seeming, but it exists as the ultimate. Therefore, it really exists.

> These three are nominally existent, substantially existent, and existent without reference points, respectively.
> They are the emptinesses of the nonexistent and of the existent, and the ultimate [emptiness].
> They are the lack of nature in terms of characteristics and arising, and the ultimate [lack of nature].
> . . .
> Therefore, it is asserted that all knowable objects are pervaded by emptiness.
> The perfect [nature]'s own essence is not connected with seeming phenomena.

> . . .
> It is free from reference points, permanent, partless, and
> omnipresent.
> . . .
> It is said that most of the other presentations of ground, path,
> and fruition accord with those of the Mere Mentalists.[513]

Differing from most Yogācāra texts, Jamgön Kongtrul explicitly states that the perfect nature is empty of both the imaginary and the other-dependent natures.[514]

> The basis of negation—the perfect [nature]—is the dhātu or suchness, which is beyond being an object that is a reference point. The object of negation consists of both the imaginary and the other-dependent characteristics. The way of being empty is that the basis of negation is empty of this twofold object of negation. Therefore, the perfect [nature] itself is empty of something other.[515]

The practical approach of determining and realizing this perfect nature is presented as the classical "four yogic practices"[516] found in many mahāyāna sūtras and Yogācāra texts. However, the fourth phase of realizing the nonduality of apprehender and apprehended (nondual dharmadhātu) is explicitly equated by Jamgön Kongtrul with recognizing buddha nature, which is said to be really established and beyond dependent origination, thus clearly differing from the unity of dependent origination and emptiness in classical Madhyamaka.

> The Yogācāra-Mādhyamikas are those among the followers of Madhyamaka philosophical systems who are adorned with many secret essential points that are special and uncommon. Their way to determine the view through studying and reflecting is described by the great regent [Maitreya as in *Mahāyānasūtrālaṃkāra* VI.8]:
>
> > The mind is aware that nothing other than mind exists.
> > Then, it is realized that mind does not exist either.
> > The intelligent ones are aware that both do not exist
> > And abide in the dharmadhātu in which these are absent.
>
> Accordingly, it is first resolved that all phenomena are not established as something other than merely mind or [as something] outside of it. Through this reason, it is established that a nature

> of the apprehended does not exist. Then, it is resolved that also a nature of the apprehender does not exist. Thus, the dharmadhātu as such, empty of the duality of apprehender and apprehended, is determined. It is without stains, its nature is luminosity, and it possesses the seven vajra points.[517] . . . This is called "suchness" or "Sugata heart." It encompasses and resides in all phenomena—sentient beings, Buddhas, and so on—as equality. However, in sentient beings, it resides as their Heart, while it does so in a directly manifest way in Buddhas. Therefore, it is also called "Buddha heart" because its nature does not change. In all regards, it is not comparable to a permanent, singular, and independent personal self, since it is free from [all] extremes of reference points. In its own nature, saṃsāra and nirvāṇa are undifferentiable, but in dependence on [certain] phases it is presented as threefold.[518] It is also free from the plain view that the lack of a personal self is [nothing but] emptiness. [Rather,] it is established as the one and only ultimate reality. It is free from appearance and nonappearance or entities and nonentities. Therefore, it is called "the actual unconditioned" or "the unconditioned that is ultimate reality." Since it is said that this ultimate is even beyond interdependence, [in this system,] the ultimate is not presented as interdependence. . . . It is said that this Heart is empty of all adventitious flaws or stains. [However,] it is not empty of the attributes of unsurpassable qualities but possesses them in a spontaneously present way. Therefore, with regard to its nature, there is nothing to be removed in terms of stains or to be added in terms of qualities. This is precisely what is not realized through mere one-sided study and reflection, but is gradually realized through the personally experienced [wisdom] that results from meditation, that is, stainless self-sprung awareness.[519]

The main difference between *shentong* and "Mere Mentalism" is explained as follows:

> In the system that is known in Tibet as that of the False Aspectarian Mere Mentalists, it is said that the nature of the ālaya-consciousness is really established. Due to this explanation, it is consciousness that is mind's object. Therefore, this is [a form of] realism. But in this system here, it is asserted that the nature of wisdom itself—which lies beyond consciousness and is free from all reference points—is really established. However, since this wisdom free from reference

points is not conditioned, it is said that ultimate reality is free from all mistakes of realists.[520]

Jamgön Kongtrul says that there are no differences between *rangtong* and *shentong* with regard to their positions on seeming reality and when resting in meditative equipoise. The differences primarily pertain to the conceptual analyses during subsequent attainment.

> Between the [two systems of] Madhyamaka that are known as self-empty and other-empty, there is no difference with regard to the manner in which they determine that all phenomena consisting of seeming [reality] are emptiness and the cessation of all extremes of reference points in meditative equipoise. But the differences lie [for one] in the way in which conventions of consciousness and expression are used during subsequent attainment, that is, during the phase when philosophical systems are clearly distinguished. As a mere conventional position at this time, it is either said that the nature of phenomena—suchness—exists or that it does not exist. [The second difference is] with regard to the view that whether, at the time of the final analysis through reasonings that analyze the ultimate, nondual wisdom is really established or not. Therefore, the followers of the other-empty [system] assert that both the imaginary and the other-dependent [natures] are seeming reality, and that the perfect [nature] is ultimate reality. As for the latter, it is asserted that the view [of regarding it] as a mere nonimplicative negation in the sense of the nonestablishment of any nature represents a dead emptiness.[521] Such is [merely] the way in which the seeming is empty, but not the basic nature of ultimate emptiness. In brief, [the latter] is presented as personally experienced wisdom empty of the duality of apprehender and apprehended. Since this system accords very much with the great tantra collections, it is also asserted as the profound view that links sūtra and mantra, that is, as the pinnacle of the doctrinal systems of Madhyamaka.[522]

Dölpopa's *Mountain Dharma* says something very similar:

> When making a combination of the latter two [turnings of the] wheel [of dharma] and the meaning of the vajrayāna a living experience, the conclusive resolve is to rest in meditative equipoise within the profound nature of phenomena in accordance with the middle

[turning of the] wheel [of dharma] in a nonconceptual manner free from reference points. After that, during subsequent attainment, when correctly discriminating phenomena at the time of clearly differentiating them, this is pointed out by distinguishing well in accordance with what is said in the final [turning of the] wheel [of dharma] and the vajrayāna. If one does so, one's entire practice of the profound meaning of all mahāyāna teachings will be unerring and completely pure.

. . . As for the meaning of being free from the extremes of existence and nonexistence, it is twofold. While deeply resting in meditative equipoise within the profound nature of phenomena, all reference points (such as existence and nonexistence) fall away and [this state] is without speech, thought, and expression. But during subsequent attainment, while determining how the basic nature is, there is no flaw in clearly deciding in accordance with that basic nature that what exists is "existent," and what does not exist is "nonexistent." In the opposite case, however, there will be the flaw of falling into extremes. As for the meaning of "buddhahood being neither existent nor nonexistent," this is stated in terms of it not being existent for [ordinary] minds and not being nonexistent for wisdom.[523]

At the behest of the Eleventh Situpa, Pema Wangcho Gyalbo[524] (1886–1952), the Kagyü scholar Surmang Padma Namgyal (twentieth century) wrote a text called *Full Moon of Questions and Answers*,[525] which lists seven different kinds of views held by various Jonang, Sakya, Kagyü, and Nyingma masters on the distinction between *rangtong* and *shentong*.[526] According to this text, (1) Dölpopa and his followers hold consciousness to be *rangtong* and wisdom to be *shentong*. (2) Śākya Chogden considers phenomena—appearances—as *rangtong* and the nature of phenomena—luminosity—as *shentong*. (3) Sabsang Mati Panchen Lodrö Gyaltsen[527] (1294–1376) maintains subject and object to be *rangtong* and expanse (*dbyings*) and wisdom to be *shentong*. (4) The Thirteenth Karmapa, Düdül Dorje, considers saṃsāra to be *rangtong* and nirvāṇa to be *shentong*. (5) The Eighth Karmapa, Mikyö Dorje, and his followers take the pure kāyas and wisdom to be *rangtong* in terms of their actual mode of being and to be *shentong* in terms of the way they appear. (6) The Eighth Situpa, Chökyi Jungné, considers the side of negation as *rangtong* and the side of affirmation as *shentong*. (7) The Nyingma master Katog Gédsé Panchen[528] (1761–1829) regards the phase of conclusive resolve during meditative equipoise to be *rangtong* and the phase of clearly distinguishing during subsequent attainment to be *shentong*.[529]

Summarizing these seven views into three, Padma Namgyal says that Dölpopa asserts wisdom to be "other-empty," Śākya Chogden holds the expanse to be "other-empty," and all others take both wisdom and expanse to be "other-empty." When summarized into two, the first five are said to present *rangtong* and *shentong* mainly by way of what is to be determined, while the latter two do so primarily by way of the means to determine that.[530] To complicate matters further, these seven distinctions are obviously based on three very different categories of comparison. The first—and most common—category takes *rangtong* and *shentong* to refer to phenomena as belonging to two different levels of reality (seeming and ultimate), underlying views (1)–(5). Category two refers to *rangtong* and *shentong* as two approaches to conceptually determine the subject in question (6). Category three considers *rangtong* and *shentong* as distinct (nonconceptual) experiences or phases in the process of attaining realization (7).

The Nyingma master Lochen Dharmaśrī's *Commentary on Ascertaining the Three Vows*[531] presents yet another way of comparing *rangtong* and *shentong*—as two ways of cutting through reference points:

> As for cutting through reference points, there are two [ways]—*rangtong* and *shentong*. *Rangtong* means to assert the emptiness that is a nonimplicative negation as the ultimate, since [all] subjects in question—no matter how they appear—are empty of a nature of their own right from the point of their mere appearance. As for the Mādhyamikas that determine *shentong*, due to the difference of asserting all knowable objects as the three characteristics [the imaginary, other-dependent, and perfect natures] or summarizing them into two—the imaginary and the perfect [natures]—there are two dissimilar ways of identifying the subject in question. In the Yogācāra scriptures, the perfect [nature] is explained as the other-dependent (the basis of emptiness) being empty of the imaginary (the object of negation). In the *Uttaratantra* and so on, it is said that the nature of phenomena—the perfect [nature]—is empty of the imaginary (the object of negation). Therefore, in the essence of this perfect [nature]—the true nature of mind, the ultimate dhātu—there are no stains to be eliminated and no previously nonexistent qualities to be accomplished newly, since it is primordially and naturally pure, and the qualities are spontaneously present.[532]

Mipham Rinpoche's *Lion's Roar Proclaiming Other-Emptiness* starts by listing the sources of the *shentong* view—the sūtras of the third turning of the wheel of dharma, which teach the definitive meaning; Maitreya's *Uttaratantra*;

the profound teachings by Asaṅga and Vasubandhu; the commentaries on the definitive meaning, such as Nāgārjuna's collection of praises; the tantras, such as the *Kālacakratantra*; and the commentaries on their intention, such as the trilogy of bodhisattva commentaries[533]—saying that they all share the same essential meaning. The *Lion's Roar* primarily explains the difference between *rangtong* and *shentong* as pertaining to seeming reality and ultimate reality, respectively, thus largely following category two above. However, Mipham Rinpoche repeatedly emphasizes that such a distinction only applies to the conventional level and not to the sphere of the nonconceptual wisdom of meditative equipoise that directly realizes what is called "ultimate reality." He says that the statement that ultimate reality "is not empty from its own side" must be understood in terms of the two realities being mutually exclusive, but definitely not as being of the same nature and just different isolates. According to his above-mentioned distinction of the two realities in terms of the way things appear and how they actually are being discordant or concordant, respectively, seeming reality is what appears from the perspective of mistakenness, thus being delusive. Ultimate reality is established as it appears from an entirely unmistaken perspective. Since this is not invalidated through valid cognition, it is said to exist ultimately and to be really established. However, this does not mean that ultimate reality has to be a really established appearance different from emptiness. Rather, it is primordially established as the emptiness endowed with the supreme of all aspects (the union of dharmadhātu and emptiness), that is, the ultimate reality that is the essential nature of all phenomena. Since this very dharmadhātu, which is directly realized in an individual's experience, is in itself beyond any negation and proof, it is simply said to be conventionally established as existing as ultimate reality. For, just as a rope and the snake for which that rope may be mistaken, seeming reality and ultimate reality should be differentiated as being conventionally established and not established, respectively, since they cannot be either both mistaken or both real. Thus, "not being empty of itself" simply means that ultimate reality is not empty of being ultimate reality, otherwise it would be seeming reality and therefore deceiving. What this ultimate reality is empty of are the subjects and objects that make up the mistaken appearances called "seeming reality." Consequently, conventionally speaking, ultimate reality is not empty of its own nature, since it entails both an unmistaken subject and object; since what exists on this level cannot be invalidated by any valid cognition; since it is what is established *after* the reasonings that establish emptiness have already been applied; and since what is established through the correct valid cognition that analyzes what is conventionally real cannot be disputed in accordance with the dharma.[534]

As for further distinctions within the *shentong* tradition, one of Tāranātha's works outlines twenty-one criteria as to how Dölpopa's (and his own) interpretation of "other-emptiness" differ from Śākya Chogden's position,[535] which provide a useful grid to compare the views of other *shentongpas* as well.

The Kagyü School sometimes distinguishes between "the other-emptiness of luminosity" (*gsal ba gzhan stong*) and "the other-emptiness of the dhātu" (*dbyings gzhan stong*). Briefly speaking, the first refers to buddha nature's wisdom being empty of adventitious stains (the "other"), and this wisdom itself not being empty but existing as the ultimate nature of luminosity. Thus, the ultimate existence of the luminous nature of mind and its innate buddha qualities are emphasized. Typical proponents are Dölpopa, Tāranātha (who even wrote two commentaries on the *Heart Sūtra* from the perspective of "other-emptiness"),[536] and Jamgön Kongtrul. "The other-emptiness of the dhātu," means that, in and as itself, the nondual nonconceptual experience of the wisdom that realizes the dharmadhātu as mind's true nature is free from reference points. This view is found, for example, in the Eighth Karmapa's commentary on the *Abhisamayālaṃkāra* and in the works of the Sixth Shamarpa.

In brief, as this by no means comprehensive sketch already shows clearly, the various takes on what *rangtong* and *shentong* mean may differ greatly, depending on which perspectives they are evaluated from to begin with. Thus, the study of the specific presentations of individual masters seems mandatory, rather than just following highly generalized doxographical schemes. In this context, one of the crucial points that often was and continues to be overlooked by later proponents of other-emptiness as well as their opponents is that Dölpopa's original presentation of *rangtong* and *shentong* (such as in his main work, *Mountain Dharma*) clearly distinguishes between a "philosophical system" (Skt. *siddhānta*, Tib. *grub mtha'*) based on certain explanations and arguments and a "point of view" in the sense of a wider outlook (Skt. *darśana*, Tib. *lta ba*). For him, the latter is understood as not only dealing with scholarly ascertainments but also—and more importantly so—including what is directly experienced in meditative equipoise (often in the context of advanced vajrayāna practices). It is the entirety of this that he calls "Great Madhyamaka" and "other-emptiness," that is, the outlook of noble beings who directly see the nature of phenomena just as it is. As such, it is clearly contrasted with Madhyamaka or "self-emptiness" as a mere philosophical system. Thus, on these two levels, the entire perspective of how mind perceives and, consequently, the way of discourse are quite different. Therefore, despite the claims of his later opponents, Dölpopa's use of this distinction is primarily epistemological in nature and not ontological or reifying. Also, Dölpopa himself never spoke about "proponents of self-emptiness" as opposed to "proponents of other-emptiness." Rather, he sees self-emptiness as a philosophical system that he accepts himself as far as it goes, that is, on the level of philosophical analysis but not as adequately portraying the level of ultimate and direct meditative insight.[537]

For a number of reasons, many later proponents of other-emptiness and their opponents do not follow the above epistemological distinction and often take both *rangtong* and *shentong* to be philosophical systems, pertaining to ontological concerns. Thus, a major part of the later *rangtong-shentong* controversies is based on the issue—and the confusion—of whether the contrast pertains to the level of philosophical systems or the level of a direct vision of true reality. Both Dölpopa and many later *shentongpa*s say that *shentong* includes and is based on *rangtong* as a form of analytical rigor, but that *shentong* supersedes this level of discourse. Nevertheless, some of these later *shentongpa*s argue for the supremacy of *shentong* even on the level of philosophical systems, which is then fiercely denied by others. Thus, it was on this level that the sometimes highly polemical disputes about this issue and the ensuing attempts to establish the supremacy of one such system over the other started to proliferate. In this process, *shentong* became a highly "loaded" term and also quite often a source of serious confusion, at least for those who try to understand the actual content of these traditions apart from the mere sectarian elements.[538]

Despite all of this, in itself, the term *shentong* does not necessarily entail any substantive ontology. The Eighth Karmapa's commentary on the *Abhisamayālaṃkāra* refers to the proper way of using the term "other-empty" primarily as a pedagogic means to point out that the nature of phenomena—the dharmadhātu—is empty of adventitious stains. But he emphasizes that the nature of phenomena itself is neither self-empty nor other-empty to start with, let alone really existent. As the following excerpt illustrates, the Karmapa's explanations in this commentary are often somewhat tantalizing, since he constantly plays with the terms "self-empty" and "other-empty," shifting their perspectives and setting up paradoxes. Being a pedagogic approach in itself, this can only be understood as cutting through any attempts to adhere to either the one or the other as something to hold onto, in order to realize what a mind free from all reference points would be like.

> There is no such flaw that the nature of other-emptiness itself is not empty, since the name "other-empty" is applied to emptiness [in the sense] that the other features within this basis [emptiness] are empty of their own respective natures. Therefore, the other-empty's own nature does not become nonempty. The reason for this is that the name "other-empty" is [only] applied to the compound meaning that this basis [emptiness] is empty of such and such [and not

> to this basis being other-empty in itself]. However, it is not asserted that this basis—the nature of phenomena—is empty of its own nature. [Likewise, as was just said,] this [basis itself] is not other-empty either. Therefore, if it is not other-empty, forget about it being self-empty [since these two are mutually dependent]. . . .
>
> There is also another reason for the other-empty's own nature being self-empty. The subject in question—the other-empty, in being empty of what is other (the adventitious bearers of the nature [of phenomena])—is what entails being empty of the adventitious stains that are other than this basis in that their own nature does not remain even for an instant, because these bearers of the nature [of phenomena] are seeming reality. For this reason, one definitely needs to accept that whatever is other-empty is necessarily self-empty. But if one claims the emptiness that is claimed to be self-empty as being the fully qualified emptiness, it is not tenable to accept some other-empty that is other than self-empty. So, this basis—the nature of phenomena—is neither other-empty nor self-empty, because [let alone being other-empty or self-empty,] it is not even suitable as a mere emptiness that is not specified as being empty or not empty of itself or something other. The reason for this is that it has the essential character of being the utter peace of all reference points in terms of being empty or not being empty. Thus, from the perspective of the [actual] freedom from reference points, no characteristics whatsoever of being empty of itself or something other transpire within the basis that is the nature of phenomena.[539]

In brief, controversies on "self-empty" and "other-empty" seem to be only a problem if these notions are regarded as belonging to the same level of discourse and realization, and to be mutually exclusive on that level. However, in pertaining to different such levels, they lack the basic criteria for meaningful comparison. As Ruegg says:

> [O]ne could assume an incompatibility, at one and the same level of reference, between two philosophical propositions, both of which cannot be true in accordance with the principle of contradiction. Alternatively, one might perhaps suppose a complementarity — perhaps even an incommensurability — between two doctrines that relate to different levels of reference or discourse, and which are accordingly not mutually exclusive or contradictory.[540]

This leads to the issue of Buddhist—and particularly Tibetan—doxographical classifications and hierarchies in general. I am fully aware that many people will hate me for saying this, but I am not the first one to caution that, despite the classical Tibetan doxographical systems usually portraying the positions and affiliations of various Indian Buddhist schools and masters as facts that are cast in stone, often going into the minutest of details of various levels of subschools, all these systems have their own agendas superimposed onto many of the historical developments, relations, and teachings of Indian "schools," thus often failing to properly describe them.[541] This is particulary obvious when one looks at the strikingly different presentations and classifications of the Yogācāra and Madhyamaka traditions (including the so-called "*Shentong*-Madhyamaka") in different Tibetan schools. Fundamentally, the very notions of different Indian Buddhist "schools" and even "subschools" are largely superimpositions in themselves, since Indian masters usually did not regard themselves as belonging to some factions with solidly established boundaries set off from others, especially within the Yogācāra and Madhyamaka traditions. Of course, different scholars had varying opinions on certain matters and engaged in debates. However, it should be more than clear to everyone who has looked just a little bit into the Indian Yogācāra tradition without Tibetan doxographical lenses that there never existed a so-called "Cittamātra School." Also, it is very hard to find any Yogācāras who considered themselves as "False Aspectarians" or "Real Aspectarians," or even any of their writings that would clearly match these terms as understood in Tibetan doxographies, let alone the (Tibetan) classifications into "subschools" such as "Half-Eggists."[542] Likewise, Indian Mādhyamikas saw themselves simply as followers of Nāgārjuna—even the terms Madhyamaka or Mādhyamika appeared rather late with Bhāvaviveka and only became common still much later—and definitely not as adherents to the later Tibetan labels *rang rgyud pa* (*Svātantrika) or *thal 'gyur pa* (*Prāsaṅgika) with all their ramifications.[543]

Moreover, since all these categorizations usually rely on just a single criterion (or a very limited set thereof), depending on which of them are employed, certain masters end up in the same or very different camps. For example, in terms of their approach to reasoning, Bhāvaviveka and Candrakīrti are considered Svātantrika and Prāsaṅgika, respectively. However, in terms of conventionally not rejecting outer objects as a part of seeming reality, they belong to the same group. Similarly, the Svātantrika Jñānagarbha and the Prāsaṅgika Candrakīrti, in terms of both explicitly saying that they follow common worldly consensus as far as seeming reality is concerned, find themselves on the same side as well. Also, just in terms of reasoning, both Bhāvaviveka and Śāntarakṣita are considered Svātantrikas (though they exhibit major differences even in this regard), but their extensive and greatly differing presentations of seeming reality (somewhat simplified, at least partly corresponding to the Sautrāntrika and Yogācāra systems, respectively) makes one wonder why a rather limited similarity should justify putting them into the same camp, thus overruling a great number of more substantial differences. One of the most striking examples here is Dharmakīrti, who has been variously classified as a Sautrāntika, Mere Mentalist, Yogācāra, Mādhyamika, or *shentongpa*, depending on which part of his work with its—as McClintock puts it—"sliding scales of analysis" one focuses. Alternatively, to do justice to each point in the usually complex and finely discriminated explanations of individual masters, one would have to string together long lists of such classifying names. For example, the writings of someone like Kamalaśīla include many Yogācāra elements, but he refutes both the Aspectarian and the Non-Aspectarian approach. He greatly employs the system of Dignāga and Dharmakīrti with regard to reasoning and epistemology, but also explicitly lists numerous cases in which the sole use of (absurd) consequences is sufficient.[544] Finally, as mentioned above, he also speaks favorably about mind's luminosity and buddha nature (and many more features could be added). So does that make him a Neither-Aspectarian-nor-Non-Aspectarian-Yogācāra-Svātantrika-Prāsaṅgika-Shentong-Mādhyamika?

To be sure, I am not saying all this to discredit Tibetan doxography altogether (it no doubt contains pedagogical value), but because there are so many—and typically always the same—misunderstandings triggered by these presentations (followed by endless and pointless discussions), when they are taken to represent actual Indian schools and masters, with each one nicely tucked into their assigned drawers. Often, this just serves as a basis for further enhancing mind's tendencies for reification and solidified belief systems, while the whole point of ascertaining the proper view is to undermine exactly these tendencies. In addition, the fact that doxographies from different Tibetan schools, depending on their own preferences and in glaringly contradictory ways, arrive at affiliating individual masters with all kinds of schools with widely differing positions, and then claim the very same teachers as being part of their own opposing camps just shows how problematic all this can be. When abstracting from the by now almost unavoidable polemics in such doxographies and the people who adhere to them as the sole truth, ideally, it seems that these systems are better understood and more helpful as retrospective pedagogical overviews and/or classifications of the immensely rich variety of Indian Buddhist thought. As such, they may range from just presenting possible or alternative ways of thinking about certain issues, over identifying progressively more subtle manners of reifying and/or relating phenomena (often embedded in the overall framework constituted by mind as the cognizing subject and the objects it perceives), up to standardized outlines of a Buddhist practitioner's progressive development of meditative experiences and realizations.

From such a more pragmatic perspective, it does not matter then whether the views presented were ever held by historical schools or persons (and who held what among these), since the main purpose is to sharpen one's own view against other, typically progressively more subtle models. Unfortunately, this important distinction with regard to such doxographical presentations is more often than not left unsaid. One of the very few positive examples is Khenpo Tsultrim Gyamtso Rinpoche's book *Progressive Stages of Meditation on Emptiness*, which lists the five meditation stages of (1) Śrāvaka, (2) Cittamātra, (3) Svātantrika, (4) Prāsaṅgika, and (5) Shentong-Madhyamaka according to classical Kagyü doxography. However, as the text says at the outset, despite these stages being given the names of these schools, in terms of actually practicing the steps of analytical meditation, the point is not to ascertain the precise positions of these schools, nor to look for the exact historical and philosophical correspondences between these five stages and the views of the schools whose names they bear. Rather, the presentation of these stages is meant as a pedagogical and soteriological model for the progressively evolving personal insights of practitioners meditating on emptiness. This is also evident from the above five "schools" actually standing for meditating on (1) personal identitylessness, (2) mere mind without the duality of an internal subject and external objects, (3) emptiness as a space-like nonimplicative negation, (4) emptiness as utter freedom from reference points, and (5) emptiness and luminosity inseparable.

Thus, such hierarchical doxographical models may either be helpful as simplified overviews of the vast diversity of the works of Indian and Tibetan masters and their views and/or for refining one's own view against the background of progressively more subtle philosophical systems. However, it cannot be overemphasized that mixing or confusing a historical account of actual Indian and Tibetan schools and teachers (based on what their texts actually present and how they interrelate), with a primarily pedagogic and soteriological approach to practice can—and constantly does—only lead to confusion. One of the most obvious reasons is that the historical evolvement of the various—particularly Indian—Buddhist schools simply does not match the progressive and hierarchical model from "lower" to "higher" views in Tibetan doxographies. Also, individual masters or developments that do not readily fit into the four standard schools of Vaibhāṣika, Sautrāntika, Yogācāra, and Madhyamaka[545] are either often omitted or made to fit into one or another category, depending on the overall hierarchy intended. As with all overly broad or schematic descriptions and classifications, there is a danger of not studying the original texts anymore but just following what the "politically correct" default schemes of the respective Tibetan schools say, often obscuring attempts to look at the more subtle aspects of the issues at hand. This does not even consider the fact that many teachers, when commenting on scriptures from different Buddhist philosophical systems, such as Yogācāra or Madhyamaka, attempt to do so by faithfully following the approaches of these very systems and not by superimposing their own agenda. Furthermore, both style and content of what individual masters teach in certain situations may vary considerably to the point of seeming mutually exclusive, since they are usually adapted to the capacities and needs of the respective audiences. This may even mean that some authors defend a certain position for rhetorical purposes or to reveal that its critiques by others do not hold water, without though holding this position themselves. Usually, in Buddhism, philosophical considerations come in response to practical and soteriological issues, that is, from the Buddha's fundamental agenda of removing afflictions and suffering, and not primarily as systems of thought to be fortified in one way or another, especially since clinging to any reference point is considered as the very problem that lies at the root of saṃsaric suffering. The most obvious example for this is the Buddha himself, who gave a vast range of teachings to many different beings in very dissimilar situations. Thus, it seems moot to classify him in any way as a Vaibhāṣika, Sautrāntika, Mādhyamika, Yogācāra, *rangtongpa*, *shentongpa*, adherent of Mahāmudrā or Dzogchen, or anything else. As Nāgārjuna's *Niraupamyastava* says:

> Nothing, not even a single syllable,
> Has been uttered by you, O lord,
> But every person to be guided
> Has been satisfied by your rain of dharma.[546]

Considering all these issues and the above-mentioned differences even within what is called "the *shentong* tradition," let alone the different approaches within the classical Madhyamaka tradition, one may wonder about the benefit of categorically classifying certain masters as *shentongpa*s or *rangtongpas*. Kapstein aptly summarizes this discussion:

> I would suggest, therefore, that . . . doxographic labels such as gzhan stong pa and rang stong pa are best avoided, except of course where they are used within the tradition itself. Our primary task must be to document and interpret precise concepts and arguments, and in many cases the recourse to overly broad characterizations seems only to muddy the waters.[547]

What Huntington says on the early Indian mahāyāna equally applies here as well:

> In working to develop a critical intellectual history of early Indian Mahāyāna, then, the focus of our attention must shift from "tenets" and "schools" . . . to individual authors and their own original words.[548]

In the end, all the various views and presentations may be taken as "role models" that serve as aids to figure out "the correct view," but the process of figuring-out can only be accomplished by relying on one's own intelligence and wisdom—simply following traditions is of no benefit (this is, by the way, what the Buddha is reported to have often said himself). Thus, if one looks at the controversies between great masters or schools in this way, they can be helpful as yardsticks to gauge and refine one's personal insights. I remember Khenpo Tsultrim Gyamtso Rinpoche engaging in formal Tibetan debate with some advanced Kagyü students from the Tibetan Institute for Higher Learning in Sarnath, India. They kept urging him to present the "official" Kagyü position on various issues. Every time Rinpoche replied that it does not matter what the commonly acknowledged stance in a certain camp is, but that they have to honestly investigate for themselves what they personally think is correct. In this vein, the function of doxographical materials and controversies resembles that of a lighthouse signaling on both sides of a dangerous maritime passage to alert us of rocks, shoals, and so on, but the task of steering clear of such obstacles still lies with ourselves alone.

To return to the question whether Rangjung Dorje is a "*shentongpa*," when considering the very distinct explanations in his above-mentioned texts and comparing them with Dölpopa's presentation, they clearly and repeatedly contradict the rather commonly held position that Dölpopa's view was greatly influenced by Rangjung Dorje's, let alone the claims that the Karmapa "invented" the *shentong* view, that Dölpopa may have received his terminology of *rangtong* and *shentong* from the Karmapa, or even that Rangjung Dorje was very much influenced by Dölpopa and his *shentong* view.[549] I could only find three passages in the Third Karmapa's works from which "typical" *shentong* statements could be pieced together. The first one appears in EDV as one of its explanations of the two aspects of the perfect nature—the unchanging and the unmistaken:

> How is the perfect [nature] to be understood as twofold? The unchanging [perfect nature] is expressed by the name "emptiness" because it is empty of the characteristics of both the imaginary and the other-dependent. Since this is never other, it is called "suchness."

> Because it is the unmistaken actuality to be realized, it is "the true end." Because the characteristics of the [above] two have ceased, it is "signlessness." Because it is the sphere of the noble ones, it is "the ultimate." Because it is the cause of the dharmas of the noble ones, it is the "dharmadhātu." . . . The unmistaken perfect nature is the nature of the wisdom of the noble ones, produced by perfect prajñā . . . In brief, they are to be understood as the following classification: the former is the dharmakāya that is the stainless dharmadhātu, and the latter is the very profound dharmakāya,[550] which is the natural outflow of this [stainless dharmadhātu].[551]

The perfect nature being not empty of itself but of both the imaginary and other-dependent natures is a classical *shentong* position. However, the above passage relates the perfect nature being empty of the other two to only one aspect of the perfect nature—the unmistaken—and makes it clear that "emptiness" (not "other-emptiness") is just one among many labels for the perfect nature and does not entail any reification. The latter is explicitly stated in the other explanations on the perfect nature in EDV, such as that its unchanging aspect—suchness—is the nature of the two realities that abides in all knowable objects, which is the lack of nature of all phenomena.[552] Also, the perfect nature is said to be absolutely without any arising or ceasing in terms of itself, others, both, or neither.[553] Elsewhere, EDV matches the three natures with the well-known example of mistaking a rope for a snake. The imaginary nature is like the snake for which the rope is mistaken, that is, a nonexistent that nevertheless seems to appear. Just as the rope, the other-dependent nature appears but is not real in the way it appears as a rope, since all that appears is a mere collection of threads with a certain color and shape. The perfect nature is the snake's and the rope's very own nature of lacking any reality as well as unmistaken self-awareness, since it is without being mistaken about what appears.[554] When establishing that phenomena and the nature of phenomena cannot be said to be different, the text gives the following reason. The direct appearance of the nature of phenomena is nothing but mere dualistic cognizance—the imaginary and the other-dependent natures—appearing without the characteristics of such cognizance, and the nature of phenomena is characterized by nothing but the lack of phenomena. In the inseparability of appearing and being empty, phenomena and their nature are not established as different.[555]

The second passage relates to the same issue, pertaining to two headings in DSC, which speak of "the manner in which [the dharmadhātu] is not empty of wisdom" and "the manner in which [the dharmadhātu] is empty of something to be relinquished and a remedy" (fols. 15b–16b). There are several passages in DSC that indirectly identify the dharmadhātu with the perfect nature, though only referring to its fruitional aspect by saying that "naturally luminous dharmakāya" (fol. 14a) or "wisdom with its enlightened activity" (fol. 21a) are the perfect nature, or that "the abode of all dharmas"—the dharmakāya—"fully bears the naturally luminous perfect nature." At one place (fol. 20a), "imaginations in terms of factors to be relinquished and remedies" are equated with both the imaginary and the other-dependent natures. Thus, put together, it may be said that the dharmadhātu as the perfect nature is not empty of wisdom but empty of the imaginary and the other-dependent natures. However, when Rangjung Dorje says that the dharmadhātu is not empty of wisdom, he immediately makes it perfectly clear that the dharmadhātu is not like the self of the tīrthikas, and that this wisdom is neither empty nor nonempty, neither arisen from itself, something other, both or neither, thus also being without abiding and ceasing and so on.

The third case is the beginning of AC's discussion of the two realities, which—when read on its own—might be regarded as another "typical" *shentong* position:

> Ultimately, what are labeled as causes, results, and the path, as well as thinking and imagining, are all merely superimpositions by our imagination—they do not exist ultimately. So what does exist ultimately? The Buddha heart—the basic element of sentient beings, which is naturally pure mind beyond the entire web of imaginations—exists. Therefore, I say:
>
> The basic element of sentient beings is the Buddha's
> Stainless Heart endowed with the two realities.[556]

The crucial point in terms of how buddha nature exists obviously lies in the phrase "endowed with the two realities," since AC continues by discussing these two realities primarily in classical Madhyamaka style. It elaborates on the above-mentioned passage from the *Vajrajñānasamucchayatantra* (also found in DSC), which speaks of ultimate reality as being free from all characteristics, its locus thus being the eighteen emptinesses.

Thus, from the above, it should be clear that Rangjung Dorje's view neither corresponds to *shentong* as understood by masters of the Jonang tradition (be they Dölpopa, Tāranātha, or others) nor to Jamgön Kongtrul Lodrö Tayé's presentation. Whether the Karmapa's view matches one or several of the other categories in terms of *rangtong* and *shentong* listed above could only be decided after a detailed study of the positions of the masters who propound them or to whom they are ascribed. However, in a sense, this is a moot point, since such comparisons could always only be made by way of terms, categories, and distinctions that Rangjung Dorje himself never used, since he does not speak about *rangtong* and *shentong*, let alone explain their differences, whether or how they exclude each other, and which one—if either—is superior. So, rather than trying to find the "right" label to put onto the Third Karmapa's view, it seems more beneficial to understand the full depth of his own distinct approach of persistently pointing out the essential points of the Buddha's teachings in both the Yogācāra and Madhyamaka systems.

Finally, it should be noted that there are many—also contemporary—so-called *shentongpa*s who emphasize that there is not only no contradiction between what the views of *rangtong* and *shentong* refer to, but that they in fact supplement each other and, ultimately, are one in terms of the definitive meaning. For example, like some others, Śākya Chogden says that the view of *rangtong* is the best for cutting through all reference points, while the view of *shentong* is more helpful for describing meditative experience and realization.[557] But he also summarizes the need for both approaches as follows:

> If there were not these texts of what Asaṅga maintains—
> The dharma system of the ālaya and the presentation of the three
> emptinesses—
> Through what could you explain the ground of purification, the
> means for purification,
> And the presentation of "outer," "inner," and "other" in the texts
> of the great mode of being?[558]
>
> If there were not the way in which nondual wisdom is empty
> of a nature,
> As elucidated by the texts of Prāsaṅgikas and Svātantrikas,
> What would relinquish our clinging to the reality of profound
> luminous wisdom
> And our conceptions of being attached to magnificent deities?[559]

On Rangjung Dorje's Commentary on the Dharmadhātustava

Among all available commentaries on the *Dharmadhātustava*, the Third Karmapa's is both the earliest and the longest, composed in either 1326 or 1327. Until the recent appearance of a single *dbu med* manuscript (fifty-two folios with eight lines each), the text had been considered lost at least since the Tibetan exodus in 1959. The title of Rangjung Dorje's commentary—*An Explanation of* In Praise of Madhyamaka-Dharmadhātu[560]—already indicates that he obviously considers Nāgārjuna's text to be a Madhyamaka work, not fundamentally different from what the latter says in his well-known collection of reasoning and elsewhere. Indeed then, considerable parts of the commentary are devoted to showing that the *Dharmadhātustava* does not conflict with Nāgārjuna's classical Madhyamaka works. Moreover, Rangjung Dorje freely uses typical terminologies from both the Indian Madhyamaka and Yogācāra traditions, such as the frameworks of the two realities, the three natures, the eight consciousnesses, the four wisdoms, and the two/three kāyas; the middle and extremes; false imagination; *tathāgatagarbha*; natural luminosity; and the fundamental change of state. Through both this and extensively quoting mainly Nāgārjuna, Maitreya, Asaṅga, and Candrakīrti, these two traditions are shown to perfectly accord in the essential points. Thus, the Karmapa's commentary often offers original interpretations and also elaborates on a number of supplementary topics, though it does not explicitly explain every single line of the *Dharmadhātustava*.

To give a brief overview of the text, its basic layout consists of the three phases of the dharmadhātu:

(1) being impure, called "sentient being" (verses 2–15; fols. 1–12b)
(2) being in the process of the elimination of its stains, called "bodhisattva on the path" (verses 16–87; fols. 12b–42a)
(3) being utterly pure, called "buddhahood" (verses 88–101; fols. 42a–52a).

According to the commentary, the first verse of the *Dharmadhātustava* introduces these three phases.

(1) As for the first phase, elaborating on verse 2, Rangjung Dorje gives an extensive presentation of the two realities in the context of Madhyamaka ground, path, and fruition. Drawing on a great number of sources from both the Yogācāra and Madhyamaka traditions, he demonstrates that these two systems are complementary and share the same essential points. He ends this topic by saying that Nāgārjuna's collection of reasoning negates the clinging to characteristics, but definitely not the teachings on the way of being of the Buddha and the dharma, wisdom, great compassion, or enlightened activity. The main part of describing the dharmadhātu in its impure phase of being obscured by adventitious stains consists of the *Dharmadhātustava*'s first six examples of butter in milk, a lamp within a vase, an encrusted gem, gold in its ore, rice in its husk, and the banana tree (verses 3–15). The commentary's detailed explanation of these examples emphasizes that the root of being mistaken is just the stainless dharmadhātu being unaware of itself, while there are not the slightest adventitious stains other than that, let alone any that are really existent. The dharmadhātu itself is the Tathāgata heart, which does not just refer to mere emptiness. Rather, it is the twofold wisdom of a Buddha that

knows both how things truly are and the infinite variety of how they appear. This nonconceptual wisdom is obtained through becoming pure of adventitious stains, which are the four characteristics of conceptualizing the factors to be relinquished, the remedies, suchness, and the fruition, as taught in the *Avikalpapraveśadhāraṇī*. It is explained how the dharmadhātu is endowed with the four pāramitās of purity, self, bliss, and permanence and how these differ from the same set of four as the mistaken notions of ordinary beings. Finally, each of the six examples is matched with certain kinds of wisdom and obscurations, respectively.

(2) As for the second phase of the dharmadhātu ("bodhisattva on the path"), the commentary explains how the notions of cause and result are to be understood with respect to the dharmadhātu and the dharmakāya—there is nothing to be newly attained and nothing to be removed. With the adventitious stains—the eight consciousnesses—being mere illusions, once they are seen through, mind's nature becomes aware of what it has always been (verses 16–19). Purification on the path only happens on the level of the factors to be relinquished and their remedies (primarily mind realizing emptiness) interacting in a mutually dependent way, but the dharmadhātu is empty of both and never affected by either. Once they both subside, the dharmadhātu simply displays its natural luminosity, similar to murky water becoming clear on its own when not stirred. In this way, it is not empty of its own wisdom-nature, which however is completely free from being empty, not empty, both, or neither (20–29). In other words, from among the three natures, the imaginary nature is in fact nonexistent, while the other-dependent nature appears like a dream but does not really exist the way it appears. Thus, the factors to be relinquished and their remedies (both consisting of the imaginary and the other-dependent natures) are just appearances as mere imaginations. They are unreal, not arising from themselves, something other, both, or without a cause. They are just dependent origination, and this is precisely what is expressed as emptiness. Through relinquishing the various kinds of clinging to extremes, one enters the middle, which is taught in both the *Madhyāntavibhāga* and the *Mūlamadhyamakakārikā*. Ultimate reality is this unity of appearance and emptiness, which is changeless and unmistaken. Thus, it is taught to be the perfect nature. In brief, the very same dharmadhātu is called "sentient being" when associated with obscurations, while it is referred to as "Buddha" once it is without obscurations (30–37).

The actual practice on the path consists of the two phases of meditative equipoise and subsequent attainment. The first is the nonconceptual samādhi of superior insight, being immersed in the suchness of the dharmadhātu, also expressed as Prajñāpāramitā and Mahāmudrā. During the time of subsequent attainment, bodhisattvas keep meditating with mindfulness by scrutinizing whatever appears to their senses and their minds. When sense perception, mental direct perception, and self-awareness are embraced by the correct samādhi, they all become yogic direct cognition, which is dharmadhātu wisdom's own nature. All phenomena—whether they seem to be outside or inside—are realized to be just mind's self-lucid appearances, which lack arising and ceasing, thus gaining certainty that they are nothing but the dharmadhātu. This section on how the nature of the mind is found within dualistic consciousnesses includes a detailed discussion of the mental consciousness, the afflicted mind, the immediate mind, and "stainless mentation" as well as their interrelations (38–45).

In brief, the difference between saṃsāra and nirvāṇa is whether the nature of mind is realized through prajñā or not (46–50). The appearance of the three jewels—which in itself is the natural outflow of the dharmadhātu—is the supporting condition for such realization. Through seeing the kāyas of Buddhas, hearing the dharmas of the mahāyāna, smelling the scent of ethics, tasting the pleasure of the dharma, and touching upon the tangible object of samādhi, finely analyzing prajñā examines all phenomena. This means to become increasingly familiar with and rest in the immediate experience of one's own awareness-wisdom, thus proceeding through the paths and bhūmis. In this way, the dharmadhātu is also the cause for everything on the path, including the enlightened activity that this path's final fruition—buddhahood—manifests at its very end (51–61). The fundamental manner of adopting and rejecting on the path is to extract wisdom from the blend of obscurations and wisdom, while leaving behind the former. This is accomplished by seeing through these adventitious obscurations by realizing twofold identitylessness as the remedy for saṃsāra. The remedy for abiding in some kind of personal nirvāṇa is to realize the nonduality of saṃsāra and nirvāṇa. This means to realize the dharmakāya, which is the nonabiding nirvāṇa that consists of the four pāramitās of genuine purity, genuine self, genuine bliss, and genuine permanence (62–65).

As the remedies for obscurations, the ten pāramitās are the dharmas that make the dharmadhātu's luminosity shine forth, just like the qualities of a gem manifesting through removing its covering. The main mental driving force for practicing these pāramitās is bodhicitta as the dharmakāya's primary cause or seed, which needs to be cultivated through the path. Due to that, it seems as if the dharmadhātu unfolds, just like the waxing moon, but this only appears that way by virtue of the obscurations gradually dissolving (66–76). The stages of this process are the paths of accumulation and preparation, as well as the ten bhūmis. Here, "nonconceptual wisdom" is used as the conventional term for the unfolding of the dharmakāya and "illusionlike wisdom" as the expression for the unfolding of the rūpakāyas (77–87).

(3) The third phase of the dharmadhātu is its full manifestation as the dharmakāya. This is the final fundamental change of state of the five skandhas, with the skandha of the eight consciousnesses changing into the four wisdoms. Being endowed with the infinite inconceivable qualities of purity and attainment, it is the support of various sambhogakāyas and nirmāṇakāyas that appear with the major and minor marks in order to mature bodhisattvas, pratyekabuddhas, and śrāvakas (88–95). Among the many enlightened activities of these kāyas, the main one is to empower the bodhisattvas on the tenth bhūmi so that these become Buddhas too, while those who dwell in arhathood are ushered onto the path of the mahāyāna. The spontaneous enlightened activity for the welfare of all sentient beings is the final consummation of the emptiness that is endowed with the supreme of all aspects. Such effortless and nonconceptual enlightened activity is illustrated through the nine examples taught in the *Uttaratantra*. A Buddha's nonconceptual prajñā is like the sun's luminosity, dispelling the darkness that obscures true reality. The engaging prajñā that knows all that can be known is similar to the sun's rays. The basis of both these prajñās—mind's nature being utterly stainless and luminous—is similar to the pure orb of the sun. Since all three are inseparable from the dharmadhātu, they are like the sun's light, rays, and orb being inseparable. In this way, buddhahood is only complete with all of these elements (96–101). Finally, the commentary explains that all great masters, such as Nāgārjuna, Maitreya, Āryadeva, Asaṅga, Buddhapālita, Bhāvaviveka, and Candrakīrti, accord in teaching this dharmadhātu wisdom. Likewise, the correct view and realization of all yānas is to be understood as just this (for the detailed outline of the Karmapa's commentary, see Appendix I).

As for quotations from Indian texts in Rangjung Dorje's commentary, given the nature of the subject of the *Dharmadhātustava*, it is not surprising that by far the most citations (forty-two verses) and references come from the *Uttaratantra*. However, Rangjung Dorje's equal emphasis on both the Madhyamaka and the Yogācāra tradition is perfectly mirrored by him quoting and referring to a wide variety of sūtras, tantras, and treatises, in particular the *Mahāyānasūtrālaṃkāra* (twenty verses), *Madhyāntavibhāga* (seventeen), *Yuktiṣaṣṭikā* (eight), *Madhyamakāvatāra* (seven; implying another twenty-nine), *Abhisamayālaṃkāra* (seven), *Bodhicittavivaraṇa* (seven), *Mūlamadhyamakakārikā* (six), and *Dharmadharmatāvibhāga* (eighteen lines). Also quoted at length are Asaṅga's *Ratnagotravibhāgavyākhyā* and *Mahāyānasaṃgraha* (both four times). The *Śūnyatāsaptati*, *Acintyastava*, and *Satyadvayavibhāga* are each represented with two verses. The *Ratnāvalī* is even quoted with forty-nine verses, but twenty-nine of them are just an elaboration on the causes of the thirty-two major marks of a Buddha, while the presentation of each one of the ten bhūmis is supported by two verses.

Other Tibetan Commentaries on the Dharmadhātustava

As for the ten Tibetan commentaries on the *Dharmadhātustava* that are known so far, it is somewhat surprising that half of them were written by Sakya authors, while there is no Nyingma commentary. Three were composed by Jonang writers, one by a Kagyüpa (Rangjung Dorje), and one by a Gelugpa.[561] What is striking about the six from among these commentaries that are available at present—and even more surprising—is that the term "other-empty" appears only one single time (in Sönam Sangbo's text), though there are indeed more than enough verses in the *Dharmadhātustava* that would lend themselves readily to an interpretation in terms of "other-emptiness." Otherwise, apart from some varying explanations on technical details or how to understand a particular line of verse, there are no fundamental disagreements throughout these commentaries, including Rangjung Dorje's. In particular, what they all share is their emphasis on the dharmadhātu—the Tathāgata heart—being the nature of the mind, which is nonconceptual wisdom. This dharmadhātu wisdom is the total absence of any obscurations in mind's nature. However, this absence and the complementary presence of enlightened mind's infinite and inseparable qualities must, and can only be, realized through personally experienced wisdom. Most of the commentaries explicitly reject the notion that the dharmadhātu is just sheer emptiness in the sense of a nonimplicative negation and also agree on the equal status of Nāgārjuna's collections of reasoning and praises. The same goes for the Yogācāra and Madhyamaka systems in general, neither of them being superior to or excluding the other but rather being complementary and essentially arriving at the same point.

To supplement the translation of Rangjung Dorje's commentary, I used all other five available commentaries, relevant excerpts from them being provided in the endnotes. Through this approach, it is hoped that the reader may gain an even richer picture of the *Dharmadhātustava* as well as a number of important related topics. These five commentaries can be described briefly as follows.

• Dölpopa Sherab Gyaltsen's (1292–1361) *[Interlinear Commentary on]* In Praise of Dharmadhātu *Composed by Noble Nāgārjuna ('phags pa klu sgrub kyis mdzad pa'i chos dbyings bstod pa ['i mchan 'grel])*

This is a short interlinear commentary (eleven folios with seven lines) that inserts brief glosses between the words of the verses but does not provide much additional information. Dölpopa starts by saying that the dharmadhātu pervades both the inanimate world and its inhabitants. Especially in his case, the complete absence of the term "other-empty," for which he is so well known and which appears frequently in his other works, is striking. Some passages in his commentary can be seen as traces of his typical approach of "other-emptiness," but they come nowhere near his full-blown presentation of this system,[562] so the text may be assumed to be one of his rather early works. The commentary ends by saying:

> The son of the victor, Nāgārjuna,
> Through this *Dharmadhātustava*, teaches the way Madhyamaka is.
> Those who accept Madhyamaka and wish to follow him
> Should henceforth understand Madhyamaka just as [presented] in this [text].

• Rongtön Śākya Gyaltsen's[563] (aka Rongtön Sheja Künrig; 1367–1449) *Commentary on* In Praise of Dharmadhātu, *Cloud in Which Elegant Sayings Stir (Chos dbyings bstod pa'i 'grel pa legs bshad rnam par g.yo ba'i sprin)*

This text (ten folios with six lines) is also just a brief interlinear commentary, not going into any details or general explanations. Rongtön is renowned as one of "the six gems of the Sakya tradition" and considered as an emanation of Maitreya. Having founded the monastery of Penbo Nalendra[564] in 1436, he taught at its famous monastic college, guiding disciples from all schools of Tibetan Buddhism, including six early abbots of the Ganden and Drebung Monasteries. The majority of the scholastic lineages of the Kagyü and Nyingma Schools also pass through Rongtön, with the Sixth Karmapa, Tongwa Tönden[565] (1416–1453), having been one of his main disciples. Thus, Rongtön and his numerous works had an immense influence on all other Tibetan schools. On the other hand, he was the first to openly criticize Tsongkhapa's novel interpretations of Madhyamaka and pramāṇa.

• Nyagpowa Sönam Sangbo's (1341–1433) *Explanation of* In Praise of Madhyamaka-Dharmadhātu, *Elucidating the Heart (Dbu ma chos kyi dbyings su bstod pa'i rnam par bshad pa snying po gsal ba)*

Sönam Sangbo is considered an emanation of the Sthavira Bakula and served as Dölpopa's attendant for some years until the latter's death, though he is not counted as one of Dölpopa's thirteen original disciples. He was also a student of the famous Sakya master Sabsang Mati Panchen and later became the abbot of Tsalchen Monastery.[566] Interestingly, in his colophon, Sönam Sangbo says that he composed this commentary at the very serious request of the great Kashmiri paṇḍita Śavari.[567]

The commentary (thirty-nine folios with six lines; written in 1418) is second in length to Rangjung Dorje's and shows several very close similarities with it, often containing literally the same passages and/or supporting quotes at the same places (in general, it abounds with quotes). Also, the entire outline (*sa bcad*) corresponds almost completely to Rangjung Dorje's. In some cases, Sönam Sangbo's text is helpful in clarifying and/or elaborating on certain points in Rangjung Dorje's comments. The only mention of the term "other-empty" occurs in the context of Sönam Sangbo's presentation that the prajñāpāramitā sūtras explain two ways of being empty. The first is that form is empty of form, which is said to pertain to all phenomena up through omniscience. The second is mainly found in the Maitreya chapter of the *Pañcaviṃśatisāhasrikaprajñāpāramitāsūtra*, which speaks about the three natures. From among these, the first two are empty of a nature of their own, while the third—the perfect nature as the nature of all phenomena—is empty of the imaginary and the other-dependent nature, which are just adventitious stains. Quoting from various sources, the ultimate existence of buddha nature's inseparable qualities is affirmed, summarizing: "Since the Tathāgata heart is empty of adventitious stains, it is other-empty, but it is never at any time empty of its unconditioned qualities, such as the powers."[568]

The text also offers insightful additional discussions of specific topics, such as the notion of "fundamental change," saying that Nāgārjuna's *Bodhicittavivaraṇa* only refutes this notion as understood by the Mere Mentalists, while he obviously accepts it as he presents it in his *Dharmadhātustava.* Sönam Sangbo rejects the categorical position that Mādhyamikas neither assert eight consciousnesses (specifically an ālaya-consciousness) nor self-awareness. He points out that both Nāgārjuna's *Bodhicittavivaraṇa* and Candrakīrti's *Madhyamakāvatāra* only refute a really existent ālaya-consciousness as held by certain Vijñaptivādins. For, the *Bodhicittavivaraṇa* continues by saying that an illusory likeness of such a consciousness appropriates the three realms. Candrakīrti's commentary on the *Guhyasamājatantra* discusses the eight consciousnesses and their purification, and also Haribhadra speaks about them in his commentary on the *Prajñāpāramitāsaṃcayagāthā*. As for self-awareness, Madhyamaka texts refute just the kind that is held to be really existent, but the *Dharmadhātustava* speaks about self-awareness in its verse 56 (for details, see the endnote on Rangjung Dorje's commentary on verse 88).

• Śākya Chogden's (1428–1507) *Explanation of the Treatise Called* In Praise of Dharmadhātu, *Certainty about the Dharmadhātu (Chos kyi dbyings su bstod pa zhes bya ba'i bstan bcos kyi rnam par bshad pa chos kyi dbyings rnam par nges pa)*

Śākya Chogden's early main teacher in the Sakya tradition was Rongtön Sheja Künrig. Throughout his career, Śākya Chogden displayed a rather strong tendency for independent, creative, and synthesizing thinking. Even in his own school, he was quite a controversial figure, which became even more the case when he chose the Seventh Karmapa as his main spiritual master and openly engaged in the view of "other-emptiness."

His commentary on the *Dharmadhātustava* (twenty-two folios with six lines; written in 1479), however, neither employs the term "other-empty" nor particularly enters this discussion, except for pointing out that buddha nature is neither sheer emptiness nor a nonimplicative negation nor some really established absolute. Śākya Chogden does not explain each and every of Nāgārjuna's verses in detail but sometimes just links them to explanatory headings in his outline. As mentioned above, the commentary's introduction provides an excellent overview of wrong ideas about "dharmadhātu wisdom," identifying the purpose of its composition as eliminating such views and then giving rise to certainty in what the essence of dharmadhātu is—luminous aware experience free from reference points. The text further discusses a number of supplementary issues, such as the manner in which nirmāṇakāyas appear to those to be guided; that dharmadhātu wisdom is not just emptiness, since pure qualities are intrinsic to the dharmadhātu, while afflicted phenomena can be separated from it; and why sentient beings possessing buddha nature are not actual Buddhas.

Similar to Sönam Sangbo, Śākya Chogden addresses Nāgārjuna's distinct treatment of the notion of "fundamental change of state" in his *Bodhicittavivaraṇa* and *Dharmadhātustava*. The former is said to refute certain Yogācāras who take "fundamental change of state" to mean that the ālaya-consciousness was first the abode of all the factors to be relinquished, but then was turned into something later that is not such an abode. The *Dharmadhātustava*, however, does not present the "fundamental change of state" as the dharmadhātu being without qualities before, while possessing qualities later. Rather, dharmadhātu wisdom is ever-present and gradually becomes manifest during the three phases of sentient beings, bodhisattvas, and Buddhas. This being the case, one may wonder why it is not taught in this way throughout all the teachings of the Buddha. For those who need to be led up to the definitive meaning gradually, in order to first establish them in virtue, the Buddah initially taught in a manner that accords with really existent persons and phenomena. Next, in order to establish the disciples in what is conducive to liberation, he taught in a manner that highlights the lack of any real personal or phenomenal identity. Finally, he taught that dharmadhātu wisdom—the basis for purifying the two obscurations and gathering the two accumulations—pervades all three phases of ground, path, and fruition. Some may mistake this dharmadhātu wisdom as being identical to a self as claimed by the tīrthikas. But since the Buddha's just-mentioned progression already covered the lack of a self before teaching dharmadhātu wisdom, it is impossible that someone who has gone through it may misconceive of it as a self or mine.

Thus, since the dharmadhātu is present throughout the three phases of ground, path, and fruition, if one employs the remedies to relinquish its stains, there is no need to search for enlightenment somewhere else. But if one does not use these remedies, Śākya Chogden cautions, buddhahood is nowhere near, since just the mere existence of the dharmadhātu does not make anybody enlightened. Though one needs to accept dharmadhātu wisdom as "natural buddhahood," this in itself does not qualify as actual buddhahood, since the three kāyas are not complete. But even though the three kāyas are in fact complete naturally, this does not qualify as actual buddhahood either, since in ordinary beings they are not the kāyas that serve as the ultimate welfare of others. Therefore, what is called "natural buddhahood" refers to the cause of actual buddhahood. Otherwise, if actual buddhahood existed only through what is called "natural buddhahood," one would simply assert the system of the Sāṃkhyas. For then, during the time of sentient beings, full buddhahood would reside in them in a nonmanifest way and would just need to be manifested at a later point through the power of the path. Also, if all sentient beings possessed the actual dharmakāya, the respective bases for applying the terms "bodhisattva," "sentient being," and "Buddha" would be indefinite. Also, the mere fact of being pure of some portion of the afflictions is not sufficient for presenting the dharmadhātu in its phase of bodhisattvas as a part of the dharmakāya, because both being pure in this way and generating bodhicitta for supreme enlightenment must come together. The reason for this is that the dharmadhātu cannot be presented as the "Buddha heart" without bodhicitta having arisen.

• Lodrö Gyatso's (born nineteenth century) *Commentary on* In Praise of Dharmadhātu, *Opening the Treasure of the Profound Definitive Meaning (Chos kyi dbyings su bstod pa'i 'grel pa nges don zab mo'i gter gyi kha 'byed)*

Lodrö Gatso was the seventh abbot of Dzongsar[569] Monastery near Derge in eastern Tibet with its college Khamje Shedra,[570] founded by the renowned Sakya master Jamyang Kyentse Chökyi Lodrö[571] (1893–1959) in 1918, thus being part of the nonsectarian Rimé movement.

His commentary (thirty-two folios with six lines) gives thorough explanations of Nāgārjuna's verses and elaborates on a number of related topics, such as how the teachings on emptiness do not invalidate what is said about buddha nature, wisdom, and the dharmakāya. Rather, the instructions on emptiness are like pointing out that both being born and dying in a dream are delusive, which is not meant to demonstrate that the appearances of the waking state are delusive. This is the reason why all affirmations and negations are shown to be delusive, but such is in no way an instruction on the nonexistence of the inconceivable wisdom, in which mistaken appearances have vanished altogether. Some people think that all phenomena are just imaginary, and thus the dharmakāya must be too. This is indeed true, as long as one clings to the latter as being existent or nonexistent, but it is a completely different story, once such clinging collapses. Otherwise, all explanations of the definitive meaning would be just as meaningless as explanations on the horns of a rabbit, since both buddha nature and its stains would be alike in just being adventitious. If the Tathāgata heart did not exist at all, since it needs to be pointed out in the end, all who do so would just create a lot of disappointment in their disciples. Also, there would be no final fruition of the Buddhist path, just as nihilists claim. Consequently, practicing such a path would be pointless. Even if it were practiced, since there is no fruition of buddhahood, one's mind stream would simply become extinct at the end of this path. However, at the same time, let alone that the Tathāgata heart is something really established, it is not even asserted to exist as something that lacks real existence. Therefore, what the *Dharmadhātustava* teaches is not like a sprout arising after its seed has ceased. Rather, all that happens during the path is the extinguishing of adventitious stains, while the Buddha heart is without increase or decrease. However, all of this is difficult to gauge for the minds of ordinary beings. Since they are already incapable of gauging the mind of the waking state while being in a dream, forget about the level of a Buddha with its wisdom. Buddhahood is the manifestation of the basic nature of one's own mind, free from the two obscurations, which is the final change of state of the five wisdoms.

Lodrö Gyatso also discusses the nature of yogic consciousness in ordinary beings and bodhisattvas, as well as its relationship to self-awareness and nonconceptual wisdom; the expedient status of the explanation of the two realities and their union; and that ultimately there is only a single yāna. He also explicitly says that buddhahood is not attained through the incomplete view of a mere nonimplicative negation, just as with any other result whose causes are incomplete. Furthermore, the text contains an interesting introduction and colophon, both on the relationship between the texts of Nāgārjuna and Maitreya, saying that there is no dispute about Nāgārjuna's scriptural tradition being Madhyamaka, while different opinions as to which Buddhist philosophical system the five texts of Maitreya represent abound (in Tibet). There follows a detailed refutation of the claim that the three middling texts of Maitreya (*Mahāyānasūtrālaṃkāra*, *Madhyāntavibhāga*, and *Dharmadharmatāvibhāga*) are just Mere Mentalism, clarifying instead that they can just as easily be explained according to Madhyamaka. The presentations by Maitreya and Nāgārjuna may appear different but are one in terms of the definitive meaning. With regard to the single essence of the path, their texts just reveal clearly the notions of lucidity and emptiness, respectively. Therefore, if one does not understand these two notions as the single inseparability of the two realities, one may assert some blank emptiness as the ultimate nature of phenomena and then explain the Buddha heart as being of expedient meaning. Or, just as the Mere Mentalists, one may take the Buddha heart as something really established, thus asserting these two aspects of lucidity and emptiness to be separate.

In any case, one falls from the path of the two realities in union, destroying the root of the path to liberation. Nāgārjuna clearly does not hold that nothing but sheer emptiness is the final view, while Maitreya's texts do not speak about something being really established. Therefore, they agree on the change of state that is nothing but the mistakenness of apprehender and apprehended having vanished within the dharmadhātu—the union of appearance and emptiness. In brief, if all the countless distinct methods, from the most basic yāna up through the vajrayāna, are not divorced from the elixir of profound means and prajñā, just as the tools of an expert craftsman, they are one in essence in that they serve as helpful means to the same end. If this essential point is realized, one can say that one has realized all intentions of the victor being without contradiction.

As said above, the remaining four of the ten known Tibetan commentaries on the *Dharmadhātustava* are not accessible at present. They were all written in a period between the mid-fourteenth and early sixteenth centuries, and there is only little information available on them and their authors.

• Sönam Gyaltsen's (1312–1375) *Commentary on* In Praise of Dharmadhātu *(Chos kyi dbyings su bstod pa'i 'grel pa.* Source: *Dkar chag mthong bas yid 'phrog chos mdzod byed pa'i lde mig:* a bibliography of Sa-skya-pa literature prepared at the order of H.H. Sakya Tridzin, based on a compilation of the Venerable Khenpo Apey and contributions by other Sa-skya-pa scholars. New Delhi: Ngawang Topgyal, 1987. TBRC no. W11903). Among the author's many teachers from several schools were Butön Rinchen Drub; the tertön Sangyé Lingba[572] (1340–1396), who was also a teacher of the Fourth Karmapa; and the renowned Bang Lotsāwa Lodrö Denba[573] (1276–1342) of the Bodong School. Sönam Gyaltsen was a prominent master and prolific writer in the Kön[574] lineage of the Sakya School, having his seat in one of the four great palaces of that tradition, called Sakya Rinchen Gang Labrang.[575] He also held the major Tibetan prajñāpāramitā transmission that came from Ngog Lotsāwa.

• Nyagpowa Sönam Sangbo's (1341–1433) *Presentation of* In Praise of Dharmadhātu, *The Essence of Amṛta (Chos kyi dbyings su bstod pa'i rnam bzhag bdud rtsi'i nying khu.* Source: TBRC no. W14074.). No further information is available, but this seems to be a second commentary by the same person as above.

• Nyendön Śākya Gyaltsen's (born fourteenth century) *Commentary on* In Praise of Dharmadhātu, *Eliminating the Darkness of Bad Views (Chos kyi dbyings su bstod pa'i 'grel pa lta ngan mun sel.* Sources: *A khu dpe tho* MHTL 11446; TBRC no. W12845). He was a student of Gyaltsab Darma Rinchen[576] (1364–1432), one of the two main disciples of Tsongkhapa, and a teacher of Jamyang Tönyö Balden[577] (1445–1524), the tenth abbot of the major Gelugpa seat of Séra.

• Lowo Khenchen Sönam Lhündrub's (1456–1532) *Explanation of* In Praise of Dharmadhātu (*Chos dbyings bstod pa'i rnam bshad.* Source: no. 188 in *Index of the Collected Works of Glo-bo Mkhan-chen*, Gelung Manuscript in Jackson 1987, vol. 2, p. 561).[578] This author was considered a reincarnation of Sakya Paṇḍita and brought up at the monastic seat of Sakya. His main teacher was Gyaltsab Tamba Kunga Wangchug[579] (1424–1478), the fourth abbot of another major Sakya seat, Ngor Evam Chöden.[580] From him, Lowo Khenchen received novice vows at age twelve, full ordination at twenty, and studied the sūtras and tantras. His other teachers included Ra Yönden Bal,[581] Yönden Chögyal,[582] Tsultrim Gyaltsen,[583] and Śākya Chogden, though he later became rather critical of the latter, especially with regard to his *shentong* view. After Kunga Wanchug's death, Lowo Khenchen had some serious disagreements with the abbot of Sakya, so he eventually moved to Evam Chöden for some years. After that abbot had passed away, upon his successor's command, Lowo Khenchen returned to Sakya and kept teaching and practicing there. He was the teacher of the Sakya head Jamyang Kunga Sönam[584] (1485–1533) and several great masters of Ngor, among them its tenth abbot, Göncho Lhündrub[585] (1497–1557). Finally, he passed away after having spent the last two years of his life in retreat. His collected works (consisting of six volumes) show that he is the most prolific author of materials related to Sakya Paṇḍita's works, such as five texts on the latter's *Differentiating the Three Vows* (*sdom gsum rab dbye*), three works each on his *Treasury of Valid Cognition and Reasoning* (*tshad ma rigs gter*) and *Illuminating the Intention of the Sage* (*thub pa'i dgongs gsal*), and one of the only two presently available commentaries on *The Entrance Gate for the Learned* (*mkhas pa'i sgo la 'jug pa*).[586] Further works include a text on *tathāgatagarbha*, a great number of praises, sādhanas, biographies, and recordings of question and answer sessions.

Translation of Rangjung Dorje's Commentary

An Explanation of *In Praise of Madhyamaka-Dharmadhātu*[587]

[1b][588] I pay homage to all gurus, Buddhas, and bodhisattvas.

I pay homage to the glorious Mighty Sage,
In whom the turbidities of mind and mental factors have completely settled,
Whose vision of suchness and variety has reached its culmination,
And whose nature is enlightenment with its qualities and activities.

I pay homage to venerable Nāgārjunagarbha,
The eldest son of all the victors,
Who sees true reality, teaches dependent origination
Without fail, and is a noble being full of compassion.

Though the *Dharmadhātustava* lies not within my reach,
Great aspiration [for it] arose in me, so I will briefly elucidate it.

The great being, noble Nāgārjuna, who possesses unassailable and marvelous knowledge and compassion, was prophesied by the completely perfect Buddha [Śākyamuni] in many sūtras and tantras. He was born four hundred years after the sun of that victor had set and illuminated the teachings for six hundred years. Then, he passed into Sukhāvatī and [eventually] will become the Tathāgata *Jñānākaraphrabha in the worldly realm *Prasannaprabhā.[589] In accordance with his [former] aspiration prayers, he composed innumerable treatises for the sake of elucidating the teachings for a long time and, by eliminating the obscurations of the ignorance of beings, illumining the principles of the supreme yāna. From among those [texts], in particular, he composed three types of commentaries on the collection of the sūtras. The [first type] consists of the collection of speeches, which is composed in such a way that the accomplishment of mundane and supramundane purposes and the definite distinction between what is to be relinquished and what is to be adopted are noncontradictory in terms of the presentations of the labels of the mahāyāna and the hīnayāna. [The second type consists of the collection of reasoning,] based on which Īśvara, puruṣa, both, . . .[590] [The third type consists of the collection of praises, . . .

1. The manner of engaging the treatise

This has two parts:

1) The meaning of the title
2) Paying homage to the dharmadhātu

1.1. The meaning of the title

In Indian language: *Dharmadhātustava*
In Tibetan: Chos kyi dbyings su bstod pa
In English: **In Praise of Dharmadhātu**

1.2. Paying homage to the dharmadhātu

> **I bow to you, the dharmadhātu,**
> **Who resides in every sentient being.**
> **But if they aren't aware of you,**
> **They circle through this triple being.** [1]]

[3a] This [verse] teaches the concise meaning of the main body of the treatise. **If they**—whichever [sentient beings]—**aren't aware of** the heart of the victors that dwells in them, this is called "ignorance." Based on this, **they** circle uninterruptedly in the form of the wheel of the twelve links [of dependent origination] and hence **circle through this triple being** [in saṃsāra]. Through not knowing that the characteristics of causes and conditions come about just as in dreams or illusions, formations—mental factors such as impulse—that derive from false imagination apprehend the naturally pure dhātu as being an "I" and input all latent tendencies [into the ālaya-consciousness]. Therefore, since that [ignorance] serves as the causal condition of all consciousnesses, it is called "mind." When that very [mind] assumes an existence that is brought about through meritorious, nonmeritorious or unmoving karma, a body and so forth is formed. Through this, it manifests in such a way as if it were bearing the distinctive features of skandhas, dhātus, and āyatanas. Since these are formed by mind or possess it, they are what we call "**sentient beings**."[591] What is naturally pure **in every** one having these obscurations and **resides** without stains in them is **the dharmadhātu**.[592] Since buddhahood is [precisely] this, **I bow** [to it]. Thus, the great being, noble Nāgārjuna sees this buddhahood as the most marvellous state, pays homage [to it], and bows down with body, speech, and mind. Thereafter, he elucidates the meaning of this.[593]

In this way, the dharmadhātu is the subject matter, and this treatise serves to discuss the meaning of it being impure, the process of its stains being eliminated, and it becoming utterly pure. Through [the treatise] stating the concise meaning [of that topic] in this single verse [above], what is called "dharmadhātu" is made understood as being related to three stages, and

[3b] the meaning of the text can be understood easily, which is its purpose. Through engaging [the text's meaning] in this way, it makes one attain the object that is unsurpassable buddhahood, by realizing and accomplishing it. This is called the "essential purpose."[594]

Having thus explained [the manner of] engaging the treatise, [there follows] now:

2. [The actual treatise to be engaged, which] demonstrates how the dharmadhātu resides during three stages

[This has three parts:
1) The way in which it resides during the stage of sentient beings
2) Instruction on the stage of those on the path
3) Praising the dharmakāya free from all stains]

2.1. The way in which [the dharmadhātu] resides during the stage of sentient beings

This has two parts:
1) Brief introduction to its nature
2) Detailed explanation by correlating this with examples

2.1.1. Brief introduction to its nature

> **Due to just that being purified**
> **What is such circling's cause,**
> **This very purity is then nirvāṇa.**
> **Likewise, dharmakāya is just this.** [2]

As for **what circles** somewhere, it is the mind, that is, the ālaya-consciousness consisting of all seeds, since it is completely impregnated by all the latent tendencies of skandhas, dhātus, and āyatanas. **Due to just that** [cause of saṃsāra] **being** fully **purified** through the dharma of the Buddha, which is the natural outflow of nonconceptual wisdom, gradually, **this very** [dharmadhātu] becomes **pure** and **is** [finally] called "**nirvāṇa.**" **Likewise**, the **dharmakāya** of all Buddhas **is just this.**

You may wonder, "Well, how could these words here that 'the fruition of nirvāṇa—dharmakāya—[becomes manifest] through the cause of saṃsāra having become pure' be appropriate? Aren't these two mutually exclusive in the sense of not coexisting? Moreover, how could it be appropriate in this [context] that saṃsāra and nirvāṇa exist? This contradicts [Nāgārjuna's] statement that all phenomena are without nature, which he makes in [his] collection of reasoning, refuting [any such nature] through enumerating many [reasonings]." What is to be explained here is as follows. [4a] [Asaṅga's *Ratnagotravibhāgavyākhyā*] says:

> Here, the ones who are outside of [the ranks of] those who see the inconceivable object of the Buddhas are ordinary childish beings, tīrthakaras who have views about a self, śrāvakas, pratyekabuddhas, and [even] beginner bodhisattvas whose minds are distracted from emptiness.[595]

You may wonder, "For those four, what are the obscurations to seeing the dharmakāya?" Childish beings who crave for what is wrong are hostile towards the dharma of the mahāyāna. Secondly, the tīrthikas have views about a self. Thirdly, the śrāvakas are afraid of saṃsāra. Fourthly, the pratyekabuddhas turn their backs to the welfare of sentient beings. Possessing [any of] these four kinds [of obscurations] represents a big adverse condition. As the *Uttaratantra* says:

> Hostility towards the dharma, views about a self,
> Fear of saṃsāra's suffering,
> And not considering the welfare of sentient beings—
> These are the four obscurations
>
> Of those with great desire, tīrthikas,
> Śrāvakas, and pratyekabuddhas.[596]

[In due order,] the remedies for these [four] are aspiring for the correct cause, the dharma of the mahāyāna; realizing the lack of a self through prajñā; cultivating [blissful] samādhis, such as [the one called] "sky-treasure"; and the great compassion of engaging in saṃsāra for as long as it lasts. As [the *Uttaratantra*] says:

> The causes of purification are the four properties
> Of aspiring and so forth.[597]

These [four], which are like the semen, the mother, the comfortable abode of the womb, and the fostering nanny, accomplish the very profound dharmakāya,[598] which is the natural outflow [of the stainless dharmadhātu]. As the *[Mahāyāna]sūtrālaṃkāra* says:

> Born from the semen of aspiration for the dharma
> And the mother that is the supreme pāramitā,

The bliss originating from samādhi is the womb,
And compassion is the nanny who nurtures.[599]

Even beginner bodhisattvas, through the characteristics of conceptualizing suchness and [4b] the fruition, are [still] obscured on the seven impure and the three pure bhūmis [respectively]. In order to relinquish their clinging to characteristics of anything, they must know the presentation of the factors to be relinquished and their remedies. This is expressed in Lama Patsab Lotsāwa's[600] *Summary of the Heart of Madhyamaka*:[601]

The union of the two realities—the object—is what is to be understood.
The union of the two accumulations—the subject—is the path.
The union of the two kāyas is the fruitional Madhyamaka.
This is found in the texts of Candrakīrti, who elucidated noble [Nāgārjuna's] intention.

Accordingly, the object—the two realities—is the basis that is to be understood. Since the assessment [of the two realities] by a correct mind that makes you understand [them] depends on conventions, they are two realities [just on the level] of conventions. Based on them, correct knowledge arises. Having realized through that what is to be relinquished and what is to be adopted, you complete the accumulations of merit and wisdom. Through this, the fruition—the dharmakāya, which is the stainless dharmadhātu, and its natural outflow, the very profound dharmakāya (the two rūpakāyas)—is accomplished. This is the intention of the great being, noble Nāgārjuna, the meaning of ground, path, and fruition.

Here, the meaning of the two realities as that which is to be understood is as follows. It is seeming dualistic appearances' own nature to appear like [a reflection of] the moon in water. This is seeming reality. Ultimate reality means that precisely these mere appearances abide naturally free from all reference points. Thus, [the two realities] are completely free from being the same or different. This is also said in the *Mūlamadhyamakakārikā*:

What is dependent origination
Is explained as emptiness.
It is a dependent designation[602] [5a]
And in itself the middle path.

Since there is no phenomenon
That is not dependently originating,

There is no phenomenon
That is not empty.[603]

This means that [any hypothetical] phenomena which have not arisen in dependence simply [would] abide by their very nature without any arising or ceasing. Therefore, all phenomena are said to "lack a nature," since the phenomena of [both] saṃsāra and nirvāṇa are free from being anything other than just mere appearances, that is, [devoid of] the eight extremes of reference points. [Also] the *Saṃdhinirmocanasūtra* speaks to this way of being:

> The defining characteristic of the realm of formations and the ultimate
> Is the defining characteristic that they are free from being one or different.[604]

The *Vajrajñānasamucchaya[tantra]*[605] [states]:

> The seeming is dualistic appearance. [Its] reality is like [a reflection of] the moon in water. Since ultimate reality is free from all characteristics, its locus is the eighteen emptinesses.[606]

Even though this is simply inconceivable for ordinary beings, in order that they engage in it and realize it by relying on the conventional, these conventional two realities have been taught in [Nāgārjuna's] *Mūlamadhyamakakārikā*.

> The teaching of the dharma by the Buddhas
> Is perfectly based on the two realities.
> These are the seeming worldly reality
> And the ultimate reality.
>
> Those who do not know the distinction
> Between these two realities,
> Do not know the profound true reality
> Of the teaching of the Buddhas.[607]

His autocommentary, the *Akutobhayā*, says [on these verses]:

> This so-called "seeming worldly reality" is the seeing that all phenomena arise, [5b] since the mistakenness of worldly [beings] does not realize that all phenomena are empty of nature. Seemingly, this is the very reality for just these [beings]. Hence, it is

> seeming reality. As for ultimate reality, since the unmistakenness of the noble ones realizes it, it is the seeing that all phenomena do not arise. Ultimately, this is the very reality for precisely these [noble ones]. Therefore, it is ultimate reality.[608]

This is equivalent to what noble Maitreya states in the *[Dharma]dharmatā-vibhāga*:

> Here, the defining characteristics of phenomena
> Are duality and how it is designated.
> What appears [as that]
> Is false imagination, because nonexistents appear.
>
> Furthermore, the defining characteristic of the nature of phenomena
> Is suchness, which is without a difference
> Between apprehender and apprehended,
> Or a designated object and what designates.[609]

Thus, [the two realities] are expressed as two conventional characteristics. But in terms of their nature, all phenomena are said to "lack a nature" and [the *Madhyāntavibhāga*] states that

> Ultimate actuality pertains to just one.[610]

Also master Jñānagarbha's [*Satyadvayavibhāga*] teaches:

> Just these very appearances, as they [appear],
> Are the seeming. The other is its counterpart.[611]

You may think, "Conventional defining characteristics also explain just the conventional, but this contradicts the very fact that, ultimately, there is nothing to be differentiated." This is a wrong idea, similar to the following statements: "This has not the slightest function, yet what is produced is impermanent," and "Since a self is not observable, one speaks of the nonexistence of a self; but if one speaks of 'self,' that contradicts [its] nonexistence." Moreover, also master Candrakīrti explained [in his *Madhyamakaprajñāvatāra*]:

> No entity whatsoever exists
> Whose being one or many is excluded,
> Because these exist by mutual exclusion.

You may object, "This contradicts perception and so on." [6a]
That is not the case. I do not negate
[Appearances] that [only] satisfy when unexamined.[612]

What is taught in detail in this text [—the *Dharmadhātustava*—] is what abides ultimately in this way, the ultimate in terms of seeing this mode of being, the ultimate in terms of practice, and the ultimate in terms of being free from stains. The *Yuktiṣaṣṭikā* says:

Between saṃsāra and nirvāṇa,
There is not the slightest difference.[613]

This is the ultimate in terms of the perfect [nature].[614]

Those who take dependent entities
As being neither real nor delusive,
Just like [a reflection of] the moon in water,
Are not carried away by views.[615]

This is the ultimate in terms of seeing and practice.

Those great beings who see
With [their] eyes of wisdom
That entities are like reflections
Do not get stuck in the mire of so-called "objects."[616]

This is the ultimate [in terms of] attainment. Moreover, the nominal ultimate is stated [in the *Vigrahavyāvartanī*]:

Since there is nothing to negate,
I do not negate anything at all.[617]

and the *Śūnyatāsaptati*:

I do not negate this worldly way
That says, "In dependence on this, that originates."
Since what originates in dependence lacks a nature,
How could it exist? [Thus,] true reality is ascertained.[618]

Thus, also the meanings of[619] what is common consensus through reasoning and what is common consensus due to worldly [conventions] are taught.

These are expressions that are synonyms. This is just as it is stated in the *Madhyāntavibhāga*:

> Object, attainment, and practice
> Are held to be the three kinds of the ultimate.
> The changeless and the unmistaken
> Are the two aspects of the perfect [nature].
>
> Common wordly consensus is due to one,
> And common consensus through reasoning is due to three.
> The domain of complete purity is twofold,
> But is expressed by just a single one.[620]

[6b] As for these [notions in the above verse,] the first three pertain to the three stages of ground, path, and fruition. The two [notions] of the unchanging and the unmistaken [perfect nature are given] in terms of the specific characteristics of the two realities.[621] Common worldly consensus and [consensus] through reasoning are instances of seeming reality. With this in mind, the *Satyadvaya[vibhāga]* says:

> Although [phenomena] are similar in appearance,
> Since they are able to perform functions or not,
> Due to being correct or false,
> The division of the seeming was made.[622]

What is able to perform a function is an undeceiving consciousness. What is not able to perform a function is what causes deception. Based on this, since there is certainty about what is deceiving and what not, one engages in actuality. Therefore, also the presentation of what is permanent is taught. The point of Madhyamaka is to bring every clinging to reality, unreality, entities, and nonentities to an end. The order of teaching the [two] realities is taught in the *Yuktiṣaṣṭikā*:

> Actions together with their results
> And also [beings'] migrations were correctly explained.
> The full knowledge of their nature
> And [their] nonarising too were taught.[623]

Without having internalized the two realities' own essences, [their] classifications, and [their] order in this way, to one-sidedly voice something [about them] is similar to some fools who take the word "ox" that is mouthed [in a debate between] a proponent and an opponent as referring to themselves and then get angry. Don't act like that![624]

Thus, when the teachings on the [two] realities in terms of subject and object are practiced as the path, they represent the two accumulations. The accumulation of merit is seeming reality and the accumulation of wisdom is based on the ultimate. Generosity and ethics are the accumulation of merit, while [7a] prajñā is the accumulation of wisdom. The three [pāramitās] of patience, vigor, and samādhi represent both [accumulations]. If embraced by prajñā, all of them are the accumulation of wisdom. This is also explained in the *[Mahāyāna]sūtrālaṃkāra*:

> Generosity and ethics are the accumulation of merit,
> While prajñā is the one of wisdom.
> The three others are [the accumulation] of both,
> And all five [can] also be the accumulation of wisdom.[625]

These are explained in detail in [Nāgārjuna's] *Madhyamaka-Ratnāvalī*, master Śūra's *Pāramitāsamāsa*, and the chapter on the parāmitās in the *[Mahāyāna]sūtrālaṃkāra*.[626] Knowing them accordingly, you should engage in the sūtras.

Having thus relied on the [two] realities of ground and path, the fruition—the union of the two kāyas—is as follows. The dharmakāya is that which is endowed with thirty-two qualities[627] and enlightened activity through the own nature of the meditative equipoise of nonconceptual wisdom. The rūpakāya is the knowledge of variety, which bears the name "the wisdom attained subsequently to this very [meditative equipoise]" and is endowed with thirty-two qualities[628] and enlightened activity. This is how they are known in the Madhyamaka texts:

> This rūpakāya of the Buddha
> Originates from the accumulation of merit.
> The dharmakāya, in brief,
> O king, originates from the accumulation of wisdom.
>
> Thus, these two accumulations
> Are the causes for attaining buddhahood.[629]

This is taught extensively in the *Uttaratantra* and also by Candrakīrti in his *Madhyamakāvatāra*.[630] In this way, since the seeming is false, impermanent, deceiving, and illusionlike, what appear as the abodes, objects, and bodies of sentient beings in the three realms, consisting of the eight collections of consciousness, are merely false imagination. This is also said in the *Madhyāntavibhāga*:

> False imagination [consists of]
> The minds and mental factors [7b] of the three realms.
> Here, consciousness is the seeing of a referent,
> While mental factors [refer to seeing] its distinctive features.
>
> One is the conditioning consciousness,
> And the second [kind] is what consumes.
> What consumes, discriminates,
> And sets the [mind] in motion are the mental factors.[631]

Since these consciousnesses arise in dependence on false imagination, they are not real. But since they originate dependently and appear, they are not nonexistent either. Hence, they are called "other-dependent." The meanings as they are designated in dependence on these [other-dependent appearances], their discriminations, their latent tendencies, and their appearing as if they were [actual] referents [all] come about like a mirage and [thus] are called "the imaginary [nature]," because what is nonexistent is imagined as existent. The root of such mistakenness is just that the stainless dharmadhātu itself is not aware of itself, while there is not the slightest thing that is really established. Therefore, the *Yuktiṣaṣṭikā* says:

> Once ignorance has ceased,
> Why should it not be clear
> That that which will cease
> Was imagined by ignorance?[632]

The *Bodhicittavivaraṇa* reads:

> The imaginary, the other-dependent,
> And the perfect, [their] nature being
> The character of emptiness alone,
> Are labels for the mind.[633]

You may wonder, "Well, how does the perfect [nature] speak about the mind?" [The answer is given in the *Bodhicittavivaraṇa*'s next verse]:

> For those whose character is delight in the mahāyāna,
> The Buddha's teaching is in brief:

Phenomena are identityless and equality,
And mind is primordially unborn.[634]

[The *Madhyāntavibhāga*] states:

Consciousness arises as the appearance of referents,
Sentient beings, a self, and cognizance,
[But] it does not have an [external] referent.
Since that does not exist, it does not exist either.

The imaginary, the other-dependent,
And also the perfect, [8a]
Are explained through referent, false imagination,
And the nonexistence of duality.[635]

Thus, this has been taught in the Yogācāra scriptures as well. Therefore, once all conceptions of apprehender and apprehended within [primary] minds and mental factors have become pure and are at peace, what is called "buddha wisdom" is made to appear. The *Acintyastava* says:

What is dependent origination
Is precisely what you maintain as emptiness.
Also the genuine dharma is like that,
And even the Tathāgata is the same.

It is also held to be true reality, the ultimate,
Suchness, and the basic substance.[636]
This is the undeceiving reality.
Through realizing it, [one] is called a Buddha.[637]

Therefore, due to [the stained dharmadhātu as] the cause of saṃsāra having become pure, there is no contradiction in referring to it with the term "nirvāṇa." In the collection of reasoning, [Nāgārjuna] negates the clinging to characteristics, but he definitely does not refute the teachings on the way of being of the Buddha and the dharma, wisdom, great compassion, or the wonderful enlightened activity of the Buddhas. Nevertheless, the blinded wisdom eyes of ordinary beings conceive of that as something else.

The presentation of the basic nature of saṃsāra being a circle,[638] of the form in which it circles, and that it is [a succession of] causes and results—which includes the pure teachings on its natural purity and that this is mutual great dependent origination—is given in detail in the *Pratītyasamutpāda-*

hṛdayavyākhyā[639] composed by noble Nāgārjuna himself. Therefore, it is not written out here and should be understood from said [text]. This [text] here occasions the teaching on the very own essence of pure consciousness that is stained by apprehender and apprehended [in just an adventitious way]. Hence, the general meaning behind this [second] verse, which is the brief introduction [to this essence], had to be discussed.

2.1.2. Detailed explanation by correlating this with examples
[8b] This has seven parts:

2.1.2.1. The way in which the dharmadhātu does not appear and then appears, exemplified by butter

[This is taught by] two verses.

> **While it's blended with the milk,**
> **Butter's essence appears not.**
> **Likewise, in the afflictions' mix,**
> **Dharmadhātu is not seen.** [3]

Mind as such that abides together with the water of afflictions is like **milk.** [In milk,] **butter** that is not enshrouded by water is just **not** observable, but it is not that butter does not exist in the milk. **Likewise**, buddhahood as such, which is expressed as **dharmadhātu, is** just **not** observable, but it is not that it does not exist in all sentient beings. That this is certain is expressed in the *Avataṃsakasūtra*:

> Within the hosts of sentient beings, there is no being whatsoever into which tathāgata wisdom has not entered in its entirety. But because of their grasping of discriminating notions, they are not aware of that tathāgata wisdom. By becoming free from their grasping of discriminating notions, the omniscient wisdom, which is self-sprung wisdom, becomes visible again in an unimpeded way. O sons of the victors, it is as follows: . . .[640]

[Following that, the sūtra] treats this in detail through the example of a [tightly folded] huge silk cloth [on which an entire] trichiliocosm [is painted]. Therefore, [the next verse] says:

> **Once you've cleansed it from the milk,**
> **Butter's essence is without a stain.**

Just so, with the afflictions purified,
The dharmadhātu lacks all stain. [4]

Through conditions such as churning [the milk], water and **butter** appear separately. **Just so**, due to the condition of practicing the path, the obscurations are cleared away, and therefore [the dharmadhātu] is said to appear as buddhahood. But this does not mean that [buddhahood] has arisen from itself, something other, both, or without a cause.

2.1.2.2. The detailed explanation through the example of a lamp inside a vase, which teaches the gradual stages of sentient beings, the path, and the appearance of wisdom in buddhahood

[This is taught by] three verses. The first [refers to] the stage of sentient beings: [9a]

Just as a lamp that's sitting in a vase
Does not illuminate at all, [5ab]

This states the example.

While dwelling in the vase of the afflictions,
The dharmadhātu is not seen. [5cd]

This teaches the meaning. Here, some may say, "It is possible to understand this term dharmadhātu as [referring to] nothing but emptiness." This is not the case. Here, the [underlying] intention of dharmadhātu refers to both the wisdom of suchness and [the wisdom of] variety. That this is certainly the case is stated in the *Uttaratantra*:

In brief, since the uncontaminated dhātu
Is classified as fourfold in meaning,
It should be known that there are four synonyms,
The dharmakāya and so forth.

[These] are the inseparable buddha qualities,
The disposition for that being obtained just as it is,
The true nature without falsity and deception,
And natural primordial peace.[641]

Under the aspect of [the dharmadhātu being] the fruition, it is taught as buddhahood that is inseparable from its qualities. Under the aspect of [it being] the cause [for that fruition, it is taught] as the natural[ly abiding] and the unfolding disposition. Under the aspect of the two realities, [it is taught] as undeceiving valid cognition without falsity. Under the aspect of relinquishment, [it is taught] as "natural peace" and "peace from adventitious [stains]." However, [these four aspects] are not different in nature. This is explained in detail in the *Anūnaṇtvāṇpūrṇaṇtvanirdeśasūtra*.[642]

In order to teach the stage of those on the path, [the next verse] says:

> **From whichever of its sides**
> **You punch some holes into this vase,**
> **From just these various places then,**
> **Its light rays will beam forth.** [6]

Due to the particular [size] of the **holes** [that you may punch into **this vase**], the lamp inside this vase emits small, medium, or great beams of **light**. Likewise, on the path of seeing, the seven impure bhūmis and the [three] pure bhūmis, through the nonconceptual and the illusionlike samādhis, the light rays of the [just-mentioned] twofold wisdom—[starting with] the twelve times hundred [qualities of the first bhūmi] up to boundless [such qualities on the tenth bhūmi]—[9b] **will** become increasingly bright, just as explained below.[643]

The stage of a Buddha [is as follows]:

> **Once the vajra of samādhi**
> **Has completely smashed this vase,**
> **To the very limits of all space,**
> **It will shine just everywhere.** [7]

At the end of the continuum of the ten bhūmis, **the vajralike samādhi smashes this vase**, [which consists of] the contaminated, uncontaminated, and formational karmas as well as the consciousnesses that originate in mutual dependence, [all stemming] from the remainders of the two obscurations, which is the so-called "ground of the latent tendencies of ignorance." **Once** that **has** [happened], the radiant light of the enlightened activity of the wisdom that is free from the two obscurations **will shine to the very limits of all space**. As the *[Mahāyāna]sūtrālaṃkāra* says:

> The attainment of the vajralike samādhi
> That cannot be destroyed by thoughts

Is the final fundamental change of state,
Unstained by all obscurations.

Omniscience is attained—
The unsurpassable state,
Abiding in which, one's activity
Is for the benefit of all sentient beings.[644]

2.1.2.3. The meaning of [the dharmadhātu] being changeless and free from arising and ceasing

In light of such differences appearing in the three stages, you may wonder, "Do the qualities and so forth newly arise?" In order to remove such wrong ideas, [the text] says:

Unarisen is the dharmadhātu,
And never cease it will.
At all times without afflictions,
Stainless through beginning, middle, end. [8]

The dharmadhātu—the Tathāgata heart—does **not** newly **arise**, since a cause [for it] is unobservable and it is devoid of [any cause]. **It will never cease**, since it is without arising and free from conditions. **At all times**, [10a] it is **without** being tainted by **afflictions**, because it serves as the remedy for all afflictions and is permanent [in its purity]. In all three times, it is naturally pure, since it is genuine purity as such.

Thus, for these four reasons, it is endowed with the following four pāramitās. What is called its "genuine purity" consists of its [timeless] natural purity (the general characteristic of the dharmakāya) and its purity due to being without stains [at the end of the path] (its specific characteristic). It is [also] the "genuine self," which means being free from conceptions about a self and conceptions about the lack of a self, that is, the extremes of tīrthikas and śrāvakas and pratyekabuddhas [respectively]. It is "genuine bliss" because it is endowed with mastery over the nonarising of suffering and [its] origin. [Finally,] it is "genuine permanence," since it is without arising and ceasing in all situations and [since its] natural enlightened activity is uninterrupted.[645] These [four notions of purity, self, bliss, and permanence are also found as] the mistaken notions of ordinary beings, who [entertain] the fourfold clinging to the five skandhas that perpetuate saṃsāra as being pure, a self, blissful, and permanent. The remedies for these [four kinds of clinging] are the four characteristics of familiarizing oneself with [the skandhas] as being repulsive, without a self, suffering, and impermanent. Since all eight of those [notions] are conceptually imputed, momentary, and [ultimately] untrue, in order to be liberated from the extremes of these [eight], buddhahood is accomplished through realizing the eight realities [of the noble ones]. This is what the *Śrīmālādevīsūtra* says.[646] Summarizing the meaning of this, the *Uttaratantra* declares:

> The fruition consists of the pāramitās—
> The qualities of purity, self, bliss, and permanence.[647]

and:

> As before, so it is after—
> It is the changeless true nature.[648]

In order to demonstrate that such can be established through an example, [the next two verses speak about a gem in its ore].

2.1.2.4. Explaining through the example of a gem that the stages of sentient beings and Buddhas are not different

From among the two verses [that explain this], the example itself is given [10b] [in verse 9]:

> **A blue beryl, that precious gem,**
> **Is luminous at any time,**
> **But if confined within its ore,**
> **Its shimmer does not gleam. [9]**

As for a great **blue beryl**'s shimmer, color, and [ability to] grant what is desired and needed, during the two [phases] of it being **confined within its ore** or being without its ore (that is, cleansed and polished), there is no difference in its essence. However, while it is confined within its ore, its **shimmer** and qualities do not appear. In accordance with this example,

> **Just so, the dharmadhātu free of stain,**
> **While it's obscured by the afflictions,**
> **In saṃsāra doesn't shine its light, [10ac]**

Since **the dharmadhātu is obscured by the** innumerable millions of cocoons of **afflictions** when [it still appears as] a sentient being, even though its nature is not tainted by these **stains**, it does not appear, and the **light** of its qualities and enlightened activity **does not shine** either. Since it does appear and shine, once its purification is completed, [the next line] says:

> **But in nirvāṇa, it will beam. [10d]**

When great **nirvāṇa**—buddhahood—is attained, [the dharmadhātu] will be very pure. This is stated in the *Avikalpapraveśadhāraṇī*, which gives the example of a gem confined in the middle of a rock. In [this example], a blue beryl becomes visible after earth and the ores of [other precious substances] like silver, gold, and various [other] gems have been removed. Likewise, nonconceptual wisdom is obtained through having become pure of the four characteristics of conceptualizing what is to be relinquished, the remedies, suchness, and the fruition.[649] In the same way, the purification of the basic element is taught through the example of [cleansing] a blue beryl [by three progressively refined methods] in the *Daśabhūmikasūtra*[650] and also in the *Buddhamahākaruṇānirdeśasūtra*.[651]

2.1.2.5. Explaining the nature of the basic element through the example of gold

> **If this element exists, through our work,**
> **We will see the purest of all gold.**
> **Without this element,** [11a] **despite our toil,**
> **Nothing but misery we will produce. [11]**

This [verse] teaches that, in a place where **the element** of gold **exists, through our work, we will see the purest of all gold**. However, even if we were [to make the effort of] digging up some earth that contains no gold, this would only [make us] suffer. Likewise, since the completely pure Buddha heart exists in the earth of the afflictions, it will appear. But if it did not exist, even if we removed the afflictions, this would be pointless. This meaning is stated in a sūtra:

> Just as the purest of all gold
> Is not seen in crumbled stones,
> But becomes visible through purification,
> So it is with the Tathāgatas in the world.[652]

2.1.2.6. The way in which the dharmakāya appears, [illustrated] by the example of rice [and its] husk

[This is taught by] two verses, first stating the example:

> **Just as grains, when covered by their husks,**
> **Are not considered rice that can be eaten,** [12ab]

Just as rice that [still] possesses its husk is [not] given the name "**rice that can be eaten,**"

> **While being shrouded in afflictions,**
> **It is not named "buddhahood."** [12cd]

During the time of being a sentient being, though the dharmakāya resides in a fully complete way within the cocoon of **afflictions, it is not** called "**buddhahood**." [Rather,] it is **named** "the basic element of sentient beings."

> **Just as rice itself appears**
> **When it is free from all its husks,**
> **The dharmakāya clearly manifests,**
> **Once it is free from the afflictions.** [13]

Through being **free from the husks** of **afflictive** and cognitive obscurations, the fruition of [the dharmadhātu] having become pure—**the dharmakāya** [with its] qualities (the ten strengths, the four fearlessnesses, and the eighteen unshared features)—will become **clearly manifest**. Thus, the *Śrīmālādevīsūtra* says:

> Since the mind is completely afflicted, sentient beings are afflicted.
> Since mind has become purified, it is completely pure.[653]

[11b] Also the *Madhyāntavibhāga* states:

> If it were not afflicted,
> All beings would be liberated.
> If it were not pure,
> Efforts would be without result.[654]

Therefore, "basic element of sentient beings," "Buddha heart," and "dharmadhātu" are synonyms. This should be understood in detail from the *Uttaratantra*.

2.1.2.7. [Explaining its] natural outflow, the very profound dharmakāya, [illustrated] through the example of a banana tree

[This is taught by] two verses, teaching first the example:

"Banana trees don't have a pith"—
That's used as an example in the world,
But their fruits—their very pith—
In all their sweetness[655] we do eat. [14]

The meaning [of this is as follows]:

Just so, when saṃsāra without pith
Is released from the afflictions' peel,
Its fruition, buddhahood itself,
Turns into nectar for all beings. [15]

This teaches which qualities of attainment one possesses through becoming free from what. When splitting up **banana trees**, they **do not have a pith, but** [still] **their fruits** first ripen, and then **we do eat** [them]. **Just so**, when examined, what is **without** the slightest **pith** is **saṃsāra**, and saṃsāra is conception. In the *Yuktiṣaṣṭikā*, we find:

Since the Buddhas have said
That the world is conditioned by ignorance,
Why should it not be justified
That this world is conception?[656]

Accordingly, conceptions definitely have no pith, being like illusions and mirages, but due to the fundamental change of state of precisely these [conceptions], the rūpakāya that benefits all sentient beings comes forth. Therefore, consciousness blended with the web of the afflictions is called "saṃsāra." Through becoming free from the afflictions, it **turns into** all-accomplishing wisdom, which is the **nectar for** [all] sentient **beings**.

[12a] Thus, this sequence of teaching the natural purity of the basic element through examples [is as follows.] (1) The example of butter teaches on the nature [of the dharmadhātu]. During the time of being a sentient being, just like butter and water appear to be blended into one in milk, what appears is this very sentient being, while buddhahood does not appear. When having become a Buddha, [the dharmadhātu] is not mingled with stains, just like the appearance of butter that is not mixed with any water at all. (2) The example of the lamp teaches on the [dharmadhātu's] intrinsic qualities. [As for them,] there is no contradiction in the light of these qualities being without

difference during all times of either being impure or pure, yet still appearing as if it were smaller or bigger due to the condition of being covered by obscurations [to a greater or lesser degree]. (3) The example of the gem teaches on the dharmakāya's own qualities, that is, possessing the qualities of being free from all obscurations and engaging in nonconceptual enlightened activity. (4) The example of gold teaches on the cause and result of the sambhoghakāya, which has the nature of being unproduced, virtuous, and completely pure mentation. (5) The example of the rice husks teaches that the mind does not see [its own nature] until it is liberated from the ground of the latent tendencies of ignorance.[657] (6) The example of the banana tree is the example for the fruition of nirmāṇakāya, which is the change of state of clinging and conception.

In brief, the natures of (1) the [dharma]dhātu, (2) wisdom, (3) mirrorlike [wisdom], (4) [the wisdom of] equality, (5) discriminating [wisdom], and (6) all-accomplishing [wisdom] are taught by (1) butter, (2) light, (3) the gem, (4) gold, (5) rice, and (6) the fruit of a banana tree. As for their [respective] obscurations, (1) being mixed with water, (2) being obscured by a vase, (3) being enveloped by a covering [of encrustments],[658] (4) earth, (5) husks, and (6) the banana tree should be understood as [symbolizing], in due order, (1) afflictive obscurations, (2) cognitive obscurations, (3) mind, (4) mentation, [(5) the ground of the latent tendencies of ignorance],[659] and (6) clinging and thoughts. [12b] For these [points], there are certainly many scriptural quotations from [both] sūtras and treatises, but I do not elaborate [on them here].[660]

2.2. Instruction on the stage of those on the path

This has three parts:
1) How the manner of it being justified to purify the stains and the sequence [of that] are to be understood
2) The way to meditate
3) The sequence of attainment

2.2.1. How the manner of it being justified to purify the stains and the sequence [of that] are to be known

This has three parts:

2.2.1.1. The way in which the basic element of the dharmakāya itself is justified as the disposition

[This is taught by] two verses. In dependence on the conventional expression of "removing the stains" of the [dharmadhātu's] nature as it has been taught [to exist] during the stage of impurity, [the dharmadhātu] with stains is taught as the cause and [the dharmadhātu] without stains as the result. In order to [do so, the text says]:

> **Likewise, from all seeds there are,**
> **Fruits are born that match their cause.**
> **By which person could it then be proved**
> **That there is a fruit without a seed? [16]**

Here, all **causes**, which are **all seeds**, are observed [to yield] their individual, specific **fruits**. A brief summary of this is as follows. The cause and seed of saṃsāra is the ālaya-consciousness. Through it functioning as the causal condition, the other seven collections of consciousness become [its] results, from which all the karmas and sufferings of the three realms individually and specifically mature. [In turn,] since they all produce the potencies of the ālaya-consciousness, it is also called [their] "result." In this way, this is dependent origination itself. The *Mahāyānasaṃgraha* calls this "the dependent origination of differentiating the nature."[661] Based on that, the twelve [links] of "the dependent origination of differentiating what is desired and undesired"[662] come about, which in their entirety are obscurations. [As for cause and result in terms of nirvāṇa,] the natural outflow that is grounded in the stainless dharmakāya refers to the qualities and enlightened activities of the very profound dharmakāya streaming forth. Therefore, the essence [of buddhahood], which is mirrorlike, [13a] is the dharmakāya. Since the [buddha]kāya [that consists] of the two kāyas is not fully complete [in being just the dharmakāya], here, [its] uncontaminated natural outflows—the pāramitās, such as generosity, and the completely immaculate dharmas—are called "the cause of buddhahood." However, these completely immaculate dharmas also stem from the dharmakāya. In this way, in terms of their natures, saṃsāra and nirvāṇa [entail] their individual, distinct [sets of] causes and results, which are the factors to be relinquished and their remedies [respectively]. This is how it is described in the *Mahāyānasaṃgraha* after [this text] has taught the manner in which the buddhadharma—the latent tendencies of listening—depends on the ālaya-consciousness and arises and ceases:

> [You may say,] "Well, if the ālaya-consciousness is the cause of the afflictions, it needs to be said from where its remedy, the seed of the supramundane mind, stems." This [supramundane mind] originates from the seeds of those latent tendencies of listening that are the natural outflow of the completely pure dharmadhātu.

You may wonder, "As for these latent tendencies of listening that are the remedy for the [ālaya-consciousness], are they of the very nature of the ground consciousness or not? If they were of the very nature of the ground consciousness, how should they be suitable as the seeds of its remedy? But if they are not of its nature, just go and look what the matrix of these seeds of latent tendencies of listening is." As for the matrix that is entered by these latent tendencies of listening in dependence on the enlightenment of Buddhas, they enter the consciousness of maturation,[663] whose mode it is to exist simultaneously [with them], just like milk and water. They are not the ālaya-consciousness, because they are the very seeds of its remedy.

Based on small latent tendencies, these turn into medium and great ones . . .

[13b] Hence, they are to be regarded as the seeds of the dharmakāya. Since they are the remedy for the ālaya-consciousness, they are not of the nature of the ālaya-consciousness. [In the sense of being a remedy,] they are something mundane, but since they are the natural outflow of the supramundane—the utterly and completely pure dharmadhātu—they are the seeds of supramundane mind. Although supramundane mind has not yet originated, they are the remedy for being entangled by the afflictions, the remedy for migrating into the lower realms, and[664] the remedy that makes all wrongdoing vanish. They are what is in complete concordance with meeting Buddhas and bodhisattvas.

Although [these latent tendencies in the minds] of beginner bodhisattvas are mundane, they should be regarded as being constituted by the dharmakāya and [those of] the śrāvakas and pratyekabuddhas as being constituted by the vimuktikāya. These [latent tendencies] are not the ālaya-consciousness but are constituted by the dharmakāya and the vimuktikāya. To the extent that they gradually increase as small, medium, and great ones, to that same extent the consciousness of maturation wanes and also changes state. Once it has changed state in all respects, the consciousness of maturation with all its seeds has no more seeds and is relinquished in all respects.[665]

Therefore, in order to teach the conventional terms of cause and result with regard to this dharmadhātu, [the next two lines] say:

> **This basic element, which is the seed,**
> **Is held to be the basis of all dharmas. [17ab]**

The basis of all uncontaminated qualities is the naturally pure dharmadhātu. **This** is also **the seed** and the **basic element** [for enlightenment]. As [Asaṅga's] commentary on the *Uttaratantra* says:

> Here, the meaning of dhātu has the meaning of cause.[666]

The *Uttaratantra*'s chapter on enlightenment states:

> Just as space, which is not a cause,
> Is the cause for forms, [14a] sounds, smells,
> Tastes, tangible objects, and phenomena
> To be seen, heard, and so on,
>
> Likewise, it is the cause for the arising
> Of uncontaminated qualities
> Within the sensory field of the stable ones
> Through being joined with the two kāyas being unobscured.[667]

For this reason, due to the obscurations of mind, mentation, and consciousness gradually becoming pure, [the dharmadhātu's] own stainless qualities appear. Hence, this is taught as "attaining great enlightenment." In order to demonstrate that, [the next two lines say]:

> **Through its purification step by step,**
> **The state of buddhahood we will attain. [17cd]**

However, there is nothing to be attained newly from something extrinsic [to the dharmadhātu], nor are there any obscurations other than being caught up in our own discriminating notions to be relinquished. Therefore, these discriminating notions' own essence is that they, just like a mirage, lack any nature of their own. To directly realize this lack for what it is and to realize and reveal the basic nature of the naturally luminous dharmakāya—the perfect [nature]—as just this perfect [nature] means to have gone to the other shore, since it cannot be gauged by the mind of any childish being. This is stated in master [Nāgārjuna]'s text on dependent origination:

There is nothing to be removed from it
And not the slightest to be added.
Actual reality is to be seen as it really is—
Who sees actual reality is liberated.[668]

2.2.1.2. Teaching an example and its meaning in order to [show] the removal of the [dharmadhātu]'s obscurations

[This is taught by] two verses, which start with an example in order to illustrate the luminosity of pure mind.

Spotless are the sun and moon, [18a]

Sun and moon are naturally luminous and do not coexist with obscurations, such as darkness. Still, [from our perspective, they may be temporarily covered by] adventitious obscurations that are nonexistent yet appear. To demonstrate this, [the next three lines] say:

But obscured by fivefold stains:
These are clouds and smoke and mist,
Rahu's face [14b] **and dust as well. [18bd]**

The meaning is stated [in the next verse]:

Similarly, mind so luminous
Is obscured by five[fold] stains.
They're desire, malice, laziness,
Agitation and doubt too. [19]

As for the naturally **luminous** essence of the Buddha heart, its very own nature **is** made invisible **by fivefold** [stains]. **Desirous** attachment is like **clouds** that moisten [saṃsāric] existence. **Malice** created by the fire of hatred is similar to **smoke. Laziness** resembles **mist** in that it makes [the dharmadhātu] invisible through mental dullness. An **agitated** mind together with pride that obscures the shine of wisdom is like **Rahu's face. Doubt** is similar to dust in being produced through the storms of various [wrong] views. Therefore, the luminosity of sentient beings is not seen. In order to make it clearly manifest, it is to be realized through studying, reflecting, and meditating on the manner in which all phenomena are dependent origination. Hence, this is taught in what follows.

2.2.1.3. Brief introduction to the modes of being of what is to be relinquished and its remedy

This has five parts:
1) [Instruction on the dharmadhātu's] nature becoming pure through the purification of stains
2) Instruction that emptiness is the remedy
3) The manner in which [the dharmadhātu] is not empty of wisdom
4) The manner in which [the dharmadhātu] is empty of something to be relinquished and a remedy
5) Detailed explanation of the [last point]

2.2.1.3.1. Instruction on [the dharmadhātu's] nature becoming pure through the purification of stains

[This is taught by] two verses, [starting with] the example.

> **A garment that was purged by fire**
> **May be soiled by various stains.**
> **When it's put into a blaze again,**
> **The stains are burned, the garment not.** [20]

[Take a piece of] cotton **that was** cleansed **by fire**,[669] or, a **garment** that is made of asbestos,[670] which then becomes tainted **by stains**. Through **putting it into a blaze, the stains are burned** and **the garment** becomes pure, being as shiny as before. Accordingly, the meaning [of this example] is stated [in the next verse]:

> **Likewise, mind that is so luminous**
> **Is soiled by stains of craving** [15a] **and so forth.**[671]
> **The afflictions burn in wisdom's fire,**
> **But its luminosity does not.** [21]

Through [mis]conceiving the Buddha heart—naturally **luminous mind**—as subject and object, we think of it as "me" and "mine." Through such mental formations, we conceive of something to be adopted and something to be rejected, which leads to **craving** for [certain] abodes and objects. The mind streams of those who entertain clinging due to this cause are ignorant. Since the stains are just this, it is also what is to be purified. If we examine and analyze through prajñā to what we are attached, through what we are attached, and the manner in which we are attached, none of these are observable. Therefore, we will realize that [the dharmadhātu] is, by its nature, unarisen, unceasing, empty, void, peaceful, and luminous. This is **wisdom's fire**. The very mind that realizes [this starts with] correct imagination, but although such correct imagination and so on are certainly presented as the path of the noble ones, once it has become free from [all] characteristics [such as the above] as well, **luminous** buddhahood is revealed, just as the garment becomes clearly visible, when [both] stains and fire have subsided. Furthermore, just as the fire blazes for as long as there are stains [to burn], the conceptions that are the remedies will blaze for as long as there are conceptions to be relinquished. Through both subsiding, [the dharmadhātu] becomes [manifestly] luminous. [672]

2.2.1.3.2. Instruction that emptiness is the remedy

You may wonder, "If both something to be relinquished and the remedy have subsided in this way, how is it that the naturally luminous basic element itself exists?"

> **The sūtras that teach emptiness,**
> **However many spoken by the victors,**
> **They all remove afflictions,**
> **But never ruin this dhātu.** [22]

The Bhagavat has **spoken** in **the sūtras** about all aspects, starting with form, being **emptiness**. [15b] The intended meaning of these [sūtras] is that they were spoken in order to **remove** the **afflictions** of sentient beings. Those [sūtras] that—in order to remove the many kinds of views in terms of prakṛti, puruṣa, time, Īśvara, minute particles, and extinction—teach on causes and results as well as on samsāra and nirvāṇa (such as [discussing] the skandhas, the āyatanas, the dhātus, and the four realities of the noble ones). By thus teaching on dependent origination, saṃsāra is conceived as what is to be relinquished, and the remedial dharmas are considered as what is to be adopted in a real sense. Therefore, in order to overcome this [initial approach], which [still] represents a [certain] clinging to an identity in phenomena, [the Buddha] taught that all phenomena are without nature. Since both types of identitylessness will be realized through that, the purpose [of the teachings on emptiness] is such [realization]. The Buddha heart—the luminous **dhātu**—is the wisdom that is completely free from being empty, an entity, both, or neither. [But] it is **never** the case that **the** [teachings on emptiness] **ruin this** [wisdom], that is, teach that it does not exist.[673] This principle is stated in many [texts], such as [Nāgārjuna's] *Mahāyānaviṃśikā*:

Identity and identitylessness are not real,
They are imputed by ordinary beings.
Happiness and suffering are interdependent,
And afflictions and liberation are just like that.[674]

Also the *Yuktiṣaṣṭikā* says:

You are neither liberated through being
Nor through nonbeing from this [saṃsāric] existence.
Great beings are liberated
Through fully understanding being and nonbeing.[675]

2.2.1.3.3. The manner in which [the dharmadhātu] is not empty of wisdom

Water dwelling deep within the earth
Remains untainted through and through.
Just so, wisdom in afflictions
Stays without a single stain. [23]

For example, the nature of **water deep within the earth remains** moist, clear, and **untainted. Just so,** [16a] the stains of the **afflictions** resemble the earth, and the nature of naturally luminous mind's **wisdom stays without a single stain.** It does exist but is just not observable. Through becoming free from [this] condition [of the afflictions], its very nature will appear. Therefore, [also] the conceptions of entities and nonentities being empty, which are like earth, are to be relinquished. In other words, you should let the silt settle. This is also said in the *[Mahāyāna]sūtrālaṃkāra*:

When murky water becomes clear,
[Its] transparency does not arise from elsewhere,
But it just becomes free from stains.
The same goes for the purity of your own mind.

Mind is held to be always naturally luminous.
It is [only] blemished by adventitious flaws.[676]

2.2.1.3.4. The manner in which [the dharmadhātu] is empty of something to be relinquished and a remedy

[This is taught by] three verses, the first of which is given in order to teach that this naturally luminous mind is without a self.

Since dharmadhātu's not a self,
Neither woman nor a man,
Free from all that could be grasped,
How could it be labeled "self"? [24]

You may say, "If the **dharmadhātu** existed as natural luminosity, it would be just like the self of the tīrthikas." It is not like that, because the luminous dharmadhātu **is not a self, neither** a **woman nor a man**, and **free from all that** grasps or could **be grasped. How could** something that is not established as what grasps or is to be grasped **be labeled "self?"** [It simply cannot,] since nothing is established that specifies it. Some may wonder, "If that is the case, then, just as these beings with their luminous mind are not really established ultimately, how could good existences and bad existences, such as men and women, appear and be labeled?" [16b]

In all the dharma that's without desire,
You see neither women nor a man. [25ab]

The entire **dharma** is contained in what is free from **desire** ([the reality of] cessation) and that through which one becomes free from desire (the reality of the path). Both of these are, in terms of their own essence, pure, lucid, and serve as remedies,[677] since these three causes bear the specific characteristics of being naturally untainted by afflictions, overcoming the darkness of the obscurations, and serving as the remedies for the clinging to identity [respectively]. **In** all phenomena, which are nothing but identitylessness, **you** can **see neither women nor men** and so forth. That is definitely how it is, but childish beings, who stand outside of seeing true actuality, are fettered through their discriminating notions. Hence, in order to teach those who are fettered in this way the conventional notions of "desire" and, in case that exists, the "freedom" [from desire, the next two lines say]:

"Men" and "women" are just taught
For guiding those plagued by desire. [25cd]

Thus, the conventional notions of seeming [reality] are taught [by Nāgārjuna] in just the way we think. Here, the root of all the characteristics that are to be relinquished is ignorance—not realizing natural luminosity, which is by nature free from anything to be adopted or to be rejected, for what it is—since all desire for [saṃsāric] existence is produced from that. Through conceiving of a self and being attached to it, we come to conceive of what is other and grasp for it. This is what the sūtras say:

> Childish beings who cling to characteristics in terms of their discriminating notions and are attached to them, delight in [saṃsāric] abodes and wish for [saṃsāric] objects.

In order to overcome these characteristics, [the instruction in the next verse] is given.

> **"Impermanence," "suffering," and "empty,"**
> **These three, they purify the mind.**
> **The dharma purifying mind the best**
> **Is the lack of any nature. [26]**

As the basis of all yānas, the victor taught: [17a] "Everything conditioned is **impermanent**. All that has come into [saṃsāric] existence is **suffering**. All phenomena are without identity [and empty]. All nirvāṇa is peace." These four seals that are the marks of his enlightened words are a synopsis of the dharma. Therefore, since [all phenomena] are impermanent, suffering, momentary, perishing, and unreal, they are **empty**. Since they are identityless and peaceful, they are free from reference points. Hence, here, for the reason that any characteristics of something to be relinquished and its remedy cannot be observed in the dharmadhātu—the Buddha heart—it is declared that all phenomena **lack a nature**, that is, are without essence.[678] The essence of naturally pure luminosity abides in just this way. With this in mind, the sūtras say:

> No matter whether Buddhas have arrived in the world or not, [this] is just what abides as the true nature of phenomena.[679]

2.2.1.3.5. Detailed explanation of the point [that the dharmadhātu is empty of something to be relinquished and a remedy]

This has eight parts:

1) [Showing that the dharmadhātu] abides within ourselves but is invisible
2) Showing that which obscures it
3) The way in which wisdom realizes it
4) The meaning of the imaginary [nature]
5) The meaning of the other-dependent [nature]
6) Dependent origination
7) The mode of being of the perfect [nature]
8) The summary of these [points]

2.2.1.3.5.1. [Showing that the dharmadhātu] abides within ourselves but is invisible

> **In a pregnant woman's womb,**
> **A child exists but is not seen.** [27ab]

This teaches through an example [that the dharmadhātu exists despite its present invisibility], with the corresponding meaning [following in the next two lines].

> **Just so, dharmadhātu is not seen,**
> **When it's covered by afflictions.** [27cd]

This mode of being is also stated in the *Tathāgatagarbhasūtra*:

> There may be a cakravartin in the womb of a destitute woman without anyone to protect her, but she does not know it [and thus suffers]. Likewise, in the cocoon of having our own afflictions, the Buddha heart exists, but we do not know it and thus are afflicted.[680] [17b]

2.2.1.3.5.2. Showing that which obscures the [dharmadhātu]

> **Through conceptions of a self and mine,**
> **Discriminations of names, and reasons,**
> **The four conceptions will arise,**
> **Based on the elements and their outcome.** [28]

As for not realizing what exists within ourselves, as taught above, based on the stirring of unceasing mentation within the naturally luminous mind of appearance and emptiness inseparable, consciousness is **conceived of** as **a self and**, due to that, form and such are conceived as mine. Through that, formations propel us [toward karmic results], **discriminations** grasp at characteristics, and through feelings, we analyze and determine pleasure and displeasure. Based on not realizing the **reasons** for these four **names,**[681] we think that what is impermanent is permanent, take suffering to be pleasure, cling to what is naturally empty as being entities, and conceive of what lacks a self as being a self. As for the **arising** of **the** [latter] **four** mistaken **conceptions**, from the perspective of being a cause, they are **the** origin[682] [of suffering], and, from the perspective of being a result, they are **their outcome** [(suffering itself)], which [both] stem from not realizing dependent origination.[683]

2.2.1.3.5.3. The way in which wisdom realizes [the dharmadhātu]

[This is taught by] one verse.

> **The Buddhas' aspiration prayers too**
> **Lack appearance and characteristics. [29ab]**

As for what consists of the paths and the cessations of those who directly see the reality of the noble ones and engage in it, it **lacks** the **appearance** of suffering and [its] origin, **and**, by its nature [or] **characteristic**, it lacks the imaginary and the other-dependent natures. Realizing this, **the Buddhas** engage in great, causeless compassion for all sentient beings.[684] Therefore, they engage in [the pāramitās of] means and **aspiration prayers too** like this:

> **Immersed in their very own** [18a] **awareness,**
> **Buddhas have the nature of permanence. [29cd]**

Due to being liberated from the bondage of conceptions and discriminations that apprehend characteristics, [Buddhas] are **immersed in** [the wisdom that is] **their very own awareness.**[685] Here, what [bodhisattvas on the path] are aware of is the naturally pure dharmadhātu, onto which the light rays of the very profound immaculate dharma—the natural outflow of the [dharmadhātu]—radiate. Through this, in the beginning, they realize [the dharmadhātu] to be just the mere elimination of adventitious stains. In between, it becomes manifest. Finally, once without any stains, they reside within wisdom together with its qualities and enlightened activity, which represents the nature of the three [kinds of] **permanence** [of the three kāyas in terms] of nature, continuity, and an uninterrupted series [respectively].[686] As the *[Mahāyāna]sūtrālaṃkāra* says:

> Through the three kāyas, the summary
> Of the buddhakāyas should be known.
> Through the three kāyas, one's own and others'
> Welfare plus its basis are taught.
>
> Through basis, intention, and activity,
> They are held to be equal.
> By nature, in terms of continuity,
> And in terms of an uninterrupted series, they are permanent.[687]

2.2.1.3.5.4. The meaning of the imaginary [nature]

> **Any horns there on a rabbit's head**
> **Are just imagined and do not exist.**
> **Just so, all phenomena as well**
> **Are just imagined and do not exist. [30]**

You may wonder, "According to what has been taught above, if the Buddhas are permanent and primordially changeless, then how could it be possible that these stains, which were explained as what is to be relinquished, and these remedies (such as [meditating on] impermanence), which were explained as the means to purify those [stains], do not exist? Do they exist in a similar way to the Buddha heart?" **On a rabbit's head, horns do not exist**, so even if you **imagine** [this nonexistence] as "horns of a rabbit," how should absolutely nonexistent horns ever come about? This is not reasonable. [18b] In this way, **all phenomena** of minds and mental factors of the impure ālaya-consciousness **as well are imagined** through false imagination. Apprehender and apprehended absolutely **do not exist** as they are imagined. To think of something nonexistent as existing is called "mistakenness." If [such a nonexistent] would exist just a little bit, this [above thought] would not be mistaken. Therefore, [from among the three characteristics—imaginary, other-dependent, and perfect—] the imaginary is designated as the characteristic that is absolutely nonexistent.

2.2.1.3.5.5. The meaning of the other-dependent [nature]

> **Also the horns of an ox do not exist**
> **As having the nature of particles. [31ab]**

You may say, "Granted, all imagined phenomena absolutely do not exist. However, just as the horns of an ox appear as existents, do not all phenomena exist as they appear as subjects and objects? Also the collection of reasoning says that, since mere appearances are not negated, other-dependent phenomena exist. If they do not exist, one must accept that path and fruition do not exist either." It is not like that. There indeed appears something that looks like an ox and horns. However, in the case of referring to all entities as being either consciousness or matter, material horns are referred to as [consisting of things] like **particles**. When divided in terms of spatial dimension, they are [found to be] partless. As for immaterial consciousness appearing as if it were horns, how could it be suitable as horns that are [outer] referents? Furthermore, "what is located on the head" is not suitable as [defining] horns, since then hairs would also be horns. [Their mere] shape is also not suitable as horns, since also wooden sticks and such appear in a similar way. Nor are their color and hardness suitable as horns, since also hoofs and stones and so on appear like horns [in that respect] and since the appearance of such aspects [of shape, color, and so on] is established to be unreal, just as in a dream. When examined correctly, [19a] in every respect, **also the horns of an ox do not exist** as something really established. Thus, the appearance of the characteristic of the other-dependent [nature] certainly exists in dependence on the triad of sense faculty, consciousness, and object, but it does not exist as something really established. This is stated in many [texts], such as Āryadeva's *Jñānasārasamucchaya*:

> A "something that has parts" does not exist,
> Minute particles do not exist,
> And what appears distinctly is unobservable—
> Experiences are like a dream.[688]

In this way, [just as the horns of a rabbit,] the imaginary is actually nonexistent. As for the other-dependent, [just as the horns of an ox,] it appears but does not exist as something real in the way [it appears]. Therefore, since all phenomena are without self and mine, they are explained as being "without nature," because this [state of being without nature] abides like that primordially.

> **Just as before, so it is after—**
> **What could be imagined there? [31cd]**

What has not arisen **before** does not arise [now]. What has arisen does not arise [either], since it has arisen already. Since the same goes for ceasing too, all phenomena—which are free from the triad of arising, abiding, and ceasing—abide, in terms of **their** own essence, as appearance and emptiness inseparable. There, anything that is **imagined** as arising or ceasing does not exist.[689]

2.2.1.3.5.6. Instruction on dependent origination

[This is taught by] seven lines of verse. [The first two lines are given] in order to teach on the nature of dependent origination.

> **Since [things] dependently originate**
> **And in dependence too will cease, [32ab]**

In terms of the nature [of phenomena], according to the labels of the conventional two realities, the nonrealization of that [nature] in the case of existing stains is suitable to be labeled "stains." Such is the dependent origination in terms of nature. [19b] [The statement,] "If that exists, this comes about" [refers to] the **dependent origination** of differentiating what is desired and undesired. If, through the latent tendencies of ignorance, both are present, saṃsāra comes about. Once they **cease**, [the spinning of] the wheel of saṃsāra will be interrupted. As for these latent tendencies of ignorance here, they are [just] the appearing of what seems to be the arising of momentarily stirring thoughts of being ignorant about natural luminosity [actually] being this very luminosity. Other than this, there is no real root [of the latent tendencies of ignorance]. Also, these thoughts have not arisen from themselves, from others, from both, or without a cause. Since they do not arise, they do not cease, and since they do not cease, they do not abide. This is just as in the example of there being a [mis]conception of a mirage as water in springtime, thus becoming mistaken and seeing it as water. This [seeming water] is without any arising, abiding, or ceasing, since it is absolutely not established as water. As for appearing despite being nonexistent, a mirage appears through dependent origination, [which involves] a mistaken sense faculty and consciousness, sunlight, vapor, and so on.

[The next two lines say that] all phenomena are just like that.

> **If not even one [of them] exists,**
> **How can fools imagine them?** [32cd]

How can mistaken **fools imagine** that phenomena without arising, abiding, and ceasing arise, abide, and cease? For as long as they imagine this, they determine it that way. When analyzed, it is the cause of craving that has them grasp, which in turn makes them afflicted, and hence they cling to extremes. Therefore, as was said above,

> **How the dharmas of the Sugata**
> **Are established as the very middle**
> **Is through the ox- and rabbit-horn examples.** [33]

[20a] Childish beings dwell on their clinging to a **rabbit** not having horns and their clinging to an **ox** having **horns**. Thus, they think, "This is real, but the other is delusive" and cling to [such] characteristics. However, when examined, both are equal in lacking real [existence]. Also, if both existence and

nonexistence are equal in just appearing as mere imaginations, to apprehend and cling to extremes through [further] imaginations is incorrect. Therefore, the learned who speak in accordance with the **dharma how** it was taught by **the Sugata** cast away the clinging to extremes and **establish** it **as the very middle**. They say that imaginations in terms of factors to be relinquished and remedies—the imaginary and the other-dependent—are just appearances as mere imaginations but not real. Rather, they are dependent origination, and precisely this is expressed as emptiness. Thus, the *Madhyāntavibhāga* says:

> [These are] the extremes of being different and one,
> [Those of] tīrthikas and śrāvakas both,
> Respectively the two extremes of superimposition
> And denial with regard to persons and phenomena,
>
> The extremes of antagonistic factors and remedies,
> And the notions of permanence and extinction;[690]
> In relation to apprehended and apprehender
> And afflicted and purified [phenomena, there are] two and three.
>
> The extremes of dual conceptions
> Are held to be of seven kinds:
> Entities and nonentities, what is to be pacified
> And what pacifies, what is to be feared and fright of that,
>
> Apprehended and apprehender, truth
> And falsity, being engaged or not,
> Nonarising and simultaneity—
> These are the extremes of dual conceptions.[691]

By thus relinquishing the twenty [kinds of] clinging to extremes, one enters the middle. The reasonings [that lead there] are discussed in detail in the *Mūla[madhyamakakārikā]prajñā[nāma]*.[692] Glorious Saraha says [in his *Dohākośagīti*]:

> Without [realizing] connateness,
> Those who familiarize themselves with nirvāṇa
> Will not accomplish the single ultimate
> By anything whatsoever.[693] [20b]

2.2.1.3.5.7. Instruction on the mode of being of the perfect [nature]

[This is taught by] two verses, which start by teaching the example.

> **The forms of sun, moon, and the stars**
> **Are seen as reflections upon water**
> **Within a container that is pure— [34ac]**

Having stated the example for emptiness (appearing, yet being without nature), which [refers to] not falling into extremes, [the last line of this verse] says:

> **Just so, the characteristics are complete. [34d]**

In terms of their own essence, the dualistic appearances of seeming [reality] are [just expressions of] mistakenness, yet they [nevertheless] appear as this duality. These appearances, which are like [a reflection of] **the moon** in **water**, are called "reality," since the supreme noble ones see them as the unmistaken reality.[694] This is also stated in great detail in the *Samādhirājasūtra*:

> Since the victors see everything in nirvāṇa
> Like [a reflection of] the moon in water, . . .[695]

Also the *Yuktiśaṣṭikā* says:

> Those who mentally see
> That existence is like a mirage and an illusion
> Are not affected by views
> [About] a previous limit or a later limit.
>
> Those who conceive of an arising and ceasing
> Of conditioned [phenomena]
> Do not understand the movement
> Of the wheel of dependent origination.
>
> What has arisen in dependence on this and that
> Has not arisen in terms of its nature.[696]
> What has not arisen by its nature,
> How can that be called "arisen"?
>
> What subsides due to its cause being extinguished
> Is understood to be "extinguished."
> [But] what is by nature not extinguished,
> How could that be expressed as "being extinguished"?

Thus, there is no arising of anything,
And nothing will cease.[697]

Thus, all illusionlike phenomena are only expressed as mere conventionalities, whereas they are without arising and without ceasing ultimately. Therefore, the bright Buddhadharma—the natural outflow of the dharmakāya—appears as if intermingled with ordinary beings, [21a] but ultimately, it remains unmingled as [pure] virtue. Hence,

Virtuous throughout beginning, middle, end,
Undeceiving and so steady,
What's like that is just the lack of self—
So how can you conceive it as a self and mine? [35]

[The dharmadhātu], which is virtuous in the **beginning**, is [also] virtuous in the **middle**, since, [during the path] between [ground and fruition], it appears to [itself] like the realization of its own nature and a remedy that overcomes the obscurations. It is **virtuous** in the **end**, since, finally, the wisdom with its enlightened activity—which bears the name "fundamental change of state"—operates until saṃsāra is emptied. This actuality represents valid cognition due to its characteristic of being **undeceiving and** it is **steady**, since it is changeless.[698] **It is the lack of self**, since it is not suitable for superimpositions through the web of thoughts. Therefore, it cannot be superimposed **as mine** [either]. It is not **conceivable** by thoughts. Thus, in this sense of being changeless and unmistaken, it is taught as the perfect [nature].[699]

2.2.1.3.5.8. The summary of those [points]

[This is taught by] two verses, the first stating the example and the latter its meaning:

About water at the time of spring,
What we say is that it's "warm."
Of the very same [thing], when it's chilly,
We just say that it is "cold." [36]

Covered by the web of the afflictions,
It is called a "sentient being."
Once it's free of the afflictions,
It should be expressed as "Buddha."[700] [37]

"Buddhas" and "sentient beings," "saṃsāra" and "nirvāṇa," "mind" and "wisdom," "phenomena" and "the nature of phenomena," "seeming" and "ultimate," [all] these expressions should be understood as synonyms. This point is stated in the *Uttaratantra*:

> The basic element is empty of what is adventitious,
> Which has the characteristic of being separable.
> It is not empty of the unsurpassable dharmas,
> Which have the characteristic of being inseparable.[701]

[21b] Its commentary [by Asaṅga] says:

> These two verses [I.154–155] unmistakenly teach the defining characteristic of emptiness, since it [thus] is free from the extremes of superimposition and denial. Here, those whose minds stray away and are distracted from this principle of emptiness, do not rest [in it] in meditative concentration, and are not one-pointed [with regard to it] are therefore called "those whose minds are distracted from emptiness." Without the wisdom of ultimate emptiness, one cannot realize and reveal the nonconceptual dhātu. With this in mind, the *Śrīmālādevīsūtra* says:
>
> > The wisdom of the Tathāgata heart is the emptiness-wisdom of the Tathāgatas. All śrāvakas and pratyekabuddhas have not seen or realized the Tathāgata heart before.[702]

Therefore, since [the dharmadhātu with stains] is disturbed by conceptions about mere imputations of distinct conventional terms, [just as calling] **water warm** or **cold**, it **should be expressed as a "sentient being"** and naturally luminous mind free from conceptions as a "**Buddha**." This explains the manner of it being not contradictory that the dharmadhātu with stains is not tainted by obscurations in its nature yet is purified [of these obscurations].[703]

2.2.2. Instruction on the way to meditate, beginning with [the paths of] accumulation and preparation and so on

This has two parts:

1) Explaining the way to make [the dharmadhātu] a living experience
2) [Explaining] the way in which the conditions [for realizing it]—the [three] jewels—appear

2.2.2.1. Explaining the way to make [the dharmadhātu] a living experience
This has seven parts:

2.2.2.1.1. How to meditate based on the five [sense] doors

[This is taught by] five verses, the first of which teaches what is to be realized based on the eyes and [visible] forms.

> **In dependence upon eye and form,**
> **Appearances without a stain occur.**
> **From being unborn and unceasing,**
> **The dharmadhātu** [22a] **will be known.** [38]

Those beings who, by having confidence in the Tathāgata, understood the dharmadhātu taught above, which is naturally luminous and the teaching of the unsurpassable yāna, immerse themselves in meditation. When doing so, they [start by] going through the preliminaries of properly training in the factors to be adopted and to be relinquished according to the common yāna. These are the factors to be relinquished in the three realms and their remedies, that is, the worldly path that entails characteristics. Through [this path, they train in] the four samādhis [of the form realm], the [four samādhis of] the formless [realm], and the four immeasurables, such as [universal] love. Thereafter, they manifest the samādhi whose nature is superior insight and which focuses on suchness, the characteristic of the dharmadhātu that is expressed by the terms prajñāpāramitā and Mahāmudrā. At the point of resting in meditative equipoise in this way, being fused with samādhi, they should meditate in a way of withdrawing all thoughts. Upon rising from that [samādhi], during the time of subsequent realization, they should meditate with mindfulness by examining and analyzing [phenomena].

In that [phase of subsequent attainment], to start with, the **eye** sense faculty, which is shaped like a flax flower and consists of subtle matter, serves as the dominant condition [of the eye-consciousness]. Mind appearing as the aspects of color and shape, which appear as if being external, serves as the object-condition. The momentary stirring of mentation that dwells in the mind serves as the immediate condition. Thus, an eye-consciousness appears to arise. From these [three conditions], **appearances without a stain occur**, which means that unmistaken perception free from thoughts takes place. The stains are mistakenness, called "that which appears to consciousness suitable to be mixed with expressions." What appears as form unaffected by superimposing conceptions is, in its own essence, both appearing and empty. In its own essence, it is **unborn and unceasing**, [22b] mere cognizance. This is also called "perceptual valid cognition [based on] the eye sense faculty," since it is both a perception and valid cognition.

This actuality appears for ordinary beings, but since they do not realize it, mentation immediately makes them superimpose [something] and has them conceive of and cling to shapes, colors, the internal, and the external, such as, "This is a pillar," "This is a vase," "This is white," or "This is black." This cause leads to grasping, which [in turn] causes arising and ceasing. Based on that, the production of the conventionalities of causes, the conventionalities of results, and the conventionalities of the three times and so on is taken up through being raised since beginningless [time] and then serves as the basis for what follows. Through causing these miragelike [processes] and more, [mentation] renders us mistaken. The noble ones who possess the eye of prajñā see just what is unmistaken and do not raise the web of thoughts. Therefore, theirs is a perception [that is based on] the sense faculties of yogins. As for those who are not noble ones but emulate their [kind of perception], their unmistaken cognizance that observes what appears as if being external is valid cognition because it is similar to yogic perception. Exactly that which resembles the true actuality [of the nature of phenomena] is the valid cognition of this [true actuality], because it is indeed established that true actuality is realized through this [fact]. This is what is maintained [here].[704]

Here, "true actuality" refers to the factor of self-lucid consciousness. Apart from [consciousness] merely appearing as if it were something external, there are no other external referents that are real as minute particles and so on. Therefore, one will realize that self-lucid appearances lack arising and ceasing and become certain that they are just **the dharmadhātu.**[705] This is the meaning of what the sūtras say:

> By knowing the suchness of forms in this way, one will know all phenomena in a nutshell and in detail. [23a]

[The following verse is given] in order to instruct on sound in the same way:

> **In dependence upon sound and ear,**
> **Pure consciousness [comes forth],**
> **All three dharmadhātu without signs.**
> **Linked with thought, this will be hearing.** [39]

The sense faculty of the **ear**, which is shaped like a twisted birch gnarl and consists of subtle matter, serves as the dominant condition [of the ear-consciousness]. **Sound**, which appears as if conjoined [with the activity of sentient beings] and not so conjoined both, serves as the object-condition. From the triad of [these two and] the immediate mind, **pure consciousness**—free from thoughts and unmistaken—arises. This is to be realized as being, in its own essence, **without signs**, that is, the **dharmadhātu** free from arising, abiding, and ceasing. What involves apprehending characteristics in sound—mistaken consciousness **linked with thought—will be hearing.**[706] This means being with stains.

The same is said [for the nose-consciousness] in dependence on smell.

> **Smelling in dependence upon nose and smell**
> **Is an example for the lack of form.**
> **Likewise, it's the nose's consciousness**
> **That conceptualizes**[707] **dharmadhātu.** [40]

The sense faculty of the **nose**, which is shaped like aligned copper needles and consists of subtle matter, serves as the dominant condition [of the nose-consciousness]. Natural and manufactured smells serve as the object-conditions. From these together with the immediate [mind], **the nose-consciousness**—free from thoughts and unmistaken—arises. In terms of [form's] own essence, this **is an example for** demonstrating **the lack of** a nature of **form. Likewise,** since [the nose-consciousness] is without arising and without ceasing, it is realized as **dharmadhātu.**

Just so, [the next verse] instructs on taste.

> **The nature of the tongue is emptiness,**
> **And the dhātu of the taste is void—**
> **Being of the dharmadhātu's nature,**
> **Consciousness is nonabiding.** [41]

The sense faculty of the **tongue**, which is shaped like [two aligned] half-moons and consists of subtle matter, serves as the dominant condition [of the tongue-consciousness]. [23b] The six **tastes**, such as sweet and sour, serve as the object-conditions. Produced by [these and] the immediate [mind], the pure tongue-consciousness arises. This is to be realized as naturally **empty and void**[708] and **being of the dharmadhātu's nature**, that is, as **consciousness** free from arising, **abiding**, and ceasing.

Likewise, [the next verse is given] in order to instruct on tangible objects.

> **From the nature of a body pure**
> **And the characteristics of the tangible conditions,**

> **What is free from such conditions**
> **Is to be expressed as "dharmadhātu." [42]**

The sense faculty of the **body**, which is shaped like the skin of the "bird that is soft to the touch"[709] and consists of subtle matter, serves as the dominant condition [of the body-consciousness]. What is **tangible**, such as softness, roughness, cold, and heat, is the object-**condition**. From the triad of [these two] and the immediate [mind], the body-consciousness arises. In its nature, it **is free from** the nature of causes and **conditions** and **is to be expressed as** the actuality of **the dharmadhātu**, appearance and emptiness inseparable.[710]

Thus, as for the three conditions of the five [sense] doors, their causal condition is indeed mind as such. However, as was taught above, consciousness too serves as the causal condition of mind. Hence, through the power of mutually dependent origination, just as in a tent [made] of spears [leaning against each other], object, sense faculty, and the immediate mind appear as if they were causes and conditions. Ultimately, however, there is no arising or ceasing through anybody in [all of] this. For example, it may appear that [a magician] causes many illusory beings to be born, some to die, some to go, and some to come. But there is no real being born, ceasing, coming, or going in this way, since these very beings are not established [in the first place]. Just like other causes, such as mantras [for producing illusory beings], the conditions of mere thoughts that do not realize their nature indeed appear. But [24a] through knowing and realizing their luminous nature as being without arising and ceasing, they become what they truly are, thus all becoming the dharmadhātu.

2.2.2.1.2. Instruction on meditating on mentation that makes the connection with all the [above], which depends on phenomena

> **Once conception and its concepts are relinquished**
> **With regard to phenomena whose principal is mind,**
> **It's the very lack of nature of phenomena**
> **That you should cultivate as dharmadhātu. [43]**

Mind (or mentation) has two aspects—(1) the one that dwells in the ālaya-consciousness and arises based on that and (2) the afflicted mind that, by looking inward, conceives [of the ālaya-consciousness] as a self.

(1) From among these, the one [discussed] here is the former, which represents the locus of the arising and ceasing of consciousness. This is the mental faculty, in other words, the dominant condition [of the mental consciousness].

The object-conditions [of the mental consciousness] are phenomena, which are twofold: conditioned and unconditioned. Among these, conditioned [phenomena] are eightfold: (1) aggregational [form], (2) circumstantial [form], (3) [form] originating from correct commitment and symbols, (4) imaginary [form], (5) [mastered form],[711] (6) the skandha of feeling, (7) the skandha of discrimination, (8) and [the skandha of] formation. Unconditioned [phenomena] are [also] eightfold: (1–3) the suchness of virtuous, unvirtuous, and neutral phenomena [respectively], (4) space, (5) the meditative absorption of cessation,[712] (6) the meditative absorption without discrimination,[713] (7) analytical cessation,[714] and (8) nonanalytical cessation.[715] These [eight can] also be summarized into four or three.[716]

As for the immediate [condition of the mental consciousness], it refers to [the state] immediately after the previous [moment of] mind and the phenomenon [that is its object] have ceased, while the next one has not [yet] arisen. Thus, from these three conditions, the mental consciousness arises. Nevertheless, what is called "the sixth, the mental consciousness," [is also taught to] represent the very motion of the six collections [of consciousness], which does not occur when discriminations have vanished, during the time of resting in the meditative absorption of cessation, [24b] when having fully entered into the meditative absorption without discrimination, in states without mind, in deep sleep, and during the state of having fainted. As the *Triṃśikā[kārikā]* says:

> The mental consciousness occurs always,
> Except for when being without discrimination,
> In the two kinds of meditative absorption,
> And during being without mind, sleeping, and fainting.[717]

Therefore, the sixth, the mental [consciousness] arises from three conditions. If someone is absorbed in cessation, the mental consciousness that represents the support and locus of the arising and ceasing of consciousness [still] exists [in such a way that it] rests in the ālaya-consciousness. Hence, [the *Abhidharmakośa*] explains:

> Mentation is the consciousness
> Immediately after [any of] the six [consciousnesses] have passed.[718]

Since it is without affliction, it is called "stainless mentation." Because it bears the nature of being without an agent, it is the "dhātu of mentation."[719] Since it functions as the door for consciousness, it is to be explained as "the āyatana of mentation."[720]

(2) As for the afflicted mind, since it is due to it that mentation is not realized [for what it actually is], it has the nature of being ignorant and clinging to "me," thus causing us to conceive of a self, be attached to a self, and crave, all of which have continued since beginningless [time]. Since this [afflicted mind] is obscured yet neutral, it is the root of the entirety of the imaginary [nature] and the afflictions. Therefore, it is also explained as "false imagination." From it, the afflictions that are to be relinquished through [the path of] meditation originate. Since the condition of this [afflicted mind] also stains the six collections [of consciousness], the afflictions to be relinquished through [the path of] seeing arise [from it] too.[721]

For this reason, there are three aspects to mentation: (a) the aspect of stains, which is produced through the afflicted mind, (b) the sixth, the mental consciousness, which specifically focuses on [the above-mentioned mental] phenomena as its objects, and [25a] (c) the immediate [mind] that serves as the momentary locus of the arising and ceasing of all consciousnesses. The first is the imaginary [nature], which is absolutely nonexistent. The second appears in accordance with the five [sense] doors but is empty of nature. The third is the mere aspect of the stirring of the consciousnesses that are either factors to be relinquished or their remedies.[722]

Since, in its nature, it is just dependent origination without conception, **mind is** also the **principal** of all **phenomena**. Hence, having realized it in this way, **conceptions and** what they **conceptualize** due to characteristics—all conceptions about the external and the internal—**are relinquished** and mind [is found to] not exist by a nature of its own. Therefore, it is to be realized as the **dharmadhātu**, which is all **phenomena**—be they conditioned, unconditioned, bright, or dark—**lacking a nature**. [On the paths of accumulation and preparation,] **you should cultivate** this through aspiring [for it]. In terms of direct perception [from the path of seeing onward], this is the samādhi of the appearance of nonconceptual wisdom, which is prajñāpāramitā.[723] Thus, the *[Prajñāpāramitā]saṃcayagāthā* says:

> When conditioned, unconditioned, bright, and dark phenomena
> Are scrutinized by prajñā and not even an atom [of them] is
> observable,
> Then, within the worlds, the ranks of prajñāpāramitā are entered.[724]

This is discussed in detail in the *Avikalpa[praveśadhāraṇī]*. By summarizing the way to mentally engage in this, noble Maitreya said in the *Dharmadharmatāvibhāga*:

Through not knowing suchness,
"That which has all seeds"—
Which are unreal but completely imaginary—
Is the cause of nonexistents appearing as duality.
Through the different causes that are based on that,
Causes together with their results
Appear but do not exist.
With that appearing, the nature of phenomena does not appear.
Through that not appearing, [25b] the nature of phenomena appears.
If they engage their minds properly in this way,
Bodhisattvas will enter
Into nonconceptual wisdom.[725]

2.2.2.1.3. The way to realize that [the nonconceptual experience of the six consciousnesses] is in itself [the inseparability of being] luminous and empty

[This is taught by] two verses.

What you see and hear and smell,
What you taste and touch, phenomena as well—
Once yogins realize them in this way,
The characteristics are complete. [44]

As taught above, in their own essence, the six objects and [their respective] consciousnesses are mere appearances of dependent origination, free from arising and ceasing. At the point when that is realized, **the characteristics** of the thought-free and unmistaken perception of **yogins are complete**.[726] Likewise,

Eyes and ears and also nose,
Tongue and body, mind as well—
The six āyatanas fully pure,
This is true reality's own mark. [45]

Also the six inner āyatanas, in their own essence, have this mark of being fully pure in that they appear yet lack a nature. Also Saraha puts it like that [in his *Dohākośagīti*]:

In front, behind, and in the ten directions,
Whatever you see is true reality.[727]

2.2.2.1.4. Instruction that the nature of saṃsāra and nirvāṇa consists in realizing or not realizing mind

[This is taught by] two verses.

> **Mind as such is seen as two:**
> **Worldly and beyond the world.** [46ab]

This is the brief introduction. Since **mind** is tainted by the latent tendencies of skandhas, dhātus, and āyatanas, it is **worldly**—saṃsāra. Once the stains of the latent tendencies have become pure, it is nirvāṇa. The detailed explanation of this [follows in the next six lines]:

> **Clinging** [**to it**] **as a self, it is saṃsāra—**
> **In your very own awareness, true reality.** [**46cd**]
>
> **Since desire is extinguished, it is nirvāṇa.**
> **Hatred and ignorance are extinguished** [**too**].
> **Since these have ceased, it's buddhahood itself,** [26a]
> **The very refuge for all beings.** [47]

If someone possesses the **clinging to** mind **as** being **a self**, the clinging to the six objects as being something other arises. Under this influence, the entirety of karma and afflictions is produced, through which the wheel of **saṃsāra** appears like an illusion. For this reason, through the **desire, hatred, and ignorance** of the six collections of consciousness having become pure, the path of seeing is actually attained. When the afflicted mind that obscures pure mentation and the ālaya-consciousness **is extinguished** [on the eighth bhūmi], great poised readiness[728] is attained. And once the ālaya-consciousness itself has become relinquished and pure, **it** becomes omniscient **buddhahood**. This is **the** genuine **refuge for all beings.**[729] As the *[Mahāyāna]sūtrālaṃkāra* says:

> Mind is what appears as twofold:
> It appears as desire and such, and likewise,
> It appears as confidence and so on.
> There is no other phenomenon that is affliction and virtue.
>
> Mind appears as variety
> And operates in various ways.
> What appears in it exists, but there is nothing [extrinsic to it].
> Therefore, this is not [an existence] of phenomena.[730]

2.2.2.1.5. Explaining the meaning of the rūpakāya

> **Due to realization and its lack,**
> **All is in this very body.**
> **Through our own conceptions, we are bound,**
> **But when knowing our nature, we are free.** [48]

Since the stains of mind have become pure in this way, it is suitable that it becomes buddhahood. However, in the common yāna, [people] think that the body, which comes forth from conditions, such as one's parents, is impure and frightening. Therefore, since it is precisely what is to be relinquished, in its own essence, the skandha of form is without any purity. In order to eliminate such mistaken [thinking], it is only **due to** the difference between **realization and its lack** that the rūpakāya of buddhahood, which is the fundamental change of state, is expressed in two [ways]—"the body with stains and without stains." [26b] However, **all** the qualities of the rūpakāya exist **in this very body** [that appears to be stained]. Just as a blue beryl within its covering, **we are bound through** the fetters of **our own conceptions** and thus do not see these qualities. **But when knowing** that we are released from the fetters of **our nature, we are** the completely **free** rūpakāya.[731] This is discussed in detail in the *Mahāyānasaṃgraha*:

> From among the fundamental changes of state, due to the skandha of form having changed its state, there is mastery over the major and minor marks, pure [buddha] realms . . .[732]

2.2.2.1.6. Explaining the meaning of enlightenment

> **Enlightenment is neither far nor near,**
> **And neither does it come nor go.**
> **It's whether it is seen or not**
> **Right in the midst of our afflictions.** [49]

Due to the stains of both body and mind having become completely pure, the conventional expression "enlightenment is attained" is applied. However, **enlightenment is neither near**—being obscured by the fetters of the afflictions of thoughts, it is as far away as light and darkness are—**nor** is enlightenment **far**, since it is the pure essence of body and mind. Therefore, the difference [between sentient beings and Buddhas] consists of nothing but the difference between **seeing** this very web **of our afflictions or not seeing** it.[733] Hence, all of saṃsāra and nirvāṇa is mere dependent origination, without arising and without ceasing, free from all reference points. As the *Śūnyatāsaptati* says:

> Since all entities are empty of nature,
> The incomparable Tathāgata
> Taught this dependent origination
> With respect to entities.[734]

2.2.2.1.7. Instruction on the meaning of the sūtras

> **By dwelling in the lamp of prajñā,**
> **It turns into peace supreme.**
> **So the collection of the sūtras says:**
> **"By exploring your self, you should rest!" [50]**

[27a] Thus, the prajñā of realization [that comes] from the power of gathering the completely pure collection of causes—the correct view (understanding the way of being of the two realities) as well as calm abiding and superior insight—is **the lamp of prajñā**. Eventually, **it turns into** the essence of buddhahood, which is **peace supreme**. [Thus,] the Bhagavat said in all **sūtras: "By exploring your** naturally pure **self, you should rest!"** Since [this verse] instructs on the way in which, **by dwelling in** nonconceptual wisdom like that, the light of wisdom arises and manifests profusely, it needs to be spoken of.[735]

2.2.2.2. Explaining the way in which the conditions [for realizing the dharmadhātu]—the [three] jewels—appear

This has five parts:
1) Brief introduction
2) The way of not seeing Buddhas
3) The way of seeing [Buddhas]
4) Inconceivable enlightened activity
5) Explaining the meaning of enlightenment being neither near nor far

2.2.2.2.1. Brief introduction

> **Children blessed by tenfold powers' force,**
> **[See them] like the crescent of the moon,**
> **But those beings with afflictions**
> **Do not see Tathāgatas at all. [51]**

[The ten powers of a Buddha are] (1) knowing what is the case and what is not, (2) knowing the maturations of karma, (3) knowing the various constitutions [of sentient beings], (4) knowing [their] inclinations, (5) knowing afflicted and purified phenomena, (6) knowing the superior and inferior faculties [of sentient beings], (7) [knowing their] former places [of rebirth], (8) [knowing their future deaths and rebirths through] the divine eye, (9) knowing the termination of contamination, and (10) knowing the paths that lead everywhere [in saṃsāra and into nirvāṇa]. Through being **blessed by the force of the ten powers** in this way, in the beginning, [ordinary beings who are like children] will see the Tathāgatas appearing as if there were a [distinct] subject and object, that is, only [as much as one sees] **the** [new] **crescent of the moon.**[736] **But those** whose minds are obscured by afflictions, **do not** even **see** the thought, "This is a reflection of the **Tathāgatas**" [cross their minds]. [27b] As Maitreya states [in his *Mahāyānasūtrālaṃkāra*]:

> Just as a container with water, when broken,
> Does not display the reflection of the moon,
> In lower sentient beings,
> The image of the Buddha does not show.[737]

2.2.2.2.2. The way of not seeing Buddhas

[This is taught by] two verses. [The first presents] the example [illustrating] that we are never separated from the Buddhas at any time but do not see them due to the bondage of the obscurations.

> **Just as ghosts with thirst and hunger**
> **See the ocean to be dry,** [52ab]

Those who are born as hungry ghosts, tormented by thirst, know that there had been an inexhaustible [quantity of] water in the ocean before when they had been born as humans. [However,] when they go there [now driven] by [this recollection], because of their obscurations, they see the ocean to be dry, but the ocean did, [of course,] not go anywhere. Likewise,

> **Those obscured by ignorance**
> **Think that Buddhas don't exist.** [52cd]

Those who do not possess the blessings of the [five] powers, such as confidence,[738] in their own continua and whose mind streams are burned by the affliction of **ignorance think that** Tathāgatas **do not exist,** whereas they are never separated from them at any time. Some may feel, "It is just fine to see them once in while." Even if you [merely] see them, what good is that? It is just like not seeing them at all. To instruct on that, [the next verse says:]

> **What's the Bhagavat supposed to do**
> **For inferiors and those whose merit's low?**
> **It's just like the supreme of jewels**
> **Put in the hand of one who's blind.** [53]

Those who are **inferior** [in general] are the childish beings in the lower realms and the pleasant realms, but **those whose merit is low** [in the human realm] are barbarians, people born blind, those who have wrong views, and so on. Even if they see the **Bhagavat, what** good is that to them? Since they will simply again entertain wrong cravings and lack confidence [upon meeting a Buddha], it is [even] possible that this turns into a condition for [them to commit] bad actions. [28a] And even if that is not the case, **just like** a blue beryl **put in the hand of one who is blind, it is** of no benefit at all and will just be a waste.[739]

2.2.2.2.3. Explaining the way of seeing Buddhas

[The next] four verses [explain] how [Buddhas] appear, [what they] do, what the purpose is [of that], and the final mode of being. Through these four, wisdom is to be understood. First,

> **But for beings who acquired merit,**
> **The Buddha dwells before their eyes,**
> **With the thirty-two marks shining bright**
> **In their luminous and glorious light.**[740] [54]

[There are also] those **beings** whose mind streams are endowed with the five dharmas, such as confidence, and [who have gathered] the accumulation of **merit**. Due to that, the **glorious** kāya that has the nature of **light** and is embellished with **the** major and minor **marks** manifests. The major marks appear as they are described in the [prajñā]pāramitā [sūtras]:

> It is (1) marked with wheels on hands and feet, and (2) has tortoiselike feet.
> (3) Fingers and toes are joined by webs,
> (4) Hands and feet are soft and supple,
> (5) The body has seven convex surfaces,

(6) Long fingers, (7) broad heels, and is (8) tall and straight.
(9) It has nonprotruding ankles, (10) body hairs that point upward,
(11) Antelopelike calves, (12) long and beautiful arms,
(13) And is the supreme of those whose sexual organ is covered by a sheath.

(14) The skin has a golden hue and (15) is delicate.
(16) It has well-grown body hairs, each one single by itself and curling to the right,
(17) The face is adorned with the ūrṇā-hair, and (18) the upper body is lionlike.
(19) It has evenly rounded shoulders, (20) with compact flesh in between,

(21) And even unpleasant tastes appear as the most delicious tastes for it.
(22) Its figure has symmetrical proportions like the nyagrodha [tree][741],
(23) It has an uṣṇīṣa on the head, (24) a large and beautiful tongue,
(25) A melodious voice like Brahmā, (26) jaws like a lion,

(27) Very white teeth of (28) equal size, (29) well arranged,
And (30) in a complete set of forty, [28b]
(31) Dark-blue eyes, and (32) eyelashes like those of a magnificent heifer.
These are the thirty-two marks.[742]

You may wonder, "What does the appearance of this [kāya] do?"

Though the protector's rūpakāya
May remain for many eons,
For guiding those in need of guidance,
This very dhātu shows as different.[743] [55]

The [rūpakāyas] appear to guide [specific beings] by **remaining** for exactly as long or short a time as it takes to mature their mind streams. In that this completely bright wisdom of their own appears as an object, there is a slight factor of dualistic apprehension. Therefore, [the rūpakāyas] indeed appear in this way, but it is not that the dharma**dhātu** and wisdom are **different** ultimately.

Therefore, [the next verse] teaches what the purpose is.

Ascertaining the object of the mind,
Consciousness will engage in it.

Once your very own awareness becomes pure,
You will dwell right in the bhūmis' nature. [56]

By seeing the kāyas of Buddhas, hearing the dharmas of the mahāyāna, smelling the scent of ethics, tasting the pleasure of the dharma, and touching upon the tangible object of samādhi, finely analyzing prajñā examines all phenomena. These six doors are **the mind's object**, which is considered to be wisdom. Therefore, **it** is what **consciousness will engage in**. Through entering into and resting more and more within this pure **awareness of your very own**, you will dwell in a completely pure [way] **in** all paths and **bhūmis**.[744] Thus, this is expressed by the conventional term "**dwelling.**"

The final mode of being [is taught in the next verse].

The great and mighty ones' supreme abode,
Akaniṣṭha that's so beautiful,
And consciousness, all three of them,
Fuse into a single one, I say. [57]

It is explained that, once self-aware wisdom—[29a] the completely pure dharmadhātu—has reached its culmination, the wisdom of the rūpakāyas and [the form of] the sambhoga[kāya] in the **abode of the great and mighty** bodhisattvas—the **Akaniṣṭha** of the form realm—appear. [This presentation] and what is said in the Buddhāvataṃsakasūtra about the great Akaniṣṭha of the dharmadhātu are indeed explained as if they were different. However, actually, [all that is spoken of here] does not [actually] exist as any external referent in the way [it is described]. Rather, it is due to the aspect of the stains on the essence of one's own mind having become pure or not that wisdom merely appears in [two] aspects, as if it were an object and a [perceiving] subject. In the final picture, since the **three consciousnesses fuse into a single one**, all Buddhas are equal through the three equalities.[745] Therefore, **I**, the noble great being Nāgārjuna, say that also the appearances in the consciousnesses of those who engage in yoga do not exist as anything other than [just these consciousnesses] themselves.

Here, the three [kinds of] consciousness are the [six] consciousnesses that operate with entities, the mentation that dwells in the ālaya[-consciousness], and the ālaya-consciousness. You may wonder, "How do they fuse?" Through [practitioners] purifying their operating consciousnesses on the bhūmi of engagement through aspiration,[746] the nirmāṇakāya is displayed [for them]. Through purifying the mentation that dwells in the ālaya-consciousness from having entered [the first of] the bhūmis of pure superior intention[747] up through the seventh bhūmi, the sambhogakāya appears. Through the ālaya-consciousness becoming pure on the three pure bhūmis, the dharmakāya appears. Thus, [the bhūmis] are attained just as [these kāyas] appear, and through such attainment, mastery is gained. This is expressed [in line 56d] as the conventional term "having arrived at their very **nature**." Therefore, the enlightened activity of the buddhakāyas and wisdoms, at the same time, appears as if it existed externally and [yet] is without any real existence in the outside. Consequently, you should know that it is the light rays and the enlightened activity of your own dharmakāya.[748] [29b] Thus, the meaning of this accords with what is stated in the *[Sarvabuddhaviṣayāvatāra]jñānālokālaṃkārasūtra*[749] and the *Uttaratantra*:

> Likewise, in those with unstained confidence and such
> By having cultivated the qualities of confidence and so on,
> What appears in their own minds are the perfect Buddhas,
> Endowed with the major and minor marks.
>
> These Buddhas] are walking, standing,
> Sitting, and sleeping,
> Performing all kinds of conduct,
> Speaking the dharma of peace,
>
> Resting in meditative equipoise in speechless reality,
> And demonstrating all kinds of miraculous displays.
> Possessed of great splendor,
> [The Buddhas] will be seen by sentient beings.
>
> Having seen them, those who have the wish
> Will devote their efforts to this "buddhahood."
> Correctly adopting its causes,
> They will attain the state they long for.
>
> These appearances are utterly
> Without thought and movement.
> Nevertheless, they manifest
> With great benefits in the worlds.
>
> Ordinary beings surely do not understand
> That these are appearances of their own minds.
> Nevertheless, seeing these forms
> Becomes fruitful for them.

By relying on gradually seeing these [forms],
Those who dwell in this principle
Will see the genuine dharmakāya
Right in their middle through the eye of wisdom.[750]

2.2.2.2.4. Explaining inconceivable enlightened activity

[This is taught by] three verses. First, in order to instruct on the meaning of omniscience, [the text says:]

As for knowing all among the childish,
The diversity among the noble, [58ab]

For the sake of sentient beings without realization, [the Buddhas] demonstrate omniscience and guide them. **Among the noble**, they show infinite displays of samādhi. [All of this] is the power of their mastery of pure mind. Furthermore,

And the great and mighty, infinite in time—
What's the cause of time in eons? [58cd]

[30a] The **time**[spans] of **the great and mighty** Akaniṣṭha and those [who dwell] in Akaniṣṭha are indeed sixty million great **eons**. [The Buddhas] also teach **what the cause of** that **is** and they teach what is even more **infinite** than that as well, which is the mode [of such timespans] as they, in particular, are found in the *Avataṃsakasūtra*. [There, a single one] of such eons is counted as one full day, and then an eon [consisting] of such [days] is again counted as [merely] one full day. This same way [of counting] is repeated thirteen times. Through having mastered [teaching like that], wisdom springs forth.[751]

For sustaining the duration,
During eons truly infinite,
Of [all] beings' outer realms
And for creatures' life-force to remain,
This is what's the inexhaustive cause. [59]

[The infinite dharmadhātu is also the cause] **that sustains** the continuum of **the duration** of the inconceivable manner in which **all outer realms of sentient beings**, due to the factor of their not realizing their own wisdom, dependently originate **during infinite**, inexpressible **eons** without showing a beginning or an end. Also, the **life-force of creatures** originates in dependence on what is called "akṣara"[752]—the principle of being unborn and unceasing. Therefore, the manner in which their life-force **remains is this** point of being **inexhaustive**. Hence, through realizing dependent origination, one should realize that the nature of saṃsāra is inseparable from nirvāṇa.[753] Therefore, [the next verse] says:

> **In that whose fruition's inexhaustible,**
> **Through the special trait of nonappearance,**
> **Engage in full for prajñā's sake. [60]**

Since the **fruition** that [comes forth] from the cause of realizing that saṃsāra and nirvāṇa do not exist as two knows **no exhaustion**, it is held to be similar [in this respect] to the end of saṃsāra, [which will never occur either]. Therefore, **through the trait of** the **non**existence of the duality of apprehender and apprehended, which was taught above, [30b] those with insight should **engage in that** [cause] **for the sake of** the **prajñā** that manifests the path of seeing. In this way, the revelation of this [fact that] inexhaustible saṃsāra—the realms of sentient beings—and inexhaustible buddha wisdom are unborn and unceasing demonstrates the inconceivability of the dharmadhātu.[754] As the *Yuktiṣaṣṭikā* says:

> [Saṃsāric] existence and nirvāṇa—
> These two are not to be found.
> It is just the true understanding of existence
> That is expressed as "nirvāṇa."[755]

2.2.2.2.5. The way in which enlightenment, due to such realization, is neither near nor far

> **Don't think enlightenment is far away,**
> **And don't conceive it as close by.**
> **With the sixfold objects not appearing,**
> **It's awareness of reality just as it is. [61]**

Since unsurpassable **enlightenment** is the realization of saṃsāra's nature, **don't think** that it **is far away**. Since there is absolutely no being enlightened in those who are involved in apprehender and apprehended, **do not conceive it as close by**. If there is **no appearing** of any characteristics of **the sixfold objects** [that would qualify them] as [external] referents, there simply are none. [Consequently,] if there is no appearance of the six apprehending consciousnesses, there is no arising and ceasing [of them]. Therefore, the seventh [consciousness]—mentation—does not exist [either]. And if [all of] those do not exist, also the ālaya-consciousness that is produced by them does not arise. Therefore, mind does not exist. The direct realization of this by being **aware** of and realizing it as **it really is** is buddhahood.[756] This is also stated in [Nāgārjuna's] *Lokātītastava*:

> Without being known, nothing is a knowable object,
> But consciousness does not [exist] without that.
> Therefore, You said that, by a nature of their own,
> Knowledge and knowable object do not exist.[757]

Master [Nāgārjuna]'s own *Bhāvanākrama* says:

> By relying on mere mind,
> One does not imagine outer objects.
> By resting in the observed object of suchness, [31a]
> One should go beyond mere mind too.
>
> Going beyond mere mind,
> One must even go beyond nonappearance.
> The yogin who rests in nonappearance
> Sees the mahāyāna.[758]

Master Candrakīrti declares [in his *Madhyamakāvatāra*]:

> The dry firewood of knowable objects having been burned entirely,
> This peace is the dharmakāya of the victors.
> At this point, there is neither arising nor ceasing.
> The cessation of mind is revealed through this kāya.[759]

The *[Mahāyāna]sūtrālaṃkāra* reads:

> The mind is aware that nothing other than mind exists.
> Then, it is realized that mind does not exist either.
> The intelligent are aware that both do not exist
> And abide in the dharmadhātu in which they are absent.[760]

All of these statements have the same meaning, which can be phrased as follows: "Once the eight collections of consciousness have become pure and relinquished, they appear as the direct perception of buddha wisdom." But it is not said [here] that "the wisdom-kāya and its enlightened activity do not exist either."

This completes the explanation of the way to meditate [section 2.2.2.], which includes the way in which the conditions [for realizing the dharmadhātu]—the [three] jewels—appear [subsection 2.2.2.2.].

2.2.3. Explaining how the manner of manifesting and attaining the path arises from having become familiar [with the dharmadhātu] in this way

This has five parts:
1) Needing to understand the manner of adopting and rejecting
2) The remedy for saṃsāra
3) The remedy for peace
4) The dharmas that make the basic element unfold
5) The sequence of the manner in which it unfolds

2.2.3.1. Needing to understand the manner of adopting and rejecting

> **Just as from a mix of milk and water**
> **That is present in a vessel,**
> **Geese just sip the milk but not the water,**
> **Which remains just as it is. [62]**
>
> **Just so, being covered by afflictions,**
> **Wisdom dwells within this body, one [with them].**
> **But yogins just extract the wisdom**
> **And leave the ignorance behind. [63]**

For example, [according to Indian tradition,] **geese** [are able to] separate **milk** from **water** [31b] and **sip** [just the milk]. **Just so,** buddha **wisdom** [in its two aspects of knowing] suchness and variety **dwells within this** mind and **body, being covered by afflictions. But** through the stains, it seems as if it is not clearly manifest and mixed [with them]. Through relying on the correct condition—hearing the dharma that distinguishes what to adopt and what to reject (the natural outflow of the compassion of the Buddhas), which is just our own stainless cognizance—it so happens that **yogins extract the wisdom and leave the** stains of **ignorance behind.**[761] This is how the manner of adopting and rejecting appears, which is called "the path of accumulation," since, based upon the accumulation of merit, the accumulation of wisdom is realized and adopted.

2.2.3.2. Instruction on the remedy for saṃsāra

As long as we still cling to "self" and "mine,"
We will conceive of outer [things] through this.
But once we see the double lack of self,
The seeds of our existence find their end. [64]

When sentient beings **cling to** a **self and** think of the person as being something real, they are mistaken. Hence, there is no self in the person.[762] Their thinking **conceives of** conditioned phenomena that appear as objects to be outer [things, saying,] "[These] are **mine**," thus clinging to all phenomena as arising and ceasing. In order to overcome this, it is taught that all phenomena **lack** a **self** [or real identity]. Through realizing this **double** [lack of identity] just as it is, **the seeds of existence** in the three realms **find their end**, and what is supramundane is realized. Therefore, this Mother that is the realization of identitylessness is the one who gives birth to all four [kinds of] noble ones. Śrāvakas realize the identitylessness of the person. [On top of that,] pratyekabuddhas realize phenomenal identitylessness with regard to the apprehended referents. Bodhisattvas realize [twofold] identitylessness, by [all of the above] plus the conceptions about the apprehender having become pure. Therefore, it is extensively stated in the [prajñā]pāramitā [sūtras] [32a] that "those who wish to train in the bhūmis of the śrāvakas should listen to just this prajñāpāramitā . . . ," [the same being repeated for] "those who wish to train in the bhūmis of the pratyekabuddhas," "in the bhūmis of bodhisattvas," and "in the knowledge of all aspects."[763] Hence, it is to be realized deeply that all phenomena are without nature, which should be done just as it is discussed in detail in [Nāgārjuna's] collection of reasoning. Thereafter, in order to relinquish being headed for the extreme of [personal nirvāṇic] peace, through the mode of being of buddhahood and great compassion and for the sake of accomplishing the wisdom-kāya, [Nāgārjuna] taught the unsurpassable attainment. Thus, he makes us realize the dharmadhātu.

2.2.3.3. Instruction on the remedy for peace

Since it is the ground for buddhahood, nirvāṇa,
Purity, permanence, and virtue too,
And because the childish think of two,
In the yoga of their nonduality, please rest. [65]

Since even the noble ones who realize the two [kinds of] identitylessness [still] have the ground of the latent tendencies of ignorance, uncontaminated karma, a body of mental nature, and the inconceivable death and transition, they fall a bit short of fully reaching the dharmadhātu, [that is, they do not realize the actual dharmakāya]. Thus, the dharmakāya is the **nirvāṇa** that consists of the four pāramitās of genuine **purity**, genuine self, genuine bliss, and genuine **permanence**. Therefore, it is taught that, in comparison with these, even [the notions of] impermanence, emptiness, suffering, and lack of self are mistaken. Hence, the actuality of the dharmakāya abides in a profound way. You may wonder, "**Because** of what is that so?" **The childish think of** saṃsāra and nirvāṇa as being **two**, whereas **buddhahood** has the nature of the **nonduality** of saṃsāra and nirvāṇa. Therefore, you should know how to **rest in the yoga of that.**[764] [32b] The great master Asaṅga reports that this is discussed in detail in the *Śrīmālādevīsūtra*:

> Since arhats, pratyekabuddhas, and bodhisattvas who have attained mastery[765] have not relinquished the ground of the latent tendencies of ignorance, they [still] possess the latent traces of the stench of the afflictions. Therefore, they have not attained the final culmination of purity. Based on that, they possess subtle [kinds of] engaging in the reference points of characteristics. Therefore, they have not attained the unconditioned pāramitā of self. Based on the uncontaminated karma that is triggered by these causes and conditions, they come to have a body whose nature is mental. Therefore, they have not attained the pāramitā of the utter bliss of such a [body] having ceased. For as long as they have not manifested the basic element of the Tathāgatas in which [all of] the [above] have ceased, they are not free from the death and transition that are inconceivable changes. Therefore, they have not attained the pāramitā of changeless permanence.[766]

Furthermore, the teachings on emptiness as the remedy for the clinging to characteristics of entities are very profound. To speak here about other-awareness, self-awareness, kāyas, and wisdom by mentally superimposing [any notions of these arising from] themselves, others, both, or without a cause and so forth, and thus clinging to them as being real is what mistakenness is all about. Therefore, such is to be put to an end in all respects. [However,] if ordinary beings, based on such teachings, fixate solely on emptiness as being the supreme and thus reject dependent origination, they are done for. As the *Mūla[madhyamakakārikā]prajñā[nāma]* says:

> By the flaw of having views about emptiness, [33a]
> Those of little prajñā are ruined,

> Just as when incorrectly seizing a snake
> Or mistakenly practicing an awareness-mantra.[767]

The *Yuktiṣaṣṭikā* states:

> Those who do not understand the meaning of voidness,
> But engage in mere studying
> Without practicing any merit,
> Such base people are ruined.[768]

Furthermore, even though they are noble ones, śrāvakas and pratyekabuddhas only like the expanse of [their own] peace. In order for them to enter the mahāyāna and take a rest from being worn out by saṃsāra, the teachings in [sūtras such as] the *[Saddharma]puṇḍarīka*[769] are given. In order for bodhisattvas on the path of seeing, on the sixth bhūmi, and also on the eighth bhūmi to not fall into [this kind of peace], the point that the Buddha Bhagavats exhort them in a single moment also represents the point of the [Buddha] heart's wisdom having to be revealed. For this reason, [a sūtra quoted in the *Ratnagotravibhāgavyākhyā*] says:

> Just as in a sky tainted by clouds, here, you are not seen completely
> Even by those noble ones who have the pure eyes of insight, [yet still] limited discernment.
> But, Bhagavat, those whose insight is infinite behold your dharmakāya in its entirety,
> Which pervades the vast space of infinite knowable objects.[770]

This topic is also extensively discussed in other [sources], but [what I said so far] is enough of an elaboration. In brief, you should not think that the dharmadhātu is nothing but empty.

2.2.3.4. Teaching that the basic element—the particularly pure abode—is to be unfolded

This has three parts:
1) Identifying the dharmas that make the basic element unfold
2) [The manner in which] enlightenment is accomplished due to that
3) Being guarded by the victors

2.2.3.4.1. Identifying the dharmas that make the basic element unfold

The next three verses teach that the ten pāramitās [33b] cause the unfolding of the nature of the basic element, which, in terms of its own essence, is [already] pure and attained. Something like the qualities of a gem unfolding through the removal of its coverings is what is referred to as "purity" [here].[771] [Also,] in the manner of dependent origination, something like a tree comes forth from a fruit, or, something like a harvest from seeds. [Here,] such is referred to by the conventional term "attainment." The inseparability of these two [—purity and attainment—] is then called "wisdom-kāya," which is nothing but the dharmakāya.

Therefore, [the line]

> **Generosity's multiple hardships, [66a]**

refers to the generation of bodhicitta endowed with aspiration, which is the activity of bodhisattvas and the principle of nonattachment in the generosity of material goods, the generosity of protecting [others], and the generosity of dharma. [The next line]

> **Ethics gathering beings' good, [66b]**

means that the **ethics** of bodhisattvas in terms of vows, their **ethics** of gathering virtuous dharmas, and their ethics of promoting the **good of beings** are not [motivated by] the wish for their own pleasures within [saṃsāric] existence.

> **And patience benefitting beings—**
> **Through these three, the dhātu blooms. [66cd]**

[This refers to the patience of] not taking offense with anyone who inflicts harm upon oneself, the **patience** of taking on the suffering that [arises through practicing] what is virtuous, and the patience of mind being certain about the dharma of emptiness, that is, not being afraid of it. [The pāramitā of patience] serves as an aide for the former two [pāramitās]. Thus, **these three**, which are called "the accumulation of merit that originates from generosity and ethics," are the dharmas that make the basic element of the rūpakāya **bloom**.[772]

> **Enthusiastic vigor for all dharmas,**
> **Mind that enters meditative poise,**
> **Prajñā as your permanent resort—**
> **These too make enlightenment unfold. [67]**

Through the armor[like] **vigor**, [the vigor] of engagement, and [the vigor] of final emancipation,[773] all qualities are brought forth. [34a] **Meditative poise** is what makes one attain mundane and supramundane samādhis, connecting with the special abode [of the form realm] and also **entering** the formless [meditative absorptions].[774] **Prajñā** is the [threefold] prajñā that thoroughly discriminates mundane and supramundane phenomena, is not attached to anything in saṃsāra and nirvāṇa, and merges into nonconceptual wisdom. **These** [three] represent the special merit that originates from meditation and the accumulation of wisdom, which **make** the basic element in terms of both kāyas **unfold**. Once these six pāramitās are embraced by prajñā, they [all] become the accumulation of wisdom. As for their essence, the two [pāramitās of] generosity and ethics are the accumulation of merit, while prajñā is the accumulation of wisdom. The three of patience, vigor, and samādhi represent both. As the *[Mahāyāna]sūtrālaṃkāra* says:

> Generosity and ethics are the accumulation of merit,
> While prajñā is the one of wisdom.
> The three others are [the accumulation] of both,
> And all five [can] also be the accumulation of wisdom.[775]

> **Prajñā that is joined with means,**
> **Aspiration prayers very pure,**
> **A firm stand in power, wisdom too—**
> **These four dharmas make the dhātu bloom. [68]**

Through being endowed with skill in **means**—the dedication [of merit], imaginative willpower,[776] and rejoicing [in others' virtue]—**prajñā** is made swifter and vaster. **Aspiration prayers** are [the pāramitā] connected to speech, in order to accomplish the skill in means for the arising and increasing [of all qualities of the path], so that they become inexhaustible. As for **power**, it is the power of discrimination and meditation that makes [the dharmadhātu] unfold. **Wisdom** accomplishes the welfare of oneself and others through [its two aspects of knowing] suchness and variety. Therefore, **these four make the** completely pure basic element **bloom**.[777]

On the paths of accumulation and preparation, through the armor[like accomplishment] and the accomplishment of engagement,[778] one engages in practicing [the pāramitās] in an approximate manner. [34b] After that, they are practiced properly. That means, on the seven impure bhūmis, [they are practiced] in a way that [still] entails some reference points and on the three [pure bhūmis], in a nonreferential manner. On the bhūmi of a Buddha, they are said to be spontaneously present without effort.

As for their functions, generosity holds all sentient beings in your care. Ethics renders all harm nonexistent. Through patience, you bear with everything. Vigor makes the qualities increase. Through meditative poise, you introduce [others to the dharma] with the help of miraculous powers and so forth. Prajñā liberates the mind streams of all [beings]. Means render [everything virtuous] inexhaustible. Through aspiration prayers, you always engage in pleasing the Buddhas. Through power, you are victorious over antagonistic factors. Wisdom brings sentient beings to complete maturity. The *Madhyāntavibhāga* says:

> The functions are holding in one's care,
> Not harming, bearing with such,
> Increase of qualities, being able to introduce,
> Leading to liberation,
>
> Being inexhaustible, always engaging,
> Securing, and enjoying as well as maturing.[779]

In [Nāgārjuna's text] here, the essences, the classification, and the functions [of the ten pāramitās] are taught in brief. In detail, these are to be understood from what is said in [his] *Ratnāvalī* and *Sūtrasamucchaya*, master Śūra's *Pāramitāsamāsa*, and the chapter on the pāramitās in the *[Mahāyāna]sūtrālaṃkāra*. In brief, since all practices of all bodhisattvas are contained in these [pāramitās], they are explained to be "the dharmas that make the basic element unfold."

2.2.3.4.2. Explaining the manner in which enlightenment is accomplished due to that

[This is explained by] four verses. The first teaches that bodhicitta is the cause of the dharmakāya.

> **"To bodhicitta,[780] I pay no homage"—**
> **Saying such means speaking badly.**
> **Where there are no bodhisattvas,**
> **There will be no dharmakāya. [69]**

Enlightenment is buddhahood [35a] and the accomplishment of a great many activities out of the wish and the striving for it is **bodhicitta**, which has the character of aspiration and application. As the *Abhisamayālaṃkāra* says:

The wish for completely perfect enlightenment
For the welfare of others is bodhicitta.[781]

Bodhisattvas are those who, by relying on [bodhicitta], engage in this means to realize the ultimate, which is to be personally experienced, and the inseparability of emptiness and compassion. Whoever has no respect and **pays no homage** to this [bodhicitta], **speaks badly** and thus abandons the enlightenment of a Buddha. Therefore, if **there are no bodhisattvas, there is no** buddhahood that is the **dharmakāya**, since there is no result without a cause.

About this reasoning, some may think, "Since aspiration and application are conceptions, they are something newly produced. Therefore, also buddha wisdom is something newly attained that did not exist before." Since this is not appropriate, I will explain. Aspiration is the very wish for buddhahood. Application means to apply oneself to the causes [of buddhahood] out of the wish for it. These causes are two: the [actual] cause and the cause that is a [contributing] condition. The actual cause is naturally luminous mind as such, which is called "the basic element." The cause that is a condition is called both "the light rays of this very [mind]" and "the enlightened activity of the compassion of Buddhas, which is free from obscurations." This refers to the pāramitās, which are to be practiced with confidence and aspiration and have the character of determination, contact, and recollection.[782] It is not justified that one of these two [causes] is realized and manifested, if the other is not present. Thus, this is the two realities' own nature. [Here,] you should understand the meaning of what [the *Uttaratantra*] says:

Through mind's natural luminosity, they see that the afflictions are without nature.
Therefore, they truly realize that all beings are at peace, the ultimate lack of identity.
They see that perfect buddhahood is all-pervading, have an unobscured mind, [35b]
And are endowed with the vision of wisdom that has limitless beings' purity as its object. I bow down to them, [the noble saṅgha].[783]

Therefore, the second [two verses] instruct on [how this] is established [through] an example.

Some dislike the seeds of sugar cane
But still wish to relish sugar.
Without seeds of sugar cane,
There will be no sugar. [70]

When these seeds of sugar cane
Are well guarded, fostered, and refined,
Molassis, sugar, candy too
Will then come forth from them. [71]

[The following verse] teaches the meaning [of this example]. If you guard bodhicitta, which is like sugar cane, all fruitions of qualities will come forth.

With bodhicitta, it is just the same:
When it's guarded, fostered, and refined,
Arhats, conditioned realizers, Buddhas too
Will then arise and spring from it. [72]

In this way, in dependence upon **bodhicitta** and bodhisattvas, the **arhats** [of the śrāvakas manifest] through their afflictions and rebirths becoming exhausted. [The arhats of] the pratyekabuddhas [manifest] due to **realizing** enlightenment through **conditions** and thus become liberated on their own. Omniscient Buddhas [manifest] through realizing the final ultimate. Thus they all **spring from** the mind of bodhicitta. This is also stated by master Candrakīrti in his *Madhyamakāvatāra*:

Śrāvakas and middling buddhas issue from the mighty sages.
Buddhas are born from bodhisattvas.
A compassionate mind, nondual insight,
And bodhicitta are the causes for the victors' children.[784]

Furthermore, you may think here, "If even śrāvakas and pratyekabuddhas spring from bodhicitta in this way, what is the reason that they are not just like bodhisattvas?" This is to be explained as follows. [The *Abhisamayālaṃkāra*] says:

It is held that perfect buddhahood is easily realized
By the sharp but difficult to realize by the dull.[785]

Master Haribhadra's *[Abhisamayālaṃkāra]vivṛti* instructs:

Implicitly, this teaches that those with inferior faculties attain arhathood, those with medium [faculties] pratyekabuddhahood, and those with sharp [faculties] buddhahood.[786]

[36a] Here, it is said that there are five differences between śrāvakas and pratyekabuddhas [on the one hand] and bodhisattvas [and Buddhas on the

other]. [Maitreya] states that Buddhas and bodhisattvas differ [from the other two] in five respects: (1) being nonconceptual, (2) unlimited, (3) nonabiding, (4) perpetual,[787] and (5) unsurpassable. The wisdom of śrāvakas and pratyekabuddhas realizes saṃsāra as what is to be relinquished and peace as what is to be adopted. Since it [only] focuses on the four realities, it is limited. [Śrāvakas and pratyekabuddhas] pass into nirvāṇa [and remain there]. Their skandhas discontinue without a remainder and [their realizations] are surpassed by buddhahood. From the perspective of what the [śrāvakas and pratyekabuddhas] realize, Buddhas and bodhisattvas are certainly similar [to them]. However, different [from them], they do not conceptualize saṃsāra and nirvāṇa, since these [two] are equal [for them]. Since they know all knowable objects, [their wisdom] is unlimited. They do not abide in either saṃsāra or nirvāṇa. Since, after having become Buddhas, their kāyas, wisdoms, and enlightened activities are inexhaustible for as long as[788] saṃsāra [lasts], they are permanent. Since there is no one above them, they are unsurpassable. These [five differences] are discussed in the *Dharmadharmatāvibhāga*.[789] As for these differences and the certainty that [bodhisattvas] promote the welfare of sentient beings, the *Sāgaramati[paripṛcchā]sūtra*[790] says:

> When compared to the example of a boy falling into a pit of filth, Sāgaramati, the meaning of this example is as follows. "The pit of filth" stands for the three realms. "The only son" is an expression for sentient beings, since bodhisattvas think of all sentient beings as if they were their only son. "Mother and friends" are the terms for those who have entered the yānas of śrāvakas and pratyekabuddhas. They are those who, seeing the suffering of saṃsāra, are in agony and wail but are incapable of making any efforts to pull sentient beings out of it. [36b] "The householder who is a merchant" is an expression for bodhisattvas. They are those who are endowed with stainless minds in relation to what is pure and free from stains, who directly realize the unconditioned dharma, and who link up with the three realms as they please in order to completely mature sentient beings. Sāgaramati, though they are utterly liberated from all linking up [with saṃsāra], this [kind of] taking rebirth in existence is [due to] the great compassion of bodhisattvas. Since they are skilled in means and fully embraced by prajñā, they are not harmed by the afflictions. They also teach sentient beings the dharma in order to set them free from all fetters of the afflictions.

For this reason, [there follows the]

2.2.3.4.3. Instruction on being guarded by the victors

Just as farmers guarding
Seeds of rice and others,
Thus, the leaders guard all those
Who're aspiring to the supreme yāna. [73]

For example, when one has put **seeds of rice** into a field, the fruits come forth from **guarding** them well. **Thus,** since **aspiring to the supreme yāna** is the seed, the Buddhas and bodhisattvas **guard those who** have it. The manner of [doing so] is discussed in detail in the [prajñā]pāramitā [sūtras].

Thus, [the next point is] the outcome of having taught the dharmas through which the basic element is to be unfolded.

2.2.3.5. The sequence of the manner in which it unfolds

This has four parts, with [the first three representing] the brief introduction:
1) The manner of seeing by way of engagement through aspiration
2) The example of unfolding in those who have entered the bhūmis
3) The example for the ultimate
4) Detailed explanation

2.2.3.5.1. The manner of seeing by way of engagement through aspiration

Just as, on the fourteenth day of waning,
Just a little bit of moon is seen,
Those aspiring to the supreme yāna
Will see a tiny bit of buddhakāya. [74]

Just as in the example of the **waning moon** on the twenty-ninth [day of a lunar cycle] barely appearing, which is how it appears when being obscured, [37a] **those** on the beginner's bhūmi of **aspiration** see the **buddhakāya** as something outside. [One may] even [speak of] nonappearance. This means that, through causes such as one's own confidence, what appears as nirvāṇa and so forth appears **just a little bit**. However, since the appearance of the wisdom of one's own basic element is not realized due to conceptual obscurations, it appears like that [external buddhakāya].[791]

2.2.3.5.2. The example of unfolding once one has entered the bhūmis

Just as when the waxing moon
Is seen more in every moment,
Those who've entered on the bhūmis,
See its increase step by step. [75]

On the first **bhūmi**, the samādhi in which one's own nonconceptual wisdom appears is the attainment of the appearance of the dharmakāya. Therefore, through the power of that, on the outside, there will be an appearance of the wisdom of subsequent attainment seeing one hundred Tathāgatas, hearing them speak the dharma, retaining it, and so on.[792] Likewise, it is said that, on the second bhūmi, [the same] appears one hundred thousand times; on the third bhūmi, ten million times; [on the fourth, a hundred billion;][793] on the fifth, ten trillion; on the sixth, a thousand times as much as that; on the seventh bhūmi, ten quadrillion times as much; on the eighth bhūmi, in a number [equal to] the minute particles in one hundred thousand trichiliocosms; on the ninth, in a number [equal to] one hundred thousand countless times that; and on the tenth, countless and inexpressibly many times that.[794]

2.2.3.5.3. Teaching the example for the ultimate

On the fifteenth day of waxing,
Eventually, the moon is full.
Just so, when the bhūmis' end is reached,
The dharmakāya's full and clear. [76]

The full **moon**'s own maṇḍala **is full** and it spreads its light rays. **Just so**, once **the end of the** ten **bhūmis** is reached, the stainless **dharmakāya is full and** [37b] becomes equal with all Buddhas through the three equalities by fusing and becoming equal with all the maṇḍalas of the victors that display [the three types of nirmāṇakāya that display] arts and crafts, rebirths, or great enlightenment to the very limits of space.[795]

2.2.3.5.4. Detailed explanation

This has eleven parts:

1) The bhūmi of engagement through aspiration
2) Utter Joy
3) Stainless
4) Illuminating
5) Radiating
6) Difficult to Master
7) Facing

8) Gone Afar
9) Immovable
10) Excellent Insight
11) Cloud of Dharma

2.2.3.5.4.1. The bhūmi of engagement through aspiration

> **Having generated this mind truly**
> **Through continuous firm aspiration**
> **For the Buddha, dharma, and the saṅgha,**
> **Irreversibility shows time and again.** [77]

This is just as it is stated in the *Uttaratantra*. **Through** taking refuge in and [cultivating] irreversible **firm aspiration for the** three unsurpassable jewels from now until enlightenment, you **generate this mind** [of bodhicitta], which has the character of aspiration and application. Then, you **truly** [engage in] the pāramitās' armor[like accomplishment] and the accomplishment of engagement. **Having** done so, you will attain the irreversibility of the paths of accumulation and preparation, and the signs of being close to the **irreversibility** of the path of seeing will **show**.[796] These [two paths] are the phases of the [four] applications of mindfulness, the [four] correct exertions, the [four] limbs of miraculous powers, the five faculties, and the five powers.[797]

2.2.3.5.4.2. Instruction on entering the first bhūmi, Utter Joy

> **Through the ground of darkness all relinquished**
> **And the ground of brightness firmly seized,**
> **It is ascertained right at this point.**
> **Therefore, it is designated "Joy."** [78]

What has the nature **of darkness** are the six primary afflictions, among which view is fivefold. Therefore, [there are] ten factors to be **relinquished** through seeing, which are relinquished through realizing the [four] realities of the noble ones. [38a] **The ground of brightness** is called "ascertainment." To rely on the sūtra collections of the mahāyāna is the cause for the calm abiding and superior insight that are proper mental engagement. **Through seizing** that, **right at this point, ascertainment** refers to attaining and experiencing suchness in the manner of the direct perception of the path of seeing. Upon such realization, a special supramundane joy about the welfare of sentient beings being accomplished [through this] is attained. Therefore, the first bhūmi is called "Utter **Joy**."[798] The *[Mahāyāna]sūtrālaṃkāra* says:

> Upon seeing that enlightenment is near
> And the welfare of sentient beings is accomplished,
> Utter joy will arise.
> Therefore it is called "Utter Joy."[799]

The meaning that is described here is the meaning of utter joy. Master [Nāgārjuna] himself explains the meaning of this [topic of the bhūmis] in detail, [that is, in terms of] the meanings of their names, their natures, their qualities, which pāramitās constitute them, and the results of maturation of the rūpakāya [in his *Ratnāvalī*,] which says:

> The first of these is "Utter Joy,"
> Since the bodhisattvas are overjoyed,
> Have relinquished the three entanglements,[800]
> And are born in the lineage of the Tathāgatas.
>
> Through the maturation of those [qualities],
> The pāramitā of generosity becomes supreme,
> They shake a hundred worldly realms,[801]
> And become great lords of Jambudvīpa.[802]

2.2.3.5.4.3. Explaining the second bhūmi, The Stainless

> **What's been tainted through all times**
> **By the stains of passion and so forth**
> **And is pure [now], without stains,**
> **That is called "The Stainless One." [79]**

[On the second bhūmi, bodhisattvas] will be **without** the **stains** of the afflictions (**passion and so forth**), which means being without distorted ethics. [The *Mahāyānasūtrālaṃkāra*] says:

> Since it is free from the efforts of distorted ethics,
> It is called "The Stainless Bhūmi."[803]

[The *Ratnāvalī* states]:

> The second is called "The Stainless,"
> Since the actions of body, speech, and mind

Are all ten without stains
And since the [bodhisattvas] naturally abide in them.[804]
Through the maturation of those [qualities], [38b]
The pāramitā of ethics becomes supreme,
They become cakravartins who benefit beings
And are masters over the glorious precious seven.[805]

2.2.3.5.4.4. Explaining the third bhūmi, The Illuminating

Once the afflictions' web pulls back,
Stainless prajñā brightly shines.
This dispels all boundless darkness
And thus is The Illuminating. [80]

On this bhūmi, **once** most of the **stains** of the afflictions that are to be relinquished through meditation have **pulled back** too, the light of wisdom without any clinging **dispels** the **darkness** of the minds of infinite [numbers of] sentient beings. **Thus**, it becomes the vast radiance of the dharma. The [*Mahāyānasūtrālaṃkāra* says]:

Since it causes the great radiance of dharma,
It is The Illuminating.[806]

[The *Ratnāvalī* states]:

The third bhūmi is The Illuminating,
Since the peaceful light of wisdom dawns,
Samādhi and supernatural knowledge are brought forth,
And desire and hatred are completely exhausted.

Through the maturation of those [qualities],
They engage most excellently in the practice of patience
And become a skillful great sovereign of the gods
Who puts an end to passionate desire.[807]

2.2.3.5.4.5. Explaining the fourth bhūmi, The Radiant

It always gleams with light so pure
And is engulfed by wisdom's shine,
With [all] bustle being fully dropped.
Hence, this bhūmi's held to be The Radiant. [81]

Through the [thirty-seven] dharmas that concord with enlightenment, [here, bodhisattvas] have far removed themselves from the **bustle** of the distractions of a mind that entails apprehender and apprehended. Therefore, they are endowed with the cause for the **radiance** of the **wisdom** that realizes that there is no difference [between apprehender and apprehended]. The [*Mahāyānasūtrālaṃkāra* says]:

> Thus, the dharmas concordant with enlightenment
> Are like intensely burning light.
> Because it is endowed with these, this bhūmi
> Burns both [obscurations], thus being The Radiant.[808]

[The *Ratnāvalī* states:]

> The fourth is called "The Radiant,"
> Since the light of true wisdom shines [39a]
> And since the [bodhisattvas] particularly cultivate
> All dharmas concordant with enlightenment.
>
> Through the maturation of those [qualities],
> They become kings of the gods in Free from Strife[809]
> Who are skilled in overcoming
> Any arising of the views about a real personality.[810]

2.2.3.5.4.6. The fifth bhūmi, The Difficult to Master

> **It triumphs in science, sports, and arts and crafts,**
> **The full variety of samādhi's range,**
> **And over afflictions very hard to master.**
> **Thus, it is considered Difficult to Master.** [82]

[The bodhisattvas on this bhūmi] perform the activities of all the means to mature sentient beings, such as **arts and crafts**, and accomplish discordant [meditative states], such as peaceful **samādhis** and cessation, at the same time. Since this is **hard to master** but is accomplished [by them, this bhūmi] is called "**Difficult to Master**."[811] As the [*Mahāyānasūtrālaṃkāra*] says:

> Since they fully mature sentient beings
> And guard their own minds,

This is difficult to master [even] by the intelligent.
Therefore, it is called "Difficult to Master."[812]

[The *Ratnāvalī* states:]

The fifth is very Difficult to Master,
Since all māras find it very difficult to overpower [them],
And since they become very skilled in knowing
The subtle meanings of the realities of the noble ones and so forth.

Through the maturation of those [qualities],
They become kings of the gods who live in Tuṣita[813]
And put an end to the foundations
Of the afflicted views of all tīrthikaras.[814]

2.2.3.5.4.7. The sixth bhūmi, The Facing[815]

The three kinds of enlightenment,
The gathering of all that's excellent,
Arising, ceasing too exhausted—
This bhūmi's held to be The Facing. [83]

Through their prajñā, [the bodhisattvas on this bhūmi] realize that **the three kinds of enlightenment** of śrāvakas, pratyekabuddhas, and bodhisattvas are equality. Therefore, by **facing** that existence and peace are without difference, they realize the very profound **arising and ceasing**.[816] [39b] [The *Mahāyānasūtrālaṃkāra*] says:

Since saṃsāra and nirvāṇa
Are both faced here,
It is said to be "the bhūmi of Facing,"
Which is based on the pāramitā of prajñā.[817]

[The *Ratnāvalī* states:]

The sixth is called "The Facing,"
Since they face the buddhadharmas
And, through familiarity with calm abiding and superior insight,
Attain cessation, by which [prajñā] unfolds.

Through the maturation of those [qualities],
They become kings of the gods [in Liking] Emanations,[818]
Are not surpassed by śrāvakas,
And pacify those with the pride of superiority.[819]

2.2.3.5.4.8. The seventh bhūmi, The Gone Afar

Since it's ever playing with a web of light
That's configurated in a circle
And has crossed saṃsāra's swampy pond,
This is labeled "Gone Afar." [84]

As the sign for having entered the secret place of the Buddhas, the [bodhisattvas] on this [bhūmi] have **configurated a circle**. This means that they **play with a web of light** that is similar to the maṇḍalas of the Buddhas and also enter, in a [single] moment, the absorption of cessation.[820] Therefore, by realizing the equality [of that], they have **gone afar** and hence **have crossed** [saṃsāra's] **swamp**. The [*Mahāyānasūtrālaṃkāra*] says:

Due to being joined with the single path to travel,
It is held to be the bhūmi Gone Afar.[821]

[The *Ratnāvalī* states:]

The seventh is Gone Afar,
Since the number [of qualities] has gone afar
And they, moment by moment,
Enter the absorption of cessation.

Through the maturation of those [qualities],
They become lords of the gods in Power [over Others' Emanations][822]
And become great leaders of masters,
Who know the clear realization of the realities of noble ones.[823]

This explanation refers to the meaning of the pāramitā of skill in means.

2.2.3.5.4.9. Explaining the eighth bhūmi, The Immovable

Being cared for by the Buddhas,
Having entered into wisdom's ocean, [40a]

Being without effort and spontaneous—
By the hordes of māras, it's Immovable. [85]

When the eighth bhūmi is attained, mentation, clinging, and conceptions have changed state. Therefore, **being cared for by the Buddhas** [refers to] what is stated in the *[Sarvabuddha]rahasyopāyakauśalyasūtra*[824]—once this [bhūmi] is attained, [bodhisattvas could] display the attainment of unsurpassable great buddhahood in seven days, if they wish. Hence, **having entered into** the secret of the Buddhas on this [bhūmi], they dwell in the **ocean of wisdom**. That all **māras** [cannot] unsettle [their] **spontaneous** enlightened activity is the attainment of the pāramitā of aspiration prayers.[825] The [*Mahāyānasūtrālaṃkāra* says]:

> Since it is unmoved by the two discriminations,
> It is named "The Immovable."[826]

The two discriminations are the discrimination of having concepts about knowable objects and the discrimination of having concepts about suchness. [The eighth bhūmi is not tainted by these], since both have become pure. [The *Ratnāvalī*] explains:

> Likewise, the eighth is the youthful bhūmi.
> It is immovable, since it is not conceptualizing.
> Just like this immovability, the spheres
> Of their body, speech, and mind are inconceivable.
>
> Through the maturation of those [qualities],
> They become a Brahmā who is the lord of a thousand [worlds],[827]
> And śrāvakas, pratyekabuddhas, and so on
> Cannot surpass them in ascertaining actuality.[828]

2.2.3.5.4.10. Explaining the ninth bhūmi, Excellent Insight

Since those yogins have completed
Their discourses teaching dharma
In all awarenesses discriminating perfectly,
This bhūmi is considered Excellent Insight. [86]

On **this bhūmi**, [bodhisattvas] demonstrate their might over all dharmas, **the completion of all perfectly discriminating awarenesses.**[829]

Since they demonstrate this in an effortless way, it is the final equality of the nature of all buddha speech. [40b] This is the pāramitā of power. The [*Mahāyānasūtrālaṃkāra*] says:

> The supreme mind of perfectly discriminating awareness
> Is the bhūmi that is Excellent Insight.[830]

[The *Ratnāvalī* states:]

> The ninth is called "Excellent Insight,"
> Since they, just like a regent,
> Have attained perfectly discriminating awareness
> And therefore have supreme insight here.
>
> Through the maturation of those [qualities],
> They become a Brahmā who is the lord of a million [worlds],[831]
> And arhats and so forth cannot surpass them
> In [answering] the questions sentient beings have in mind.[832]

2.2.3.5.4.11. Explaining the tenth bhūmi, Cloud of Dharma

> **The kāya with this wisdom's nature,**
> **Which is stainless, equal to the sky,**
> **Holds [the dharma] of the Buddhas.**
> **From it, the "Cloud of Dharma" forms. [87]**

[The bodhisattvas on] **this** [bhūmi] will be endowed with the enlightened activity that equals [the activity of] the **kāyas of** all **Buddhas** whose **wisdom** has reached its culmination. [Their enlightened activity] consists of the incessant twelve deeds [of a supreme nirmāṇakāya], which are the limitless abundance to guide disciples. This means that [their wisdom of knowing] suchness and variety has become **equal to the sky**. Therefore, this is called "the pāramitā of wisdom." [The *Mahāyānasūtrālaṃkāra*] says:

> The two that are like clouds pervade the space[like] dharma.
> Therefore, it is the Cloud of Dharma.[833]

[The *Ratnāvalī* states:]

> The tenth is the Dharma Cloud,
> Since it pours down a rain of dharma

And since the Buddhas bestow empowerment
Upon these bodhisattvas through light rays.

Through the maturation of those [qualities],
They become the lord of the gods in Pure Abode,
The lord of the sphere of inconceivable wisdom,
Who is supreme Maheśvara.[834]

[Throughout this presentation of the ten bhūmis,] the respective first quotes came from the *Mahāyānasūtrālaṃkāra*, and the latter are found in the *Ratnāvalī*.

As for briefly teaching these ten bhūmis' own essences, what obscures them are [ten aspects of] nonafflicted ignorance about ten aspects of the dharmadhātu, such as its actuality of being omnipresent. [41a] In due order, these obscure the ten bhūmis of bodhisattvas, since they are the antagonistic factors of these [bhūmis]. As the *Madhyāntavibhāga* [says]:

[They are] the actuality of omnipresence, the actuality of the highest,
The natural outflow as the highest to be strived for,
The actuality of the lack of clinging,
The actuality of mind streams not being different,
The actuality of being neither afflicted nor pure,
The actuality of nondifference,
The actuality of being without decrease and increase,
And the matrix of fourfold power.

Ignorance about the dharmadhātu
[Consists of] the ten nonafflicted obscurations.
The bhūmis are the remedies
Of the antagonistic factors of the ten bhūmis.[835]

[These ten kinds of nonafflicted ignorance] are the cognitive obscurations. The thorough purifications to purify them are taught in detail in the [prajñā]pāramitā [sūtras].[836]

In brief, the intense rising of desire, hatred, and ignorance that brings about the desire realm is to be relinquished through the remedies of [meditating on] repulsiveness and so forth. The latencies of the three poisons that bring about [the realm of] form and the formless [realm] are to be relinquished through the supramundane paths. The ground of the latent tendencies of ignorance that exists in the mind streams of śrāvakas and pratyekabuddhas, the factors to be relinquished through seeing, the factors to be relinquished through meditation, as well as the factors to be relinquished on the seven impure bhūmis and on the three pure bhūmis are discussed by summarizing them into afflictive [obscurations], cognitive [obscurations], and obscurations of meditative absorption. The remedies [for these obscurations] are taught through the sequence [as presented in the *Avikalpapraveśadhāraṇī*] of [not mentally engaging in] the four characteristics of factors to be relinquished, their remedies, suchness, and fruition.

Here, "nonconceptual wisdom" is used as the conventional term for the unfolding of the dharmakāya and "illusionlike wisdom" as the conventional term for the unfolding of the rūpakāyas. [41b] In terms of their own essence, they are said to be inseparable dependent origination. As for the rūpakāyas being taught to be similar to the bodies of kings, [it is to be] understood that such is taught with the implication of [referring to] the aspect of the features of form that appear in the three realms, whereas the five powers are not like that. The **Vimalatejasvargaparipṛccha[sūtra]*[837] and the *Śilākṣipta[sūtra]* speak of the following five[838] powers: (1) the prajñās of bodhisattvas and Buddhas, (2) their wisdoms, (3) the samādhis in which they meditate, (4) their merits of having gathered the accumulations, and (5) their pure bodies.

From among these, the power of their bodies is discussed as follows. [Take the power of] ordinary elephants, puruṣa[-elephants], white [elephants], lotus[-elephants], white water-lily[-elephants], wool-elephants, perfume-elephants, Vindhya-elephants,[839] those who have weapon[like] claws; ordinary lions and great lions; divine beings above the earth, Garland-Holders, Basin-Holders, Always Intoxicated Ones, Vinā-Possessors,[840] Kubera, and the gods from "the Thirty-Three." Then multiply [the power of all] these by ten and multiply that by seven, all of which [equals the power of] a single Indra. Again, multiply [the power of] the gods from Free from Strife, Tuṣita, Liking Emanations, and Power over Others' Emanations by seven, all of which equal a single Māradeva. All of the above [together equal] half [the power of] Nārāyaṇa,[841] and two of these [equal the power of] a Mahāpuruṣa.[842] Ten of the latter [make up the power of] arhats in their last existence, and one hundred thousand of them [equal the power of] one rhinoceroslike pratyekabuddha.[843] One hundred eons after having attained the path of seeing, bodhisattvas [possess the power of] ten pratyekabuddhas. In the same way, infinite multiplications are described in terms of [their having stayed on this path for] one thousand, ten thousand, hundred thousand, a million, ten million, a billion, ten billion, a hundred billion, a trillion, and countless eons; the eighth, ninth, and tenth bhūmi; and their last existence [as a bodhisattva]. [42a] In a similar way, merit is described in detail [in the *Ratnāvalī*]:

The merits that come from pratyekabuddhas,
Those from learners and nonlearners,
And those of all worlds without exception
Are as infinite as these worlds.

Through multiplying that much by ten,
Just a single pore [of a Buddha] is accomplished.
. . .[844]

However, since I am afraid of being [too] wordy, I will not explain this here. [Those interested] should look it up in the *Daśabhūmikasūtra* and other [texts].

2.3.[845] Praising the dharmakāya free from all stains

This has four parts:
1) The dharmakāya's own essence that is a change of state
2) [Its] inconceivability
3) The qualities of realization
4) Explaining enlightened activity

2.3.1. The dharmakāya's own essence that is a change of state

The abode of buddhadharmas
Fully bears the fruit of practice.
This fundamental change of state
Is called the "dharmakāya." [88]

Once all ten bhūmis have been completed, the vajralike samādhi destroys the ālaya-consciousness, which is the ground of the latent tendencies of ignorance. At that point, [bodhisattvas] receive the empowerment of great light rays bestowed [by all Buddhas] and become **Buddhas** [themselves]. As for this stage, **the abode of** all **dharmas'** ultimate own essence, once the miragelike afflictive obscurations and cognitive obscurations are purified through the infinite **practices** of the activities [of bodhisattvas] on many bhūmis, it **fully bears the** naturally luminous perfect nature. This is taught to be "**the fundamental change of state**," which **is called the "dharmakāya."**[846] This point is discussed in detail in the *Mahāyānasaṃgraha*:

> First, how is this dharmakāya attained through contact? Through excellently cultivating the five aspects[847] of the nonconceptual and

the subsequently attained wisdoms that have the dharmas belonging to the mahāyāna as their objects, on all [bhūmis], the accumulations [42b] are well gathered. Then, through the vajralike samādhi ([which bears that name], since it destroys the subtle obscurations so difficult to destroy), one becomes free from all obscurations right after [coming out of] that samādhi. Hence, [the dharmakāya] is attained due to the change of state through those.

By how many kinds of masteries is the mastery of the dharmakāya attained? In brief, mastery is attained through five kinds. (1) Through the change of state of the skandha of form, mastery over [pure buddha] realms, kāyas, the excellent major and minor marks, infinite voices, and the invisible mark on the crown of the head [is attained]. (2) Through the change of state of the skandha of feelings, mastery over infinite and vast blissful states without wrongdoing [is attained]. (3) Through the change of state of the skandha of discrimination, mastery over the teachings [is attained] through all groups of words, groups of phrases, and groups of letters. (4) Through the change of state of the skandha of formation, mastery over creation, transformation, gathering retinues, and gathering the immaculate dharmas [is attained]. (5) Through the change of state of the skandha of consciousness, mastery over mirrorlike [wisdom], [the wisdom of] equality, discriminating [wisdom], and all-accomplishing [wisdom] is attained.[848]

In how many ways is the dharmakāya to be understood as a support? In brief, it is a support in three ways. (1) As for it being the support of the various [accomplished] states of a Buddha, [I offer two] verses here:

> Since the Buddhas' own dhātu has been found,
> The joy with a fivefold nature is found,
> But those who have not attained that [dhātu] are deprived
> of such joy.
> Therefore, those who wish for that, should attain it.
>
> Power, all-accomplishment, the taste of dharma,
> And the consummations of [its] meanings and qualities
> [43a] are boundless.
> Through seeing this eternal inexhaustibility,
> The Buddhas find supreme joy without wrongdoing.

(2) It is the support of various sambhogakāyas, since it brings bodhisattvas to maturity. (3) It is the support of various nirmāṇakāyas, since it mainly brings the śrāvakas to maturity.

How many buddhadharmas constitute the dharmakāya? In brief, it is constituted by six. [It is constituted] (1) by the buddhadharma of purity, since the dharmakāya is attained by the ālaya-consciousness having changed state; (2) by maturation, since the wisdom of maturation is attained by the material sense faculties having changed state; (3) by abiding, since the abiding through boundless wisdom is attained by our abiding in enjoying sense pleasures and so on having changed state; (4) by mastery, since mastery over the wisdom of supernatural knowledges that is unimpeded throughout all worldly realms is attained by our various purposeful activities having changed state; (5) by conventionalities, since mastery in knowing the teachings that satisfy the minds of all sentient beings is attained by the expressions of the conventionalities of what is seen, heard, asserted, and [perceived by] consciousness having changed state; (6) by removal, since the wisdom of knowing how to remove all misfortunes of all sentient beings is found by the removal of all misfortunes and flaws. One should know that the dharmakāya of the Buddhas is constituted by these six buddhadharmas.[849]

2.3.2. Its inconceivability

[This is explained by] two verses.

Free from latent tendencies, you're inconceivable. [89a]

[43b] Since the root of saṃsāra consists of **latent tendencies**, being **free from** them is to be free from what is conceivable. Therefore, [the dharmakāya] is taught to be **inconceivable**. [The next lines are given] in order to explain this in detail.

Saṃsāra's latent tendencies, they can be conceived.
You're completely inconceivable—
Through what could you be realized? [89bd]

Beyond the entire sphere of speech,
Outside the range of any senses, [90ab]

Saṃsāra [consists of] the five appropriating skandhas.[850] When evaluating their **latent tendencies** through thinking, they are dependent origination, which has the defining characteristics of causes and conditions. This **can** indeed **be** examined and **conceived** by those who have the minds of ordinary beings, but **you**, buddha wisdom, **are completely inconceivable**. Though you have stains in the beginning, are in the process of removing these stains in between, and, finally, are free from [all] stains, you are unconditioned, not newly arisen, not something formed, nor a basis for stains,[851] [yet] of unlimited power and compassion. Therefore, **through what could you be realized**, since knowable objects and knower have fused into being equal? If knowable objects and knower are not different, words, phrases, and letters[852] do not arise. Therefore, you are **beyond the sphere of speech**. What is not the sphere of mind and speech[853] is not a part of the body [either]. Hence, you are **outside the range of** the **senses** (the [five physical] sense faculties, such as the eye, up through the mental one), since these are empty. The same is found in the *Uttaratantra*:

> Since it is subtle, it is not an object of study.
> Since it is the ultimate, it is none of reflection.
> Since it is the profound nature of phenomena,
> It is none of worldly meditation [44a] and so forth,
>
> Because childish beings have never seen it before,
> Just like a person born blind [has never seen] form.[854]

You may wonder, "If [the dharmakāya] is like that, is it then not something that cannot be realized at all?" [The answer] is stated [in the next line].

> **To be realized through mental knowing—[90c]**

It is through the stains of **mentation** having become pure and it having become stainless mentation that [the dharmakāya] is something **to be realized** and to be aware of through your own personal experience, just as it was taught above. Therefore, [the Buddhas know] that the inexpressible [can be] expressed through anything possible, and they know all thinking about the unthinkable. Also, all of saṃsāra and nirvāṇa is enacted in what is without action.

> **I bow to and praise whatever's suitable.**[855] **[90d]**

Likewise, [the *Uttaratantra*] says:

> Even noble ones [see it] as a baby [would glimpse]
> The form of the sun from within its house of birth.[856]

Glorious Saraha declares [in his *Dohākośagīti*]:

> If the stains of mind have become pure, it is connateness.
> At that point, nothing antagonistic can enter it.[857]

2.3.3. Explaining the qualities of the final realization of this

This has four parts:
1) The way in which mind becomes pure
2) The completeness of the body of wisdom
3) The qualities of purity
4) The qualities of attainment

2.3.3.1. The way in which mind becomes pure

> **In this manner of gradual engagement,**
> **The highly renowned children of the Buddhas,**
> **Through the wisdom of the cloud of dharma,**
> **See phenomena's empty nature. [91]**
>
> **Once their minds are cleansed completely,**
> **They have gone beyond saṃsāra's depths. [92ab]**

Through bodhisattvas having **gradually** and excellently **engaged** in and attained all ten bhūmis, they [finally] attain the bhūmi of a Buddha through being granted empowerment. At that point, since they are praised by all **Buddhas** throughout the infinite reaches of space, they are **highly renowned.** [44b] From **the cloud** of the [Buddhas'] enlightened activity of the immaculate **dharma**—their compassion that equals space—the rain of the enlightened activity of great enlightenment and so on pours forth effortlessly, and nonconceptual **wisdom** becomes **empty** of the four characteristics of conceiving of factors to be relinquished, remedies, suchness, and fruition. Immediately at that point, the mind that is the support of the ground of the latent tendencies of ignorance—the ālaya-consciousness—becomes pure and accomplished. This means that, since it has ceased, there is freedom from all factors to be relinquished. This is called "the peace of the Buddha Bhagavats." Since mind has ceased in this way, [the next six lines teach]

2.3.3.2. The way in which the body of wisdom is complete

> **They rest calmly on a throne,**
> **Whose nature is a giant immense lotus. [92cd]**
>
> **Everywhere they are surrounded**
> **By lotuses that number billions,**
> **In their many jewelled petals' light,**
> **And with anthers of enthralling beauty. [93]**

Once their minds have ceased, they are liberated from **saṃsāra's depths**. Then, the **throne** upon which their body of wisdom rests is as follows. It is made of the boundless aspiration prayers of the Buddhas, with the stainless jewel of the heart of enlightenment at its heart. It is endowed with the **light** of inconceivably boundless [precious substances], such as the mighty king,[858] the wish-fulfiller,[859] the one held by Indra,[860] blue beryl, sapphire, ruby, diamond, crystal, gold, coral, emerald, and gold from the river Jambu, which reach beyond all worlds and completely fill up the infinite reaches of space. [In addition, this throne is] embellished with all [kinds of] ornaments. In brief, even if one were to proclaim its praise and its arrangement with ten septillions of mouths for as many eons [45a] as there are sand grains in the river Gaṅgā, one would never reach an end. So [the wisdom-bodies of the Buddhas] reside on such a [lotus that is] **surrounded everywhere by lotuses that number billions**. In detail, this [arrangement] is as described in the *Avataṃsaka[sūtra]*. As for the display of their bodies, it is like the display [of the body] that Samantabhadra, the son of the victors, saw under the bodhi-tree, but there is no room to speak about it here.[861]

2.3.3.3. Instruction on the qualities of purity

> **They overflow with tenfold power,**
> **Immersed within their fearlessness,**
> **Never straying from the inconceivable**
> **Buddhadharmas without reference point. [94]**

This is the instruction on the thirty-two qualities of the dharmakāya: **the ten powers, the** four **fearlessnesses**, and the eighteen unshared qualities. I will describe them here in the way in which the great noble Maitreya puts them succinctly in his *Uttaratantra*. The ten powers:

What is the case and not the case,
Maturation of karma, faculties,
Constitutions, inclinations,
The paths that lead everywhere,

Samādhi and so forth when afflicted or stainless,
Recollection of [former birth]places,
The divine eye, and peace—
Knowing these are the ten kinds of power.[862]

The four fearlessnesses:

All phenomena being completely realized,
Putting an end to obstacles,
Teaching the path, and teaching cessation—
Fearlessness about these is fourfold.[863]

These [four statements] are [expressions of a Buddha's] fearlessness,[864] since they cannot be disputed by others, be they gods, demons, śramaṇas,[865] or brahmans, by saying, "This is not the case."

He lacks mistakenness and chatter.
The teacher's mindfulness never deteriorates.
He lacks a mind not resting in meditative equipoise,
Lacks all kinds of discriminations,

And lacks nonexamining indifference. [45b]
His striving, vigor, mindfulness,
Prajñā, complete liberation, and the vision
Of the wisdom of complete liberation never deteriorate.

Actions are preceded by wisdom,
And wisdom is unobscured with regard to time.
These eighteen are the qualities
Unshared by the teacher with others.[866]

These [eighteen] are said to be the supreme [qualities], of which [a Buddha] does not even share an atom with others. Since these are described in detail in the *Tathāgatamahākaruṇānirdeśasūtra*,[867] you should look [them up there].[868]

2.3.3.4. The qualities of attainment

> **Through all their actions of outstanding conduct,**
> **Their merit and their wisdom are complete—**
> **This full moon's surrounded everywhere**
> **By the stars that are its retinue. [95]**

[The Buddhas'] **outstanding conduct** means that they have **completely** gathered the utterly bright **actions** that consist of the accumulations of **merit and wisdom**. Therefore, they appear [in this way, being endowed with] the thirty-two excellent marks [of the rūpakāyas]. The enumeration [of these] has already been taught above,[869] but here, master [Nāgārjuna] relates them to their causes. [In detail,] his *Ratnāvalī* says:

> Through properly honoring stūpas,
> Those to be worshipped, noble ones, and elders,
> You will become a cakravartin,
> Your glorious hands and feet marked with wheels.
>
> O King, always firmly keep
> Your commitment to the dharma.
> Through this, you will become a bodhisattva
> Whose feet are very well planted.
>
> Through generosity, pleasant words,
> Benefitting, and conduct that matches [your words],[870]
> You will come to have long[871] hands
> Whose glorious fingers are joined by webs.
>
> Through abundant giving
> Of the choicest foods and drinks,
> Your glorious hands and feet will be supple.
> Your hands, feet, shoulders,
> And the nape of your neck will protrude,[872]
> So that your body will be large, with these seven [areas] protuberant.
>
> Through never doing harm and liberating those to be killed,
> Your body will be beautiful, upright, large, [46a]
> And very tall, with long fingers
> And broad heels.

Through making the dharmas to which you committed flourish,
You will have the marks of looking splendidly,
Excellent [skin] color, your ankles not protruding,
And your body hairs pointing upwards.

Through respectfully assimilating and passing on
Activities such as science, arts, and crafts,
You will have the calves of an antelope,
A sharp mind, and great knowledge.

Through the spiritual discipline of swift generosity,
When [others] seek your wealth and possessions,
You will have large and pleasant arms
And become the leader of the world.

Through perfectly reconciling
Friends who have become divided,
You will become the foremost of those
Whose glorious sexual organ is withdrawn in a sheath.

Through providing palaces
And excellent comfortable carpets,
Your [skin] color will be very soft,
Just like stainless refined gold.

Through bestowing the unsurpassable powers [of a kingdom]
And following a guru properly,
You will be adorned with a glorious strand of body hair [in] each [pore]
And the ūrṇā-hair on your face.

Through speaking in nice and pleasing ways
And acting in accord with excellent speech,
You will have round shoulder joints
And a lionlike upper body.

Through nursing and healing the sick,
You will have broad shoulders,
Rest in natural ease,
And [all food] will be of finest taste.

Through encouraging activities
In accordance with the dharma,
Your uṣṇīṣa will be positioned well
And [your body] well proportioned like a Nyagrodha [tree].

Through pronouncing true and soft words
For a long time, O lord of humans,
Your tongue will be long,
And you will have the voice of Brahmā. [46b]

Through always and continuously[873]
Speaking words of truth,
You will have jaws like a lion,
Be glorious, and hard to overcome.[874]

Through showing excellent respect and service
And following what is appropriate,
Your teeth will be very white,
Shining, and even.

Through being used to true and nondivisive
Words over a long time,
You will have a complete set of forty glorious teeth,
Which are excellent and set evenly.

Through looking upon sentient beings with love
And without desire, hatred, or ignorance,
Your eyes will be bright and dark-blue,
With eyelashes like a heifer.

Thus, in brief, know well
These thirty-two [marks] with their causes,
Which are the marks
Of a lion[like] Mahāpuruṣa.[875]

Here, it is taught that [these marks] appear in accordance with the attire of the pure aspect of the mind, which is their actual cause. Through the conditioning causes [just described], this purity just becomes more and more consummate. As the [*Ratnāvalī*] explains:

The merits that come from pratyekabuddhas,
Those from learners and nonlearners,
And those of all worlds without exception
Are as infinite as these worlds.

Through multiplying that much by ten,
Just a single pore [of a Buddha] is accomplished.
All the pores of a Buddha
Come about in this same way.

It is held that multiplying one hundred times
The merit that produces
All the pores of a Buddha
[Brings about] a single minor mark.

O king, through just that much merit,
A single minor mark is completed.
The same applies to [each of them]
Up through the eightieth.

Through multiplying a hundred times
The accumulation of merit that accomplishes
The eighty minor marks,
A single major mark of a Mahāpuruṣa [is obtained].

Through multiplying a thousand times
The vast merit that is the cause
Of accomplishing thirty of the major marks,
The ūrṇā-hair, resembling the full moon, [comes forth].

Through adding up a hundred thousand times
The merit of the ūrṇā-hair,
A protector's uṣṇīṣa is produced,
Which rests invisibly on the crown of his head.[876]

One should understand this detailed instruction on the qualities of the rūpakāyas. Here, [lines 95cd] refer to them by saying, "**This full moon is surrounded by the stars.**"[877] The same manner of appearance [of the rūpakāyas] is also found in the *Uttaratantra*:

Just as the form of the moon in a cloudless autumn sky [47a]
Is seen in the blue waters of a lake,
So the form of the sovereign of the assemblies of the victors' children
Is seen in the maṇḍala of complete buddhahood.[878]

This is discussed in detail in the *Ratnādārikāparipṛcchasūtra*[879] and in the *Samādhirājasūtra*['s section on] recollecting the Buddha.

2.3.4. Explaining enlightened activity

This has five parts:

1) The main enlightened activity of bestowing empowerment upon the children of the victors
2) The manner of performing enlightened activity in saṃsāra
3) Exhorting those [dwelling in] peace
4) The meaning of nirvāṇa
5) Instruction on the meaning of effortless enlightened activity

2.3.4.1. The main enlightened activity of bestowing empowerment upon the children of the victors

In the sun that is the Buddhas' hands,
Stainless jewels shine their light.
Through empowering their eldest children,
They bestow empowerment on them. [96]

The deeds and enlightened activities of those who have become completely perfect **Buddhas** are indeed boundless, but the main one is the following. Without moving away from the dharmakāya, the sambhogakāya is displayed. An emanation that springs forth from the latter shows in the [heavenly] abode of Tuṣita as someone like Śvetaketu.[880] This one, in the form of a certain emanation of a bodhisattva and in the manner of [performing] the twelve deeds [of a Buddha], simultaneously promotes infinite welfare in a billion four-continent worlds. Nevertheless, the main [enlightened activity of these Buddhas] is to **empower their eldest children**, such as the bodhisattva Maitreya.[881] The *Avataṃsaka[sūtra]* says:

> [Through deeds] such as the display of bestowing empowerment by placing his hands on the crown of the head of the bodhisattva Samantabhadra, and through the blazing jewels free from all obscurations in the sun of wisdom of the Buddha's hands, he bestows empowerment upon the ocean of the children of the victors continuously.

[47b] [The *Uttaratantra*] states:

Without moving away from the dharmakāya,
Through various [forms] that have the nature of emanations,

He takes a [divine] rebirth,
Leaves the abode of Tuṣita,
Enters the womb, is born,
Becomes skilled in the sciences of arts and crafts,

Enjoys amusements among his retinue of spouses,
Experiences renunciation, practices austerities,
Proceeds to the heart of enlightenment,[882]
Vanquishes the hosts of Māra,

Becomes completely enlightened, [turns] the wheel of dharma,
And passes into nirvāṇa.
He shows these deeds in impure realms
For as long as existence lasts.[883]

2.3.4.2. The manner of promoting the welfare of sentient beings in saṃsāra

Abiding in this yoga that's so great,
With divine eyes, they behold
Worldly beings debased by ignorance,
Distraught and terrified by suffering. [97]

From their bodies, without effort,
Light rays are beaming forth,
And open wide the gates for those
Who are engulfed in ignorance's gloom. [98]

Through having reached the culmination of calm abiding and superior insight, the **great yoga** [is attained]. **With** their unobscured **divine** Buddha **eyes,** the Buddhas who **abide in this** [yoga] **behold** [the beings in] in the lower realms who are **debased by ignorance**—not knowing their own Buddha heart—and **terrify**ing [in that they are] **distraught by suffering. From the bodies of** these great supreme emanations, six sextillion **light rays are beaming forth and open wide the gates** of the path to liberation **for those who are engulfed in the gloom of ignorance,** thus causing them to travel on the path to peace. This is to be known in detail as [it is presented] in the sūtra that teaches on the accomplishment of a hundred quadrillions of light rays.[884] [48a]

2.3.4.3. Instruction on the enlightened activity of exhorting those [dwelling in] peace

> **It's held that those in the nirvāṇa with remainder**
> **Into the nirvāṇa without remainder pass. [99ab]**

This [verse] here is not [about] the śrāvakas' assertion of [nirvāṇa] with remainder or without remainder.[885] Here, "with remainder" refers to attaining the arhathood of śrāvakas or the self-enlightenment of pratyekabudhas. You may wonder, "In what way are these with remainder?" Since the ālaya-consciousness that contains all seeds is not [completely] relinquished [by śrāvakas and pratyekabudhas], there is [still] this very remainder. Through their prajñā, they have eradicated [the portion of] this [ālaya-consciousness that constitutes] the afflictions, in the form of possessing the seeds for being born in the three realms. Consequently, [they dwell in] a peaceful samādhi in the uncontaminated expanse, due to which they [still] have a body that is of mental nature. Therefore, [this state] is both something **with remainder** and **nirvāṇa**. The *Bodhicittavivaraṇa* instructs:

> So that those weary with the path of existence
> [Can] take a rest, the two wisdoms [of śrāvakas and pratyekabuddhas],
> Which [eventually] merge into the mahāyāna,
> Were discussed [by the Buddha], but they are not the ultimate.
>
> For as long as they are not exhorted by the Buddhas,
> Existing in a body of wisdom,
> The śrāvakas stay in a swoon,
> Intoxicated by samādhi.
>
> Upon being exhorted, in various forms,
> They will become devoted to the welfare of sentient beings,
> Gather the accumulations of merit and wisdom,
> And attain the enlightenment of Buddhas.[886]

Upon this, you may wonder, "Well, how could the eradicated[887] seeds for being born in existence be reborn as a body in existence?" This is possible due to two [factors]: (1) the cause that is the support of latent tendencies—

[the ālaya-consciousness] that contains all seeds—and (2) the condition that consists of the Buddhas' light rays, [which make the arhats rise from their samādhi and enter the mahāyāna]. [The *Bodhicittavivaraṇa*] continues:

> Since there are the latent tendencies of those two, [48b]
> [Their] latent tendencies are said to be the seeds.
> These seeds, coming together with the [conditioning] entities,
> Produce the [various] sprouts of [persons in] existence.[888]

The *Uttaratantra* states:

> Through the terms "impermanence," "suffering,"
> "Lack of self," and "peace," the [Buddhas] who know [all] means
> Produce weariness for the three realms in sentient beings
> And cause them to enter into nirvāṇa.
>
> Those who have fully entered the path to peace
> Have the notion that they attained nirvāṇa,
> [But] in the *Saddharmapuṇḍarīka[sūtra]* and others
> The true reality of phenomena is taught.
>
> Through this, [the Buddhas] put their previous clinging to an end,
> Make them fully adopt means and prajñā,
> Thus mature them in the mahāyāna,
> And prophesy [their] supreme enlightenment.
>
> These [kāyas] are profound and of perfect power,
> Thus guiding childish beings in tune with their welfare.
> Therefore, in due order, they are called
> "Profound," "vast," and "great being."[889]

Therefore, this [kind of] nirvāṇa without remainder is buddhahood, and what places you there is the enlightened activity [of the Buddhas].[890]

2.3.4.4. Explaining the meaning of nirvāṇa that is peace

> **But here, the actual nirvāṇa**
> **Is mind that's free from any stain. [99cd]**
>
> **The nonbeing of all beings—**
> **This nature is its sphere.**

The mighty bodhicitta seeing it
Is fully stainless dharmakāya. [100]

Here, the actual [nirvāṇa] that is called "the **nirvāṇa** of the Buddha Bhagavats" is to be understood as follows. This "**mind free from any stain**" [first seems to be] ensnared by the infinite millions of cocoons of the afflictions and [then] undergoes a fundamental change of state as taught above. Its nature dwells in all sentient beings, but the **nature** of this **being**, which is inconceivable for the thinking and evaluating **of all beings**, is like [a reflection of] the moon in water. Since **this is the sphere of the** supreme state of mind, the time of reaching final consummation by **seeing it** [49a] is called "attaining the **fully stainless dharmakāya**." As [the *Hevajratantra*] says:

Mind is perfect buddhahood itself.
There is no teaching of buddhahood as anything else.[891]

This teaches [mind's] stainlessness through the name "mind." What is expressed by the terms "mind," "mentation," and "consciousness" is stainless in every repect. Therefore, once the [adventitious stains] have become nonexistent, it is called "buddhahood."[892]

2.3.4.5. Instruction on the meaning of effortless enlightened activity

In the stainless dharmakāya,
The sea of wisdom finds its place.[893]
Like with variegated jewels,
Beings' welfare is fulfilled from it. [101]

The change of state in dependence on **the stainless dharmakāya** does not refer to having become nothing whatsoever. Rather, the oceans of the hordes of thoughts have changed state into **the sea of wisdom**,[894] which is the final consummation of the emptiness that is endowed with the supreme of all aspects. As for "all aspects" in this [expression], they are all the above-mentioned dharmas, such as generosity, that make the basic element unfold. Through "the supreme" of these [aspects, their] unsurpassable consummation [is expressed]. [These aspects are] "emptiness," since they, in terms of their own essence, are nothing but purity itself and thus inseparable [from emptiness]. This is described in detail in the *Uttaratantra* through the example of the portrait [of a king], which will not become completely finished without all painters—each of whom knowing [how to paint] a particular part—coming together.

The painters of these [parts]
Are generosity, ethics, patience, and so on.
Emptiness endowed with the supreme of all aspects
Is said to be the form [of the king].

Since prajñā, wisdom, and complete liberation
Are illuminating, radiating, pure,
And not different, they are similar to
The light, the rays, and the orb of the sun. [49b]

Therefore, without attaining buddhahood,
Nirvāṇa is not attained,
Just as you cannot see the sun,
Once you take away its light and its rays.[895]

Thus, in the final picture, the nonconceptual prajñā that the mind stream of a Buddha possesses is similar in its features to [the sun's] luminosity, since it dispels the darkness [that obscures] the genuine true reality of [all] knowable objects. Since [the prajñā] that is attained subsequently to this [nonconceptual prajñā] engages all knowable entities without exception in every respect, it is similar in its features to a radiating web of light. Due to the basis of both these [prajñās]—the completely liberated nature of the mind—being utterly stainless and sheer luminosity, it is similar in its features to the completely pure orb of the sun. Through all three [—nonconceptual prajñā, subsequently attained prajñā, and the liberated nature of the mind—] having the nature of being inseparable from the dharmadhātu, they are similar to the feature of the triad [of the sun's light, rays, and orb] being inseparable. Consequently, complete liberation is not tenable, if just a single one [of the above three elements] is not realized. For this reason, [the *Uttaratantra*] teaches the example of not [being able to] see the sun, once its light and its rays are taken away.

When [the Buddhas'] way of performing the enlightened activities of their ocean of wisdom operates like that, their displays of great supreme nirmāṇakāyas are like the reflections of Indra that appear in the blue beryl [of his palace and inspire the beings on earth who see them]. Their speech is like the drum of the gods [that resounds with the four seals of the dharma without anyone playing it]. Their omniscience and loving-kindness that pervade the entirety of existence are like clouds. The example of Brahmā [illustrates that] nirmāṇakāyas radiate from the sambhogakāyas. The example of the sun [illustrates that] wisdom illuminates [the stains] by radiating [everywhere] but is untainted by these stains. Since enlightened activity that fulfills the hopes of sentient beings happens without [the Buddhas'] minds entertaining any thoughts, it is **like** a wish-fulfilling **jewel**. The example of an echo [illustrates that] they do not utter any speech as such, but [50a] [what appears as their speech] is something that accords with the individual [kinds of] cognizance [of beings to be guided]. Since their bodies are all-pervading, permanent, and unobstructed, they are like space. Since [the Buddhas] serve as the basis for all sentient beings giving rise to the completely bright [dharmas], they are like the earth. This is a brief instruction on the nine aspects through which the *[Sarvabuddhaviṣayāvatāra]jñānālokālaṃkārasūtra* describes [enlightened activity] in detail.[896] Maitreya summarizes this [in his *Uttaratantra*]:

> That which, similar to Indra, the drum, clouds,
> Brahmā, the sun, the royal gem of a wish-fulfilling jewel,
> An echo, space, and the earth, promotes the welfare of others
> Effortlessly until [the end of] existence is [only] known by yogins.
>
> [Bodies] are displayed like the lord of gods appearing in the gem.
> [Their] excellent instructions resemble the drum of the gods.
> The cloud-banks of the sovereigns' great knowledge and loving-kindness
> Pervade infinite numbers of beings up through the peak of existence.
>
> Like Brahmā, without moving from their uncontaminated abodes,
> They display many kinds of emanations.
> Like the sun, wisdom radiates its brilliance.
> [Their] minds resemble the gem of a pure wish-fulfilling jewel.
>
> Like an echo, the speech of the victors is without articulation.
> Just as space, their bodies are pervasive, formless, and permanent.
> Like the earth, the buddhabhūmi is the ground for the medicinal herbs
> Of the immaculate dharmas of beings without exception and in all respects.[897]

Here, people with inferior intelligence may think, "Master Candrakīrti does not assert these wisdoms," but this is not the case. The *Madhyamakāvatāra* says:

> The cessation of mind is revealed through this kāya.[898]

You may wonder what this is about. [The *Madhyamakāvatāra* continues]:

> This kāya of peace is lucidly manifest like a wish-fulfilling tree
> And nonconceptual like a wish-fulfilling jewel. [50b]

For the sake of the world's affluence and until beings are liberated,
It appears permanently within the freedom from reference points.[899]

Thus, [Candrakīrti] teaches on the utterly stainless dharmakāya through its four [features] of being lucid, nonconceptual, permanent, and appearing. Thereafter, he also instructs in detail on the [dharmakāya]'s natural outflow, that is, the rūpa[kāya]s that are called "the profound dharmakāya." [He does so in the next thirty-one verses,] from [XI.19] up through [XI.49]:

In its natural outflow, a single rūpakāya,
The Mighty Sage displays simultaneously his own states of rebirth,
Which have ceased before, in a clear and ordered way,
Without exception, and very lucidly.
. . .
O victor, for as long as all worlds do not pass into supreme peace,
[All] beings are not ripened, and space has not perished,
Since you were born by the mother of prajñā, and the nanny of loving-kindness
Provides you with this approach [of remaining for that long], how could you ever be at peace?

In brief, it can be shown in detail how the positions of all great masters, such as Āryadeva, Śūra,[900] Buddhapālita, Bhāvaviveka,[901] and Jñānagarbha, are in accord on these [points], but I do not present [them here] out of fear of [too] many letters. Also noble Asaṅga has spoken in accord with this.[902] [However,] among others—the Mere Mentalists—there is the assertion that the wisdom of a Buddha is really [existent as mere] cognizance. This is refuted by noble master [Nāgārjuna] with [verses] such as the following [from his *Bodhicittavivaraṇa*]:

When considering that there is
No consciousness without a body,
You must tell us of what kind
Its own self-awareness is![903]

Temporarily, [51a] there may be dissimilar statements [by these masters], but in terms of their meaning, they do not differ as to the basic nature. Likewise, the correct view of all yānas and what is to be realized and attained in them is to be explained and understood as just one. The *Samādhirājasūtra* says:

In those with supernatural prajñā,
Buddha wisdom is inconceivable.
In those who remain in clinging,
Wisdom will not be found.

As for the many inconceivable dharmas
That are taught by terms,
Those who fixate on terms
Do not understand what is explained with [certain] intentions.

Those who do not understand the intentions
Of explanations given with certain intentions,
Not being trained in the nature of phenomena,
Explain nondharma as dharma.

The sūtra collections that I taught
In thousands of worldly realms
Have different letters but one meaning—
[All of] them cannot be proclaimed everywhere.

If you meditate on the meaning of a single word,
You meditate on all of those
Many dharmas that were explained
By all the Buddhas, however many there are.

For people who are learned in the meaning
Of the emptiness of all dharmas,
Once they have trained in this word,
The buddhadharmas are not hard to attain.

All dharmas are buddhadharmas,
So those who have trained in the nature of phenomena
Fully know the nature of phenomena
And do not go against the nature of phenomena.[904]

In brief, what you should do is as follows. Examine your own body and mind that are covered by the cocoon of ignorance and understand the intention of the victors, the basic nature of the two realities. [51b] Train in the two accumulations in union and attain the fruition of the inseparable two kāyas.

This completes the *Dharmadhātustava* composed by the great being, **noble Nāgārjuna.**

[The last sentence] was added by the translators. Thus, [the entire text] has been taught without remainder. **The *Dharmadhātustava***—[a praise to] the marvelous Buddha heart—was **composed by the great** being, **noble Nāgārjuna**. Through relying on the power of aspiration and to the best of his abilities, it was elucidated through this detailed explanation by Rangjung Dorje, who was born in the northern snowy ranges during this degenerate age.

The profound and vast teachings of the victor
Are held by the sons of the victor, Mañjughoṣa and Ajita,[905]
In a dimension equaling that of space.
There are infinite numbers of scholars and siddhas here in Jambudvīpa,

But those who were prophesied by the victor as the supreme
Are the two noble ones Nāgārjuna and Asaṅga.
Their followers are the supreme ornaments of Jambudvīpa, the friends of the teachings,
And they are the glory of sūtra, abhidharma, vinaya, and [all] beings.

They dispel the gloom of plain dialectics through the light of scripture and reasoning.
A fraction of [their] enlightened compassion has dawned upon the snowy ranges,
Making persons with insight practice and into bodhisattvas,
And causing chatter even among childish students.[906]

This praise to the Heart of the victors—the Heart without stains— [52a]
Is understood by all the mighty ones on the ten bhūmis.
But for [scholars of] the five sciences, gods, śrāvakas, and pratyekabuddhas,
Even devotion [for it] is difficult, let alone understanding.
Though it lies not within the sphere of fools like me,
Who bears the name Rangjung [Dorje], great aspiration [for it] arose in me.
Thus, I have explained it according to the vast sūtras and treatises.
Through this virtue, may all beings become just like the Mighty Sage.

Appendix I: Outline of Rangjung Dorje's Commentary

[1. The manner of engaging the treatise
1.1. The meaning of the title
1.2. Paying homage to the dharmadhātu
2. The actual treatise to be engaged, which] demonstrates how the dharmadhātu resides during three stages
2.1. The way in which [the dharmadhātu] resides during the stage of sentient beings
2.1.1. Brief introduction to its nature
2.1.2. Detailed explanation by correlating this with examples
2.1.2.1. The way in which the dharmadhātu does not appear and then appears, exemplified by butter
2.1.2.2. The detailed explanation through the example of a lamp inside a vase, which teaches the gradual stages of sentient beings, the path, and the appearance of wisdom in buddhahood
2.1.2.3. The meaning of [the dharmadhātu] being changeless and free from arising and ceasing
2.1.2.4. Explaining through the example of a gem that the stages of sentient beings and Buddhas are not different
2.1.2.5. Explaining the nature of the basic element through the example of gold
2.1.2.6. The way in which the dharmakāya appears, [illustrated] by the example of rice [and its] husk
2.1.2.7. [Explaining its] natural outflow, the very profound dharmakāya, [illustrated] through the example of a banana tree
2.2. Instruction on the stage of those on the path
2.2.1. How the manner of it being justified to purify the stains and the sequence [of that] are to be known
2.2.1.1. The way in which the basic element of the dharmakāya itself is justified as the disposition
2.2.1.2. Teaching an example and its meaning in order to [show] the removal of the [dharmadhātu]'s obscurations
2.2.1.3. Brief introduction to the modes of being of what is to be relinquished and its remedy

2.2.1.3.1. Instruction on [the dharmadhātu's] nature becoming pure through the purification of stains
2.2.1.3.2. Instruction that emptiness is the remedy
2.2.1.3.3. The manner in which [the dharmadhātu] is not empty of wisdom
2.2.1.3.4. The manner in which [the dharmadhātu] is empty of something to be relinquished and a remedy
2.2.1.3.5. Detailed explanation of the point [that the dharmadhātu is empty of something to be relinquished and a remedy]
2.2.1.3.5.1. [Showing that the dharmadhātu] abides within ourselves but is invisible
2.2.1.3.5.2. Showing that which obscures the [dharmadhātu]
2.2.1.3.5.3. The way in which wisdom realizes [the dharmadhātu]
2.2.1.3.5.4.The meaning of the imaginary [nature]
2.2.1.3.5.5. The meaning of the other-dependent [nature]
2.2.1.3.5.6. Instruction on dependent origination
2.2.1.3.5.7. Instruction on the mode of being of the perfect [nature]
2.2.1.3.5.8. The summary of those [points]
2.2.2. Instruction on the way to meditate, beginning with [the paths of] accumulation and preparation and so on
2.2.2.1. Explaining the way to make [the dharmadhātu] a living experience
2.2.2.1.1. How to meditate based on the five [sense] doors
2.2.2.1.2. Instruction on meditating on mentation that makes the connection with all the [above], which depends on phenomena
2.2.2.1.3. The way to realize that [the nonconceptual experience of the six consciousnesses] is in itself [the inseparability of being] luminous and empty
2.2.2.1.4. Instruction that the nature of saṃsāra and nirvāṇa consists in realizing or not realizing mind
2.2.2.1.5. Explaining the meaning of the rūpakāya
2.2.2.1.6. Explaining the meaning of enlightenment
2.2.2.1.7. Instruction on the meaning of the sūtras
2.2.2.2. Explaining the way in which the conditions [for realizing the dharmadhātu]—the [three] jewels—appear
2.2.2.2.1. Brief introduction
2.2.2.2.2. The way of not seeing Buddhas
2.2.2.2.3. Explaining the way of seeing Buddhas
2.2.2.2.4. Explaining inconceivable enlightened activity
2.2.2.2.5. The way in which enlightenment, due to such realization, is neither near nor far
2.2.3. Explaining how the manner of manifesting and attaining the path arises from having become familiar [with the dharmadhātu] in this way
2.2.3.1. Needing to understand the manner of adopting and rejecting

2.2.3.2. Instruction on the remedy for saṃsāra
2.2.3.3. Instruction on the remedy for peace
2.2.3.4. Teaching that the basic element—the particularly pure abode—is to be unfolded
2.2.3.4.1. Identifying the dharmas that make the basic element unfold
2.2.3.4.2. Explaining the manner in which enlightenment is accomplished due to that
2.2.3.4.3. Instruction on being guarded by the victors
2.2.3.5. The sequence of the manner in which it unfolds
2.2.3.5.1. The manner of seeing by way of engagement through aspiration
2.2.3.5.2. The example of unfolding once one has entered the bhūmis
2.2.3.5.3. Teaching the example for the ultimate
2.2.3.5.4. Detailed explanation
2.2.3.5.4.1. The bhūmi of engagement through aspiration
2.2.3.5.4.2. Instruction on entering the first bhūmi, Utter Joy
2.2.3.5.4.3. Explaining the second bhūmi, The Stainless
2.2.3.5.4.4. Explaining the third bhūmi, The Illuminating
2.2.3.5.4.5. Explaining the fourth bhūmi, The Radiant
2.2.3.5.4.6. The fifth bhūmi, The Difficult to Master
2.2.3.5.4.7. The sixth bhūmi, The Facing
2.2.3.5.4.8. The seventh bhūmi, The Gone Afar
2.2.3.5.4.9. Explaining the eighth bhūmi, The Immovable
2.2.3.5.4.10. Explaining the ninth bhūmi, Excellent Insight
2.2.3.5.4.11. Explaining the tenth bhūmi, Cloud of Dharma
2.3. Praising the dharmakāya free from all stains
2.3.1. The dharmakāya's own essence that is a change of state
2.3.2. Its inconceivability
2.3.3. Explaining the qualities of the final realization of this
2.3.3.1. The way in which mind becomes pure
2.3.3.2. The way in which the body of wisdom is complete
2.3.3.3. Instruction on the qualities of purity
2.3.3.4. The qualities of attainment
2.3.4. Explaining enlightened activity
2.3.4.1. The main enlightened activity of bestowing empowerment upon the children of the victors
2.3.4.2. The manner of promoting the welfare of sentient beings in saṃsāra
2.3.4.3. Instruction on the enlightened activity of exhorting those [dwelling in] peace
2.3.4.4. Explaining the meaning of nirvāṇa that is peace
2.3.4.5. Instruction on the meaning of effortless enlightened activity

Appendix II: Existing Translations of the Praises Attributed to Nāgārjuna in the Tengyur

From among the eighteen praises attributed to Nāgārjuna in the Tibetan *Tengyur*, to my knowledge, eleven have been translated into Western languages so far.[907]

- ***Dharmadhātustava***
  J. Scott in *Shenpen Ösel*, vol. 3, no. 2 (1999): 6–16
  D. Lopez in Lopez 2004: 464–77
  French:
  Paraphrase in Ruegg 1971
  German:
  Brunnhölzl 2004, Nitartha Institute Hamburg (unpublished draft)

- ***Catuḥstava***
  G. Tucci in "Two Hymns of the *Catuḥstava*," *Journal of the Royal Asiatic Society*, 1932: 309–25 (*Niraupamyastava* and *Paramārthastava*)
  C. Lindtner 1982: 128–61 (*Lokātītastava* and *Acintyastava*)
  F. Tola and C. Dragonetti 1985 (*Lokātītastava*, *Niraupamyastava*, *Acintyastava*, *Paramārthastava*)[908]
  B. Shakya in *Buddhist Himalaya* 1, no. 2 (1988), (*Niraupamyastava* and *Paramārthastava*)
  Brunnhölzl 2007: 14–17 (*Niraupamyastava*)
  French:
  La Vallée Poussin in "Quatre Odes," in *Muséon* 14 (1913): 4–16 (*Niraupamyastava*, *Lokātītastava*, *Paramārthastava*, and *Cittavajrastava*)
  Silburn in *Le Bouddhisme*. 1977: 201–9 (*Niraupamyastava* and *Paramārthastava*)
  Italian:
  R. Gnoli in *Nāgārjuna*. 1961: 157–79 (*Niraupamyastava*, *Paramārthastava*, *Lokātītastava*, and *Acintyastava*)

Spanish:
C. Dragonetti in "*Niraupamyastava* y *Paramārthastava*," in *Oriente Occidente*. 1982: 259–71
F. Tola and C. Dragonetti in *Boletin de la Asociacion Española de Orientalistas* 24 (1988): 29–68; 25 (1989): 175–98
Danish:
C. Lindtner in *Juwelkaeden og andre skrifter*. 1980 (*Niraupamyastava* and *Paramārthastava*) and *Nāgārjuna's filosofiske Vaerker*. 1982: 55–66 (*Lokātītastava* and *Acintyastava*)[909]

- ***Cittavajrastava***
  F. Tola and C. Dragonetti 1985
  Brunnhölzl 2007: 17–18
  Spanish:
  F. Tola and C. Dragonetti 1989

- ***Kāyatrayastotra***
  G. Roerich in *The Blue Annals*, p. 2
  Brunnhölzl 2007: 18–21 (including major parts of the autocommentary)

- ***Dvādaśakāranayastotra***
  Nālandā Translation Committee 1983 (as "Praise to the Buddha")
  T. Dewar in *Bodhi*, vol. 5, no. 1 (2002): 33–34

- ***Aṣṭamahāsthānacaityastotra***
  H. Nakamura in *Indianisme et Bouddhisme. Mélanges offerts à Mgr. Étienne Lamotte*. 1980: 264–65[910]

- ***Narakoddharastava***
  C. Lindtner in *Acta Orientalia* 40 (1979): 146–55[911]

- ***Prajñāpāramitāstotra*** (as a work by Rāhulabhadra)
  E. Conze in Conze et al. 1999: 147–49
  Brunnhölzl 2007: 4–7
  French:
  E. Lamotte in *Le Traité de la Grande Vertu de Sagesse de Nāgārjuna*. Tome 3: 1374

Appendix III: Translations of the Remaining Praises

In Praise of Paying Homage to Sentient Beings (*Sattvārādhanastava*)[912]

To have respect for me means [to act for] the welfare of beings, not any other [kind of] respect.
Those who do not abandon compassion are the ones who have respect for me.
Those who have fallen, being in a state of abandoning compassion,
Can be uplifted from that [state only] through compassion but not through anything else. [1]

Those who take care of sentient beings with compassion
Both please me and carry the load of the teachings.
Those who possess ethics, erudition, compassion,
Insight, and clarity always venerate the Tathāgata. [2]

I reached accomplishment because I benefited sentient beings—
It is only for the welfare of sentient beings that I have assumed this body.
Those who harbor harmful intentions toward sentient beings,
Why would they resort to me, being the ones who disrespect me? [3]

Looking after the benefit of sentient beings is veneration—
It offers joy to [my] mind as the one being venerated.
But any veneration whose nature is harmful or which hurts others
Is not, even if well performed, as it does not comply with [me as] the one being venerated. [4]

My wives, children, riches, grandeur, kingdom,
Flesh, blood, fat, eyes, and body
I sacrificed out of loving-kindness for these [beings]—
So if you harm them, you harm me. [5]

To promote the welfare of beings is the supreme way to venerate me,
But to inflict harm on beings is the supreme way to harm me.
Since sentient beings and I experience happiness and suffering in the same way,
How could someone who is hostile toward beings be my disciple? [6]

It was for sentient beings that I achieved virtuous deeds, pleased the protectors,
And attained the pāramitās, solely being grounded in the welfare of the assembly of beings.
Through my mind being eagerly engaged in the welfare of beings, I vanquished Māra's power.
It was by virtue of how sentient beings acted in all kinds of ways that I became a Buddha. [7]

If there had been no beings, cherished like friends, through all my lifetimes,
On what basis had loving-kindness been established here, what had compassion focused on,
What had been the object of equanimity, joy, and so forth, for whom had liberation and such occurred,
And for whose sake had patience been cultivated for a long time with a mind set on compassion? [8]

It was precisely those wandering through [various] forms of existence, such as elephants, to whom I showed generosity many times.
It was these very sentient beings who approached me as the vessels for my gifts and whom I had take them.
By virtue of these sentient beings wandering through various forms of existence, my compassion flourished.
If I were not[913] protecting these sentient beings, for whose sake was this welfare provided? [9]

If there were no beings in saṃsāra—which abounds with [situations of them] heading for disaster—
Who have grown so accustomed to arriving [nowhere but] in the realm of Yama through playing their parts in spinning through their lives,
Why would I—the Sugata, this amazing great being—wish to liberate them from saṃsāra,
If there were no sentient beings whom I cherish? [10]

For as long as my teachings that instruct the world are shining brilliantly
You people who long to benefit others should remain.
Studying again and again what I did for the sake of sentient beings, you who never grow weary of it,
Without becoming exhausted, should apply this body [so that it embodies] the essence of my words. [11]

This completes what the Bhagavat spoke to the sixteen great śrāvakas in the passage called "Alkaline River"[914] *in the* Bodhisattvapiṭaka[sūtra], *summarized in verses by master Nāgārjuna as* In Praise of Pleasing Sentient Beings.[915]

In Praise of The One Beyond Praise *(Stutyatītastava)*

The Tathāgata who has traveled
The unsurpassable path is beyond praise,
But with a mind full of respect and joy,
I will praise the one beyond praise. [1]

Though you see entities being devoid
Of self, other, and both,
Your compassion does not turn away
From sentient beings—how marvelous! [2]

Not arisen by any nature
And in the sphere beyond words—
The dharmas that you taught
Represent your being marvelous. [3]

The skandhas, dhātus, and āyatanas
You have indeed proclaimed,
But any clinging to them too
You countered later on. [4]

Not coming from conditions,
How could entities arise from conditions?
Through saying so, O wise one,
You cut through reference points. [5]

Coming about due to a collection [of causes],
[Entities] originate from this collection as their cause—
That those who see it that way rely on the two extremes
Is what you see very clearly. [6]

That entities [just] come about in dependence on conditions
Is what you have maintained indeed.
But it being a flaw that they are [truly] produced that way
You, O teacher, have seen like that. [7]

Neither coming from anywhere,
Nor going anywhere,
All entities are similar to reflections—
This is what you held. [8]

In order to relinquish all views,
O protector, you declared [entities] to be empty.
But that too is an imputation,
O protector—you did not hold that this is really so. [9]

You assert neither empty nor nonempty,
Nor are you pleased with both.
There is no dispute about this—
It is the approach of your great speech. [10]

"There are no entities that are not other,
Nor any that are other, nor both," you said.
Since being one or other is abandoned,
No matter which way, entities do not exist. [11]

If the triad of arising and so on existed,
The characteristics of conditioned phenomena would exist,
And all three of them, such as arising,
Would be different as well. [12]

On its own, each one of the three, such as arising,
Is incapable of conditioned functioning.
Also, there is no meeting
Of one coming together with another. [13]

Thus, neither characteristics nor their basis exist.
Since they are not established this way,
Conditioned phenomena are not established,
Let alone unconditioned phenomena being established. [14]

O lion of speech, your speaking like that
Is just like a lion['s roar] dispelling
The self-infatuation of Vindhya-elephants
With their trumpeting. [15]

Just as people embarked on a path
Do not rely on various harmful things
Or bad paths of [wrong] views, through relying on you,
We rely on neither existence nor nonexistence. [16]

Those who understand properly
What you said with implications
Need not understand again
What you said with implications. [17]

In those who understand
All entities to be equal to nirvāṇa,
How could any clinging to "me"
Arise at such a point? [18]

Through my merit of praising you,
The supreme of knowers,
The knower of true reality,
May [all beings in] the world become supreme knowers. [19]

In Praise of The Unsurpassable One (*Niruttarastava*)

Having left behind this and yonder shore,
You illuminate the supreme nature of all that can be known
Through the power of your miraculous display of wisdom—
To the unsurpassable, I pay homage. [1]

In you, there is neither knowing nor nonknowing,
Neither a yogin nor an ordinary person,

Neither meditation nor nonmeditation—
To the unsurpassable, I pay homage. [2]

Your luminous single wisdom
Determines all knowable objects without exception,
Thus being unequalled and immeasurable—
To the unsurpassable, I pay homage. [3]

Without any coarse or subtle,
Heavy or light particles,
Not having the nature of snake-feet—[916]
To the unsurpassable, I pay homage. [4]

Just as when someone proceeds through a desert
Through the power of fireflies,
You eliminate our darkness through your light—
To the unsurpassable, I pay homage. [5]

For the dancers who move their feet
Through the miraculous power of magical creation,[917]
You are the guide who sees the path—
To the unsurpassable, I pay homage. [6]

Nothing in you is fractional or meaningless,
Rather, having relinquished both,
You are the omniscient mighty sovereign—
To the unsurpassable, I pay homage. [7]

All flaws utterly relinquished,
Far away from what has the nature of stains,
Free from being and nonbeing—
To the unsurpassable, I pay homage. [8]

In Praise of Venerable Noble Mañjuśrī's Compassion (*Āryamañjuśrībhāṭṭa-rakakaruṇāstotra*)

You have eliminated all flaws without exception,
And your fame, sage, pervades the entire world.
Endowed with an utterly firm and glorious body,
O glorious one, I always pay homage to you. [1]

The whole world keeps crying out to you,
And you protect it from all kinds of being destitute.
Though I am suffering, I [must be] lowly—
You, why do you not dispel it? [2]

Bhagavat, it's unfair that you always and everywhere
Are of service to everybody in all respects,
But do not favor me even with a glance—
Therefore, I'm indeed of very low fortune. [3]

If you who are endowed with qualities and dispel flaws
Make efforts in protecting all beings with good minds,
Though my mind holds on to you so tightly,
How come I am tortured by being destitute? [4]

You with the nature of compassion,
With your two eyes, pure like lotuses,
You benefit beings, but that you do not see
That I am suffering, alas, this is so painful! [5]

Those with devastated minds you always comfort
For a long time with the lotuses of your hands,
But through the heat of my faulty fortune,
They remain invisible, so far away. [6]

With your two ears, so sharp and pure,
Though I lament loudly right in front of you,
Agonized by the suffering in my body,
Why do you not hear of my lowliness? [7]

If you who you guide with compassion in every situation,
Make [even] the kinds of beings who went to the hells happy,
Couldn't you have some compassion and kindness,
O Bhagavat, for me, an evil one, as well? [8]

If you, who benefit the lowly world,
Are endowed with such youthful play
And yet do not protect me, tormented here by suffering,
It is the flaw of my evil thinking. [9]

"Who is suffering here?
Which fools have used up their prosperity?"
[Asking like this,] you keep roaming and protecting,
But that you still do not see my destitution is most amazing. [10]

"Some, I should favor with words,
Others, with temporary vast prosperity"—
Why does your superior knowledge
That makes efforts in such ways not protect me? [11]

Whoever has confidence in you is not unhappy.
There is no one who has confidence in you and yet is low in merit.
I have confidence in you [too], but why is it that I suffer?
This is the birth of a real miracle! [12]

O great physician who cuts through suffering,
If you abandon me as well,
With all my merit being crushed, to whom else
Should I turn for refuge then—you tell me! [13]

Your mind is always full of loving-kindness for beings,
As if they were an only child, and you engage in liberating them.
If even you don't dispel what harms me,
I am without protector, simply trounced. [14]

Bhagavat, if you, just by thinking of them,
Shower all matchless fruitions upon beings,
Though I serve you and pay every respect,
Why do you always procrastinate on my side? [15]

Through whatever virtue I have accumulated by expressing
A mere fraction of your qualities through such lamentations,
[May I become] the excellent vase of accomplishing
The possession of the nature of vast merit by all beings. [16]

May I turn into your youthful body,
Which is like a wish-fulfilling tree, with its two feet moving
As belonging to a rūpakāya resembling a wish-fulfilling jewel,
And in all lifetimes be the one in charge [of beings]. [17]

In Praise of the Stūpas of the Eight Great Places *(Aṣṭamahāsthānacaitya-stotra)*

Having first generated bodhicitta,
You gathered the accumulations for three countless eons,
Became a Buddha at enlightenment's heart,[918] and tamed the māras—
To the stūpa of great enlightenment, I pay homage. [1]

In the city of Kapilavastu, the foundation of the dharma,
You were born by your mother Māyā into the Śākya clan of Śuddhodana.
Upon raising your body, your right hip was supported by Brahmā—
To the stūpa of auspiciousness, I pay homage. [2]

You went to Vārāṇasī and so on for alms
And tamed the mad elephants of [king] Bimbisāra
Through the power of a finger on your hand—
To the stūpa of taming the city, I pay homage. [3]

While resting[919] on a lawn,
Halumañju offered you honey,
Passed away in a well, and was born in the Trayastriṃśa [heaven]—
To the stūpa of compassion arising, I pay homage. [4]

Upon Brahmā having offered a wheel, you turned the wheel [of dharma],
Tamed the six tīrthika teachers through your power,
And satisfied gods and humans through a [great] number of emanations—
To the stūpa of displaying miracles, I pay homage. [5]

With hosts of nāgas, such as Nanda,
Paying their respects and girls providing milk,
You subjugated all difficulties and the world without exception—
To the stūpa of peaceful victory, I pay homage. [6]

Being surrounded by bodhisattvas,
Pratyekabuddhas, and śrāvaka arhats,
You established them in the vows and ethics—
To the stūpa of complete purity, I pay homage. [7]

[Having fulfilled] your intention to guide impermanent beings
And having descended from the gods, at the end of all your deeds,
Being supplicated by Cunda, you completed [your life] three months later—[920]
To the stūpa of entering nirvāṇa, I pay homage. [8]

A Praise by Paying Homage (*Vandanāstotra*)

You have relinquished the web of harming, desire, hatred,
And what bewilders in the wheel of existence.
Bestower of boons, supreme victor,
Supremely born Buddha—I pay homage to you. [1]

Perfect knower, complete Buddha,
Worshipped by gods and nongods,
Guru of the three worlds,
Invincible and unequalled,
Vanquishing māra's power—I pay homage to you. [2]

Born as the son of the king of Śākyas,
Your dynasty is known as the lineage of the sun.
Heroic and wonderful Buddha,
Embodying the entire host of qualities—
Gods, humans, and the wind-deities pay homage to you. [3]

Your body resembles the tops of the golden mountains,[921]
Is endowed with eyes [like] the petals of a lotus,
Possesses a golden hue,
And has the thirty-two marks,
The excellent auspicious signs—I pay homage to you. [4]

Possessing an orb [emitting] fire, lightning,
Sparks, and a thousand sun rays,
You are adorned with power,
Endowed with unequalled strength—I pay homage to you. [5]

Highest glorious one, perfectly endowed
With blazing merit and discipline,
Supreme lord of sages,

Having found perfect enlightenment,
You are venerated [even] by the very haughty—I pay homage to you. [6]

For the sake of benefitting beings and their happiness,
You deal with them with compassion.
Since you entered true reality,
You proceeded to the city of nirvāṇa—I pay homage to you. [7]

Through whatever merit I have accumulated
By my praising the victor—
Venerated by uragas, kinnaras,[922]
Gods, and asuras—in this way,
May all sentient beings
Come to realize enlightenment. [8]

Glossary: English–Sanskrit–Tibetan

English	***Sanskrit***	***Tibetan***
adventitious stains	āgantukamala	glo bur gyi dri ma
afflicted ignorance	kliṣṭāvidyā	nyon mongs can gyi ma rigpa
affliction	kleśa	nyon mongs
afflictive obscuration	kleṣāvaraṇa	nyon mongs pa'i sgrib pa
basic element	dhātu	khams
bhūmi of engagement through aspiration	adhimukticaryābhūmi	mos pas spyod pa'i sa
calm abiding	śamatha	zhi gnas
causal condition	hetupratyaya	rgyu rkyen
clinging to reality/real existence	*satyagrahaṇa	bden 'dzin
cognition	buddhi	blo
cognitive obscuration	jñeyāvaraṇa	shes bya'i sgrib pa
cognizance	vijñapti	rnam par rig pa
conception	kalpanā, vikalpa	rtog pa, rnam rtog
consciousness	(vi)jñāna	(rnam par) shes pa
correct imagination	bhūtaparikalpa	yang dag kun rtog
definitive meaning	nītārtha	nges don
dharmas that concord with enlightenment	bodhipakṣadharma	byang chub phyogs chos
disposition	gotra	rigs
emptiness endowed with the supreme of all aspects	sarvākāravaropetāśūnyatā	rnam kun mchog ldan gyi stong pa nyid
entity	bhāva/vastu	dngos po
expedient meaning	neyārtha	drang don

false imagination	abhūtaparikalpa	yang dag ma yin kun rtog
four realities of the noble ones	caturāryasatya	’phags pa’i bden pa bzhi
freedom from reference points	niṣprapañca	spros bral
(fundamental) change of state	āśrayaparivṛtti	gnas (yongs su) gyur pa
ground of the latent tendencies of ignorance	avidyāvāsanābhūmi	ma rig bag chags kyi sa
identity	ātman	bdag
identitylessness	nairātmya	bdag med
imaginary (nature)	parikalpita(svabhāva)	kun brtags (kyi rang bzhin)
immediate condition	samanantarapratyaya	de ma thag rkyen
implicative negation	paryudāsapratiṣedha	ma yin dgag
innate	sahaja	lhan skyes
latent tendencies of listening	śrutavāsanā	thos pa’i bag chags
latent tendency	vāsanā	bag chags
meditative absorption of cessation	nirodhasamāpatti	’gog pa’i snyoms ’jug
meditative absorption without discrimination	asaṃjñisamāpatti	’du shes med pa’i snyoms ’jug
meditative equipoise	samāhita	mnyam bzhag
mental consciousness	manovijñāna	yid kyi rnam shes
mentation	manas	yid
mere cognizance	vijñaptimātra	rnam rig tsam
Mere Mentalist	—	sems tsam pa
mere mind (Mere Mentalism)	cittamātra	sems tsam
mind	citta	sems
mindfulness	smṛti	dran pa
natural outflow	niṣyanda	rgyu mthun pa
naturally abiding disposition	prakṛtisthagotra	rang bzhin gnas rigs
nature	svabhāva	rang bzhin/ngo bo nyid
nature of phenomena	dharmatā	chos nyid
nirvāṇa with remainder	sāvaśeṣanirvāṇa	lhag bcas myang ’das
nirvāṇa without remainder	nirupadhiśeṣanirvāṇa	lhag med myang ’das
nominal ultimate	paryāyaparamārtha	rnam grangs pa’i don dam

nonabiding nirvāṇa	apratiṣṭhitanirvāṇa	mi gnas pa'i mya ngan las 'das pa
nonafflicted ignorance	akliṣṭāvidyā	nyon mongs can ma yin pa'i ma rig pa
nonconceptual wisdom	nirvikalpajñāna	rnam par mi rtog pa'i ye shes
nonentity	abhāva/avastu	dngos med
nonimplicative negation	prasajyapratiṣedha	med dgag
nonnominal ultimate	aparyāyaparamārtha	rnam grangs ma yin pa'i don dam
nonreferential	anupalambha, anālambana	mi dmigs pa, dmigs med
object generality	arthasāmānya	don spyi
other-dependent (nature)	paratantra(svabhāva)	gzhan dbang (gi rang bzhin)
other-empty	—	gzhan stong
perfect (nature)	pariniṣpanna(svabhāva)	yongs grub (kyi rang bzhin)
personal identitylessness	pudgalanairātmya	gang zag gi bdag med
personally experienced (wisdom)	pratyātmavedanīya(jñāna) (svapratyātmāryajñāna)	so so rang rig (pa'i ye shes)
phenomenal identitylessness	dharmanairātmya	chos kyi bdag med
philosophical system	siddhānta	grub mtha'
reality	satya	bden pa
reference point	prapañca	spros pa
reification	bhāvagrāha	dngos 'dzin
seeming (reality)	saṃvṛti(satya)	kun rdzob (bden pa)
self-aware(ness)	svasaṃvedana, svasaṃvitti	rang rig
self-empty	—	rang stong
subsequent attainment	pṛṣṭhalabdha	rjes thob
superior insight	vipaśyanā	lhag mthong
three natures	trisvabhāva	ngo bo nyid/rang bzhin gsum
three spheres	trimaṇḍala	'khor gsum
true reality	tattva	de (kho na) nyid
ultimate reality	paramārthasatya	don dam bden pa
unfolding disposition	paripuṣṭagotra	rgyas 'gyur gyi rigs

unity	yuganaddha	zung 'jug
views about a real personality	satkāyadṛṣṭi	'jig tshogs la lta ba
wisdom that knows suchness	yathāvatjñāna	ji lta ba mkhyen pa'i ye shes
wisdom that knows variety	yāvatjñāna	ji snyed mkhyen pa'i ye shes

Glossary: Tibetan–Sanskrit–English

Tibetan	*Sanskrit*	*English*
kun brtags (kyi rang bzhin)	parikalpita(svabhāva)	imaginary (nature)
kun rdzob (bden pa)	saṃvṛti(satya)	seeming (reality)
khams	dhātu	constituent, basic element
'khor gsum	trimaṇḍala	three spheres
gang zag gi bdag med	pudgalanairātmya	personal identitylessness
grub mtha'	siddhānta	philosophical system
glo bur gyi dri ma	āgantukamala	adventitious stains
rgyas 'gyur gyi rigs	paripuṣṭagotra	unfolding disposition
rgyu mthun pa	niṣyanda	natural outflow
nges don	nītārtha	definitive meaning
ngo bo nyid	svabhāva	nature
dngos po	bhāva/vastu	entity
dngos med	abhāva/avastu	nonentity
dngos 'dzin	bhāvagrāha	reification
chos kyi bdag med	dharmanairātmya	phenomenal identitylessness
chos nyid	dharmatā	nature of phenomena
ji snyed mkhyen pa'i ye shes	yāvatjñāna	wisdom that knows variety
ji lta ba mkhyen pa'i ye shes	yathāvatjñāna	wisdom that knows suchness
'jig tshogs la lta ba	satkāyadṛṣṭi	views about a real personality
nyon mongs	kleśa	affliction
nyon mongs can gyi ma rig pa	kliṣṭāvidyā	afflicted ignorance

nyon mongs can ma yin pa'i ma rig pa	akliṣṭāvidyā	nonafflicted ignorance
nyon mongs pa'i sgrib pa	kleṣāvaraṇa	afflictive obscuration
mnyam bzhag	samāhita	meditative equipoise
rtog pa	kalpanā	conception
thos pa'i bag chags	śrutavāsanā	latent tendencies of listening
de (kho na) nyid	tattva	true reality
de ma thag rkyen	samanantarapratyaya	immediate condition
don dam bden pa	paramārthasatya	ultimate reality
don spyi	arthasāmānya	object-generality
drang don	neyārtha	expedient meaning
bdag	ātman	identity
bdag rkyen	adhipatipratyaya	dominant condition
bdag med	nairātmya	identitylessness
bden pa	satya	reality
bden 'dzin	*satyagrahaṇa	clinging to reality/ real existence
'du shes med pa'i snyoms 'jug	asaṃjñisamāpatti	meditative absorption without discrimination
gnas (yongs su) gyur pa	āśrayaparivṛtti	(fundamental) change of state
rnam kun mchog ldan gyi stong pa nyid	sarvākāravaropetāśūnyatā	emptiness endowed with the supreme of all aspects
rnam grangs pa'i don dam	paryāyaparamārtha	nominal ultimate
rnam grangs ma yin pa'i don dam	aparyāyaparamārtha	nonnominal ultimate
rnam rtog	vikalpa	conception
rnam par rig pa	vijñapti	cognizance
rnam par shes pa	vijñāna	consciousness
rnam rig tsam	vijñaptimātra	mere cognizance
spros pa	prapañca	reference point
spros bral	niṣprapañca	freedom from reference points
'phags pa'i bden pa bzhi	caturāryasatya	four realities of the noble ones

bag chags	vāsanā	latent tendency
byang chub phyogs chos	bodhipakṣadharma	dharmas that concord with enlightenment
ma yin dgag	paryudāsapratiṣedha	implicative negation
ma rig bag chags kyi sa	avidyāvāsanābhūmi	ground of the latent tendencies of ignorance
mi gnas pa'i mya ngan las 'das pa	apratiṣṭhitanirvāṇa	nonabiding nirvāṇa
med dgag	prasajyapratiṣedha	nonimplicative negation
mos pas spyod pa'i sa	adhimukticaryābhūmi	bhūmi of engagement through aspiration
dmigs rkyen	ālambanapratyaya	object condition
dmigs med	anupalambha, anupalabdhi	nonreferential
zhi gnas	śamatha	calm abiding
gzhan stong	—	other-empty
gzhan dbang (gi rang bzhin)	paratantra(svabhāva)	other-dependent (nature)
zab mo lta rgyud	—	lineage of profound view
zung 'jug	yuganaddha	unity
yang dag kun rtog	bhūtaparikalpa	correct imagination
yang dag ma yin kun rtog	abhūtaparikalpa	false imagination
yid	manas	mentation
yid kyi rnam shes	manovijñāna	mental consciousness
yongs grub (kyi rang bzhin)	pariniṣpanna(svabhāva)	perfect (nature)
rang stong	—	self-empty
rang bzhin	svabhāva	nature
rang bzhin gnas rigs	prakṛtisthagotra	naturally abiding disposition
rang bzhin gsum	trisvabhāva	three natures
rang rig	svasaṃvedana, svasaṃvitti	self-aware(ness)
rang sangs rgyas	pratyekabuddha	pratyekabuddha
rigs	gotra	disposition
shes bya'i sgrib pa	jñeyāvaraṇa	cognitive obscuration
sems	citta	mind
sems tsam	cittamātra	mere mind,

		Mere Mentalism
sems tsam pa	—	Mere Mentalist
so so rang rig (pa'i ye shes)	pratyātmavedanīya(jñāna) (svapratyātmāryajñāna)	personally experienced (wisdom)
lhag bcas myang 'das	sāvaśeṣanirvāṇa	nirvāṇa with remainder
lhag mthong	vipaśyanā	superior insight
lhag med myang 'das	nirupadhiśeṣanirvāṇa	nirvāṇa without remainder
lhan skyes	sahaja	innate

Bibliography

Canonical Works

Āryadeva. *Jñānasārasamucchaya*. (Ye shes snying po kun las btus pa). P5251. ACIP TD3851.

Āryaśūra. *Pāramitāsamāsa*. (Pha rol tu phyin pa bsdus pa). P5340.

Asaṅga. *Abhidharmasamucchaya*. (Mngon pa kun btus). P5550.

——. *Mahāyānasaṃgraha*. (Theg chen bsdus pa). P5549.

——. *Ratnagotravibhāgavyākhyā* or *Mahāyānottaratantraśāstravyākhyā*. (Theg pa chen po'i rgyud bla ma'i bstan bcos rnam par bshad pa). Sanskrit edition by E. H. Johnston. Patna: Bihar Research Society, 1950. P5526.

——. *Yogācārabhūmi*. (Rnal 'byor spyod pa'i sa). P5536. ACIP TD4035.

Atiśa. *Bodhipathapradīpapañjikā*. (Byang chub lam gyi sgron ma'i dka' 'grel). P5344. ACIP TD3948.

——. *Dharmadhātudarśanagīti*. (Chos kyi dbyings la lta ba'i glu). P3153/5388.

——. *Madhyamakopadeśa*. (Dbu ma'i man ngag). P5324/5326/5381.

——. *RatnakaraṇḍodghātanāmaMadhyamakopadeśa*. (Dbu ma'i man ngag rin po che'i za ma tog kha phye ba). P5325.

Bhāvaviveka. *Madhyamakahṛdayakārikā*. (Dbu ma'i snying po'i tshig le'ur byas pa). P5255. ACIP TD3855.

——. *Madhyamakaratnapradīpa*. (Dbu ma rin po che'i sgron ma). P5254. ACIP TD3854.

Candrakīrti. *Catuḥśatakaṭīkā*. (Bzhi brgya pa'i rgya cher 'grel pa). P5266. ACIP TD3865.

——. *Madhyamakaprajñāvatāra*. (Dbu ma shes rab la 'jug pa). P5264. ACIP TD3863.

——. *Madhyamakāvatāra*. (Dbu ma la 'jug pa). Sanskrit edition with *Madhyamakāvatārabhāṣya* by L. de La Vallée Poussin. Bibliotheca Buddhica 9. St. Petersburg, 1907–12. P5261/5262. ACIP TD3861.

——. *Madhyamakāvatārabhāṣya*. (Dbu ma la 'jug pa'i bshad pa). P5263. ACIP TD3862.

——. *Mūlamadhyamakavṛttiprasannapadā*. (Dbu ma'i rtsa ba'i 'grel pa tshig gsal ba). Sanskrit edition with Nāgārjuna's *Mūlamadhyamakakārikā* by L. de La Vallée Poussin. Bibliotheca Buddhica 4. St. Petersburg, 1903–13 (Corrections publ. by J. W. de Jong, *Indo-Iranian Journal* 20 (1978): 25–59, 217–52). P5260. ACIP TD3860.

——. *Śūnyatāsaptativṛtti.* (Stong nyid bdun cu pa'i 'grel pa). P5268. ACIP TD3867.

——. *Yuktiṣaṣṭikāvṛtti.* (Rigs pa drug cu pa'i 'grel pa). P5265. ACIP TD3864.

Dharmakīrti. *Pramāṇavārttika.* (Tshad ma rnam 'grel). P5709. ACIP TD4210.

Haribhadra. *Abhisamayālaṃkāranāmaprajñāpāramitopadeśaśāstravivṛtti.* (Shes rab kyi pha rol tu phyin pa'i man ngag gi bstan bcos mngon par rtogs pa'i rgyan ces bya bai 'grel pa). P5191. ACIP TD3793.

——. *Aṣṭasāhasrikāprajñāpāramitāvyākhyānābhisamayālaṃkārālokā.* (Shes rab kyi pha rol tu phyin pa brgyad stong pa'i bshad pa mngon par rtogs pa'i rgyan gyi snang ba). Sanskrit ed. U. Wogihara. Tokyo 1932–35. P5189.

Jayānanda. *Madhyamakāvatāraṭīkā.* (Dbu ma la 'jug pa'i 'grel bshad). P5271. ACIP TD3870.

Jñānagarbha. *Satyadvayavibhāga.* (Bden gnyis rnam 'byed). [Not in P.] T3881. ACIP TD3881.

Kamalaśīla. *Bhāvanākrama.* (Sgom pa'i rim pa) Sanskrit edition of First *Bhāvanākrama* by G. Tucci. *Minor Buddhist Texts*, Part 2. Serie Orientale Roma 9/2, 1958 (Delhi: Motilal Banarsidass, reprint 1986, pp. 497–539). Third *Bhāvanākrama* by G. Tucci. *Minor Buddhist Texts*, Part 3. Serie Orientale Roma 43, 1971. P5310–5312. ACIP TD3915–3917.

——. *Madhyamakālaṃkārapañjikā.* (Dbu ma rgyan gyi dka' 'grel). P5286. ACIP TD3886.

Maitreya. *Abhisamayālaṃkāra.* (Mngon rtogs rgyan). P5148. ACIP TD3786.

——. *Dharmadharmatāvibhāga.* (Chos dang chos nyid rnam par 'byed pa). P5523/5224.

——. *Madhyāntavibhāga.* (Dbus dang mtha' rnam par 'byed pa). P5522.

——. *Mahāyānasūtrālaṃkāra.* (Theg pa chen po'i mdo sde rgyan). P5521.

——. *Ratnagotravibhāgamahāyānottaratantraśāstra.* (Theg pa chen po'i rgyud bla ma). Sanskrit edition by E. H. Johnston. Patna, India: The Bihar Research Society, 1950 (includes the *Ratnagotravibhāgavyākhyā*). P5525. ACIP TD4024.

Nāgārjuna. *Acintyastava.* (Bsam gyis mi khyab par bstod pa). P2019.

——. *Āryamañjuśrībhāṭṭarakakaruṇāstotra.* (Rje btsun 'phags pa 'jam dpal gyi snying rje la bstod pa). P2023.

——. *Bhāvanākrama.* (Sgom pa'i rim pa). P5304.

——. *Bodhicittavivaraṇa.* (Byang chub sems kyi 'grel pa). P5470.

——. *Cittavajrastava.* (Sems kyi rdo rje bstod pa). P2013.

——. *Dharmadhātustava.* (Chos dbyings bstod pa). P2010.

——. *Kāyatrayastotra.* (Sku gsum la bstod pa). P2015.

——. *Lokātītastava.* ('jig rten las 'das pa'i bstod pa). P2012.

——. *Mahāyānaviṃśikā.* (Theg pa chen po nyi shu pa). P5465. ACIP TD3833.

——. *Mūlamadhyamakavṛttyakutobhayā.* (Dbu ma rtsa ba'i 'grel pa ga las 'jigs med). P5229.

——. *Niraupamyastava*. (Dpe med par bstod pa). P2011.

——. *Niruttarastava*. (Bla na med pa'i bstod pa). P2021.

——. *Paramārthastava*. (Don dam par bstod pa). P2014.

——. *Prajñānāmamūlamadhyamakakārikā*. (Dbu ma rtsa ba'i tshig le'ur byas pa shes rab ces bya ba). P5224. ACIP TD3824.

——. *Pratītyasamutpādahṛdayakārikā*. (Rten cing 'brel bar 'byung ba'i snying po'i tshig le'ur byas pa). P5236/5467.

——. *Pratītyasamutpādahṛdayavyākhyāna*. (Rten cing 'brel bar 'byung ba'i snying po'i rnam par bshad pa). P5237/5468.

——. *Rājaparikathāratnāvalī*. (Rgyal po la gtam bya ba rin po che'i phreng ba). P5658.

——. *Sattvārādhanastava*. (Sems can la mgu bar bya ba'i bstod pa). P2017. Sanskrit edition in Lévi 1929, p. 264.

——. *Stutyatītastava*. (Bstod pa las 'das par bstod pa). P2020.

——. *Suhṛllekha*. (Bshes pa'i springs yig). P5682.

——. *Śūnyatāsaptati*. (Stong nyid bdun cu pa). P5227. ACIP TD3827.

——. *Sūtrasamucchaya*. (Mdo kun las btus pa). P5330. ACIP TD 3934.

——. *Vandanāstotra*. (Phyag 'tshal ba'i bstod pa). P2027.

——. *Vigrahavyāvartanīkārikā*. (Rtsod pa bzlog pa'i tshig le'ur byas pa). Sanskrit edition by E. H. Johnston and A. Kunst in Bhattacharya 1978. P5224. ACIP TD3828.

——. *Yuktiṣaṣṭikā*. (Rigs pa drug cu pa). P5225. ACIP TD3825.

Nāropa. *Paramārthasaṃgrahanāmasekoddeśaṭīkā*. (Dbang mdor bstan pa'i 'grel bshad don dam pa bsdus pa zhes bya ba). Sanskrit edition by M. Carelli. Baroda: Gaekwad Oriental Series, 1941. P2068. D1351.

Saraha. *Dohākośagīti*. (Do hā mdzod kyi glu; "People's Dohā"). P3068.

——. *Dohākośopadeśagīti*. (Mi zad pa'i gter mdzod man ngag gi glu; "Queen's Dohā"). P3111.

Vasubandhu. *Abhidharmakośa*. (Mngon pa mdzod). P5590. ACIP TD4089.

——. *Dharmadharmatāvibhāgabhāṣya*. (Chos dang chos nyid rnam par 'byed pa'i 'grel pa). P5529. ACIP TD4028.

——. *Madhyāntavibhāgabhāṣya*. (Dbus mtha' rnam 'byed kyi 'grel pa). P5528. ACIP TD4027.

——. *Triṃśikākārikā*. (Sum cu pa tshig le'ur byas pa). P5556.

Tibetan Works

Bdud 'joms 'jigs bral ye shes rdo rje. 1991. *The Nyingma School of Tibetan Buddhism*. Trans. Gyurme Dorje and M. Kapstein. 2 vols. Boston: Wisdom Publications.

Blo gros grags pa, 'dzam thang mkhan po. 1993. *Fearless Lion's Roar*. (Rgyu dang 'bras bu'i theg pa mchog gi gnas lugs zab mo'i don rnam par nges pa rje jo nang pa chen po'i ring lugs 'jigs med gdong lnga'i nga ro). Dharamsala: Library of Tibetan Works and Archives.

Blo gros rgya mtsho. 1984. *Chos kyi dbyings su bstod pa'i 'grel pa nges don zab mo'i gter gyi kha 'byed*. (*Dbu med* manuscript). Bylakuppe: Publ. by Ven. Pema Norbu Rinpoche. TBRC no. W27521.

Bsod nams bzang po, gnyag pho ba. n.d. *Dbu ma chos kyi dbyings su bstod pa'i rnam par bshad pa snying po gsal ba*. (*Dbu med* manuscript). 'Dzam thang edition: 605–81. TBRC no. W27553.

——. n.d. *Chos kyi dbyings su bstod pa'i rnam bzhag bdud rtsi'i nying khu*. n.p. TBRC no. W14074.

Bsod nams rgyal mtshan. 1987. *Chos kyi dbyings su bstod pa'i 'grel pa*. In *Dkar chag mthong bas yid 'phrog chos mdzod byed pa'i lde mig*: A bibliography of Sa-skya-pa literature prepared at the order of H. H. Sakya Tridzin, based on a compilation of the Venerable Khenpo Apey and contributions by other Sakyapa scholars. Publ. by Ngawang Topgyal. New Delhi. TBRC no. W11903.

Bu ston rin chen grub. 1931. *History of Buddhism*. Trans. E. Obermiller. Heidelberg: Otto Harrassowitz.

Chos grags rgya mtsho (Karmapa VII). 1985. *The Ocean of Texts on Reasoning. Tshad ma legs par bshad pa thams cad kyi chu bo yongs su `du ba rigs pa'i gzhung lugs kyi rgya mtsho*. 4 vols. Publ. by Karma Thupten Chosphel and Phuntsok. Rumtek (Sikkim, India).

——. n.d. *Mngon rtogs rgyan gyi 'grel pa 'jig rten gsum gyi sgron me*. Unpublished Nitartha *international* File (jigsumsgronmeK7).

Chos kyi 'byung gnas (Situpa VIII). n.d. *Nges don phyag rgya chen po'i smon lam gyi 'grel pa grub pa chog gi zhal lung*. Rumtek Monastery (Sikkim, India).

Chos kyi 'byung gnas (Situpa VIII) and *'Be lo tshe dbang kun khyab. 1972. Sgrub brgyud karma kaṃ tshang brgyud pa rin po che'i rnam par thar pa rab 'byams nor bu zla ba chu shel gyi phreng ba*. 2 vols. Publ. by Gyaltsan and Kesang Legshay. New Delhi.

Chos kyi rgyal mtshan, Se ra rje btsun pa. 2004. *Kar lan klu sgrub dgongs rgyan*. Sarnath: Vajra Vidya Library.

Dbu ma gzhan stong skor bstan bcos phyogs bsdus deb dang po. 1990. Rumtek (Sikkim, India): Karma Shri Nalanda Institute.

Dkon mchog yan lag (Shamarpa V). 2005. *Mngon rtogs rgyan gyi 'grel pa nyung ngu rnam gsal*. Sarnath: Vajra Vidya Library. Also *dbu med* manuscript, n.p., n.d.

Dngul chu thogs med bzang po dpal. 1979. *Theg pa chen po mdo sde rgyan gyi 'grel pa rin po che'i phreng ba*. Bir, India: Dzongsar Institute Library.

Dol po pa shes rab rgyal mtshan. 1988. *The Mountain Dharma Called The Ocean of Definitive Meaning*. (*Ri chos nges don rgya mtsho*). Beijing: Mi rigs dpe skrun khang.

——. n.d. *'phags pa klu sgrub kyis mdzad pa'i chos dbyings bstod pa ('i mchan 'grel)*. Collected Works. Vol. 8. 'Dzam thang edition: 137–57. Also in Dpal brtsegs bod yig dpe rnying zhib 'jug khang 2005 (no. 015689). TBRC no. W21209.

Dpa' bo gtsug lag phreng ba. 2003. *History of the Dharma, A Feast for the Learned.* (Dam pa'i chos kyi 'khor lo bsgyur ba rnams kyi byung ba gsal bar byed pa mkhas pa'i dga' ston). 2 vols. Sarnath: Vajra Vidya Library.

Dpal brtsegs bod yig dpe rnying zhib 'jug khang. 2005. *'Bras spungs dgon du bzhugs su gsol ba'i dpe rnying dkar chag.* 2 vols. Beijing: Mi rigs dpe skrun khang.

Dpal sprul 'jigs med chos kyi dbang po. 1997. *Shes rab kyi pha rol tu phyin pa'i man ngag gi bstan bcos mngon par rtogs pa'i rgyan ces bya ba'i spyi don dang 'bru 'grel.* Beijing: Mi rigs dpe skrun khang.

Dvags po rab 'byams pa chos rgyal bstan pa. 2005. *Dpal rdo rje' tshig zab mo nang gi don gyi 'grel bshad sems kyi rnam par thar pa gsal bar byed pa'i rgyan.* Seattle: Nitartha international.

Glo bo mkhan chen bsod nams lhun grub. *Chos dbyings bstod pa'i rnam bshad don dam snying po* (listed in Jackson 1987, vol. 2, p. 561).

Go bo rab 'byams pa bsod nams seng ge. 2004. *Dbu ma'i spyi don nges don rab gsal. In Go bo rab 'byams pa bsod nams seng ge'i bka' 'bum.* Vol. 5. Dehradun: Sakya College, 1–417.

'Gos lo tsā ba gzhon nu dpal. 1996. *The Blue Annals.* Trans. G. N. Roerich. Delhi: Motilal Banarsidass.

——. 2003a. *Deb ther sngon po.* 2 vols. Sarnath: Vajra Vidya Library.

——. 2003b. *A Commentary on the Uttaratantra.* (Theg pa chen po'i rgyud bla ma'i bstan bcos kyi 'grel bshad de kho na nyid rab tu gsal ba'i me long). Ed. by Klaus-Dieter Mathes (Nepal Research Centre Publications 24). Stuttgart: Franz Steiner Verlag.

'Ju mi pham rgya mtsho. 1975. *A Synopsis of the Heart of the Sugatas, Called Lion's Roar.* (Bde gshegs snying po stong thun chen mo seng ge'i nga ro). In *Collected Writings of 'Jam-mgon 'Ju Mi-pham-rgya-mtsho.* Vol. pa. Ed. by Sonam T. Kazi. Gangtok: fols. 282–304.

——. c. 1990. *The Lion's Roar Proclaiming Other-Emptiness.* (Gzhan stong khas len seng ge'i nga ro). *Collected Works (gsungs 'bum).* Sde dge dgon chen edition. Vol. ga. Ed. by Dilgo Khyentse Rinpoche. Kathmandu: 359–99.

——. 1992. *Dbu ma rgyan rtsa 'grel.* Chengdu, China: Si khron mi rigs dpe skrun khang.

Kong sprul blo gros mtha' yas. 2005. *Rnal 'byor bla na med pa'i rgyud sde rgya mtsho'i snying po bsdus pa zab mo nang don nyung ngu'i tshig gis rnam par 'grol ba zab don snang byed.* Seattle: Nitartha *international.*

——. 1982. *The Treasury of Knowledge.* (Theg pa'i sgo kun las btus pa gsung rab rin po che'i mdzod bslab pa gsum legs par ston pa'i bstan bcos shes bya kun khyab; includes its autocommentary, Shes bya kun la khyab pa'i gzhung lugs nyung ngu'i tshig gis rnam par 'grol ba legs bshad yongs 'du shes bya mhta' yas pa'i rgya mtsho; abbr. Shes bya kun kyab mdzod). 3 vols. Beijing: Mi rigs dpe skrun khang.

——. 1990a. *A Commentary on the Treatise That Points Out the Heart of the Tathāgatas, Called Illuminating Rangjung Dorje's Intention.* (De bzhin gshegs pa' i snying po bstan pa'i bstan bcos kyi rnam 'grel rang byung dgongs gsal). In *Dbu ma gzhan stong skor bstan bcos phyogs bsdus deb dang po*. Rumtek (Sikkim, India): Karma Shri Nalanda Institute, 63–129.

——. 1990b. *A Commentary on the Treatise on The Distinction between Consciousness and Wisdom, Called Ornament of Rangjung Dorje's Intention*. (Rnam par shes pa dang ye shes rnam par 'byed pa'i bstan bcos kyi tshig don go gsal du 'grel pa rang byung dgongs pa'i rgyan). In *Dbu ma gzhan stong skor bstan bcos phyogs bsdus deb dang po*. Rumtek (Sikkim, India): Karma Shri Nalanda Institute, 130–90.

——. n.d. *A Commentary on the Uttaratantra, Called The Unassailable Lion's Roar*. (Theg pa chen po rgyud bla ma'i bstan bcos snying po'i don mngon sum lam gyi bshad srol dang sbyar ba'i rnam par 'grel ba phyir mi ldog pa seng ge nga ro). Rumtek Monastery (Sikkim, India).

Lo chen Dharmaśrī ngag dbang chos 'phel. n. d. *Commentary on Ascertaing the Three Vows*. (Sdom pa gsum rnam par nges pa'i 'grel pa legs bshad ngo mtshar dpag bsam nye ma). Bylakuppe, India: Ngagyur Nyingma Institute.

Mi bskyod rdo rje (Karmapa VIII). 1990. *The Lamp That Excellently Elucidates the System of the Proponents of Other-Empty Madhyamaka*. (Dbu ma gzhan stong smra ba'i srol legs par phye ba'i sgron me). In *Dbu ma gzhan stong skor bstan bcos phyogs bsdus deb dang po*. Rumtek (Sikkim, India): Karma Shri Nalanda Institute.

——. 1996. *The Chariot of the Tagbo Siddhas*. (Dbu ma la 'jug pa'i rnam bshad dpal ldan dus gsum mkhyen pa'i zhal lung dvags brgyud grub pa'i shing rta). Seattle: Nitartha *international*.

——. 2003. *The Noble One Resting at Ease*. (Shes rab kyi pha rol tu phyin pa'i lung chos mtha' dag gi bdud rtsi'i snying por gyur pa gang la ldan pa'i gzhi rje btsun mchog tu dgyes par ngal gso'i yongs 'dus brtol gyi ljon pa rgyas pa). 2 vols. Seattle: Nitartha *international*.

Ngag dbang kun dga' dbang phyug. 1987. *Shes rab kyi pha rol tu phyin pa'i man ngag gi bstan bcos mngon par rtogs pa'i rgyan 'grel pa dang bcas pa'i tshig don snying po gsal ba'i me long*. Bir: Dzongsar Institute Library.

Ngag dbang yon tan bzang po. 2000. *Jo nang chos `byung dang rje jo nang chen po'i ring lugs*. Beijing: Mi rigs dpe skrun khang.

Rang byung rdo rje (Karmapa III). 1990a. *The Treatise That Points Out the Heart of the Tathāgatas*. (De gshegs snying po bstan pa'i bstan bcos). In *Dbu ma gzhan stong skor bstan bcos phyogs bsdus deb dang po*. Rumtek (Sikkim, India): Karma Shri Nalanda Institute.

——. 1990b. *The Treatise on the Distinction between Consciosuness and Wisdom*. (Rnam shes dang ye shes rnam par 'byed pa'i bstan bcos). In *Dbu ma gzhan stong skor bstan bcos phyogs bsdus deb dang po*. Rumtek (Sikkim, India): Karma Shri Nalanda Institute.

——. 2006a. *Collected Works*. (Dpal rgyal dbang ka rma pa sku phreng gsum pa rang byung rdo rje'i gsung 'bum). 11 vols. Lhasa: Dpal brtsegs bod yig dpe rnying zhib 'jug khang.

——. 2006b. *Explanation of the Dharmadharmatāvibhāga*. (Chos dang chos nyid rnam par 'byed pa'i bstan bcos kyi rnam par bshad pa'i rgyan). In *Collected Works*, vol. cha, 488–613.

——. n.d. *Aspiration Prayer of Mahāmudrā*. (Nges don phyag rgya chen po'i smon lam). Rumtek (Sikkim, India).

——. n.d. *Autocommentary on The Profound Inner Reality*. (Zab mo nang gi don gsal bar byed pa'i 'grel pa). Rumtek (Sikkim, India).

——. n.d. *An Explanation of In Praise of Madhyamaka-Dharmadhātu*. (Dbu ma chos dbyings bstod pa'i rnam par bshad pa; *dbu med* manuscript). n. p. Republished in (a) *Mdo sngags mtshams sbyor*. 2003. Lan kru'u: kan su'u mi rigs dpe skrun khang: 219–321. (b) *Mngon rtogs rgyan gyi sa bcad snang byed sgron me dang skabs brgyad kyi stong thun dang dbu ma chos dbyings bstod pa rnam bshad*. 2004. Sarnath: Vajra Vidya Institute: 157–312. TBRC no. W24267.

——. n.d. *The Profound Inner Reality* (Zab mo nang gi don). Rumtek (Sikkim, India).

Rma bya ba byang chub brtson 'grus. 1975. *Dbu ma rtsa ba shes rab kyi 'grel pa 'thad pa'i rgyan*. Rumtek Monastery (Sikkim, India): Publ. by Rang byung rig pa'i rdo rje, Karmapa XVI.

Rong ston shes bya kun rig. n.d. *Chos dbyings bstod pa'i 'grel pa legs bshad rnam par g.yo ba'i sprin*. In *Rong ston śākya rgyal mtshan gyi gsung 'khor*. Dehradun: Sakya College, 629–48.

Sa bzang ma ti paṇ chen blo gros rgyal mtshan. 1977. *Dam pa'i chos mngon pa kun las btus pa'i 'grel pa zhes bya ba rab gsal snang ba*. Gangtok: Gon po Tseten.

Śākya mchog ldan. 1975a. *Chos kyi dbyings su bstod pa zhes bya ba'i bstan bcos kyi rnam par bshad pa chos kyi dbyings rnam par nges pa. The Complete Works (gsuṅ 'bum) of gSer-mdog Paṇ-chen Śākya-mchog-ldan*, vol. 7. Ed. by Kunzang Tobgey. Thimpu, Bhutan: 303–92.

——. 1975b. *The Origin of Madhyamaka*. (Dbu ma'i 'byung tshul rnam par bshad pa'i gtam yid bzhin lhun po). *The Complete Works (gsuṅ 'bum) of gSer-mdog Pan-chen Śākya-mchog-ldan*, vol. 4. Ed. by Kunzang Tobgey. Thimpu, Bhutan: 209–48.

——. 1975c. *Distinction between the Two Traditions of the Great Charioteers*. (Shing rta chen po'i srol gnyis kyi rnam par dbye ba bshad nas nges don gcig tu bsgrub pa'i bstan bcos kyi rgyas 'grel). *The Complete Works (gsuṅ 'bum) of gSer-mdog Pan-chen Śākya-mchog-ldan*, vol. 2. Ed. by Kunzang Tobgey. Thimpu, Bhutan: 471–619.

Śākya rgyal mtshan. n.d. *Chos kyi dbyings su bstod pa'i 'grel pa lta ngan mun sel*. In *A khu dpe tho* MHTL 11446.

Sgam po pa. 1990. *The Jewel Ornament of Liberation*. (Thar pa rin po che'i rgyan). Chengdu, China: Si khron mi rigs dpe skrun khang.

Tāranātha. 1980. *History of Buddhism in India*. Trans. Lama Chimpa and Alaka Chattopadhyaya. Calcutta: Bagchi.

——. 1983. *The Collected Works of Jo-nang rje-btsun Tāranātha*. Leh, Ladakh: Smanrtsis Shesrig Dpemdzod.

——. n.d. *Collected Works*. 'Dzam thang edition. TBRC no. W22276.

Tshal pa kun dga' rdo rje. 1981. *Deb ther dmar po*. Beijing: Mi rigs dpe skrun khang.

Zur mang padma rnam rgyal. n.d. *Full Moon of Questions and Answers*. (Dri lan tshes pa'i zla ba). n.p.

Modern Works

Bareau, André. 1955. *Les sectes bouddhiques du Petit Véhicule*. Saigon: L'École Française d'Extrême-Orient.

Bhattacharyya, Bhaswati. 1978. *The Dialectical Method of Nāgārjuna (Vigrahavyāvartanī)*. Delhi: Motilal Banarsidass.

Brunnhölzl, Karl, trans. 2002a. *The Presentation of Grounds, Paths, and Results in the Causal Vehicle of Characteristics in The Treasury of Knowledge* (*Shes bya kun khyab mdzod*, ch. 9.1 and 10.1). Mt. Allison, Canada: Nitartha Institute.

——, trans. 2002b. *The Presentation of Madhyamaka in The Treasury of Knowledge* (*Shes bya kun khyab mdzod*, selected passages from ch. 6.3, 7.2, and 7.3). Mt. Allison, Canada: Nitartha Institute.

——. 2004. *The Center of the Sunlit Sky*. Ithaca: Snow Lion Publications.

——. 2007. *Straight from the Heart: Buddhist Pith Instructions*. Ithaca: Snow Lion Publications.

Burchardi, Anne. 2002. "Towards an Understanding of *Tathāgatagarbha* Interpretation in Tibet with Special Reference to the *Ratnagotravibhāga*." In Henk Blezer et al., eds., *Religion and Secular Culture in Tibet*. Tibetan Studies 2. Proceedings of the Ninth Seminar of the International Association for Tibetan Studies, Leiden 2000. Leiden: Brill, 59–77.

——. 2007. "The Diversity of the *gzhan stong* Madhyamaka Tradition." *Journal of the International Association for Tibetan Studies* no. 3. www.thdl.org.

Corless, Roger. 1995. "The Chinese Life of Nāgārjuna." In Donald Lopez Jr., ed., *Buddhism in Practice*. Princeton: Princeton University Press, 525–29.

Davidson, Ronald M. 1985. "Buddhist Systems of Transformation: Asraya-parivrtti/-paravrtti among the Yogacara." Ph.D. diss., University of California.

Dragonetti, Carmen. 1979. "Some Notes on the *Pratītyasamutpādahṛdayakārikā* and the *Pratītyasamutpādahṛdayavyākhyāna* Attributed to Nāgārjuna." *Buddhist Studies* 6 (Delhi): 70–73.

Dreyfus, Georges B. J., and Sara L. McClintock, eds. 2003. *The Svātantrika-Prāsaṅgika Distinction*. Boston: Wisdom Publications.

Duckworth, Douglas S. 2005. "Buddha-Nature and a Dialectic of Presence and Absence in the Works of Mi-pham." Ph.D. diss., University of Virginia.

Frauwallner, Erich. 1951. "Amalavijñānam und Ālayavijñānam." *Beiträge zur indischen Philosophie und Altertumskunde. Walther Schubring zum 70. Geburtstag dargebracht.* Alt- und Neu-Indische Studien 7. Hamburg: 148–59.

Gyamtso, Tsultrim, Khenpo Rinpoche. 1988. *Progressive Stages of Meditation on Emptiness*. Trans. Shenpen Hookham. Oxford: Longchen Foundation.

——. 1999. "Commentary on In Praise of Dharmadhātu." *Shenpen Ösel* 3 (2): 17–91.

——. 1999–2000. "In Praise of Dharmadhātu." *Bodhi*, no. 4: 6–16 (verses 38–40); no. 5: 6–29 (verses 41–43).

Harris, Ian Charles. 1991. *The Continuity of Madhyamaka and Yogācāra in Indian Mahāyāna Buddhism*. Leiden: Brill.

Hayashima, Satoshi. 1987. "Sanhokkaijuko." In *Nagasakidaigaku Kyōikugakubu Shakaikagakuronsō*, Nr. 36: 41–90.

Hookham, S. K. 1991. *The Buddha Within*. Albany: State University of New York Press.

Hopkins, Jeffrey. 1983. *Meditation on Emptiness*. Boston: Wisdom Publications.

——. 1998. *Buddhist Advice for Living and Liberation*. Ithaca: Snow Lion Publications.

——. 2002. *Reflections on Reality*. Berkeley: University of California Press.

——. 2006. *Mountain Doctrine*. Ithaca: Snow Lion Publications.

Huntington, C. W. 1995. "A Lost Text of Early Indian Madhyamaka." *AS* 49 (4): 693–767.

Jackson, David P. 1987. *The Entrance Gate for the Wise (Section III)*. 2 vols. Vienna: Arbeitskreis für Tibetische und Buddhistische Studien Universität Wien.

Kano, Kazuo. 2006. "rNgog Blo-ldan Shes-rab's Summary of the *Ratnagotravibhāga*." Ph.D. diss., University of Hamburg.

Kapstein, Matthew T. 2000. "We Are All Gzhan stong pas." *Journal of Buddhist Ethics* 7: 105–25.

Karma Thinley. 1980. *The History of the Sixteen Karmapas of Tibet*. Boulder: Prajñā Press.

Keenan, John P. 1989. "Asaṅga's Understanding of Mādhyamika." *JIABS* 12 (1): 93–107.

King, Richard. 1994. "Early Yogācāra and Its Relationship with the Madhyamaka School." *PEW* 44 (4): 659–83.

Lévi, Sylvain M. 1929. "Autour d'Aśvaghoṣa." *Journal Asiatique* 215: 255–85.

Lindtner, Christian. 1982. *Nāgārjuniana*. Indiske Studier 4. Copenhagen: Akademisk Forlag.

——. 1992. "The *Laṅkāvatārasūtra* in Early Indian Madhyamaka Literature." *AS* 46 (1): 244–79.

——. 1997. "Cittamātra in Indian Mahāyāna until Kamalaśīla." *WZKS* 41: 159–206.

Lopez, Donald S., ed. 2004. *Buddhist Scriptures*. London: Penguin Books.

Mathes, Klaus-Dieter. 1996. *Unterscheidung der Gegebenheiten von ihrem wahren Wesen (Dharmadharmatāvibhāga)*. Swisttal-Odendorf, Germany: Indica et Tibetica Verlag.

——. 1998. "Vordergründige und höchste Wahrheit im *gZhan stong*-Madhyamaka." Annähenrung an das Fremde. 26. Deutscher Orientalistentag vom 25. bis 29.9. 1995 in Leipzig. Ed. by H. Preissler and H. Stein. *Zeitschrift der Deutschen Morgenländischen Gesellschaft* 11: 457–68.

——. 2000. "Tāranātha's Presentation of *trisvabhāva* in the *gŹan stoṅ sñiṅ po.*" *JIABS* 23 (1): 195–223.

——. 2002. "'Gos Lo tsâ ba gZhon nu dpal's Extensive Commentary on and Study of the *Ratnangotraṇvibhāgavyākhyā.*" In Henk Blezer et al., eds., *Religion and Secular Culture in Tibet.* Tibetan Studies 2. Proceedings of the Ninth Seminar of the International Association of Tibetan Studies, Leiden 2000. Leiden: Brill, 79–96.

——. 2004. "Tāranātha's 'Twenty-one Differences with regard to the Profound Meaning'—Comparing the Views of the Two gzhan stoṅ Masters Dol po pa and Śakya mchog ldan." *JIABS* 27(2): 285–328.

Meinert, Carmen. 2003. "Structural Analysis of the *Bsam gtan mig sgron*: A Comparison of the Fourfold Correct Practice in the *Āryāvikalpapraveśanāmadhāraṇī* and the Contents of the Four Main Chapters of the *Bsam gtan mig sgron.*" *JIABS* 26 (1): 175–95.

Murti, T. R. V. 1955. *The Central Philosophy of Buddhism, A Study of the Madhyamika System*. London: George Allen and Unwin.

Pettit, J. W. 1999. *Mipham's Beacon of Certainty*. Boston: Wisdom Publications.

Rawlinson, Andrew. 1983. "The Ambiguity of the Buddha-nature Concept in India and China." In W. Lai and L. Lancaster, eds., *Early Ch'an in China and Tibet.* Berkeley: Asian Humanities Press, 259–79.

Ruegg, David Seyfort. 1969. *La théorie du tathāgatagarbha et du gotra.* Paris: L'École Française d'Extrême-Orient.

——. 1971. "Le Dharmadhâtustava de Nâgârjuna." In *Études Tibetaines: Dediées à la Mémoire de Marcelle Lalou (1890–1967).* Paris: Librairie d'Amérique et d'Orient, 448–71.

——. 1976. "The Meanings of the Term Gotra and the Textual History of the *Ratnagotravibhāga.*" *Bulletin of the School of Oriental and African Studies* 39: 341–63.

——. 1981. *The Literature of the Madhyamaka School of Philosophy in India.* Wiesbaden: Otto Harrassowitz.

Schaeffer, Kurtis R. 1995. "The Enlightened Heart of Buddhahood. A Study and Translation of The Third Karma pa Rang byung rdo rje's Work on Tathagatagarbha, The *De bzhin gshegs pa'i snying po gtan la dbab pa.*" M.A. thesis, University of Washington.

Schmithausen, Lambert. 1971. "Philologische Bemerkungen zum Ratnagotravibhāga." *WZKS* 15: 123–77.

——. 1973. "Zu D. Seyfort Rueggs Buch 'La théorie du *tathāgatagarbha* et du gotra' (Besprechungsaufsatz)." *WZKS* 22: 123–60.

——. 1981. "On Some Aspects of Descriptions of Theories of 'Liberating Insight' and 'Enlightenment' in Early Buddhism." In K. Bruhn and A. Wezler, eds., *Studien zum Jainismus und Buddhismus: Gedenkschrift für L. Alsdorf. Alt- und Neu-Indische Studien* 23. Wiesbaden: 199–250.

——. 1987. *Ālayavijñāna: On the Origin and the Early Development of a Central Concept of*

Yogācāra Philosophy. 2 vols. Tokyo: International Institute for Buddhist Studies.

Schuh, Dieter. 1977. *Erlasse und Sendschreiben Mongolischer Herrscher für Tibetische Geistliche*. Monumenta Tibetica Historica, Band 1. St. Augustin: VGH Wissenschaftsverlag.

Sparham, Gareth. 1993. *Ocean of Eloquence. Tsong kha pa's Commentary on the Yogācāra Doctrine of Mind*. Albany: State University of New York Press.

——. 2001. "Demons on the Mother: Objections to the Perfect Wisdom Sūtras in Tibet." In Guy Newland, ed., *Changing Minds. Contributions to the Study of Buddhism and Tibet in Honor of Jeffrey Hopkins*. Ithaca: Snow Lion Publications, 193–214.

Stearns, Cyrus. 1995. "Dol-po-pa Shes-rab rgyal-mtshan and the Genesis of the *gzhan stong* Position in Tibet." *AS* 49 (4): 829–52.

——. 1999. *The Buddha from Dolpo*. Albany: State University of New York Press.

Takasaki, Jikido. 1966. *A Study on the Ratnagotravibhāga*. Serie Orientale Roma 33. Roma: Istituto Italiano per il Medio ed Estremo Oriente.

Tillemans, Tom J. F., and Toru Tomabechi. 1995. "Le *Dbu ma'i byuṅ tshul* de Śākya mchog ldan." *AS* 49 (4): 891–918.

Tola, Fernando, and Carmen Dragonetti. 1985. "Nāgārjuna's *Catuḥstava*." *Journal of Indian Philosophy* 13: 1–54.

Tucci, Giuseppe. 1986. *Minor Buddhist Texts, Parts 1 and 2*. (Indian reprint. Originally published as Serie Orientale Roma 9 [1956/58]). Delhi: Motilal Banarsidass.

Walser, Joseph. "Nāgārjuna and the *Ratnāvalī*. New Ways to Date an Old Philosopher." *JIABS* 25 (2): 209–62.

Wangchuk, Dorji. 2004. "The rÑiṅ-ma Interpretations of the *Tathāgatagarbha* Theory." *WZKS* 48: 171–213.

Wayman, Alex, and Hideko Wayman. 1974. *The Lion's Roar of Queen Śrīmālā*. New York: Columbia University Press.

Zimmermann, Michael. 2002. *A Buddha Within: The Tathāgatagarbhasūtra. The Earliest Exposition of the Buddha-Nature Teaching in India*. Bibliotheca Philologica et Philosophica Buddhica 6. Tokyo: International Research Institute for Advanced Buddhology, Soka University.

Endnotes

1 Tib. bstod tshogs.

2 The clearest passages that are usually quoted as prophesying Nāgārjuna are found in the *Laṅkāvatārasūtra* (X.163–66; P775, p. 74.3.6–8) and the *Mañjuśrīmūlatantra* (P162, p. 259.3.8–259.4.2; see also Bu ston 1931, vol. 2, p. 111). Two further sūtras are often mentioned as giving such prophecies. In the *Mahāmeghasūtra* (P898, pp. 253.4.8–255.3.2), Nāgārjuna's actual name is not found in either of the translations of this sūtra in the Tibetan and the Chinese canons, but appears in Candrakīrti's autocommentary on the *Madhyamakāvatāra* (ACIP TD3862@245A), when he quotes the *Mahāmeghasūtra in Twelve Thousand Stanzas* (see also Bu ston 1931, vol. 1, p. 129, who is skeptical about that). The *Mahābherīsūtra* (P888, pp. 88.2.4, 97.5.4, and 98.5.7) likewise does not mention Nāgārjuna by name, but refers to him as a reincarnation of a certain Licchavi youth in the same way as the *Mahāmeghasūtra* does (another version is found in the *Suvarṇaprabhāsottamasūtra*, ed. Johannes Nobel, pp. 12–17).

3 Unlike any Sanskrit and Chinese sources, almost by default, Tibetan accounts associate every great Indian master with the famous university of Nālandā, including also Rāhulabhadra and Nāgārjuna (usually, this university is said to only have flourished from the fifth century onward).

4 The Chinese sources speak of King "Righteous" and the Tibetan ones have *bde spyod*, which are understood variously as Sātavāhana (the name of the dynasty), or the personal names Udayāna (there is, however, no king with that name in the said dynasty) or Jantaka (this may rather refer to the place name Dhānyakataka), etc. Walser 2002 identifies Yajña Śrī Sātakarṇi (c. 175–204) of the Sātavāhana dynasty in the eastern Deccan as the most likely candidate.

5 Tibetan sources usually give Nāgārjuna's lifespan as about six hundred years due to his accomplishment of rasāyana (the practice to extract nutrients even from stones or space). He is also presented as a great alchemist, turning rocks into gold and so on.

6 This place is located in the southeast of India near the delta of the river Kṛṣṇa (present-day Amaravati in Andhra Pradesh). The Buddha is said to have taught the *Kālacakratantra* and other tantras there.

7 The account of Prince Śaktimān first appears in the *Kathāsaritsāgara*, a collection of Indian tales.

8 An asterisk * before a word indicates a Sanskrit reconstruction from the Tibetan.

9 Given Nāgārjuna's long life, the Tibetan tradition also lists Śavaripa as his main tantric student. In the Chinese sources, such a lifespan is not found and Western scholars usually distinguish two Nāgārjunas (the early Mādhyamika and the later tantric siddha in the sixth century).

10 He is the third of the five Pandava sons, who are the heroes of the ancient Indian epic *Mahābhārata*.

11 Tib. gtam tshogs.

12 Tib. (dbu ma) rigs tshogs.

13 The same list is found at the end of the *Prasannapadā*, adding the *Akṣaraśataka* (P5234).

14 Both Avalokitavrata's *Prajñāpradīpaṭīkā* (ACIP TD3859@05B) and Atiśa's *Bodhipathapradīpapañjikā* (ACIP TD3948@280B) explicitly identify the text as Nāgārjuna's autocommentary on the *Mūlamadhyamakakārikā*. In both the Tibetan tradition and Western scholarship, his authorship is often denied, mainly on the grounds that the text quotes a verse that is also found in Āryadeva's *Catuḥśataka*. However, given the well-known tendency of Indian texts to freely use verses from other authors, Āryadeva's text may also have incorporated it from some common earlier source. In addition, Tsongkhapa (1357–1419) says that it cannot be Nāgārjuna's work, since if it were, it would have to be quoted by later Mādhyamikas, such as Buddhapālita, Bhāvaviveka, and Candrakīrti, which it is not. In itself, this does not seem to be a very conclusive argument, since it (a) contradicts the above attribution by at least two—generally considered reliable—Indian masters, and since (b) Buddhapālita's commentary on the *Mūlamadhyamakakārikā*—which is referred to and quoted at length in Bhāvaviveka's and Candrakīrti's commentaries—incorporates large parts of the *Akutobhayā* (see the excellent work by Huntington 1995 on this; of course, (b) in itself is no proof that the text was authored by Nāgārjuna). Thus, the *Akutobhayā* no doubt existed in the mainstream of early Madhyamaka exegesis and, via Buddhapālita's text, exerted a considerable influence upon later commentators as well. Hence, a more thorough study of the *Akutobhayā* and its influence on the Madhyamaka approach to reasoning seems overdue.

15 The authorship of this text has been disputed by many, mainly based on the grounds that it speaks about the three natures and the ālaya-consciousness, which are assumed by these critics to be later Yogācāra notions. However, that Nāgārjuna was familiar with the three natures is also evidenced by his *Acintyastava*, which mentions the first two natures in verses 44–45. As Lindtner 1992 (p. 253) points out, lines 45cd are moreover identical to *Laṅkāvatārasūtra* II.191ab. His article presents detailed evidence throughout Nāgārjuna's texts that the latter not only knew but also greatly relied on an early version of the *Laṅkāvatārasūtra*—which despite, no doubt, being a major source for later Yogācāras also criticizes (earlier) reifying versions of Yogācāra/Vijñānavāda. Furthermore, verses 33–35 of the *Bodhicittavivaraṇa* on the ālaya-consciousness almost literally correspond to three verses from the *Ghanavyūhasūtra* (P778, fols. 49b7–50a2), which is also a major Yogācāra source.

16 Chin. pu ti zi liang lun (Taishō 1660). The text is quoted twice in Candrakīrti's *Catuḥśatakaṭīkā* (P5266, fols. 103a and 215b) and also in Asvabhāva's *Mahāyānasaṃgrahopanibandhana* (P5552, fol. 329b). It is listed as one of Nāgārjuna's texts by Butön (see below) and quoted with its title in Tsongkhapa's *lam rim chen mo* (fol. 414b). For details, see Lindtner 1982.

17 This text is not preserved, except for six verses in Śāntarakṣita's *Madhyamakālaṃkāravṛtti* (P5285, fol. 69b.1–5). Kamalaśīla's *Madhyamakālaṃkārapañjikā* (P5286, fols. 123a–124b) states their source to be the *Vyavahārasiddhi* and comments on them in detail.

18 Tib. rnam par mi rtog pa'i bstod pa. This refers to the *Prajñāpāramitāstotra*, which is quoted under this name also in Vibhūticandra's *Bodhicaryāvatāratātparyapañjikāviśeṣadyotanīnāma* (see below). As Gorampa says below, Nagtso Lotsāwa (born 1011)—who closely collaborated

with Atiśa—also referred to the *Prajñāpāramitāstotra* by this name, obviously following a not uncommon Indian tradition.

19 P5388, fol. 128a.6–7.

20 P5254, fols. 358a–b (verses 91–96); 361a (101).

21 Verses 18–23 (Ed. Carelli, p. 66; D1351, fol. 281a.7–b4).

22 D3935, fol. 296b.7 (verse 27).

23 P4534, fol. 102a (verse 8).

24 These are verses 1–10, 12–13, 22, 24, 26–27, 30–32.

25 There are several Sanskrit editions of the *Catuḥstava* (Tucci 1932, Sakei 1959, and Dragonetti 1982). Though there has been some dispute among modern scholars as to which four praises it contains, all Sanskrit manuscripts agree on the *Lokātītastava* (P2012), *Niraupamyastava* (P2011), *Acintyastava* (P2019), and *Paramārthastava* (P2014). These are also the four on which Amṛtākara comments (on this author, no further information is available). The Sanskrit edition of his text is found in Tucci 1986, pp. 238–46.

26 Ed. La Vallée Poussin, pp. 420, 488, 533, 573.

27 Ibid., pp. 359, 415, 417, 476, 489, 533, 583, and 587.

28 Ibid., pp. 420, 489.

29 Ibid., pp. 375, 528, 573.

30 ACIP TD3875B@143B (verse 7); @148B (9).

31 P4534, fols. 92b; 95a; 97a; 98b; 102a; 105a.

32 Ed. La Vallée Poussin, pp. 55, 64, 234, 413.

33 Ibid., pp. 23, 200, 310.

34 Ibid., pp. 299, 348, 381, 405, 441, 482, 490, 536.

35 ACIP TD3870–1@190B (verse 10); @214A (5); @293A/B (23).

36 P3099, fol. 182a (verse 15).

37 Ed. La Vallée Poussin, p. 215.

38 P5259, fol. 315a.

39 ACIP TD3948@259A (verse 21).

40 ACIP TD3870-2@302A (verse 7); @353 (21).

41 Verses 7 and 21 (in Shastri 1927, p. 22).

42 Ed. La Vallée Poussin, p. 36 (verses 18–19).

43 P5254, fol. 372.

44 P4531, fol. 39b.

45 Lines 43ab (ibid., p. 24). The Sekanirdeśa (p. 28) also has two lines that correspond to *Lokātītastava* 12ab but are explicitly said to come from a tantra.

46 P3099, fols. 176b; 177b; 181b–182a; 182b; 184b–185a (verses 22; 13; 10–11 (9); 43; 37–42).

47 P5254, fols. 358a–b (verses 91–96); 361a (101).

48 ACIP TD3854@283B (verse 8).

49 Ed. La Vallée Poussin, p. 27 (III.1cd: *evam stute namas te 'stu kaḥ stotā kaś ca saṃstutaḥ*). Without giving any details, Tucci 1986 (p. 236) also mentions that there are quotations of the praises in the *Pañcakrama*. Lindtner 1982 (p. 180) says, "It is my general impression that YṢ [*Yuktiṣaṣṭīkā*], CS [*Catuḥstava*], and BV [*Bodhicittavivaraṇa*] are the most frequently quoted among all works ascribed to Nāgārjuna in later Indian literature." For a detailed list of quotations from the *Catuḥstava* in Indian works, see ibid., pp. 125–27.

50 Ed. La Vallée Poussin, p. 200 (verse 3).

51 Carelli, p. 57. Nāropa attributes the *Kāyatrayastotra* to Nāgāhvaya ("the one called Nāga"), which is not very specific, and exactly how Nāgārjuna is referred to in the above prophecy in the *Laṅkāvatārasūtra*. Tāranātha 1980 (p. 126) has the same attribution, obviously considering Nāgāhvaya to be a different person.

52 Ed. A. Thakur (Patna: K.P. Jayaswal Research Institute, 1959), p. 503.

53 P5282 (ACIP TD3880@256B, verse 8; @266A, verse 17).

54 P4534, fol. 102b.

55 ACIP TD3948@285A.

56 Ed. La Vallée Poussin, p. 36 (*nirālamba namo 'stu te*); the three stanzas appear right after the above-mentioned two verses from the *Niraupamyastava*, further suggesting their relation to Nāgārjuna.

57 The Chinese Buddhist canon is comparatively very modest with its twenty-four works ascribed to Nāgārjuna. Among these, the most important ones not contained in the *Tengyur* are the **Bodhisaṃbhāraśāstra* (Taishō 1660), *Mahāprajñāpāramitāśāstra* (1509), *Daśabhūmivibhāṣāśāstra* (1521), *Dvādaśanikāya(mukha)śāstra* (1568; one of the three main texts of the Chinese Madhyamaka School), and *Ekaślokaśāstra* (1573).

58 The three collections and their correspondence to the three wheels of dharma may indeed be seen to have a scriptural basis in the *Mahābherīsūtra* (p. 98.5.7), which says, ". . . initially, he will eradicate the great foundations of what is improper, proclaiming the great sound of the dharma. . . . Secondly, he will propound the sūtras of the mahāyāna that discuss emptiness. Thirdly, he will give discourses that examine the basic element (*dhātu*) of sentient beings."

59 These are the *Prajñāśatakanāmaprakaraṇa* (P5820), *Nītiśāstraprajñādaṇḍanāma* (P5821), and *Nītiśāstrajantuposaṇabindunāma* (P5822).

60 Almost all Indian, Chinese, and Tibetan sources attribute this text to Rāhulabhadra. It is found as authored by him at the beginning of three prajñāpāramitā sūtras in Sanskrit: the *Aṣṭasāhasrikā* (ed. R. Mitra), *Pañcaviṃśatisāhasrikā* (ed. N. Dutt), and *Suvikrāntavikrāmiparipṛcchā* (ed. R. Hikata; neither the Tibetan nor the Chinese translations of these sūtras contain that praise). In 1907, Haraprasad Shastri found an undated Nepali manuscript of the text, which also gives Rāhulabhadra as its author *(kṛtir iyaṃ rāhulabhadrasya; Journal of the Proceedings of the Asiatic Society Bengal* 6, no. 8 (1910); pp. 425ff.). The praise is quoted almost in its entirety (nineteen stanzas) in the *Mahāprajñāpāramitāśāstra* attributed to Nāgārjuna (trans. Lamotte, vol. 2, pp. 1363–65), but Lamotte (p. 1060) reports that Chi-tsang's (549–623) *Tchong kouan*

louen chou (Taishō 1824, k. 10, p. 168c4–5) says, "The stanzas of the *Prajñāpāramitāstotra* found in the 18th scroll of Nāgārjuna's *Ta tche tou louen* are the work of the dharmācārya Lo ho (Rāhula)" (as per H. Ui, *Indo-Tetsugaku-Kenkiu*, 1 [1934]: pp. 431ff. and Matsumoto, *Die Prajñāpāramitā Literatur*, p. 54). Buddhapālita's *Mūlamadhyamakavṛtti* (P5242, fol. 275b) quotes the praise with its name as being authored by Rāhulabhadra. *The Blue Annals* (*'Gos lo tsā ba gzhon nu dpal* 1996, pp. 35, 344), Butön's *History of Buddhism* (*Bu ston rin chen grub* 1931, p. 123), and Rongtön Sheja Künrig's (1367–1449) commentary on the text also agree that its author was Rāhulabhadra. The later Tibetan tradition rather tends to attribute this praise to Nāgārjuna (see Gorampa and Jamgön Kongtrul below).

61 This text is mostly verbatim the same as P2014, thus obviously being just another version of it.

62 Despite the identical title, P2024 and 2025 are two different compositions (see below).

63 The available Sanskrit manuscripts of this text and the Derge and Cone *Tengyurs* have either *-stava* or *-stotra* (P has just *-zhes bya ba*). The above eighteen praises correspond to P2010–2028 (P2016 is the autocommentary on the *Kāyatrayastotra*). Obviously, besides the texts in the three collections mentioned, there are quite a number of other works attributed by the Tibetan tradition to Nāgārjuna that do not belong to any of these three collections, such as his *Bodhicittavivaraṇa* and **Bodhisaṃbhāraśāstra*, as well as the many tantric works attributed to him, foremost among them the *Pañcakrama* (P2667), a commentary on the *Guhyasamājatantra*.

64 As for the praises, by now, the only full agreement seems to be that the *Catuḥstava* is by Nāgārjuna and that the *Prajñāpāramitāstotra* (P2018) is considered to be a work by Rāhulabhadra. For further details on all the texts mentioned and the question of their authorship, see Ruegg 1981 and Lindtner 1982.

65 See the section "Who or What Is Praised in Nāgārjuna's Praises?"

66 XVIII.9; see also XXIV.8–10, 18.

67 Verse 35.

68 Verses 69cd–71, 109.

69 Verses 15–16.

70 Verse 3.

71 Verses 19–20, 22–23, 25. Verse 21 even speaks about a nocturnal emission due to a dream, without having actual intercourse, just as Vasubandhu's *Viṃśatikā* (verse 4) does.

72 Verses 19–20.

73 Ibid., verse 34.

74 Lindtner 1982, pp. 264–65.

75 For details, see below.

76 Ibid., p. 279.

77 P5265, fol. 2b.

78 P5325, fols. 127b.2–128a.4.

79 The last two commentaries as well as the **Bodhisattvāvatāraprakāśa* and **Guhyasamājamaṇḍalābhiṣekavidhi* are not preserved.

80 ACIP TD3948@280B.

81 Tib. rma bya ba byang chub brtson 'grus. Note that he is not to be confused with his contemporary Majaba Jangchub Yeshe (Tib. rma bya pa byang chub ye shes), one of the four main disciples of Patsab Lotsāwa (Tib. pa tshab lo tsā ba; born 1055). Often, however, Jangchub Dsöndrü is listed instead of Jangchub Yeshe as one of the four sons of Patsab Lotsāwa. In any case, Jangchub Dsöndrü first was a student of Chaba Chökyi Senge (Tib. phyva pa chos kyi seng ge; 1109–1169). Later, he became a disciple of Patsab Lotsāwa, the main person to translate and introduce Candrakīrti's Madhyamaka texts in Tibet. Consquently, as a Mādhyamika, Jangchub Dsöndrü followed the Prāsaṅgika approach and became an important figure in the early dissemination of this system in Tibet. This is also evidenced by his becoming a disciple and collaborator of two of Patsab Lotsāwa's contemporaries, the Kashmiri Mādhyamika Jayānanda and his Tibetan disciple Ku Lotsāwa Dode Bar (Tib. khu lo tsā ba mdo sde 'bar). Majawa Jangchub Dsöndrü's surviving commentary on Nāgārjuna's *Mūlamadhyamakakārikā* is an important, though hitherto largely unstudied, testimony of early Tibetan interpretations of Madhyamaka, especially in its Prāsaṅgika form.

82 As presented above, Candrakīrti speaks only about the relationship between the *Mūlamadhyamakakārikā* and the *Yuktiṣaṣṭikā* on the one hand (main texts) and the *Vigrahavyāvartanī* and the *Śūnyatāsaptati* on the other (elaborations), but does not mention the *Vaidalyaprakaraṇa* and the *Vyavahārasiddhi* (this is also pointed out in Gorampa's presentation below).

83 Rma bya ba byang chub brtson 'grus 1975, pp. 13–17.

84 Rang byung rdo rje n.d., fol. 1b. Unfortunately, folio 2 of the text with its discussion on the remaining two collections is missing. The last words on folio 1 are "based on which Īśvara, puruṣa, both, . . ." probably indicating that the collection of reasoning refutes arising from others, self, both, and neither. See the text's following statements on the collections of reasoning and praises and their relationship.

85 Ibid., fol. 3b. What follows is an extensive explanation on Nāgārjuna's understanding of ground, path, and fruition, how that is in harmony with what Yogācāra texts teach, and that there is no contradiction between the collection of reasoning and the collection of praises (see the translation of DSC below).

86 Verses 40–41.

87 Ibid., fol. 8a.

88 ACIP buston chosbyung@019B (my translation; see Bu ston rin chen grub 1931, vol. 1, pp. 50–51).

89 Tib. theg chen blo sbyong. There is no text by this name; Butön may refer here to the *Mahāyānaviṃśikā*.

90 Ibid., @100A (Bu ston, vol. 2, pp. 125–27).

91 Tib. gnyag pho ba bsod nams bzang po.

92 Tib. dol po pa shes rab rgyal mtshan. He is considered to be the one who coined the terms "other-empty" (*shentong*) and "self-empty" (*rangtong*) and one of the most outspoken proponents of the superiority of the view of "other-emptiness."

93 Bsod nams bzang po n.d., p. 606.

94 It is not clear whether this is taken to consist of five or six texts or exactly which these are. A list on p. 947 (*'Gos lo tsā ba gzhon nu dpal* 2003; 1996, p. 808) lists the collection of reasoning and the *Ratnāvalī* separately, thus indicating that the latter is not considered a part of the former.

95 Tib. shākya mchog ldan, aka gser mdog pan chen/zi lung pan chen.

96 *Dbu ma'i 'byung tshul rnam par bshad pa'i gtam yid bzhin lhun po*, pp. 219–20.

97 *Shing rta chen po'i srol gnyis kyi rnam par dbye ba bshad nas nges don gcig tu bsgrub pa'i bstan bcos kyi rgyas 'grel*, fol. 6a–b (for details, see below).

98 Tib. go rams pa bsod nams seng ge. Both masters were fellow students of Rongtön Sheja Künrig (1367–1449) but later went different ways.

99 Here, Gorampa correctly quotes Majawa's above presentation in abbreviated form.

100 Here, Gorampa again incorporates exactly what is said in the corresponding part of Majawa's outline.

101 P760.12.

102 Go bo rab 'byams pa bsod nams seng ge 2004, fols. 7a.1–10a.3.

103 Tib. dpa' bo gtsug lag phreng ba.

104 Dpa' bo gtsug lag phreng ba 2003, p. 1442.

105 Tāranātha 1980, pp. 108 and 126.

106 Tib. grub mtha'i rnam bshad rang gzhan grub mtha' kun dang zab don mchog tu gsal ba kun bzang zhing gi nyi ma lung rigs rgya mtsho skye dgu'i re ba kun skong. Musoorie: Dalama, 1962), vol. ca, fols. 4a.2–6b.7.

107 Tib. 'jam dbyangs bzhad pa.

108 See also Hopkins 1983 (pp. 356–57) and 1998 (pp. 16–17).

109 The actual name of this text is *Ratnagotravibhāga* ("Elucidating the Disposition of the [Three] Jewels"). However, in nonacademic circles and among Tibetans, it is better known by the above name, so I will use it throughout. I refrain from reentering the historically undecidable dispute about whether Maitreya is really the author of this text and Asaṅga the composer of its *Vyākhyā* (the main Indian commentary), but follow the Tibetan tradition on this (the Chinese has a certain *Sāramati, whom modern scholars try to identify in various ways). However, that Maitreya's authorship is not just a Tibetan invention is corroborated by the fact that the *Ratnagotravibhāga* is quoted several times as the work of the bodhisattva Maitreya in a Khotan-Saka script fragment (Stein CH 0047). As Takasaki 1966 (p. 7) points out, this shows that Maitreya was regarded as its author not only in Tibet but also in Central Asia and probably in India too, at least between the eighth and twelfth centuries. That there actually were at least some late Indian masters who explicitly considered Maitreya as this text's author is evident from Ratnākaraśānti's *Sūtrasamucchayabhāṣya* and Abhayākaragupta's *Munimatālaṃkāra*. The former quotes and attributes verse I.27 to Ārya Maitreya (D3935, fol. 296b.5–7) and also explains a part of the *Ratnagotravibhāgavyākhyā* (ibid., fol. 325b; [J 67.9–68.6]). The latter also attributes the text (with the name *Mahāyānottaratantra*) to Maitreya, while quoting a verse from the *Vyākhyā* (D3903, fol. 150a.6 [J 71.1–4]). The colophon of Ngog Lotsāwa's translation of both texts in the *Tengyur* attributes the verses of the *Ratnagotravibhāga* to Maitreya and the *Vyākhyā* to Asaṅga. In this, he most probably relied on an Indian tradition, since the translation was accomplished in Kashmir under the guidance of the local paṇḍita Sajjana.

110 Tibetan edition in Hopkins 1983, pp. 9–10 (English, ibid., p. 590).

111 Tib. grub pa'i mtha' rnam par bzhag pa bsal bar bshad pa thub bstan lhun po'i mdzes rgyan.

112 ACIP lcang-grubmtha.4@03B–4A.

113 As explained above, Gorampa identifies this as the *Cittavajrastava.*

114 Gorampa identifies these two as the *Sattvārādhanastava* and the *Prajñāpāramitāstotra*, respectively.

115 As Gorampa says, this is the *Kāyatrayastotra.*

116 As mentioned above, this list is found in both the *Madhyamakaśāstrastuti* and at the end of the *Prasannapadā.*

117 Tib. khu lo tsā ba mdo sde 'bar. He was a student of the Kashmiri Mādhyamika Jayānanda, both collaborating with Majawa Jangchub Tsöndrü.

118 As for these arguments here, as mentioned above, there are many other texts—also accepted by Tsongkhapa and others as authentic works by Nāgārjuna—that are not in this list in the *Prasannapadā* either. There is indeed no known quote from the *Vyavahārasiddhi* by Nāgārjuna's direct disciples. However, both Śāntarakṣita and Kamalaśīla—whom nobody in Tibet considers as unreliable—cite six verses from it, the latter explicitly attributing it to Nāgārjuna and even giving an extensive commentary.

119 TOK vol. 1, pp. 404–6.

120 Tib. blo gros rgya mtsho.

121 Blo gros rgya mtsho 1984, p. 9.

122 Ibid., p. 62.

123 As presented above, Gorampa indicates that others seem to add four more praises, thus making fifteen.

124 However, as mentioned above, the former is just another version of the *Paramārthastava.*

125 S. Lévi edited the Sanskrit of this praise under Aśvaghoṣa's name (see Bibliography), while Lindtner 1982 (p. 17) says that its style is most reminiscent of Mātṛceṭa.

126 Skt. *vaśita* can also mean "void." The translation was chosen, since the Tibetan has *gzhan dbang* and the next term in the verse is "empty" (*śūnya*).

127 Verses 13, 17, 21–24.

128 Verses 13–14.

129 Verses 3, 13, 22, 23, 37–40, and 43.

130 Verse 3.

131 Verse 2.

132 Verses 24, 26, 35, 64–65, 89, and 100.

133 VIII.15.

134 Verses 4, 9–10.

135 Verse 8.

136 Verses 1 and 3.

137 Verses 6, 15, 21–22. Interestingly, except for "yāna" being replaced with "disposition" (*gotra*), lines 15ab correspond almost literally to *Abhisamayālaṃkāra* I.39ab.

138 Verse 41 and lines 45ab (*svabhāvaḥ prakṛtis tattvaṃ dravyaṃ vastu sad ity api*).

139 Verses 1–2.

140 Verses 20–21.

141 Verse 88. It should be noted that the mere occurrence of the term "fundamental change of state" in a text by Nāgārjuna and especially its equation with the dharmakāya is quite remarkable. For, usually not even the term is used in the Madhyamaka tradition, let alone it being explained in this way, which is found in some sūtras, but otherwise is a typical Yogācāra presentation. For more details on the notion of fundamental change of state, see the section "A Terminological Map for the *Dharmadhātustava* and Its Commentaries."

142 Verse 22. For more details, see below and the translation of DSC.

143 For further examples of Nāgārjuna's texts using positive and affirmative terminologies, see below in the section "An Overview of the Basic Themes of the *Dharmadhātustava*."

144 *Shing rta chen po'i srol gnyis kyi rnam par dbye ba bshad nas nges don gcig tu bsgrub pa'i bstan bcos kyi rgyas 'grel*, fol. 6a–b.

145 I translated the term *sugata* here in an attempt to retain the alliterative play on words.

146 Verses 9–11.

147 Murti 1955, p. 90.

148 Of course, this is a textual history and not one in terms of experience. From the latter point of view, any "history" of luminous mind and its adventitious stains is quite boring and in fact obsolete, since it is always the same and happens only in the present moment.

149 As quoted in Ngag dbang yon tan bzang po 2000, p. 115.

150 Literally, *kliṣṭamanas* means "defiled mind," but here I follow the Tibetan (lit. "plagued mind"), since it is not just a question of mind being defiled like a dusty but insentient mirror. Rather, as the above process shows, mind experiences mental and physical suffering through such defilement.

151 It can also refer to intellect, intelligence, perception, spirit, opinion, intention, inclination, and more.

152 Matters are somewhat complicated by "mentation" sometimes being used for the sixth—the mental— consciousness as well and there being overlapping descriptions of and relationships between the afflicted mind, the immediate mind, pure mentation, the mental sense faculy, and the mental consciousness.

153 Webster's *Third New International Dictionary* says that "concept" comes from Latin conceptus (collection, gathering, fetus) and is "something conceived in the mind : THOUGHT, IDEA, NOTION: as a philos : a general or abstract idea : a universal notion: (1) : the resultant of a generalizing mental operation : a generic mental image abstracted from percepts; also : a directly

intuited object of thought (2) : a theoretical construct . . ." About "conceive," Webster's says, "to take into one's mind . . . to form in the mind . . . evolve mentally . . . IMAGINE, VISUALIZE . . ." Thus, somewhat differing from "concept," when "conceive" is understood in these latter senses in a very general way, it comes closer to the above meanings of *kalpana* and its related terms.

154 Tib. sgo ba. Here, this term may very well be understood in its double sense of making pregnant and being suffused or imbued with something.

155 As for the last term, most translations from the Tibetan say "thoroughly established nature" or the like. This is usually based on too literal an understanding of the Tibetan (while disregarding the original Sanskrit) and on certain Tibetan doxographical hierarchies, which consider this term as an exclusive feature of so-called "Mere Mentalism" with its alleged assertion of some ultimately existing consciousness. However, neither the Sanskrit term nor its understanding by all major Yogācāra masters justifies any such wrongly reifying rendering. Also, it is misleading to say "perfected nature," since there is nothing to be changed, let alone perfected, in this nature, its whole point being rather to signify primordial perfection and completeness.

156 Chos grags rgya mtsho 1985, vol. 1, pp. 192–94.

157 These are the impulses and habits of listening to and engaging in the dharma that are the natural expression of one's own buddha nature. Thus, the facts of the dharma, teachers, and texts appearing for oneself as well as being attracted to and engaging them come about through the main cause that is the revival of these internal tendencies appearing as if external, with the compassion and manifestations of Buddhas aiding as contributing conditions.

158 Skt. ṣaḍāyatanaviśeṣa, Tib. skye mched drug gi khyad par.

159 For more details on this, see the section "Luminous Mind and *Tathāgatagarbha*" below as well as the translation of DSC.

160 This is already found in the *Trikāyanāmasūtra* and the *Suvarṇaprabhāsottamasūtra*. Presenting the dharmadhātu as a fifth wisdom—dharmadhātu wisdom—has its origin in the tantras but later, especially in Tibet, became the predominant presentation. If the dharmadhātu wisdom is added, it usually represents the svabhāvakāya.

161 This is basically the way it is presented in AC (fols. 99a–103b). NY and its commentaries treat this process in great detail (for further details/refinements, see below).

162 That said two terms were understood differently is also evident from several scriptures that deny the former, while frequently speaking about the latter, such as the *Laṅkāvatārasūtra* (X.568: "Mind cannot see mind, just as a sword cannot cut its own blade or a finger touch its own tip").

163 See Zimmermann 2002, p. 90.

164 H. Isaacson (in Zimmermann 2002, p. 41, note 58) identifies at least three examples in rather late Indian commentaries (two on the *Hevajratantra*, one on the *Tantrāloka*) that gloss *garbha* in this sense as *hṛdaya* and *sāra*, respectively.

165 For a detailed analysis of the term *tathāgatagarbha*, see Zimmermann 2002, pp. 39–46.

166 See also the discussion of buddha nature in the Eighth Karmapa's commentary on the *Abhisamayālaṃkāra* below.

167 The two examples of a seed in its husk and a cakravartin-baby in the womb seem to suggest some development or growth, but as their various sources and commentaries show, the meaning

emphasized in both is something being enclosed in a covering, from which it must be freed (see also Zimmermann 2002, pp. 62–65).

168 One of the cuter anecdotes here (it actually happened) is the one of an enthusiastic Buddhist freshman, who—inspired by having been H.H. the Dalai Lama's driver during a visit—returned to his apartment and set up with great care a nice Tibetan shrine with all its rich arrangements. He lit the incense and the candles, and solemnly sat down to meditate, his eyes closed. After a while he thought, "Wow, that's it, I'm getting it, the clear light is dawning on me!"—just to open his eyes and see his shrine in flames.

169 To be sure, it is not being suggested here that this theme is understood in exactly the same way in all the sources to follow.

170 I.10 (*pabhassaram idaṃ bhikkhave cittaṃ/ taṃ ca kho āgantukehi upakkilesehi upakkiliṭṭhaṃ/ taṃ assutavā puthujjana yathābh taṃ nappajānāti/ tasmā assutavato puthujjanassa cittabhāvanā natthī ti vadāmī ti/ pabhassaram idaṃ bhikkhave cittaṃ/ taṃ ca kho āgantukehi upakkilesehi vippamuttaṃ/ taṃ sutvā ariyasāvakō yathābh taṃ pajānāti/ tasmā sutavato ariyasāvakassa cittabhāvanā atthī ti vadāmī ti/*).

171 III.151.22–23; 31–32; and 152.8–9 (*cittasaṃkilesā bhikkave sattā saṃkilissanti, cittavodānā sattā visujjhanti*).

172 See Bareau 1955, pp. 294–95.

173 Taishō 2031, p. 15c27.

174 Trans. La Vallée Poussin, pp. 109–11.

175 P. 615.

176 *Manorathapūraṇī* (*Aṅguttaranikā-atthakathā*) I.60; *Dhammasaṅghanī-atthakathā* 140; Buddhaghoṣa's *Kathāvatthu-atthakathā* 193.

177 Ed. Wogihara, pp. 5 and 644. The Sanskrit for "element" here is again *dhātu*, which in its original sense can refer to a metal or mineral contained in ore. The *dhātu* as seed is also common (see the recurring example in the *Tathāgatagarbhasūtra*, *Dharmadhātustava*, *Uttaratantra*, and the explanation in Asaṅga's *Ratnagotravibhāgavyākhyā* on I.26).

178 XXV.1 (P783, p. 238.5.6; ACIP KD0095@305B–306A). A similar verse is also found in the Pāli canon.

179 Ibid., @270A.

180 Ibid., @345A–B.

181 Ed. Vaidya, p. 3.18 (ACIP KD0012@03A).

182 Ibid., @142B.

183 Ed. Dutt, p. 121.14–122.3 (ACIP KD0009-1@169A). The *Śatasāhasrikāprajñāpāramitā* (p. 495) contains a parallel passage.

184 ACIP KD0009-2@252B–253A.

185 Ed. Hikata, p. 85.

186 Ed. Dutt 1941–54, vol. 2.2, pp. 300.9–10 (*yasya co mṛdukī saṃjñā nāmarūpasmi vartate/ agṛdhraṃ nāmarūpasmi cittaṃ bhoti prabhāsvaram*). "Name and form" is an expression for the five skandhas, the four mental skandhas being without form, just suitable to be named.

187 Ed. Rahder, p. 74D.

188 ACIP KL0107@135B.

189 ACIP KD0113@35A.

190 Ibid., @193B.

191 Ibid., @218B–219A.

192 As quoted in J, p. 49.9–12.

193 I.63.

194 I.17 and I.22.

195 XIII.19ab.

196 Lines 128–32 and 306–7 (ed. Mathes).

197 P5529 (ACIP TD4028@038B).

198 Sanskrit quoted in Ruegg 1969, p. 427.

199 J6 (P5526, fol. 77b.5–6).

200 This is the fourth point in the text's first chapter on the knowledge of all aspects (verses I.38–40).

201 Some say this text was composed by Daṃṣṭrāsena.

202 D3791, fol. 204b.3–5.

203 P5536–8 (ACIP TD4035@257A).

204 P5539 (ACIP TD4038-1@044A; further examples @005A and 058A).

205 P5213, fol. 7a.7–7b.7 (see also fols. 6b.7 and 7a.7).

206 P5866, verses 5, 23, 177–78.

207 Verses 37–38.

208 Taishō 1584, 1616 (esp. pp. 863b20f and 864a28), 1617 (esp. p. 872a1f).

209 P5709, II.208cd.

210 P5710, I.38 (ACIP TD4211@164B).

211 Ed. A. Thakur, pp. 405, 411, 431, 432, 491, 496, 530, 540.

212 III.279–80ab.

213 ACIP TD3854@279.

214 Ibid., @281A–B.

215 Ibid., @272A and 281A.

216 ACIP TD3859-3@83B.

217 Ibid., @283B.

218 P5764 (ACIP TD4266@125A and 129A).

219 P5285 (ACIP TD3885@81A).

220 ACIP TD3915@034B.

221 D3887, fol. 242b.4–7. To note, this text is the first one to incorporate the teachings on *tathāgatagarbha* with a more positive meaning into the Madhyamaka tradition. Later, the same is done in Dharmamitra's (eighth/ninth century) commentary on the *Abhisamayālaṃkāra* (quoting the above-mentioned phrase of all beings possessing the Tathāgata heart from the *Adhyardhaśatikaprajñāpāramitāsūtra*) and Abhayākaragupta's *Munimatālaṃkāra* (D3903, fol. 150a.6–7; quoting the same passage as the *Madhyamakāloka*, with an interspersed verse from the *Ratnagotravibhāgavyākhyā* [J71.1–4]). Earlier, Bhāvaviveka's *Tarkajvālā* (D3856, fol. 169a.1–2), referring to the *Laṅkāvatārasūtra*, says that "possessing the Tathāgata heart" refers to emptiness, signlessness, and wishlessness (the three doors to liberation) existing in the continua of all beings, but does not indicate something like an inherent, eternal, and all-pervading person (*puruṣa*) as held in certain non-Buddhist Indian schools. The text also speaks about bodhisattvas having respect even for beings with no qualities, since they think that these beings will come to possess all qualities in the future due to being endowed with the Tathāgata heart (fol. 50b.3–4). Candrakīrti's *Madhyamakāvatārabhāṣya* (ACIP TD3862@281Af), by also quoting the *Laṅkāvatārasūtra*, clearly states that the teachings on the Tathāgata heart are of expedient meaning, given for people who are afraid of emptiness and in order to guide the tīrthikas who believe in an ātman. Interestingly, the *Madhyamakāloka* (ibid., fol. 162b.3–7) quotes the same passage of the *Laṅkāvatārasūtra* as Candrakīrti but only says that, depending on the different ways of thinking of those to be guided, the Buddha taught nothing but the dharmadhātu through a variety of means. Jayānanda's *Madhyamakāvatāraṭīkā* stands somewhat in between, since it refers to the Tathāgata heart (quoting the *Uttaratantra*) as authoritative in establishing that there is only a single yāna (D3870, fol. 354b.1–2), but otherwise equates its meaning with emptiness and, like Candrakīrti, considers it to be of expedient meaning (fol. 213a.4–5).

222 Lines 12ab. This text is listed under Candrakīrti's works in the *Tengyur* and appears as an appendix to his *Madhyamakāvatārabhāṣya*. Its colophon gives "the great master Candrakīrti" as its author, but also says that it was translated into Tibetan by the author himself and the translator 'gos khug pa lha btsas (eleventh century). There was indeed an eleventh-century master by the name Candrakīrti (Tibetan tradition calls him "the lesser Candrakīrti") who was a disciple of Jetāri (tenth/eleventh century), one of the teachers of Atiśa.

223 P4535; 5573; 5579; 5586; D1424 (esp. fol. 153b).

224 Ed. La Vallée Poussin, p. 448.10 (missing in the Tibetan); ACIP TD3865@273B.

225 ACIP TD3862@322A–B.

226 Ibid., @343A.

227 ACIP TD3870-1@051A.

228 Ibid., @306A–307A.

229 ACIP TD3870-2@342A.

230 P5273 (ACIP TD3872@59B).

231 Ibid., @118B.

232 The last two lines allude to the above-mentioned verse in the *Lalitavistarasūtra*.

233 P5325, fols. 107b.8–108a.2.

234 P5324, fols. 105b.7–106a.6. It may be added here that Atiśa's *Bodhipathapradīpapañjikā* (ACIP TD3948@258B) speaks about all beings without exception possessing a single disposition, that is, the Tathāgata heart, the disposition of the mahāyāna. His *Ratnakaraṇḍodghāta-nāmamadhyamakopadeśa* (P5325, fols. 116b.8–117a.3) says the same and further explains that beings are thus naturally endowed with great compassion and the qualities of the pāramitās, meaning they possess natural ethics.

235 P5282 (ACIP TD3880@264A).

236 Skt. ed. B. Lal (Sarnath: Central Institute for Higher Tibetan Buddhist Studies, 1994), p. 136.26–28.

237 Lines 20–23.

238 Tib. lta ba mdor bsdus.

239 Lines 43–49.

240 Bka' brgyud mgur mtsho. Rumtek ed. n.d., fol. 53b.

241 Mi la ras pa'i rnam mgur. 1981. Beijing: mi rigs dpe skrun khang, p. 466.

242 Verse 7.

243 Chos grags rgya mtsho 1985, vol. 1, pp. 196–97.

244 According to Pawo Tsugla Trengwa's *History of the Dharma*, the Eighth Karmapa considered Saraha and Nāgārjuna as the final authorities to clarify the view (pp. 1254–55), which accords with what Mikyö Dorje himself says in his *Chariot of the Tagbo Siddhas*. Pawo Rinpoche also reports a statement by the Karmapa that it is not reasonable for the view of all teachings on valid cognition, abhidharma, Madhyamaka, and the Vajrayāna to be other-emptiness (p. 1236). Still, Pawo Rinpoche says, the Karmapa's early teacher Chödrub Senge (who fully ordained him and gave him extensive instructions on the view of "other-emptiness") had requested the Karmapa to uphold this view (p. 1240). Thus, before his outspoken rejection of any kind of "other-empty" Madhyamaka in the *Chariot*, his first major commentary—on the *Abhisamayālaṃkāra*—uses the term "other-emptiness" (and also Mahāmudrā) frequently, but one looks in vain for any reifying or absolutist interpretation of that term. Especially in comparison with other texts on "other-emptiness" (such as Dölpopa's), one is tempted to call the Karmapa's presentation "*Shentong* Lite." In fact, his commentary presents the hidden meaning of the prajñāpāramitā sūtras mainly in classical Yogācāra terms, while emphasizing that this is not what Tibetans call "Mere Mentalism." In general, it is regarded as one of the signs of a commentator of the highest caliber to expound each scripture according to its own system and context, without mixing different traditions or imposing one's own "highest" view. Pawo Rinpoche says that this approach is reflected in all commentaries by the Eighth Karmapa, since he always taught in accordance with the propensities of his disciples and by keeping to the principles that apply to the specific texts of sūtras and tantras and not by just clinging to a single meaning throughout (p. 1254). Mikyö Dorje himself states that the systems of Madhyamaka and Yogācāra must be treated independently in their own contexts. So far, there are hardly any systematic studies of the Eighth Karmapa's scriptural legacy. Instead, unfounded claims about his view are often repeated (by both Tibetans and Westerners), such as that he was one of the greatest proponents of the system of other-emptiness in the Kagyü lineage. Even a brief overview of the Karmapa's texts shows that this is definitely not the case. What is certain, though, is that he went to considerable pains to employ the language and technique of debate used by his opponents (often Tsongkhapa and his followers). In good Prāsaṅgika style, he often flings their

own approach back at them to reveal its internal inconsistencies. This is also evidenced by his following presentation of buddha nature.

245 In terms of the meaning (if not the words), the same distinction is also made in Asaṅga's *Mahāyānasaṃgraha*, upon which the presentation by the Eighth Karmapa here greatly relies. Asaṅga distinguishes between the "ālaya-consciousness" and "the supramundane mind" (Skt. lokottaracitta, Tib. 'jig rten las 'das pa'i sems), which is said to come from the latent tendencies of listening that are the natural outflow of the very pure dharmadhātu (which is said to be equivalent to the dharmakāya). The supramundane mind is equivalent to nonconceptual wisdom (see the quote from the *Mahāyānasaṃgraha* below). In Tibet, the explicit distinction between "ālaya-consciousness" (Tib. kun gzhi'i rnam shes) and "ālaya-wisdom" (Tib. kun gzhi'i ye shes) seems to have been made first in the texts of Dölpopa (such as his *Mountain Dharma, Fourth Council,* and *Kun gzhi'i rab tu dbye ba khyad par du 'phags pa*; see also Stearns 1995). Also Dölpopa's disciple Sabsang Mati Panchen (1294–1376)—an early teacher of Tsongkhapa—refers to these two types of ālaya in his commentary on the *Abhidharmasamucchaya* at length (Sa bzang ma ti pan chen 1977, fols. 85b6–86a1 and 86a6–86b2). Sparham 2001 says on this: "[His] contribution is to show how such a doctrine, explicit in several sūtra passages, is also implicit in the writings of Asaṅga." Likewise, the Sakya master Śākya Chogden accepts this terminology in his *Shing rta chen po'i srol gnyis kyi rnam par dbye ba*. The Third Karmapa's AC (fols. 13bff.) also describes such a distinction—though without using the specific terms "ālaya-consciousness" and "ālaya-wisdom." His EDV (pp. 501.4–502.2) says that "ālaya" is a general label for the three natures, while the imaginary and other-dependent natures are referred to as "ālaya-consciousness." The eight consciousnesses are the obscurations, while the four wisdoms are the stainlessness of these consciousnesses, thus being the perfect nature, with dharmadhātu wisdom being the matrix of all of these. Jamgön Kongtrul Lodrö Tayé's commentary on ZMND quotes some passages from AC and elaborates on this topic (Kong sprul blo gros mtha yas 2005, pp. 23–27). He says, "Ālaya-wisdom is the Sugata heart, which was discussed above. It is taught to be the nature of mind in the prajñāpāramitā [sūtras] and the *Uttaratantra*." In terms of meaning, Lodrö Tayé makes the same distinction also in his commentary on Rangjung Dorje's NY (Kong sprul blo gros mtha yas 1990, pp. 101–2). In his *Treasury of Philosophical Systems* (p. 145), Longchen Rabjam distinguishes between "the ālaya of the actual real nature, which is the dharmadhātu, natural luminosity, the Tathāgata heart" and "beginningless basic unawareness . . . which is called 'the ālaya of various latent tendencies.'" In an exposition of the Jonang School (Ngag dbang yon tan bzang po 2000, pp. 113, 230–33), it is said that the actual ālaya-consciousness is the support for all tendencies of afflicted phenomena that constitute saṃsāra. It exists in ordinary beings and ceases as such a support in the case of arhathood as well as on the first bodhisattva bhūmi. From this bhūmi onwards, when one speaks about the ālaya, what is meant is not the ālaya-consciousness but the support for all tendencies of completely purified phenomena (the remedies). This support is ālaya-wisdom. Thus, in the most general sense, ālaya-wisdom—or buddha nature—is the fundamental basis for the ālaya-consciousness too. This is to be understood in the sense that it accommodates all phenomena of saṃsāra and nirvāṇa, just as the sky accommodates a greater or lesser density of clouds.

246 The three characteristics are the same as the three natures (imaginary, other-dependent, and perfect nature).

247 Lines 294–303.

248 ACIP TD4028 @037B.

249 That means being actual effective causes and results and not just nominal ones.

250 The verse gives suchness, the true end (*bhūtakoṭi*), signlessness, the ultimate, and dharmadhātu as the synonyms of emptiness.

251 Skt. vipākavijñāna, Tib. rnam smin gyi rnam shes (another name for the ālaya-consciousness).

252 Asvābhava's commentary (P5552, fol. 262a; Taishō 1598) gives the further example of the ālaya-consciousness being like an attic in which all kinds of things are jumbled up, such as a panacea amidst all kinds of poison. Although these might abide next to each other for a long time, the medicine is not identical with the poison, nor are any of the poisons its seed. The same applies for the latent tendencies of listening.

253 In this distinction here between dharmakāya and vimuktikāya, the latter designates the removal of only the afflictive obscurations, as it is attained by the arhats of the śrāvakas and pratyekabuddhas too. The dharmakāya refers to the removal of the cognitive obscurations. (Without relating these two kāyas to the distinction between bodhisattvas and arhats, the *Uttaratantra* describes them as the two aspects of the relinquishment of these two obscurations in complete buddhahood. When talking about the dharmakāya as the actual state of buddhahood in general, it is understood that both types of obscurations have been relinquished in it. In this sense, it then includes the vimuktikāya.)

254 Often this term is translated as "swan," but the Sanskrit *haṃsa* clearly refers to a special type of white wild goose that is common in India.

255 I.45–49 (P5549, fols. 11b.1–12a.6).

256 Verses 62–63.

257 I.56–57. These verses say that the skandhas and so on rest on karma and afflictions, these on improper mental engagement, and the latter on the purity of mind, which does not rest on any of them.

258 Both Dölpopa's *Mountain Dharma* and *The Fourth Council* speak about buddha nature or the naturally abiding disposition as being unconditioned and a support for buddha qualities.

259 According to Dzogchen Ponlop Rinpoche, "these" refer to the nature of phenomena (in general) and the dharmadhātu (the disposition in specific) two sentences above.

260 Skt. vyatireka, Tib. ldog pa (a technical term for a conceptual mental image).

261 In the above, the Karmapa has presented the three criteria to identify a teaching as being of expedient meaning: the intention behind it, its purpose, and the explicit statement being refutable through reasoning.

262 These and their relation to the disposition are taught under this fourth point of the disposition in the first chapter of the *Abhisamayālaṃkāra*.

263 For further details on the ālaya being conditioned or unconditioned, its relation to buddha nature, and the "distinctive feature of the six āyatanas," see the introduction of Sparham 1993 (esp. p. 33).

264 The second aspect of purity means being pure of all adventitious stains.

265 These are the only two types of connection that Buddhist epistemology and logic allow. Below, the Karmapa discusses their applications in "nature reasons" and "result reasons," respectively.

266 This refers to *Uttaratantra* I.105–7 and I.136 and Asaṅga's commentary (J61; neither, however, has the explicit word "imputed").

267 This is how the dharmakāya is often explained—as the kāya of the nature of phenomena (dharmatākāya). For example, see Ārya Vimuktisena's *Abhisamayālaṃkāravṛtti* (D3787, fol. 192a.7–8).

268 AC fols. 13bff. (for more details, see the endnote on DSC's comments on verse 1 of the *Dharmadhātustava*).

269 Jamgön Kongtrul's commentary on ZMND (Kong sprul blo gros mtha' yas 2005, p. 183) says: "The Omniscient [Seventh Karmapa,] Chötra Gyatso, maintains that the emptiness endowed with the supreme of all aspects and the Sugata heart are equivalent. That the Sugata heart actually possesses the sixty-four superior qualities of freedom and maturation means that it is endowed with the supreme of all aspects. That these are not established as anything identifiable or any characteristic is the meaning of emptiness. Therefore, he holds that making this a living experience—cultivating [mind] as being lucid, yet nonconceptual—is Mahāmudrā meditation." (The thirty-two qualities of freedom are the ten powers, the four fearlessnesses, and the eighteen unshared qualities of the dharmakāya. The thirty-two qualities of maturation are the thirty-two major marks of the rūpakāyas.)

270 In Buddhism, an entity is defined as "something that is able to perform a function," which includes not only material things but also all types of mind as well as processes that are neither matter nor mind (such as persons and continua).

271 Just to note, that the Karmapa for the second time here refutes both this position—which is no doubt still maintained by many Kagyüpas today and regarded as the epitome of the view of "other-emptiness"—and the claim further above that the ālaya-consciousness is refined into mirrorlike wisdom is quite remarkable (to say the least) for a text that is supposed to be written to uphold the view of "other-emptiness."

272 Interestingly and unlike with other opponents, the Eighth Karmapa uses honorific terms when he quotes Dölpopa.

273 Now, the Karmapa shifts into debate mode, which becomes a bit technical but very interesting, since it leads up to the analysis of *Uttaratantra* I.28 on all sentient beings having buddha nature. A simple example for a "nature reason" would be "A squirrel is an animal because it is a mammal." Mammals (the reason) and animals (the predicate) share the same nature, in this case fulfilling the definition of an animal. An example of the second reason—a "result reason"—would be "Behind this house, there exists a fire, since there exists smoke." Here, one infers the existence of the cause, fire (the predicate), from the existence of smoke as its result (the reason).

274 In nature reasons, both verbs must be *is* (or *are*) and may never be *exist* (obviously, one cannot say something like "A squirrel *is* an animal because mammals *exist*"). In the above case, the full reasoning that the Karmapa refers to would run, "Sentient beings are Buddhas, since buddhahood exists in them."

275 Skt. pakṣadharmatā, Tib. phyogs chos. This is the first criterion for a correct reason—the set expressed by the reason must include the set expressed by the subject (for example, squirrels are included in mammals). In the above case, if being a sentient being and being a Buddha are held to be mutually exclusive, any reason that uses Buddha or buddhahood contradicts the above criterion and can never establish that the one is the other either.

276 Skt. anvayavyatireka, Tib. rjes su 'gro ldog. These refer to the second and third criteria for a correct reason—the set of the reason must be included in the set of the predicate and may never be outside of it (for example, all mammals are necessarily animals, and there is no mammal that is not an animal).

277 I.28 (Skt. *saṃbuddhakāyaspharaṇāt tathatāvyatibhedataḥ/ gotrataś ca sadā sarve buddhagarbhāḥ śarīraṇaḥ*; Tib. *rdzogs sangs sku ni 'phro phyir dang/ de bzhin nyid dbyer med phyir dang/ rigs yod phyir na lus can kun/ rtag tu sangs rgyas snying po can*).

278 This refers to the paths of accumulation and preparation.

279 As mentioned before, this triad represents the criteria qualifying a statement as being of expedient meaning.

280 There are many volumes in Tibet as well as by Japanese and Western scholars on how *Uttaratantra* I.28 and the compound *buddhagarbhāḥ* in it can be interpreted, so I will highlight just a few things here. As for the somewhat differing Sanskrit and Tibetan versions (see the above verse), *spharaṇa* literally means "quivering," "throbbing," "vibration" or "penetration." *Vyatibheda*, rendered as "undifferentiable" above (which corresponds more to the Tibetan *dbyer med*), literally means "pervading." The third line in the Tibetan says "because the disposition *exists*." The fourth line ends in *can*, which literally means "to possess," but is also a common way to indicate a *bahuvrīhi* compound in translations from Sanskrit, as in this case here. The two most basic renderings of the Sanskrit of this line with its compound *buddhagarbhāḥ* are "all beings are always such that they contain a Buddha/have a Buddha as their core" (thus, my above translation factually renders *garbha* twice in order to cover both facets). Interestingly, in the early Tibetan translations, the verse ended in *yin* ("are"), which was only replaced by *can* at a rather late point. The most obvious reason for this is trying to avoid the reading "all beings *are* the Buddha heart," which is immediately suggested to readers of Tibetan unfamiliar with the underlying Sanskrit. Nevertheless, especially some later Tibetan (and Western) commentators make a big point out of beings actually possessing the Buddha heart or even full-fledged buddhahood. This is a point evidently denied by the Eighth Karmapa here and is even contradicted by the preceding verse I.27 in the *Uttaratantra* (the order of the two verses being reversed in the Tibetan):

> Since buddha wisdom enters into the hosts of beings,
> Since its stainlessness is nondual by nature,
> And since the buddha disposition is metaphorically referred to [by the name of] its fruition,
> All sentient beings are said to contain the Buddha [heart].

This explicitly says that the disposition is *not* actual buddhahood or dharmakāya—the fruition—but a case of labeling the cause with the name of its result. So, one way to look at these two verses is in terms of cause, fruition, and their fundamental equality. In this way, the disposition is the cause for the fruition of the buddhakāya, with suchness indicating that this "cause" is not different from the result (the nature of the mind being always the same in sentient beings and Buddhas or throughout ground, path, and fruition). This is underlined by *Uttaratantra* I.144ab:

> Its nature is the dharmakāya,
> Suchness, and the disposition.

As the Eighth Karmapa demonstrates, it is impossible to establish verses I.27–28 as strict logical proofs for buddha nature actually existing in all beings (they may only serve as indications or metaphors). This is also highlighted by the fact that, in the Tibetan tradition, buddha nature is typically considered as a "very hidden phenomenon," which by definition does not lie within the reach of inferential valid cognition but can only be approached through valid Buddhist scriptures. As for other explanations on *Uttaratantra* I.27–28, there is hardly anything in the three known Indian commentaries. Neither Asaṅga's commentary nor Vairocanarakṣita's (eleventh century) very brief *Mahāyānottaratantraṭippaṇī* (eight folios) elaborate at all on these verses. Sajjana's *Mahāyānottaratantraśāstropadeśa* just glosses the first line of I.28 by saying that the dharmakāya is twofold: (a) the completely unstained dharmadhātu and (b) its natural outflow, the instructions on the principles of the profound and the manifold (this distinction being based on *Uttaratantra* I.145). Line I.28 should be understood as (b) (*dharmakāyo dvidhā jñeyaḥ dharmadhātuḥ sunirmalaḥ/ tann iṣyandaś ca gambhīravicitranayadeśaneti/ saṃbuddhakāyaspharaṇāt iti jñeyam/*). Among Tibetan texts, there are a few that go into the details of explaining and justifying the "proofs" in I.28 on a more conventional level. Mipham Rinpoche's *Synopsis of the Sugata Heart* (fols. 282–94) says rightly that the usual brief glosses on the three parts of this "proof" do not penetrate the essential point of the *Uttaratantra's* explanation of buddha nature. A common interpretation is that the dharmakāya—whether it is regarded as emptiness or wisdom—pervades all phenomena, that the suchness of Buddhas and sentient beings is of the same type in being nothing but emptiness, and that the existence of the disposition refers to nothing but being suitable to become a Buddha. However, with regard to both the first and the second lines, since both omniscient wisdom or emptiness equally pervade all phenomena without a mind too, it is hard to see that point as a specific reason for the mind of sentient beings having the potential to become Buddhas, while other phenomena don't. As for the third line, the disposition cannot just be a mere potential that may evolve into the result of buddhahood, since then that result would actually be produced by impermanent causes and conditions and thus—by definition—be impermanent too. (As the Karmapa explained above, this is impossible for something like buddhahood, since Buddhas would then inevitably fall back into saṃsāra at some point, and there would be huge differences between ground, path, and fruition, contradicting a primordially pure nature of the mind that does not change from sentient beings to Buddhas.) In explaining the first three lines of verse I.28, Mipham Rinpoche joins them with the Buddhist standard set of the four reasonings of (1) dharmatā, (2) dependence, (3) performing a function, and (4) justification. As for the first line, he says that, though there is actually no earlier cause or later result as far as buddha nature is concerned, from the perspective of how things (mistakenly) appear, the result of the manifestation of the dharmakāya proves the cause of the disposition (see also below in this introduction), thus applying reasoning (2). On the second line, the text says that the basic nature of all phenomena in saṃsāra and nirvāṇa—emptiness—is primordially inseparable from great luminosity, due to which Buddhas and sentient beings too are equal ultimately. Therefore, reasoning (1) establishes that what is projected by adventitious delusion and looks like a sentient being never moves an inch from this ultimate nature of phenomena, thus having buddhahood as its Heart. Also the sūtras say that all phenomena have the nature of primordial luminosity (see the above quote from the *Pañcaviṃśatisāhasrikāprajñāpāramitā*). Of course, this seems to invite the above-mentioned consequence that stones and such would also have the disposition. Thus, Mipham Rinpoche says, what is called "disposition" must be presented as the infallible cause for buddhahood, that is, the unfolding of the mind that is unmistaken about the nature of all knowable objects, once the two obscurations that have arisen by virtue of mind's power are relinquished. But since what is not mind (such as stones) is without any process of accomplishing this through the path, despite it being inseparable in terms of suchness conventionally, there is no need to present it as having the disposition. Also, stones and such equally appear by virtue of the power of the mind—it is not that they are mental appearances by virtue of the power of external stones and the like. This is to be understood through the example of the relationship between what appears in a dream and the consciousness that dreams. As for the third line, sentient beings have the disposition of being suitable to become Buddhas, since the adventitious stains are established to be relinquishable, while the dharmakāya with its primordial qualities is established to exist without any difference throughout all phases from an ordinary being up through becoming a Buddha. That sentient beings have such a disposition of being suitable to become Buddhas means that they definitely have the Buddha heart, since it is only for *them* that there is a phase of actually becoming Buddhas, while the unconditioned nature of the dharmakāya is without any differences in terms of before and after or better and worse. Through this third reasoning, one understands that a result is produced from a cause, thus applying reasoning (3). This is not just inferring that a result comes forth through the mere existence of the cause, which is due to the following essential points: The disposition that is suchness (the nature of phenomena) is changeless; at the time of fruition, its nature is still without being better or worse; since the adventitious stains are always separable from it, no matter how long they have been around, it is impossible that the disposition ever loses its capacity for becoming a Buddha. The Kagyü scholar Surmang Padma Namgyal's *Full Moon of Questions and Answers* (Zur mang padma rnam rgyal, pp. 32–33) explains verse I.28 through linking it with the same four reasonings and even adding the nine examples for buddha nature in the *Uttaratantra*. It says that the first line proves the cause by way of the result, applying reasoning (3) and examples 1–3. As for the second line, the true nature of Buddhas and sentient beings is the same and without any distinction of purity and impurity, referring to reasoning (1) and example 4. The third line shows that the result of the three kāyas depends on both the naturally abiding and the unfolding disposition, thus applying reasoning (2) and examples 5–9 (reasoning (4) is said to be contained implicitly in all three lines). Pöba Tulku's (1900/1907–1959) Notes on the *Essential Points* of Mipham Rinpoche's above *Synopsis* (Stong thun gnad kyi zin thun; photocopy of a digital file from Shechen Monastery, p. 17.5–18.1) follows the latter's matching of the three lines with reasonings (2), (1), and (3), referring to result, nature, and cause, respectively. He adds that the first one is a result reason (*'bras bu'i rtags*), while the latter two are nature reasons (*rang bzhin gyi rtags*). Also, when it is said that "sentient beings are Buddhas," this only refers to buddhahood in the sense of natural purity (but not in the sense of being endowed with twofold purity). Therefore, it speaks about the true nature of the mind but not its result. Hence, there is no flaw of the result already abiding in the cause (as in the Sāṃkhya system). A Sakya commentary on the *Abhisamayālaṃkāra* by Ngag dbang kun dga' dbang phyug (1987, pp. 197–98) says that the first three lines of I.28, in due order, refer to that which is suitable for (a) the condition of the Buddha's enlightened activity engaging it, (b) relinquishing the adverse conditions of the obscurations, and (c) the arising of all buddha qualities as the fruition. Thus, the Sugata heart at the time of it being a cause for buddhahood is defined as the dharmadhātu that has these three features. The Third Karmapa's AC (fols. 43b–44a) refers to this verse in the context of explaining that the stained minds of ordinary beings, which appear as the five skandhas, are tainted forms of the buddhakāyas. Thus, upon the stains disappearing, the dharmakāya as well as, physically, the supreme nirmāṇakāya of a Buddha radiate. Differing from the Eighth Karmapa's presentation here and without going through all the technicalities of reasoning, his *Lamp That Elucidates Other-Empty Madhyamaka* (pp. 14–31) justifies the three reasons at length. To summarize, as for "the buddhakāya radiating," it says that the stained minds of sentient beings change state into stainless wisdom due to the power of both the blessings of the already stainless wisdom of all Buddhas and the factor of wisdom within the stainless aspect of their own minds. As for "suchness being undifferentiable," "the Tathāgata heart," "dharmakāya," and so on are just different names with the same meaning. It is just the unobscured manifestation of the Tathāgata heart that is called "dharmakāya." This is found in the three phases of sentient beings (impure), bodhisattvas (pure and impure), and Buddhas (completely pure), but in itself is never tainted by any stains and is pure by nature. Thus, it is taught that, in the Tathāgata heart, there is neither any being tainted by stains in the beginning nor any relinquishment of them later. In this way, the Tathāgata heart is what appears as the three jewels (Buddha, dharma, saṅgha), since it is capable of bringing forth the accumulations of merit and wisdom on a temporary level as well as the excellence of self-sprung wisdom ultimately. Thus, throughout all these phases, in the Tathāgata heart, there is never any difference in terms of it being a cause that can be separated from its result. As for "the disposition," strictly speaking, the support of the path is the Tathāgata heart with stains, the supports of practicing this path are the persons in the three yānas, and the nature of the path is the disposition. If it did not exist, even if Buddhas have arrived in the world, there would be no basis for the growth of the roots of true reality and thus no attainment of perfect buddhahood. Without going into further details (which are indeed infinite in this issue), I would like to present another more path-oriented example that adds to the perspective on the three "proofs," especially "the buddhakāya radiating." As we saw, the respective first lines in the above three verses I.27, I.28, and I.142 of the *Uttaratantra* equate buddhakāya, buddha wisdom, and dharmakāya, clearly indicating that the dharmakāya is not just mere emptiness but—as buddha wisdom—actively engages and communicates with sentient beings (this is also clearly suggested by the above gloss on the first line of I.28 in Sajjana's *Mahāyānottaratantraśāstropadeśa*). Also, as mentioned above, the Sanskrit term for "radiates" literally means "vibrates." So, as far as the "awakening" of buddha nature in sentient beings is concerned, one may think of both Buddhas and sentient beings as violins, with the "Buddha violins" being in perfect tune and playing (teaching the dharma in various ways), while the strings of the "sentient being violins" are covered by various kinds of cloth and are somewhat out of tune. Still, as we know, all strings with the same tuning start to vibrate if just one of them resounds. Even if some strings are a little bit out of tune and/or are covered by a very light cloth, they still vibrate slightly. Of course, the better they are tuned and the less they are covered, the louder and clearer they resound. So one may say that proceeding on the path is a matter of progressively uncovering and tuning the strings, but they already have the perfect capacity to resound properly and thus make themselves noticeable by vibrating right at the very beginning of the play of the "Buddha violins" (which is a 24/7 display anyway), even if ever so inconspicuously. Thus, the path is basically a matter of sentient beings tuning in to the concert of all Buddhas. In brief, the first line of *Uttaratantra* I.28 refers to the "Buddha violins" vibrating and the third line to the "sentient being violins." The fact that the former can actually make the latter vibrate too is shown by the second line, which states that their strings are of the same nature. For further discussions of *Uttaratantra* I.28, see Jamgön Kongtrul's commentary on that text (Kong sprul blo gros mtha' yas n.d., fol. 44a–b), which also briefly presents Ngog Lotsāwa's explanation, Mipham Rinpoche's *Lamp of Certainty* (Pettit 1999, pp. 384–87), and especially Kano 2006.

281 P5550, fol. 62b.4.

282 According to *Uttaratantra* I.14–18, the three qualities of awareness are (1) the wisdom that knows suchness, (2) the wisdom that knows variety, and (3) internal personally experienced wisdom. The three qualities of liberation are (1) freedom from afflictive obscurations, (2) freedom from cognitive obscurations, and (3) being unsurpassable in terms of irreversible realization.

283 Tib. bsam gtan sa drug. These refer to the preparatory and main stages of the four mundane dhyāna levels of the form realm, which are temporarily also cultivated on Buddhist paths.

However, it is only their aspect of calm abiding that is used as a support for the cultivation of supramundane superior insight into identitylessness.

284 Tib. 'od gsal chub pa'i byang bya yin. Mikyö Dorje plays here on the two syllables of the Tibetan word *byang chub* (enlightenment, buddhahood), *byang* meaning "to purify" and *chub* "to fully realize."

285 Mi bskyod rod rje 2003, vol. 1, pp. 208–29.

286 As was said above, both Vairocanarakṣita's *Mahāyānottaratantraṭippaṇī* and Sajjana's *Mahāyānottaratantraśāstropadeśa* are just very brief summarizing commentaries.

287 SC, p. 329.

288 Tib. dbu ma rgyan gyi rnam bshad (in 'Ju mi pham rgya mtsho 1992, pp. 471–72). In this context, compare also sūtra 7 of the *Māṇḍūkya Upaniṣad*, characterizing the supreme Brahman in its ultimate aspect: "Fourth, it is considered to be invisible, beyond the conventional, ungraspable, without characteristics, inconceivable, undefinable, the single essential ground, the utter subsiding of reference points, peace, bliss, nonduality—it is to be understood as ātman" (*adṛṣṭam avyavahāryam agrahyam acintyam avyapadeśyam ekātmapratyayasāraṃ prapañcopaśamaṃ śāntaṃ śivam advaitaṃ caturthaṃ manyate sa ātmā sa vijñeyaḥ*).

289 This is another name of the Jainas.

290 As quoted in 'Ju mi pham rgya mtsho 1975, fol. 287a–b.

291 Schmithausen 1973, p. 136 (the English translation is mine); see also pp. 131–35 and 137–38. For further references see Takasaki 1966, Schmithausen 1971, Hookham 1991, Mathes 1996 and 2002, Stearns 1999, Zimmermann 2002, and Brunnhölzl 2004.

292 The following is just a brief sketch (for more details, see Brunnhölzl 2004, pp. 186–93, 308–20, and 576–84).

293 Zimmermann 2002, pp. 64–65.

294 In an attempt of addressing this dilemma and its consequences—and contrary to what even the Gelugpa system itself says about nonimplicative negations everywhere else—the nonimplicative negation that is the lack of real existence is then assigned a unique dual status of being suitable as an object of both a conceptual consciousness and yogic perception. That this creates more problems than it solves is obvious, but another issue (see Brunnhölzl 2004).

295 Mi bskyod rdo rje 1990, pp. 45–46.

296 Quoted in Tulku Thondup, *Practice of Dzogchen* (Snow Lion Publications 1996, pp. 245–46) in an excerpt from Longchenpa's *Tshig don mdzod* (ed. Tarthang Tulku, fols. 897.4–899.2).

297 There may be Sanskrit manuscripts, but I was unable to evaluate the possible sources. *A Descriptive Bibliography of the Sanskrit Buddhist Literature, Vol. III: Abhidharma, Madhyamaka, Yogācāra, Buddhist Epistemology and Logic* (K. Tsukamoto, Y. Matsunaga, and H. Isoda, 1990, Kyoto: Heirakuji-Shoten, p. 148) mentions a Sanskrit manuscript of the *Dharmadhātustava* (located at the Institute for Advanced Studies of World Religions, New York, MBB-II-292, Nepali paper, nine fols.). Also the microfilm title list of the NGMPP (Nepal-German Manuscript Preservation Project; title list on CD available at www.uni-hamburg.de/ngmpp) contains several titles that bear the names *Dharmadhātustava* and/or *-stotra* (however, these titles obviously were also used for other texts than the one by Nāgārjuna and at least some of the manuscripts in this list are much longer).

298 Tib. nag tsho lo tsā ba tshul khrims rgyal ba.

299 I am indebted to Mr. Kazuo Kano for drawing my attention to this and translating the relevant points from the Japanese and Chinese in Hayashima 1987.

300 Just to note, the Derge *Tengyur* contains a *Dharmadhātugarbhavivaraṇa* (D4101, fols. 222b.1–223a.4) attributed to Nāgārjuna. However, it neither comments on *dharmadhātu* nor *garbha*, but only very briefly on the famous formula of the Tathāgata having taught the causes as well as the cessations of phenomena that arise from causes (*ye dharmā hetuprabhavāḥ* . . . ; already found in *Dīgha Nikāya* I.40).

301 The translation is based on a careful edition of the text based on the *Tengyur* versions DNP and the various Tibetan commentaries, with reference to the Sanskrit of verses 18–23 (as quoted in Nāropa's *Sekoddeśaṭīkā*). Significant variants from D in NP will be footnoted as in this case: D *stava* NP *stotra*.

302 This is is the homage by the Tibetan translator.

303 This example is also found in the *Mahābherīsūtra* (N mdo tsa, fols. 181a–182b) and the *Aṅgulimālīyasūtra* (N mdo ma, fol. 310a).

304 This example is found in the *Dhāraṇīśvararājasūtra* (P814, fol. 176b), which is also quoted in Asaṅga's *Ratnagotravibhāgavyākhyā* on I.2 (J 6).

305 This is the third of the nine examples for buddha nature in the *Tathāgatagarbhasūtra* (D258, fol. 250a.2–b.2) and the *Uttaratantra* (I.105–7).

306 D/DSC *sangs rgyas* NP *snying po* (core, essence).

307 Buddha nature as a seed is also described as the sixth of the nine examples in the *Tathāgatagarbhasūtra* (D258, fol. 252a.1–b.3) and the *Uttaratantra* I.115–17.

308 This is the order of this line in N, P, and DSC, with most commentaries matching it with the order of afflictions in the next verse. D has *sprin dang khug rna du ba dang*, which corresponds to the order of this line in Sanskrit.

309 In ancient Indian cosmology, solar and lunar eclipses are regarded as the sun or moon being swallowed by the demon Rahu, since he envies them for their light. However, he is not able to retain them in his body and thus has to release them very quickly.

310 Interestingly, the *Aṅguttaranikāya* (I, pp. 253–54, 275; III, p. 16) also speaks about mind needing to be freed from the same five obscuring stains in order to regain its natural state. Also, Vasubandhu's *Mahāyānasūtrālaṃkārabhāṣya* says that mind is similar to the sky by virtue of its luminosity, since all manifold phenomena are as adventitious with regard to the mind as are dust, smoke, clouds, and mist with regard to the sky (ed. Nagao, p. 18.43–44).

311 DNP *nyon mongs* DSC *dri ma* (stains).

312 NP/DSC *gdungs* D *ldongs* (blinded).

313 This corresponds to the eighth of the nine examples for buddha nature in the *Tathāgatagarbhasūtra* (D258, fols. 253b.1–254a.5) and the *Uttaratantra* (I.121–23).

314 The Tibetan of this verse is somewhat ambiguous. Hayashima 1987 offers a helpful Sanskrit reconstruction (without considering the meter) based on both the Tibetan and the Chinese, with the Sanskrit terms for the four conceptions being sufficiently obvious from the Chinese: *ahaṃkāra-mamakāra-vikalpābhyāṃ, nāmasaṃjñā-nimittābhyāṃ ca/ catuḥvikalpā bhavanti,*

bhūtabhautikaiś ca [rūpāṇi bhavanti] (the last two words having no correspondence in the Tibetan). *Nimitta* can mean "sign," "characteristic," "cause," or "reason." The Tibetan has the latter (*rgyu mtshan*), while the Chinese has "object/referent." For the different interpretations of this verse by the commentators, see below.

315 The Tibetan for "very own awareness" in verses 29, 46, and 56 is *so sor rang rig* (Skt. pratyātmavedanīya), otherwise translated here as "personally experienced (wisdom)."

316 NP/DSC *yod* D *dmigs*.

317 Tib. dbu ma nyid.

318 D *yin* NP *yis*. Following PN, this line would translate as "Through dharmadhātu being their nature, . . ."

319 D *brtags pas* NP *rtag par* (most commentaries agree with D). Following PN, this line would translate: "Always rest in your self!"

320 See Asaṅga's *Mahāyānasaṃgraha* I.49.

321 NP/DSC *gnas* D *nas*.

322 D/DSC *'phel* NP *rgyas*.

323 Literally, "black."

324 Literally, "white."

325 NP, DSC, and SS *zab*; D and all other commentaries *zad*.

326 After this, NP mistakenly repeat line 92d of the translation (line 92c: *pad ma chen po'i rang bzhin gyis*).

327 NP/DSC *las* D *lam*.

328 Tib. sna tshogs nor bu (probably Skt. nānāratna, which means "various gems"). Traditionally, in India, the oceans were regarded as the source of a great variety of precious gems. Texts such as the *Uttaratantra* (I.42–43) apply this metaphor to the dharmadhātu or buddha nature, saying that its jewel-like qualities of buddha wisdom and samādhi resemble the ocean's immeasurable precious qualities (the same metaphor is also applied to the ten bhūmis and their enlightened activities in IV.8–9). However, at least the Tibetan term *sna tshogs nor bu* seems to bear the same ambiguity as the English word "variegated" (meaning both various and multicolored). Thus, it can also be taken to suggest a "wish-fulfilling jewel" (Skt. cintāmaṇi), which is exactly what all commentaries except LG do (there are, however, no Sanskrit sources for corresponding terms, such as *citramaṇi).

329 NP add 'phags pa (noble).

330 NP add dge slong (monk).

331 Tib. tshul khrims rgyal ba.

332 P5254, fols. 358a–b. Note that Bhāvaviveka refers here to the typical (Yogācāra) triad of mind, mentation, and consciousness (representing the eight consciousnesses).

333 Ibid., fol. 361a.

334 Ed. Carelli, p. 65–66 (D1351, fol. 281a3–b5).

335 As mentioned above, this verse is also quoted in Asaṅga's *Ratnagotravibhāgavyākhyā*.

336 D3935, fol. 296b.5–7.

337 P5866, verse 13.

338 P4534, fols. 101b–102b.

339 P5388, fol. 128a.6–7.

340 Verses 46–47; 65–66 (the last verse condenses *Uttaratantra* I.94cd and II.21cd–23ab). Just as an aside, at least in this text, Atiśa speaks far too much about the luminous nature of the mind and its qualities to qualify as an exclusive and "pure" Prāsaṅgika (as he is claimed to be in most of the Tibetan tradition). In addition, he also speaks quite favorably of other elements of the Yogācāra tradition. For more details on Atiśa's view and a translation of the *Dharmadhātudarśanagīti*, see Brunnhölzl 2007, pp. 75–91.

341 Rang byung rdo rje n.d., fol. 19b.

342 Ibid., fols. 76a–77a (for more details, see the endnote on verse 47 in the translation of DSC below).

343 Ibid., fols. 119b–120b.

344 Ibid., fol. 168a–b.

345 Rang byung rdo rje 2006b, pp. 555–56.

346 'Gos lo tsā ba gzhon nu dpal 2003b, p. 7.

347 Ibid., pp. 12 (verse 2); 33 (17ab, 66–68); 46 (38–43); 47 (30–33, 18–22); 72 (78–87); 103 (22); 119 (17); 121 (75–76, 5–7); 122 (8); 181 (10c); 215 (36–37); 260 (82); 323 (2); 445 (75–76); and 456–57 (43–45). For some of Gö Lotsāwa's comments, see the endnotes to the translation of DSC.

348 Chos grags rgya mtsho n.d., p. 31.

349 Chos grags rgya mtsho 1985, vol. 2, pp. 516–19.

350 Tib. karma phrin las pa phyogs las rnam rgyal.

351 Rang byung rdo rje 2006a, vol. traṃ, pp. 36 and 50.

352 Mi bskyod rdo rje 1990, pp. 41–42.

353 Mi bskyod rdo rje 2003, vol. 1, pp. 33–34.

354 Ibid., p. 349.

355 Ibid., vol. 2, p. 423.

356 Mi bskyod rdo rje 1996, pp. 537–40. For a detailed treatment of this, the Karmapa refers to his own massive commentary on the Drikung master Jigden Sumgön's (1143–1217) famous *Single Intention of the Genuine Dharma* (dam chos dgongs gcig).

357 Tib. dkon mchog yan lag.

358 Dkon mchog yan lag 2005, pp. 94–95. This is very similar to what the Eighth Karmapa's above discussion of the disposition says. In brief, sentient beings neither *have* the nature of a Buddha, nor *are* they Buddhas. Since sentient beings are nothing but illusory adventitious stains that—other than as the delusions of a mistaken mind—never existed in the first place, how could such nonexistents possess anything, let alone buddha nature? Also, since the char-

acteristics of such adventitious stains and buddha nature are contrary in every respect, the one possessing the other would be like darkness possessing light or hatred possessing love. Sentient beings cannot be said to *be* Buddhas either, because sentient beings—as adventitious stains—are impermanent and disintegrate, whereas buddhahood is unconditioned, thus absolutely changeless, and can never become nonexistent. Thus, they cannot be the same.

359 Ibid., p. 291.

360 Ibid., pp. 296–97.

361 Tib. chos kyi byung gnas (aka bstan pa'i nyin byed).

362 Chos kyi 'byung gnas n.d., pp. 24–26.

363 Ibid., pp. 30–31.

364 Ibid., pp. 38–39.

365 Ibid., pp. 41–42.

366 According to the "official" Tibetan account of the "debate at Samyé" between the Indian master Kamalaśīla and the Ch'an master Hvashang Mahāyāna from Tun-huang, the latter was refuted by the former. Hvashang is said to have advocated an exclusive cultivation of a thought-free mental state—as representing realization of the ultimate—along with a complete rejection of the aspect of means, such as the accumulation of merit and proper ethical conduct. However, there are at least two indigenous Tibetan versions of the "debate at Samyé," with the more verifiable one presenting a different account of Hvashang's position. Also, Tibetan and Chinese documents on this debate found at Tun-huang differ greatly from the "official" Tibetan story, eventually presenting Hvashang as the winner and not Kamalaśīla. In any case, in Tibet, Hvashang's name and view became the favorite polemical stereotype that continues to be freely applied—justified or not—to the views and meditation instructions of other Tibetan schools.

367 Ibid., pp. 52–55.

368 Kong sprul blo gros mtha' yas 1990a, pp. 135–36.

369 Ibid., p. 140.

370 Ibid., pp. 146–48.

371 Ibid., pp. 157–58.

372 Ibid., pp. 160–61.

373 Ibid., p. 167.

374 Ibid., p. 173.

375 Ibid., p. 181. The annotations to NT by the Fifth Shamarpa, Göncho Yenla, (in *Selected Writings on Vajrayana Buddhist Practice* [1979], vol. 1, pp. 459–74) quote the same verse here. The term *tīrthika* (lit. "forders") was originally a neutral expression in India, meaning "follower of a spiritual system." Specifically, the Jainas refer to their founding gurus by the name *tīrthakara* ("ford-builder"). In Buddhist texts, the term came to be a general—and rather pejorative—term for non-Buddhist schools. TOK (vol. 2, p. 335) explains its Tibetan equivalent *mu stegs pa* in a more positive way as referring to those who dwell within a part (*mu*) of liberation or on a stepping-stone (*stegs*) toward it, although their paths are not sufficient to grant actual liberation from saṃsāra.

376 Kong sprul blo gros mtha' yas 1990b, pp. 123 and 124. For further details, see my forthcoming translations of said two commentaries.

377 Kong sprul blo gros mtha' yas n.d., fols. 11a–12b.

378 Ibid., fol. 29b.

379 Tib. sa skya pan ḍi ta kun dga' rgyal mtshan.

380 Tib. rin po che'i phreng ba dri ma med pa zhes bya ba'i rgya cher 'grel pa (aka dri ma med pa'i rgyan).

381 *Sa pan kun dga' rgyal mtshan gyi gsung 'bum* (bod ljongs bod yig dpe rnying dpe skrun khang, Hsinhua 1992), vol. 3, pp. 392–93.

382 X.5 (P5549, fol. 44a.8–45b.5).

383 The wisdom that knows suchness sees how all phenomena actually are, while the wisdom of variety sees suchness as it appears as all kinds of different phenomena.

384 Ibid., pp. 409–12.

385 *Lta ba'i shan 'byed theg mchog gnad kyi zla zer* (Sa skya pa'i bka' 'bum, vol. 13 [Tokyo: The Tōyō Bunko 1969], p. 18).

386 Tib. re mda' ba gzhon nub lo gros.

387 Sdom pa gsum gyi rab tu dbye ba'i kha skong gzhi lam 'bras gsum gsal bar byed pa'i legs bshad 'od kyi snang ba (ibid., vol. 14). *Differentiating the Three Vows* is one of Sakya Paṇḍita's most famous texts (trans. by Jared Rhoton as *A Clear Differentiation of the Three Codes*, State University of New York Press 2005).

388 Tib. rong ston shes bya kun rig.

389 Tib. bsod nams rgyal mtshan.

390 Tib. glo bo mkhan chen bsod nams lhun grub. Other sources give his dates as 1441–1525 (for more details, see the section "Other Tibetan Commentaries on the *Dharmadhātustava*").

391 SC, pp. 304–6.

392 For further details on these and the other commentaries on the *Dharmadhātustava* mentioned just below, see the section "Other Tibetan Commentaries on the *Dharmadhātustava*" and the endnotes to the translation of DSC.

393 Dol po pa shes rab rgyal mtshan 1998, pp. 45–46 and 411.

394 Tib. bstan pa spyi 'grel (verse 11; Bhutanese ed. 1984, vol. 1, p. 688).

395 Tib. bka' bsdu bzhi pa (ibid., p. 398).

396 Tib. gzhan stong dbu ma'i rgyan gyi lung sbyor (Tāranātha 1983, vol. 4, pp. 539–40).

397 As in this case, the *shentong* tradition is also often referred to as "Great Madhyamaka," further names being "Yogācāra-Madhyamaka," "Vijñapti-Madhyamaka," and "the meditative tradition of the dharmas of Maitreya" (*byams chos sgom lugs*). However—and this is often a source of confusion—the first three of these terms are equally applied to various Buddhist systems other than *shentong*. For example, Atiśa speaks about "the Great Madhyamaka beyond existence and nonexistence" as referring to the meaning of prajñāpāramitā as taught by Nāgārjuna as opposed to its meaning taught by Asaṅga (*Bodhipathapradīpapañjikā*, fol. 280a.4–7), while

Tsongkhapa uses Great Madhyamaka to refer to his own interpretation of Madhyamaka. The term "Yogācāra-Madhyamaka" started as one of the earliest subdivisions of the Madhyamaka School in general, later being widely used for the approach of Śāntarakṣita and Kamalaśīla. "Vijñapti-Madhyamaka" is often understood as a name for Ratnākaraśānti's later synthesis of Yogācāra and Madhyamaka.

398 Tib. gzhan stong snying po (ibid., p. 499).

399 Tib. 'dzam thang mkhan po blo gros grags pa. Dzamtang is an area in far eastern Tibet, where a few monasteries of the Jonang tradition, including its scriptural legacy, survive to the present day.

400 Blo gros grags pa 1993, pp. 94–95.

401 This is Dölpopa's specific term for the Buddhist teachings that present true reality just as it is. Judging from the quotes throughout his texts, for him, these include many scriptures, such as the Anuttarayogatantras, the sūtras that teach buddha nature, and—among treatises—the works of Maitreya, Nāgārjuna, Asaṅga, Vasubandhu, Nāropa, and Saraha.

402 Lo chen Dharmaśrī n. d., p. 377.1–4. *Ascertaining the Three Vows* is a text by Ngari Panchen Bema Wangyal (Tib. mnga' ris pan chen pad ma dbang rgyal; 1487–1542), translated into English as *Perfect Conduct* (Wisdom Publications 1996).

403 Ibid., 296.1–5.

404 *Dbu ma sogs gzhung spyi'i dka' gnad* (*Collected Works*, vol. 22, p. 450.3).

405 Tib. dam chos dogs sel (in 'Ju mi pham rgya mtsho 1992, p. 521).

406 Tib rong zom chos kyi bzang po.

407 'Ju mi pham rgya mtsho c. 1990, pp. 361–63. For a translation of this text, see Pettit 1999.

408 This kind of result is defined as "the exhaustion or relinquishment of the specific factors to be relinquished through the force of the remedy that is prajñā." It thus refers not to the usual notion of a result as some phenomenon that is produced by causes and conditions but to the absence of afflictive and cognitive obscurations. In this context of buddha nature here, it specifically refers to the absence of adventitious stains, which reveals the buddha qualities, thus emphasizing that these qualities are not conditioned or newly produced.

409 'Ju mi pham rgya mtsho 1975, fol. 286a.2–b.1. For a translation of this text, see Duckworth 2005.

410 Ibid., fol. 286b.3–6.

411 Tib. klong chen rab 'byams.

412 Ibid., fols. 293b.2–294a.2.

413 Tib. nges shes sgron me.

414 Tib. khro shul 'jam rdor.

415 See Pettit 1999, pp. 364–65.

416 Ibid., pp. 284–85.

417 Tib. bod pa sprul sku mdo sngags bstan pa'i nyi ma.

418 Stong thun gnad kyi zin thun (photocopy of a digital file from Shechen Monastery, pp. 14.4–15.3).

419 Tib. dag gzigs tshad ma. This is one of the two conventional kinds of valid cognition introduced by Mipham Rinpoche, the other being "valid cognition of seeing only what is right in front of one's eyes" (*tshur mthong tshad ma*). The two ultimate valid cognitions are to realize the nominal and the nonnominal ultimate, respectively.

420 To wit, following Mipham Rinpoche's above statements, Pöba Tulku says elsewhere *(lta grub shan 'byed gnad kyi sgron me'i grel pa*, Si khron mi rigs dpe skrun khang 1996, pp. 92, 120ff.) that the general feature of Nyingma scriptures is that both the second turning of the wheel of dharma (including the Madhyamaka scriptures related to it) and the third one (including texts like the *Uttaratantra*) are of definitive meaning—the former due to teaching the ultimate as the union of appearance and emptiness and the latter through teaching the ultimate as the concordance between the way things appear and how they actually are.

421 Bdud 'joms 'jigs bral ye shes rdo rje 1991, p. 211.

422 Ibid., pp. 173 and 265.

423 Ibid., p. 196.

424 Ibid., pp. 930–31.

425 Ibid. p. 207.

426 Ibid., p. 216.

427 Ibid., p. 301–2.

428 Tib. nyan ston shākya rgyal mtshan.

429 Tib. mkhan zur pad ma rgyal mtshan.

430 Tib. zab don gdams pa'i mig 'byed gser gyi thur ma. Mundgod: Drepung Loseling Printing Press, 1984, vol. 3, p. 147.

431 The same goes for the other praises by Nāgārjuna—if any of their verses are quoted in Gelugpa sources at all, then only those that speak about typical Madhyamaka notions, such as emptiness, nonarising, or interdependence.

432 Chos kyi rgyal mtshan 2004, pp. 40–48 (verses 1, 20–21, 26, 30, 43–44, 101).

433 For details, see my forthcoming translation of the Fifth Shamarpa's commentary *A Concise Elucidation of the Abhisamayālaṃkāra*, which also includes the crucial parts of the Eighth Karmapa's commentary.

434 Tib. mang yul ding ri glang 'khor.

435 Tib. ston pa chos dpal.

436 Tib. jo mo g.yang 'dren.

437 Tib. u rgyan pa rin chen dpal.

438 Tib. khro phu ba kun ldan shes rab.

439 Tib. gnyan ras dge' 'dun 'bum.

440 Tib. slob dpon shes rab dpal.

441 Tib. rgya sgom ye shes 'od.

442 Tib. gnam mtsho ba mi bskyod rdo rje. In particular, the Karmapa received the transmission of Cutting Through (Tib. gcod) from him.

443 Tib. gzhon nu byang chub.

444 Tib. dge 'dun rin chen.

445 Tib. gsang phu.

446 Tib. shākya gzhon nu.

447 Tib. snye mdo ba kun dga' don grub.

448 Tib. tshul khrims rin chen.

449 Tib. sba ras.

450 Tib. bi ma snying thig. These are the main Dzogchen teachings by Vimalamitra.

451 Tib. ka rma yang dgon.

452 Tib. ka rma snying thig.

453 Tib. g.yag ston sangs rgyas dpal.

454 Tib. sgam po zang lung.

455 Tib. dvags po.

456 Tib. kong po.

457 Tib. rkungs (Chos kyi 'byungs gnas 1972 has *spungs*).

458 Tib. bde chen steng.

459 The only source that reports a meeting between the Karmapa and Dölpopa at all is Chos kyi 'byung gnas 1972 (p. 208.1–2), but there is no mention of the latter being a disciple of Rangjung Dorje.

460 Tib. lkog phreng.

461 Tib. ka rma dgon. The main Karma Kagyü seat in Kham, established in 1173 by the First Karmapa.

462 Tib. sog chu.

463 Tib. ri bo rtse lnga.

464 Tib. phyag rgya chen po'i smon lam.

465 Tib. phyag rgya chen po lhan cig skyes sbyor khrid yig.

466 Tib. sku gsum ngo sprod.

467 Tib. rlung sems gnyis med.

468 For extensive bibliographies, see www.tbrc.org and Schaeffer 1995, pp. 14–18 and 136–39.

469 Tib. rgyal ba g.yung ston pa.

470 Tib. grags pa seng ge.

471 1981, p. 200.

472 Rang byung rdo rje n.d., fol. 12b (NT) and fol. 18a–b (NY).

473 As for commentaries by others on Rangjung Dorje's above works, there are several on his ZMND, including those by the Fifth Shamarpa, Tsurpu Jamyang Chenpo, Tagbo Rabjampa Chögyal Denba, the First Karma Trinlépa, Jamgön Kongtrul Lodrö Tayé, and the Fifteenth Karmapa. The latter two and the Fifth Shamarpa also wrote commentaries on NT and NY. Finally, there is a commentary by the Eighth Situpa on MM (see also the bibliography).

474 1332 was another Monkey Year, but Rangjung Dorje was on his long journey to and stay at the Chinese court at that time and not in Upper Dechen.

475 In *The Blue Annals* (p. 492), Chos kyi 'byung gnas 1972 (p. 210.7), and Tshal pa kun dga' rdo rje 1981 (p. 100), the entry of the year 1326 is followed by a number of events, the last one being the composition of DSC. The next explicit dates are 1328 in the first two texts and 1329 in the latter.

476 There is some unclarity here, since both the commentaries by Jamgön Kongtrul and the Fifteenth Karmapa (the latter basically throughout copying the former) gloss this as the Pig Year of the sixth sixty-year cycle of the Tibetan calendar, which would make it 1335, since this is the only Pig Year within that cycle during Rangjung Dorje's lifetime. However, as this date is clearly contradicted by NY being explicitly referred to in AC, the only Pig Year before the AC's indubitable composition in 1325 and after ZMND's in 1322 is 1323, which fits well with the overall chronology. Of course, there are still earlier Pig Years in Rangjung Dorje's life (1311 and 1299), but it seems highly unlikely that he composed NY eleven or even twenty-three years (at age fifteen) before ZMND. Also, while NY says itself that it was composed at Upper Dechen in Tsurpu (Central Tibet), all sources agree that, upon his return from the Chinese court, Rangjung Dorje went through Minyag and other areas of Kham in eastern Tibet in 1335, teaching the dharma extensively. Tshal pa kun dga' rdo rje 1981 (p. 103), Dpa' bo gtsug lag phreng ba 2003 (vol. 2, p. 941), and Situ Chos kyi 'byung gnas (fol. 111a) all say that he returned to Tsurpu only during the ninth month of that Pig Year (November/December) and then stayed at Chimpu in Samyé during that winter for six months.

477 Since this was written before the time of Tsongkhapa and his followers (who are well known to hold that buddha nature is nothing but sentient beings' emptiness in the sense of a nonimplicative negation), it refers to the position of Ngog Lotsāwa and some of his followers, explicitly appearing in the former's *Theg pa chen po'i rgyud bla ma'i don bsdus pa* (Dharamsala 1993, fol. 4a2–3).

478 AC fols. 10a–12b (the last line refers to NT).

479 Here, AC quotes the same passage from this text (P5549, fols. 11b.1–12a.6) as Mikyö Dorje's above discussion on buddha nature.

480 AC fols. 13a–23b.

481 Ibid., fols. 25b–28b.

482 Ibid., fols. 116b–120b.

483 For a list and explanation of the eighteen emptinesses, see Brunnhölzl 2004, pp. 117–22.

484 There is a nice ambiguity about this "distraction" here. In all the passages of Asaṅga's commentary where this expression appears, it is always the compound *śūnyatāvikṣiptacitta*,

which can mean either a mind distracted by emptiness, from emptiness, or toward emptiness. From the various contexts in this commentary, it can be gathered that the ambiguity of this compound is probably not by chance. For, the point is always that beginner bodhisattvas are distracted *by* a wrong understanding of emptiness (either misconceiving it as destroying phenomena or as some separate entity to be focused on deliberately) and thus distracted *from* its correct understanding, which is explicitly identified as the principle of what emptiness means in terms of the Tathāgata heart. This ambiguity is reflected in the various Tibetan versions of Asaṅga's commentary in the *Tengyur* and its quotations in other texts (such as AC), which—in a rather inconsistent manner—take this Sanskrit compound to have either the one or the other meaning (respectively using *la, las,* or *gyis* after *stong pa nyid*).

485 Ibid., fols. 122a–124a.

486 It is interesting to note here that later commentators on ZMND, such as Tagramba and Jamgön Kongtrul, elaborate on a typical *shentong* doxographical hierarchy of Vaibhāṣikas, Sautrāntikas, Mere Mentalists, and Mādhyamikas (*rangtong*), with the Great (Yogācāra-) Mādhyamikas (alias *Shentong*-Mādhyamikas) at the top, while AC does not make any such distinctions beyond the first two schools. Rather, the text just refers to the Buddha's teachings and presents exemplifying quotes from both Nāgārjuna's *Bodhicittavivaraṇa* and Maitreya's *Mahāyānasūtrālaṃkāra* on equal footing, thus highlighting the fundamental unity of Yogācāra and Madhyamaka also with respect to this gradual approach. That this is nothing new or unusual can be clearly shown through the ample scriptural evidence that, at least in terms of the progressive stages of meditation in the mahāyāna, this approach is shared by almost all Indian Mādhyamikas and Yogācāras (see Brunnhölzl 2004, pp. 295–310).

487 Rang byung rdo rje 2006b, p. 600.3–4 and n.d., fols. 99a–103b.

488 This means mental direct cognition, which perceives outer objects just like the five sense consciousnesses.

489 As mentioned before, depending on the perspective, the relationships and classifications of "immediate mind," "afflicted mind," and "stainless mentation" with regard to the sixth and the seventh consciousness vary (for more details, see the translation of DSC below).

490 In other texts, there are also explanations of the empty aspect of the ālaya-consciousness changing state into the dharmadhātu wisdom and its lucid aspect into mirrorlike wisdom.

491 It may be noted that Jamgön Kongtrul's commentary on NT supports this by frequently quoting the *Uttaratantra* (eleven times), the *Mahāyānasūtrālaṃkāra* (ten), the *Dharmadhātustava* (eight), and the ZMND (five).

492 This is also evidenced by Jamgön Kongtrul's commentary relating the above texts to the respective passages in NY by quoting the *Mahāyānasūtrālaṃkāra* twenty-three times and the *Mahāyānasaṃgraha* five times (the *Uttaratantra* also appears five times).

493 Interestingly, Düjom Rinpoche explicitly confirms that Rangjung Dorje's presentation of the naturally abiding and unfolding disposition (the Tathagāta heart), wisdom, and the eight consciousnesses in his AC, NT, and NY accords with the *Uttaratantra*, the *Mahāyānasaṃgraha*, and also the *Madhyāntavibhāga* (Bdud 'joms 'jig bral ye shes rdo rje 1991, p. 202).

494 The Eighth Situpa's commentary on this verse says that the ground for everything in saṃsāra and nirvāṇa is the purity of mind, that is, the basic element or Tathāgata heart. This is the ground of purification but not what is to be purified, since in its own essence, there is nothing whatsover to be purified (quoting *Dharmadhātustava* verses 17 and 19). Also, mind's

nature is the unity of being lucid and empty, since there is no being lucid apart from being empty and no being empty apart from being lucid. Those who explain lucidity and emptiness as two separate things and their union as these two things becoming associated stand outside the teachings of the Tathāgata. In terms of Mahāmudrā, Situ Rinpoche justifies the Kagyü approach of pointing out instructions with or without tantric empowerment and clarifies that it is in full accord with Madhyamaka. Adventitious stains are identified as the dualistic phenomena of apprehender and apprehended produced by the adventitious mistakenness of mind about itself. The dharmakāya is the manifestation of the fundamental nature of the ground in which all such adventitious dualistic phenomena are relinquished (quoting *Dharmadhātustava* verse 37). This is followed by the description of the eight consciousnesses changing state into the four wisdoms and the three kāyas as explained in AC and NY (Chos kyi 'byung gnas n.d., pp. 24–31. To note, this commentary also often refers to ZMND and AC, particularly to their above description of how mind is deluded about itself).

495 Rang byung rdo rje 2006b, pp. 527, 525.5, and 528.4.

496 AC fols. 166a–169a.

497 See Kambala's Ālokāmālā and *Prajñāpāramitānavaślokapiṇḍārthaṭīkā*; Ratnākaraśānti's *Triyānavyavasthāna*, *Madhyamakālaṃkāravṛtti-Madhyamapratipadāsiddhi*, *Prajñāpāramitopadeśa*, and *Madhyamakālaṃkāropadeśa*; Jñānaśrīmitra's *Sākarasiddhiśāstra* (esp. p. 506.9) and *Sākarasaṃgrahasūtra* (verse 2); and Abhayākaragupta's *Munimatālaṃkāra*.

498 Many of Śāntarakṣita's and Kamalaśīla's texts attempt to integrate Yogācāra into Madhyamaka (and not the other way round, as Kambala and Ratnākaśānti usually did), fitting the model of the three natures into the presentation of the two realities. The main feature of this approach is to equate the imaginary and the other-dependent natures with false and correct seeming reality, respectively (done before already by Bhāvaviveka and Jñānagarbha). For details, see Śāntarakṣita's *Madhyamakālaṃkāra* and its autocommentary, in which he speaks about the existence of self-aware mind, as opposed to external objects, on the level of seeming reality (even quoting *Yuktiṣaṣṭikā*, verse 34 as support). In the famous verses 92–93, he declares a true follower of the mahāyāna to be one who rides the chariots of both Yogācāra and Madhyamaka (quoting *Laṅkāvatārasūtra* X.256–57). His *Tattvasiddhi*—not only assimilating Yogācāra but also vajrayāna to Madhyamaka—moreover says that mind is pure by nature and naturally luminous, like a crystal, which is to be personally experienced through self-awareness (*svasaṃvedya*). Ultimately, consciousness is unarisen, neither having nor lacking aspects (ākāra), since it is not the result of any inferior type of cognition under the sway of normal causality. In line with *Laṅkāvatārasūtra* X.257f, the highest cognition as the final result is wisdom that lacks appearance (*nirābhāsajñāna*), being at the same time nondual in terms of any subject and object of awareness. Kamalaśīla's *Madhyamakālokā* equates the other-dependent nature with all three characteristics of correct seeming reality (P5287, fol. 162b.6–7) and says that mere mind, being established through itself, exists on the level of seeming reality, while external objects do not, being just mental aspects (fol. 185a.4–b.5). The text moreover reconciles the stances of the two classical sūtras on which Mādhyamikas and Yogācāras respectively rely in order to distinguish between the expedient and the definitive meaning (fol. 162a.7–b.6): "Nonarising and so forth have been taught as being the definitive meaning in the noble *Akṣayamatiṇnirdeśa[sūtra]*. Therefore, it is certain that precisely these [statements] of nonarising and so on are called 'ultimate.' You may wonder, 'If this is the case, then how could the Bhagavat teach in the noble *Saṃdhinirmocana[sūtra]* that all phenomena lack a nature by intending the three natures, that is, the threefold lack of nature?' There is no fault in this. . . . A mind that has fallen into [either

of] the two extremes of superimposition and denial does not enter the very profound ocean of the way of being of the ultimate, which is free from the two extremes. Consequently, for that purpose, through pronouncing the teaching of nonarising and so forth exclusively in terms of the ultimate and [also] teaching [its underlying] intention of the threefold lack of nature, the Bhagavat taught the middle path free from the two extremes. Therefore, he established nothing but the definitive meaning in his scriptures. [Thus,] it is not the case that Mādhyamikas do not accept the presentation of the three natures." For further details on all this, see Lindtner 1997 (esp. pp. 192–97, 199–200).

499 Tib. gar dbang chos kyi dbang phyug.

500 Tib. rtogs brjod lta sgom spyod 'bras kyi glu (lines 132–35).

501 Tib. bdud 'dul rdo rje.

502 Tib. go nyams lta ba'i glu (lines 73–90). For complete translations of these two songs, see Brunnhölzl 2007, pp. 344–57 and 430–40.

503 Tib. bkra shis 'od zer.

504 Rang byung rdo rje 2006a, vol. ja, p. 128.

505 AC fols. 13bff. (for more details, see the endnote on DSC's comments on verse 1 of the *Dharmadhātustava*).

506 Mi bskyod rdo rje 2003, vol. 1, p. 221.

507 Ibid., pp. 33–34.

508 TOK, vol. 3, p. 24.

509 Ibid., vol. 1, p. 461; vol. 2, p. 544.

510 In this context, it is interesting to note that Hopkins 2002 (pp. 308–9) reports H.H. the Dalai Lama having said that "the fundamental innate mind of clear light—a topic only of Highest Yoga Mantra—is what Maitreya is finally getting at in his *Sublime Continuum of the Great Vehicle* [*Uttaratantra*]" and that this "fundamental innate mind of clear light can be considered an **other-emptiness** [bold by Hopkins] in that it is empty of being any of the coarser levels of consciousness."

511 Phyi nang grub mtha'i rnam bzhag bsdus don blo gsal yid kyi rgyan bzang (*Collected Works,* 'Dzam thang ed., vol.10, fols. 243.7–244.1 and 270.6–7).

512 Blo gros grags pa 1993, p. 88.1–2.

513 TOK, vol. 2, pp. 546–49.

514 Yogācāra texts usually say that the perfect nature is the other-dependent nature being empty of the imaginary. However, when considering their detailed descriptions of what exactly this means, the two statements often come down to the same purport (for more details, see Brunnhölzl 2004, pp. 462–71 and esp. 485–86).

515 TOK, vol. 3, p. 61.

516 Skt. prayoga, Tib. sbyor ba. These four are as follows:
(1) outer objects are observed to be nothing but mind (*upalambhaprayoga/dmigs pa'i sbyor ba*)
(2) thus, outer objects are not observed (*anupalambhaprayoga/mi dmigs pa'i sbyor ba*)
(3) with outer objects being unobservable, a mind cognizing them is not observed either

(*upalambhānupalambhaprayoga/dmigs pa mi dmigs pa'i sbyor ba*)

(4) not observing both, nonduality is observed (*nopalambhopalambhaprayoga/mi dmigs dmigs pa'i sbyor ba*).

These four steps are found in *Laṅkāvatārasūtra* X.256–57, Maitreya's *Mahāyānasūtrālaṃkāra* VI.8 and XIV.23–28, *Dharmadharmatāvibhāga* (lines 182–85, 264–75), *Madhyāntavibhāga* I.6–7ab, as well as in Vasubandhu's *Triṃśikākārikā* 28–30 and *Trisvabhāvanirdeśa* 36–37ab. Ratnākaraśānti's explanations in his *Prajñāpāramitopadeśa* (P5579, fols. 236.4–250.1), *Prajñāpāramitābhāvanopadeśa* (P5580, fols. 250.1–251.2), *Madhyamakālaṃkāravṛtti* (D4072, pp. 234–37), *Kusumāñjali* (D1851, fols. 82.7–84.3), and *Bhramahāra* (D1245, fols. 378.7–379.3) resemble these four steps more or less closely (he sometimes refers to them as the four *yogabhūmis*). In addition to the *Laṅkāvatārasūtra*, he also relates them to the *Avikalpapraveśadhāraṇī* (P810; Meinert 2003 confirms this as referring to fols. 5a.3–6b.2) and a verse from the *Guhyasāmajatantra*. Also some other Yogācāra-Madhyamaka texts quote the *Laṅkāvatārasūtra* and refer to these four stages, commenting on the last one from a Madhyamaka perspective, such as Śāntarakṣita's autocommentary on his *Madhyamakālaṃkāra* (ACIP TD3885@079A–B) as well as Kamalaśīla's *Madhyamakālaṃkārapañjikā* (P5286, fols. 137a–138a) and first *Bhāvanākrama* (ACIP TD3915@033A–B).

517 These are the seven topics of presenting buddha nature in the *Uttaratantra*—Buddha, dharma, saṅgha, the basic element, enlightenment, its qualities, and its enlightened activity.

518 This refers again to buddha nature's impure phase in sentient beings, its partly pure and partly impure phase in bodhisattvas, and the completely pure phase of Buddhas.

519 Ibid., vol. 3, pp. 81–82.

520 Ibid., vol. 2, pp. 549–50. Interestingly, it is precisely this common distinction by *shentongpas*—Mere Mentalists asserting consciousness to be ultimately existent, while *shentongpas* hold wisdom to be ultimately existent—that Pawo Rinpoche Tsugla Trengwa's commentary on Śāntideva's *Bodhicaryāvatāra* considers as just an attempt to sell brass as gold, since it still means to entertain some reference point for the clinging to real existence, which does not get any better by just giving it a more sophisticated name. See also the above quote from Mipham Rinpoche's *Commentary on the Madhyamakālaṃkāra* on just using sophisticated labels without realizing the actual Dzogchen—personally experienced luminosity.

521 Tib. bem stong (lit. "material emptiness"). This refers to a mere blank nothingness as opposed to mind's nature as the union of awareness and emptiness.

522 Ibid., vol. 2, pp. 550–51. The Jonangpa Lodrö Tragba's *Fearless Lion's Roar* says that, since the ultimate reality from the perspective of the wisdom of the noble ones is the primordially unchanging essence of the inseparability of dhātu and awareness, it is really established in the sense of being permanent, stable, and solid (Blo gros grags pa 1993, p. 50). Also Mipham Rinpoche's *Dbu ma sogs gzhung spyi'i dka' gnad* (*Collected Works*, vol. 22, p. 450.2–3) says that, in the *rangtong* system, it is impossible for anything to exist ultimately. In the *shentong* system, if something does not exist ultimately, it is the seeming, while what exists ultimately is the ultimate as such.

523 Dol po pa shes rab rgyal mtshan 1998, pp. 138–39 and 255.

524 Tib. padma dbang mchog rgyal po.

525 Thanks to Anne Burchardi for directing my attention to this rare text and providing me with a copy.

526 Zur mang padma rnam rgyal, pp. 60.3–61.6.

527 Tib. sa bzang ma ti pan chen blo gros rgyal mtshan.

528 Tib. kaḥ thog dge rtse pan chen. His personal name was Gyurmé Tsewang Chogdrub (Tib. 'gyur med tshe dbang mchog grub), and he was considered a reincarnation of several Nyingma masters, foremost of Katog Chenga Jambabum (Tib. kaḥ thog spyan lnga byams pa 'bum; twelfth century), a teacher of the Second Karmapa. Among his many teachers were Jigmé Trinlé Öser (Tib. 'jigs med phrin las 'od zer; 1745–1821)—one of the four main disciples of the great tertön Jigmé Lingba (1729–1798)—and the famous Gelugpa master Janggya Rölpé Dorje. Having been educated at Katog—one of the six main seats of the Nyingma School—he later founded Gédsé Dralé (Tib. dge rtse bkra legs) Monastery with a thousand monks in northern Tibet, spread the Katog tradition in Golog and numerous other parts of eastern Tibet, and restored many Nyingma monasteries there. Being a very prolific author on sūtras, tantras, and termas (his collected works fill ten volumes) and having flourished at an important time of Nyingma revival, his writings indeed deserve close study.

529 This clearly echoes the statement in Dölpopa's *Mountain Dharma* just above. In terms of the relation of *rangtong* and *shentong* to the two latter turnings of the wheel of dharma, Gédsé Panchen's *Rgyal bstan 'khor lo gsum dgongs pa gcig tu rtogs pa rton pa bzhi ldan gyi gtam* (Sichuan ed., vol. 1, fol. 116) says that the second turning teaches the self-empty seeming (*kun rdzob rang stong*), while the third turning teaches the other-empty ultimate, the profound nature of phenomena (*don dam gzhan stong chos nyid zab mo*).

530 Padma Namgyal explicitly considers views (4), (6), and (7) to be good positions.

531 Lo chen Dharmaśrī n.d., pp. 373.5–374.5.

532 Apart from presenting both *rangtong* and *shentong* as ways to eliminate reference points (which—as can be seen below—is usually only said about *rangtong*), this passage is remarkable in several other ways. First, the text makes a distinction between Yogācāra texts and the *Uttaratantra*, while most *shentongpas* take at least all works by Maitreya, Asaṅga, and Vasubandhu as a unit, though they often split the Yogācāra tradition into "Mere Mentalists" (who are said to assert self-aware consciousness as ultimately existent) as opposed to the actual *shentongpas* (Maitreya and so on). That the latter approach is obviously not Lochen's is indicated by the fact that he considers both kinds of texts as the works of *Shentong*-Mādhyamikas, though his above twofold distinction of what is empty of what in terms of the three natures closely resembles the way in which most *shentongpas* set off Mere Mentalism from *shentong* proper.

533 These are by Kalkin Puṇḍarīka's commentary on the *Kālacakratantra*, called *Vimalaprabhā* (Tib. 'grel chen dri med 'od); Vajragarbha's commentary on the *Hevajratantra*, called *Hevajrapiṇḍārthaṭīkā* (Tib. rdo rje'i snying 'grel); and Vajrapāṇi's commentary on the *Cakrasaṃvaratantra*, called *Lakṣābhidānāduddhṛtalaghutantrapiṇḍārthavivaraṇa* (Tib. phyag rdor stod 'grel).

534 'Ju mi pham rgya mtsho c. 1990, pp. 361–64. As mentioned above, despite treating the topic of *shentong* in several of his texts, Mipham Rinpoche declared himself repeatedly to be a *rangtongpa*/Prāsaṅgika. The issue of his affiliation with one or the other side—or simply lack thereof—is highly complex and hotly disputed among both Tibetan and Western scholars. However, in his case more than in anybody else's, only a careful and exhaustive study of his works and the way in which he uses the terms *rangtong* and *shentong* can shed light on this. For, as Duckworth 2005 (p. 140) points out, according to the definitions of these terms by Dzamtang Khenpo Lodrö Tragba, Mipham Rinpoche is neither a *rangtongpa* nor a *shentongpa*, while

according to the definitions by Lochen Dharmaśrī, he can be said to be both. For further details on Mipham Rinpoche's position, see Pettit 1999, Duckworth 2005, and the English translations of his commentaries on the *Madhyamakāvatāra* and *Madhyamakālaṃkāra*.

535 Tib. zab don khyad par nyer gcig pa (for a translation, see Mathes 2004). Not that Gelugpa scholars are the final authority on this, but it should be noted that, while they all agree on Dölpopa's view being completely off the mark, there are some who say that Śākya Chogden's approach of "other-emptiness" cannot be refuted.

536 Tāranātha n. d., vol. 17: *Shes rab kyi pha rol tu phyin pa'i snying po'i don rnam par bshad pa sngon med legs bshad* (pp. 571–759) and *Sher snying gi tshig 'brel* (pp. 759–83).

537 It is interesting to note here that even someone like J. Hopkins, who so closely followed the Gelugpa tradition almost exclusively for nearly four decades, lately seems to have developed great fascination with Dölpopa's view, speaking very favorably about it, showing that its usual Gelugpa critique often misses the point, and even translating Dölpopa's *Mountain Dharma* (Hopkins 2006).

538 That some of the reasons to engage in such disputes were not only philosophical in nature or about "finding the truth" is another story. Apart from the mere doctrinal differences between the increasingly predominant Gelugpa tradition on the one side and the other Tibetan schools on the other, also as a result of hegemonic conflicts, the *rangtong-shentong* controversy sometimes came to be a strange mix of philosophical and political issues, including vying for significant sponsors for one's own monastic seat. In this situation, the *shentong* view often served as a kind of common "corporate identity" for those who were opposed—both doctrinally and politically—to the Gelugpa hegemony. It would certainly go too far to say that the nineteenth-century nonsectarian Rimé movement in eastern Tibet, which included many Sakya, Nyingma, and Kagyü masters, was a political movement or even "*shentong*-only," but the sense of a common doctrinal ground was definitely one of its underlying forces.

539 Mi bskyod rdo rje 2003, vol. 1, pp. 313–14.

540 Ruegg 2000, pp. 80–81.

541 It should be noted that the very early Tibetan doxographies are more faithful to the Indian tradition, while they tend to become more and more removed, schematized, and ramified the later they are.

542 Even Jamgön Kongtrul Lodrö Tayé's *Treasury of Knowledge* says that the conventional terms "real aspect" and "false aspect," which are based on the system of the Mere Mentalists, are just applied by Tibetans as they please. All that is found in the original texts are the two types of passages that establish the consciousness that appears as an outer referent as being a real or a false aspect of consciousness (TOK, vol. 2, p. 545; Elizabeth Callahan informed me that a similar statement is found in Śākya Chogden's *Nges don gcig tu grub pa*, p. 538.2–4). In Indian philosophy in general, the distinction between "Aspectarians" (*sākāravādin*) and "Non-Aspectarians" (*nirākāravādin*) is very common. Somewhat simplified, the former assert that mind apprehends an object via or as a mental "aspect" or image that appears to consciousness, thus being mind's actual cognitive content. Non-Aspectarians deny such an aspect (or at least its real existence). The Tibetan tradition often refers to the former as "Real Aspectarians" (*rnam bden pa*) and the latter as "False Aspectarians" (*rnam brdzun pa*). Among Buddhist schools, the Sautrāntikas and certain Yogācāras are usually said to be Aspectarians, while the Vaibhāṣikas and certain other Yogācāras are held to be Non-Aspectarians (or False Aspectarians). With regard to the Yogācāras, however, the situation is rather complex and there are vari-

ous (later) interpretations as to what exactly the terms Aspectarian and Non-Aspectarian refer to. Often, Yogācāras such as Dignāga and Dharmapāla are classified as the former and Asaṅga, Vasubandhu, Sthiramati, Kambala, and so on as the latter (for further details on the distinction, see Lindtner 1997, pp. 175–82, 198–99). However, there is no mention of either such names or the corresponding positions in their own writings, and it is highly questionable whether the standard descriptions of these terms adequately represent their view (for example, Asaṅga, Vasubandhu, and others say that, in being the imaginary nature, both the apprehended and apprehending aspects are equally unreal, while not asserting any ultimately real or independent kind of consciousness). Also, it seems that, in their treatment of all beings except Buddhas, all Yogācāras must be considered Aspectarians, just differing as to whether they take these aspects to be conventionally real as a part of consciousness (that is, as part of the other-dependent nature) or not even conventionally real (in being just the imaginary nature). Later Indian Mādhyamikas, such as Jñānagarbha, Śāntarakṣita, Kamalaśīla, and Haribhadra, refer to the notion of a really existent consciousness or self-awareness in both the Aspectarian and Non-Aspectarian versions and unanimously refute them (without, however, mentioning specific persons). It is mainly in a number of late Indian works dating from the eleventh and twelfth centuries—usually written as or containing doxographies from a Madhyamaka point of view—that the explicit distinction between Aspectarians and Non-Aspectarians with regard to the Yogācāras is found (though by no means always described in the same way). These texts include Jitāri's *Sugatamatavibhāgabhāṣya* (D3900, fols. 46a.8ff.), Bodhibhadra's *Jñānasārasamucchaya-nibandhana* (P5252; ACIP TD3852@43B), Maitrīpa's *Tattvaratnavālī* (P3085, fols. 128a.1–129a.3), Sahajavajra's *Sthitisamucchaya* (P3071, fols. 100b.3–101b.5) and *Tattvadaśakaṭīkā* (P3099, fol. 179b.3–4), Ratnākaraśānti's *Prajñāpāramitopadeśa* (P5579, fol. 168a.4f), and Mokṣākaragupta's *Tarkabhāṣā* (P5762; ed. R. Iyengar 1952, pp. 69.11–19: despite not explicitly mentioning the names Aspectarian and Non-Aspectarian, the text distinguishes them in almost literally the same way as Jitāri's *Sugatamatavibhāgabhāṣya* and also includes parts of Jñānaśrīmitra's *Sākarasiddhi*, followed by a Madhyamaka refutation). Both the *Tattvadaśakaṭīkā* (P3099, fols. 180a.5–181b.1) and the *Prajñāpāramitopadeśa* (P5579, fol. 168a.4f) apply this distinction not only to the Yogācāras but even to the Mādhyamikas. The *Nirākārakārikā* (P5294)—a Madhyamaka text by the Nepalese paṇḍita Nandaśrī—is devoted solely to a refutation of consciousness without aspects. However, when looking at the ways in which the distinction between Aspectarians and Non-Aspectarians is described in some of these texts, one wonders what fundamental difference is at stake here, since they rather seem to represent just two slightly different ways of describing the same fact—pure self-aware consciousness being ultimately free from all stains of the imaginary aspects of both apprehender and apprehended. For example, the above-mentioned passage in both the *Sugatamatavibhāgabhāṣya* and the *Tarkabhāṣā* says, "Here, some say that everything that is commonly known as the natures of the body and objects is this very consciousness. Since this [consciousness] is self-awareness, it is in no way apprehender and apprehended. Rather, the natures of apprehender and apprehended are superimposed through imagination. Therefore, the consciousness free from the natures of imaginary apprehender and apprehended is real. Others say that, ultimately, consciousness is unaffected by all the stains of imagination, resembling a pure crystal. These [imaginary] aspects are nothing but mistaken, appearing [only] due to being displayed through ignorance. Thus, a so-called 'apprehended' is entirely nonexistent. Since this does not exist, an apprehender does not exist either." In any case, apart from all such doxographical references in Madhyamaka texts, there is only one explicit and rather late (eleventh century) Indian dispute about various issues within the distinction between Aspectarians and Non-Aspectarians that is actually recorded. Here, the Non-Aspectarian stance is advocated by Ratnākaraśānti in his *Madhyamakālaṃkāropadeśa*

(P5586), *Triyānavyavasthāna* (P4535), and *Prajñāpāramitopadeśa* (to wit, just as Asaṅga and others, he considers both the apprehended and apprehending aspects as false, while saying that it is solely mind's underlying sheer lucidity—*prakāśamātra*—free from these two that is real; P5579, fol. 161a.5–161b.4). The Aspectarian position is mainly represented by Jñānaśrīmitra's *Sākarasiddhi* and *Sākarasaṃgraha* (ed. A. Thakur, mainly pp. 368.6–10 and 387.8–23) and also by Ratnakīrti's *Ratnakīrtinibandhāvalī* (ed. A. Thakur, 1976, esp. p. 129.1–12; none of the texts in these two editions are contained in the *Tengyur*), both quoting and rejecting Ratnākaraśānti's Non-Aspectarian approach in the *Prajñāpāramitopadeśa*. However, it is hard to regard this as a dispute purely within the Yogācāra School itself, since at least Ratnākaraśānti consistently exhibits a clear synthesis of Yogācāra and Madhyamaka, being more often than not considered as a Mādhyamika. Also, it should be noted that the issues at stake in all these texts are rather complex and not just a matter of whether consciousness has aspects or not (which might be real or illusory). Thus, much more research needs to be done to correctly understand such debates within their respective contexts and perspectives. For example, as the title of Ratnakīrti's *Citrādvaitaprakāśavāda* (Thakur, pp. 129–44) suggests, it elaborates on mind's lucidity (*prakāśa*) manifesting or appearing in both a nondual (*advaita*) and a manifold way (*citra*). It says that whatever appears within a nonconceptual consciousness (*nirvikalpajñāna*) is nondual or one, but at the same time is a complex and ever-shifting collection of diverse aspects (*vicitrākārakadambakam*), such as the color white, the sound "ga," a sweet taste, a fragrant smell, a soft tangible object, and a feeling of happiness or its opposite. In other words, both awareness and what appears in it—which are essentially not separable in terms of a nonconceptual experience—are nondual and manifold (p. 129.19–21). As this shows, the meaning of Ratnakīrti's term *citrādvaita*—despite it literally corresponding to the Tibetan *sna tshogs gnyis med pa* (nondual variety)—obviously does not really match what Tibetan doxographers understand by it as characterizing one of the "subschools" of "Real Aspectarian Mere Mentalists" (Tib. sems tsam rnam bden pa), that is, perceiving consciousness being one, while the aspects of its perceived object are many. Another example is Śāntarakṣita's autocommentary on his *Madhyamakālaṃkāra* (verses 22–60), which extensively refutes both the Aspectarian and the Non-Aspectarian stances. This includes the three possible epistemological relationships among Aspectarians (a single coarse object being perceived by a single consciousness, all the many distinct aspects of that coarse object being perceived by a single consciousness, and these many objective aspects being perceived by a corresponding number of aspects of consciousness). Throughout, however, Śāntarakṣita never refers to his refutations as applying only to Yogācāras (in fact Kamalaśīla's *Madhyamakālaṃkārapañjikā* relates a great number of the above verses to various other Buddhist and non-Buddhist schools), let alone taking said three relationships between subject and object as Yogācāra "subschools" with distinct names. In any case, the much later Tibetan labels "Real/False Aspectarian Mere Mentalists"—with all their respective subclassifications—refer to the objective aspect that appears to consciousness as being really existent as mind or just being an illusory and mistaken appearance, respectively. However, there are numerous discrepancies in various Tibetan doxographies as to which Indian masters belong to these categories and their supposed subschools (moreover, the adduced scriptural sources—especially for the latter—are usually rather flimsy).

543 To be sure, all of the above are commonplace in Western and Japanese academia, of course with the exception of those—mostly American—scholars who just copy and repeat the default positions of Tibetan (in particular Gelugpa) doxographies with their own agendas like mantras. This fact can hardly be overemphasized, especially since there are still reputed scholars who—despite ample historical and scriptural evidence to the contrary—rely on ramified artificial distinctions of subschools of Madhyamaka and "Mind-Only" (understood as the "idealist"

school that asserts mind or the other-dependent nature to be ultimately really existent), even claim that such a "school" was founded by Asaṅga, and use unattested fantasy terms such as "Cittamātrin" for the followers of such a "school" as if all such imputations were hard and fast facts accepted by everyone (for more details, see Brunnhölzl 2004, pp. 333–73 and 457–501).

544 *Madhyamakālaṃkārapañjikā* (ACIP TD3886@88A).

545 To be sure, there are some (late) Indian precursors who divide all Buddhist views into these four schools, but this is by no means the only classification (and arguably not even the main one) found in Indian texts.

546 Verse 7.

547 2000, p. 122.

548 In Dreyfus and McClintock 2003, p. 71.

549 Apart from Rangjung Dorje not even using the terms *rangtong* and *shentong*, while they are *the* cornerstones of Dölpopa's discussions, there are many other differences between the views of these two masters. For details, see Schaeffer 1995 (esp. pp. 25–36), Stearns 1995 and 1999, Hopkins 2002 (pp. 273–315) and 2006, Mathes 1998 and 2004, Burchardi 2007, and my forthcoming more extensive study of the Third Karmapa's view (titled *Luminous Heart*).

550 As is explained below in DSC, "the very profound dharmakāya" refers to the two rūpakāyas.

551 Rang byung rdo rje 2006b, pp. 509.2–510.3.

552 Ibid., p. 501.5.

553 Ibid., p. 611.3.

554 Ibid., p. 497.2–3.

555 Ibid., p. 514.4–6.

556 Rang byung rdo rje n.d., fol. 116b.

557 This is amply documented in works such as his *Distinction between the Two Traditions of the Great Charioteers* and *The Origin of Madhyamaka*. Similar statements are found in TOK and, for Prāsaṅgika-Madhyamaka and the Madhyamaka taught in the third turning of the wheel of dharma, respectively, in Lo chen Dharmaśrī n.d., pp. 377–78.

558 This refers to the tantras.

559 As quoted in TOK vol. 2, p. 553. For more details on the *shentong* issue, see Brunnhölzl 2004, pp. 445–526.

560 The same expression is found in the title of Sönam Sangbo's commentary too.

561 It would be especially interesting to gain access to the latter commentary to see how someone during the very formation of the Gelugpa School explains the *Dharmadhātustava* and whether this might differ from the other commentaries and/or the fully established stance of the later Gelugpa tradition.

562 For details, see Stearns 1999.

563 Tib. rong ston shākya rgyal mtshan.

564 Tib. 'phan po na len dra.

565 Tib. mthong ba don ldan.

566 Tib. mtshal chen dgon pa.

567 Tib. ri khrod pa. It is not clear who this paṇḍita was. There is mention of a Śavari dbang phyug in the biography of Paṇḍita Vanaratna as one of the teachers of the latter, but to my knowledge there are no records of a Śavari ever having come to Tibet or Sönam Sangbo having traveled to India (there is also no mention of any Śavari in the extensive list of Indian paṇḍitas who visited Tibet in Dpa' bo gtsug lag phreng ba 2003, p. 510ff.). Vanaratna himself only came to Tibet in 1426, that is, eight years after Sönam Sangbo wrote his commentary. Incidentally, in 1418, another Indian paṇḍita—Śāriputra from Bodhgayā —is reported to have visited Tibet.

568 Bsod nams bzang po n.d., p. 631.

569 Tib. rdzong sar.

570 Tib. khams bye bshad grva.

571 Tib. 'jam dbyangs mkhyen brtse chos kyi blo gros.

572 Tib. sangs rgyas gling pa.

573 Tib. dpang lo tsā ba blo gros brtan pa.

574 Tib. 'khon.

575 Tib. sa skya rin chen sgang bla brang.

576 Tib. rgyal tshab dar ma rin chen.

577 Tib. 'jam dbyangs don yod dpal ldan.

578 Mr. Kazuo Kano reported that this commentary also is listed in Dpal brtsegs bod yig dpe rnying zhib 'jug khang 2005 (unfortunately, he did not record the entry no.), so it might be published in the not so distant future.

579 Tib. rgyal tshab dam pa kun dga' dbang phyug.

580 Tib. e vaṃ chos ldan.

581 Tib. r(v)a yon tan dpal.

582 Tib. yon tan chos rgyal.

583 Tib. tshul khrims rgyal mtshan.

584 Tib. 'jam dbyangs kun dga' bsod nams.

585 Tib. dkon mchog lhun grub.

586 The other commentary is by Śākya Chogden.

587 The translation of this commentary is based on a careful edition (published in a separate volume) of the single extant *dbu med* manuscript, comparing it with the various available typeset or digitized versions, which are all based on that manuscript (see Bibliography). However, the quotes in the text often vary considerably from what is found in the Tibetan canon (in some cases, they are completely corrupted). Thus, if not otherwise indicated, in translating them, I follow DP, only indicating significant variants in DSC (for all these variants, see the Tibetan editions in the bibliography, which usually just reproduce whatever is said in the manuscript).

588 Numbers in [ ] refer to the folio numbers of the manuscript.

589 The last two sentences correspond to the *Mahāmeghasūtra* (except for the reference to Sukhāvatī, which is only found in the other three sūtra sources mentioned in the introduction).

590 In all available editions of DSC, fol. 2 is missing in its entirety. Thus, everything that follows in [ ] up through the first verse of the *Dharmadhātustava* is inserted here, with the outline and its wording being inferred with the help of Dzogchen Ponlop Rinpoche from the traditional style of Tibetan commentarial outlines and from what follows below in the text.

591 All Tibetan versions of DSC have just *sems*, but the context and the root text clearly suggest *sems can*, which literally means "one who has a mind" or "mind-bearer."

592 As presented above, Rangjung Dorje's ZMND (ch. 1, lines 1–12) explains the whole process of delusion—mind being unaware of its own nature—in a similar way. Jamgön Kongtrul's commentary on this section of ZMND (pp. 27–28) elaborates: What is [mind as such] ignorant of? It is ignorant of mind as such, the Buddha heart, which just resides as the play of the three kāyas. Through what is it ignorant? Through mind as such itself. With regard to mind's own essence, which is not established as anything whatsoever, its [two] facets that [actually] are a union—the unborn fundamental ground and its unceasing radiance—are [mis]conceived as self and other [respectively]. Therefore, [mind] is ignorant [of this essence] through [its own] unimpeded creative display of appearing as if it were [distinct] subjects and objects. In which way is it ignorant? The ālaya is stirred through mind being formed [in a way that it moves] toward objects, which is [done by] the seventh [consciousness] of mentation. This movement, which is like water and waves, gives rise to the afflicted mind, which is always embraced by the set of four afflictions that are associated with it—self-conceit, attachment to the self, the views about a real personality, and ignorance. Thus, saṃsāra appears for false imagination. . . . The repetitive formation through this movement of the afflicted mind and the ālaya stirring each other mutually is false imagination. Since the phenomena of saṃsāra, which do not exist by their nature yet appear as if they were solidly real, are brought about due to that [process], it is the way in which [mind] is ignorant. Therefore, the lucid aspect of mind as such is referred to here by the term "the seventh [consciousness] of mentation," and the aspect of not recognizing its own essence is taught to be ignorance, which identifies innate ignorance. Thus, through the movements of the seventh [consciousness] of mentation, [also] the bright [remedial] actions are formed, which represent correct imagination. What abides as its own unstained essence is "stainless mentation," which is contained in the unfolding disposition and represents the wisdom of equality at the time of the ground, as well as the cause of a Buddha's qualities of freedom {the phrase starting with "as well" is inserted here from below, when this point is discussed again}. . . Therefore, the seventh [consciousness] of mentation that is explained here [in the ZMND] and shapes mind [in such a way that it moves] toward objects is presented as mentation [in general], without differentiating it into the afflicted mind and stainless mentation. When the other six collections [of consciousness] arise and cease, it inputs their potencies into the ālaya . . . Therefore, the autocommentary repeatedly refers to it as the "immediate mind" as its synonym. . . . In brief, out of the ocean of the ālaya, mentation moves like waves on water and shapes [the mind], which brings about saṃsāra. So the ālaya is saṃsāra's basis or cause, while mentation is its condition. For more details on the process of delusion in terms of the eight consciousnesses, especially on the two aspects of mentation—afflicted and immediate mind—see also below.

593 SC (pp. 306–7) glosses "dharma" in "dharmadhātu" as nonabiding nirvāṇa and the "dhātu" of that as its cause, that is, the wisdom that is ever-present throughout all the phases of ground, path, and fruition. If this wisdom is not seen, the cart of the afflictions draws it onto the paths of saṃsāra. However, if the dharmadhātu is explained to be just a nonimplicative negation, its

being identified here as circling in existence and residing in all beings is meaningless, since a nonimplicative negation cannot be drawn into saṃsāra by karma and afflictions and pertains equally to everything that is not a sentient being. On the opposite pole, Döl (p. 138)—of course being far from identifying the dharmadhātu as a nonimplicative negation—glosses it as pervading all of the inanimate world and its inhabitants.

594 Traditionally, every Indo-Tibetan Buddhist treatise has to fulfill four criteria, the first three of which are explicitly stated here. (1) Proper subject matters from a Buddhist point of view are as described in Asaṅga's *Viniścayasaṃgrahaṇī* (fol. 205a.3–7). He speaks about six types of specious and three kinds of proper treatises. The former include meaningless texts (such as on whether crows have teeth), those with wrong meanings (from a Buddhist perspective, such as discussing an eternal soul), treatises on cheating others, heartless ones (such as on warfare or killing animals), and those that mainly focus on study or debate. Proper treatises are meaningful ones (in a Buddhist sense), those that lead to relinquishing suffering, and those that mainly focus on practice. (2) The purpose of the text means that it must serve as a convenient avenue for penetrating the intended meaning of the teachings. (3) The essential purpose is to engage in this meaning with enthusiasm and eventually attain a Buddha's omniscience. (4) The proper connection refers to the one between the purpose and the essential purpose. Also, in terms of the subject matter, the earlier parts of the contents of the text must be properly connected with the following ones.

595 This is a paraphrase that combines parts of Asaṅga's commentary on *Uttaratantra* I.32–33 and I.153–55 (J29, 74, 76; P5526, fols. 92a.6–b.3, 117a.1–3, 118b.4–8). The immediately following passages in DSC on the four obscurations and their four remedies are paraphrases of fol. 92b.1–6.

596 I.32–33ab. As for my translations from the *Uttaratantra* and the *Ratnagotravibhāgavyākhyā*, if the English varies from the Tibetan, I have followed the Sanskrit in J.

597 I.33cd.

598 As mentioned before and just below, "the very profound dharmakāya" refers to the two rūpakāyas.

599 IV.11 (the same four are found in *Uttaratantra* I.34).

600 Tib. pa tshab lo tsā ba (born 1055). As mentioned in the introduction, he was the main person to translate and introduce Candrakīrti's Madhyamaka texts in Tibet.

601 Tib. dbu ma'i snying po bsdus pa. Apart from what is available in a few quotations, this text is not preserved.

602 Due to a scribal error in the manuscript, fol. 5 has been numbered no. 6. The same continues for fols. 6 and 7. After this, the mistake was obviously noticed, with fol. 8 being numbered as "upper 9" (*dgu gong ma*). From fol. 9 onwards, the correct numbering is resumed. I abstained from repeating this confusion here.

603 XXIV.18–19.

604 P774, III.6 (ACIP KD0106@14B).

605 This is an explanatory tantra of the *Guhyasamājatantra* (P84).

606 The same quote is also given—sometimes slightly differing—in ZMND (lines IX.6–9), AC (fols. 117b–118a), TOK (vol. 3, p. 40), and Kong sprul blo gros mtha' yas 1990a (p. 76) and 2005

(p. 227).

607 XXIV.8–9.

608 ACIP TD3829@89A.

609 Lines 19–22 and 26–29 (ed. Mathes 1996). DSC has a paraphrase in prose in a different order, somewhat corresponding to the prose version of the text in the *Tengyur* (P5523; lines 13–14 and 16–17, ed. Mathes): *gnyis dang ji ltar mngon par brjod pa ni yang dag ma yin pa'i kun tu rtog pa ste chos kyi mtshan nyid do/ gsung ba dang/ 'dzin pa dang/ brjod par bya ba dang/ brjod par byed pa khyad par med pa ni de bzhin te chos nyid kyi mtshan nyid do.*

610 III.10d.

611 Lines 3cd.

612 Lines 7bd–8ac. In the Tibetan *Tengyur*, this text is listed under the well-known master Candrakīrti's (sixth/seventh century) works and appears as an appendix to his *Madhyamakāvatārabhāṣya*. However, the text itself says that it was translated into Tibetan by Candrakīrti himself and the translator 'Gos khug pa lha btsas, who lived in the eleventh century. There was indeed an eleventh-century master by the name Candrakīrti (the Tibetan tradition calls him "the lesser Candrakīrti"), who was a disciple of Jetāri (tenth/eleventh century), one of the teachers of Atiśa.

613 The quote is actually *Mūlamadhyamakakārikā* XXV.19a.

614 The Tibetan *yongs su grub pa* usually renders the Sanskrit *pariniṣpanna*—the "perfect [nature]" that stands for the ultimate reality among the three natures presented in the Yogācāra teachings, the other two being the "imaginary nature" and the "other-dependent nature." Just above, the Third Karmapa lists "what abides ultimately, the ultimate in terms of seeing this mode of being, the ultimate in terms of practice, and the ultimate in terms of being free from stains," which he then below equates to the three kinds of the ultimate—in terms of object, practice, and attainment—as presented in Maitreya's *Madhyāntavibhāga*. Moreover, he uses the terminology of the three natures throughout DSC in an extensive way. Given this, the most natural reading here is to understand *yongs su grub pa* as referring to the perfect nature in the sense of the actual ultimate. However, literally, that Tibetan term means "perfectly established" and thus could also be understood as being established by reasoning. Taking into account the above considerations and that Rangjung Dorje here quotes from a Madhyamaka text, the obvious pun may very well be intended. In other words, the ultimate may be seen as being perfectly established in the sense of being the perfect nature and/or as being perfectly established by reasoning.

615 *Yuktiṣaṣṭikā*, verse 45.

616 Ibid., verse 54.

617 Lines 63ab. The first line in DSC varies (*nga la bsgrub bya med pas na*), saying, "Since I have nothing to prove, . . ."

618 Verse 71.

619 DSC *don dam*, which is strange. Also, just below, DSC clearly says that these two are instances of seeming reality.

620 III.11–12. In Vasubandhu's commentary on the *Madhyāntavibhāga* (Sanskrit ed. Nagao 1964, p. 41, lines 18–21. ACIP TD4027@012A–B), the "ultimate" (lit. "supreme object or goal"; Skt. *paramārtha*) is shown to have three different meanings that depend on the three possible

ways of analyzing this compound in Sanskrit. (1) Tatpuruṣa: "The ultimate in terms of the object is suchness in the sense of being the object of supreme wisdom." (2) Karmadhāraya: "The ultimate in terms of attainment is nirvāna in the sense of being the supreme object." (3) Bahuvrīhi: "The ultimate in terms of practice is the path in the sense that the supreme is its object." Here, the path is primarily understood as nonconceptual wisdom. This corresponds exactly to Bhāvaviveka's presentation of the meaning of *paramārtha* found in his *Tarkajvālā* (ACIP TD3856@59B).

621 Usually, the unchanging perfect nature is said to be the nature of phenomena and the unmistaken perfect nature the nondual nonconceptual wisdom that realizes it.

622 Verse 12 (DSC line 2: *nus pa'i phyir dang don byed dag*).

623 Verse 32 (DSC *las kyi 'bras bu yod pa dang/ 'gro ba dag kyang shin tu brjod/ de'i rang bzhin yongs shes dang/ rnam par dben pa dag kyang bstan*).

624 For the discussion of the two realities in Rangjung Dorje's AC (fols. 116b–124a), see the above introductory section on his view.

625 XVIII.39.

626 This is Chapter XVI of that text.

627 These are the ten powers, the four fearlessnesses, and the eighteen unshared qualities of a Buddha (for details, see below).

628 This refers to the thirty-two major marks of a Buddha (for details, see below).

629 *Ratnāvalī*, III.12–13ab.

630 In the latter, this is found mainly in Chapter XI on the fruition.

631 I.9–10.

632 Verse 38.

633 Verse 28.

634 Verse 29 (DSC omits line 1).

635 I.4 and I.6.

636 Skt. dravya, Tib. rdzas.

637 Verses 40–41 (line 4 in DP has *de rdzogs pas* instead of *de rtogs pas*, but Skt. *tadbodhād* confirms the latter).

638 DSC *'khor ba'i gnas lugs 'khor ba*. This could also be read as "The basic nature of saṃsāra, saṃsāra, . . ."

639 This is Nāgārjuna's autocommentary on his *Pratītyasamutpādahṛdayakārikā*.

640 P761. This passage is also quoted in Asaṅga's *Ratnagotravibhāgavyākhyā* (J 22; P5526, fol. 88a.2–4).

641 I.85–86.

642 This sūtra is only preserved in Chinese translation (Taishō 668).

643 The nonconceptual and the illusionlike samādhis refer to the mind of a bodhisattva in meditative equipoise and subsequent attainment, respectively. The latter term is usually trans-

lated as "postmeditation," which at best seems to be too neutral a word and has the connotation of just taking a break. Rather, "subsequent attainment" refers to the level of realization of emptiness that is attained as a result of having rested in meditative equipoise. Subsequent to rising from such equipoise, the realization of emptiness that has been gained while resting in it informs and enhances the seeing of the illusionlike nature of all appearances and experiences while actively engaging in the six pāramitās during the time between the formal sessions of meditative equipoise. This is the reason why "illusionlike samādhi" is often used as a synonym for this phase. For more details on the bhūmis and their qualities, see verse 75ff.

644 XIV.45–46.

645 Mikyö Dorje 1990 (p.33) agrees on the first two pāramitās and explains the latter two as follows. The meaning of bliss is to be free from all aspects of movements of body and mind [that occur] for as long as one is an ordinary being all the way through the end of the mind stream [of a bodhisattva] on the tenth bhūmi. The meaning of permanence is to neither cling to the impermanent and deceiving world nor to solely conceive of permanent nirvāṇa.

646 P760.48 (for parts of the above paragraph, see Wayman, trans. 1974, pp. 101–2 and 97). "The eight realities of the noble ones" refer to two ways—produced (*kṛta*) and unproduced (*akṛta*)—of explaining the usual four realities of the noble ones. Unlike śrāvakas and pratyekabuddhas, the Tathāgatas also accomplish the unproduced set of these four realities, which is based on buddha nature and culminates in the full revelation of all its qualities (ibid., pp. 96–98).

647 I.35ab.

648 I.51cd.

649 P810 (DSC *rnam par mi rtog pa la 'jug pa'i mdo*), fol. 4a.4–5a.1. The *Avikalpapraveśadhāraṇī* itself uses the example of a wish-fulfilling jewel instead of a beryl, and the first and fourth of the four characteristics are called "nature" (Skt. prakṛti; indicating the five skandhas as what is to be relinquished) and "attainment" (Skt. prāpti), respectively. For more details, see below.

650 P761.31.

651 P814, fol. 176ff. The actual name of that sūtra is *Tathāgatamahākaruṇānirdeśasūtra*, but it is usually better known as the *Dhāraṇīśvararājaparipṛcchasūtra*. In that text, the coarsest stains of the beryl are removed with a woven cloth and by soaking it in an alkaline solution. The next layer is cleansed through soaking it in an acid solution and wiping it with a woolen towel. Finally, the most subtle stains are removed through soaking it in pure water (or a herbal solution) and polishing it with the finest cotton. In due order, these steps correspond to the Buddha first teaching the vinayadharma to make beings who are fond of saṃsāra renounce it; secondly teaching on emptiness, signlessness, and wishlessness; and finally teaching the irreversible wheel of dharma free from the three spheres (agent, recipient, and action) in order to make beings engage the actual object of the Buddhas. This passage is also quoted in Asaṅga's *Ratnagotravibhāgavyākhyā* on I.2 (J 6) and Nāgārjuna's *Sūtrasamucchaya* (ACIP TD3934@189B–190A).

652 This quote is also found in *Ratnagotravibhāgavyākhyā* on I.2 (J 6; P5526, fol. 77b.5–6).

653 I could not locate the quote as it stands, but the sūtra abounds with statements of the same meaning.

654 I.22.

655 DSC *dang po* DNP *mngar po*.

656 Verse 37.

657 DSC *ma rig bag chags kyis*; em: *ma rig bag chags kyi sa (las)*.

658 According to what was said before, one would rather expect "being confined in ore" here.

659 DSC omits the fifth obscuration.

660 Details on this can, for example, be found in the *Uttaratantra's* first chapter.

661 Skt. *svabhāvavibhāgaḥ pratītyasamutpādaḥ, Tib. ngo bo nyid rnam par 'byed pa can gyi rten 'brel (I.19).

662 Skt. *prīyāprīyavibhāgaḥ pratītyasamutpādaḥ, Tib. sdug pa dang mi sdug pa rnam par 'byed pa can gyi rten 'brel. The *Mahāyānasaṃgraha* (I.28) mentions a third kind of dependent origination, "the dependent origination of experience" (Skt. *upabhogaḥ pratītyasamutpādaḥ, Tib. nyer spyod can gyi rten 'brel) without elaborating on it. According to TOK (vol. 2, pp. 427–28), this describes the way in which the six consciousnesses (the primary minds) arise and cease based on the four conditions. Here, the experiencer is the mental factor of feeling, and what is experienced is the mental factor of contact between object and consciousness. Feeling further produces the mental factor of impulse in the following way. In the case of a pleasant object, a pleasant feeling arises, which in turn leads to desire and the impulse of not wishing for the mind to become separated from that object. In the case of unpleasant or neutral objects, respectively, aversion and the wish to be separated from such objects or indifference and no such wish arise. Together, the three mental factors of feeling, contact, and impulse are said to blemish the primary minds.

663 Skt. vipākavijñāna, Tib. rnam par smin pa'i rnam par shes pa. This is another term for the ālaya-consciousness.

664 In DSC, the passage from here up to the end of this paragraph is erased. It is inserted from *Mahāyānasaṃgraha* I.48.

665 The above is an abridged paraphrase of I.45–48 (P5549, fols. 11b.1–12a.4).

666 J 72 (P5526, fol. 116a.4–5).

667 II.27–28. In DSC, line 2 of the second verse says *sbyor bstan pa'i dbang don la*, and DP also have *bstan pa'i*. However, the Sanskrit reads *dhīrānām*, suggesting *brtan pa'i,* which is confirmed by Jamgön Kongtrul's commentary on the *Uttaratantra*.

668 *Pratītyasamutpādahṛdayakārikā*, verse 7. Some scholars hold that verses 6–7 are not part of the original stanzas but were added later. In any case, both verses are found in Nāgārjuna's text as it appears in the Tibetan canon and in an eighth-century Tibetan manuscript from Tun-huang (PT 769), with verse 6 being identical to *Yuktiṣaṣṭikā* 12. In general, the above verse is among the most famous and often-cited ones in the literature of the mahāyāna. Gampopa's *Ornament of Precious Liberation* (Sgam po pa 1990, p. 289) says that it originally stems from the *Gaganagañjaparipṛcchāsūtra* (P815). Except for the third line, it is also found in the *Śrīmahābalatantra* (P36, fol. 34a.6–7). It features as one of the most essential verses in both Maitreya's *Uttaratantra* (I.154) and *Abhisamayālaṃkāra* (V.21). To my knowledge, there are at least nine more works in which it appears: Buddhaghoṣa's *Sumaṅgalavisāraṇī* I.12 (in Pāli; attributes the contents to the Buddha); Nāgārjuna's *Kāyatrayastotranāmasyavivaraṇa* (P2016, fol. 83a.7); Aśvaghoṣa's *Saundarananda* (paraphrase XIII.44) and *Śuklavidarśana* (a summary of the *Śālistambasūtra* that begins with this verse); Nāgamitra's *Kāyatrayāvatāramukha*

(paraphrase verse 106); the *Bodhisattvabhūmi* (Wogihara ed., p. 48; prose); Sthiramati's *Madhyāntavibhāgaṭīkā* (P5534, fol. 36a.5); the *Nāmasaṃgītiṭīkā* ad VI.5 (which attributes it to Nāgārjuna); and the *Mahāyānaśraddhotpāda* (Suzuki'sūtrans., p. 57; prose).

669 The Tibetan literally says "washed," so this may refer to cleansing cotton (LG silk) with hot steam.

670 Skt. khaṭikā, Tib. rdo rgyus. Monier Williams has "chalk" and *Bod rgya tshig mdzod chen mo* says "a mineral that, when beaten, becomes like vulture downs." All this matches the features of asbestos, which is a white, fibrous mineral that is fire-resistant and can easily be spun into yarn (see also *Webster's International Dictionary*, p. 126). RT (p. 633) also has *rdo rgyus*, Döl (p. 142) has *rdo dreg* (pitch).

671 DSC *'dod chags las skyes dri ma can* DNP *'dod chags la sogs dri ma can.*

672 As mentioned before, "correct imagination" refers to increasingly more refined—but still more or less dualistic—mental processes or creations that serve as the remedies for respectively coarser kinds of obscuring mental creations and misconceptions (false imagination). Initially, on the paths of accumulation and preparation, such remedial activities are conceptual in a very obvious way, such as meditating on the repulsiveness of the body as an antidote against desire. More subtle approaches would include meditating on momentary impermanence or on personal and phenomenal identitylessness. From the path of seeing onward, all coarse conceptions of ordinary sentient beings (even the remedial ones) have ceased. However, as mentioned above, during the first seven bhūmis, there are still subtle concepts about suchness, and on the last three bhūmis, about attaining the final fruition of buddhahood. In other words, to realize that the dharmadhātu is naturally unarisen, unceasing, empty, peaceful, and luminous is the remedial fire of wisdom that consumes any ideas to the contrary. However, since that fire of wisdom still depends on what it relinquishes (and still has some reference points with regard to the dharmadhātu), it must eventually and naturally subside too, once even its most subtle fuel (the apprehending of said characteristics on the bhūmis) is burnt up. At this point, buddhahood—complete freedom from all reference points—is revealed, unblurred by anything to be relinquished or a remedy. (In the example of washing a stained garment, remedial wisdom would correspond to the detergent used to wash away the dirt. Obviously, after the detergent performed its function, both it and the dirt would be removed from the garment in order for it to be clean.)

673 LG (pp. 20–22): You may wonder, "Since what is to be relinquished and the remedies are equally nonexistent, why is it not the case that there is no basic nature at all [either]?" It is [like] demonstrating that both being born and dying in a dream are delusive, which does not [serve to show] that the appearances of the waking state are delusive. Just as in this example, all affirmations and negations from the perspective of mistaken minds have never been objects to be negated that are established by a nature of their own in the first place. It is for this reason that they are demonstrated to be delusive, but how could that be a teaching on the nonexistence of the inconceivable wisdom, in which mistaken appearances have become exhausted through the fundamental change of state? Otherwise, . . . all the explanations in the sūtras and tantras of the definitive meaning including the commentaries on their intention would be just as meaningless as explanations about the horns of a rabbit, since both the basic element and the stains would be alike in being adventitious. . . . They are [also] not [just some expedient means to] temporarily produce certain reference points . . . in those to be guided. If the basic nature did not exist at all, since it needs to be pointed out in the end, at that point, [nothing but] disappointment would be created. Therefore, to conceive [of it that way] is just a joke. Therefore, the point to demonstrate

that both what is to be relinquished and the remedies do not exist is that the modes of apprehending existence and nonexistence, which are contrived by [dualistic] mind, are empty. But this is not a demonstration that the dharmakāya beyond [such a] mind is nonexistent. "Well, then it exists as something that is really established." Forget about it being really established, it is not even asserted to exist as something that lacks real [existence]. No matter whether it is accepted to be existent, nonexistent, real, delusive, or anything else, that can be invalidated through reasoning. Since all of these are mutually dependent, none whatsoever can be asserted. [Saraha's] *Dohā[kośopadeśagīti* ("Queen's Dohā"), lines 21–22] says:

> Whoever clings to entities is like cattle,
> But who clings to the lack of entities is even more stupid.

. . . If the basic element too did not exist, there would be no final fruition [of the path], just as the [nihilistic] Lokāyatas assert. Consequently, having practiced the path would be pointless, and since there is no fruition of buddhahood, one's mind stream would afterwards simply become extinct. Such and many other flaws would accrue. Therefore, what is taught here is that this is not like a sprout arising after its seed has ceased, but that [what happens] during the phase of the path is merely the extinguishing of the stains, while the basic element is without increase or decrease. SS (pp. 626–31) explains that, in the prajñāpāramitā sūtras, there are two manners of being empty. The first is that form is empty of form, which is said to pertain to all phenomena up through omniscience. The second is (mainly, but not exclusively) found in the Maitreya chapter of the *Pañcaviṃśatisāhasrikaprajñāpāramitāsūtra*, which uses the terms "imaginary form" (Skt. parikalpitarūpa, Tib. kun tu brtags pa'i gzugs), "conceived form" (Skt. vikalpitarūpa, Tib. rnam par brtags pa'i gzugs), and "form in terms of the nature of phenomena" (Skt. dharmatārūpa, Tib. chos nyid kyi gzugs). In due order, these terms correspond to the imaginary nature, the other-dependent nature, and the perfect nature. From among these, the first two are empty of a nature of their own, while the nature of phenomena—the perfect nature—is empty of the imaginary and the other-dependent natures, that is, adventitious stains. In this context, SS says, to state that what does actually exist is existent and what does not exist is nonexistent is not equivalent to the extreme views of permanence or extinction. Rather, to hold what does actually exist to be nonexistent and what does not exist to be existent is what characterizes such views. Through quotes from various sources, SS affirms the ultimate existence of buddha nature's inseparable qualities, summarizing: "Since the Tathāgata heart is empty of the adventitious stains, it is other-empty (*gzhan stong*), but it is never at any time empty of its unconditioned qualities, such as the powers." GL (pp. 47–50) comments on verses 18–22 as follows. No matter how the dharmadhātu is labeled as emptiness through teaching the lack of any nature in the collection of reasoning, the luminosity that is inextinguishable despite its being associated since beginningless time with the afflictions cannot be negated through all the many sūtras and reasonings that teach it as emptiness. Therefore, the view here is as follows. Without considering the actual way of being of phenomena, if one takes just the way they appear as what is valid, they indeed exist in the form of saṃsāra and nirvāṇa, matter and consciousness, the world and its inhabitants, and so on. However, if one takes their actual way of being as what is valid, this is the prajñā that knows that there is absolutely nothing other than mind, and that this mind itself is "ordinary mind" (*tha mal gyi shes pa*), which is not established as a phenomenon that has any characteristics. What abides as the emptiness [arrived at through] reasoned analysis and as luminosity, and what cannot be destroyed by anything is the Tathāgata heart. The reasonings that establish the lack of any essence whatsoever and the fact of mind abiding in the manner of luminosity indeed appear in many teachings of the Buddha, but especially in the detailed explanations in the *Ghandavyūhasūtra* and the *Laṅkāvatārasūtra*. The teachings on being empty of any nature as found in the Madhyamaka treatises no doubt apply here in just the same way too. However, [consider that] a cloud that appears like a mountain [from afar] does not exist that way, once you have arrived at it. The flickering of a mirage is not observable, once you have reached it. There is no person in a cairn, once you have come close to it. In just the same way, if minds and mental factors that consist of afflictions and conceptions are thoroughly examined through direct perception, even without relying on reasoning, they are nothing whatsoever. Therefore, even the features of a correct and false seeming reality are difficult to distinguish. Still, if one takes the world as what is valid, they can be distinguished. These points were also taught by the gurus of old . . . [There follow extensive quotations from three early Kagyü masters.] Mind's not being established as either affirmation or negation is not a nonimplicative negation but mind as such that is not established as any characteristic whatsoever. . . . The clinging to a personal identity is explained in the great treatises to be clinging to the mind. But since one clings to nothing but this very mind that appears in various ways as being a self, and since this variety is nothing other than [mind's] very lack of characteristics, any basis or root of a self is cut through. As for the clinging to a phenomenal identity, if it is any clinging to the existence of mind's nature, it is said that "luminous mind is without basis or root." . . . Since mind that has no characteristics and appearances that are unceasing arise together, this is called "connate."

674 Verse 5.

675 Verse 4.

676 XIII.18–19ab.

677 These three characteristics of the Buddha's teachings are described in detail in *Uttaratantra* I.10–12.

678 SC (p. 312) says that the prajñā that realizes that the skandhas are impermanent, suffering, and empty (which includes being identityless) purifies the afflictive obscurations, since it overcomes their root, the clinging to a personal identity. The remedy for the cognitive obscurations is the prajñā that realizes that all phenomena lack a nature, since it overcomes the clinging to phenomenal identity. RT (p. 634) and SS (p. 634) basically agree with this.

679 This is, for example, found in the *Pañcaviṃśatisāhasrikaprajñāpāramitāsūtra* (ACIP KL0009-2@289A), the *Daśabhūmikasūtra* (ACIP TD3915@26B; Rahder ed., p. 65), and the *Tathāgatagarbhasūtra*.

680 The above is a summary of D258, fol. 253b.1–5. This is the eighth of the well-known nine examples in this sūtra for how buddha nature is present in all beings. These examples are also found in the *Uttaratantra*, the example above being described in I.121–23.

681 "The four names" is a common term for the four mental skandhas (except form) mentioned just before.

682 Tib. kun byung.

683 As mentioned above, the Tibetan of this verse being somewhat ambiguous, various commentators offer different interpretations. As for the way of glossing "reasons" in the second line, it seems that both meanings of Skt. *nimitta* are retained, since the "reasons" for certain names are the "characteristics" or definitions of what these names refer to. Obviously, DSC speaks not only about one but two sets of four conceptions. Though not as explicit as in SS (see below), the first set consists of conceptions about (1) a self, (2) mine, (3) the names of the four skandhas except form, and (4) the reasons for these names (thus not referring to the term "discrimina-

tions" in line 2 of verse 28 and relating (4) "reasons" directly to "names"). From these four, the second set of the four well-known mistaken conceptions of ordinary sentient beings arises. As for DSC's interpretation of the last line of verse 28, comparison with the other commentaries confirms that it is not the most obvious one. SS (p. 635) largely follows DSC in this (and not his teacher Dölpopa), speaking of the same two sets of four conceptions but spelling out (3) and (4) more clearly: "(1) We **conceive of** consciousness as **a self and** (2) conceive of form and such as **mine**. (3) We conceive of the nature of the four **names**—feelings, formations, discriminations, and consciousness—and (4) we conceive of the **reasons** of these four names: feelings [are so called], since they experience pleasure and displeasure; formations [have their name], since they propel us toward [karmic] results; discriminations [are so named], since they apprehend characteristics; and consciousness [has its name], since it apprehends objects. Based on these four conceptions, . . ." Thereafter, SS follows DSC's remaining explanation almost verbatim. Döl (p. 144), RT (p. 635), and SC (pp. 312–13) all identify just one set of four conceptions—those about (1) a self, (2) mine, (3) discriminations of names, and (4) reasons. Here, SC replaces "afflictions" in verse 27 with "conceptions" and says that there are two kinds—conceptions that are discriminations of names (such as, "This is a vase") and conceptions that are discriminations of the reasons for these names (such as, "It has a round belly"). These obviously refer to conceptions (3) and (4) in verse 28. LG (p. 25) has also just a single set of four conceptions about (1) self, (2) mine, (3) names, and (4) conceptions due to the reason of discriminating these names. Döl, SC, and LG all take "The elements and their outcome" to refer to the four elements of earth, water, fire, and wind and their derivatives, that is, the various kinds of material forms. RT takes it to mean past and future events (the Tibetan expressions for both are almost the same).

684 Again, "lacking appearance and characteristics" is interpreted in different ways by the commentators. Döl (p. 144) says, "The aspiration prayers of the Buddhas lack the appearance of a self and the clinging to a self as well as the characteristics of conceptions." SC (p. 313) explains, "The aspiration prayers of the Buddhas as well as the form kāyas and the various [buddha] realms arising under their influence do not appear within a Buddha's own appearances and lack any characteristics that would characterize [anything]." LG (p. 26) states, "The appearance of the form kāyas due to the power of the aspiration prayers of the Buddhas lacks any specifically characterized appearance and is not in the slightest way established as any characteristics." SS (p. 636) comments, "The aspiration prayers of the Buddhas . . . lack the appearance of self and mine as well as the characteristics of apprehender and apprehended." RT does not comment on this.

685 As mentioned before, the Tibetan for "very own awareness" in some of the verses (29, 46, 56) and the corresponding passages of DSC is *so sor rang rig* (Skt. pratyātmavedanīya), otherwise translated here as "personally experienced (wisdom)."

686 The dharmakāya is said to be permanent by nature, since its essential character is the ultimate freedom from arising and ceasing. The sambhogakāya is permanent through its inexhaustible continuum, since the enjoyment of dharma is a continuous stream. The nirmāṇakāya is permanent due to its uninterrupted continuum of performing altruistic activity despite the appearance and disappearance of its various manifestations.

687 IX.65–66.

688 Verse 26.

689 SC (p. 314) presents the objection that the example of the horns of a rabbit does not apply to the phenomena of saṃsāra and nirvāṇa, since—as a nonexistent—it lacks any specific char-

acteristics, while the specific characteristics of those phenomena exist. However, any specific characteristics of the horns of an ox are not observable either, since they cannot be found as being of the nature of minute particles. For the very same reason, these horns also do not exist as coarse objects, since there cannot be any specific characteristics of a phenomenon that is just imputed onto a nonexistent basis of imputation. LG (p. 28) has someone object that, if all phenomena are just imagined and imputed, then the basic nature—the dharmakāya—would be superimposed as well. He answers that this is true, if you cling to it as existent or nonexistent, but it is a different situation, once such clinging collapses.

690 DSC omits lines 1–2 of this verse.

691 V.23–26 (note that the Tibetan translation of the *Madhyāntavibhāga* inserts three verses from Vasubandhu's commentary before these verses, thus counting them as V.26–29). These verses list twenty-eight conceptions about extremes (two sets of seven pairs) to be avoided on the middle path (that DSC speaks of twenty extremes just below seems to be based on a different way of counting). The commentaries by Vasubandhu (P5528; ACIP TD4027@023B–025B) and others extensively quote the well-known passages from the *Kāśyapaparivartasūtra* (P760.43, §§52–71), which are also the standard source in the Madhyamaka tradition for "practicing the middle path of eliminating all extremes." The gist of this is that the "middle" is not *something between* these extremes, but simply stands for the very freedom from any possible extremes or reference points, which include the notion of a "middle."

692 SC (p. 315) comments that the mere imputations made by consciousness and expressions exist even for nonexistents like the horns of a rabbit, while an intrinsic nature of its own does not even exist in the horns of an ox. Finally, when having deeply reflected with Madhyamaka reasonings, there is nothing whatsoever that could be called "a phenomenon that is established through valid cognition." For that reason, it is nothing but being free from the two extremes of permanence and extinction that is labeled by the conventional term "middle." GL (p. 47) has a unique variant of verse 33 in four lines (*skye bar brtags pa'i mtshan nyid dag/ ri bong ba lang rva yi dpes/ dbu ma ru ni rtogs bya ste/ bde gshegs chos nyid ji bzhin no*):

> The characteristics imputed as arising,
> Through the examples of rabbit and ox,
> Are to be realized as the middle,
> Just as the Sugata's true nature is.

(The last line could also be read as "Just as the Sugata [realized] the nature of phenomena.")

GL's comment on verses 30–33 is that the bodhisattvas' generation of ultimate bodhicitta greatly enhances their practice through the view. Thus, what is taught in Nāgārjuna's collection of reasoning is also asserted here—all phenomena of saṃsāra and nirvāṇa are primordially without any nature of their own, free from the eight extremes of reference points.

693 Lines 47–51 (DSC omits the first line).

694 RT (p. 636) says that, from the perspective of their appearing, reflections are not something extinct, while from the perspective of their essence, they are not permanent. This provides the complete picture of the characteristics of all phenomena as well. Döl (p. 145) states that the complete seeing of the characteristics of the middle is like that. LG (p. 29) explains that, from the very moment of its appearing, a reflection of the moon in the water never exists as a specifically characterized phenomenon in the first place, yet the mere appearance of the moon's color and shape is unimpeded. So if we realize that this reflection is appearance and emptiness inseparable, and that the characteristics of the moon in the water are empty, our clinging to

that moon there is liberated in its own place. Likewise, from the very moment of their appearing, the characteristics of saṃsāra and nirvāṇa, which are complete and appear unmixed and distinctly on the level of seeming reality, never really exist in the first place. Still, while lacking any reality, they appear unimpededly as mere appearances. So if we realize that they are appearance and emptiness inseparable, and that their characteristics are empty, our clinging to these appearances is liberated in its own place. Therefore, realizing the nature of phenomena is just as in this example. SS (p. 638) summarizes this as being the complete characteristics of the union of appearance and emptiness. SC (p. 315) explains that, when we see a reflection of the moon, all we see is a mere reflection but not its actual nature, just as it is. Likewise, the fully complete characteristics of the phenomena of seeming reality are something to be experienced through meditation but cannot be fully demonstrated as objects of ordinary consciousness.

695 P795. I could not locate these lines in the sūtra.

696 DSC omits this line.

697 Verses 17–21ab.

698 RT (p. 636) glosses "virtuous through beginning, middle, end" as the generation of bodhicitta, the actual path, and the fruition of that path, respectively. SC (pp. 315–16) says that the dharmadhātu is undeceiving, since it is in perfect harmony with what the noble ones see. It is a steady continuum throughout all the phases of ground, path, and fruition. You may wonder, "If it is the case that the dharmadhātu wisdom pervades all these three phases, why is it not taught that way in all the teachings of the Buddha?" For those who need to be led up to the definitive meaning gradually, he needed to teach through the progression of initial, intermediate, and final instructions. First, in order to establish them in the virtue that is conducive to merit, he taught in a manner that accords with the existence of a personal identity and an identity of phenomena. In the middle, in order to establish them in the virtue that is conducive to liberation, he taught in the manner of both these identities not existing. Finally, he taught that the basis for purifying the two obscurations and gathering the two accumulations—this very dharmadhātu wisdom—pervades all three phases of ground, path, and fruition. Since this teaching is pure through the three kinds of analysis [through perceptual, inferential, and scriptural valid cognition], it is undeceiving. "If something like that is taught in the end, it is the same as the teaching on a self as imputed by the tīrthikas, since there is no difference to the way of explaining such [a self]." How could the dharmadhātu wisdom taught by the Buddha be conceived of as a self or mine, since there is this progression in the way the victor taught the dharma, and within this virtue of beginning, middle, and end, the lack of a self has been taught already?

699 This refers again to the two aspects of the perfect nature, with the unchanging perfect nature being the nature of phenomena and the unmistaken perfect nature the nondual nonconceptual wisdom that realizes it.

700 DSC omits the last two lines.

701 I.155.

702 J 76; P5526, fol. 118b.4–8 (for the quote from the *Śrīmālādevīsūtra*, see Wayman, trans. 1974, pp. 99–100).

703 GL (pp. 215–16) comments on verses 36–37 that nothing but the basic element or Heart of sentient beings is ignorance, desire and so on—desire does not exist anywhere else than in this Heart. Therefore, for those who are skilled in the path, this Heart is to be searched for right within desire—it is not that pure phenomena are obtained from anywhere else than just such

afflicted phenomena. Therefore, the statement, "The essence of desire is the Heart, but desire is adventitious" is truly inconceivable.

704 This paragraph addresses the manner in which practitioners on the path of preparation realize ultimate reality. The Eighth Karmapa's commentary on the *Abhisamayālaṃkāra* (Mi bskyod rdo rje n.d., pp. I.182–83) elaborates on this as follows. The point when the freedom from all characteristics of apprehender and apprehended is directly realized in this way is the path of seeing, which has the character of yogic direct valid cognition. These meditative equipoises of the path of preparation are unmistaken self-aware direct valid cognitions that are approximately concordant with the unmistaken wisdom that lacks the duality of apprehender and apprehended. . . . During the [path of preparation], these meditative equipoises are not something other than self-aware direct valid cognition, because both what is aware and what it is aware of arise as the nature of a single clear and aware experience. AC (fol. 163b) says that, when embraced by the correct yoga, sense perception, mental direct perception, and self-aware direct perception are all yogic direct perception, connate wisdom's own nature (for further details, see the comments on verses 43–47 and 74 below).

705 SS (p. 640) comments that when yogins whose familiarization with samādhi is stable, in dependence on their eyes, form, and mental engagement, directly see some form with their eye-consciousness, right upon such seeing, that form appears as appearance-emptiness, lucidity-emptiness, and awareness-emptiness and is directly seen as the unborn and unceasing basic nature. Therefore, the superior insight of directly seeing the dharmadhātu dawns on its own. Based on that, during subsequent attainment, appearances are known to be without reality, just like a city of gandharvas. LG (p. 31) says that while form is appearing, it is emptiness. It comes about due to conditions, such as the dominant condition and the object condition, but upon analysis, the nature of dependent origination is established as emptiness—being unarisen and unceasing. From this, the dharmadhātu is known. Döl (p. 146) has someone ask, "From what is the nature of phenomena known?" In dependence upon the eye and form of the nature of phenomena, the appearance of luminosity without a stain occurs for the yogin. Due to seeing the unborn and unceasing luminous mind, it will be known from the dharmadhātu, that is, through nonconceptual wisdom.

706 SC (p. 318) says that, based on sound and ear, the nonconceptual consciousness that appears lucidly as sound is the dharmadhātu, which has no other characteristic than pointing out true reality. However, through being linked with subsequent thought, we cling to that dharmadhātu as being us having heard a sound. SS (p. 641) and LG (p. 31) agree with that. LG explicitly confirms that "three" in line 3 refers to sound, ear, and consciousness, while Döl (p. 146) explains this as the three aspects—object, subject, and pure self-awareness—of a consciousness that is pure of apprehender and apprehended.

707 DNP *chos kyi dbyings la rtog par byed.* Due to the unfortunate and frequent confusion of *rtogs pa* (realize) and *rtog pa* in Tibetan texts, the commentators differ here according to which version they adhere to. DSC has *chos kyi dbyings su rtogs par byed* in both line 4 of verse 40 and its commentary (which in itself makes perfect sense and is in line with DSC's manner of commenting on the other verses on sense perception here). SC (p. 318) and SS (p. 641), following their comments on the other verses here, confirm "conceptualizes" (*rtog pa*). LG (p. 32) states that the nose-consciousness serves as an aid for realizing the dharmadhātu; Döl (p. 146) says that the dharmadhātu is realized through discriminating wisdom by way of the nose-consciousness; and RT has *rtogs pa* in both verse 39 and 40 (it is to be noted that LG, Döl, and RT all have *chos kyi dbyings la rtogs par byed*, which suggests *rtogs pa* just being a typo for *rtog pa* in the root texts they used, since *rtogs pa* is never connected with *la* to its object).

708 This could also be read as "empty and void of nature."

709 Some other sources speak of the fine down on such a bird.

710 Döl (p. 146) says that the eighteen ultimate dhātus, (the six objects, six sense faculties, and six consciousnesses) free from the conditions of seeming reality, are the dharmadhātu.

711 Together, these five kinds of form are also referred to as "imperceptible form" (Skt. avijñaptirūpa, Tib. rnam par rig byed ma yin pa'i gzugs) or as parts of the "form of the āyatana of phenomena" (Skt. dharmāyatanarūpa, Tib. chos kyi skye mched kyi gzugs). They are phenomena that appear as aspects of form that are solely experienced by the mental consciousness, not demonstrable to the eye consciousness, and intangible. Aggregational form refers to the form of the minutest material particle. Circumstantial form includes, for example, the space in between things or reflections. Form originating from correct commitment and symbols refers to vows. Imputed form includes, for example, appearances in a dream or skeletons appearing through the samādhi of repulsiveness. Mastered form appears through mastery over certain samādhis, for example, the entire universe appearing as earth or red due to the samādhi of the totality (Skt. kṛtsnāyatana, Tib. zad par kyi skye mched) of earth or red and such.

712 This is the meditative absorption that stops coarse discriminations and feelings. It represents the cessation of all primary minds and mental factors with an unstable continuum as well as some with a stable continuum, that is, the first seven consciousnesses (except the ālaya-consciousness) and their mental factors. This absorption is used as the culminating meditative absorption in the process of ninefold progressive abiding (various alternating ways of entering in and rising from the four samādhis of the form realm, the four formless ones, and this meditative absorption).

713 This is the highest type of meditative absorption within the fourth dhyāna of the form realm, during which primary minds and mental factors with an unstable continuum (the five sense consciousnesses, the mental consciousness, and their accompanying mental factors) temporarily cease. However, the latent tendencies for the arising of these consciousnesses are not eliminated. Thus, mistaken appearances will occur again, once one rises from this meditative absorption. When performed for a long time, it leads to rebirth in the highest level of the gods of the form realm.

714 Skt. pratisaṃkhyānirodha, Tib. so sor brtags pa'i 'gog pa. This refers to the result of freedom from the factors to be relinquished on the path of seeing through thoroughly analyzing all the aspects of the four realities of the noble ones.

715 Skt. apratisaṃkhyānirodha, Tib. so sor brtags pa ma yin pa'i 'gog pa. This refers to something not happening due to its specific causes and conditions not being complete. Instead of these two cessations, DSC reads *so sor brtags pa ma yin pa'i snyoms 'jug.*

716 In accordance with the Sarvāstivāda system, Vasubandhu's *Abhidharmakośa* lists only (4), (7), and (8), while his *Pañcaskandhaprakaraṇa* gives the same plus suchness. The above list of eight unconditioned phenomena originated with the Mahīśāsakas and is later found in the *Yogācārabhūmi* and the *Abhidharmasamucchaya.*

717 Verse 16.

718 I.17ab.

719 Skt. mano dhātu, Tib. yid kyi khams.

720 Skt. mana āyatana, Tib. yid kyi skye mched.

721 There are very detailed and complex presentations on the factors to be relinquished through

seeing and meditation in texts such as the *Abhidharmakośa*, the *Viniścayasaṃgrahaṇī*, and the *Abhisamayālaṃkāra* and their commentaries. Basically, there are ten afflictions to be relinquished in general: ignorance, desire, anger, pride, doubt, and the five wrong views (the views about a real personality, the views about extremes, wrong views, the views to hold a view as paramount, and the views to hold ethics and spiritual conduct as paramount). These are then relinquished as they relate to the three realms and in terms of being imputed (path of seeing) and connate (path of cultivation). For detailed charts, see Brunnhölzl 2002a (Appendices I–II).

722 As mentioned in the introduction, the Sanskrit word *manas* (Tib. *yid*) is used to refer to both the sixth and the seventh consciousnesses (strictly speaking *manovijñāna*; Tib. *yid kyi rnam shes*). Thus, not only terminologically but also in terms of content, depending on the perspective, one finds overlaps between the descriptions of these two consciousnesses with regard to the "immediate mind," "afflicted mind," and "stainless mentation." Rangjung Dorje's AC explains the following about the various aspects of mentation: This [immediate mind] . . . operates by being based on the ālaya, and when the other six collections of consciousness arise and cease, it inputs their potentials into the ālaya. Therefore, it is called "mental consciousness." [In his *Pramāṇaviniścaya*,] Dharmakīrti states that its own essence is valid cognition . . . [The other aspect of] "mentation," which focuses on the [ālaya-consciousness], has the character of regarding the ālaya as "me" and is called "afflicted mind." Since [this aspect of] mentation thinks of the ālaya as a self and is always tainted by a set of four afflictions, it is the locus of the afflictedness of consciousness. Therefore, it lacks any valid cognition and gives rise to all minds that are nonvalid cognition. This ["mentation" in general has] both [aspects]: the one [—the immediate mind—] is said to be consciousness' own essence and the other [—the afflicted mind—] is expressed from the perspective that, based on it, mistakenness is caused. Thus, they are said to be like a rope and taking that [rope] to be a snake [respectively]. Here, others explain the immediate [mind] as a part of the sixth, the mental [consciousness], and some explain that, ultimately, it does not exist. However, those [people], by clinging to the presentation of the śrāvakas who assert that there are only six collections [of consciousness], do not understand the mahāyāna's presentation of the eight collections [of consciousnesses], which is given in detail in the *Mahāyānasaṃgraha*: "Among those, mentation is twofold. Since it is the support that acts as the immediate condition, the 'mentation that is the consciousness that has just ceased' is the support for consciousness. The second is the afflicted mind, which is always associated with the four afflictions of the views about a real personality, self-conceit, attachment to the self, and ignorance. This is the support for the afflictedness of consciousness. [Thus,] consciousness is produced by virtue of the first [aspect of mentation] as its support, while the second one makes it afflicted. [Mentation] is a consciousness because it cognizes objects. Since it is [both] immediately preceding and self-centered, mentation has two aspects." [I.6 (D4048, fols. 3b.5–4a.1)] "Afflicted" is a term of possession. For this reason, this is the root of all mistakenness of circling in the three realms. Therefore, this [afflicted mind] neither exists in the meditative absorption of cessation that transcends the three realms, nor in the meditative equipoises of the paths of arhats and supramundane bodhisattvas. [However,] in the meditative absorption without discrimination, which is the cause for being born as long-living [gods] without discrimination, the afflicted mind exists. Thus, one will understand the difference. Furthermore, if one takes the immediacy of the arising and ceasing of the consciousnesses that dwells in the ālaya to be a part of the sixth, the mental [consciousness], then at the time of being able to dwell in the meditative absorption of cessation, since there is nothing except the ālaya and the six [other] collections [of consciousness], there would only be seven collections [altogether], since the afflicted mind does not exist [in that meditative absorption]. If [some people then think] that thus the "stainless mentation" taught by the Bhagavat must be presented as a ninth collection

[of consciousness], this is not justified either. {As mentioned in the introduction, this refers to the *amalavijñāna* held by the Indian Yogācāra Paramārtha and some of his Chinese followers. Since there are no Indian but only Chinese scriptural sources for this, the Tibetans seem to have obtained their informations on this from the latter, including the Chinese commentary on the *Saṃdhinirmocanasūtra*—translated into Tibetan (P5517)—by the Korean master Wonch'uk (aka Yüan-ts'e; 613–696). Following AC's above quote from the *Pramāṇaviniścaya*, Tagramba Chögyal Denba's commentary on the ZMND explicitly equates the immediate mind with nonconceptual mental direct valid cognition, which perceives outer objects (Dvags po rab 'byams pa chos rgyal bstan pa 2005, p. 104).} You may wonder then, "Due to what is this seventh consciousness of mentation that is [also] explained as the immediate [mind] presented as the afflicted mind and due to what is it presented as stainless?" It is good [to say that] it becomes afflicted, once it is embraced by the four afflictions [mentioned above], but to express it as stainless mentation, once it is embraced by the immaculate dharma that is grounded in the enlightenment of the Buddha. It is said that, as long as these two have not undergone the completely pure change of state, they stay mixed together (fols. 20a–22a). Jamgön Kongtrul's commentary on the ZMND (Kong sprul blo gros mtha' yas 2005, p. 28) says: The seventh lord [Karmapa] holds that [mentation] has three parts. From the perspective of immediacy, it is presented as the seventh [consciousness] of mentation; from the perspective of being embraced by the set of four afflictions, it is the afflicted mind; and from the perspective of being embraced by the immaculate dharma, it is stainless mentation. The relationships between the three aspects of mentation as well as between the sixth and the seventh consciousness are also described in the Third Karmapa's NY and its commentary by Jamgön Kongtrul Lodrö Tayé (Kong sprul blo gros mtha' yas 1990, pp. 90–97). The latter says: As for what is called "immediate mind," whenever the six collections of consciousnesses arise, it functions as the condition for their immediate arising, and whenever the six collections cease, it functions as the condition for immediately planting the seeds, which are the potentials of these six collections, into the ālaya. Due to this, it is the immediate condition for both the arising and ceasing [of the six consciousnesses]. When the six collections cease, the immediate consciousness—which is explained to be the same as the dhātu of mentation—carries them into the ālaya and immediately, just like the condition of waves [arising] from water, from the ālaya which possesses all the seeds, mentation that abides in the ālaya stirs again and operates, and in that way the immediate mind arises. . . . Thus, once the earlier [instances of] the six collections have ceased, it immediately triggers their following [instances]; hence, it is the immediate [mind]. Therefore, matching the number of moments that cause the arising and ceasing of the six collections, the immediate [mind] arises in a way of being connected to them by equaling their number. If one were to ask where knowledge of these principles comes from, this mentation is realized through the direct perception of a mind immersed in the yoga of the unity of calm abiding and superior insight, and through the inferences based on the principles [presented in] the profound and vast words of the victor. . . . If the immediate mind produces a purified [instance of] consciousness, such as devotion, then the afflicted [mind] does not move. Therefore, the [immediate mind] is called "stainless mentation" in the sūtras (p. 93–96).

723 Döl (p. 147) explains that once conceptions and what they conceptualize—which entail characteristics with regard to ultimate phenomena, the principal among which is ultimate mind (Samantabhadra)—are relinquished in the state of profound meditative equipoise, these ultimate phenomena lack a nature of reference points. Through apprehending it as anything whatsoever becoming exhausted, this should be cultivated as the dharmadhātu. LG (p. 32) says that once all reference points of a thinker—the mind—and the objects it thinks about are relinquished, one should rest effortlessly by conducting one's analysis right within the state of being free from ref-

erence points and thus cultivate phenomena's lack of nature—emptiness—as the dharmadhātu. SS (pp. 641–42) explains that the mental consciousness free from thought arises in dependence on three conditions—the immediate condition being a sense consciousness, the dominant condition being the mental sense faculty, and the object-conditions being form and so on. GL (pp. 46–47) comments as follows on verses 38–43. When one trains in the conduct of bodhisattvas by relying on having generated ultimate bodhicitta, this training becomes very much advanced. Once one has familiarized oneself with [ultimate bodhicitta]—mind focusing on the nature of mind—the nature of the six operating consciousnesses will be realized to be luminosity. [Here follows the quote of verses 38–43.] When the eighteen kinds of movement of mind toward the eighteen dhātus—the six consciousnesses, six sense faculties, and six objects—occur, one familiarizes oneself with these very movements being luminosity. Due to being familiar with this, these very eighteen dhātus appear as luminosity. Once they appear that way, this is called "accomplishment." Based on this, one attains the qualities of the completely pure [six sense] āyatanas as taught in the *Saddharmapuṇḍarīkasūtra* [ACIP KD0113@218B–219A; see Introduction], which says that there arise twelve times hundred or eight times hundred qualities in each of these āyatanas. It may be noted here that also Kambala's *Prajñāpāramitānavaślokī* (P5210) and its autocommentary (for a translation, see Brunnhölzl 2007, pp. 60–62) mainly consist of similar instructions on a progressive meditation on emptiness that focuses on the six kinds of consciousness and their objects, culminating in spacelike wisdom free from any subject-object duality, which is just mind's natural luminosity.

724 Lines VII.3bd.

725 Lines 252–63. DSC again has prose in slightly different order, somewhat similar to the text's prose version (P5523; lines 133–39, ed. Mathes): *yang dag pa ma yin pa'i kun tu rtog pa sa bon thams cad pa med pa gnyis snang ba'i rgyu de la brten pa'i rgyud gzhan de bzhin nyid ma shes pa las yin te/ de'i phyir rgyu dang bcas pa'i bras bu ni/ snang du zin kyang yod pa ma yin no/ 'di snang ba las chos nyid mi snang zhing/ 'di mi snang ba las ni chos nyid snang ba yin no/ zhes de ltar yid la byed pa'i byang chub sems dpa' ni rnam par mi rtog pa'i ye shes la 'jug pa yin no.*

726 LG (p. 33) says that once yogins realize all phenomena in this way, the ultimate characteristics of meditation are complete (SS agrees in slightly different words). RT (p. 638) glosses that such yogins completely realize the basic nature that is phenomena's very own characteristic. Döl (p. 147) states that then the characteristics of the dharmadhātu, true reality, are complete. SC (p. 319) says that when all inner and outer phenomena are realized to be empty of an essence of their own, phenomena are realized to be of one taste as the dharmadhātu. At that point, the characteristic of phenomena is seen in a complete way.

727 Lines 114–15.

728 Skt. kṣānti, Tib. bzod pa (lit. "patience," "endurance"). In a general sense, this refers to being mentally ready for the direct realization of emptiness, aka "the dharma of nonarising" (Skt. anutpattidharmakṣānti, Tib. mi skye ba'i chos la bzod pa). Thus, in this context, "poised or open readiness" does not mean passively enduring or bearing something but rather indicates an active openness and receptiveness to integrate the experience of emptiness into one's mind stream and to be able to live within this utter groundlessness. In a more specific sense, "poised readiness" stands for reaching the level of poised readiness among the four levels—heat, peak, poised readiness, and supreme dharma—of the path of preparation. Here, the practitioner newly attains some degree of poised readiness—or openness in the sense of lack of fear—with respect to profound emptiness. Strictly speaking, the complete extent of this kind of poised readiness is only attained from the path of seeing onward, when the nature of phenomena is

directly seen, and then an increasing familiarity with that is gained on the path of cultivation.

729 SC (p. 321) says that the two aspects of mind are clinging to a self and natural luminosity. Once personally experienced wisdom is aware of the latter, it becomes that very wisdom. SS (p. 643) explains that once one is aware of the nature of phenomena through personally experienced meditative equipoise, this is the mind beyond the world. This remedial wisdom extinguishes all three types of obscurations—afflictive obscurations, such as desire, hatred, and ignorance; cognitive obscurations, such as conceptions about the three spheres; and obscurations to meditative absorption, such as dullness and agitation. Due to that, the final fruition of buddhahood is attained. LG (pp. 33–34) elaborates that śrāvakas relinquish only the afflictive obscurations, pratyekabuddhas the afflictive obscurations and the one half of the cognitive obscurations that pertains to apprehended objects (but not the apprehending subject), and bodhisattvas have to relinquish both types of obscurations fully. AC (fols. 76a–77a) quotes verses 43–47 as support for the following. The connate wisdom of our own mind is empty in essence, lucid in nature, and unimpeded in its manifestation. All these three being free from reference points is the dharmakāya, lucidity is the sambhogakāya, and the compassionate display that can show as anything is the nirmāṇakāya. The indications that the three kāyas in this sense are present right now are as follows. The indication of the dharmakāya is that all entities appear as empty now too, since their nature does never go beyond emptiness. The indication of the sambhogakāya is the appearance of the ten signs of expanse and awareness inseparable as visual objects. The indication of the nirmāṇakāya is that the distinct energies of the appearances of the objects of the six consciousnesses are manifested individually. The indication that all three are undeceiving appears in objects right now, since wisdom (the perceiving subject) is the very nature of the consciousnesses connected with these objects. Nonconceptual yogic direct perception right within these consciousnesses means to sustain the continuum of nonconceptual direct perception, which is given the conventional term "meditation." Later, AC (fol. 163b) elaborates that when sense perception, mental direct perception, and self-aware direct perception are embraced by the correct yoga, they all are yogic direct perception, connate wisdom's own nature. Through all aspects of knowing and what is to be known being embraced by the perfect view, in terms of its functions, this wisdom then manifests as the five wisdoms. These are the wisdom that discriminates all causes and results; the wisdom of being empty of a nature of its own (mirrorlike wisdom); all-accomplishing wisdom, which displays wisdom's power due to having gained mastery over it; the wisdom of seeing the equality of all this; and the principle of not moving away from suchness, which pervades all of this (dharmadhātu wisdom).

730 XI.34–35.

731 SS (p. 643) and Döl (pp. 147–48) both gloss "realization" as wisdom and "its lack" as consciousness. Since there is no difference apart from that, all of saṃsāra and nirvāṇa is complete within this body. Nirvāṇa is fettered by our thoughts, but when nirvāṇa's nature is known through personally experienced wisdom, we are free from these thoughts.

732 Paraphrase of the beginning of X.5 (P5549, fol. 44b.1).

733 SS (p. 644) says that enlightenment is neither near to a Buddha's rūpakāya nor far from someone in saṃsāra. Nevertheless, since sentient beings are overpowered right in the midst of their afflictions, they do not see it, but once they become free from afflictions, they do. Therefore, enlightenment appears as if it were near or far. Döl (p. 148) explains that enlightenment is not far, since it exists in sentient beings' own mind stream. Nor is it said to be near, since it is buddhahood itself. It neither goes somewhere else outside of sentient beings' mind stream, nor does it come in front of what is buddhahood itself. The only difference in speaking about

Buddhas and sentient beings is that the former clearly see that enlightenment exists in the midst of the afflictions within this body, while the latter do not. SC (p. 323) comments that enlightenment is not near to sentient beings, since the dharmadhātu of mind does not become enlightenment for as long as its stains have not become pure. Nor is it far, since they need not search for it outside of mind's dharmadhātu. Rather, once it has become pure of those stains, it is presented as enlightenment.

734 Verse 68.

735 LG (p. 35) explains buddhahood as the "supreme peace" by saying that it is unlike the realization of śrāvakas and pratyekabuddhas, which is a mere negation of existence. Rather, bodhisattvas need to meditate in a way that is free from all reference points, be they existence, nonexistence, or whatever. Through the incomplete view of a mere nonimplicative negation, buddhahood is not attained, just as with any result whose causes are not complete. LG, SS (p. 644), and RT (p. 639) take "self" to mean our ordinary mistaken notion of a self, while Döl (p. 148) glosses it as "buddhahood that exists in our own body." SC simply omits it.

736 SS (p. 644) identifies those who see the Buddhas in this way as practitioners on the greater path of accumulation, having purified their karma a little bit.

737 IX.16.

738 The other four are vigor, mindfulness, samādhi, and prajñā. They specifically pertain to the latter two of the four stages (heat, peak, poised readiness, and supreme dharma) of the path of preparation. During its first two stages, the same group of five is practiced as the "five faculties," the difference being that they can still be overpowered by their opposites.

739 SC (p. 325) adds that, for such beings, the Buddhas may appear in the form of Brahmā, Viṣṇu, or Mañjuśrī to benefit them. In order to benefit those for whom they cannot even appear like that, they show as ordinary spiritual friends, merchants, ferrymen, and so on. It is not that the Buddhas simply give up on such beings.

740 DSC and SS *'od kyi rang bzhin dpal ldan pa'i.*

741 This is the Indian fig tree, also called banyan.

742 *Abhisamayālaṃkāra* VIII.13–17. Note that this is just one from among a considerable number of more or less differing lists of these thirty-two marks that are found in various sūtras and treatises.

743 DNP, SS, LG, and Döl all have *tha dad gyur pa lags*. DSC and RT have *tha dad gyur ma lags* ("not different") and comment accordingly. LG (p. 37) says that the dharmadhātu, in its essence, is inconceivable as one or different, but in terms of its mode of appearing, may show as various differences. SC (p. 325) obviously saw both versions, thus commenting on both. First, he says, the dharmadhātu wisdom itself appears as different, that is, arising and ceasing upon entering nirvāṇa, but that the Tathāgatas possess neither arriving nor abiding. Secondly, the Tathāgatas appear as if arising and ceasing from the perspective of those to be guided, but the dharmadhātu itself, the actual Tathāgata, does not possess any differences in terms of arising or ceasing. According to SC, the gist of this is as follows. When a nirmāṇakāya appears to śrāvakas, pratyekabuddhas, or ordinary sentient beings, the aspects that appear as form and speech are a part of the dharmadhātu of the mind of the person to whom they appear, having been unfolded through their merit. Therefore, these aspects are included in the phenomena of their own minds. But the dominant condition that displays these appearances in that way, is the very dharmadhātu of the Buddha, which is without any arriving, departing, increase, or

decrease. Therefore, from the perspective of those who see the dharmadhātu directly, there is no appearance of a rūpakāya passing into nirvāṇa. That it may appear that way from the perspective of those who do not directly see the dharmadhātu is just due to the fluctuations in their individual merits, such as having confidence.

744 The six doors are the six consciousnesses as just mentioned, with the sixth, the mental consciousness, being specifically referred to as prajñā. As shown in detail in verses 38–45, the true nature of both these consciousnesses and their objects is the dharmadhātu or nonconceptual wisdom. Thus, it is said here that this wisdom is the actual object of the mind—the latter being understood as personally experienced self-aware wisdom—no matter how this may appear superficially, such as sense consciousnesses seeming to dualistically apprehend forms or sounds. Thus, Döl (p. 149) says, "Ascertaining the object of ultimate bodhicitta, one engages in the wisdom that is the object to be realized in a way that this is of equal taste with the consciousnesses of the other objects. Once your very own pure awareness—the wisdom that engages in the [wisdom that is the object]—has become pure, you dwell in the nature of the wisdom of the bhūmis. SC (pp. 326–27) agrees with that. LG (p. 38) says that mind's object or basic nature is the dharmadhātu, in which the consciousness that realizes identitylessness engages. Once that personally experienced wisdom has become pure, finally, it abides as the nature of all bhūmis. SS (p. 648) gives a different interpretation, saying that the Buddhas first ascertain the objects for which the minds of those to be guided aspire, and then, in accordance with the mind-set of these beings, the wisdom of the Buddhas—the consciousness that promotes the welfare of beings—engages them. Once the personally experienced wisdom in the meditative equipoise of these beings has purified their stains, they dwell on the paths and bhūmis, whose nature is the nature of phenomena. In essence, dhātu and awareness are inseparable, but from the perspective of those to be guided, they may appear as if they were different.

745 The dharmakāyas of all Buddhas are equal, since their support—the dharmadhātu—is not different. Their sambhogakāyas are equal, since their intention is not different. Their nirmāṇakāyas are equal, since they serve as a common enlightened activity.

746 This is a term that may designate either the phase of both the paths of accumulation and preparation or just the latter.

747 Tib. adhyāśayaviśuddhibhūmi, Tib. lhag pa'i bsam pa dag pa'i sa. This is a collective term for the first seven bhūmis of bodhisattvas.

748 Being somewhat cryptic and multi-layered, verses 57–60 indeed enjoy the greatest diversity of comments. As for verse 57, RT (p. 640) says that the triad of the bhūmis, the state of buddhahood (the supreme abode of the great and mighty ones), and Akaniṣṭha fuse as the single dharmadhātu. Döl (p. 149) takes the supreme abode to be the dharmakāya, while Akaniṣṭha stands for the sambhogakāya and the nirmāṇakāya. The three consciousnesses of the three kāyas fuse into a single taste. SS (pp. 648–49) speaks of the beautiful dharmakāya in the dharmadhātu (the supreme abode), the beautiful sambhogakāya in Akaniṣṭha, and implicitly, the nirmāṇakāya. These three consciousnesses or kāyas fuse into the nature of the wisdom that is single. SC (p. 327) says that the triad of the sambhogakāya (the supreme abode), the richly adorned buddha realm of Akaniṣṭha, and the consciousnesses of the dharmadhātus of bodhisattvas on the ten bhūmis fuse into one. The gist of this, SC says, is that the aspect that appears as the sambhogakāya and its abode is contained in the nature of the wisdom of those very ones for whom it appears. The reason it appears fragmented is that it happens under the influence of this wisdom being contaminated by the latent tendencies of dualistic appearances.

The causal condition for its appearing that way is one's own wisdom, but the dominant condition for it is the wisdom of the Buddhas. On the eleventh bhūmi, since one's own wisdom and the wisdom of all Buddhas fuse into one, there are no distinctions in the ultimate kāya. However, under the influence of different previous aspiration prayers, the appearances of the rūpakāyas appear differently. LG (p. 38–39) explains that the supreme abode is the place where a Buddha's sambhogakāya is surrounded by bodhisattvas on the tenth bhūmi, which is also known as Akaniṣṭha. There, in bodhisattvas at the very end of their path, immediately upon having engaged in the vajralike samādhi, the threefold consciousness that involves agent, object, and action becomes of a single taste in that these three spheres are not observable anymore, with meditative equipoise and subsequent attainment thus fusing. This is called "the final realization of the dharmakāya." In general, when the path of seeing is attained, the clinging to real existence is ended; on the three pure bhūmis, the clinging to characteristics; and on the bhūmi of buddhahood, all conceptions about the three spheres in dualistic appearances.

749 P768.

750 IV.20–26. DSC omits lines 20d and 21c.

751 Döl (pp. 149–50) says that the first line of verse indicates the appearance of the nirmāṇakāya, the second that of the sambhogakāya, and the third that of the dharmakāya, infinite in time. The fourth line represents a question about the cause for the lifetimes of rūpakāyas lasting many eons (which is the dharmakāya). RT (p. 640–41) agrees on the first two lines but says that the great and mighty one in line three is Amitāyus. The cause for their lifespans lasting many eons is the realization of the dharmadhātu. SC (p. 328) explains that the first line indicates whichever qualities of merit and wisdom there are in the mind streams of ordinary sentient beings; the second line refers to the features of the paths and bhūmis in the mind streams of noble ones; and the third line to the dharmakāya of a perfect Buddha. The cause for these three extending over eons is the wisdom of the dharmadhātu, which is an ever-unbroken continuum. LG (p. 39) says that the dharmakāya dwells among ordinary sentient beings by way of the all-pervasive nature of the wisdom of the dharmakāya, since they do not realize the dharmakāya in its manifest way. Among noble ones, it manifests in various ways, such as the śrāvakas directly realizing personal identitylessness; the pratyekabuddhas, in addition to that, the one half of phenomenal identitylessness that pertains to apprehended objects; and the bodhisattvas the freedom from all reference points of apprehender and apprehended, either partially or fully. The dharmakāya free from stains, which is endowed with twofold purity, is also the cause for the great and mighty sambhogakāya with its duration of infinite eons. SS (pp. 648–50) comments on verses 58–60 together, agreeing with Döl and RT on the first two lines of verse 58 but saying that the cause for these two to abide many eons is the great and mighty one. The causes for beings with great desires to live for eons are that they previously have protected other beings' lives, refrained from killing them, and given them food and medicine. Thus, by way of not observing these causes, one should engage for the sake of attaining the prajñā that is aware of suchness and variety.

752 This Sanskrit word has a wide range of meanings, such as imperishable, unalterable, syllable, letter, word, vowel, sound, and, in particular, the syllable OṂ.

753 LG (p. 40) and SC (p. 328) agree that, in brief, the dharmadhātu (wisdom) is the nature or very life-force of all phenomena in saṃsāra (afflicted phenomena) and nirvāṇa (pure phenomena). SC adds that pure phenomena are inseparably mingled with the dharmadhātu, thus being incorporated in it, whereas afflicted phenomena are present in it in a manner of being separable from it.

754 SC (pp. 328–29) says that both inexhaustible fruitions—saṃsāra and nirvāṇa—come from the inexhaustible cause that is the dharmadhātu. Under the influence of the condition of ignorance, one engages oneself for the sake of saṃsāra. But through the particular trait of the prajñā that realizes that nothing whatsoever appears, one engages oneself for the sake of pure phenomena, the inexhaustible fruition of the dharmadhātu. RT (p. 641) explains that one engages in realizing the dharmadhātu for the sake of the prajñā during subsequent attainment, which discriminates all phenomena that bear the nature of the dharmadhātu. Due to the particular trait of the degree of being able to realize the dharmadhātu without appearance, there is the trait of the degree of that discriminating wisdom unfolding. Döl (p. 150) states that the cause for the inexhaustible enlightened activity that engages in saṃsāra is the dharmakāya without appearance. Through that particular trait, the rūpakāyas engage in their activities for the sake of bringing forth the prajñā of those to be guided. LG (p.40) comments that the dharmadhātu free from stains, which is the fruition of the Tathāgata heart—the nature of phenomena without exhaustion or increase—is without the appearance of the latent tendencies of apprehender and apprehended. It is just through the particular trait of realizing this well or not that prajñā engages in an object that seems to have three degrees in terms of being superior or inferior (corresponding to the prajñās of śrāvakas, pratyekabuddhas, and bodhisattvas).

755 Verse 6.

756 Döl (p. 150) says it is not that Buddhas earlier have cast away saṃsāra and gone off somewhere far way, just to return later for the sake of sentient beings. Rather, not moving away from the world even a little bit, yet lacking the appearances of the six kinds of objects of the mistakenness of apprehender and apprehended, they are aware of reality just as it is—the true nature of saṃsāra. According to LG (p. 40), the first two lines of this verse teach that there is only one yāna ultimately. Apart from just the temporary fact that realization is gained in a swifter or slower way by bodhisattvas, śrāvakas, or pratyekabuddhas, in the end, they all attain buddhahood. On the latter two lines, LG and RT (p. 641) basically comment in the same way as Döl. SS (p. 650) states that the prajñā that is aware of suchness and variety does not conceive of near or far. It is nonconceptual and the six kinds of objects are not appearing or observable for it, being aware that they are empty of essence, just as it accords with the correct view. According to SC (p. 329), the gist of this is as follows. If one has the remedies to relinquish the stains, there is no need to search for enlightenment somewhere outside or far away. But if one does not use these remedies, enlightenment is not near, since the mere existence of the dharmadhātu is not enlightenment. You may wonder, "But isn't it necessary to assert this dharmadhātu wisdom as natural buddhahood?" That is indeed so, but this in itself does not qualify as actual buddhahood, since the three kāyas are not complete. "But aren't the three kāyas complete naturally?" They are indeed complete, but that too does not qualify as actual buddhahood, since these are not the kāyas that serve as the ultimate welfare of others. Therefore, what is called "natural buddhahood" refers to the cause of actual buddhahood. Otherwise, if actual buddhahood existed just through what is called "natural buddhahood," one would assert the philosophical system of the Sāṃkhyas. For then, during the time of sentient beings, buddhahood would reside in them in a nonmanifest way and would need to be made clearly manifest later through the power of the path.

757 Verse 10.

758 Verses 54–55. As Lindtner 1997 (p. 164) points out, all the verses of this text (with some interesting variants) are found in Chapter X of the *Laṅkāvatārasūtra* (the two verses above are X.256–57; ACIP KL0107@270A). As for the last line of verse 55, Nāgārjuna's *Bhāvanākrama*

says *de yis theg pa chen po mthong* ("sees the mahāyāna"), while DSC has *de yis theg chen mi mthong ngo* (the Tibetan versions of the *Laṅkāvatārasūtra* also have this negative). In his translation of the sūtra, Suzuki (1979, Prajñā Press, p. 247) says that most Sanskrit manuscripts have *na* ("not"), but that one has *sa* ("he"). B. Nanjio's edition (Bibliotheca Otaniensis 1. Kyoto: Otani University Press, 1923) also has *sa*. The above two verses are also quoted in Śāntarakṣita's own *Madhyamakālaṃkāravṛtti* (P5285; ACIP TD3885@79B) as well as in Kamalaśīla's *Madhyamakālaṃkārapañjikā* (P5286, fols. 137a–138a) and his first *Bhāvanākrama* (ACIP TD3915@033A), the latter two giving a detailed explanation (see Brunnhölzl 2004, pp. 300–302). In these three texts too, the last line appears and is commented on as in Nāgārjuna's *Bhāvanākrama*.

759 XI.17.

760 VII.8.

761 As was said before, to meet, study, and practice the dharma is just an expression of the latent tendencies of listening that are a natural outflow of one's own buddha nature, the causal condition. The teaching of the dharma is the natural outflow of the compassion of the Buddhas, the dominant or contributing condition. Fundamentally, all of this happens nowhere else and as nothing else than appearances in our own mind, which in this case are not stained by afflictions. As for wisdom dwelling in this body, the *Hevajratantra* (part 2, I.12) says:

> In the body, great wisdom dwells,
> Which has abandoned all thoughts,
> Pervades all entities,
> Dwelling in the body, yet not born from the body.

The Tantra of the *Completion of the Lion's Prowess* (Tib. seng ge rtsal rdzogs kyi rgyud; not in *Tengyur*) declares:

> In the bodies of all sentient beings,
> The shine of pure wisdom dwells.

The *Laṅkāvatārasūtra* (ACIP KL0107@135B) states: "As for the Tathāgata heart that the Bhagavat taught in the sūtra collection, the Bhagavat said that it is completely pure natural luminosity. Thus, since it is completely pure right from the beginning, this primordial complete purity is endowed with the thirty-two major marks and exists within the bodies of all sentient beings."

762 Buddhism makes a clear distinction between "person" (Skt. pudgala, Tib. gang zag) and "self" (Skt. ātman, Tib. bdag), which is important for understanding the notion of "lack of self." The "person" is understood to be just a label imputed onto the five skandhas, which is in itself not a problem or to be refuted. The notion of a "self," however, refers to a completely fictitious entity that we relate in one way or the other to the five skandhas. The root of saṃsāra is the clinging to that notion, which makes us behave accordingly in terms of what seems to benefit or harm this self, thus leading to karmic actions and suffering. Therefore, it is the clinging to a self that is to be scrutinized and relinquished.

763 For example, this is stated in the *Aṣṭāsāhasrikaprajñāpāramitāsūtra* (ACIP KD0012@3B; byang chub as the last entry) and the *Pañcaviṃśatisāhasrikaprajñāpāramitāsūtra* (ACIP KL0009-1@171A; *sangs rgyas kyi sa* as the last entry).

764 SC (p. 330) comments that one must rest in the yoga of realizing the two [kinds of] identitylessness, because childish beings think of the dharmadhātu—which serves as the ground for buddhahood, nirvāṇa, purity, permanence, and virtue—as the twofold ignorance of clinging to

an identity. LG (p. 41) glosses buddhahood as the nirvāṇa of the mahāyāna, which is the ground of purity, since the latent tendencies of the two obscurations are relinquished; of permanence, since the equality of saṃsāra and nirvāṇa is realized; and of virtue, since uncontaminated bliss arises. Childish beings think of apprehender and apprehended as two, but yogins of the mahāyāna rest in the yoga of their nonduality. For SS (pp. 651–53), the reason why yogins adopt wisdom is that buddhahood is the ground for purity, permanence, and virtue (the first two are glossed as in LG, and the third refers to natural virtue and purity). The reason why ignorance is to be left behind is that childish beings, despite the nonexistence of the two kinds of identity, superimpose and cling to them. Therefore, yogins rest in the wisdom that realizes the two kinds of identitylessness. The four notions of ordinary beings, who take the five skandhas to be pure, permanent, pleasant, and a self, are mistaken. Compared with these, the opposite notions of śrāvakas and pratyekabuddhas are unmistaken. But compared to the dharmakāya of the Buddhas, the latter are mistaken too, since the dharmakāya is endowed with the four pāramitās of genuine purity, permanence, bliss, and self. You may object that the dharmakāya is not tenable as a self, since it is taught that all phenomena are without a self. This is taught while having personal and phenomenal identitylessness in mind, but it is also stated that the dhātu free from the reference points of a self existing or not is the genuine self. As the *Uttaratantra* says: "The reference points of self and no self being utterly at peace is the genuine self" (I.37cd). SS adds further similar quotes from the *Mahāparinirvāṇasūtra* and the *Mahāyānasūtrālaṃkāra*.

765 Skt. vaśitāprāpta, Tib. dbang thob pa. This refers to the ten masteries of bodhisattvas over (1) lifespan, (2) mind, (3) necessities, (4) karma, (5) birth, (6) imaginative willpower, (7) aspiration prayers, (8) miraculous powers, (9) wisdom, and (10) dharma.

766 This is an abridged passage from the *Ratnagotravibhāgavyākhyā* (J 33; P5526, fol. 95a.5–b.2). The *Śrīmālādevīsūtra* is not mentioned by name there, and the passage as it stands in Asaṅga's text is not found in the available Tibetan and Chinese versions of that sūtra. It does, however, speak about all the topics mentioned in the above passage in different places (see Wayman, trans. 1974, pp. 87, 102, and so on).

767 XXIV.11. Awareness-mantras (Skt. vidyāmantra, Tib. rig sngags) can be used to propitiate mundane and supramundane deities in order to partake of their activity. If these mantras are used improperly, however, these deities might turn against the person who supplicates them.

768 Verse 31.

769 P781.

770 J 77; P5526, fol. 119a5–6.

771 SS (p. 654) says that this refers to what is called "unfolding/blooming" here.

772 Döl (p. 151) says that, since the dharmadhātu free from adventitious stains is nirvāṇa, the naturally abiding disposition—the dharmadhātu—growing and unfolding more and more through the progression of the ten bhūmis (the virtuous conditions of practicing the ten pāramitās), is the unfolding disposition. Therefore, just as the factors that obscure the new moon dwindle to the very same extent that it grows and unfolds, this is the reason for the dharmadhātu being referred to as the unfolding disposition. SS adds that this does not refer to some phase during which the dharmadhātu's essence would grow. GL (p. 33) says that the expansion that comes about through the roots of virtue that concord with the ten pāramitās is called "the unfolding disposition" or "correctly adopted disposition."

773 Skt. niryāṇa, Tib. nges par 'byung ba.

774 The phrase starting with "connecting" is tentative, since the Tibetan seems to be corrupt (DSC *gnas khyad par can dang/ 'brel pa gzugs med pa yangs mal 'jug pa*; emended to *gnas khyad par can dang 'brel la gzugs med pa la yang 'jug pa*). "The special abode" probably refers to any one of the five pure abodes of noble bodhisattvas above the three levels of mundane gods dwelling in the fourth dhyāna of the form realm. Since the uppermost of these five is the highest state within the form realm, it is called Akaniṣṭha (however, this is not to be mixed up with the "Richly Adorned Akaniṣṭha" just above it, which is a sambhogakāya realm). Or, "special abode" may indicate the mental state of this fourth dhyāna in general. The fourth dhyāna of that realm is the main meditative concentration cultivated by bodhisattvas, since it is special in not only being tranquil but also very lucid. Thus, it represents the kind of calm abiding that is most suitable as a foundation for performing the Buddhist vipaśyanā meditations on the two kinds of identitylessness. Since the formless absorptions are much more dull, they are normally not cultivated as supports for such vipaśyanā meditations. However, in order to enhance their skill in samādhi and the stability of their insights, advanced bodhisattvas on the bhūmis train in accomplishing vipaśyanā even in such dull samādhis.

775 XVIII.39.

776 Tib. mos pa. In the context of the pāramitā of power, this term probably refers to one of the ten masteries of bodhisattvas mentioned above. It means that they can manifest whatever is beneficial to others through their sheer mental power, including filling the entire universe with an infinite number of Buddhas.

777 SC (p. 331) summarizes verses 66–68 by saying that the first three pāramitās unfold the accumulation of merit. Through that, temporarily, bodhisattvas see rūpakāyas, and finally, their own rūpakāyas are accomplished. The second three pāramitās unfold the accumulation of wisdom. Through that, temporarily, bodhisattvas see the dharmakāya pure of adventitious stains within their own mind streams, and finally, their ultimate kāya is accomplished. The last four pāramitās unfold the accumulation of the full capacity of the wisdom of dharmadhātu. Through that, temporarily, bodhisattvas do not become weary of promoting the welfare of others, and finally, their own full-fledged enlightened activity is accomplished. These ten pāramitās are called "the unfolding disposition" because they are the disposition that makes the full capacity of the naturally abiding disposition unfold.

778 These two accomplishments are explained in detail as the seventh and eighth points of the first topic—the knowledge of all aspects—of the *Abhisamayālaṃkāra*.

779 V.6–7ab.

780 Except for DSC and RT, all other commentaries interpret this to mean bodhisattva.

781 I.19ab.

782 In due order, these three terms (as explained in *Dharmadharmatāvibhāga* lines 276–87) refer to the practice of the pāramitās on the paths of accumulation and preparation ("determination" there is *nges par 'byed ba*; DSC *nges par rtogs pa*), the first bhūmi (the path of seeing), and the remaining nine bhūmis (the path of cultivation).

783 I.13.

784 I.1.

785 IV.34cd.

786 ACIP TD3793@113B (DSC paraphrase).

787 DSC *gzhan du ba nyid; Dharmadharmatāvibhāga*/DP *gtan du.*

788 DSC *ji snyed.*

789 Lines 228–33.

790 P819.

791 Döl (p. 153), SS (p. 657) and RT (p. 643) all agree that bodhisattvas on the path of preparation see a tiny bit of the dharmakāya, since they have a tiny bit of a clear appearance of the dharmadhātu. SC (p. 333) comments on "seeing a tiny bit of buddhakāya" as meaning that ordinary beings, śrāvakas, pratyekabuddhas, and bodhisattvas who have newly entered the path see the dharmakāya just in the manner of an object-generality (that is, a conceptual mental image), since they have confidence in the qualities of the Tathāgata. LG (p. 44–48) agrees that bodhisattvas on the paths of accumulation and preparation see the dharmakāya just in that manner. He then elaborates that the type of mind that arises in meditative equipoise during these two paths is self-awareness but not yogic valid cognition. On these paths, similar to seeing [a part of] the sun between clouds, it is possible to realize a mere absence of thoughts free from reference points, but this is not capable of stopping one's clinging to real existence during the phase of subsequent attainment. Therefore, this kind of realization is not yogic direct valid cognition, since it is unlike the yogic valid cognition of the noble ones (which is capable of stopping such clinging to real existence). Since ordinary beings have to rely mainly on conceptions, they work with object-generalities involving great aspiration. As for noble ones, during subsequent attainment, they too need to evaluate the nature of phenomena through aspiring for it by way of object-generalities, but it is not that they realize the nature of phenomena only through object-generalities. LG also refers to Sakya Paṇḍita and other early scholars and siddhas as having stated that the realization of someone on the path of preparation is self-awareness. When most of these masters refute other assertions, this is in order to put an end to the wrong ideas of those fools who, by explicitly asserting that this realization on the path of preparation is already yogic direct cognition, consequently just point to a path of seeing that lacks any qualities of relinquishment and realization. However, it is not that these masters absolutely do not assert any nonconceptual wisdom in ordinary beings. The Eighth Karmapa's commentary on the *Abhisamayālaṃkāra* (Mi bskyod rdo rje n.d., pp. I.182–83) says something very similar: The point when the freedom from all characteristics of apprehender and apprehended is directly realized in this way is the path of seeing, which has the character of yogic direct valid cognition. These meditative equipoises of the path of preparation are unmistaken self-aware direct valid cognitions that are approximately concordant with the unmistaken wisdom that lacks the duality of apprehender and apprehended. This is as it is taught in the [*Madhyāntavibhāga*]: "Approximately concordant and yet mistaken, . . ." [IV.12] During the [path of preparation], these meditative equipoises are not something other than self-aware direct valid cognition, because both what is aware and what it is aware of arise as the nature of a single clear and aware experience. The way in which such wisdom that lacks the duality of apprehender and apprehended is more eminent than the view of the pratyekabuddhas is stated by the earlier Tibetan masters as follows: "It has to be explained that the pratyekabuddhas realize merely the emptiness of an apprehender and apprehended that are substantially other. However, they do not realize true reality that is empty of [any] duality of apprehender and apprehended."

792 On the first bhūmi, bodhisattvas attain twelve times a hundred qualities: In one single moment, (1) they see the faces of one hundred Buddhas, (2) are blessed by them, (3) send forth one hundred emanations, (4) live for one hundred eons, (5) engage through wisdom from beginning to end of one hundred eons, (6) are absorbed in and rise from one hundred samādhis,

(7) mature one hundred sentient beings, (8) shake one hundred realms of existence, (9) illuminate one hundred realms of existence with light, (10) open one hundred doors of dharma, 11) display one hundred of their own body, and (12) display one hundred excellent retinues that surround each of these bodies. Here, "to engage from beginning to end of one hundred eons" (5) means that bodhisattvas, for the sake of helping sentient beings to become free from their negative actions, demonstrate the way in which ordinary beings wander in saṃsāra through their karma. Through shaking worldly realms (8), they induce aspiration in those to be guided. Through seeing the illumination of realms (9), sentient beings are matured. Opening one hundred doors of dharma (10) means that bodhisattvas, for the sake of ripening their own insight, reflect about the meaning of the various specifications of dharma (Dpal sprul 'jigs med chos kyi dbang po 1997, p. 162).

793 DSC omits the fourth bhūmi.

794 These numbers vary greatly in different sources, the main sūtras being the *Buddhāvataṃsakasūtra* and the *Daśabhūmikasūtra*. SS (p. 657) says that, though the dharmakāya's own essence is without increase or decrease, it is seen by bodhisattvas on the bhūmis as if it gradually increases. However, what increases is just the mind that sees the dharmakāya but not the dharmakāya itself. RT (p. 643) comments that, here, "dharmakāya" refers to the relinquishment of obscurations, which is the manner of seeing the nature of phenomena becoming free from adventitious stains but not the way of seeing its natural purity.

795 SC (pp. 333–36) summarizes as follows. The phase when dharmadhātu wisdom is not purified from any afflictions at all is called "sentient being." The phase when it has become pure to some degree but the aspiring bodhicitta has not arisen, is called "śrāvaka" or "pratyekabuddha." The phase when this bodhicitta has arisen and the dharmadhātu is realized merely through confidence but not seen directly, is called a "person who aspires to the supreme yāna." The phase of the process of eliminating a part up to all of the cognitive obscurations that obscure the dharmadhātu is called "bodhisattva." Once all obscuring stains have been completely purified, this is called "perfect buddhahood." Therefore, it is from the phase when a part of the dharmakāya has been attained onward that the name "bodhisattva" is applied. Otherwise, if all sentient beings had the actual dharmakāya, the individual bases for applying the terms "bodhisattva," "sentient being," and "Buddha" would be indefinite. Also, merely being pure of some portion of the afflictions is not sufficient for presenting the phase of bodhisattvas as a part of the dharmakāya, because both this kind of purity and generating bodhicitta for supreme enlightenment must come together. The reason for this is that one is not able to present the basic element as "the Buddha heart" if bodhicitta has not arisen. This is because there are still the four obscurations—aversion to the dharma, views about a self, fear of saṃsāra's suffering, and not considering the welfare of sentient beings—that prevent the basic element being presented as this Heart. Starting with the phase when this Heart is seen directly, one can be said to possess it because from that point onward, the true nature of one's mind may be presented as "Tathāgata" and "dharmakāya." The meaning of "Tathāgata" refers to having realized suchness directly. Therefore, it is only those persons for whom buddhahood and being a Tathāgata have become their Heart that can be said to "possess that Heart." However, to give the nature of buddhahood and the Tathāgata—emptiness—the name "the Heart of buddhahood and the Tathāgata," and then to explain that the inseparability of this and the true nature of sentient beings is the sense in which the statement "All sentient beings have the Tathāgata heart" is to be understood, is the great Ngog Lotsāwa's position. But I do not think it is a good one, since through this alone all five purposes of teaching that all sentient beings have the Buddha heart are not realized. You may wonder, "But is it not noble Asaṅga's explanation that, from the first bhūmi onward, one sees that all sentient beings too possess the Buddha heart?"

What he expresses by that is the following. From the first bhūmi onward, when one sees a part of the dharmakāya in one's own mind stream, one sees that the dharmadhātu of the minds of all sentient beings, just like one's own true nature, is suitable to become free from stains, because at that time, one sees that they all have the disposition for that. Otherwise, if one always just takes the above explanation literally, then perfect buddhahood would actually dwell in all sentient beings, because it is seen from the first bhūmi onward that it dwells in them. You may object, "But in that case, it is not justified to explain that the dharmadhātu, when pure of stains, is that Buddha heart and when impure is not." This is not unjustified, because in order for the dharmadhātu to be presented as the "Buddha heart," all ten aspects of its presentation that are given in (the first chapter of) the *Uttaratantra* must be complete; and for them to be complete, it must already be pure of a part of the four stains mentioned above, and the conditions that awaken the basic element's power must have caused that element to unfold somewhat. Thus, during the phase of the ten bhūmis, there are distinct portions of dharmakāya, Tathāgata, and buddhahood, but they are not fully complete. Therefore, it is difficult to present this phase as the fully qualified dharmakāya and so on. For example, in the one portion of the moon that appears on the first day of a lunar month, all its fifteen portions that appear until the full moon are not complete. Hence, it cannot be presented as the full orb of the moon. "However, isn't it explained that all sentient beings have the Buddha heart but just don't see it by themselves?" For as long as they do not see that it exists in them, it cannot be presented as their having it, just like the honey in a lotus garden. GL (p. 122) comments on verses 75–76 that it is only the factor of the dharmadhātu being more or less pure of adventitious stains that accounts for the seeming increase in qualities while progressing on the path, but the dharmadhātu itself never turns into something whose nature undergoes any change. This is just as when the space confined within a house becomes vast unrestrained space once this house collapses. However, just through that, space does not become something whose nature changes.

796 All these signs on the paths of preparation, seeing, and meditation are discussed in detail in the eighth point ("the signs of irreversible learners") of the fourth topic ("the training in completing all aspects") of the *Abhisamayālaṃkāra*.

797 Skt. Catuḥsmṛtyupasthāna (Tib. dran pa nye bar bzhag pa bzhi), catvāri samyakprahāṇāni (Tib. yang dag spong ba bzhi), catvāra ṛddhipādāḥ (rdzu 'phrul gyi rkang pa bzhi), pañcendriyāṇi (dbang po lnga), and pañcabalāni (Tib. stobs lnga). The first three sets belong to the path of accumulation and the latter two to the path of preparation. Together with the seven branches of enlightenment (Skt. saptasaṃbodhyaṅgāni, Tib. byang chub kyi yan lag bdun) on the path of seeing and the eightfold path of the noble ones (Skt. āryāṣṭāṅgamārga, Tib. 'phags pa'i lam yan lag brgyad) on the path of cultivation, they make up the thirty-seven dharmas that concord with enlightenment.

798 LG (p. 49) glosses "the ground of darkness" as a portion of the ālaya-consciousness, the ground of the latent tendencies of saṃsāra. "The ground of brightness" is a portion of mirror-like wisdom, the ground of all excellent qualities.

799 XX.32.

800 Skt. saṃyojana, Tib. kun sbyor. These are the views about a real personality, the view of holding ethics and spiritual conduct as paramount, and doubt.

801 This refers to the above-mentioned twelve times a hundred qualities.

802 V.41–42. The last line means that bodhisattvas on the first bhūmi usually take rebirth as a cakravartin king that rules over the southern continent of Jambudvīpa in the ancient Indian

four-continent world (in translating DSC's quotes from the *Ratnāvalī*, I have generally followed the text's critical edition in Hopkins 1998).

803 XX.33ab.

804 DSC omits this line.

805 IV.43–44. The precious seven attributes of a cakravartin are his precious wheel, jewel, minister, horse, elephant, queen, and general. On the second bhūmi, bodhisattvas usually take birth as cakravartin kings who rule over all four continents of the ancient Indian world-system.

806 XX.33cd.

807 IV.45–46. Bodhisattvas on the third bhūmi mostly take rebirth as the god Indra, who rules over the second heaven of the desire gods called "The Thirty-three" (Skr. trayastriṃśā, Tib. sum cu rtsa gsum).

808 XX.34.

809 This is the third heaven of the desire gods (Skr. yāmā, Tib. 'thab bral).

810 IV. 47–48.

811 GL (p. 259) comments that the reason for the name of this bhūmi is that bodhisattvas engage in all kinds of activities, such as sciences and sports, but still manage to triumph over the afflictions difficult to overcome that proliferate [during such activities].

812 XX.35.

813 This the fourth heaven of the desire gods.

814 IV. 49–50.

815 Skt. abhimukhī, Tib. mngon du gyur pa/mngon du phyogs pa.

816 In line four, SS (p. 661) also has "profound arising and ceasing," commenting that there is no arising and ceasing ultimately, but on the level of seeming reality, phenomena cease right upon having arisen. Since this is difficult to realize, profound actuality is faced. All other commentators have "arising and ceasing exhausted." SC (p. 338) glosses this as the bodhisattvas having gained mastery over the principle of dependent origination, which is difficult to fathom, thus facing both saṃsāra and nirvāṇa on this bhūmi. LG (p. 50) says that all mundane and supramundane excellences are gathered in such a manner that the progressively superior realizations incorporate the inferior. Through realizing the equality of saṃsāra and nirvāṇa, the arising and ceasing of saṃsāra are exhausted, and the bodhisattvas directly face the qualities of the level of buddhahood.

817 XX.36.

818 Skr. nirmāṇarati, Tib. 'phrul dga.' The fifth heaven of the desire gods, where the gods enjoy the sense pleasures that they themselves have emanated at will.

819 IV.51–52.

820 SC (p. 338) says that, on this bhūmi, the bodhisattvas' incessant flow of entering into and rising from the dharmadhātu resembles a wheel. Ever playing with a web of wisdom-light means that they have attained the unimpeded power to perform such entering and rising.

821 XX.37ab.

822 Skr. paranirmitavaśavartin, Tib. gzhan 'phrul dbang byed. The sixth heaven of the desire gods, in which the gods have the power to even enjoy the sense pleasures emanated by their fellow gods.

823 IV. 53–54.

824 P760.38.

825 SC (338–39) says here: On this bhūmi, if bodhisattvas do not rise from resting in meditative equipoise within the dharmadhātu, they have the power to manifest the dharmakāya, in which the cognitive obscurations are relinquished (that is, the completion of their own welfare). However, since they have not yet fully completed the accumulation of merit, they do not have the power to promote the welfare of others through the two rūpakāyas in an effortless, spontaneous, and uninterrupted way. By considering this possible flaw, the Buddhas make these bodhisattvas rise from their meditative equipoise of cessation. This flaw exists already from the first bhūmi onward, if bodhisattvas do not rise from the dharmadhātu. But since they always have some unrelinquished afflictions on the impure bhūmis, despite not needing to rise from the dharmadhātu, bodhisattvas are always capable of doing so. On the eighth bhūmi, since all afflictive obscurations are relinquished, without any prior impulse of thinking, "I should rise from this meditative equipoise," it is possible that these bodhisattvas cannot rise from it through their own power. Therefore, the Buddhas need to make them come out of it.

826 XX.37cd.

827 Here, this name does not refer to the well-known god (Mahā)brahmā himself, but to those gods who are rulers over one thousand four-continent worlds (a chiliocosm) and reside in the heaven called "Brahmā." This is the first of the three heavens of the first dhyāna level in the realm of form gods, with all three of these heavens being part of Mahābrahmā's retinue.

828 IV.55–56. DSC mistakenly replaces these last two lines by the last two lines of IV.58.

829 Skt. pratisaṃvedanā, Tib. so so yang dag par rig pa. These are usually presented as a set of four. (1) The discriminating awareness of the dharma is to teach the eighty-four thousand doors of dharma as various remedial means in accordance with the different ways of thinking of sentient beings. (2) The discriminating awareness of meaning is to know the meanings that are expressed by the words and statements about the general characteristics of phenomena—impermanence, suffering, emptiness, and identitylessness—and their ultimate characteristic—the lack of arising and ceasing. (3) The discriminating awareness of semantic explanation (Skt. nirukti, Tib. nges tshig) is not to be ignorant about any of all beings' designations and languages as well as their meanings. (4) The discriminating awareness of self-confidence (Skt. pratibhāna, Tib. spobs pa) is to be unobstructed in teaching the dharma and cutting through doubts.

830 XX.38ab.

831 This refers to those gods who are rulers over one million four-continent worlds (a dichiliocosm), residing in "Brahmāpurohita," the second of the three heavens of the first dhyāna level.

832 IV.57–58. DSC omits the last two lines of IV.58.

833 XX.38cd.

834 IV.59–60. Bodhisattvas on this bhūmi usually take birth in one of the five pure abodes (Skt. śuddhāvāsa, Tib. gnas gtsang)—the highest heavens of the form realm—as the god Maheśvara (better known as Śiva), who rules over a trichiliocosm.

835 II.14–16 (note that the Tibetan translation of the *Madhyāntavibhāga* inserts two verses from Vasubandhu's commentary before these verses, thus counting them as II.16–18).

836 These are treated in detail as one of the difficult subjects under point eight ("the accomplishment of engagement") of the first topic ("The knowledge of all aspects") of the *Abhisamayālaṃkāra* (I.49–71).

837 There is no sūtra with this name in the *Kangyur*. However, in the *Sarvapuṇyasamucchaya-samādhisūtra* (P802), there is the story of the super-athlete Vimalatejasvarga, who attempts to challenge the physical powers of the Buddha.

838 DSC *bzhi.*

839 Vindhya is the range of hills that separate northern and middle India from the Deccan, and the elephants there are considered to be especially powerful.

840 All of the above are names of certain divine beings in the first heaven of the desire realm, called "The Four Great Kings."

841 In Hindu cosmology, this is the son of Mahāpuruṣa, the latter being the primeval man as the soul and original source of the universe. Also, Nārāyaṇa is variously identified as Brahmā, Viṣṇu, or Kṛṣṇa.

842 In general, the term *mahāpuruṣa* also designates someone who has the thirty-two major marks (such as the rūpakāyas of a Buddha and cakravartins), but here it specifically refers to said primeval man.

843 There are two kinds of pratyekabuddhas, the parrotlike and the rhinoceroslike. Similar to these animals, the former live and practice together in groups, while the latter stay alone.

844 III.2–3ab. DSC omits lines III.2ab.

845 DSC *bzhi pa.*

846 Döl (p. 155) comments that the state of the dharmadhātu being with stains has changed into its being without stains. LG (p. 52) says that the first two lines of verse refer to bearing the ultimate fruit of enjoying the abode of the buddhadharmas, such as the ten powers. The final fundamental change of state of the entire ālaya-consciousness including its accompanying mental factors is called the "dharmakāya of a Buddha." Someone may argue, "Does the omniscient wisdom of Buddhas exist or not? If it exists, does it know the phenomena of saṃsāra? If it does know them, it follows that it entails mistakenness, but if it does not, the Buddhas would not be omniscient." Though this wisdom is beyond any reference points ultimately, conventionally, it needs to be asserted as belonging to the set of existents. However, it is difficult to gauge through the minds of ordinary beings. If they are already incapable of, for example, gauging the mind of the waking state through being in a dream, forget about the level of a Buddha with its wisdom of the fundamental change of state. SC (p. 340) glosses the first line of verse as the dharmakāya of the buddhadharmas that are profound and the second as the rūpakāyas enjoying the dharmas that are vast. He then discusses the difference between the notion of "fundamental change of state" being refuted in Nāgārjuna's *Bodhicittavivaraṇa* and being explained here. The *Bodhicittavivaraṇa* (verses 32–35) refutes the ālaya-consciousness, which is the abode of all that is to be relinquished, thus refuting the explanation of certain Yogācāras that the meaning of "fundamental change of state" is that the ālaya-consciousness was the abode of these factors before, but then has turned into something that is not their abode later. In this text here, Nāgārjuna does not say that "change of state" refers to being without qualities before, while pos-

sessing qualities later. In brief, the essence of the ten bhūmis is the dharmakāya being pure of the respective portions of adventitious stains, and the essence of that is dharmadhātu wisdom. SS (pp. 665–68) agrees with DSC and Döl and then also discusses the notion of "fundamental change of state." Quoting the *Suvarṇaprabhāsottamasūtra* (P174–176), the *Uttaratantra*, and Candragomin, he says that the dharmakāya is obtained from the naturally abiding disposition and the two rūpakāyas from the unfolding disposition. Implicitly, these sources speak about a fundamental change of state in terms of relinquishment and a fundamental change of state in terms of nature. The fundamental change of state of the ālaya-consciousness, mentation, and the six operating consciousnesses in the above texts is of the latter kind. Upon the objection that Nāgārjuna does not assert the notion of "fundamental change of state," since his *Bodhicittavivaraṇa* refutes it, SS (like SC) says that this is just a refutation of said notion as held by the Mere Mentalists, while Nāgārjuna obviously speaks about a "fundamental change of state" here in his *Dharmadhātustava*. Another objection adduced is that Mādhyamikas do not assert an ālaya-consciousness and that the assertion of eight consciousnesses is the system of the Mere Mentalists, it thus being untenable that the fundamental change of state of the ālaya and so on is taught here. SS says this is not correct, since Nāgārjuna's *Bodhicittavivaraṇa* refutes a really existent ālaya as held by the Vijñaptivādins, but then says that an illusionlike likeness of it appropriates the three realms (verses 32–35). Also, since Candrakīrti's *Madhyamakāvatāra* refutes an ālaya that resembles the notion of a creator like Īśvara, it is well known everywhere that master Candrakīrti does not assert an ālaya-consciousness. However, he just does not assert an ālaya-consciousness that is a real entity as held by the Vijñaptivādins. But that does not mean that he asserts that there is absolutely no ālaya-consciousness, for his commentary on the *Guhyasamāja*—which is the central yidam-practice of master Nāgārjuna and his spiritual heirs—speaks about the eight consciousnesses and their purification. Also, master Haribhadra says in his commentary on the *Prajñāpāramitāsaṃcayagāthā* (P5196): "The essence of the ālaya-consciousness, which serves as the cause, is the kāya that has the nature of mirrorlike wisdom." {I could not locate this sentence in Haribhadra's text, but it does speak about the ālaya-consciousness (ACIP TD3972@069B) in the context of the "momentary training" (topic 7 of the *Abhisamayālaṃkāra*).} Therefore, it is not necessarily the case that Mādhyamikas do not assert an ālaya-consciousness. {In this context, it may be added that Bhāvaviveka's *Madhyamakaratnapradīpa* (P5254, fol. 358b.3–4), in the context of bodhisattvas passing from the tenth bhūmi to buddhahood (quoting *Dharmadhātustava* 91–96), uses the typical (Yogācāra) triad of mind, mentation, and consciousness, which represents the eight consciousnesses. He says: Right upon that, . . . being free from mind, mentation, and consciousness, in the expanse of suchness, everything without exception is nondifferent and of one taste. This is called "buddhahood."} The final objection here is that Mādhyamikas do not assert self-awareness (rang rig), as it is refuted in the *Bodhicittavivaraṇa* (verses 36–39), the *Bodhicaryāvatāra* (IX.17–24), and other texts. SS says that all of these refutations negate the position of the Vijñaptivādins, who assert a really existent consciousness that is aware of itself, but that does not mean that Mādhyamikas absolutely do not assert self-awareness, since Nāgārjuna speaks about it in verse 56 of our text here. {The last comment needs to be taken with a grain of salt, since the Tibetan of Nāgārjuna's text—also in verses 29 and 46—consistently says *so so rang rig* and never just *rang rig*. As explained in the introduction on terminology, these two terms cannot simply or necessarily be equated, especially not in the case of a translated Sanskrit original.}

847 These are nonarising, nonceasing, primordial peace, natural nirvāṇa, and lack of nature.

848 The change of state of the eight consciousnesses into the four wisdoms (or five, if the dharmadhātu is presented as dharmadhātu wisdom) is treated in detail in Rangjung Dorje's NY

and its commentaries as well as, more briefly, in his AC (fols. 99a–103b).

849 X.4–7; P5549, fols. 44a.6–45a.6 (the translation follows DP, DSC slightly varies).

850 Skt. upādānaskandha, Tib. nyer len gyi phung po.

851 DSC *dri mas gtan ma yin pa* (em. *dri ma'i rten ma yin pa*).

852 DSC *ye shes* (em. *yi ge*).

853 DSC *gang* (em. *ngag*).

854 II.32–33ab.

855 SC (p. 340) says that the latent tendencies of saṃsāra are conceivable, since upon consideration with discriminating prajñā, one is able to understand that they are of one taste with emptiness. The dharmadhātu is inconceivable, since it is beyond the range of speech and the senses. Nevertheless, this does not stand in the way of praising it. Conventionally, one may bow to and praise whatever of the following two is suitable—either the conventional term "dharmadhātu" that is to be realized through the mental consciousness by way of an object-generality or the actual dharmadhātu that is beyond all knowing and expression. So this verse does not teach that the dharmadhātu is to be realized by the mental consciousness, since the latter only knows generalities, which is not what is to be realized here. In brief, the words "whatever is suitable" stand for both the dharmadhātu during the phase of engagement through aspiration, which can be realized by way of mere confidence, and the dharmadhātu once the bhūmis have been attained, which is directly seen by way of personally experienced wisdom. LG (pp. 52–54) comments that buddhahood—the freedom from latent tendencies—is inconceivable, while apprehender and apprehended—the latent tendencies of saṃsāra—can be grasped by the minds of ordinary beings. Thus, buddhahood means that all mistakenness has stopped. Someone may argue, "Then it would not be omniscience, [since it does not perceive saṃsāra]." [Merely] seeing that mistakenness, which is not established ultimately, does not exist is not the realization of true reality. But on the other hand, if mistaken appearances existed even from the perspective of a Tathāgata's seeing, they would not be established as mistaken appearances. "This is just the meaning of apprehender and apprehended being without difference [as in Yogācāra] but not the meaning of the lack of appearance [as in Madhyamaka]." Well, then it would follow that for persons who are freed from the disease of blurred vision, the strands of hair that they saw before now appear as the nonduality of apprehender and apprehended. Also, take those beings who have just awoken from sleep or been freed from the disease of blurred vision and happen to see in a [—relatively speaking—] unmistaken way [that is, not seeing dream appearances or strands of hair]. It would absurdly follow [from your objection] that they all go blind right at that moment, since they do not see any [dream appearances or] strands of hair. "In that case, this contradicts what is taught as the union of appearance and emptiness, which means that being empty is not obscured by appearance and appearance is not obscured by being empty." There is no contradiction. As for the meaning of what is taught as union—in the sense of the aspect that is the inseparability of the aspect of appearance (saṃsāra) and the aspect of being empty (nirvāṇa)—when taking the perspective of sentient beings on the level of seeming reality, for their minds, which sometimes grasp the two realities, appearance and emptiness appear as different. But this is just their subjective mode of apprehension, since neither empty nor nonempty are established ultimately. When having the basic nature (the nonnominal ultimate) in mind, what is taught as union (the aspect of being inseparable) is taught with the implication that, during the time of meditative equipoise [of noble ones], all reference points of any mode of apprehension have ceased. However, this does not mean that they cognize mistaken appear-

ances. This is just as in the example of people with blurred vision. While these persons are not yet freed from this disease, when a physician points out that the strands of hair that they see are just due to this disease, at times, the persons may already think, "These strands of hair do not exist ultimately." However, once they are relieved from that disease, they are also liberated from any mode of apprehension as to whether such strands of hair exist or not. As Candrakīrti says in his commentary on the *Yuktiṣaṣṭikā*: "Also the two realities are [presented] from the perspective of the seeming." His *Madhyamakāvatāra* (VI.29) declares:

> Some mistaken nature, such as strands of hair,
> Is imagined under the influence of blurred vision,
> While its actual nature, as seen by pure eyes, is true reality.
> You should understand this [distinction between the two realities] in the same way.

A sūtra says:

> The ultimate nature is just a single reality,
> But some call it "the four realities."

{One could add here verse 17 of Nāgārjuna's *Mahāyānaviṃśikā*:

> Just as when awakening, one does not see
> The objects experienced in a dream,
> Upon awakening from the sleep of the darkness of ignorance,
> Saṃsāra is no longer seen.}

As the dharmadhātu is beyond the range of speech and senses, through relying on the stainless words of the Tathāgata, it is something to be realized as a mere object-generality by the mental consciousness. Thus, I bow to and praise whatever is suitable—either what is inconceivable (the dharmadhātu just as it is), or what is conceivable (its mere object-generality).

As for line 90c, RT (p. 646) quotes Nāgārjuna's *Ratnāvalī* IV.64ab:

> You may wonder, "Through what is [true reality] seen?"
> Conventionally, it is said to be the mind.

On line 90d, RT comments that both the dharmadhātu (the cause for attaining buddhahood) and its result (buddhahood) are worthy of praise. Döl (p. 155) says that there is nothing in the dharmakāya that is unsuitable, such as ultimate worlds and their inhabitants.

856 II.33cd.

857 Lines 493–94.

858 This refers to the king of all gems, the wish-fulfilling jewel.

859 This is both a name for the wish-fulfilling jewel and the wish-fulfilling tree.

860 A particular precious gem.

861 Döl (p. 155) says that the giant lotus is the flower of the dharmadhātu, that is, a pure self-appearance of wisdom. SC (p. 342) and LG (p. 56) provide an abbreviated version of the explanation in the *Daśabhūmikasūtra* (P761.31; a part of the *Avataṃsakasūtra*), which says that the bodhisattvas on the tenth bhūmi dwell on a throne that has the size of a million trichiliocosms and is ornamented by many jeweled lotuses. This throne is surrounded by as many lotuses as there are atoms in a million trichiliocosms, on which the bodhisattvas on the other nine bhūmis sit.

862 III.5–6.

863 III.8.

864 The Sanskrit *vaiśāradya* means self-confidence, expertise, wisdom, or infallibility.

865 Lit. "those who toil" (Tib. dge sbyong). Originally, this was a term for all mendicants of nonbrahmanic origin who followed any kind of spiritual path not relying on the Vedas. In Buddhist literature, it came to be mainly used for Buddhist monks, whether mendicants or not.

866 III.11–13.

867 This sūtra is better known under the latter part of its title, that is, the *Dhāraṇīśvararājaparipṛcchāsūtra* (P814).

868 SC (p. 342) relates all the qualities described in verses 94–95 to bodhisattvas on the tenth bhūmi. Both SC and SS (p. 673) gloss "buddhadharmas without reference points" as the qualities of a Buddha lacking any identifiable characteristics.

869 See under verse 54.

870 These are the four means to attract the beings to be guided on the path (Skt. Catuḥsaṃgrahavastu, Tib. bsdu ba'i dngos po bzhi).

871 DSC *phyag ring* PD *phyag ris.*

872 DSC omits lines 4–5 of this verse.

873 DSC omits this line.

874 DSC conflates the last two lines into the single line *seng ge'i 'gram 'dra thub dkar 'gyur.*

875 II.77–96. Unlike in the context of describing the physical strength of a rūpakāya above, here, the term Mahāpuruṣa refers to a being who possesses these thirty-two marks.

876 III.2–8.

877 As for "the full moon surrounded by stars," Döl (p. 156) identifies it as the two accumulations of merit and wisdom; SC (p. 342) as the bodhisattvas on the tenth bhūmi, being surrounded by a retinue of bodhisattvas on the other nine bhūmis; SS (p. 674) as the kāya that is adorned with the major and minor marks and surrounded by pure retinues as the recipients of its enlightened activity, such as teaching them the dharma; LG (p. 57) as the Buddha's qualities of perfect relinquishment and realization, surrounded by the bodhisattvas on the tenth bhūmi; and RT (p. 647) as buddhahood—the fruition of the two previously gathered accumulations—surrounded by these two.

878 III.26.

879 DSC has *khye'u rin chen gyi zhus pa'i mdo* instead of the usual *bu mo rin chen gyi zhus pa'i mdo* (the *Ratnādārikāsūtra* is the *Uttaratantra's* main source for the qualities of a Buddha).

880 This was the name of Buddha Śākyamuni while dwelling in the heaven of Tuṣita before his birth on earth.

881 Döl (p. 156) and SS (p. 674) say that the Buddha's hands in this empowerment are like a sun that dispels the darkness of ignorance. Based on the *Daśabhūmikasūtra*, SC (pp. 342, 343), SS (pp. 671–73), and LG (pp. 57–58, 59) elaborate that countless light rays radiate from the soles, the kneecaps, the navels, the ribs, and the palms of these bodhisattvas on the tenth bhūmi, which gradually illuminate the realms of hell-beings, hungry ghosts, animals, humans,

gods, and asuras, pacifying their sufferings. Countless light rays from the bodhisattvas' shoulders, backs, necks, and mouths illuminate the śrāvakas, pratyekabuddhas, and bodhisattvas—from those who generate bodhicitta for the first time up to those on the ninth bhūmi—in the ten directions, making them gradually practice the gate that illuminates the dharma, peaceful samādhis, and the various approaches of means and prajñā. The countless light rays that issue from the ūrṇā-hair of the bodhisattvas outshine all māras in the ten directions and illuminate the bodhisattvas that receive empowerment, melting into their bodies. Then, from the crowns of the heads of these bodhisattvas, light rays equal in number to the atoms of countless millions of trichiliocosms radiate, illuminating all the maṇḍalas of the Tathāgatas in the ten directions, circling the universe ten times, and forming a maṇḍala of a web of light rays in the sky above, thus venerating all Tathāgatas, promoting the welfare of sentient beings, and finally melting into the soles of the Tathāgatas. Through this, the victors and their children see that the time for the empowerment of these bodhisattvas has come. All the countless bodhisattvas on the first nine bhūmis approach, gaze at, and venerate these bodhisattvas, entering many thousand samādhis. From the endless knots, the vajras, and the auspicious signs of the bodhisattvas who are to receive empowerment, a single light ray—called "victory over the enemies of the māras"—streams forth, surrounded by many millions of light rays, all illuminating the ten directions and displaying infinite magical feats. Through these rays melting back into the bodhisattvas' endless knots, vajras, and auspicious signs, their power increases greatly. From the ūrṇā-hairs of the Tathāgatas, a single light ray—called "being endowed with the clairvoyance of omniscience" and surrounded by countless other light rays—illuminates the ten directions, circles the universe ten times, pacifies the lower realms, and outshines all māras. Finally, it melts simultaneously into the crowns of the heads of the bodhisattvas on the tenth bhūmi, with its surrounding light rays melting into the crowns of the heads of the bodhisattvas in their retinues. All these bodhisattvas thus attain many thousands of samādhis that they had not attained before. As mentioned above, Bhāvaviveka's *Madhyamakaratnapradīpa* (fol. 358a.1–358b.8) quotes verses 91–96 in the context of bodhisattvas passing from the tenth bhūmi to buddhahood. He says: When mighty [bodhisattvas] in their last life on the tenth bhūmi look at sentient beings, they see that there is no decrease [in their number] and think . . . "Without having manifested the dharmakāya, I am not able to lead sentient beings out [of saṃsāra]. Therefore, I will manifest the dharmakāya." After that [thought], they are empowered by the Tathāgatas of the ten directions and thus attain the qualities of a Buddha, such as the ten powers, in a complete way. This very point is stated by master [Nāgārjuna in his *Dharmadhātustava*] . . . Right upon that, just as the sunlit autumn sky at noon free from dust, all the dust of characteristics is no more. Being free from mind, mentation, and consciousness, in the expanse of suchness, everything without exception is nondifferent and of one taste. This is called buddhahood. . . . Buddhahood means to have awoken from the sleep of ignorance, while the bodhicitta of the nature of phenomena—great self-sprung wisdom—knows and fully realizes the entire maṇḍala of knowable objects in a single instant.

882 DSC omits this line.

883 II.53cd–56.

884 The *Kangyur* does not contain a sūtra by this name, only three dhāraṇīs whose titles contain the words "light rays," called *Mārīcīnāmadhāraṇī* (P182/613), *Raśmivimalaviśuddhaprabhānāmadhāraṇī* (P218/607), and *Samantamukhapraveśaraśmivimaloṣṇīṣaprabhāsasarvatathāgatahṛdayasamayavilokatenāmadhāraṇī* (P206/608/3512/3892). According to SC (p. 343), Döl (p. 156), and LG (p. 59), those who "abide in this great yoga" and so on are the bodhisattvas on the tenth bhūmi. Döl adds that, through abiding in the state of being empowered by the Buddhas, these bodhisattvas radiate light, thus opening the pure gates of worldly beings. LG states

that, during the tenth bhūmi's phase of subsequent attainment, the manner in which bodhisattvas promote the welfare of beings is almost the same as the one of Buddhas. Like DSC, SS (p. 675) says that these two verses refer to Buddhas. He glosses the gates of the path to liberation as the teachings on the four seals of the dharma and so on.

885 Usually, the nirvāṇa with remainder refers to the analytical cessation in the mind stream of an arhat who is still endowed with the five skandhas that are the remainder impelled by former karma and afflictions. Analytical cessation means that all karmas and afflictions as well as their root—the clinging to a personal self—that could serve as causes for further rebirth have been eradicated through a thorough meditative analysis of all the aspects of the four realities of the noble ones. The nirvāṇa without remainder is then reached at death, that is, upon leaving the skandhas of one's last existence in saṃsāra behind. Thus, practitioners may attain arhathood while still being alive and then just shed their skandhas at death, passing from the nirvāṇa with remainder into the nirvāṇa without remainder. There are also people who attain arhathood at the moment of death and do not go through the phase of the nirvāṇa with remainder.

886 Verses 94–96.

887 DSC has *spyad pa* (em. *chad pa*).

888 Verse 97.

889 II.57–60. DSC omits lines 57c and 59c, while line 59b is inserted between 58b and c.

890 RT (p. 647) says that enlightened activity first places beings in the nirvāṇa with remainder and later in the one without remainder, nirvāṇa being identified as a mind free from stains. According to SC (p. 344), it is held that the nirvāṇa without remainder is manifested, if all the karmic formations of one's last lifetime have been relinquished. However, this is just a case of applying the conventional term "nirvāṇa" to nothing but the extinction of saṃsāra, but it is not the actual nirvāṇa, since it is not the dharmakāya. To speak of the dharmakāya, the mere relinquishment of the afflictions is not sufficient. The reason is that, though saṃsāra has ceased through just that relinquishment, if the dharmadhātu has not become pure of the second kind of obscurations—the cognitive ones—it is not seen; and one cannot speak of "not seeing the dharmadhātu" as being the dharmakāya. SS (pp. 676–77) explains the difference between the nirvāṇas with and without remainder as described above. He says that the latter is not the fully qualified nirvāṇa either, since the arhats who dwell in the uncontaminated expanse are exhorted by the light rays of the Buddhas at some point to enter the path of the mahāyāna and promote the welfare of sentient beings. According to LG (p. 60), it is held that the bodhisattvas at the end of the tenth bhūmi, who have not yet fully completed relinquishment and realization, are those in the nirvāṇa with remainder. Right after the vajralike samādhi in the last moment of the tenth bhūmi, they attain the dharmakāya of a Buddha, which is the nirvāṇa without remainder.

891 Part 2, IV.77cd.

892 RT (p. 647) says that the nature of the nonbeing of sentient beings' afflictions is the actual nirvāṇa, which is the basic nature of mind. Döl (pp. 156–57) explains that the actual nirvāṇa is the mind free from stains, which has undergone its fundamental change. The nature of the nonbeing of all seeming sentient beings is mind's natural luminosity, which is nirvāṇa's sphere. Those who fully see this luminosity are the mighty bodhisattvas on the tenth bhūmi who are empowered. Upon having reached the very end of the tenth bhūmi, this is the fully stainless dharmakāya. SC (pp. 344–45) states that, here, the dhātu of mind having become free from stains is called "nonabiding nirvāṇa," since it is the wisdom that, due to being free from the stains of the afflictions, does not abide in saṃsāra and is also liberated from the obscuration of not con-

sidering sentient beings [with compassion]. The nature of this dharmadhātu wisdom—the total nonbeing of any obscurations of sentient beings—is the sphere of this very wisdom. Therefore, it can only become a living experience by personally experienced wisdom but is beyond any object of terms or thoughts. Those who directly see this dharmadhātu that is endowed with twofold purity are the mighty bodhisattvas. The dharmadhātu endowed with twofold purity is also called "dharmakāya," since it is the body of all qualities such as the powers. SS (pp. 677–78) says that the actual nirvāṇa of the mahāyāna is the mind that is free from all adventitious stains, through these having been vanquished by remedial wisdom. This mind has the character of the kāyas and wisdoms. Once this manifests, in accordance with the thinking of all sentient beings and following the progression of the yānas, the Buddhas see that these beings are to be guided in terms of whether their sphere is the nonbeing of self and mine, the nonexistence of real outer entities, or the nature of the nonbeing of apprehender and apprehended and so on. Through teaching them the dharma accordingly, they lead them to maturation and liberation. Finally, the mighty supreme bodhicitta that is the ultimate bodhicitta—the fully stainless union of the two realities—is the dharmakāya. LG (pp. 60–61) states that there is no final nirvāṇa other than buddhahood, and that the manifestation of the basic nature of one's own mind, free from the two obscurations and their latent tendencies, is the final change of state of the five wisdoms. In addition, the nature of the nonbeing of all sentient beings—the profound basic nature that is emptiness—is the fundamental state of phenomena, the equal taste of saṃsāra and nirvāṇa. As Buddhas realize this, it is their sphere, since the nature of phenomena is without difference, and, upon becoming a Buddha, saṃsāra and nirvāṇa are inseparable. When this basic nature is seen, the mighty bodhicitta is the final consummation of mind's full capacity to generate bodhicitta. Since its nature is primordially pure, without any stains ever having entered this fundamental state, it is the fully stainless dharmakāya, which resembles space and is inseparable from the final consummation of the two accumulations.

893 DSC first two lines: *dri ma med pa'i chos sku las/ ye shes rgya mtshor gnas gyur nas* (this phrasing is repeated in the commentary just below) DNP *dri ma med pa'i chos sku la/ ye shes rgya mtsho gnas gyur nas.*

894 DSC uses the expression "change of state" (*gnas gyur pa*) twice here, obviously interpreting *gnas gyur nas* in line 101b of DSC's version of Nāgārjuna's text in this sense. The standard version of lines 101ab as found in DNP is explained by all other commentaries (except SS, who follows DSC's version of lines 101ab but gives a different commentary) as the sea of wisdom abiding/resting (*gnas par gyur nas*) in the dharmakāya, which also seems to be a more natural reading. Following this, DSC's above sentence could also be read: "Rather, the oceans of the hordes of thoughts find their place/have come to rest in the sea of wisdom." In any case, both come down to the same meaning.

895 I.92–94.

896 Döl (p. 157) comments that the sea of wisdom always abides in the stainless dharmakāya in such a way that it fills all of space and is inexhaustible. Like a variegated jewel that showers down everything desired like rain, from the dharmakāya, enlightened activities issue that fulfill the welfare of all sentient beings in a simultaneous and spontaneous manner for as long as saṃsāra lasts. SC (p. 345) says that the sea of wisdom, such as the powers, rests within the dharmakāya free from adventitious stains. From this, the two rūpakāyas incessantly fulfill the welfare of sentient beings, just like a wish-fulfilling gem with its variegated color and shape. LG (p. 61) explains that the stainless dharmakāya is like the ground, in which the oceanlike two wisdoms that know suchness and variety abide. From that state, just as all kinds of various jewels come forth from the ocean,

while not moving away from the single dharmakāya, the sambhogakāyas and nirmāṇakāyas fulfill the welfare of pure and impure beings in a permanent, all-pervading, and spontaneously present manner. According to SS (p. 678), the manner in which enlightened activity issues from the stainless dharmakāya is as follows. By way of abiding in the sea of the wisdom that knows suchness and variety, without conceiving of anything or relying on efforts, variegated enlightened activities appear. Just as is the case with a wish-fulfilling jewel or a wish-fulfilling tree, from the dominant condition that is the dharmakāya, what appears as the two rūpakāyas is produced. Through that, the welfare of beings is fulfilled spontaneously and incessantly.

897 IV.85–88 (verses IV.13–84 and 89–98 explain all of these examples in great detail).

898 XI.17d. RT (p. 648) points out that some people's assertion that Buddhas do not have wisdom, which they try to base on *Madhyamakāvatāra* XI.17ab ("The dry firewood of knowable objects having been burned entirely, this peace is the dharmakāya of the victors"), is untenable, since it contradicts the last verse of Nāgārjuna's text here. RT declares, "Keep it very well in mind that this text here states that an ocean of wisdom dwells in the dharmakāya!" The colophon of RT says that Nāgārjuna's *Dharmadhātustava* properly explains the meaning of all vast and profound dharmas in a condensed way. Since it is difficult to understand, not a single explanation on it has appeared in Tibet. This last statement seems strange, since at least the commentaries by Rangjung Dorje, Dölpopa, and Sönam Gyaltsen (1312–1375) had been written long before Rongtön wrote his (according to the colophon, it was composed in the year of his ordination, which took place when he was about twenty-one, thus around 1387). One can hardly imagine that Rongtön was unaware of these commentaries.

899 XI.18.

900 In the Tibetan tradition, Ācārya Śūra (Tib. slob dpon dpa' bo) is considered to be just another name of Aśvaghoṣa.

901 DSC *bhyakara*. In terms of the historical order of the above masters, taking the unclear Tibetan to mean Bhavya seems to make the most sense (Bhavya probably was the actual name of Bhāvaviveka, who is often referred to by that name). Verse 101 is also quoted in Bhāvaviveka's *Madhyamakaratnapradīpa* (P5254, fol. 361a) in the context of outlining the three kāyas: In brief, what consists of the buddha qualities (such as the powers, the fearlessnesses, and unshared [qualities]) and is nondual with and not different from prajñāpāramitā is the dharmakāya. What springs from its blessings and is supported by that basis of the [dharmakāya] is the sambhogakāya. What comes from its blessings and appears in accordance with the inclinations of those to be guided is the nirmāṇakāya.

902 LG's colophon (pp. 62–63; paraphrase of the original verses) agrees that the oral streams of explanations on the Buddha's intention by Maitreya and Nāgārjuna may appear different but gather and fuse into one in the ocean of definitive meaning. This is what all honest scholars and siddhas assert. If the ocean of the Buddha heart, in which the two realities are of one taste, fits into the hub of analysis, which is as wide open as the sky, this is called "realizing that the two traditions are not contradictory." But this is not seen by the biased eyes of those who say that Nāgārjuna does not assert the change of state of the Tathāgata heart being purified of stains, that the middling three texts of Maitreya are Mere Mentalism, and so forth. Rather, the *Abhisamayālaṃkāra* and the collection of reasoning teach the inseparability of the two realities, being just like space free from reference points. The three middling texts of Maitreya [*Mahāyānasūtrālaṃkāra*, *Madhyāntavibhāga*, and *Dharmadharmatāvibhāga*], the collection of speeches, and the collection of praises teach the union of the two accumulations, being just like

two wings. The collection of praises and the *Uttaratantra* mainly teach the notion of the basic element of the two kāyas, the result of union. Therefore, with regard to the single essence of the path, these texts just bring out clearly the notions of lucidity and emptiness, respectively. Nāgārjuna does not hold that nothing but plain emptiness is the final view, and Maitreya's texts do not speak about something being really established. Therefore, they agree on the change of state that is nothing but the mistakenness of apprehender and apprehended vanishing within the dharmadhātu—the union of appearance and emptiness. In addition, it is impossible for Madhyamaka and Mere Mentalism to be contradictory with regard to the aspect of vast means. Any remaining root of phenomenal identity that may not be severed in Mere Mentalism is cut into pieces through the weapons of Madhyamaka reasoning. In brief, if all the countless various methods, from the most basic yāna of gods and humans up through the fruitional vajrayāna, are not divorced from the elixir of profound means and prajñā, just as the tools of an expert craftsman, they are one in essence in that they serve as helpful means to the same end. If this essential point is realized, the conventional term "realizing that all intentions of the victor are without contradiction" applies. But since this point is difficult to evaluate, while attempting to affirm the basic nature, one may go astray into what is conceptual in nature; while trying to cut through reference points, one may fall into the extreme of extinction and get lost in the conventional words "freedom from reference points"; and even if one speaks of "union," it may just be an object of conceptual understanding. Also, LG's introduction (pp. 3–6) says that there is no dispute about Nāgārjuna's scriptural tradition being Madhyamaka, while different opinions as to which Buddhist philosophical system the five texts of Maitreya represent abound. He then goes into the details of refuting the claim that the three middling texts of Maitreya are just Mere Mentalism and makes it clear that these texts can be explained very well according to Madhyamaka. {By the way, this also is the position of most Kagyü and Nyingma masters (in particular Ju Mipham Rinpoche), as well as Śākya Chogden's.} Thus, when Maitreya teaches the manner of affirming the Tathāgata heart, he does so by mainly teaching on the notion of lucidity—the seeming—while Nāgārjuna's cutting through all reference points by way of "nonarising from the four extremes" and so on mainly teaches the notion of emptiness—the ultimate. Therefore, if one does not understand these two notions as the single inseparability of the two realities, one may assert some blank emptiness as the fundamental nature of phenomena and then explain the Buddha heart as being of expedient meaning. Or, just as the Mere Mentalists, one may take the Buddha heart as something really established, thus asserting these two aspects [of lucidity and emptiness] to be separate. In any case, one falls from the path of the two realities in union, hence destroying the root of the path to liberation.

903 Verse 36.

904 XXXII.2bd–8 (the translation mainly follows the Sanskrit); DSC omits the first line.

905 Lit. "the invincible," an epithet of Maitreya.

906 This line could also be understood as "causing chatter even among childish beings who hear [about it]."

907 If no language is mentioned, the translation is into English. For publication details not mentioned here, see the bibliography.

908 As mentioned above, the *Āryabhāṭṭarakamañjuśrīparamārthastuti* (P2022) is almost identical to the *Paramārthastava* and thus can be counted as translated too.

909 There is also a Japanese translation of the *Catuḥstava* (including Amṛtākara's *Catuḥstavasamāsārtha*) by S. Sakei in "Ryūju ni kiserareru Sanka" (*Hymns Attributed*

to Nāgārjuna). The Journal of the Nippon Buddhist Research Association 24 (1959): 6–9 (*Lokātītastava*), 10–16 (*Niraupamyastava*), 29–33 (*Acintyastava*), 38–41 (*Paramārthastava*).

910 Nakamura's article also includes a translation of the *Chinese Sūtra That Describes the Names of the Eight Spiritual Stūpas* (Taishō 1685), which contains some similar passages.

911 Lindtner says that there are neither external nor internal criteria to support this text's attribution to Nāgārjuna. His edition is based on several Sanskrit manuscripts (none of which mention an author), "a fact which indicates that it has had a certain popularity."

912 Except for the first two verses (which are not available in Sanskrit) and the colophon, the translation follows the Sanskrit. Like most praises by Nāgārjuna in the *Tengyur*, all of the following save the last one start with the translator paying homage to Mañjuśrī. The *Vandanāstotra* begins by paying homage to all Tathāgatas.

913 Unlike the Tibetan, the Sanskrit has no negative here.

914 Skt. kṣāranadī, Tib. ba tshva'i chu klung. This is a river in one of the hells.

915 This is the colophon found in the *Tengyur*. The Sanskrit merely says, "This concludes the mahāyāna sūtra spoken by the completely perfect Buddha, called *Paying Homage to Sentient Beings*."

916 This is an Indian metaphor for something delusive—when certain snakes are squeezed, little protrusions appear that may be mistaken for feet.

917 This obviously refers to illusionlike beings swirling through saṃsāra like apparitions created by a magician, in this case their own mind.

918 This refers to the bodhi tree in Bodhgayā.

919 Since DP *bsnyel so* ("remembering/reminding") does not make much sense here, I took it to be *ngal gso*.

920 This refers to Cunda—one of the Buddha's disciples—supplicating him not to pass away, upon which he extended his lifespan for another three months.

921 In the ancient Indian four-continent world, the central Mount Meru is surrounded by seven ranges of golden mountains.

922 Uragas are serpent demons living below and on the earth. Kinnaras usually have a human body with the head of a horse and live at the court of Kubera (the god of wealth). Together with the gandharvas, they are the celestial musicians of Indian mythology.

Index